DATE DUE			

AFFECT, COGNITION, AND PERSONALITY
Empirical Studies

The authors

PAUL EKMAN

RALPH V. EXLINE

O. J. HARVEY

CARROLL E. IZARD

PETER B. LENROW

HOWARD LEVENTHAL

ROBERT MCCARTER

SAMUEL MESSICK

GARDNER MURPHY

VINCENT NOWLIS

MILTON J. ROSENBERG

ELIZABETH SHARP

SILVAN S. TOMKINS

AFFECT, COGNITION, AND PERSONALITY

Empirical Studies

Edited by

SILVAN S. TOMKINS
City University of New York

CARROLL E. IZARD
Vanderbilt University

SPRINGER PUBLISHING COMPANY, INC., NEW YORK

Copyright © 1965

SPRINGER PUBLISHING COMPANY, INC.
200 Park Avenue South   New York, N.Y. 10003

All Rights Reserved

Library of Congress Catalog Card Number: 65-17489

Type set at The Polyglot Press, New York
Printed in U.S.A.

PREFACE

This book is an expanded version of a symposium on affect held at the 1964 meeting of the American Psychological Association. The symposium was organized by Silvan Tomkins and Carroll Izard and included Paul Ekman, Peter Lenrow, Howard Leventhal, and Gardner Murphy. (Tomkins' introduction to the symposium follows the Preface.) Since each contributor's paper to the symposium was limited in detail and in depth by the time constraints of a professional meeting, and since similar constraints are more and more imposed on the papers which are published in our professional journals, the editors proposed book publication of the expanded versions of the papers.* It was our intention to accelerate the growing interest of numerous investigators in the feasibility and significance of the empirical study of affect. In order to more fully represent contemporary efforts in this field, several additional investigators were invited to contribute papers to this volume. These are Milton Rosenberg, O. J. Harvey, Ralph Exline, Vincent Nowlis, and Samuel Messick.

It was our intention to present an adequate sampling of contemporary research in affect. Rather than briefly describing all the work now going on in this field, we felt it was important to present in depth the work of some of the major investigators.

The studies were written especially for this volume, and their primary emphasis is on empirical investigation. However, contributors were also encouraged to relate their empirical findings to their own theoretical orientations, as well as to the theoretical and empirical work of others.

It is clear that there is no consensus among the theoretical positions of the contributors to this volume. Similarly, within the field as a whole, there appears to be much more variance than communality of theoretical assumptions. This lack of communality was a major consideration in the editors' decision not to exercise the editorial prerogative of connective and interpretive commentary. The decision was governed also by the conflict in roles of the editors, who acted both as contributors and as

* Silvan Tomkins' work was supported in whole by a Public Health Research Career Award from the National Institute of Mental Health, 1-K6-MH-23, 797-01.

editors. We owe a special debt of gratitude to Gardner Murphy for assuming the responsibilities of commentator and critic.

The readers, including the contributors, will note the complex relationships between all of the positions presented. It is our hope that there will emerge from such confrontation both an increased differentiation and some increase in communality in professional opinion concerning the problem of affect.

December 1, 1964

SILVAN S. TOMKINS
Director, Center for Research
   in Cognition and Affect
City University of New York

CARROLL E. IZARD
Professor of Psychology
Director, Clinical Program
Vanderbilt University

INTRODUCTION TO AFFECT SYMPOSIUM, A.P.A. 1964

Silvan S. Tomkins

Since psychology committed itself to behavior without benefit of consciousness it has been walking in an untroubled, dreamless sleep now for over half a century. It is being aroused from this state and slowly regaining consciousness. In its journals one learns that the patient has first recovered his cognition—his ability to think, to dream and even to daydream. And now the patient shows signs that he is recovering not only his mind, but also his heart, his feelings, his affects.

For the past fifty years a handful of early experiments in the judgment of emotion in the face, which had yielded negative results, plus a continuing fruitless search in the guts and bowels of man for distinctive emotional responses have been sufficient to reinforce the belief that affect is a hopeless will-o'-the-wisp, essentially recalcitrant to scientific psychological investigation.

This symposium is dedicated to the disproof of several old, and young, wives' tales; and to affirmation of the following propositions: (1) that *affects are the primary motives of man;* (2) that affects are not private obscure internal intestinal responses but facial responses that communicate and motivate at once both publicly outward to the other and backward and inward to the one who smiles or cries or frowns or sneers or otherwise expresses his affects; (3) that these communications are more often *understood* than misunderstood; (4) that affects have profound effects on cognition and action, and conversely both cognition and action have profound effects on affect. Therefore the problem of measurement involves the measurement of both the *awareness* of affect by the *observer* and by the *self* and also the measurement of the impact of affect on cognition and action, and the measurement of the impact of cognition and action on affect; (5) that, in addition to the affects of anxiety and anger about which we have heard so much, so long—too long, there are also the affects of excitement and enjoyment, and distress, and contempt, and shame, and surprise.

It is to one or another of these propositions that each of the participants will address himself.

CONTRIBUTORS

THE AUTHORS

Paul Ekman, Ph.D., Assistant Professor of Psychology, San Francisco State College; Research Associate, Political Science Department, Stanford University

Ralph V. Exline, Ph.D., Associate Research Professor, Center for Research on Social Behavior, University of Delaware

O. J. Harvey, Ph.D., Professor of Psychology, University of Colorado

Carroll E. Izard, Ph.D., Professor of Psychology, Director of Clinical Program, Vanderbilt University

Peter B. Lenrow, Ph.D., Assistant Professor of Psychology, University of California, Berkeley

Howard Leventhal, Ph.D., Assistant Professor of Psychology, Yale University

Robert McCarter, Ph.D., Associate Professor of Psychology, University of South Carolina

Samuel Messick, Ph.D., Chairman, Personality Research Group, Educational Testing Service, Princeton, New Jersey

Gardner Murphy, Ph.D., Director of Research, Menninger Foundation, Topeka, Kansas

Vincent Nowlis, Ph.D., Professor of Psychology, University of Rochester

Milton J. Rosenberg, Ph.D., Professor of Psychology, Dartmouth College

Elizabeth Sharp, M.S.N., Research Assistant in Nursing at Yale University, now at Johns Hopkins University

Silvan S. Tomkins, Ph.D., Director of the Center for Research in Cognition and Affect, City University of New York

ASSOCIATE AUTHORS

Jean Fox, Research Associate, Vanderbilt-ONR Project 2149(03)

J. Rex Jennings, Major, U.S. Army, Instructor, West Point

William J. Livsey, Major, U.S. Army, Instructor, West Point

Sylvain Nagler, Teaching Assistant and Ph.D. Candidate, Department of Psychology, Vanderbilt University

Allison Peebles, Research Assistant, Philadelphia Psychiatric Center

Don Randall, Chief Psychologist, Mental Health Center, Marion, Indiana

Gerald M. Wehmer, Counselor, Vanderbilt Counseling Center and Ph.D. Candidate, Department of Psychology, Vanderbilt University

Lewis C. Winters, M.S., Senior Research Associate, Associates for Research in Behavior, Philadelphia

CONTENTS

PART ONE

AFFECT AND
LEARNING

Affect, awareness, and performance

Carroll E. Izard
with Gerald M. Wehmer
William J. Livsey
J. Rex Jennings

Until recently, the epistemology and experimental methodology of American psychology has been largely dominated by classical and neo-Behaviorism. Since objectivism, with its emphasis on observable behavior, is the central feature of this approach, one consequence has been the eclipse of interest in affect and emotion—dimensions of experience not readily amenable to S-R methodology. Behaviorism has exerted less controlling influence in recent years, and so the interests of psychologists in affect and emotion are again finding expression in theory and research.

This contemporary resurgence of interest in the area of affect derives from two quite different, although complementary, sources. One is physiological psychology and is represented by such people as P. T. Young who states that "Eventually affective process will be described in physiological terms; current research indicates that their bodily nature and locus will some day be known" (1959, p. 104). The other source is phenomenologically oriented psychology and is represented by Magda B. Arnold who states that "A phenomenological analysis of emotional experience can guide us in identifying the brain structures and pathways that mediate feelings and emotions" (1960, p. V). Both groups have brought the insides of the organism back into the picture; but the first group maintains that a valid description and understanding of affective processes must come through objective measurement and control of physiological variables, whereas the second group insists that emotion is primarily and most importantly a subjective experience and it is through the subject's immediate experience that it can best be understood, though they do not always explicitly deal with it. The two groups differ in another highly important matter—the role of awareness and/or cognition in affect. Of course the phenomenological approach would rely heavily on conscious experience in the investigation of affect, while those approaching the sphere through the study of activation or arousal would

The research reported in this chapter was supported by Vanderbilt-ONR Contract Nonr 2149 (03), Carroll E. Izard, Principal Investigator. The opinions and conclusions do not necessarily reflect those of the United States Department of the Navy.

not. The first group searches for meaning; the latter for mechanisms. The two groups differ widely in the number of dimensions used to describe affect. The phenomenologically oriented recognize many qualitatively distinct emotions; the physiologically oriented recognize two or three quantifiable, scalable dimensions.

The extent to which major theories of emotion or affect use conscious experience (e.g., self-report, self-ratings) in their research and the role they assign to awareness and cognition in affectivity are quite separate issues. It will be helpful in gaining perspective for the empirical research to be reported later if we review some of the current affect theories, with special attention to the place each gives to awareness and cognition.

THEORIES EMPHASIZING PHYSIOLOGICAL CONSTRUCTS
AND QUANTITATIVE DIMENSIONS

Activation as a Substitute for Affect

Duffy (1962) maintains that behavior varies in only two dimensions—direction and intensity. Thus we have a beguilingly simple structure for a theory of behavior; but as Duffy elaborates on the constructs of direction and intensity, the complexities implicit in her definitions are not dealt with at the level of personality functioning and interpersonal behavior. She pays her respects to the complexity of the human organism in her thinking on the neurological aspects of activation, but even here she makes things seem relatively simple.

The direction of behavior. The direction of behavior can be defined in terms of selectivity of response. To maintain direction in behavior, the organism must respond to relationships—to relationships between stimuli and past experiences and between stimuli and present goals. Such behavior requires discrimination, though neither the discriminations nor the goals need be conscious. Duffy equates her construct of direction with Tolman's cognitive maps and Hebb's cue functions.

The direction of behavior is basically goal-direction. Describing the direction of behavior means describing movements in space, sets, or cognitive plans. Habits, interests, attitudes, and values describe persistent direction of behavior. The persistent direction of behavior constitutes "a significant part of what is referred to as 'personality'" (Duffy, p. 9). This is the extent of Duffy's explanation of the dynamics of individual behavior, other than what she has to say about neurophysiological processes. However, Duffy does propose, though without explication, that the concepts of perceiving and thinking can be described fully in terms of behavior direction. Arousal may result from perceiving and thinking, but apparently Duffy believes the converse is not true. Perceiving and thinking, then, are conceived as matters of selectivity, patterning, and response to relationships.

The intensity of behavior. Intensity of behavior depends basically upon degree or kind of activation. "The level of activation of the organism may be defined, then, as the extent of release of potential energy, stored in the tissues of the organism, as this is shown in activity or response" (Duffy, p. 17). The energy released is a result of metabolic activity in the tissues. Duffy's concept of activation is organismic arousal, not merely brain wave activity as registered in the EEG. If the many factors (metabolic conditions, hormones, products of fatigue) affecting activation are held constant and the experimenter varies only the incentive value of the situation, measurement of the degree of activation is a measure of the significance of the situation, of the intensity of "motivation."

Interaction between direction of behavior and degree of activation. Duffy recognizes only two dimensions of behavior, and since one of these (degree of activation) is exclusively concerned with the internal processes it would appear that she would give much attention to the dimension of direction and its interaction with intensity; this would be her only means of describing the complex cognitive and overt behavioral activities of the human being. But she devotes very little space to the dimension of direction and to the interaction of the two dimensions.

Duffy's formula for the interaction of direction of behavior and degree of activation results in an inverted U-shaped curve. In general, extremely high and extremely low degrees of activation are less likely to result in consistent, goal-directed, integrated behavior. Duffy believes there is sketchy evidence for exception to this general rule—"even during the excitement of 'emotion,' there may be good organization of behavior on occasion" (Duffy, pp. 10, 11).

Duffy states that the resources of the individual for dealing with a stimulus constitute a significant factor in an individual's response to stress, "defined as degree of activation by stimulus when other relevant factors are held constant" (Duffy, p. 52). Duffy's brief allusion to the role of cognitive processes appears in a statement which also shows her belief in the "reactive" nature of the human organism: she concludes that "the degree of activation is in general finely adjusted to the demands of the situation, as interpreted by the individual, and within his capacity for response" (Duffy, p. 52). Here she gives a place to the individual's interpretation of the situation, but she fails to explain the relationship of cognition and arousal or how the individual comes to this or that interpretation. She recognizes individual differences in capacity for response (presumably in ability to cope with the environment); but, for explication of this notion, she turns to individual differences in activation patterns.

Affect as Contingency for Motives

The key term in McClelland's system (1953) is affective-arousal. In simplest terms, affective-arousal is what is commonly called emotion. The direct effects of affective-arousal are not the subject of study, though an affect state may be observed through autonomic reactions, direction of behavior (approach, avoidance), or verbal reports. The importance of affective-arousal is its role in the development of motives. Motive is defined as "the redintegration by a cue of a change in an affective situation" (McClelland, p. 28). Affect is an innate, diffuse reaction of the autonomic nervous system to certain stimuli or situations. The model here is similar to the paradigm for releasing stimulus → consummatory behavior in lower animals. The main difference is that in man the consummatory responses are much less specific and rigid and, indeed, are usually attenuated to the point that they occur only as affect (McClelland, p. 31). Cues associated with such affect acquire the power to evoke a facsimile of the original affect or affective situation; hence, such cues become motives, and, for McClelland, all motives are learned in this way. Two alternative hypotheses are that the cue may be associated with the affective state or with a change in affect, but "both hypotheses assume that the redintegrated affect *at the time of arousal* must represent a change over the present affective state of the organism" (McClelland, p. 29).

McClelland's theory is unabashed hedonism. Positive and negative affect are inexorably identified with subjective pleasure and pain and functionally linked with approach and avoidance behavior. The antecedent condition for affective-arousal is a discrepancy between adaptation level (after Helson, 1948) and a sensation or event. Adaptation level is synonymous with (or defines) the organism's expectation regarding affect (pleasure or pain). Sensations or events lead to perceptions. "Positive affect is the result of smaller discrepancies of a sensory or perceptual event from the adaptation level of the organism; negative affect is the result of larger discrepancies" (McClelland, p. 43).

The diffuse reactions which McClelland calls affect are for him the base on which man constructs the wide variety of motives that prompt his behavior. It is, he believes, the same base that is responsible for guiding and directing the behavior of lower animals.

McClelland's distinction between the effects of affect and motive is important for his theory of motivation. The three events necessary for the development of a motive may have quite different effects on behavior. The three events in the order of occurrence are:

A. The situation producing affect
B. Redintegration of (A)
C. Response learned to (B).

Affect is by definition diffuse autonomic reaction; hence, its effect on behavior can be observed via bio-electric measures of skin conductance and temperature, heart rate, muscle potential, and the like. McClelland distinguishes primary (or unlearned) affect from redintegrated (learned) affect by showing the difference between pain (primary affect) and fear (redintegrated affect). Pain is the innate reaction to certain traumatic stimuli; fear is the "anticipatory redintegration of the pain response" (McClelland, p. 36). Pain (the original affect) is assumed to be innate, automatic, requiring no interpretation by the S. On the other hand, fear is a learned response which results from the development of an associative link between a cue and an affective state or affective change.

McClelland does not deal explicitly with the role of awareness or of the perceptual-cognitive system in affective-arousal or motivation. However, it seems apparent that "redintegration" is a cognitive function. The redintegration process may conceivably be at a low level of awareness (functionally unconscious), but this does not rule out cognition. Certainly "*anticipatory* redintegration" (italics ours) implies a conscious cognitive process.

McClelland's theory is essentially a learning theory, though its emphasis is on acquisition of motives rather than on acquisition of habits. It is in the tradition of associationism and hedonism, but it differs in one important respect from other theories in this tradition. Innate affect (pleasure, pain) is placed at the beginning rather than at the end (consummatory phase) of a response sequence that results in acquisition. A stimulus—object, event, situation—acquires its cue function (power to evoke a facsimile of the original innate affect) through association with the unlearned affect, i.e., via the perceptual-cognitive system.

Affect As a Function of Changes in Activation Level

In the homeostatic theory of Fiske and Maddi (1961), affect is also a function of the discrepancy between actual and characteristic levels of activation. Large discrepancies or sharp increases are ordinarily associated with negative affect, while positive affect usually is experienced when such discrepancies are reduced and there is a shift toward the characteristic level of activation. It is important to note that Fiske and Maddi say that affect is influenced by the meaning of stimuli, by their specific cue-function. They have also given a place to awareness and cognition, but they do not expand on this.

The activation theory of Schlosberg (1954) locates emotional behavior on a continuum that includes all behavior, and thereby rejects the idea that emotion should be treated as a special state, differing qualitatively from other states. In addition to his fundamental dimension of intensity, which he terms sleep-tension, two other dimensions are added: pleasantness-unpleasantness and attention-rejection.

Young (1961) insists that affective processes can be quantitatively defined in terms of their attributes: sign, intensity, and duration. He offers what he terms the "hedonic continuum" (Figure A) as a way of illustrating these measurable attributes. Young (1959), in his discussion of affective processes as motivational in nature, states that affect regulates and directs behavior according to the principle of maximizing the positive and minimizing the negative. In his scheme, positive affective processes also have the role of organizing approach motives, with the strength of a motive depending upon the intensity of the affective processes.

Figure A: Hedonic continuum.

A Theory of Perception and Its Relation to Affect

The relation of affect to awareness and cognition is dealt with from another vantage point by Solley and Murphy. In their *Development of the Perceptual World* (1960) they have not written an affect theory as such, but they have assigned affect a central role in their theory of perceptual learning. They hold that perception is both a process and a product. The process is the act of perceiving; the product is the percept. The process has five stages. The first is the preparatory stage which consists of the set, hypothesis, and sensoritonic state of the individual prior to proximal stimulation. The second stage is the "moment before stimulation and the activities which prepare the organism for receiving stimuli" (Solley & Murphy, p. 19). In the searching-attending aspects of this second stage, affect plays an important role.

> "The affects are organic expressions of the approach and avoidance reactions which prepare the individual to select from the multitude of stimuli about him. It follows, therefore, that the condition of these preparatory, searching responses represents a molding of the attentive-preparatory processes by affective stimulation; and consequently the individual's expectancies or hypotheses lead to a selectivity in reception" (Solley & Murphy, p. 20).

There is no sharp dividing line between expectancy (stage one), attending (stage two), and the third stage, the reception phase. The fourth stage of Solley and Murphy is termed a trial-and-check phase; it is characterized by a time-lag between reception and final percept. Affect can also play a role in this stage of perception. It is during this stage that autonomic activity is triggered which subsequently feeds back into the perceptual process both by (a) raising or lowering the overall level of sensibility and (b) functioning as a stimulus in a background context just as other stimulus traces do. The fifth stage consists of the consolidation of the stimulus trace. Solley and Murphy believe that only a sample of the input is consolidated. While they do not make it explicit, here again is a place where affect could play a role. It is possible that affect furnishes the emphasis for the aspect of the input that is consolidated.

In order to compare Solley and Murphy's position with that of affect theorists it is necessary to see how they define affect, motivation, and reinforcement, and the relationships that they see between these concepts. It is difficult to get an understanding of what they mean by affect or to find a clear definition of it. It appears that, for them, affect is an aspect of motivation. They consider the primary motives to be hunger, thirst, sex, curiosity, and a need to maintain exteroceptive contact with the environment. They see motivation as regulating perceptual search and hence partially governing the probability of sensory reception. In operational terms, motivation may be set up either by deprivation techniques or stimulation techniques. When an individual experiences food deprivation he is made aware of the stimulation produced by his stomach contractions. The stimulation or internal stimuli are one aspect of motivation. The stomach contractions are equated by Solley and Murphy with emotional-affective responses and are considered as one aspect of motivation. These emotional-affective responses may have various effects on the autonomic system including speeding up of heart beat, increasing adrenalin flow, etc. Motivation also involves an energization of the organism. Thus motivation involves internal stimulation, emotional-affective responses, and energization. Solley and Murphy are not equating affect and biological needs, but they are definitely making affect a part of motivation, and they are defining motives primarily in terms of biological needs.

Solley and Murphy indicate that they "accept the Guthrie-Skinner-Estes concept of a reinforcement stimulus as one which preserves some act and by so preserving alters the probability of that act occurring again." This sets the stage for affect to play a prominent part in the reinforcement situation. They interpret some of the results of Miller and Olds as pointing "more and more to affect arousal as the event most worthy of emphasis in the ultimate construction of a strong law of effect" (Solley & Murphy, p. 29).

It should be clarified that the two aspects of motivation, internal stimulation and internal response, refer to distinctly different phenomena. Internal stimulation (or deprivation) triggers internal responses (e.g., stomach contractions), and it is the latter that constitute the affective aspect of motivation. The important thing here is that the authors are assigning affect to the category of response, although in their scheme they recognize that this response may set off stimulation and subsequent behavior.

"There is no doubt that the sensory aspects of motivation play an important role in perceiving, but the sensory input supplied by motivation operations is only half the picture. Let us now look at the emotional affective response r_e aspect of motivation and examine how it can influence or enter into perceiving. Some or all of these r_e's 'feed back' still other stimuli into the perceptual field. We believe this is the basis for an individual's ability to perceive such responses. In fact, we believe this may be the basis for qualitative differences in affect. We also believe that this feed-back can either facilitate or interfere with an ongoing perceptual act" (Solley & Murphy, p. 49).

The emotional affective responses can set off internal stimuli consisting of interoceptive and proprioceptive stimulation. The emotional affective responses may also bring about discharge of hormones into the blood stream. "All of these sources of stimulation, including hormonal changes, ascend to stimulate the reticular system of the brain stem" (Solley & Murphy, p. 51).

In the following quote it is clear that Solley and Murphy are attributing to motivation much of what we attribute to affect alone.

"Motivation raises or lowers the level of consciousness with which perceptual acts are carried out; it functions to guide the selectivity that we observe in perception; it serves both a facilitative and inhibitory function. In short, motivation does govern the direction and strength of perceptual acts; indeed, without motivation effects it is doubtful that we would perceive at all (Solley & Murphy, p. 52).

Solley and Murphy differ in one important respect from the other theories considered in this section. The other theories have placed activation or arousal as the immediate antecedent of affect. Solley and Murphy reverse the order of these phenomena and add some other steps to the process. First there is a need (set up by deprivation or stimulation), then internal stimulation. The latter triggers affective responses which in turn produce interoceptive and proprioceptive stimulation and hormonal changes. Finally, all of these sources of stimulation "ascend to stimulate the reticular system of the brain stem." It is possible that some of the difference in Solley and Murphy's position is due to the fact that they have differentiated the steps between initial stimulation and activation. Yet, the fact remains that they do not speak of affect as a *result* of activation or changes in activation, but just the contrary.

Solley and Murphy's work does not deal directly with the interrelations of affect and cognition. However, they see affect as significantly influencing perception, hence awareness and cognition.

THEORIES EMPHASIZING THE ROLE OF AWARENESS AND COGNITIVE PROCESSES

Affect (Emotion) as a Function of Perception and Appraisal

Arnold (1960) maintains that there are numerous qualitatively different emotions, each with its own neurophysiological reaction pattern and behavioral manifestation. Duffy, on the other hand, uses two quantifiable dimensions to explain all behavior and maintains that there is no evidence for differential neurophysiological responses among emotions. Arnold believes in the existence of qualitatively distinct emotions partly because common sense and common experience tell us that this is the case. Any individual knows that he has experienced emotion. What is more, he is capable of naming a number of emotions that he has known. The person's emotional experience may not be identical with that of another person, but it is analogous to it. Arnold holds that we shall make progress in our study of emotion and its role in behavior when we investigate this factor of analogous subjective experience. The phenomenology of emotion must include a description of the common factors in emotion that occur in every person's emotional life under given conditions, without maintaining that every person under a given condition will experience identical emotion.

Arnold defines emotion as "the felt tendency toward anything intuitively appraised as good (beneficial), or away from anything intuitively appraised as bad (harmful). This attraction or aversion is accompanied by a pattern of physiological changes organized toward approach or withdrawal. The patterns differ for different emotions" (Arnold, p. 182). To understand Arnold's concept of emotion, it is necessary to see how she relates it to feeling, perception, drive, homeostasis, and motive.

Emotion and feeling. For Arnold, feeling is a positive or negative reaction to some experience. Feeling is a reaction to something that affects our functioning. Positive feeling welcomes something sensed and appraised as beneficial and indicates enhanced functioning. There are but two classes of feeling, pleasant and unpleasant, or positive and negative, Negative feeling (unpleasantness, pain) is the response to something sensed and appraised as harmful and indicates impaired functioning. For the most part, feelings are reactions to sensory experience; but in addition to sense-bound feeling there is feeling in relation to motion and mental activity, to physical conditions, and to emotion. Mood is explained as a feeling response to an extended and continued change in organismic functioning.

Arnold's distinction between feeling and emotion appears somewhat labored and moot. "Both feeling and emotion are based upon an intuitive estimate that something is 'good or bad for me.' But emotion is aroused by an object or situation as a whole, rather than by a specific aspect of it (as is the case with feeling); and in emotion this object is appraised as good *for a specific action*, as good to eat or drink or embrace" (Arnold, p. 80). Pleasant and unpleasant feelings, on the other hand, have general effects on the motor system but do not, as in the case of emotion, lead to specific actions.

Emotion, perception, and appraisal. Arnold uses the term perception to mean "simple apprehension of an object." Apprehension of something is to know what it is like as an object independent of any effect on the perceiver. Before emotion comes into the picture, the object must be perceived and appraised as having an effect on the perceiver. Arnold also maintains that emotion is distinct from appraisal. She implies that emotion may include the appraisal as an integral or necessary part, but suggests the possibility that the emotion proper is the nonrational attraction or repulsion that follows upon the appraisal of something as good or bad for the perceiver. These rather fine distinctions between emotion, perception, and appraisal are maintained despite the fact that the appraisal itself is characterized as direct, immediate, and intuitive. Appraisal is not the result of reflection or deliberation. Appraisal is almost as direct as is perception, immediately follows and completes it, and can be recognized as a separate process only upon reflection. The "sequence perception-appraisal-emotion is so closely knit that our everyday experience is never the strictly objective knowledge of a thing; it is always a knowing-and-liking, or a knowing-and-disliking. . . . The intuitive appraisal of the situation initiates an *action tendency that is felt as emotion,* expressed in various bodily changes, and that eventually may lead to overt action" (Arnold, p. 177).

Emotion has important residual or continuing effects. The action tendencies that follow an emotion organize and bias later perception and appraisal; the emotion "fascinates us and takes us captive" (Arnold, p. 182). Appraisal and emotional reaction to a given object tend to be generalized to the whole class of objects. Further, the intuitive appraisal and emotional response tend to have constancy, so that the object or situation so appraised and responded to tends to evoke this appraisal and response "for all time to come" (Arnold, p. 184).

It is quite clear that Arnold is giving perceptual and cognitive processes top billing in her presentation of the dynamics of emotion. First, there is perception of the object or situation, then appraisal of the object or situation, and finally emotion. This appraisal directly determines the emotion or, more specifically, the action tendency that is felt as emotion. Note that emotion is only an action tendency (or the feeling of an action tendency) and, as will be seen in a later section, this is distinct from a motive.

Emotion and drives. Arnold maintains that the drive theorists have failed to bridge the great gap between the so-called basic drives and adult human motives. The attempt to span the gap by postulating secondary drives which originate and get their propulsion from primary drives has been unsuccessful. The mechanism for the development of secondary drives has never been adequately explained.

Even need as deficiency must "register in some way" (Arnold, p. 220) before it leads to action. Thus it is the organismic reaction to the deficiency, not the need *per se* that leads to overt activity. Thus on the psychological level a need "must be consciously felt as want or desire before the individual will react. . . . Action is dictated by what is wanted, not by what is actually needed" (Arnold, p. 220). Arnold points out that a need may be a requirement without being a lack of something. Such needs as the need to think, reason, talk, work or love are "naturally determined because they require the exercise of inherent capacities . . . muscles, for instance, need to be exercised . . . the same is true for sensory functions" (Arnold, pp. 220-221).

Emotion and motives. Arnold assumes that the organism is active by nature. Consequently she eliminates the need to look for special driving forces whether they are called instincts, needs, drives, motives, or what have you. "The motives that arouse, sustain and direct such specific action are not just the motors proposed in drive theories but something over and above internal drives or instincts" (Arnold, p. 224). Arnold believes that motivated action is explained by both emotional and cognitional processes . . . "a motive seems to be an action impulse (a want) that is appraised as good for action" (Arnold, p. 233). This want is typically an emotional response, and the wanting becomes a motive "when we endorse it and let it lead us to action" (Arnold, p. 238). Thus motive—action impulse plus cognition—develops only after an emotion has been favorably appraised.

Arnold thinks that emotions, wants, and physiological appetites fall short of explaining an important segment of human behavior. Thus "some impulse other than emotion is needed to move us to an action that is not itself pleasant and leads to a goal that promises neither emotional gratification nor satisfaction of a physiological appetite" (Arnold, p. 234). This is where man's rational motives come into play. "The act of choice (the will impulse) is an inherent action tendency like any other; it is set in motion by an intuitive appraisal, like emotion, but requires a deliberate decision before it will lead to action" (Arnold, p. 245).

Animal behavior that has foundation in instinct or biological need requires yet another concept, that of appetite. Appetite is what is frequently called tension: "hunger tension, sexual tension, and the like." Appetite is a felt urge toward a specific object. The behavior sequence is as follows: "physiological state induces a felt urge that is focused on the appropriate object (appetite), sensitizes appraisal, and so triggers off the wanting that leads to action" (Arnold, p. 227). Emotional wanting or desire follows the appetite. "Emotions themselves are action tendencies like physiological appetites, but they are not activated by a physiological state, nor do they aim toward a specific naturally determined object" (Arnold, p. 228).

But for the human being, instinct or biological need is "supplemented by reflection, understanding and deliberate choice" (Arnold, p. 231). Arnold's Thomistic and rationalist leanings become most apparent when she relates pleasure and motive. She maintains that pleasure cannot be the motive for action since she maintains that the more one intends and pursues pleasure, as such, the more it eludes him. Thus pleasure and delight are the result or accompaniment of activity, not the motive for it. The same kind of reasoning leads to her criticism of McClelland's conclusion that a motive stemming from a positive affective-arousal should always lead to action when it is strong enough, since it would result in something beneficial and pleasurable, or at least pleasurable. "McClelland's theory does not allow him to distinguish between a wanting that is emotional in nature and a wanting that comes from the reflective estimate that a particular attraction is contrary to our best interests. With the second kind of wanting there will be an action that is not dictated by emotion, a state of affairs that is completely inexplicable on McClelland's premises" (Arnold, p. 241).

After Arnold's extensive analysis of emotion and its relation to other functions of the personality, one is sometimes puzzled as to the importance of emotion in her theory of behavior. She recognizes several distinguishable determinants of behavior, e.g., physiological appetites, rational motives. Emotion is seen only as one component of a certain class of motives (non-rational?), a component that is apparently impotent without cognition or favorable appraisal.

Affect As a Result of Cognition

Schachter and Singer (1962) advance the theory that cognitive factors are the major determinants of emotional states. In their research they produced a single state of epinephrine-induced sympathetic activation and, by means of cognitive manipulations, were able to produce very different states: euphoria and anger. Another finding supported the possibility of having "very high degrees of activation without a subject either appearing to be or describing himself as 'emotional' " (Schachter & Singer, p. 398). They conclude that emotional states may be generally characterized by a high level of sympathetic activation with few, if any, physiological distinguishers among the many emotional states. Here they are in agreement with such writers as Duffy (1962), who states that the search for such differential physiological responses has proved to be fruitless. Others, such as Arnold (1960), point to some of the studies of brain stimulation as good evidence that this conclusion is not justified. Schachter and Singer believe that cognitions arising from the immediate situation as interpreted by past experience provide the framework within which one understands and labels his feelings.

Affect as Oriented Awareness of a Motor Attitude

Bull's theory of emotion is a modification of the familiar James-Lange formulation (Bull, 1951). The James-Lange position is that affect is brought about by actual behavior; e.g., feeling sorry is a result of crying. Bull maintains that affect in this instance is mediated by the attitude of readiness to cry, not by the act of crying. Affect results from an "involuntary *motor* attitude, maintained as readiness or wish" (Bull, pp. 5-6). This motor attitude is described as incompleted movement or movement in suspense. The attitude underlying affect occurs in an irreversible sequence: (1) latent (predisposing neural organization), (2) motor (bodily readiness, action set), (3) mental (oriented awareness of motor attitude). The affect is reduced by action, particularly consummatory activity.

Bull (p. 9, fig. 3) shows the sequence from stimulus to action in form of a diagram:

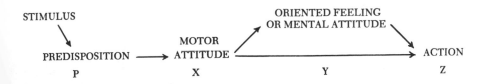

The Stage Y is the feeling or affect stage. Affect proper is an awareness, an oriented awareness, of the motor attitude.

Bull places a sharp limitation on what she considers as affect. Interestingly, the limit is set by cognition or by the level of awareness characterizing the interoceptive and proprioceptive cues stemming from the underlying motor attitude. Affect obtains only when the individual is less than fully conscious of the motor attitude. When oriented awareness of the motor attitude becomes a fully conscious mental attitude, the result is "the feeling of purpose and is not, as a rule, called affect" (Bull, p. 9). This fixes a severe restriction on the motivational properties of affect. In this framework, consciousness is supreme; it acts as regulatory mechanism for affect; without some level of conscious awareness of the motor attitude, there is no affect. Yet when this awareness becomes a fully conscious mental attitude, the result is intention or purpose, not affect. This means that Bull rules out affect as a determinant of higher order functioning— purposive behavior, propriate striving, creative endeavor.

A THEORY STRESSING BOTH INNATE AND LEARNED AFFECT
AND COGNITIVE-AFFECTIVE INTERACTION

Tomkins has presented a general model of the human being in a four volume work "Affect Imagery Consciousness" (of which two volumes have been published). The scope and complexity of argument presented there does not lend itself readily to summary and the interested reader is referred to these volumes for the detailed exposition of what is briefly summarized here.

Tomkins argues that the affect system is the primary motivational system and that the drive system is a secondary motivational system because the drives necessarily require amplification from the affects, but the affects are sufficient motivators in the absence of drives. This is because the drive in the absence of concurrent affect is too weak in motivational power. He argues that much of the apparent urgency of a drive is an artifact of the combined strength of both affect and drive. Thus if one is excited and sexually aroused the excitement (which is in the chest and face, and not in the genitals) sustains potency, but if one is guilty or afraid about sexuality the individual may lose his potency. Thus one needs to be excited to enjoy the sexual drive, but one need not be sexually aroused to be excited. One can be excited about anything under the sun.

Second, in contrast to the specificity of the space time information of the drive system, the affect system has those more general properties which permit it to assume a central position in the motivation of human beings. Thus, the affect system has generality of time rather than the rhythmic specificity of the drive system. Because the drive system is essentially a transport system, taking material in and out of the body, it must impose its specific temporal rhythms. But the affect system is under no such constraint. One can be anxious for just a moment or for half an hour, or for a day, or for a month, or for a year, or a decade, or a lifetime, or *never*, or only occasionally now though much more frequently some time ago, in childhood but not as an adult, or conversely. The affect system permits generality not only of time, but of intensity. One can feel strongly about this and weakly about that. It also permits generality of density of affect investment. One can feel strongly about something for a little while, or less intensely for a longer while, or very intensely all one's life. Thus, affects are capable of both insatiability and finickiness as well as extreme lability.

Tomkins conceives of affects as primarily facial responses (such as the smile, and cry) the feedback of which, when transformed into conscious form, have self-rewarding and self-punishing characteristics—that these responses are inherently acceptable or inherently unacceptable. These organized sets of responses are triggered at subcortical centers where specific "programs" for each distinct affect are stored. These programs are innately endowed and have been genetically inherited. They are capable, when activated, of simultaneously capturing such widely distributed organs as the face, the heart, and the endocrines and imposing on them a specific pattern of correlated responses. One does not learn to be afraid, or to cry, or to startle, any more than one learns to feel pain or to gasp for air.

Most contemporary investigators have pursued the inner bodily responses, after the James-Lange theory focused attention on their significance. Important as these undoubtedly are, Tomkins regards them as of secondary importance to the expression of emotion through the face. He regards the relationship between the face and the viscera as analogous to that between the fingers and forearm, upper arm, shoulders, and body. The fingers do not "express" what is in the forearm, or shoulder, or trunk. They rather lead than follow the movements in these organs to which they are an extension. Just as the fingers respond both more rapidly and with more precision and complexity than the grosser and slower moving arms to which they are attached, so the face expresses affect, both to others and to the self via feedback, which is more rapid and more complex than any stimulation of which the slower moving visceral organs are capable. It is the very gross and slower moving characteristic of the inner organ system which provides the counterpoint for the melody expressed by the facial solo. In short, affect is primarily facial behavior. Secondarily, it is bodily behavior, outer skeletal and inner visceral behavior. When we become aware of these facial and/or visceral responses we are aware of our affects. We may respond with these affects, however, without becoming aware of the feedback from them. Finally, we learn to generate, from memory, images of these same responses which we can become aware of with or without repetition of facial, skeletal, or visceral responses.

If the affects are primarily facial responses—what are the major affects? Tomkins has distinguished eight innate affects. There are three positive affects: First, interest or excitement, with eyebrows down, stare fixed or tracking an object. Second, enjoyment or joy, the smiling response. Third, surprise or startle, with eyebrows raised and eyeblink. There are five negative affects: First, distress or anguish, the crying response. Second, fear or terror, with eyes frozen open in fixed stare or moving away from the dreaded object to the side, and with skin pale, cold, sweating, trembling, and hair erect. Third, shame or humiliation, with eyes and head lowered. Fourth, contempt or disgust with the upper lip raised in a sneer. Fifth, anger or rage, with a frown, clenched jaw and red face.

He would account for the differences in affect activation by three general variants of a single principle: the density of neural firing or stimulation. By density he means the number of neural firings per unit time. His theory posits three discrete classes of activators of affect, each of which further amplifies the sources which activate them. These are stimulation increase, stimulation level, and stimulation decrease. Thus, there are guaranteed three distinct classes of motives—affects about stimulation which is on the increase, stimulation which maintains a steady level of density, and stimulation which is on the decrease. With respect to density of neural firing or stimulation, then, the human being is equipped for affective arousal for every major contingency. If internal or external sources of neural firing suddenly increase, he will startle, or become afraid or become interested, depending on the suddenness of increase of stimulation. If internal or external sources of neural firing reach and maintain a high, constant level of stimulation, he will respond with distress or anger, depending on the level of stimulation. If internal or external sources of neural firing suddenly decrease, he will laugh or smile with enjoyment, depending on the suddenness of decrease of stimulation. The general advantage of affective arousal to such a broad spectrum of levels and changes of level of neural firing is to make the individual care about quite different states of affairs in different ways. It should be noted that, according to Tomkins, both positive and negative affects (startle, fear, interest) are activated by stimulation increase, but only negative affects are activated by a continuing unrelieved level of stimulation (distress, anger), and only positive affects are activated by stimulation decrease (laughter, joy). Stimulation increase may, in his view, be punishing or rewarding depending on whether it is a more or less steep gradient and therefore activates fear or interest. A constantly maintained high level of neural stimulation is invariably punishing inasmuch as it activates the cry of distress or anger, depending on how high above optimal levels of stimulation the particular density of neural firing is. A suddenly reduced density of stimulation is invariably rewarding, whether the stimulation which is reduced is itself positive or negative in quality. Stated another way, such a set of mechanisms guarantees sensitivity to whatever is new, to whatever continues for any extended period of time, and to whatever is ceasing to happen, in that order.

Tomkins distinguishes sharply what he calls non-specific amplification from affects. He conceives of the reticular formation as a general amplifier which boosts the gain of *any* message, be it a sensory, motor, memory or affect message transmitted by the nervous system. In general it is conceived to sustain the state of alertness by generally amplifying all messages, and to stand in the same relationship to affect as affects do to drives.

According to Tomkins the ultimate combinations (in the human being) of affect with the receptor, analyzer, storage and effector systems produces a much more complex set of combinations than could have been built into the affect system alone, or into any predetermined affect "program."

The gain in information from the interaction of relatively independent parts or subsystems within the organism he has likened to the gain in information from a set of elements when they are combined according to the rules of a language.

Since he has argued for a sharp distinction between affects as the primary motives and the "aims" of the feedback system, let us examine what he means by these aims. The purpose of an individual is a centrally emitted blueprint which Tomkins calls the *Image*. This Image of an end state to be achieved may be compounded of diverse sensory, affective and memory imagery or any combination or transformation of these.

In many Images what is intended is not conceived as the maintenance or reduction of any affect but rather as doing something (such as taking a walk) or achieving something (such as writing a book). Despite the fact that there may be intense affect preceding and following the achievement of any Image, there may yet be a high degree of phenomenological independence between what is intended and the preceding, accompanying and consequent affect. Indeed, an individual may intend something non-affective and experience quite unintended and unexpected affect upon the achievement of his purpose or Image. In the case of predominantly habitual action it is the rule rather than the exception that affect plays a minimal role. Driving an automobile while engaged in conversation represents the operation of an Image which is minimally represented in awareness. In the Image the individual is conceived to project a possibility which he hopes to realize and that must precede and govern his behavior if he is to achieve it.

Feedback and affect, Tomkins argues, are two distinct mechanisms which may operate independent of each other. The infant passively enjoys or suffers the experience of his own affective responses long before he is capable of employing a feedback mechanism in instrumental behavior. He does not know "why" he is crying, that it might be stopped, or how to stop it. Even many years later he will sometimes experience passively, without knowledge of why or thought of remedial action, deep and intense objectless despair. Without initial awareness that there might be a specific cause that turns affect on and a specific condition which might turn it off, there is only a remote probability of using his primitive capacities to search for and find these causal conditions. The affect system will remain independent of the feedback system until the infant discovers that something can be done about such vital matters. Even after he has made this discovery it will be some time before he has achieved any degree of control over the appearance and disappearance of his affective responses. Indeed, most human beings never attain great precision of control of their affects. The individual may or may not correctly identify the "cause" of his fear or joy and may or may not learn to reduce his fear, or maintain or recapture his joy. Although his affects constitute the basic wants and don't wants of the human being, it is only gradually that they can become the targets for the feedback control system. It is a long step from the consummatory pleasure of eating and the affect of joy at the sight of the mother's face to the "wish" for these, and a still longer step to the instrumental behaviors necessary to satisfy any wish. Nonetheless, there is a high probability that the human being will ultimately utilize his feedback mechanisms to maximize his positive affects, such as excitement and joy, and to minimize his negative affects, such as distress, fear and shame, and maximize his drive pleasure and minimize his drive pain.

Affect is conceived of as a motive, by which Tomkins means immediately rewarding or punishing experience mediated by receptors activated by the individual's own responses. Motives may or may not externalize themselves in purposes. Ordinarily they do and generally tend to support strategies of maximizing reward and minimizing punishment. Human beings are so designed that they prefer to repeat rewarding affects and to reduce punishing affects, but they may or may not act on these preferences.

Concerning the relationship between learned and unlearned activators of affect, Tomkins argues that this system is the primary provider of blueprints for cognition, decision and action. The human being's ability to duplicate and reproduce himself is guaranteed not only by a responsiveness to drive signals but by a responsiveness to whatever circumstances activate positive and negative affect. Some of the triggers to interest, joy, distress, startle, disgust, aggression, fear and shame are unlearned. At the same time the affect system is also capable of being instigated by learned stimuli. In this way the human being is born biased toward and away from a limited set of circumstances and is also capable of learning to acquire new objects of interest and disinterest. By means of a variety of unlearned activators of these wanted or unwanted responses and their feedback reports, the human being is urged to explore and attempt to control the circumstances which seem to evoke his positive and negative affective responses.

No sooner do memory and analysis come into play than they too become activators of affect as potent as any of the inherited mechanisms. Indeed, it is the inheritance of a flexible, varying central assembly structure capable of activating and combining affect with varying components of this assembly that, he proposes, guarantees the basic freedom of the human being.

Problem of Definition

The area of emotional experience and behavior is one of the most confused and ill-defined in psychology. As Young puts it, "While everybody talks about emotion no one seems to know exactly what emotion is nor what to do about it. There is much confusion and uncertainty about fundamental concepts and definitions" (Young, 1961, p. 351). In the words of English and English, "*Emotion* is virtually impossible to define . . ." (1958, p. 176). This state of affairs has led some writers such as Duffy (1962) to suggest the abandonment of the term altogether.

One source of this confusion is the abundance of terms such as affect, emotion, feeling, mood, sentiment, etc., which are sometimes used inter-changeably and sometimes as distinct, separate concepts. This issue is brought up here to point out that some of the disagreement apparent in the preceding analysis of theories can be traced to this confusion in terms and definitions.

We have chosen to use the term affect. We will occasionally point up tentative distinctions or relationships among the commonly used terms in this field, but we do not believe that the present state of our knowledge permits systematic differentiation.

Affect As a Subsystem of Personality

Most of the theories considered in the foregoing pages view affect or emotion as a *response caused* by something: by changes in the nervous, glandular, or motor systems or by cognitive processes such as perception and appraisal. We believe it would be more accurate to view each of these classes of behavior as associated responses in a variable sequence. Change in activation may be frequently observed as an antecedent of affect (though in empirical studies activation is usually established as a concomitant of affect). Few would argue with the common observation that certain cognitive data lead to changes in affect. At one level of de-scription, it is permissible to speak of affect as a function of neuro-physi-ological changes which in turn result from stimulation. But to conceive of affect as a function of some organismic subsystem or as a response caused by an external or internal stimulus is a narrow, if not incorrect, conception of the "cause" of affect. Affect is a major personality subsystem with self-generating motivational properties. Affect is indigenous to the living person, but many things may amplify or attenuate affects or cause a particular affect to become predominant. Affect always has motivational properties but not necessarily a reinforcing characteristic. Conceiving of affect as inexorably rewarding or punishing puts us back in the restricting fold of ancient hedonism.

Functioning as a major subsystem of the personality, affect plays a prominent role in behavior. Integrated behavior (including productivity and creativity) is accomplished when the various subsystems of the per-sonality are functioning harmoniously. Personality disorder, breakdown in interpersonal relations, and ineffective functioning result when there is dissonance or disjunctiveness among personality subsystems.

We postulate, as does Tomkins (1962), that the affect system is the primary motivational system. Further, we believe that the perceptual-cognitive system is an excellent vehicle for modifying the affect system, thus influencing its regulatory and motivational relation to performance. We maintain that positive affect generally enhances harmonious function-ing of the personality subsystems, while negative affect tends to create dissonance among the various subsystems. In general, positive affect leads to integrative behavior and effective functioning. We do not mean that any kind of positive affect (or positive affective stimulus) will facilitate any kind of performance which the experimenter may choose to measure (Izard, 1963).

In general, negative affect leads to discordance among personality subsystems, non-integrated behavior, less effective functioning. This does not mean that any negative affect always results in psychological entropy. Certainly, prolonged negative affect would have an adverse effect; but negative affect appropriately expressed might have a net positive effect (as frequently observed in the psychotherapeutic process).

Defining affect simply in terms of the internal processes of activation or arousal results in a highly restricted view of affect (Izard, 1964). A complete definition of affect must take into account all aspects of the person's subjective experience, in particular, the way the person represents internal and external events to himself.

Subjective experience can be considered on two levels. At the first level, the experience of affect is pleasant or unpleasant feeling, according to our immediate "sense" perception or awareness of internal (neurophysiological) processes. Affect at this level typically relates to rather brief transitory states (e.g., the emotions of anger and fear), and its influence tends to be confined to behavior-of-the-moment or some *aspect* of immediate behavior. At the second level, affect is positive or negative according to its meaning for the individual, the way it is *perceived* or *conceptualized.* Affect at this level is often related to a sustained, purposive effort, and its influence tends to continue over a long period. Such affect may be likened to a mood, sentiment, or interest. Especially at this second level, it is important to consider the perceptual-cognitive framework of the affect— the way the individual experiences or maintains awareness of the affect, the internal frame-of-reference, the representational process. Acceptance of this position, in varying degrees, is evident in a number of theoretical formulations. Solley and Murphy (1960) maintain that affective stimulation results in a molding of the attentive-preparatory process in perception such that "the individual's expectancies or hypotheses lead to a selectivity in reception" (p. 20). Duffy (1962) acknowledges that "the degree of activation is in general finely adjusted to the demands of the situation, as interpreted by the individual" (p. 52).

We are saying that the neurophysiological processes described as activation or arousal are not in any sense synonymous with affect. Nor do we see a one-to-one relationship between changes in activation or arousal and changes in the quality or intensity of affect. We believe that important positive affects obtain and continue for long periods with little or no change in activation. Some instances of productive and challenging work illustrate this situation. Consistent with Murphy's (1958) position, we believe that positive affect is an important determinant and accompaniment of creative behavior. We doubt seriously that the intensity or direction of *arousal* can explain sustained creative endeavor. There is considerable doubt as to the uniqueness of the neurophysiological processes underlying effective functioning but little doubt as to the presence of affect. The quality of the affect and its role in behavior depend in large measure on the interaction of the affective and cognitive systems, on how the individual represents to himself his internal processes and the rest of his perceived world. The case for assigning a key role to the perceptual or representational process in a general theory of personality has been cogently presented by Combs and Snygg (1959), Leeper and Madison (1959), and others. Its role in affect dynamics is equally important. This perceptual-representational process is in part a function of the degree to which internal events demand awareness. The inner processes may be perceived as very vague happenings; or they may be in sharp focus, at the center of attention.

A full explication of the role of affect must also take into account the individual, group, object, or event that evokes the affect. When, for example, the affect is experienced in a social context, the other persons influence the affect and are influenced by the affect. Affect is not just what goes on within the individual's central nervous system and viscera; it also includes behavioral expression.

The expression of affect has both personal and extra-personal aspects. The personal facet relates to the manner or style of affect manifestation—facial expression, tone of voice, gestures, and other actions. The extra-personal facet relates to the object of the affect, e.g., other persons, inanimate objects, processes, goals.

There are dynamic interrelationships (or feedback processes) between the dimensions of inner experience and outward expression, but the relationships are not simple or one-to-one. Subjective experience is an important determinant of expressed behavior, but for a particular experience, such as joy or anger, there is no universal pattern of expression. Conversely, affect expression influences subjective experience in two ways. First, "acting-out" an affect (e.g., anger) changes the subjective feeling-state, or experiencing, of the affect. Secondly, a person's affect expression is a potent social stimulus, tending to evoke affective responses from the object, and these in turn tend to facilitate or impede the person's affect expression and experience.

Defining *positive affect* simply as pleasant bodily feeling is also unduly restricting. Pleasant bodily feeling is only one kind of positive affect, that which results from pleasant sensory stimulation. In everyday language, we speak of feeling good (or bad) about the way our work is going. This simple description of our internal state may actually refer to a highly important motivational construct. To *feel* good about our work may mean that the affect system is functioning harmoniously with other subsystems of the personality, and that organismic energy is being used efficiently; to *feel* bad about our effort may mean that the subsystems are functioning inharmoniously, and that energy is being used inefficiently. The affect or feeling that sustains productive work and creative activity is *positive* but not necessarily *pleasant* in the hedonistic sense or in terms of pleasurable sensory stimulation. Kierkegaardian anxiety and Murphy's urge-to-discover are positive affects but not necessarily pleasant sensation. As a man breaks out of the comfortable cultural mold and ventures into the unknown toward discovery or the creative act, he experiences anxiety. But because anxiety has been confused with negative affect (or affect that degrades the quality of behavior), a host of misconceptions has arisen as to which tensions (feelings, affects) should be reduced or suppressed and which should be freely accepted and encouraged.

STUDIES OF AFFECTIVE AND COGNITIVE FACTORS AS SIMULTANEOUS, INDEPENDENT VARIABLES

Any stimulus (object, event, situation) which involves a given individual will initiate a sequence of perceptual-cognitive and affective responses. Often the interaction of the cognitive and affective systems is sufficiently concordant to produce a seemingly unitary (perceptual-affective) response which may be described phenomenologically as the way the individual *sees* and *feels* about the stimulus. Yet, it is important to emphasize that both the affective and cognitive systems play a role in defining the impact and meaning of the stimulus.

Although the interactions and interrelations of cognitive and affective responses are undoubtedly highly complex, it is practicable to delineate the affective and cognitive components of the response sequences at both the theoretical and empirical levels (cf. Rosenberg's work on attitude change, 1956, 1960, 1963). We maintain that the affective component is the primary motivational variable and that behavior (learning, perception, performance) is altered only if the relevant affect is altered. In a situation where an individual is required to respond to positive or negative affective stimuli, cognitive data may alter the affect system by: (1) amplifying or attenuating ongoing affect or (2) instigating a competing or complementary affect.

I shall describe two studies in which we attempted to alter affect—and hence subsequent performance—via the perceptual-cognitive system. It is important to note that in our studies "cognitive data" for a given subject included his perceptions and representations of affect expressed by the experimenter.

THE EFFECT OF INTERPERSONALLY INDUCED AFFECT ON STEREOSCOPIC SELECTIVE PERCEPTION

The purpose of this study was to test whether interpersonally induced positive and negative affect would have different effects on stereoscopic selective perception. We have found that for normal subjects this technique, which involves presentation of pictures of people in a modified stereoscope, yields scores that are rather highly correlated with an independent measure of person-oriented perceptions and feelings—the positive factor of the *FIRS* (see Chapter II). Also, we wanted to see if there would be a significant interaction between personality (or adjustment) factors and the inter-personal (or treatment) conditions.

Method

Selection of adjusted and maladjusted subjects. The maladjusted group consisted of 30 confined military prisoners who had been convicted of two or more offenses and who were judged by prison guards to have demonstrated the poorest conduct during confinement. The well adjusted group consisted of 30 soldiers who had been selected by their superior officers as the best all around soldiers in an airborne division. They were judged to be self-reliant, aggressive, in excellent physical condition and to possess all the desired skills of a superior soldier. At the time of the experiment, they were instructors in a school noted for its rugged training schedule for hand-to-hand combat and other techniques of guerrilla warfare.

Interpersonal treatment. Each group of subjects was evenly divided into positive and negative treatment subgroups. The positive treatment subgroup received a "red carpet" treatment during the experimental session. They were praised for their performance on the perceptual task, and special effort was made to make them feel appreciated and worthy of respect. The experimenter attempted to create a warm, friendly relationship with each subject.

Individuals in the negative treatment subgroup were treated by the experimenter so that unpleasant feelings would be aroused between the examiner and the subject during the experimental session. Past performances of the subjects were criticized, and their abilities as subjects were questioned. The actions of the experimenter throughout the experiment were intended to be curt and irritating.

The technique for measuring stereoscopic selective perception. The measure of stereoscopic selective perception (SP) was accomplished in three steps: the development of a research stereoscope, the development of techniques for controlling differential visual acuity and convergence, and the development of suitable stimuli for stereoscopic presentation.

The stereoscope. The stereoscopic apparatus was adapted from drawings supplied by Hadley Cantril (personal communication) and the description reported by Engel (1956). The present model consists of a specially designed prism stereoscope enclosed in a light-tight box. The box is divided by a fixed partition to insure the separation of the two visual targets. This arrangement also allows for the independent illumination of the stimulus cards. Each side of the box is illuminated by a small bulb, the intensity of which can be independently varied by power stats. The lights can be placed in a circuit with a potentiometer in order to set or record the illumination level. The brackets for the stimulus cards are mounted on a movable platform which slides under the center partition. This platform can be moved by an external knob which provides a means of focusing the stereoscope. The card holders accomodate a 2 x 2 stimulus card with a viewing area of 1 3/4 in. x 1 3/4 in. Located in front of the openings are shutters operated by instantaneous solenoids. Two identical white circles are mounted, one in the center of each shutter. With the shutters closed the circles appear as one to the subject, and they keep the subject's eyes from straying between exposures. The shutter position eliminates any need for the subject to adapt to changes in illumination and focus. The controls for the lights and shutters are located in a separate box which can be kept out of the viewing range of the subject. This control box contains two power stats, a voltage meter, a power switch for placing the potentiometer in one of the light circuits, a push-push switch for operating the shutters, a red warning light to indicate the shutter position and an on-off switch for the entire unit.

Controlling for differential acuity and convergence. After the subject has focused on the white circles, the shutters are opened and two stimulus cards are exposed. One card contains a line drawing of a circle three-fourths inch in diameter and the other card a similar circle one inch in diameter. The subject is instructed to adjust the distance between his eyes and the circles until the small circle is exactly centered within the big circle. After these checks on convergence the subject is tested for differential acuity of the two eyes. This is accomplished by showing the subject a series of stimulus cards, one pair at a time. Each of the cards contained a two-digit number. Numbers were randomly placed on the cards and cards were paired at random. After the subject is in position, the shutter is opened for about one second, and the subject is asked to report the numbers he saw. If the subject reported the number on either side too frequently, light was reduced on that side. This procedure was continued for each subject until a balance of right-left responses was achieved. The subject might give a right response, a left response, or a fusion—one number from each card. Balance was arbitrarily defined as eight of ten responses that were fusions or fusions plus an equal number of right and left responses.

The stereoscopic picture stimuli. Over 50 people were photographed while attempting to portray a positive affect (enjoyment-joy) and a negative affect (anger). Photography was carefully executed to insure that the subject was essentially in the same position for both poses. From this pool of pictures, judges selected individuals whose poses best portrayed contrasting pleasant and unpleasant expressions and which could be mounted in such a way that each would stimulate virtually identical areas of the retina. There were 26 pairs in the final series. The pleasant and unpleasant expression of the same individual made up a stimulus pair or stereograph. Similar procedures were followed in developing a second type of stereograph. The 22 stereographs of the second type consisted of two pictures of an interpersonal scene, each involving the same two people; one scene displayed positive affect (friendly interaction), the other negative affect (hostile interaction). Administering the stereoscopic stimuli consisted of (a) placing the stereograph in the stereoscope, (b) opening the shutters for approximately one second, and (c) having the subject indicate what he saw.

Results

Since both the adjusted and maladjusted groups were randomly halved for the positive and negative treatments, the data on stereoscopic selective perception were handled as a 2 x 2 factorial. The responses to the two kinds of stereographs (faces, interpersonal scenes) were considered separately. The analyses of variance for both sets of responses are presented in Table 1.

Table 1 Analysis of variance for the data on stereoscopic selective presentation

		Faces		Scenes	
Source	df	MS	F	MS	F
Groups (Adjusted & maladjusted)	1	.13	2.16	.01	.20
Treatment (Positive & negative)	1	.56	9.31**	.37	7.70**
Groups x treatment	1	.13	2.16	.09	1.87
Error	26	.06		.05	

** $F_{.99}$ (1, 26) = 7.72

There was no difference between the adjusted and maladjusted groups in the selective perception of faces or scenes manifesting positive affect. However, the effect of treatment (positive or negative interpersonal interaction) was significant well beyond the .01 level for the facial stereographs and at approximately the .01 level for the interpersonal scenes. The effect of the interaction between adjustment and interpersonal treatment was not significant.

Discussion

In attempting to manipulate the subjects' affect, we thought there might very well be an interaction between groups and treatment. Particularly since the maladjusted group was substantially lower on self-esteem, it was expected that individuals in this group might respond in a more extreme fashion to the negative treatment. The lack of a significant interaction effect indicates that this was not the case. Indeed we feel that it is quite worth noting that groups differing widely on ratings of adjustment and psychometric measures of person evaluation and self-esteem (see Chapter II) did not respond differently to positive and negative interpersonal treatment on the measure of stereoscopic selective perception.

One might wonder why there was not a difference between the adjusted and maladjusted groups on our measure of stereoscopic selective perception. (Both groups saw considerably fewer positive percepts than the college female subjects described in Chapter II). Some light may be thrown on this if we reconsider the nature of the stereograph, the stereoscopic response and the constituency of our well-adjusted group. A stereograph consisted of a pleasant, friendly pose (or interpersonal interaction) and an unpleasant, hostile pose. The subject looked into the stereoscope and indicated which pose or scene he saw. We believe this response reflects a readiness to achieve positive or negative person percepts. A low score (few positive percepts) can be interpreted as high sensitivity to unfriendly or hostile faces. The adjusted soldiers obtained their high behavioral ratings partly on the basis of their aggressiveness. As already noted, they were instructors in a school known for its rugged training in hand-to-hand combat and other techniques of guerrilla warfare. These facts may account for the relatively low score of the well-adjusted group and its lack of difference from the maladjusted group on this particular measure.

THE EFFECT OF SELF-ESTEEM AND INDUCED AFFECT ON INTERPERSONAL PERCEPTION, OPINION CHANGE, AND INTELLECTIVE FUNCTIONING

We have defined interpersonal positive affect as favorable personal feeling, interest, acceptance, or esteem directed toward another person (Izard, 1960). The basic postulate relating to this construct is that positive affect is a significant determinant of positive perception and effective functioning.

The positive affect postulate derives from the field of psychotherapy. The major approaches to psychotherapy recognize the significance of some factor such as we have described as interpersonal positive affect—transference (Freud), respect, esteem (Jung), social interest (Adler), love (Rank, Fromm), or positive regard (Rogers). An essential ingredient of psychotherapy is interpersonal behavior based on positive affect. The therapist's expression of positive feeling, self-involving interest, and esteem is an essential ingredient in the patient's development of more positive perceptions of self and others and of more effective use of his capacities. Our basic postulate is an extension of this psychotherapeutic principle: behavioral expressions of positive affect tend to enhance positive perception and effective behavior in any situation (Izard, 1959). The aim of this study was to examine the effects of interpersonally induced affect and self-esteem on interpersonal perception, opinion change, and intellective functioning in a two-person interaction.

Four specific hypotheses were tested: (1) Experimentally induced positive and negative affect have differential effects on intellective functioning; (2) both induced affect and self-esteem are significantly related to interpersonal perception in the experimental situation; (3) induced affect and self-esteem are significantly related to opinion change, positive affect being positively related to change, and self-esteem being negatively related to change; (4) there is a significant interaction between induced affect and self-esteem on the measures of intellective functioning and interpersonal perception.

Method

The procedure consisted of three steps. Self-ratings were administered in order to level subjects on self-esteem or positive self-related perceptions and feelings. The experimenter, acting as another student member of a dyad, attempted to induce positive and negative affect by means of a role-playing technique. The experimenter and the subject alternated in administering the eight tasks which constituted the experiment proper. During this period the affect induction procedure was continued.

Leveling subjects on self-esteem. In an introductory course in psychology, 72 white male students were initially administered the Tennessee Self-Concept Scale (TSCS) (Fitts, 1954) and the Self Related Positive Affect Scale (SRPAS). The SRPAS is a 24 item polar adjective scale designed specifically to measure positiveness of self-related perceptions and feelings. Fitts (1954) has demonstrated satisfactory reliability for the TSCS. The correlation between the TSCS and the SRPAS was .64 for the present sample.

The subjects were rank ordered on the TSCS and SRPAS separately. The ranks were combined, and the subjects were then divided into four levels of self-esteem. They were randomly assigned within levels to the positive and negative treatments.

Affect induction. The appropriate affect for the two experimental treatments was induced by the use of a structured role-playing technique in which the experimenter followed a prepared protocol. This procedure was supplemented by instructions and prescribed handling of the subject by an assistant before the subject met the experimenter.

Upon entering the building, the student was greeted by the experimenter's assistant, who presented himself as the person conducting the experiment. As he was being taken to the experimental room, affect induction was begun by creating a set to expect a compatible or incompatible "partner" for the positive or negative conditions, respectively. In both cases the subject was asked to wait, and five minutes were allowed to lapse before the assistant introduced the experimenter as the other subject. After being introduced, the partners were left alone for five minutes to "get acquainted" while the assistant went across the hall to prepare the experimental materials.

At the conclusion of this five-minute interval the assistant returned with the materials, read the instructions for alternating administration of the tasks, and informed the partners that if they had any trouble or did not understand anything they were to work it out for themselves, and left. From this point on, the positive or negative affect was induced by the prepared statements which the experimenter introjected at various places in the tasks and by false ratings presumably made by the experimenter on the spot, but which were actually based on the subject's self-ratings.

The experiment. The experimenter and subject alternated as administrator: reading the instructions, timing the tasks, and collecting and checking the responses of each other. This gave a "natural" reason for the subject to look at the ratings made by the experimenter on the SRPAS. This was set up as task 1 for the dyad. The experimenter rated the subject on the spot, but he handed the subject a contrived rating which had been prepared previously and which deviated from the subject's self-rating in a positive or negative direction, depending on the condition to which he had been assigned. Having the subject administer one-half of the tasks was intended to involve him more as a contributing member of the team. Of the total of eight tasks, four were measures of perceptions of self, experimenter, and the experiment (tasks 1, 6, 7, 8). Task 1 required the subject to rate the experimenter on the SRPAS after five minutes of interaction during which the experimenter began the affect induction procedure. Task 8 was a repeated measure of the subject's perception of the experimenter on the SRPAS after the full hour of affect induction. Task 7 was a rating of the experimenter as a "team member" and of the experiment. Task 6 was a repeated measure of the subject's self-perception on SRPAS. This allowed us to examine self-esteem as a dependent measure. The pre-experimental SRPAS was obtained a month before the experiment.

Task 5 was an opinion change measure. Both members read a brief "clinical report" about a juvenile offender, Johnny Rocco, and a list of seven alternative approaches for treatment. The seven treatments were ordered in the amounts of love or punishment necessary to change the behavior of Johnny Rocco. The experimenter attempted to change the opinion of the subject. It was arranged so that the subject always revealed his opinion first, and then the experimenter chose a treatment two steps away from that chosen by the subject. If an initial compromise was made, the experimenter "changed his mind" and moved a step farther away so that "compromise" was now necessary at a new level. This process continued for ten minutes.

Tasks 2, 3, and 4 were measures of intellective functioning or productivity. Task 2 was a form of multiple uses task similar to that developed by Guilford (1956). Task 3 was the digit span subtest of the WAIS. Task 4 consisted of verbalizing solutions to four problems of ingenuity.

All task variables were analyzed using a treatment by levels analysis of variance, except task 5, which was analyzed by chi square.

Results

The pre- and post-treatment self-esteem (SRPAS) scores correlated .751 for the subjects given the positive affect treatment, and .743 for the subjects in the negative affect treatment group. Further, the analysis of variance showed that the experimental treatment had no effect on self-esteem scores.

Table 2 summarizes the analyses of the subjects' ratings of the experimenter and the experiment. These results support the hypothesis that both induced affect and self-esteem are significantly related to the subjects' perception of the experimenter (affect inducer) and the experiment.

Table 2 Treatment (induced affect) by levels (self-esteem) analysis of variance of
measures of interpersonal perception

Source	df	(a) Task 1 (SRPA) Ss' early perception of E		(b) Task 8 (SRPA) Ss' later perception of E		(c) Task 7 Ss' over-all perception of experiment	
		MS	F	MS	F	MS	F
Treatment	1	1720.92	6.55*	5618.00	18.92**	506.69	14.13***
Level	3	1651.31	6.28**	1705.57	5.74**	77.50	2.16+
T x L	3	419.85	1.60	237.00	.80	312.08	.34
Error	64	262.83		296.93		35.87	

+, *, **, *** indicate $p < .06, .05, .01, .001$, respectively

The results do not support the hypothesis of a treatment and self-esteem interaction effect on interpersonal perception.

The role-playing technique was efficacious within five minutes in influencing the subjects' interpersonal perceptions. More positive ratings were given the experimenter by the positive treatment group (task 1). That these "first impressions" were confirmed and strengthened as the hour proceeded was shown by the greater effects in the interpersonal perception measures taken at the end of the hour (tasks 7 and 8).

Self-esteem was related to the subjects' perception of the experimenter. The relationship was about the same for the measures taken early (task 1) and late (task 8) in the experimental session. The rating of the performance of the dyad, of the experimenter as a partner, and of the experiment (task 7) was significantly influenced by the induced affect but only marginally related to self-esteem.

Chi square was used for the analysis of task 5, the measure of opinion change. Significant chi squares were obtained for treatment and self-esteem. That is, more subjects changed their opinion in the positive condition than in the negative condition; and the higher their self-esteem, the less willing they were to change their opinion.

Table 3 summarizes the results for the measures of intellective functioning. These results supported hypothesis 1, showing that experimentally induced positive and negative affect had differential effects on intellective functioning and productivity. Each of these three intellective measures was influenced by the affect-induction techniques, higher productivity being related to the positive affect condition. Intellective functioning was not related to level of self-esteem.

The hypothesized interaction between induced affect and self-esteem on the measures of productivity, was partially supported. Interaction effects were present in two of the intellective tasks, multiple uses and problem solving, which intercorrelated .55 in the present sample. There was no interaction effect on the WAIS digit span, a task which did not correlate significantly with the other two intellective tasks.

Table 3   Treatment (induced affect) by levels (self-esteem) analysis of variance of measures of intellective functioning

Source	df	(a) Task 2 Multiple uses		(b) Task 3 Digit span		(c) Task 4 Problem solving	
		MS	F	MS	F	MS	F
Treatment	1	210.12	10.70**	45.13	8.54**	154.00	9.79**
Levels	3	7.87	.40	2.50	.47	14.53	.89
T x L	3	43.42	2.21+	5.05	.96	63.94	3.94*
Error	64	19.64		5.25		16.24	

+, *, **, indicate $p < .06, .05, .01$, respectively

Discussion

Self-esteem considered as a dependent variable supported the contention that it was a relatively enduring aspect of personality which was uninfluenced by the affect-induction treatment. The two sets of SRPAS scores correlated in the 70's with an intervening hour of affect induction. A previous test-retest reliability check showed a correlation of .77 for 38 female undergraduates and a correlation of .84 for 25 male undergraduates. This supported the findings of no treatment effects on self-esteem scores in the analysis of variance. The subjects' self-esteem as we measured it was not appreciably influenced by the affect induction; however, their intellective performance, their perception of others,, and their willingness to change opinion were influenced by the role-playing technique. This suggests that subjects interact in a way that maintains their self-perceptions at the expense of other-perception. That is, when treatment conditions were aimed at decreasing or increasing the subject's self-esteem, his self-esteem remained the same while the positiveness of his perception of the experimenter decreased or increased according to the particular condition.

The fact that the subjects' perceptions of others, as well as their overall feelings of accomplishment, are directly influenced by level of self-esteem supports findings in the literature which suggest that perceptions of productivity are influenced by the interpersonal perceptions of members in a group—Mussen & Porter (1959), Porter & Kaufman (1959). Willingness to change opinion was also directly related to self-esteem. This is consistent with Rasmussen and Zander's (1954) finding that subjects tend to interact in a manner that maintains their level of self-esteem. Level of self-esteem was not related to actual level of intellective functioning.

The most consistent results in the study were those that indicated that induced positive or negative affect were important factors in intellective functioning, interpersonal perceptions, and willingness to change opinion. Positive affect was associated with increased intellective functioning, more positive interpersonal perceptions, and greater willingness to change opinions. This extends the work of several investigators, Rosenthal & Cofer (1948), Fiedler (1961), Pepinsky (1961), who have successfully used role-playing techniques to induce change in affective variables. The earlier studies utilized one role player in a multi-person interaction in contrast to this study's two-person group.

The hypothesized interaction effects were not supported by the data related to interpersonal perception but were partially supported by the indices of intellective functioning. There were no interaction effects for the digit span test, but induced affect had differential effects on subjects at different levels of self-esteem for the multiple uses and problem solving tasks.

For the purposes of studying the interaction effects, an analysis of the means of the four groups was made. It showed that persons in the positive affect condition with high self-esteem (levels I and II) were more influenced by the treatment than were subjects with low self-esteem (levels III and IV). Interpreting this in the framework of the positive affect postulate, the subjects with high self-esteem had greater capacity to receive and respond to positive interpersonal treatment. For them such treatment was more in line with self-related perceptions and feelings and hence more believable. They could be more acceptant, in the psychotherapeutic sense of this term, and, consequently, more affected. In the negative treatment condition the extremes (levels I and IV) were more influenced by the treatment than were the others (levels II and III). The fact that the two treatment effects interacted differently with self-esteem is consistent with another line of research where we found relatively independent positive and negative factors in person evaluation, as measured by responses to pictures of people (see Chapter II). The negative treatment may have been effective by removing positive affect, by creating negative affect, or more likely by doing both. For the high self-esteem group it was probably a matter of removing interpersonal positive affect, decreasing their self-involvement and motivation. For the more vulnerable low self-esteem group it was probably more a matter of creating negative affect with its consequent debilitating effects.

THE EFFECTS OF EXPERIMENTER ATTITUDES AND AFFECTS
ON RESPONSE TO PAINFUL STIMULATION

Considering the affect system as the primary motivational system presents a challenge to prevalent conceptions of the role of the stimulus in instigating and altering behavior. Perhaps it was the influence of physics and physiology from without and of psychophysics and S-R theory from within that made pervasive the concept of the stimulus as the real and sufficient cause of behavior. Textbooks in general psychology attest to the predominance of this position: a stimulus is any "physical energy that can excite a receptor and produce an effect on the organism" (Krech & Crutchfield, 1958, p. 54); and "Activity and experience occur in response to external and internal excitation or stimuli" (Sells, 1962, p. 29). Helson

(1964) has given impetus to this view of the stimulus, maintaining that even in the study of personality and interpersonal relations it is possible and most profitable to establish functional relations between intensity of stimulation and magnitude of response. He assumes that it is the intensity of the stimulus, not its bene- or nociceptive nature, that determines its effectiveness in altering behavior.

Conceptualizations of the role of the stimulus (physical energy) in instigating and altering behavior have shifted somewhat with the recent work on activation and the advent of affective-arousal theory (Hilgard, 1963). The shift for some theorists was from stimulus intensity to intensity of organismic arousal—from amount of energy emanating from the stimulus-object to amount of energy released in the tissues via metabolic processes (Duffy, 1962, p. 17).

Although the tendency to ascribe a crucial role to the stimulus (excitation, physical energy) is quite pervasive, considerable strength is accruing to the contrasting position which holds that the critical determinant is the individual's interpretation of the stimulus. A thorough-going acceptance of this latter view leads to a phenomenological or perceptual framework like that of Combs and Snygg (1959) and calls for behavioral analysis from the standpoint of the behaving organism. Acceptance of this position in varying degrees is evident in a number of theoretical formulations. Solley and Murphy (1960) maintain that "the individual's expectancies or hypotheses lead to a *selectivity* in reception" (p. 20). Duffy (1962) acknowledges that "the degree of activation is in general finely adjusted to the demands of the situation, as *interpreted* by the individual. . . ." (p. 52). Tomkins (1962) has said that the "real" causes of affect (the primary motivational system) are patterns of neural stimulation, but "the individual's *interpretations* . . . of these causes . . . are responsible for transforming motives into governing images" (p. 248, italics ours).

Helson (1964), though his emphasis is clearly on the stimulus and stimulus intensity, has actually made a strong case for rejecting absolute stimulus intensity as a meaningful variable. He maintains that intensity is always relative to the individual's own adaptation level. He emphasizes the importance of evaluating reinforcing stimuli by reference to internal norms. Drawing on Helson's work, Fiske and Maddi (1961) went a step further in recognizing that stimulation has two properties in addition to intensity: variation and meaning.

Our own studies have supported the position that the way an individual perceives and represents the stimulus to himself is the critical determinant of subsequent behavior (Izard, 1964). They have suggested that for complex human behavior a phenomenological analysis of stimulation may have greater explanatory power than strictly quantitative indices of the density of neural firing or energy release within the tissues. We have shown that experimenter expression of positive affects and attitudes resulted in more pleasant subjective experience, more favorable interpersonal perceptions and feelings, and greater performance efficiency than did the expression of negative affect. The present study was designed to test whether the experimenter's expressed attitudes and affects could alter subjects' interpretation of painful stimulation as well as their concomitant learning efficiency. The hypothesis was that the more positive the experimenter's attitude and expressed affect, the less negative the subjects' subjective experience and the more efficient their learning in the shock-induced pain condition.

Method

Subjects. The subjects were 48 undergraduate males enrolled in a general psychology course.

Materials. Words used in the paired-associate learning task were selected from the Condensed Semantic Atlas (Jenkins, 1960) with neutrality as the criterion.

An apparatus was specially designed for presenting the words during the association task. The device was such that exposure time of the stimulus and response words could be electronically controlled.

An apparatus for administering a shock consisted of an adjustable DC power supply (0-500 volts) which charges a capacitor which drains when the switch is closed by an electrical relay. The shock cannot be maintained longer than the fraction of a second that it takes the capacitor to discharge.

Procedure

The principal dependent variables were total correct responses on the paired-associate learning task, recall, and subjective ratings of anxiety and hostility.

The subjects participated in the experiment one at a time and were randomly assigned to one of three groups, a positive treatment group, a neutral treatment group, and a negative treatment group. The procedure for the groups was identical except that attitudes and feelings (interpersonal affect) expressed by the experimenter were different for each group.

The experimenter for the positive group was relaxed and friendly and the instructions gave a good rationale for subjecting the participant to painful shock. The subject was told that he would not be shocked unless it was important to the study for which the experimenter expressed enthusiasm. The experimenter told the subject that he might be able to capitalize on the shock to facilitate learning by using it as a signal to focus his attention. Between trials the experimenter was encouraging, using statements such as "fine" and "I can see you are using the shock to advantage."

The experimenter for the negative group behaved in a cold and formal manner. The experimenter implied that the decision to include shock in the procedure was completely arbitrary but indicated that nothing the subject could do would stop or alter the shock routine. Between trials the experimenter was discouraging, using statements such as "not so good" and "I can see that shock disorganizes you."

The experimenter for the neutral group was, insofar as possible, only an apparatus operator. All instructions were written down on cards and handed to the subject. The experimenter answered questions only if they were essential to the running of the experiment. The content of the instructions was the same for all groups except for the affect-manipulation phrases mentioned above.

The subject's main task was to learn 10 word-word associations, five of them under a condition of shock-induced pain. Six trials were used with three randomizations. The stimulus word was presented for two seconds, and then after a 1.5 second interval the stimulus word and the response word were presented together for two seconds. The shock (as much as the subject was willing to take) was administered 1.8 second after the first word of the pair was presented. Each subject was shocked on five of the 10 word pairs on each of the 6 learning trials. Shock was administered in a fixed random order, regardless of whether the response was correct or incorrect.

After the learning trials, the subject was asked to write down as many of the pairs as he could recall. At the end of 1.5 minutes he was asked to add any additional words that he could remember from the associations regardless of whether he could complete a pair. A two minute time limit was used for the complete recall task.

Table 4a   Analysis of variance for the learning scores: main effects

Source	SS	df	MS	F	p
Between Ss	535.781	47			
Instructions	69.087	2	34.544	3.331	.05
Positive vs. neg.	65.703	1	65.703	6.335	.025
Remainder	3.384	1	3.384	< 1	
Ss w. groups	466.694	45	10.371		
Within Ss	802.700	432			
Shock-nonshock	91.002	1	91.002	61.157	.005
Instr. x Sh-NSh	4.330	2	2.165	1.455	.10
Sh-NSh x Ss w. groups	66.968	45	1.488		
Trials	397.533	4	99.383	176.524	.005
Instr. x trials	8.330	8	1.041	1.849	.10
Trials x Ss w. groups	101.337	180	.563		
Sh-NSh x Trls	7.675	4	1.919	2.793	.05
Instr. x Sh-NSh x Trls	1.836	8	.230	< 1	
Sh-NSh x trials x Ss w. groups	123.689	180	.687		
Total	1338.481	479			

Finally, the subject was asked to complete a short scale designed to measure extent of anxiety and hostility feelings during the experiment.

Results

Scores on the learning task were subjected to a Lindquist Type VI analysis of variance. The results of this analysis, presented in Table 4a, supported the main hypothesis. The effect of the instructions (cognitive data, including the experimenter's expressed attitudes and affects) produced different rates of learning for the three groups ($p<.05$). The orthogonal comparisons between groups showed a highly significant difference in learning efficiency attributable to the contrasting positive and negative instructions ($p<.025$). An inspection of Figure 1 shows that the learning curve for the neutral group was approximately halfway between the curves for the positive and negative groups, although it did not differ significantly from either (Newman-Keuls procedure; Winer, 1962, p. 309).

The significant shock-nonshock x trials interaction indicates that the shock did not have the same average effect at every trial. Inspection of

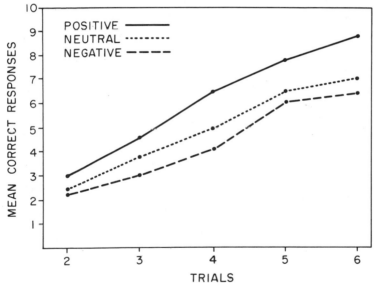

Figure 1.   Learning trials of affect groups. $N = 16$ subjects each group.

the shock and nonshock learning curves shown in Figure 2 shows that the difference between the two decreased substantially on the last trial.

The fact that the instructions x shock-nonshock interaction term approached significance ($p<.10$) justified a look at the simple effects of instructions and shock separately (Table 4b). The analyses of the learning scores for shock words alone showed that the effect of the instructions was highly significant even for the specific part of the learning task that was accomplished under shock-induced pain. For the nonshock words the

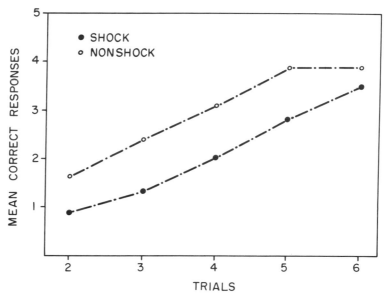

Figure 2. Learning trials of shock and nonshock words (affect groups combined). $N = 48$ subjects.

effect of instructions was also highly significant. Inspection of the shock and nonshock learning curves for the three groups separately (Figure 3) showed that the instructions separated the three groups more evenly during shock than nonshock. Figure 3 shows, as was expected, the least separation between shock and nonshock learning curves for the neutral or no-instruction group. The group that received the positive treatment

Table 4b Analysis of variance for the learning scores: simple effects

Source	SS	df	MS	F	p
Shock words only					
Instructions	26.408	2	13.204	7.767	.005
Trials	221.684	4	55.421	32.600	.005
Instr. x trials	6.966	8	.871	< 1	
Error	382.438	225	1.700		
Total	637.496	239			
Nonshock words only					
Instructions	47.008	2	23.504	14.057	.005
Trials	183.525	4	45.881	27.441	.005
Instr. x trials	3.200	8	.400	< 1	
Error	376.250	225	1.672		
Total	609.983	239			

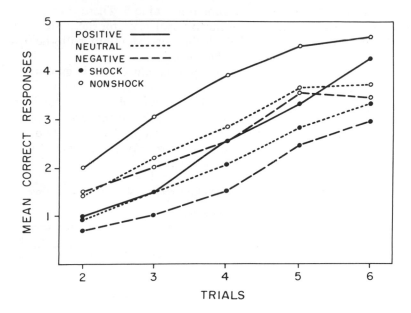

Figure 3.   Shock and nonshock word learning trials of the three affect groups. $N = 16$ subjects each group.

and good rationale for the shock learned the shock words about as rapidly as the negatively treated group learned the nonshock words.

The analysis of variance and the new Duncan Multiple Range Test

Table 5   Analysis of variance and multiple range test for total recall scores

Analysis of variance

Source	df	MS	F	p
Instructions	2	53.58	3.51	.05
Error	45	15.26		
Total	47			

Multiple range test

Means	Negative 12.62	Neutral 14.00	Positive 16.25	Shortest significant ranges p = .05
Negative 12.62		1.38	3.63	$R_2 = 2.79$
Neutral 14.00			2.25	$R_3 = 2.94$
	Negative	Neutral	Positive	

(MRT) for the recall scores are shown in Table 5. These results parallel those for the learning scores. The mean recall score for the positive group was significantly greater than that for the negative group, with the neutral group mean falling between the other two.

An analysis of the ratings of the subjects' anxiety feelings during the experiment revealed no significant differences among groups, but the means were in the predicted order. The analysis of variance for hostility feelings (see Table 6) showed that the negative group was significantly more hostile than the neutral and positive groups. The latter two groups had identical means, their magnitude indicating a very low degree of hostility.

Table 6 Analysis of variance and multiple range test for hostility scores

Analysis of variance

Source	df	MS	F	p
Instructions	2	11.00	4.68	$<.025$
Error	37	2.35		
Total	39			

Multiple range test

	Negative	Neutral	Positive	Shortest significant ranges
Means	1.21	2.77	2.77	p = .05
Negative 1.21		1.56	1.56	R_2 = .69
Neutral 2.77			0	R_3 = .73
	Negative	Neutral	Positive	

Discussion

Our previous research has shown that the experimenter's attitudes and feelings influence the subject's perception of the experimenter as well as the subject's own feelings and performance on experimental tasks. The present study demonstrated that experimenter-expressed attitudes and affects can alter the subjects' subjective experience and performance efficiency during painful stimulation. The results lend further support to the view that the subject's perceptual-affective appraisal of the stimulus, the way he represents it to himeslf, is a critical factor in altering subsequent behavior.

It seems reasonable to assume that subjective experience during learning under pain was dynamically related to the learning performance. The negatively treated subjects were the most hostile and at the same time the least efficient learners. The interpersonal treatment was effective in altering both affective and cognitive responses during painful stimulation.

As Tomkins has pointed out, pain is a potent and certain instigator of affect. Despite the great individual differences that occur in response to pain (Tomkins, 1962, p. 193 ff.), we showed differences in affective reactions between the positively and negatively treated groups. If we accept the subjects' retrospective report of hostility feelings as a valid index of subjective experience during the experiment, we can infer that the experimenter altered the subject's affect, at least for the negatively treated group.

The fact that the effects of shock and interpersonal treatment on affective reactions are confounded restricts the inferences we can draw regarding the dynamics of the experimenter-subject interaction. All we can say is that shock administered under neutral and positive conditions generated the same amount of hostility, and that the amount was very small.

Since the degree of hostility generated by shock under the neutral condition was so slight, it was hardly possible for the positive condition to effect a decrease in hostility. If we take shock under the neutral condition as the standard, these results argue for the unimportance of the physical stimulus of shock as a cause of anger or hostility.

On the other hand, the administration of shock under the negative condition created a significant amount of hostility. This suggests that for the negatively treated group the experimenter increased the frustration of shock and in other ways thwarted the subjects and made them less comfortable. Further, we believe that within the negative group the experimenter-subject interactions resulted in different conscious attitudes and feelings toward the experimenter, the experiment, and participation in the research. In particular, the rationale, attitude, and affect expressed by the experimenter gave the shock a different *meaning* than it had for the positively and neutrally treated subjects. It is reasonable to assume that the painful shock had rather negative connotations for the subjects who were treated coolly, given to understand that shock was used arbitrarily, and disparaged during the learning trials. The significantly higher hostility scores for the negative group support this line of reasoning.

The lack of difference between the positive and neutral groups on either anxiety or hostility limits what we can say about the role of affect in the learning situation. The neutral group differed significantly from the negative group on hostility but not on performance. The neutral group learned faster but not significantly so. We feel confident in attributing the observed differences in learning to the interpersonal treatment conditions—the experimenter's expressed attitudes and affects. We feel fairly certain, too, that the interpersonal treatments were successful in inducing or altering affects. Indeed, a number of subjects volunteered post-experimental reports that suggested that the positive, negative, and neutral groups were widely separated on some affective reactions not measured by the anxiety and hostility scales. Thus, we can make a reasonable guess that other affects contributed to the differences in the learning curves for the three groups.

SUMMARY

We have set forth the basic postulate that the affect system is a major subsystem of the personality, the primary motivational system. Considerable attention was given to the problem of defining affect, particularly positive affect. We emphasized the highly important role of the perceptual-cognitive system as a vehicle for modifying the affect system: amplifying, attenuating, instigating affect. The three studies reported have shown how cognitive data, especially data that include perceptions of expressed affect, can effectively alter affective response, subjective experience, and performance.

REFERENCES

Arnold, Magda B. *Emotion and personality*. New York: Columbia Univer. Press, 1960.

Bull, Nina. The attitude theory of emotion. New York: *Nervous and Mental Disease Monogr.*, 1951, No. 81.

Combs, A. W., & Snygg, D. *Individual behavior*. New York: Harper, 1959.

Duffy, Elizabeth. *Activation and behavior*. New York: Wiley, 1962.

Engel, E. The role of content in binocular resolution. *Amer. J. Psychol.*, 1956, *69*, 87-91.

English, H.B., & English, Ava C. *A comprehensive dictionary of psychological and psychoanalytical terms*. New York: McKay, 1958.

Fiedler, F. E. Interpersonal perception and psychological adjustment of group members. Annual Report. Contract DA 49-007-MD-2000. Urbana, Ill., January, 1961.

Fiske, D. W., & Maddi, S. R. *Functions of varied experience*. Homewood, Ill.: Dorsey, 1961.

Fitts, W. H. The role of the self concept in social perception. Unpublished doctoral dissertation, Vanderbilt Univer., 1954.

Guilford, J. P. The structure of intellect. *Psychol. Bull.*, 1956, *53*, 207-293.

Helson, H. Adaptation-level as a basis for a quantitative theory of frames of reference. *Psychol. Rev.*, 1948, *55*, 297-313.

Helson, H. Current trends and issues in adaptation-level theory. *Amer. Psychologist*, 1964, *19*, 26-38.

Hilgard, E. R. Motivation in learning theory. In S. Koch (Ed.), *Psychology: a study of a science*, Vol. 4. New York: McGraw-Hill, 1963.

Izard, C. E. Positive affect and behavioral effectiveness. Duplicated manuscript, Vanderbilt University, 1959.

Izard, C. E. Personality similarity and friendship. *J. abnorm. soc. Psychol.*, 1960, *61*, 47-51.

Izard, C. E., Livsey, W. F., Cherry, E. S., Hall, G. F., Wall, Pat, & Bacon, Ruth. Effects of affective picture stimuli on the learning, perception, and affective scale values of previously neutral words. ONR Technical Report No. 19, Vanderbilt Univer., 1963.

Izard, C. E. The effects of role-played emotion on affective reactions, intellective functioning, and evaluative ratings of the actress. *J. clin. Psychol.*, 1964, *20*, 444-446.

Jenkins, J. J. Degree of polarization and scores on the principal factors for concepts in the semantic atlas. *Amer. J. Psychol.*, 1960, *73*, 274-279.

Krech, D., & Crutchfield, R. *Elements of psychology.* New York: Knopf, 1958.

Leeper, R. W., & Madison, P. *Toward understanding human personalities.* New York: Appleton-Century-Crofts, 1959.

McClelland, D. C., Atkinson, J. W., Clark, R. H., and Lowell, E. L. *The achievement motive.* New York: Appleton-Century-Crofts, 1953.

Murphy, G. *Human potentialities.* New York: Basic Books, 1958.

Mussen, P. H., & Porter, L. W. Personal motivation and self-conceptions associated with effectiveness and ineffectiveness in emergent groups. *J. abnorm. soc. Psychol.*, 1959, *59*, 23-27.

Pepinsky, P. N. Originality in group productivity. Contract Nonr 495 (15) (N12 170-396), Ohio State University, 1961.

Porter, L. W., & Kaufmann, R. A. The relationship between a top-middle management self-description scale and behavior in a group situation. *J. appl. Psychol.*, 1959, *43*, 345-348.

Rasmussen, G., & Zander, A. Group membership and self-evaluation. *Human Rel.*, 1954, *7*, 239-251.

Rosenberg, M. J. Cognitive structure and attitudinal affect. *J. abnorm. soc. Psychol.*, 1956, *53*, 367-372.

Rosenberg, M. J. An evaluation of models for attitude change. Presented at APA, 1963.

Rosenberg, M. J., Hovland, C. I., McGuire, Abelson, R. P., & Brehm, J. W. *Attitude organization and change.* New Haven: Yale Univer. Press, 1960.

Rosenthal, D., & Cofer, C. N. The effect on group performance of an indifferent and neglectful attitude shown by one group member. *J. exp. Psychol.*, 1948, *38*, 568-577.

Schachter, S., & Singer, J. E. Cognitive, social, and physiological determinants of emotional state. *Psychol. Rev.*, 1962, *69*, 379-399.

Schlosberg, H. Three dimensions of emotion. *Psychol. Rev.*, 1954, *61*, 81-88.

Sells, S. B. *Essentials of psychology.* New York: Ronald Press, 1962.

Solley, C. M., & Murphy, G. *Development of the perceptual world.* New York: Basic Books, 1960.

Tomkins, S. S. *Affect, imagery, consciousness.* Vol. I. *The positive affects.* New York: Springer, 1962.

Winer, B. J. *Statistical principals in experimental design.* New York: McGraw-Hill, 1962.

Young, P. T. The role of affective processes in learning and motivation. *Psychol. Rev.*, 1959, *66*, 104-125.

Young, P. T. *Motivation and emotion.* New York: Wiley, 1961.

The effects of affective picture stimuli on learning, perception and the affective values of previously neutral symbols

Carroll E. Izard
with Sylvain Nagler
Don Randall
Jean Fox

PART A

The use of carefully scaled affective stimuli as a variable in human learning is relatively unexplored. We were, in fact, unable to find any published research bearing directly on the problem and procedures presented in this chapter. There are, however, numerous studies in verbal learning and perception which have some relevance. For one thing, there is evidence that words associated with unacceptable needs or values have higher visual recognition thresholds and are learned more slowly than are neutral or valued words—Bruner & Postman (1947), Postman & Schneider (1951). In line with this, Worchel (1955) found that once new associations are established with negatively affective material, retention for such associations are poorer than for associations with neutral material. Data of a similar nature can be found as early as 1938 when Sharp (1938) found that unpleasant materials exhibited a considerable amount of repression (less recall) relative to neutral materials. McGeoch and Irion (1952) state that the consensus is that affectively colored experiences are recalled more readily than neutral ones, and pleasant more readily than unpleasant. Bugelski (1956) concludes that "There appears to be no serious reason for doubting that when the learning material is repugnant or otherwise 'unacceptable' or actually disturbing *at the time of learning* that the learner should have some difficulty about learning, and if learning is difficult, retention should be correspondingly difficult" (p. 333).

Kleinsmith and Kaplan (1963, 1964) used GSR measures to define conditions of high arousal and low arousal, and found that nonsense syllable paired associates learned under low arousal exhibited high immediate recall and rapid forgetting. High arousal associates exhibited a marked reminiscence effect—low immediate recall and high permanent memory. In a variation on their experimental design, they used meaning-

The research reported in this chapter was supported by Vanderbilt-ONR Contract Nonr 2149 (03), Carroll E. Izard, Principal Investigator. The opinions and conclusions do not necessarily reflect those of the United States Department of the Navy.

ful paired associates as stimuli and found that high arousal associates showed stronger permanent memory and weaker immediate memory than low arousal associates. They interpret their findings in terms of the hypothesis of perseverative consolidation which predicts that under conditions of high arousal the rapidly reverberating neural trace will be relatively unavailable immediately after a response is learned.

STUDY I

The position of the present writers (Izard, 1959, 1960, 1963) is that both quality and intensity of affect are important determinants of cognitive processes. In our first study an attempt was made to study the differential effect of positive and negative affect with degree of affective arousal equated for the two conditions. The basic procedure was a paired associates learning task, in which affective picture stimuli were associated with neutral words.[1] After the learning trials we obtained a total learning score, the Ss' perceptual threshold for the neutral words, the effect of these words on a new paired associates learning task, and the effect of the pictures on the affective scale values of the neutral words.

The results of this study showed that (a) positive and neutral pictures were learned at about the same rate; (b) both positive and neutral pictures were learned more rapidly than negative pictures; and (c) the neutral syllables associated with positive pictures received significantly higher post-experimental affect scale ratings than did the syllables associated with the neutral or negative pictures.

Post-Hoc Analyses

When data from subsequent studies employing different sets of stimulus materials failed to confirm the finding that syllables for "positive" pictures were learned faster than syllables for "negative" ones, we took a second look at our original positive picture category. We found that we had six positive pictures which could be described as nature scenes and four pictures of attractive young women. The mean affect scale ratings for these two subsets of positive pictures were approximately equal (girls 3.88, scenes 3.60, a non-significant difference). Separate analyses comparing the learning curves for the girl (positive), scene (positive), and negative pictures revealed that we had significantly different learning rates for the two subsets of positive pictures. The syllables for scenes were learned faster than those of any other group; they were learned significantly faster than those of the extremely positive (girls) and extremely negative pictures. However, the post-experimental affect ratings of the syllables assigned to scenes did not differ.

STUDY II

In order to clear up some of the questions raised by the initial experi-

[1] A detailed description of the experimental procedure is given in our report of Study II.

ment, we planned an extensive study of three categories of affective stimuli: extremely positive pictures (attractive young women), slightly positive (no attractive young women included), and extremely negative pictures (individuals with diseases of the face and head, typically advanced carcinoma).

Although the second study was similar to the first, there were some important additions and modifications. One of these involved taking one-half the subjects in each treatment condition to two consecutive perfect trails for the picture syllable learning task. According to Underwood (1963) practically all of the variance in recall and other learning-related measures can be attributed to different amounts of learning. One purpose for this procedure, then, was to equate the amount of learning for all treatment groups and see if there are different effects on the other dependent variables. If different effects do appear, then they can be said to be a function of qualitatively different affective arousals and not a function of differing amounts of learning.

In his research on verbal learning, Underwood (1957, 1962) has been able to demonstrate that the amount of learning on the criterion trial is not a valid measure of original learning. "It can be shown logically and empirically that two lists learned at different rates to the same criterion do not exhibit the same degree of learning" (Underwood & Keppel, 1962, p. 1). This is illustrated by the fact that the more slowly the learning approaches a given criterion, the greater the drop on the trial immediately after the criterion trial. As a remedy for this, he offers two methodological improvements, both involving the utilization of control subjects whose performance on the trial following the criterion trial serves as a base measure of learning. In this study the continuous learning trials method was used; this involves taking the control subjects through one learning trial beyond criterion. The recall scores of independent groups of subjects were then compared with these base values obtained from the control groups to derive measures of rentention.

Hypotheses

The specific hypotheses are as follows:

Learning. Hypothesis 1: Based on the post-hoc analyses of the data from the first study, we would expect the slightly positive pictures to be learned the fastest and no significant difference between the learning rates for the two extreme groups.

Recall. Hypothesis 2: We would expect the hierarchy of recall scores to be the same as that for the learning scores.

Subjects

Ninety male students drawn from four introductory psychology classes at Vanderbilt University served as subjects. Participation was required as part of course obligations. The subjects were systematically assigned to each of the 18 cells in the design on the basis of the order of their appearance for the first experimental session.

Experimental Design

The first column in Figure 1 refers to the two levels of learning for the picture syllable paired associates task; the first group was required to achieve 100% learning (two consecutive perfect trials).

The second column refers to the counterbalancing of stimulus and response syllables in the syllable syllable paired associates task involving picture treated and new neutral syllables; for each learning condition (60% or 100%) half of the subjects were shown the picture-associated syllables as the stimuli and the other half were shown the new syllables as the stimuli. All subject in the syllable syllable learning task were taken to a 50% learning criterion.

The third column refers to the utilization of control subjects for the purpose of deriving a more valid base measure of original learning; in this case the control subjects had one extra trial beyond the criterion trial.

1	2	3	4		
Levels of learning	Counterbalancing of S & R syllables	C/E	Affective treatment conditions		
			(a) positive	(b) slightly positive	(c) negative
Sixty per cent learning	(S) picture-assoc. syllables (R) new neutral syllables		7 Ss	7	7
	(S) new neutral syllables (R) picture-assoc. syllables		7	7	7
One hundred per cent learning	(S) P-A syllables (R) N syllables	Control	4 Ss	4	4
		Exper.	4	4	4
	(S) N syllables (R) P-A syllables	Control	4	4	4
		Exper.	4	4	4

Figure 1. Experimental design of Study II.

For the subjects in the 60% learning condition, the control measure was obtained from the subjects in the 100% learning condition by noting the trial at which they got six out of ten correct and then recording the number of the trial immediately following. From within the subjects in the

100% learning condition, a separate control group was designated for deriving the base measure of original learning, and the recall scores of the "experimental" subjects were then compared against this score in order to derive the retention measures. Although the control condition of the two perfect trials group directly affected only the procedure of the picture syllable learning task, these subjects were equally subdivided between the two stimulus response conditions so that these latter conditions would not be differentially influenced by this variable.

The fourth column refers to the three different picture syllable affective treatment conditions. A "positive" group is one which learned the neutral syllables in association with the positive pictures, etc.

Selection and Development of Materials

Pictures. Sixty-six 5 x 7 chromatic photographs of people were selected from two general sources: magazines and hospital files. There were 22 pictures judged by the researchers to fall in each affective category. Each picture was numbered, mounted on a plain white 5 x 8 card, and then placed in a plastic card-holder.

The 66 pictures were then administered to an introductory psychology class for the purpose of obtaining affective scale ratings. The first step in rating procedure was to distribute the pictures in the front of the classroom, and have the students file by and glance at each picture. The purpose for this was to help the student anchor his frame of reference for making the ratings. The pictures were then distributed around the class so that each picture was the first picture rated by some student. Thus, although all students rated the pictures in the same sequential order, each student began his ratings with a different picture. This procedure controlled any possible adaptation effects. The experimenter paced the ratings, allowing 15 seconds for each rating. At his signal, the student passed the picture on to the next person and then rated the picture handed to him. In this manner, 49 male students rated the pictures on a 12 point bipolar scale of pleasantness—unpleasantness.

On the basis of these ratings (means and variances), 15 positive, 15 negative, and 17 more neutral pictures were selected for the purpose of obtaining the indices of discriminability. The need for controlling stimulus discriminability has been brought out in various studies, such as that of Marston, Kanfer, & McBrearty (1963). These measures of discriminability were obtained by employing a paired comparison method of stimuli presentation with a rating scale method for obtaining responses. First the student looked at all of the pictures within one affective category, and then he was asked to rate every combination of two pictures, so that he made either 105 or 136 ratings, depending on which affective category he was rating. Thirty-seven male students were used to obtain these ratings: 10 for the positive pictures, 11 for the negative pictures, and 16 for the slightly positive pictures. The student used a 4 point rating scale with an anchor point range from "very easy" to "very difficult" to answer the question of "How difficult is it for me to tell these two pictures apart?" The order of pairings was varied so that different pairs were rated first by different students.

Ten pictures were finally selected from each affective category on the basis of both the affective scale ratings and the discriminability ratings (for results, *see* Tables 1-3). The positive pictures are typically of attractive females, the slightly positive pictures are typically of males, and the negative pictures are typically of faces of patients with advanced untreated carcinoma.

Syllables. The syllables were CVC trigrams selected from Noble (1961) in terms of scaled meaningfulness (m'). Three lists of 10 syllables each were derived, with an attempt being made to equate them in terms of m'. Every syllable within each list began with a different consonant and the number and use of vowels was approximately the same for the three lists.

Equipment. A standard two-field Gerbrands tachistoscope served two functions in this study. The first was its normal tachistoscopic function, and the second was as a two-field viewer. In this latter function the timing and lighting system of the tachistoscope was not employed; only the enclosed viewing box was used, together with an adapted timing and lighting system which allowed the two fields to be illuminated either separately or together for varying intervals of time. This was achieved by positioning a 100-watt light over each of the top lighting apertures; these lights, in turn, were controlled by a simple RC-type electronic timer which provided for the timing of three intervals: first light, interval between lights, and second light (or first and second lights together).

Independent and Dependent Variables

The independent variable was affective arousal as elicited by affectively loaded pictures in a picture syllable association task. The dependent measures were (a) learning neutral label (CVC trigrams) for the positive, slightly positive, and negative pictures, and (b) recall of picture-associated syllables (neutral labels).

Experimental Procedure

Since approximately two hours were required to run a subject, the experiment was divided into two one-hour sessions. For every subject the second session was conducted 48 hours after the first session.

First session. Step 1: The subject was admitted to the testing room and shown to his seat, where he found a copy of the instructions for the first session. He was told to begin reading the instructions for the first task. The goal in using detailed written instructions was to keep the experimenter as inconspicuous and affectively neutral as possible so that his contribution to the subject's affective arousal would be minimized. Other than when he gave rating forms to the subject and answered questions, the experimenter remained unseen behind a screen.

Step 2: After the subject had read the preliminary and Task 1 instructions and signalled to the experimenter that he was ready to begin, he was presented the first paired associates learning task using pictures and syllables. Depending upon the condition to which the subject had been assigned—whether positive, slightly positive, or negative—he was presented that set of ten pictures with their accompanying syllables (the syllables were randomly matched with the pictures). The picture was shown first for two seconds, then the picture in combination with the word for two seconds. The subjects were required to spell the syllables and, in order to be credited with a correct response, had to be sounding the last letter of the syllable before the syllable was illuminated. The pictures with their corresponding syllable labels were presented in one random order for the first three trials and then presented in a new random order every two trials after that. Subjects in the 100% learning condition had to reach that criterion within 17 trials or they were discarded from the study. Three subjects were discarded for this reason.

Step 3: Each subject wrote down all of the picture associated syllables he could remember. He was allowed 90 seconds to complete this task.

Step 4: Two additional trials of the picture syllable association task. This task was given in the fifth randomized order.

Second session. Step 1: The subject wrote down all of the picture-associated syllables he could remember in 90 seconds.

Step 2: Two additional trials of the picture syllable association task. This task was given in the second randomized order.

Results

RATINGS OF PHOTOGRAPHIC STIMULI

The mean affective scale values and mean discriminability ratings are given in Tables 1, 2, and 3. In addition, the variance and the extent to

Table 1 Means and variances of the positive pictures

Picture number	Mean affect rating	Deviation from midpoint (neutrality)	σ^2	Mean discriminability rating
24	11.00	4.50	2.33	1.188
19	10.84	4.34	1.31	1.133
21	10.69	4.19	1.38	1.144
10	10.65	4.15	1.98	1.177
8	10.63	4.13	1.86	1.100
15	10.61	4.11	1.62	1.244
56	10.55	4.05	1.38	1.078
50	10.08	3.58	2.08	1.111
53	10.02	3.52	2.65	1.056
45	9.65	3.15	2.48	1.144
Mean of means		3.97	1.91	1.138

which each picture deviates from the midpoint of the scale are also given for the affective ratings.

An analysis of variance for the affect rating means showed that they were significantly different ($F=514.60$ $(2,27)$, $p<.001$). Duncan's Mul-

Table 2 Means and variances of the slightly positive pictures

Picture number	Mean affect rating	Deviation from midpoint (neutrality)	σ^2	Mean discriminability rating
38	6.45	-.05	2.67	1.089
29	6.65	.15	2.69	1.067
3	6.33	-.17	1.52	1.050
33	6.84	.34	1.97	1.120
48	7.24	.74	2.90	1.156
7	7.35	.85	1.40	1.170
36	7.37	.87	2.78	1.022
23	7.49	.99	1.38	1.210
63	7.55	1.05	2.00	1.170
11	7.59	1.09	2.04	1.130
Mean of means		.59	2.14	1.118

tiple Range Test (MRT) was applied to these means and it was found that each was significantly different from the other considerably beyond the .01 level. Thus, in terms of affect scale values, it was concluded that

Table 3 Means and variances of the negative pictures

Picture number	Mean affect rating	Deviation from midpoint (neutrality)	σ^2	Mean discriminability rating
37	1.65	-4.85	1.11	1.121
35	1.78	-4.72	1.26	1.152
25	1.90	-4.60	3.09	1.101
41	2.49	-4.01	1.63	1.162
46	2.61	-3.89	1.99	1.131
39	2.86	-3.64	1.88	1.172
34	3.18	-3.32	2.32	1.162
30	3.27	-3.23	2.16	1.192
44	3.35	-3.15	3.44	1.152
62	3.59	-2.91	2.95	1.131
Mean of means		-3.83	2.18	1.148

each group of photographic stimuli was significantly different from the other and elicited different affective responses.

A comparison of the positive and negative affective rating in terms of their deviation from the midpoint of the scale yielded a t of .515, which does not approach significance. The positive and negative pictures, then, were considered equivalent in terms of affective arousal.

The difference between the slightly positive affective rating mean and the scale midpoint was submitted to a t-test of significance, yielding $t=3.69$, $p<.005$. Statistically, then, this middle group of pictures were slightly positive, rather than "neutral.".

An analysis of variance for the discriminability rating means did not yield a significant F value. Thus the three sets of picture stimuli were considered equivalent in terms of confusability.

LEARNING SCORES

Picture Syllable Learning

An analysis of variance of the mean number of trials taken to reach the learning criterion for the 60% learning condition showed that the difference between the means was significant at the .05 level. The MRT showed that the labels to the slightly positive pictures were learned significantly faster than the labels for either the positive or negative pictures. The

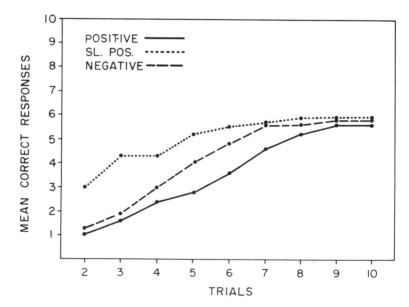

Figure 2.   Learning trials of the 60% criterion condition of Study II. Affect means of picture groups on a −6 to +6 scale: positive M = +3.97, slightly positive M = +.59, negative M = −3.83. N = 10 pictures, 14 subjects each group.

learning curves of the picture groups are shown in Figure 2. These differences were significant at the .01 level between slightly positive and positive subjects, and significant at the .05 level between slightly positive and negative subjects. ("Positive" subjects, etc., will be used as a shorthand way of referring to the affective treatment conditions). Thus, Hypothesis 1, that the subjects in the slightly positive treatment condition would learn significantly faster than the subjects in the positive and negative treatment condition, was supported; and, as expected, the latter two groups did not differ.

An analysis of variance of the mean number of trials taken to reach the learning criterion for the 100% learning condition showed that, although all of the differences among the means of the three groups are in the same direction as for the 60% learning condition (slightly positive>negative >positive), none of the differences were significant.

By way of replication of the results for the 60% learning condition, an analysis of variance of the mean number of trials taken to reach a 60% learning criterion for the 100% learning condition showed that the differ-

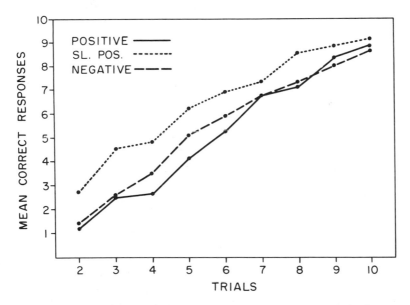

Figure 3. Learning trials of the 100% criterion condition of Study II. Affect means of picture groups on a −6 to +6 scale: positive M = +3.97, slightly positive M = +.59, negative M = −3.83. N = 10 pictures, 16 subjects each group.

ence between the means was significant at the .05 level. Further, the MRT showed that the slightly positive picture labels were learned significantly faster than the positive picture labels.

An analysis of variance for the 100% learning condition of the mean number of correct anticipations on each trial through the 10th learning trial showed that the differences among the three means were not significant. However, when the MRT was applied to the means for each trial, it was found that there were significant differences in the early trials (slightly positive>negative>positive) which wash out in later trials. As before, the slightly positive subjects always had the highest mean (significantly higher, $p<.01$, than the positive and negative subjects for each of the first four trials), followed by the negative subjects with the next highest mean. In the second and third learning trials the positive and negative subjects were not significantly different, but by the fourth and fifth trials the negative subjects began doing significantly better than the positive subjects.

Since the positive and negative subjects had significantly lower means on the initial trial than the slightly positive subjects, an analysis of covariance was used to control for difference in initial performance between the experimental groups. This analysis was done only for the 60% learning condition. An insignificant F value between the adjusted treatment mean squares was found, indicating that over-all group differences in learning were due largely to marked discrepancies in initial performance.

RETENTION MEASURES

Analyses of variance for the free recall measures for both the 60% and 100% (experimental) learning conditions failed to yield significant F values. However, when the MRT was applied to the mean differences for the 60% condition, some significant differences were found. For the first recall score, the negative subjects had a significantly higher ($p<.05$) recall score than the positive subjects. For the second recall score (from the second experimental session), both the slightly positive and negative subjects had significantly higher scores than the positive subjects.

As was discussed in the procedure section, all of the subjects were twice taken through two picture syllable relearning trials, once in the first session and then again in the second session. These scores were considered a recognition type of retention measure and used as a second method for determining amount of forgetting. The means of these relearning trials were entered into an analysis of variance for the 60% learning condition, and a significant F value ($p<.05$) was found. The MRT for the first relearning score showed that both the slightly positive and negative groups gave significantly more ($p<.01$) correct responses than the positive group. The MRT for the second relearning score showed precisely the same thing.

An analysis of variance of the relearning means for the 100% learning condition did not yield a significant F value. However, the MRT for the first relearning score showed that the positive subjects gave significantly ($p<.05$) more correct responses than the slightly positive subjects.

In Study II we again obtained post-experimental affect scale ratings on the pictures and the syllables associated with the pictures in the learning task. The analysis of the data from these scales confirmed the findings of Study I. Highly significant differences in the expected direction (positive>slightly positive>negative) were found for pictures. Similar results were obtained for the syllables. The syllables associated with positive pictures received significantly higher (more positive) affect scale ratings than the syllables associated with slightly positive pictures, and these in turn received significantly higher ratings than the syllables associated with the negative pictures.

CORRELATIONS

Correlations of Affect Scale Scores and Learning

Using the number of trials taken to reach a 60% learning criterion, learning was correlated with the various affect scale scores (Table 4). Not only the learning conditions but also the affective treatment conditions were collapsed for the correlations discussed here ($N=90$).

Table 4 Significant correlations of affect scale scores and learning

Scale A_1		Scale A_2			
Positive affect		Positive affect		Negative affect	
Item no.	r	Item no.	r	Item no.	r
2 -	-.26**	12 -	-.18*	1 -	.21*
6 -	-.23*			6 -	.27***
Σ -	-.21*			11 -	.18*
				Σ -	.25**

Of the 24 correlations between affect scale scores and learning, eight (ranging from .18 to .27) were significant in the expected direction. These correlations between affect scale scores and learning were generally consistent with the basic hypothesis that the more positive the affect aroused by the experimental treatment, the faster the subject would learn to associate the labels to the pictures.

One possible explanation for the group differences on the learning and recall measures involved differences in intellectual ability. To check this out, the Verbal and Total scores from the Scholastic Aptitude Test of the CEEB were averaged for each of the groups and entered into an analysis of variance. Neither analysis yielded a significant F value, indicating that group differences in intellectual ability could not be used to explain the marked superiority of the slightly positive subjects in the learning tasks.

Summary of Results: Study II

1. On the pre-experimental ratings, the three groups of picture stimuli were significantly different from each other in terms of affective scale values, and they were approximately equal in terms of discriminability. The positive and negative pictures were statistically equivalent in terms of departure from the middle of the affect scale.

2. In the 60% criterion condition of the picture syllable paired associates learning, the slightly positive subjects learned significantly faster than either the positive or negative subjects, supporting Hypothesis 1. These results, for the most part, were not confirmed in the 100% learning condition; however, comparisons of the groups in this condition at the 60% criterion were consistent with those above.

3. The differences in the group means on the free recall measure did not consistently support Hypothesis 2. In the 60% learning condition the positive subjects did have significantly lower recall scores than the other two groups. These results from the free recall measure were generally confirmed by a second measure of retention: relearning of picture syllable associates. However, in the 100% learning condition the positive subjects in this relearning task gave significantly more correct responses than the slightly positive subjects.

4. In both learning conditions, the positive subjects rated the picture-associated syllables significantly more positive than did either the slightly positive or negative subjects; and the slightly positive subjects, in turn, rated these syllables significantly more positive than did the negative subjects.

5. Although the highly positive (girl) pictures were learned least rapidly, the correlations between affect scale scores and learning were generally consistent with the original basic hypothesis that the more positive the affect aroused by the experimental treatment, the faster the subject would learn to associate the labels to the pictures.

STUDY III

This study was undertaken to accomplish three things. First, we wanted to use a Cardmaster to automate presentation of stimuli and to permit precise control of exposure time so it could be studied as an independent variable. Secondly, we wanted to introduce a set of pictures representing "moderate" deviation from the midpoint of the affect scale. Finally, we wanted to use an A x B x S design wherein we expose all subjects to all subsets of pictures, permitting us to make within-group comparisons of the learning curves.

METHOD

Subjects. The Ss were 28 undergraduate males enrolled in introductory psychology courses at Vanderbilt University.

The two sets of "extreme" pictures were matched for deviation from neutrality, and the intraset range of affect ratings was minimized. The two sets of "moderate" pictures were similarly matched, but selected so that their deviation means were approximately midway between neutrality and the deviation means of the extreme pictures. The affect means and the mean deviations for all the pictures are presented in Table 5.

Selection of the stimuli. From the pool of pictures used in Study II, we selected four sets of three pictures each. We labelled these sets *Extremely Positive, Moderately Positive, Moderately Negative,* and *Extremely Negative.* The extremely positive set was composed of pictures of very attractive and sexually arousing girls in lingerie; the moderately positive group were girls less attractive and in less suggestive wear. The extremely negative set of pictures was composed of people with severe facial and upper body diseases; in the moderately negative set, the disfigurations were less obvious and repugnant.

Table 5 Mean affect ratings of the picture stimuli

Affect group	Mean affect rating	Deviation from midpoint (neutrality)
Extremely positive	11.00	+4.50
	10.84	+4.34
	10.69	+4.19
Mean of means	10.84	+4.34
Moderately positive	9.08	+2.58
	8.80	+2.30
	8.43	+1.93
Mean of means	8.77	+2.27
Moderately negative	3.94	-2.56
	4.08	-2.42
	4.78	-1.72
Mean of means	4.27	-2.23
Extremely negative	1.90	-4.60
	1.78	-4.72
	2.49	-4.01
Mean of means	2.06	-4.44

Procedure

A Cardmaster was used to present the picture stimuli and the trigram responses. The stimuli were 2 x 3" photographic reproductions mounted on both right and left sides of the standard white presentation card to correspond with the shutters of the apparatus. A pair of identical pictures was placed on each card. Each picture had a surrounding white border of about 3/8"; the response trigram was mounted in this border beneath the picture on the right. The trigram was lettered in bold black print so that it stood out clearly and distinctly. The trigrams were from the list used in Study II. The presentation card is illustrated in Figure 4.

Prior to the learning phase of the experiment the subjects were instructed to rate the twelve pictures. The following instructions were presented.

We want you to rate your reactions to some pictures of people. First you will be shown a set of pictures one at a time in the Cardmaster. Look at each picture carefully. After you have seen the entire set of pictures, each will be presented again so that you will be able to rate them on the answer sheets provided, one page for each picture. When you have completed the ratings for a picture, let the experimenter know and the next picture will be shown.

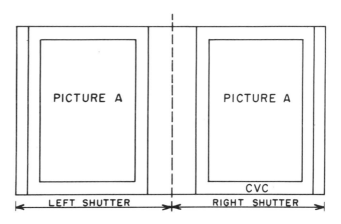

Figure 4. The presentation card. During the initial phase of the presentation (2 or 4 sec.) the left shutter opened and exposed the left side of the card, the picture. At the end of this interval, the left shutter remaining open, the right shutter opened and exposed the right side of the card, the *same* picture and the trigram CVC, for the same time interval (2 or 4 sec.).

The subjects had as much time as was necessary to complete the ratings. The Cardmaster was controlled so that only the left shutter opened; in this way, the subjects did not see the trigram during the rating of the picture. The five 12-point bipolar scales were: (a) pleasant–unpleasant, (b) comfortable–uncomfortable, (c) no feelings of guilt–guilt feelings, (d) attractive–unattractive, (e) no feeling of shame–shame.

After the ratings the subjects were read the following instructions:

We will now proceed to the learning part of the experiment. This is not a personality or intelligence test. The machine on the table is a Cardmaster; it is a device for presenting psychological stimuli. The machine will present cards on which you will see two identical pictures, the same ones you just rated. One picture will be on the left and one on the right. At first the left shutter will open and you will see the picture on the left. A few seconds later, the shutter on the right will open and you will see the same picture but with a label beneath it. Your job will be to learn to pair the picture with its label. That is, to anticipate which label goes with the picture.

We will go through the set of cards once. When the left shutter opens, look carefully at the picture. Then, when the right shutter opens you are to say the label aloud. At the end of this practice set of cards you will see a blank card. At that time I will instruct you to begin responding. By that I mean that thereafter when the left shutter opens, look at the picture and try to remember its label and say it aloud before the right shutter opens. At first you may have some difficulty remembering the label that goes with the picture, but as you become more familiar with the pictures and labels the task will become easier. Your job is to beat the right shutter—make the correct response before the right shutter opens. You will be marked correct if you correctly guess the label before the right shutter opens.

If you do not know the response, or if you should make a mistake by guessing the wrong label, be sure to say the label aloud when the right shutter opens. This will help you learn the pairs. There will be several sets of cards. Each set will contain the same pictures you will see in the practice trial. Each set will contain the same labels. The picture and label making a pair will always occur together, but a given picture label pair will not always appear in the same position in the series.

Now remember, each label is associated with a particular picture. You must learn to anticipate what label follows a given picture.

Four copies of each stimulus presentation card were made, permitting four randomizations. At the end of the fourth trial the Cardmaster recycled and presented again the first randomization. There was a 2 second interval between cards, and after 12 cards a blank card was exposed for 4 seconds to signal the end of the trial. Subjects were randomly assigned to the 2 or 4 second exposure condition, i.e., the exposure of the stimulus and the response cards were each 2 or 4 seconds.

Results: Study III

Learning

The learning curves for the picture sets for the two exposure conditions are presented in Figure 5.

The analysis of variance for the 2 second condition indicated a significant difference between learning for the picture sets ($F=3.48$ (3,39), $p<.025$). A Newman-Keuls multiple comparison test ($p=.05$) demonstrated a separation between sets as follows (variables within brackets do not differ significantly):

Moderately Positive
Moderately Negative
Extremely Negative
Extremely Positive

Inspection of the learning curves revealed that the same separation of curves that existed in Study II (extremely positive separating from all others) was also present here at some points. The Newman-Keuls comparison test ($p=.05$) for each separate trial revealed that there was statistically significant separation for trials 5-7:

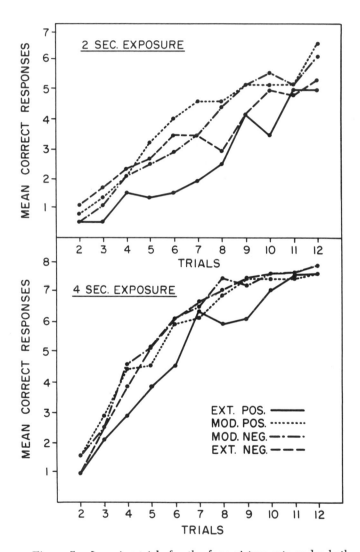

Figure 5.   Learning trials for the four picture sets under both
2 and 4 sec. exposure-interval conditions of Study III. Affect
means of picture sets on a —6 to +6 scale: extremely positive
M = +4.34, moderately positive M = +2.28, moderately
negative M = —2.23, extremely negative M = —4.44. N = 3
pictures each set, 14 subjects.

For the 4 second condition the overall comparison was again significant ($F=3.01$ (3,39), $p<.05$). Multiple comparison ($p=.05$) results were as follows:

> Moderately Negative ⎫
> Extremely Negative ⎬
> Moderately Positive ⎭
> Extremely Positive

Affect Ratings and Learning

Product-moment correlations between the subjects' affect ratings of the pictures and their total earning scores were not significant.

The hierarchy of learning curves in Study III corresponds with that found in Studies I and II, i.e., the extremely positive picture set was the slowest to be learned.

The differences between the multiple comparison tests for the two exposure interval conditions can be best explained by the relative magnitude of the error variances, i.e., the groups x subjects variance for the 2 second group was more than twice that of the 4 second group.

The scatter diagrams, plotting affect rating vs. learning, indicate that the negative correlations resulted primarily from the slow learning of the extremely positive pictures.

Discussion and Conclusions: Studies I, II, and III

The results of the three studies do not consistently support the general hypothesis that positive affect facilitates effective functioning. The data do not make the reasons for this failure clear, but they enable us to raise some questions and to make some observations that may point the way to solution. In this discussion we shall, for the most part, speak in (or have in mind as referents) operational terms (e.g., positive affective stimuli as determined by our scaling procedure) rather than refer to general states or constructs (e.g., affective arousal).

What conditions constitute the standard or "norm" for behavioral effectiveness? When we speak of positive affect facilitating or improving learning efficiency, what is the appropriate standard of comparison? As already indicated, cooperative college students participating in a brief experimental task may learn at or near their maximum rate when the task consists of neutral stimulus materials and is given under ordinary research conditions. Is it appropriate, then, to expect positive affective stimuli to be learned significantly faster than neutral stimuli in this kind of laboratory study?

Different classes (qualities) of positive affect? Quantitatively, or in terms of our scaling procedures, our extremely positive picture stimuli were one category (or one scale position). The pretty girls and nature scenes of Study I received approximately equal affect scale ratings. According to the affect scale ratings, the girls and scenes do not differ in their power to evoke "pleasant feeling." The post-experimental affect scale ratings of the labels associated with girls were not significantly different from the post-experimental ratings given to the scene labels. Thus, the pictures of girls and scenes evoked the same (pleasant—unpleasant) affect scale ratings and they had the same effect on the post-experimental affect scale ratings of the previously neutral labels.

Despite the fact that the two subsets of positive pictures (girls, scenes) had the same effect on the affect scale ratings and on the affective valence of the previously neutral labels, they did not necessarily evoke the same kind of positive affect. Labels for the scenes were learned significantly faster than for the girls.

Except for the lack of pictures of nature scenes, the findings of Studies II and III confirm those of Study I. Again, the pictures of pretty girls received significantly more favorable ratings, this time on more extensive measures of affective reaction. The positive pictures (girls) had a significantly greater effect on the affective scale values of the picture-associated labels.

The learning curves for the three groups of pictures in Study II were what we expected from the post-hoc analyses of the data from Study I. The slightly positive pictures (nearest to neutral on the affect scale) were learned fastest, while the extremely positive and negative pictures were learned at about the same rate.

These results run counter to the hypothesis regarding the facilitating effect of positive affect. The feelings aroused by the positive pictures (girls) are clearly positive, according to the data from our affect reaction scales. The post-experimental affective ratings of the picture-associated labels suggest that the positive affect aroused by the pictures was sustained for some time. Yet, the labels for the positive pictures (pretty girls) were learned no faster than the negative picture labels. There are three possibilities: our hypothesis is wrong; the positive affect aroused was not relevant to the learning task and hence was not a motivational variable in performance; the positive (girl) pictures aroused competing affects or drives leading to intra- and intersubsystem discord that interfered with learning. We think the third alternative is most probably the correct one.

For one thing, we now believe that the sex drive was more of a factor than we expected. In selecting our pictures of girls, we tried to use as primary criterion esthetic appeal rather than sex appeal. We excluded obvious sexy poses. We never doubted that the pictures had some sex stimulus value, but we hoped this would be overshadowed by the positive affect aroused.

In retrospect, we decided that our "cold, scientific planning" (or wishful thinking) had affected our common sense. We now believe that the pretty girl pictures aroused the sex drive and that this drive was completely irrelevant to the learning of "nonsense" labels. As Tomkins (1962) points out, sex involves both drive and affect, and the drive can instigate the negative affects of fear, shame, guilt, or anger.

PART B

In view of the results of Studies I, II, and III and the relationship of their results to the original hypotheses, we began to suspect that the experimental procedures may not have provided a fair or adequate test of our underlying assumptions. In fact, the possibility occurred to us that the structure of the experiment was not completely in keeping with our general theoretical formulations, from which the hypotheses were drawn. If we look again at the learning task we can see that what we had set up in the classical paired associate paradigm as stimuli and what we had set up as responses are highly disparate classes of materials. The stimuli are affect inducers. They have proved to be capable of evoking affect powerful enough to influence performance and powerful enough to change the affective valence of previously neutral stimuli. On the other hand, the responses which subjects were asked to learn were "cognitive stimuli" of the purest variety. Considering both stimulus and response in a paired associates paradigm as "stimuli" in the sense that both evoke some change in the organism, we can see that the stimulus half of the pair acts primarily on the affect system, while the response half of the pair acts primarily on the cognitive system.

The task given our subjects was a cognitive task by definition; they were required to learn something. Further, our procedure forced the subject to use an affect inducer as stimulus (or cue) for a strictly cognitive response. In retrospect, we consider that a learning task which so integrates an affective and a cognitive element has a high probability of setting up some degree of discord within and between major systems of the personality. For example, we thought (also in retrospect) that in the picture syllable paradigm, interest affect or sex drive related to the picture as a pretty girl would interfere with interest in the picture as a part of the learning task (stimulus for a nonsense syllable response).

In line with the foregoing discussion, we decided that some modification of our experimental procedure would have to be undertaken. The question remained whether to alter the learning paradigm and perhaps introduce a totally different task or to use a different sample of affective picture stimuli. Changing our pictures in favor of others would seem to be of no avail in explaining the unexpected hierarchy of learning curves in the first study.

We decided that a more appropriate test of our original hypothesis could be made by separating the affective stimuli from the cognitive stimuli. Procedurally, this would mean that we would place the picture stimuli in the background and a pair of trigrams in the foreground and that the learning task would now become the more or less standard paired associate problem: learning to associate one trigram with another. The design would be such that pictures could not possibly serve as cues in successful performance on the learning task.

Our new experimental procedure makes it possible to conduct studies substantively comparable to the previous studies and examine the differences in the learning rates between the various affect picture-groups. Differences between the two series of studies should be attributable primarily to the differences in the method of presenting the affect inducer (picture), either as an inherent part of the learning task (stimulus) or as "background" with a standard syllable pair as figure (learning task). Two such studies were carried out; one employing a between Ss design (parallel to Study II) and one employing a within Ss design (parallel to Study III).

STUDIES IV AND V

Method

Subjects. Subjects for Studies IV and V were male undergraduates secured from introductory psychology classes at Vanderbilt University.

Thirty subjects participated in Study IV. The statistical design was a simple between groups design like that of Study II. Subjects were randomly assigned to one of three groups: one group was presented the positive pictures, one the negative pictures, and one the trigram pairs with no background pictures.

Twenty-nine subjects participated in Study V which employed the same statistical design as that of Study III but time was not studied as a separate independent variable.

Selection of stimuli. Study IV employed the positive and negative sets of pictures used in Study II, and Study V employed pictures identical with those used in Study III.

Procedure

The Cardmaster was used to present the picture stimuli and the trigrams. The pictures were of the same size and mounted on the presentation card in the same way as described for Study III. The only difference was that CVC trigrams (drawn from the list described in Study II) were mounted beneath *both* pictures, one beneath the left picture and one beneath the right picture. The usual precautions were taken in making up the trigram pair combinations.

The instructions for the learning task for Studies IV and V were the same. The control group in Study IV received standard paired associates instructions, since no pictures were involved.

The instructions are presented below.

This is a verbal learning experiment. It is not an intelligence or personality test. We are interested in investigating a general psychological phenomenon.

The machine on the table in front of you is a Cardmaster. It is a machine for presenting verbal stimuli materials. Notice the window. Through this window you will see some cards which will be presented to you with photographs on them. Each card will have two identical pictures on it, one picture on the right and one picture on the left. Beneath each picture you will see a nonsense syllable. Your task will be to pair the nonsense syllables;

that is, to learn which syllable on the right hand side of the card goes with the syllable on the left hand side.

At first the shutter on the left will open and you will see the picture and a nonsense syllable beneath it. A few seconds later the shutter on the right will be raised and you will see the identical picture you just saw but with a different nonsense syllable beneath it. Your job will be to learn to respond with the nonsense syllable on the right each time you see the one on the left.

First we will go through all the cards once to give you a chance to become acquainted with them. When the shutter on the left opens, you are to say the syllable *aloud,* then when the shutter on the right opens say the syllable on the right *aloud.* At the end of this practice set of cards, you will see a blank card. At that time I will instruct you to begin responding —by that I will mean that the next time the cards come up when the left shutter raises say the syllable you see *aloud* and quickly try to anticipate the syllable which you recall having occurred with it on the right. You are to do this quickly, before the right shutter raises. At first you may find it difficult to remember which syllable on the right goes with the syllable on the left, but as you become more familiar with the syllables the task will become easier. It is important that you say the syllables aloud, for this will help you learn the pairs.

Thus, your job is to beat the right shutter—that is, say the syllable on the right before the right shutter raises. If you do not know the correct response, when the right shutter opens say the syllable on the right *aloud;* also, if you should happen to make the wrong response, be sure to correct yourself and say the correct syllable *aloud* once it appears in the window.

There will be several sets of cards. Each set is composed of the same pictures you saw on the first trial. However, the nonsense syllables which are paired below the pictures on the right and left will *not* always occur beneath the same photographs, although the syllables will always occur together as pairs.

We will go through these sets of cards a certain number of times. Try to learn the pairs as quickly as possible.

In Study IV there were four randomizations repeated twice, resulting in one familiarization trial and seven learning trials. In each series of randomizations (four trials) no trigram pair was presented below the same picture, making it impossible for the subject to associate a trigram pair with any particular picture. There were a total of ten trigram pairs and ten pictures in each treatment group. The stimulus half of the card was exposed for 2 seconds followed by a 2 second exposure of the response half of the card. There was a 2 second interval between each card. A blank card was exposed for 4 seconds between each trial.

The treatment groups consisted of (1) subjects in the positive picture condition, and (2) subjects in the negative picture condition. There was also a control group in which no pictures were presented at all. For each of these three groups, the same trigram pairs were used and were presented in the identical sequence, so that the only difference between groups was the presence of either positively or negatively rated pictures, or no pictures at all. In the latter case, the trigrams were placed in the same position on the presentation card as they were in the two affect conditions.

Study V repeated the within-subjects design of Study III, employing four sets of stimuli (extremely positive, moderately positive, moderately negative, and extremely negative). A stimulus set consisted of three pictures and three trigram pairs; each picture trigram pair combination appeared only once in a series of randomizations (three trials), and each picture and each trigram pair appeared only once in a trial.

There were three randomizations repeated four times, resulting in one familiarization trial and 11 learning trials. Each half of the presentation card was exposed for 3 seconds, with a 2 second interval between each card. A blank card was presented for 6 seconds between each learning trial (twelve cards).

At the conclusion of the learning phase of the experiment the subject was administered a series of rating scales.

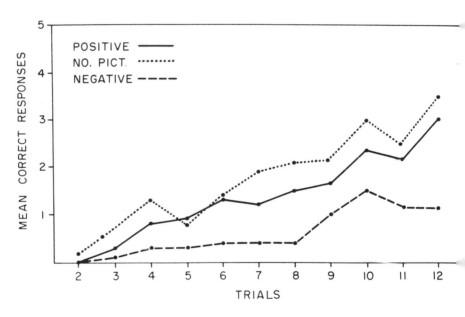

Figure 6. Learning trials of Study IV. Affect means of picture groups on a —6 to +6 scale: positive M = +3.97, negative M = —3.83; remaining group saw no pictures. N = 10 pictures or word pairs, 10 subjects trials 2-8, 6 subjects trials 9-12.

RESULTS

Learning. The learning curves for the three groups in Study IV are presented in Figure 6. The control group (exposed to no pictures) had the fastest rate of learning, followed by the positive group and, finally, the group exposed to negative pictures. The analysis of variance computed revealed that the differences in learning were significant ($F=7.569$ $(2,27)$, $p<.01$). A Newman-Keuls multiple comparison test ($p=.05$) disclosed that the negative group was significantly different from both the control group and the positive group, but that the control group and positive group did not statistically separate (variables within a bracket do not statistically differ):

Control Group ⎱
Positive Group ⎰
Negative Group

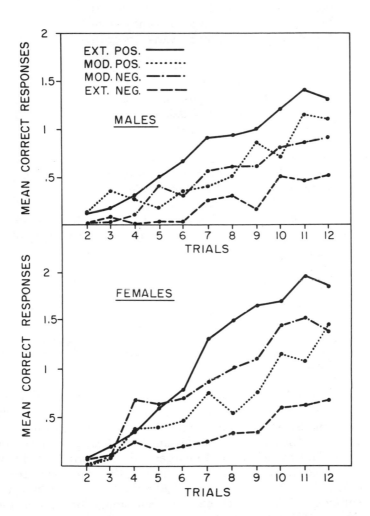

Figure 7. Learning trials for the four picture sets of Study V. Affect means of picture sets on a −6 to +6 scale: extremely positive M = +4.34, moderately positive M = +2.28, moderately negative M = −2.23, extremely negative M = −4.44. N = 3 pictures each set, 29 subjects.

Similar results were obtained from Study V. The learning curves for the four affect picture sets are presented in Figure 7. The extremely positive pictures were learned at the fastest rate, followed by the moderately positive and moderately negative picture sets. The negative set was the slowest learned. The analysis of variance revealed that the differences between the four groups were significant ($F=18.34$ (3,84), $p<.001$). The Newman Keuls multiple comparison test was used to test the differences between the total learning scores for the four picture sets. At $p=.05$ the moderately positive and moderately negative curves did not differ from each other, but they both differed significantly from the extremely positive and extremely negative groups (variables within a bracket do not statistically differ):

> Extremely Positive
> Moderately Positive ⎫
> Moderately Negative ⎰
> Extremely Negative

Affect ratings. The ratings completed by the subjects at the conclusion of Study IV, measuring their reactions to an entire set of either positive or negative pictures, revealed that those subjects exposed to the positive set of pictures gave higher positive ratings than those exposed to the negative set of pictures. Table 6 presents the mean affect ratings to the pictures of the two experimental groups (no ratings could be obtained for the control group).

Table 6 Study IV: Subjects' affect ratings

Affect group	Mean affect rating
Positive group	28.6
Negative group	19.9

F btn = 33.18 (1,18), p< .005

As Study V employed a within Ss design, it was not appropriate to have the Ss complete a rating scale similar to the one used in Study IV. In its place, the Ss were asked to rate each individual picture on a 12 point continuum "pleasant . . . unpleasant," identical to that continuum originally used for the selection of pictures. The results indicated that the Ss' ratings placed the pictures at approximately the same four affect scale positions as did the ratings which we had initially obtained from the independent judges. Table 7 presents the mean ratings for the four picture sets by the Ss in Study V and compares them to our original ratings obtained from independent judges.

Affect ratings vs. learning correlations. The six scale items rated by subjects in Study IV were summed and correlated with the learning scores for both the positive and negative groups. The product-moment correla-

Table 7 Study V: Mean affect ratings

Affect picture set	Ss' ratings	Deviation from midpoint (neutrality)	Judges' ratings	Deviation from midpoint (neutrality)
Extremely positive	10.50	+4.50	10.84	+4.34
Moderately positive	8.83	+2.23	8.77	+2.27
Moderately negative	4.83	-1.67	4.27	-2.23
Extremely negative	3.06	-3.44	2.06	-4.44

tion coefficient was .845 (18df), $p<.005$, indicating that the higher the affect rating, the better the learning.

Five scale items were used in the ratings for Study V. Three correlations were found to be significant ($p<.005$). The individual correlations are presented in Table 8.

Table 8 Correlation of scale items and learning

Item high score indicates, on scale 1 . . . 12	r	p
pleasant	.374	.005
comfortable	.360	.005
no guilt	.097	-
attractive	.366	.005
no shame	.084	-

SUMMARY AND DISCUSSION

The investigations of the impact of affect on cognitive processes yielded several reliable findings.

1. Picture stimuli can be reliably rated on a simple bipolar (positive-negative) affect scale.

2. Pictures with different affect scale ratings evoke significantly different cognitive performances (learning rates) and different cognitive-affective responses (affective ratings of picture-associated, previously neutral trigrams).

3. Both intensity *and* quality of affect are significant factors in altering behavior, contrary to most theoretical positions where the construct of adaptation level is pivotal.

4. The relationship or relevance of the affect-inducing stimuli (e.g., whether they are figure or ground) to concomitant or subsequent cognitive processes (e.g., learning) is of great importance in determining the influence of affect on performance.

The results of Studies I-III (picture trigram procedure) and those of Studies IV and V (trigram trigram, affective picture in background procedure) are dramatically different. In the picture trigram learning paradigm only one set of pictures results in a learning curve that differs reliably from all others: the extremely positive (pretty girl) pictures are learned significantly more slowly than any other set.

The usual paired associates learning task presented with affective pictures as background gave distinctly contrasting results. The extremely positive pictures resulted in significantly faster learning than moderately rated pictures and these in turn yielded significantly faster learning than the extremely negative pictures.

Explaining or reconciling the contrasting findings is difficult because the general relationships between affect, cognition, and performance are so complex. For reasons which we will presently clarify, the relationships between affect, cognition, and performance that obtain in the trigram trigram learning experiments, *with affective pictures in the background*, approximate real life conditions. In the picture trigram learning experiments a very special bind was created by the experimental design, which resulted in the paradox that the most pleasant pictures produced the worst learning.

Let us first consider the general case. Any cognitive learning task demands not only the affect of interest to sustain the continuing exploration of the problem but also a tolerance for one or more of a group of negative affects such as distress, shame, disgust or anger, which may be evoked by task difficulties or frustrations. To the extent to which the individual concurrently experienced free floating positive affect that was phenomenologically "objectless" there could be synergistic summation so that cognition and learning was improved. In part this might happen by successful interference with the evocation of competing negative affects (through the principle of a finite channel capacity). On the other hand, if the concurrently experienced free floating affect (that was phenomenologically "objectless") were negative in nature, it might sufficiently attenuate or even swamp the positive affect connected with cognition and the learning task to deteriorate such performance, depending upon either the absolute intensity of the negative affect or upon the relative intensity of both the negative affect and the positive affect. On the other hand, if the absolute intensity of the competing negative affect were low enough, or if the relative intensity of the positive affect about the learning task was sufficiently greater than the intensity of the free floating negative affect, then in either case the competition between these affects might be such that the positive affect successfully excluded the negative affect from consciousness or at least changed it from figure to ground in the conscious field. Further, the negative affect might be attenuated from a figural to a ground-like position in the conscious field but become much amplified and figural as soon as a critical difficulty was experienced in the task which itself activated negative affect, which then summated with the background negative affect, to swamp first the sustaining interest in the task, and then radically impoverish learning performance.

Learning, in short, occurs in a highly labile psychological field in which the interplay of positive and negative affects, both those evoked by the task itself and those evoked by either internal or external (non-task relevant) stimuli, can: (a) summate positive affects and enrich or facilitate performance; (b) through interference exclude competing negative affect and not change performance; (c) through interference exclude positive affect and deteriorate performance; or (d) summate negative affects and deteriorate performance.

If we consider the case in which the competing affects are *not* phenomenologically objectless but are experienced as related to competing objects of cognition (either external perceptual competition or internal daydreams or ideas which instigate competing affect) then there is a more complex affect-cognition affect-cognition interference. In the classic clinical case of the TAT card #1, the child doesn't want to play the violin because he would rather go out and play with the boys. Out of this conflict between a mild positive and an intense positive affect, intense *additional* negative affect is generated so that neither activity can be truly enjoyed or successfully pursued.

If now we look at the case of the extremely positive pictures in the picture trigram learning experiments of this type of affect-cognition affect-cognition conflict is further complicated by making the *non-task relevant* cognition, which evokes positive affect (the pretty girl), act in a second capacity: it must become a cue to the *task relevant* cognition. It is very likely that the dissonance and increased complexity of the particular experimental design generates additional negative affect sufficient to attenuate both the original positive affect evoked by looking at a pretty girl and the positive affect evoked by the learning task.

In contrast the trigram trigram learning task is structured in such a way that the positive affect evoked by the pretty girl can serve as background affect which can summate with the positive affect of the learning task because it can be experienced without the additional strain of transforming the stimulus into a cue for a trigram to be learned.

We believe that the foregoing analysis is consistent with our earlier speculation that the extremely positive pictures in the picture trigram paradigm created intra- and inter-subsystem discord. Interest in the pretty girl as an esthetic and sexual object could have conflicted with interest in he picture as *cue* (affect affect interference). Attention to the picture as cue could have conflicted with interest affect aroused by the picture (affect cognition interference). These two types of dissonance could occur virtually simultaneously resulting in the complex affect-cognition affect-cognition interference.

REFERENCES

Bruner, J. S., & Postman, L. Emotional selectivity in perception and reaction. *J. Pers.*, 1947, *16*, 69-77.

Bugelski, B. R. *The psychology of learning.* New York: Holt, 1956.

Izard, C. E. Positive affect and behavioral effectiveness. Mimeographed, Vanderbilt Univer., 1959.

Izard, C. E. Personality similarity and friendship. *J. abnorm. soc. Psychol.*, 1960, *61*, 47-51.

Izard, C. E. Dimensions of affect: some theoretical and methodological issues. ONR Technical Report No. 17, Vanderbilt Univer., 1963.

Kleinsmith. L. J., & Kaplan, S. Paired-associate learning as a function of arousal and interpolated interval. *J. exp. Psychol.*, 1963, *65*, 190-193.

Kleinsmith, L. J., & Kaplan, S. Interaction of arousal and recall interval in nonsense syllable paired-associate learning. *J. exp. Psychol.*, 1964, *67*, 124-126.

Marston, A. R., Kanfer, F. H., & McBrearty, J. F. Stimulus discriminability in verbal conditioning. *J. Psychol.*, 1962, *53*, 143-153.

McGeoch, J. A., & Irion, A. L. *The psychology of human learning.* New York: Longmans, 1952.

Noble, C. E. Measurements of association value (a), rated associations (a′), and scaled meaningfulness (m′) for the 2100 CVC combinations of the English alphabet. *Psychol. Rep.*, 1961, *8*, 487-521.

Postman, L., & Schneider, B. Personal values, visual recognition and recall. *Psychol. Rev.*, 1951, *58*, 271-284.

Sharp, Agnes A. An experimental test of Freud's doctrine of the relation of hedonic tone to memory revival. *J. exp. Psychol.*, 1938, *22*, 395-418.

Tomkins, S. S. *Affect, imagery, consciousness.* Vol. I. *The positive affects.* New York: Springer, 1962.

Underwood, B. J. Interference and forgetting. *Psychol. Rev.*, 1957, *64*, 49-60.

Underwood, B. J. Paper read at Institute in Psycholinguistics, Peabody College, Nashville, June 1963.

Underwood, B. J., & Keppel, G. An evaluation of two problems of method in the study of retention. *Amer. J. Psychol.*, 1962, *75*, 1-17.

Worchel, P. Anxiety and repression. *J. abnorm. soc. Psychol.*, 1955, *50*, 201-205.

PART TWO

AFFECT AND
COGNITION

Affect and the psychology of knowledge

Silvan S. Tomkins

Proud and aloof on the banks of the mainstream of human history, American psychology guards its virginity. It will give itself to the laboratory but not to man in real time. It is haunted by the vision of exposing the causal roots of things. But effects are epiphenomena, important only because they are produced by first causes. And so human responses are degraded to the status of operational criteria for the presence of some prior stimulus. This is but one of the many sources of the chaste indifference of American psychology to human history.

We will argue that a complete science of man must focus not only on the causal mechanisms underlying cognition, affect and action, but also on the cultural *products* of man. Man is to be found as much in his language, his art, in his science, in his economic, political and social institutions, as he is to be found in his cerebrum, in his nervous system, and in his genes. We would urge that the biopsychological mechanisms and the social products be integrated into a science of man and not polarized as competitors for the attention of psychology. Further, the psychologist should be equally at home in the laboratory as in the library, as in the armchair, as in the computer room, as on the streets, or in the field. McClelland (1961) has provided a critical model in his study of the achievement motive, moving back and forth, with minimal embarrassment and with great profit, from the experimental study of the achievement motive to the historical study of the relationship between the achievement motive and economic growth and finally to the application of this theory in changing the rate of economic growth in one of the emerging nations. We too will attempt to show that some of the same phenomena which are invariant in the history of western thought can also be brought under experimental scrutiny in the laboratory. We do *not* intend by this however to argue for the superiority of one method over the other. Invariances found in the library through an examination of beliefs which men have

Invited Address to Division 8, American Psychological Association, September 7, 1964.

held over centuries of time are not necessarily any less lawful than those found in the laboratory.

If we enlarge our spectrum of methods and the sites of investigation, a new field becomes possible and, we think, profitable for psychology, which we would call the psychology of knowledge. Such a field would concern itself first of all with the structure of man's knowledge. This would include both knowledge which is demonstrably valid and knowledge which is demonstrably invalid, and knowledge which is gray and especially knowledge which is based on faith. It would also concern itself with the ebb and flow of affect investment in ideas and ideology, in methods and styles of investigation, and in what is considered acceptable criteria of evidence. It would concern itself with the matches and mismatches between the ideologies which individuals and societies believed, and their needs. It would concern itself with the dynamics of initial resonance to ideology, of seduction by ideas, of disenchantment with ideas, of addiction to ideas and the abstinence symptoms of ideological deprivation, of commitment to ideas and the integration of both individuals and societies through commitment. It would concern itself with the role of violence and suffering in either discouraging or encouraging commitment to and deepening of ideology, as for example in the deepening and strengthening of both the anti-democratic and the democratic ideology by the threat of fascism and again by the challenge of the Negro for integration into American society.

We have presented such theory and some supporting evidence in "The Psychology of Commitment" in this volume and in the third and fourth volumes of *Affect Imagery Consciousness*. Here we wish to present another part of such a psychology of knowledge in a theory of the structure of ideology.

The Structure of Ideology

I will use the word ideology in a restricted and somewhat special sense. By ideology I will mean any organized set of ideas about which human beings are at once most articulate and most passionate, and for which there is no evidence and about which they are least certain. The foundations of mathematics, the philosophy of science, metaphysics, theology, epistemology, the theory of value, ethics, aesthetics, jurisprudence, government, theory of education, and finally, theories about child rearing, more recently called socialization—these have all evoked the most coherent and passionate controversy. When the same ideas are firmly established and incorporated into the fabric of a science or tested and found wanting, they cease to constitute an ideology in the sense in which we are using the term. At the growing edge of the frontier of all sciences there necessarily is a maximum of uncertainty, and what is lacking in evidence is filled by passion and faith, and hatred and scorn for the disbelievers. Science will never be free of ideology, though yesterday's ideology is today's fact or fiction. Ideology appears in many domains, but it is found in its purest form in those controversies which are centuries old, and which have never ceased to find true believers, whether the issue is joined in mathematics or in aesthetics or in politics. Over and over again, whether theorists address themselves to one or another of these domains, they appear to become polarized on the same issues.

Now let me introduce the concepts of ideo-affective postures, ideological postures and ideo-affective resonance. (1) By ideo-affective postures I mean any *loosely organized* set of feelings and *ideas about feelings*. (2) By ideological postures I refer to any *highly organized* and articulate set of *ideas about anything*. A generally tolerant or permissive attitude would be an instance of an ideo-affective posture, whereas a progressive or democratic political position would be an example of an ideological posture. All individuals have ideo-affective postures, but not all attain an organized ideological posture. (3) By ideo-affective resonance we mean the engagement of the loosely organized beliefs and feelings (of the ideo-affective postures) by ideology (as we have defined it), when the ideo-affective postures are sufficiently similar to the ideological posture, so that they reinforce and strengthen each other. Ideo-affective resonance to ideology is a love affair of a loosely organized set of feelings and ideas about feelings with a highly organized and articulate set of ideas about anything. As in the case of a love affair the fit need not at the outset be perfect, so long as there is sufficient similarity between what the individual feels and thinks is desirable and the characteristics of the love object, to set the vibrations between the two entities into sympathetic coordination with each other. Once a critical degree of similarity has been reached, a way will be found to heighten the communality. It is possible and indeed common for different individuals to resonate in different manners to the same ideology, just as it is possible for two individuals to fall in love with different aspects of the same person for different but somewhat similar reasons. Resonance is a relationship between *families* of ideas and feelings. If each family has many similar members but no two members exactly alike, and if there is as much resemblance between members of one family and another family (e.g., between a grandmother and her grandchild, as between this child and a sibling), then resonance may produce a sub-set of ideo-affects (composed of parts of the original ideo-affects and parts of the ideology) which resemble each other more than the members of the total original set of ideo-affects resembled each other, and more than the original members of the ideology resembled each other. By virtue of this new tighter organization the formerly loosely organized personality may become extraordinarily integrated, with varying degrees of exclusion of non-fitting components of the former personality. The concept of families of ideo-affects and families of ideas organized into an ideology also enables us to account for many alternative equivalent families. It is like a large family which is married off to another large family, with a common set of ancestors not too far back. The families of such families, if they continue to intermarry, will produce tantalizing communalities which will be filtered through most conceptual nets except those designed to catch family resemblances. Stated more precisely, if there exists a set of families of ideo-affective postures of the form a, b, c, ... a_n, b_n, c_n, and a set of families of ideological postures of the form A, B, C, ... A_n, B_n, C_n, then there will be ideo-affective resonances of the following types: (a, b, c, A, B, C,) or (a, b, A, B) or (a, A, B,) or (a, b, A,) in which all members of one set are mapped on to analogues in the other set, or some are, or some are mapped on to more or less analogues in the other set. Thus one individual exposed primarily to literary controversy might resonate to romanticism rather than classicism, whereas the same kind of person exposed to both politics and literature might resonate to revolutionary ideas in both domains. Further, of two individuals, both romantic in ideo-affective posture, one might resonate to the emphasis on feeling in ideology and the other resonate to the emphasis on the unconscious forces within the individual and still another resonate to the anti-traditionalism of the romantic ideology.

Further, there will be resonances of the types (a_1, b_1, c_1, A_2, B_2, C_2,) or (a_1, b_2, c_3, A_4, B_4, C_4) in which the fit between the components of the two sets is not so close as it is in other cases. This can happen because of historical accident. If the prevailing ideologies are restricted in range, individuals may resonate to ideologies which are not quite so congenial as another member of the ideological family might have been, had the individual lived a century earlier when this might have been an available alternative. Thus a politically conservative ideology in a democratic society might be much less conservative than the ideo-affective resonance would have made attractive had the individual lived in a feudal society.

A very special case of such historically produced and limited resonance occurs in the life history of all creative artists and scientists. Ordinarily the artist or scientist as a young man will resonate to that one ideology, among those available, which is closest to the ideology which he will later create to give expression to what is unique in his own ideo-affective posture. At that earlier time he may also engraft onto the contemporary organized ideology, toward which he is then most resonant, certain characteristics which will later become the central features of his later ideology. My own work offers an illuminating instance. As a young man, the two ideologies toward which I resonated, due to my own ideo-affective postures, were the theories of Freud and Murray. I was not aware at that time of any lack of fit between my own ideo-affective posture and these ideologies. But despite this I constructed, with the aid of my colleague Daniel Horn, a test of personality (the PAT) which was focussed on the problems of affect and affect investment, in work, in people, and in the body. These are the focus of my present ideology as it is expressed in *Affect Imagery Consciousness* some twenty years later. What is of interest here is the alien quality of these concepts to their originator because of their lack of fit with the dominant ideologies which were totally accepted because of the great congeniality of both Freud's and Murray's ideologies to my own ideo-affective posture. It was not until some twenty years later when I completed my theoretical work that I could understand how and why I wrote, in *The Tomkins-Horn Picture Arrangement Test*

(Tomkins & Miner, 1957, p. 27): "Why did we choose these variables rather than others? Prejudice and hunch, both personal and professional. The PAT continues the empirical tradition begun by Rorschach and Murray in utilizing dimensions that the test constructor and his colleagues think worth measuring. Ten years from today personality theorists may regard these questions as not worth answering." Clearly I had a hunch, but since I could not rationalize the hunch, it could not be defended, and the inference that it might therefore not be worth defending had to be confronted. It should also be noted that the development of the theory later developed could indeed, by that time, have provided some theoretical justification for the variables measured on the PAT. However the better total fit between Freud and Murray's ideology and my own ideo-affective posture prevented these links' being forged at that time. As in science generally, one theory is displaced only by another theory, and my own theory was still too inarticulate to be used as a support for conceptual decisions and actions which were in fact taken, unconsciously prompted by this embryonic theory and the ideo-affective posture behind it.

One may generalize the questions raised by this particular instance to that of the congruence for large masses of individuals between the ideologies open to them and the ideo-affective postures generated by their socialization and by the circumstances of the historical period in which they live. One would suppose there to be a reasonably good fit between the ideology and myths in a society and the general feelings and ideas generated by the particular schedules of socialization and the particular way of life in a society with its special social structure. In many historical periods the ideology to which most members of a society resonate is in fact as much an outcome of that society as is its institutions. The ideology is a part of the social whole which not only expresses the feelings and ideas of its present members but helps to create in the next generation the same kind of socialized human beings through influencing the socialization and social structure to either maintain or to better approximate the general ideology.

In a relatively static society one would suppose that ideology and society would achieve a relatively stable equilibrium so that the experiences one had from birth to death predisposed one to resonate to the prevailing ideology of that society. To the extent to which there was a lack of fit, either the ideology might change the society or the society might change the ideology so that there was a better fit. But over the long term there would tend to be an accommodation between life in a society and the ideology which summarized and symbolized that life.

When societies change, however, they are confronted with the problem which every creative individual faces alone. How shall a society create the myths towards which it can resonate when its own experience has changed, but when it in fact resonates to ideologies of the past because these are better than no ideologies at all? We must then anticipate a great unwillingness to relinquish the older ideology and an unrest produced by such commitments which do not completely satisfy, a flirtation with novelties of all kinds, including an ultra-reactionary component and a permanent openness to any hint of the new ideology and mythology which will express enough of the essential feelings and ideas of life as it is being lived to excite the imagination to resonance.

If the distance between the ideology and the ideas and feelings of a people, particularly of the elite, grows too far apart too quickly, then in such an ideological vacuum we may expect a vulnerability to any ideology which fits better than the rejected older ideology. Such would appear to be the circumstance today. As Black (1965) has shown, there is in all the underdeveloped countries of the world a yearning for rapid modernization. We may expect that Marxist ideology will prove particularly congenial to any elite group which is impatient to pull itself by its bootstraps quickly into twentieth century modern industrial civilization. This is not to say that there may not be ideologies which would be better suited both to realize the wish to modernize quickly and to preserve components of the older society, but it may be that the Marxist ideology is in fact the only presently available alternative which is sufficiently visible to be adopted. If these rapidly changing societies are not to adopt a Marxist ideology then there must be ideological invention. As Black has suggested, each country does in fact face somewhat different problems, and there is no reason to believe that a blanket solution or a blanket ideology will work equally well for all these societies. Further, there are models other than either the Russian or American experiments which might be more appropriate for these societies groping for ideologies with which to identify. Japan in particular might provide a model for many presently underdeveloped countries with aspirations for rapid modernization. We are not here concerned with the larger question of the rational means to rapid modernization but rather with the more restricted question of what kind of ideology will be acceptable to a society which has ideas and feelings which no longer resonate to the traditional ideologies. There is no reason to believe that the fit between the ideology to which such a society is vulnerable and its own affective and ideological needs may not be quite gross, in the absence of a more congenial alternative. The danger of such a circumstance is that the modernization of a society under the directive of a poorly fitting ideology may subject the members of that society as well as other societies to excessive strain in the attempt to accommodate to the somewhat alien ideology. Commonly this strain is greatly reduced for the first generation reared under the new ideology since their socialization will be more influenced by the new ideology than by the older ideology of their parents. It is our belief that ideology is the major organizing force within any society, and that in modern times the concentration of power and the means of communication in the hands of an elite enables the control of society through the dissemination of the revolutionary ideology. Whereas in the Middle Ages religion constituted the major ideology, today the major ideology is Marxism. The ideology which powered the American and French Revolutions has yet to be modernized and is we think the major reason for the loss of nerve in

Western Europe and America in the face of the Marxist ideology.

It is also the case that large masses of Americans and Europeans have within their basic ideo-affective postures many loosely organized components which might with some reorganization constitute a more articulate, tightly organized ideology. In America such components are "freedom," "the rights of the individual," "freedom of speech," which predispose Americans to resonate toward a competitive capitalism and away from a Marxist dictatorship. These fragments of their collective ideo-affective postures would also however predispose Americans to resonate to an as yet unformulated ideology for modern times for a highly industrialized society, in which additional ideo-affective components generated by modern civilization might be incorporated. These would include the extraordinary increase in communion, intimacy and extended identification made possible by modern communication techniques, as well as by the radical increase in physical mobility into space and over the face of the earth. It would include an extension of the collective consciousness and concern away from national states to a world order. It would include an active concern for the economic and psychological well being of citizens of the world society, now within reach through the utilization of atomic energy for the benefit of all mankind. It would include a commitment of major energies, under forced draft, to the world-wide study of man in a war of man against those aspects of man which restrict his freedom and development. A sense of urgency about the possible benefits of self-knowledge achieved through the scientific study of man is needed as much and as urgently as the atomic bomb was needed in the second World War. These benefits include the control of war and discrimination but they also include the possibility of the radical enrichment of experience in ways remote from our present aspirations, as atomic energy is remote from the discovery of fire. It would include a renewal of the awareness of the significance of the individual as an innovator on the extended frontier which reaches from the virgin land to the endless frontiers of art and science. It would also include a renewal of the awareness of one's identification with all human beings in a common effort to solve our collective human problems, a renewal of the sense of solidarity and the pride of being a member of the human race. These are but a few of the ideas and feelings about human potentialities at this point in human history which all Americans have sensed dimly and sometimes obliquely, in part because of the glare from an outmoded ideology which was radical when the colonists first achieved a sense of nationality. Before America can provide a revolutionary ideology for the world it must provide an ideology for itself which will express and integrate the loosely knit residues of the past and the intimations of the future American dream. The distinction which we have drawn between the basic ideo-affective postures and ideology proper is a fundamental one, and societies can and do die when their ideologies atrophy through increasing irrelevance to the changing ideo-affective postures. Yet it should be noted that the ideo-affective postures contain all the components which will be expressed more articulately in the organized ideology, even if this latter is never attained.

Not all human beings attain an ideological commitment, nor the same commitment in all the fields where it is represented. Thus many human beings never attain sufficiently intimate acquaintance with the realm of philosophy, art and science to resonate to one or another ideological posture. Even more individuals who resonate to one ideological domain fail to do so to another. If our theory is correct, however, it should be possible to predict from the basic ideo-affective postures to what ideological postures the individual would resonate if he were to be sufficiently exposed to these domains. Our evidence suggests that this can be done and that if one knows what an individual believes about the nature of literature, one would also know what he would believe about the nature of mathematics if he were to be confronted with the latter problems. It also appears that, even if the individual is completely innocent of any ideology, if one knows his general ideo-affective posture one can predict what his ideological posture will be if one asks him to consider an ideological question. Thus the completely ideologically innocent layman will not be indifferent to the ideological question in mathematics, "Do you think numbers are real or do you think someone invented them?"

Ideological Polarity in Western Thought

Let us now briefly examine some general features of what I regard as the basic ideological polarity in Western thought. In the foundations of law, or mathematics, or science, or art, or child rearing, theorists who address themselves to one or another of these domains appear to become polarized on the same issues. The issues constitute a polarity extending from the extreme left through a middle of the road position to the extreme right wing position. The issues are simple enough. Is man the measure, an end in himself, an active, creative, thinking, desiring, loving force in nature? Or must man realize himself, attain his full stature only through struggle toward, participation in, conformity to a norm, a measure, an ideal essence basically prior to and independent of man. In Greek philosophy this is the polarity between Protagoras and Plato, between the conception of man as the measure of all things and the conception of Ideas and Essences as the realm of reality and value. When man has thought about man he has either glorified himself or derogated himself. He has judged himself to be inherently good or basically evil, to be the source of all value or to be worthless.

Let us now examine this polarity as it appears first in the foundations of *mathematics*. For Poincaré and others, mathematics is the finest type of human play. Man is most free in this domain because he constructs the entities of mathematics entirely from his imagination. Because of the delight in play, Poincaré defends mathematics as an end in itself. "Mathematics for mathematics sake! People have been shocked by this formula, and yet it is as good as life for life's sake, if life is but misery." Courant

(1941, p. 521), among others, equates such a view with childish caprice. It would be a mere game, lacking contact with reality and of interest to no one.

"A serious threat to the very life of science is implied in the assertion that mathematics is nothing but a system of conclusions drawn from definitions and postulates that must be consistent but otherwise may be created by the free will of the mathematician. If this description were accurate, mathematics could not attract any intelligent person. It would be a game with definitions, rules and syllogisms, without motive or goal. The notion that the intellect can create meaningful postulational systems at its whim is a deceptive half-truth. Only under the discipline of responsibility to the organic whole, only guided by intrinsic necessity, can the free mind achieve results of scientific value."

The bipolar attitude towards games and play and man find their clearest expression in the foundations of mathematics. When everyone was congratulating Lindemann in 1882 over his proof that pi is transcendental, Kronecker said, "Of what value is your beautiful proof, since irrational numbers do not exist?" "God created the natural numbers; everything else is man's handiwork." Courant's comment is: "In these words Leopold Kronecker pointed out the safe ground on which the structure of mathematics can be built."
Bell (1951, p. 437) is a representative of the other pole.

"In the older books on geometry, postulates were sometimes called axioms, and it was gratuitously added that 'an axiom is a self-evident truth' (which must have puzzled many an intelligent youngster). Modern mathematics is concerned with playing the game according to the rules; others may inquire into the 'truth' or mathematical propositions, provided they think they know what they mean.
"The rules of the game are extremely simple. Once and for all the postulates are laid down. These include a statement of all the permissible moves of the 'elements' or 'pieces.' It is just like chess.

"Only a very original philosopher would dream of asking whether a particular game of chess was 'true.' The sensible question would be, 'was the game played according to rules?'"

Laplace's comment on Leibnitz is the other orientation: "Leibnitz saw in his binary arithmetic the image of creation. He imagined that unity represented God, and zero the void, that the Supreme Being drew all beings from the void, just as unity and zero express all numbers in his system of numeration."
In an investigation of the determinants of the attraction to mathematics as a career, I have also noted that there is a polarization between right wing mathematicians who were originally attracted as children to mathe-

matics by its certainty and discipline, that they knew what the right answer was and whether they had attained it, and left wing mathematicians who were attracted by its novelty and promise of excitement, and its "wild, unaccountable spaces."

In the *philosophy of science*, there is the same polarization. On the one hand science is understood as correspondence with reality and facts. Measurement is the most direct route to physical reality, and inference is the danger which must be held in check lest fancy run away with reality. Thus Verplanck, Collier and Cotlow (1952, p. 273) among many other psychologists reveal, in an aside, their suspicion of inference running wild.

> "The sensory, neural, photochemical, or physical processes that have been postulated to generate the observed functions have been inferred from the functions themselves, and have seldom, if ever, been available to direct or collateral observation. Limits have been placed on such inference by information obtained in other disciplines. Physiological, biochemical, and histological evidence, often scanty, have served to keep in check the variety of inferences drawn."

Most American sciences were governed by such a philosophy until the 1930's when refugee scientists from Europe began to assume a more important role in American thought. Contrast such an attitude with that of Einstein (1942, p. 313):

> "The formulation of a problem is often more essential than its solution, which may be merely a matter of mathematical or experimental skill. To raise new questions, new possibilities, to regard old problems from a new angle, requires creative imagination and makes a real advance in science.
> "Physical concepts are free creations of the human mind, and are not, however it may seem, uniquely determined by the external world."

The importance of play in science is affirmed by Newton as it was by Poincaré for mathematics. "I do not know what I may appear to the world but to myself I seem to have been only like a boy playing on the seashore, and diverting myself in now and then finding a prettier shell, or a smoother pebble than ordinary, whilst the great ocean of truth lay all undiscovered before me."

Perhaps the classic statements of the extreme left wing of philosophy of science are from Russell. Russell, in *Our Knowledge of the External World* said, "Things are those series of aspects that obey the laws of physics."

In *metaphysics*, it is the contrast between a realistic and an idealistic conception of the relation of man to reality. In the extreme right wing metaphysics, as in Platonism, both man and nature are pale copies of Ideas or Essences which exist prior to and independent of man. Man and nature alike owe whatever significance they attain to their participation in, their approximation to, the ideal essences which alone are truly real and important. A less extreme right wing metaphysics conceives nature as more real, prior to and independent of man. The extreme left wing metaphysician conceives the world to be constructed by man or some form of mind. In its extreme form, as in Fichte and in Berkeley, the world is created by mind, and is an idea. In its less extreme form, nature is a dull affair, enlivened only by the mind of man. Listen to Whitehead (1926, p. 296) in *Science and the Modern World:*

> "These sensations are projected by the mind so as to clothe appro-priate bodies in external nature. Thus the bodies are perceived as with qualities which in reality do not belong to them, qualities which in fact are purely the off-spring of the mind. Thus nature gets credit which should in truth be reserved for ourselves: the rose for its scent, the nightingale for his song, and the sun for its radiance. The poets are entirely mistaken. They should address their lyrics to themselves, and should turn them into odes of self-congratulation on the excellency of the human mind. Nature is a dull affair, soundless, scentless, colorless; merely the hurrying of material, endlessly, meaninglessly."

In *epistemology*, it is reality as grasped immediately by the senses con-trasted with reality as an idea constructed by the perceiving mind. In a second cousin to epistemology, the psychological theory of *perception*, it is the contrast between stimulus-bound theory such as that of Gibson and the constructivist position of Cassirer and the transactionalist theory of Cantril and Ames.

In the *general theory of value*, it is value defined as any object of any interest contrasted with value as an external quality of reality.

In the *theory of politics*, it is the view of the state as a creation of the people, by the people, for the people, and the view of the state as a superordinate entity through which the people attain such freedom as is possible. It is the difference between the conservative emphasis on tradition and conformity to the status quo, and the progressive's emphasis on change, in the interests of the people.

In *jurisprudence*, it is the interpretation of law as man made or law as transcendental.

In *art*, there is the recurrent polarity between romanticism and classi-cism, between conservation of tradition and radical experimentation, between emphasis on the personal, the irrational, on human feeling versus the emphasis on control, on restraint, on reason.

M. H. Abrams (1958, p. 406) in his analysis of romantic theory and the critical tradition in the book *The Mirror and the Lamp* also finds evidence of a recurrent polarity between the right and left wing.

> "The title of the book identifies two common and antithetic metaphors of mind, one comparing the mind to a reflector of external objects, the

other to a radiant projector which makes a contribution to the objects it perceives. The first of these was characteristic of much of the thinking from Plato to the eighteenth century: the second typifies the prevailing romantic conception of the poetic mind."

In *educational theory*, there is a perennial polarity between a left wing progressive theory which stresses the wishes of the child and a more conservative authority-oriented emphasis on moral or achievement norms to be achieved by education.

In *psychology*, our own discipline, the conflict between experimental psychology and clinical psychology is a derivative of a philosophy which stresses feeling and thinking rather than perceiving or acting and which stresses theory and observation rather than experimental control. It is also a conflict between being good (in the achievement or moral sense) and doing good. In the authority ideology, God helps those who help themselves. The same phenomenon of revulsion at the "do-gooders" appears among the conservatives in psychology and in politics.

One of the extraordinary characteristics of this polarity is its appearance even within domains that appear at the outset to be primarily right or left wing in orientation. Thus within the field of clinical diagnosis by the Rorschach method, an essentially left wing method, we are confronted with the unrelenting antithesis of a free-wheeling Klopfer and a norm-oriented Beck.

The same polarity breaks out within *psychiatry*, a left wing profession in its insistence on the value of the individual and on the legitimacy of his claim to be helped rather than rejected. Yet Strupp has shown that there is a radical difference among psychiatrists which is very similar to the general right wing left wing polarity we have postulated. In studying the performance of psychotherapists under comparable controlled conditions, Strupp (1960) used a sound film of an initial interview. The film was prepared for "audience participation" (therapists in the audience) by interrupting the interview sequence at predetermined points with the uniform question "What would you do?"—giving the audience therapist an opportunity to indicate what he could have done had he been the interviewer. Strupp's investigation rested on the assumption that the simulated interviewer behavior of the therapist bears a relationship to his performance in similar real-life therapy situations, and that valid inferences can be drawn from this sample of his behavior.

Following the film showing, the therapists were requested to complete a comprehensive questionnaire on diagnostic impressions, treatment plans and goals, formulations of the patient's dynamics, problems in treatment, estimates of the patient's anxiety, emotional maturity, social adjustment, prognosis with and without therapy, the respondent's attitude toward the patient and the therapist in the film, and an evaluation of the latter's performance. Strupp found that clinical impressions and therapeutic planning are influenced by attitudinal variables within the therapist. Group I therapists appear to be more tolerant, more humane, more permissive, more "democratic" and more "therapeutic." Group II therapists emerge as more directive, disciplinarian, moralistic, and harsh. This contrast suggested the hypothesis that Group I therapists are "warmer" in their communications to the patient and that "cold" rejecting comments will be less frequent.

"On the one hand, it is a basic attitude of understanding, respect, and compassion—what Albert Schweitzer calls 'reverence for life.' It is the ability to listen to the patient's story without preconception, prejudgment, or condemnation. It is the ability to pierce the neurotic distortions, the socially unacceptable attitudes and acts, the more unsavory aspects of his personality, and to see behind it a confused, bewildered and helpless individual trying to shape his destiny, hampered and hindered by his neurotic conflicts and maladaptations. On the other hand, it is an attitude of coldness, calculation, 'clinical evaluation,' distance, 'objectivity,' aloofness, moral judgment, and condemnation. It is a readiness to take the neurotic defenses and the patient's character structure at face value, and to react to them with irritation, impatience, annoyance, and anger. It is also an attitude of forming a judgment about the patient's illness, almost from the beginning of the interview, often accompanied by a diagnostic label of 'psychopathic,' 'paranoid,' etc." (Strupp, 1960, p. 338).

The analyses also suggested that the empathic as well as the unempathic approach was in part a reflection of the therapist's conscious attitude. That is, to some extent at least, therapists were aware of their positive or negative reaction to the patient and their willingness or unwillingness to enter into a therapeutic relationship.

Finally this same polarity appears in the popular *child rearing* literature of America, according to C. B. Stendler (1950). In this literature, there is a polarization between loving and controlling the child. In the child rearing theory based on Calvinism, methods were consciously related to the type of adult desired: a moral, honest, religious, independent individual who would take his proper place in society. It was assumed that the child was doomed to depravity throughout his life unless given careful and strict guidance by the parents and ultimately saved through Grace. Complete obedience and submission were thus required, and achieved, by "breaking the will" of the child.

Sooner or later the child would refuse to obey a command, and the issue of "will" was at hand. It was considered fatal to let the child win out. One mother, writing in the *Mother's Magazine* in 1834, described how her sixteen-month-old girl refused to say "dear mama" upon the father's order. She was led into a room alone, where she screamed wildly for ten minutes; then she was commanded again, and again she refused. She was then whipped, and asked again. This was kept up for four hours until the child finally obeyed. Parents commonly reported that after one such trial the child became permanently submissive . . . However, many mothers seemed to find it hard to follow such prescriptions and the *Mother's Magazine* carried many exhortations to mothers to their duty toward their children. For parents of this group, indulgence was to be shunned.

Another theory which stressed conformity to a norm, the norm of the achievement and competence, centered around "hardening" the child. Children should become strong, vigorous, unspoiled men like those in the early days of the country. Cold baths and cold plunges were considered necessary, in the manner of the Indians. The implication derived from Rousseau was that the external environment of civilization was dangerous to the child and so required a long period of "training" of an athletic sort.

The other chief competitor for the attention of mothers in the child rearing literature of the nineteenth century was the delicate flower theory that rejected hardening altogether. As Stendler (1950, p. 122) reports: "In 1890 one editor wrote, 'Love, petting and indulgence will not hurt a child if at the same time he is taught to be unselfish and obedient. Love is the mighty solvent.' Another writer outlined her plan for treating a boy who was labeled lazy, careless, and good-for-nothing: 'I thought I would try to win him with love alone, and never strike him . . . Mothers who have trouble with their children, bring them up the Christian way . . . with a loving and tender heart, and you will surely succeed.' "

The child was to be led, not driven; persuaded to the right, not commanded. Consistency and firmness are counselled but with understanding and justice to the child. Corporal punishment was undesirable. The child was likened to "an immortal bud just commencing to unfold its spotless leaves . . . a beautiful flower opening to the sunshine." The child was ignorant of right rather than bent to wrong. Stendler mentions that a verse dating from an earlier day was often quoted during this period. It reflects the orientation of the nineties:

> "If a babe sucks his thumb
> 'Tis an ease to his gum:
> A comfort, a boon, a calmer of grief,
> A friend in his need affording relief,
> A solace, a good, a soother of pain,
> A composer to sleep, a charm and a gain."

As Stendler has shown in her study, there have been regular swings of the pendulum from the tender to the tough-minded treatment of the child. From 1890-1900 there was a highly sentimental view. From 1910-1930 there was an increasing emphasis on rigid scheduling and disciplinary fervor. From 1940 to the present, the pendulum swung back again—and there is now appearing evidence for a swing in the other direction again.

The same polarity concerning child rearing is found in the old and the new testaments. The difference between the God of Love and the God of

Authority is reflected in the assumed relationship between parent and child.

In the Old Testament we find:

> "He that hateth reproof is brutish."   Proverbs 13:1

> "The eye that despiseth to obey his
> mother, the ravens of the valley shall
> pluck it out."   Proverbs 30:17

> "He that curseth Father or Mother,
> let him die the death."   Leviticus 20:9

But in the New Testament:

> "And ye Fathers provoke not your
> children to wrath, lest they be
> discouraged."   Ephesians 6:2 & 3

We have thus far considered the left and right wing ideologies. What of the middle of the road? This position exists, and indeed one might defend the thesis that the middle of the road represents the most radical ideology rather than a compromise. This is so because the tension between the right and left wing in ideology has been perennial, and a creative synthesis evokes some resonance from both sides. It is not accidental that the most influential modern philosopher, Kant, represents a synthesis of the right and the left, and that the giant of modern music, Beethoven, also achieved a creative synthesis of the right and left wing musical forms.

Consider Kant. He affirmed both that reality, the *Ding an sich*, exists independent of and prior to man, that it is forever unknowable, but that what man does know he has in large part created, the categories of the mind through which alone nature can be experienced. Kant achieved the same synthesis in his ethical theory. Let us suppose that Kant was torn between the demands of the right and the left. How could one synthesize a foundation for morality which was personal and subjective and at the same time universal and objective? Kant's solution was extraordinarily creative: one should act in such a way that what one did could be universalized. Be yourself, find morality within, but let it be possible that your morality is capable of serving as a norm for mankind. As in his metaphysics and epistemology, Kant unites the creative and subjective with the universal and objective. It is an extraordinary tour de force, and all philosophy thenceforth has been more or less "critical." In contemporary value theory the word commitment is an analogous synthesis which attempts to avoid both the pitfalls of "caprice" and the harshness of external "demands." It is a modern version of willing the obligatory.

Where one would speak of "demands," or with a less strident voice of "responsibilities," the modern Kantian speaks of commitment.

In music Beethoven stands between the classical and romantic styles. Form never becomes an end in itself as in much classical music, and expression never completely overflows form and constraint as in much romanticism. It is because Beethoven, like Kant, struggled to join the right and the left that his interpreters, the conductors, have been able to transform him into a romantic or into a classic composer.

In recent philosophy Whitehead is perhaps the principal representative of the creative synthesis of the right and the left. In his recipe for a viable society he insists that loyalty to tradition must be combined with a willingness to experiment. The revolutionary is like a child with an arrow in his hand who brings his society to the brink of its destruction but without whom that society would perish.

The Origins of Polarity

What might be the origins of such a duality in man's view of himself? Consider the basic alternatives open to parents interacting with their children. At one pole is a return of the parent to his own golden age through identification with the child in play and shared delight. The child's zest for life and obvious joy in simple human interaction and in elementary curiosity and attempted control over his own body, and the world in general, can revitalize the adult personality. Such a parent bestows on the child the feeling that he is an end in himself and that shared human interaction is a deeply satisfying experience. Further, such a parent will not puncture the child's conception of his ability to control his parent. Eventually such a child must come to the awareness that the world presents endless opportunities for the experience of varied positive affects—joy, excitement, love of people, of places, of activities, and of things. He becomes addicted to creating satisfaction for himself and for others.

There is another possibility open to any parent. This is the conjoint opportunity and obligation to mold the child to some norm. The norm may be a moral norm, a norm of "manners," a norm of competence, a norm of independence. In any case, the parent sets himself in opposition to the child and bestows upon the child the sense that positive satisfaction is necessarily an epiphenomenon, consequent to effort, to struggle, to renunciation of his own immediate wishes. The child's feelings and wishes are devalued in favor of some kind of behavior which is demanded of him. When the child wishes to do one thing and the parent wishes him to do another, the normative parent must set himself in opposition to the child's wishes. He must convey to the child that what he wants to do is of no consequence when it is in opposition to the norm. What is expected of him, in opposition to his own wishes, may be presented with all possible attractiveness and positive sanctions, but the fundamental necessity of renunciation and devaluation of his own wishes, thereby of his self, cannot in a normative socialization be sidestepped.

There are three alternative types of the middle of the road socialization. First, one parent socializes according to the left and the other parent socializes in the right wing manner. A person growing up this way becomes exquisitely aware of the clash of ideologies, living as he does at the intersection of opposites. He is likely to be concerned with the reconciliation of opposites. He is concerned too with the problem of communication, between his divided selves and between the left and right wing ideologists who have little or no understanding of each other and who therefore cannot communicate.

The second type of socialization which produces a resonance with the middle of the road ideology is by parents who are themselves mixed in their own ideo-affective posture or in their own ideology. Such parents may swing from loving and playing with the child to a very stern, demanding insistence on norm compliance.

In the third type of socialization the parents do not swing from the right to the left, but stiffen their left wing attitudes with right wing overtones, and temper their right wing strictures with left wing softening. Thus such a parent may say "You and your friend can play and have as much fun as you would like so long as you don't make too much noise. If you do you will have to stop and your friend will have to go home." Again, "I want you to clean up your room, and I'm not going to let you do anything else until you do that. Do you understand? I know that you and your friend have a date to play together this afternoon and I would hate to have you miss that, but if you hurry and finish up with your room I'll take you over to see your friend."

EMPIRICAL STUDIES OF THE POLARITY

Let us turn now to our empirical studies of the polarity. The first empirical study was undertaken by Dr. Michael Nesbitt (1959) as his doctoral dissertation and was published as an ETS Research Bulletin. Since then, Edward Engel, Robert McCarter, Margaret Stewart and I have been engaged in the intensive study* of several samples now totalling approximately 500 subjects. These include high school students, university students, older normals aged 45 to 60, psychotic depressives and schizophrenics. Both males and females are included at all ages. All of these subjects have also been given a brief intelligence test and the Tomkins-Horn Picture Arrangement Test. Approximately 250 of these subjects were studied more intensively with an extended battery of procedures. We will here report the results of one of these procedures, the integration of conflicting information presented in a stereoscope, as well as the results on the Tomkins-Horn Picture Arrangement Test.

To test the basic theory we have constructed a 57-item Polarity Scale

* These studies have been supported in part by a grant from the National Institute of Mental Health (MH-04685-03) which is gratefully acknowledged. I am also indebted to Dr. Al Friedman for much help and advice in the testing of psychotic depressives at the Philadelphia Psychiatric Center.

(more recently expanded to 59 items). If the theory reasonably approximates the structure of ideology then the correlations between all items, whether they deal with science or child rearing or democracy or sympathy, should be positively correlated. Such is the case. The intercorrelations are predominantly positive on a combined sample of about 500 subjects. Ninety-seven percent of all possible intercorrelations between items are positive when keyed as humanistic for one option and normative for the other. Further, the few negative correlations are very low whereas the average positive intercorrelation is $+.30$.

A detailed examination of this matrix will be presented elsewhere. Here we will examine the most general trends. We have said that human beings tend to idealize themselves or to derogate themselves and that if one knows which of these options is elected one will know a great many other ideological options which will be elected.

In Item 38 we have confronted the individual with one form of this question. "Human beings are basically good" versus "Human beings are basically evil."

If an individual agrees with the proposition "human beings are basically good" and disagrees with the proposition "human beings are basically evil" what else does he believe or say he believes? Using a criterion of a positive correlation of .30 or better, he agrees with 80% of all the other items keyed as humanistic if he thinks human beings are basically good, or with 80% of all the other items keyed normatively if he thinks human beings are basically evil. That is 80% of all the items in the test correlate .30 or better with this item. If we use as a criterion a positive correlation of .40 or better he agrees with 55% of all the other appropriate items. If we use as a criterion a positive correlation of .50 or better he agrees with 32% of all the other appropriate items.

Let us examine some of these relationships in detail. First, is there such a relationship as we have posited between an individual's belief in the worth of human beings and his philosophy of science? Following are the relevant items and the magnitude of their intercorrelations with Item 38, on the goodness or evil of human beings. (The humanistic choice has been sifted to the left hand side whereas it is randomized in the test itself).

Item 4 $(r+.48)$

The most important aspect of science is that it enables man to realize himself by gaining understanding and control of the world around him.

The most important aspect of science is that it enables man to separate the true from the false, the right from the wrong, reality from phantasy.

Item 5 $(r+.55)$

The fact that people once believed the world was flat is just one in a long series of errors which shows how much progress human beings have made and will continue to make.

The fact that people once believed the world was flat is just one in a long series of errors which show how foolish human beings have been and will continue to be.

Item 22   (r+.40)

The main purpose of education should be to enable the young to discover and create novelty.

The main purpose of education should be to teach the young the wisdom of the remote and recent past.

Item 25   (r+.28)

The important thing in science is to strike out into the unknown—right or wrong.

The important thing in science is to be right and make as few errors as possible.

Item 26   (r+.34)

Great achievements require first of all great imagination.

Great achievements require first of all severe self discipline.

Item 29   (r+.55)

The beauty of theorizing is that it has made it possible to invent things which otherwise would never have existed.

The trouble with theorizing is that it leads people away from the facts and substitutes opinion for truth.

Item 30   (r+.53)

Imagination frees people from the dull routines of life.

Imagination leads people into self deception and delusions.

Item 31   (r+.55)

Thinking is responsible for all discovery and invention.

Thinking keeps people on the straight and narrow.

Item 32   (r+.45)

Observing the world accurately provides a human being with constant excitement and novelty.

Observing the world accurately enables human beings to separate reality from imagination.

Item 43   (r+.39)

Truth is found only by those who immerse and lose themselves in what they are studying.

Truth is found only by those who are objective and detached from what they are studying.

Item 44   (r+.40)

No one can understand another human being unless he has loved and been intimate with that person.

No one can understand another human being until he has achieved some distance from that person.

Item 45   (r+.37)

Reason is the chief means by which human beings make great discoveries.

Reason has to be continually disciplined and corrected by reality and hard facts.

Second, those who believe that human beings are basically good also believe that government is for the people and that man can govern himself democratically:

Item 3   (r+.63)

If an individual breaks the law, it is not always to his advantage or to the advantage of society that he be punished.

If an individual breaks the law, he should be punished for the good of society.

Item 7 (r+.30)

Promotion of the welfare of the people is the most important function of a government.

The maintenance of law and order is the most important duty of any government.

Item 13 (r+.30)

A government should allow freedom of expression even though there is some risk in permitting it.

A government should allow only such freedom of expression as is consistent with law and order.

Item 28 (r+.36)

The trouble with democracy is that it too seldom represents the will of the people.

The trouble with democracy is that it too often represents the will of the people.

Item 41 (r+.42)

Anger should be directed against the oppressors of mankind.

Anger should be directed against those revolutionaries who undermine law and order.

Third, the individual who believes human beings are basically good is sympathetic, responding to distress with distress, expects help from others, trusts and likes other human beings:

Item 2 (r+.70)

To every lover, his beloved is the most beautiful person in the world.

Love is blind. Otherwise no one would ever fall in love.

Item 8 (r+.61)

To assume that most people are well-meaning brings out the best in others.

To assume that most people are well-meaning is asking for trouble.

Item 16 (r+.33)

When people are in trouble, they need help and should be helped.

When people are in trouble, they should help themselves and not depend on others.

Item 17 (r+.63)

Little white lies are justified when the truth might hurt the feelings of a close friend.

Little white lies in the long run lead to big black lies.

Item 19 (r+.41)

When a person is in trouble, friendship can become much deeper and closer.

When a person is in trouble, he runs the risk of losing his friends.

Item 20 (r+.36)

The most important characteristic of a friend is that he is warm and responsive to one.

The most important characteristic of a friend is that he is worthy of our admiration and respect.

Item 27 (r+.29)

If human beings were really honest with each other, there would be a lot more sympathy and friendship in the world.

If human beings were really honest with each other, there would be a lot more antipathy and enmity in the world.

Item 33   (r+.45)
It is distressing to see an adult cry.   It is disgusting to see an adult cry.

Item 34   (r+.58)
Fear can make the bravest man trem-   Cowardice is despicable and in a
ble. We should not condemn failure   soldier should be severely punished.
of nerve.

Item 35   (r+.21)
When a person feels sorry for him-   When a person feels sorry for himself, he really needs more sympathy   self, he really should feel ashamed of
from others.   himself.

Item 39   (r+.39)
Those who err should be forgiven.   Those who err should be corrected.

Item 42   (r+.25)
Familiarity like absence makes the   Familiarity breeds contempt.
heart grow fonder.

Item 44   (r+.40)
No one can understand another hu-   No one can understand another human being unless he has loved and   man being until he has achieved some
been intimate with that person.   distance from that person.

Item 48   (r+.43)
Human beings should be loved at all   Human beings should be loved only
times, because they want and need   if they have acted so that they de-
to be loved.   served to be loved.

Item 55   (r+.42)
Human beings should be treated with   Human beings should be treated with
respect at all times.   respect only when they deserve re-
                                             spect.

Fourth, there is, as a special case of a general human sympathy, a love
of children and of childish play:

Item 1   (r+.16)
Children should be encouraged to ex-   Children should be taught to obey
press themselves even though parents   what is right even though they may
may not always like it.   not always feel like it.

Item 6   (r+.79)
Play is important for all human be-   Play is childish. Although it is proper
ings. No one is too old to enjoy the   for children to play, adults should
excitement of play.   concern themselves with more serious
                                             matters.

Item 10   (r+.30)
Parents should first of all be gentle   Parents should first of all be firm
with children.   with children.

Item 12   (r+.55)
A child must be loved so that he can   A child must be taught how to act
grow up to be a fine adult.   so that he can grow up to be a fine
                                             adult.

Item 15 (r+.66)

What children demand, parents should take seriously and try to satisfy.	What children demand should be of little consequence to their parents.

Item 23 (r+.49)

Juvenile delinquency is due to factors we do not understand. When we do understand these we will be able to prevent it in the future.	Juvenile delinquency is simply a reflection of the basic evil in human beings. It has always existed in the past and it always will.

Item 50 (r+.48)

Children are entirely delightful.	Children should be seen and not heard.

Item 54 (r+.46)

To act on impulse occasionally makes life more interesting.	To act on impulse is to act childishly.

Fifth is a correlated cluster of attitudes in favor of feelings as such. Their lability is valued and they are presumed to offer a special avenue to reality:

Item 46 (r+.54)

The changeableness of human feelings makes life more interesting.	The changeableness of human feelings is a weakness in human beings.

Item 47 (r+.33)

When God created man in his own image, he gave him both a heart and a head. His feelings and his reason are both important.	If there is anything like a divine spark in a human being, it is the faculty of reason by which he can control his passions and feelings.

Item 52 (+.33)

Mystical experiences may be sources of insight into the nature of reality.	So-called mystical experiences have most often been a source of delusion.

Item 53 (r+.50)

Man must always leave himself open to his own feelings—alien as they may sometimes seem.	If sanity is to be preserved, man must guard himself against the intrusion of feelings which are alien to his nature.

Item 56 (+.68)

There is a unique avenue to reality through the feelings, even when they seem alien.	There is no surer road to insanity than surrender to the feelings, particularly those which are alien to the self.

Sixth, there is a bias in favor of pluralism and plenitude rather than of hierarchical selectivity:

Item 49 (r+.50)

There are a great many things in the world which are good for human beings and which satisfy them in different ways. This makes the world an exciting place and enriches the lives of human beings.	There are a great many things which attract human beings. Some of them are proper, but many are bad for human beings, and some are very degrading.

Seventh, we have employed a somewhat disguised, indirect measure of the individual's tolerance for or rejection of human beings and of life generally. This is:

Item 57   (r+.49)
Life sometimes leaves a bad taste in   Life sometimes smells bad.
the mouth.

In both cases the individual is confronted with what is negative in his experience in general and in his interpersonal relationships. In one choice (bad taste) another human being or any bad experience has been permitted to come close, to enter the body through the mouth. In the other choice (bad smell) the bad other person or experience has been kept at a distance. In terms of the underlying affects one is a response of shame, the other of disgust and contempt.

This covert measure is related to all the expected ideological options in much the same way as the more explicit statement of ideological posture.

Summarizing, we have seen that if one believes human beings are good there is a cluster of attitudes about science which stresses man's activity, his capacity for invention and progress, the value of novelty and the excitement of discovery, the value of immersion and intimacy with the object of study. If one believes human beings are basically evil there is a cluster of attitudes about science which stresses its value in separating truth from falsity, reality from phantasy, the vulnerability of human beings to error and delusion, the wisdom of the past, the importance of not making errors, the value of thought to keep people on the straight and narrow, the necessity for objectivity and detachment, for discipline and correction by the facts of reality.

Second, there is an associated cluster of attitudes about government— that welfare of the people is the primary aim, that freedom of expression should be permitted even if there is risk in it, that democracy should strive to increase the representation of the will of the people, that anger should be directed against the oppressors of mankind, not against revolutionaries, and punishment for violation of laws is not always to the advantage of the individual or his society.

If the individual believes human beings are basically evil the associated cluster of attitudes on government are that the maintenance of law and order is primary, that offenders should always be punished, that freedom of expression should be allowed only in so far as it is consistent with law and order, that the trouble with democracy is that it too often represents the will of the people and that revolutionaries should be the targets of anger, not the oppressors of mankind.

Third, the individual who believes human beings are basically good is generally sociophilic. The human being who believes human beings are basically bad is generally sociophobic. One likes, trusts, and is sympathetic, the other dislikes, distrusts and responds to the distress of the other with contempt.

Fourth, there is particular sympathy and love of children, and of childish play.

Fifth, there is a cluster of attitudes in favor of feelings as such. Their lability is valued and they are presumed to offer a special avenue to reality.

Sixth, there is a bias in favor of pluralism and plenitude rather than of hierarchical selectivity.

Finally, a covert measure of taste versus smell correlates both with the more explicit ideological option as well as with its correlates.

In our next series of studies, on the same 500 subjects, we compared the humanistic and normative ideological positions with the scores on the Tomkins-Horn Picture Arrangement Test. This is a broad spectrum projective type personality test which has been standardized on a representative sample (1500) of the American population and which is computer scored. Separate norms for age, intelligence and education permit us to compare the polarity scores of young and old, dull and bright subjects on a wide variety of personality measures.

The results for the entire group confirm our expectations. The humanistic ideology is significantly related to general sociophilia (key 97), whereas the normative ideology is significantly related to sociophobia in which there is avoidance of physical contact between men (key 120) and to the expectation of high general press of aggression from others (key 124) and finally to social restlessness (key 149).

Sociophilia is measured by the predominance of arrangement of three pictures which shows the hero both alone and together with others so that in the last picture the hero is with others rather than alone. Sociophobia is measured by the predominance of the last picture showing the hero alone rather than with people. It should be noted that the humanistic orientation is much more generally related to sociophilia than the normative orientation is related to sociophobia, since it is avoidance of physical contact with men (a special case of the more general sociophobia) which is elevated, whereas general sociophilia is elevated in the humanist orientation. The second finding sheds some additional light on this avoidance of contact, since here (key 124) there is a predominance of arrangements in which the hero is placed in a final position of being insulted or aggressed upon. The third finding, social restlessness (key 149), is measured by a maximizing of the number of changes from social to non-social situations, as in the sequences alone-together-alone, or together-alone-together rather than the sequences together-alone-alone (or alone-alone-together) or together-together-alone (or alone-together-together). This finding tells us that the individual cannot tolerate for long either being by himself or with others. It is in marked contrast to the general sociophilia found in the humanist orientation.

These more indirect measures of personality are entirely consistent with the structure of explicit beliefs defended by these subjects in the polarity scale. They raise a serious question about the assumed generality of discrepancies between direct statements about own beliefs and covert indirect measures. It would appear that if one asks the right questions about matters which deeply concern the individual that he will give valid answers.

In the final series of studies the total number of subjects was 247. We will discuss here 87 of these who were high school students of both sexes. (The same set of procedures was also administered to psychotic depressives and schizophrenics, but these results will be discussed elsewhere). In this procedure we first posed and took facial photographs of several professional models, both adults and children, to simulate the eight primary affects. We then presented a set of the 69 best photographs to a group of untrained subjects, whose task it was to identify the affect in the photograph. The average intercorrelation between the judgments of the subjects and the affects which the models had been posed to simulate was .85 for all affects and all photos. These intercorrelations ranged from .63 for surprise to .98 for enjoyment. The best set of photos of all affects for any one subject, a young girl, was selected for presentation in a stereoscope. The same face, showing one of six affects (surprise and interest were excluded) was used throughout the experimental series. The subject was presented on each trial with one affect on the right eye and another affect on the left eye. In addition, each affect was also randomly presented simultaneously to both eyes as a check on how the face would be seen if it were not in conflict with a different face. Each affect was pitted in turn against every other affect, e.g., the sad face of the subject was presented to one eye while the other eye saw a happy face, on another trial an angry face, on another trial an ashamed face, on another trial a contemptuous face, and a frightened face. Each affect was put into conflict with every other affect. In all there were 32 pairs of stimuli shown to each subject. After the presentation of a pair of slides the subject was asked to describe the posed affect he had just perceived. Then one of the two slides was shown separately to him and he was asked whether it resembled the face he had just seen (when in fact each eye had been shown a different face). Next, the other slide was shown to him and he was again asked whether it was like what he saw before or not. A score of one was given to the posed affect which subject stated was more like his percept of the stereoscopically presented pair of affects, and a score of zero was assigned to the other posed affect. Whenever the two separate affects contributed equally to the combined percept, they each received a score of one-half. Since each affect was matched once with the other five, it would thus earn five independent scores. Summing over all five generated a single score for each affect. These scores were then correlated with the humanist score and the normative score of each subject.

It is our assumption that the same attitudes and expectancies which operate at the cognitive level in responding to the polarity scale, and to the Picture Arrangement Test, will also be activated in the resolution of the perceptual conflict in the stereoscope, when the brain is confronted with two incompatible faces and thereby produce either a fusion of both faces or a suppression of one affect in favor of the other.

On the basis of our theory we predicted that the humanistic orientation would result in a dominance of the smiling face over all other affects. We predicted that the normative orientation would produce a dominance of the contemptuous face. Both predictions were confirmed. The correlation of the dominance of the smiling face with the humanistic orientation was .42. The correlation of the dominance of the contemptuous face with the normative orientation was .60. These findings are consistent not only with the structure of explicit ideology as it is affirmed within the polarity scale, but also with the findings of sociophilia and sociophobia as revealed in the Picture Arrangement Test.

In summary, we believe that how positively or how negatively a human being learns to feel about himself and about other human beings will also determine his general posture toward the entire ideological domain.

REFERENCES

Abrams, M. H. *The Mirror and the Lamp*. New York: Norton, 1958.

Bell, E. T. *Mathematics*. New York: McGraw-Hill, 1951.

Black, C. E. *Modernization: Essays in Comparative History*. Forthcoming, 1965.

Bronowski, J., & Mazlish, B. *The Western Intellectual Tradition*. New York: Harper, 1960.

Camus, A. *The Myth of Sisyphus*. New York: Knopf, 1955.

Courant, R., & Robbins, H. *What Is Mathematics?* New York: Oxford University Press, 1941.

Einstein, A., & Infeld, L. *The Evolution of Physics*. New York: Simon and Schuster, 1942.

Fromm, E. *Man for Himself*. New York: Holt, Rinehart and Winston, 1947.

Hadas, M. *Humanism*. New York: Harper and Brothers, 1960.

Locke, J. *Some Thoughts Concerning Education*. New York: Scribner, 1928.

McClelland, D. C. *The Achieving Society*. Princeton: D. Van Nostrand, 1961.

Nesbitt, M. D. Friendship, love and values. ETS Research Bulletin, 1959.

Russell, B. *On Education*. London: Allen & Unwin, 1930, 250.

Stendler, C. B. Sixty years of child training practices. *Journal of Pediatrics*, 36. C. V. Mosby Company, 1950, 122-134. Quoted with permission from C. B. Stendler.

Strupp, H. H. *Psychotherapists in Action*. New York: Grune and Stratton, 1960.

Tomkins, S. S. *Affect Imagery Consciousness*. New York: Springer, 1962.

Tomkins, S. S., & Miner, J. B. *Tomkins-Horn Picture Arrangement Test*. New York: Springer, 1957.

Verplanck, W. S., Collier, G. H., & Cotlow, J. W. Non independence of successive responses in measurements of the visual threshold. *J. exp. Psychol.*, 44, 1952, 273-282.

Whitehead, A. *Science and the Modern World*. New York: Macmillan, 1926.

IV

The impact of negative affect on cognition and personality

Samuel Messick

On Saturday, November 23, 1963, the day after John F. Kennedy had been assassinated, a six-hour battery of cognitive and personality measures was to have been administered, by prior arrangement, to a sample of approximately 60 undergraduates at a small eastern college. As far as could be ascertained and much to the surprise of the examiners, all of the scheduled subjects arrived for the appointed session. At the time of testing, most of the subjects seemed manifestly distressed by the assassination, but they agreed to participate in the experiment anyway. Perhaps they agreed out of loyalty to their fraternity or sorority (through which the subjects had been recruited and to which payment would be made for their services). Perhaps they welcomed the opportunity to leave their television sets and turn their attention to mental exercises far removed from the events of Dallas and Washington. In any event, the subjects had come to participate in a psychological study, so the measures were duly administered and the data collected.

Three months later, on Saturday, February 29, 1964, another sample of fraternity and sorority members from the same college was administered the same battery of cognitive and personality measures for comparison purposes. The present paper compares the mean performances of these two samples on the measures in question, in an effort to appraise the impact on personality and cognitive dimensions of the negative affect produced by the violent death of the President. The differential reactions

This research was supported by the National Institute of Mental Health, United States Public Health Service, under Research Grant M-4186, as part of a research program on "Personality Organization in Cognitive and Social Processes." The test battery used in this study was developed jointly with Harold Schiffman of Duke University in connection with an investigation of cognitive styles in scanning and focusing. The author wishes to acknowledge a special debt to Diran Dermen for his assistance in all phases of this research, but particularly for his major role in recruiting the subjects, in administering the test battery, and in setting up scoring procedures. The author also wishes to thank Mrs. Geraldine A. Nagy for assisting in the test administration, and Miss Henrietta Gallagher for supervising the scoring and statistical analyses.

of males and females and of first-born and youngest offspring will also be investigated.

METHOD

Subjects

The sample tested the day following the assassination, hereafter called the "experimental group," consisted of 58 undergraduate college students, 25 males and 33 females. At the time of testing, the males had a mean age of 21.2 years and the females a mean age of 20.6 years.

The sample tested in February, 1964, hereafter called the "comparison group," consisted of 55 undergraduates from the same college, 27 males and 28 females. At the time of testing, the males had a mean age of 21.7 years and the females a mean age of 20.0 years.

Although no attempt was made to match the two samples (other than by recruiting them from similar fraternities and sororities at the same college), several measures of educational, socioeconomic, and family characteristics were obtained so that the comparability of the samples in these regards might be evaluated. These measures included:

1. Sex of subject (0 = male, 1 = female).

2. Subject's age, scored as year of birth.

3. Subject's educational level (1 = freshman, 2 = sophomore, 3 = junior, 4 = senior).

4. Father's occupation, scored on a seven-point scale modified from Warner, Meeker, and Eells (1949), with 1 representing "unemployed, no occupation, or on relief" and 7 representing "profession requiring a postgraduate degree."

5. Parental income, scored on a 10-point scale: 1) less than $2,000, 2) $2,000 to $4,000, 3) $4,000 to $6,000, 4) $6,000, to $8,000, 5) $8,000 to $10,000, 6) $10,000 to $14,000, 7) $14,000 to $20,000, 8) $20,000 to $26,000, 9) $26,000 to $32,000, 10) over $32,000.

6. Father's education, scored on a 10-point scale ranging from 1 (no formal schooling) through 5 (finished high school) to 10 (attained a graduate or professional degree).

7. Mother's education, scored on the same 10-point scale.

In addition, the following measures of birth order and family size were obtained:

8. First born, scored dichotomously (1 = first born including "only" child, 0 = not first born).

9. Last born, scored dichotomously (1 = last born but not "only" child, 0 = not last born).

10. Number of siblings older than the subject.

11. Number of siblings younger than the subject.

Means and standard deviations for these 10 measures are presented in Table 1 for the two samples separately, along with t-values from significance tests for the differences in means. Since none of these mean differences proved to be statistically significant, the two samples turned out on the average to be roughly comparable with respect to educational level, socioeconomic status, birth order, and family size. [1]

Table 1 Means and standard deviations for Experimental and Comparison Groups on educational, socioeconomic and family characteristics, along with t-values from significance tests of mean differences

Variable	Experimental Group (N = 58)		Comparison Group (N = 55)		
	Mean	σ	Mean	σ	t
1. Sex (M = 0, F = 1)	.57	.50	.51	.50	.64
2. Youth (Year of birth)	43.03	1.08	43.33	1.34	1.26
3. S's year in college	2.67	.90	2.60	1.11	.38
4. Father's occupation	4.45	1.49	4.55	1.50	.34
5. Parental income	5.24	1.53	5.22	1.83	.07
6. Father's education	5.66	2.06	5.65	2.19	.00
7. Mother's education	5.40	1.60	5.42	1.52	.07
8. First born	.59	.49	.47	.50	1.20
9. Last born	.34	.48	.44	.50	.99
10. Number of older siblings	.53	.72	.85	1.15	1.74
11. Number of younger siblings	.72	.92	.53	.85	1.17

Procedure

A battery of personality and cognitive measures was administered to the experimental group on November 23, 1963, the day after President Kennedy had been assassinated, and to the comparison group on February 29, 1964. This battery was developed originally as part of a study of stylistic consistencies in perception, with emphasis upon individual differences in scanning and focusing as characteristic modes of spontaneous attention deployment—Gardner et al. (1959), Gardner & Long (1962), Schlesinger (1954), Silverman (1964). What has become the "experimental group" in the present study was originally intended, until

[1] The two samples were found to differ on a few of these measures, however, in their interaction with sex of subject. In 2 x 2 factorial analyses of variance, significant interactions were obtained between type of sample (experimental vs. comparison groups) and sex of subject for measures of age, educational level, and mother's education: Females were found to be significantly younger than males as a main effect $(F = 30.20, p < .01)$, and the difference in age between males and females was sufficiently larger in the comparison group than in the experimental group to produce a significant interaction $(F = 7.57, p < .01)$. As might be expected, females were also found to be significantly lower in educational level (year in college) than males $(F = 41.71, p < .01)$, and again the difference in education was sufficiently larger in the comparison group than in the experimental group to produce a significant interaction $(F = 6.05, p < .05)$. Although neither main effect was significant, the mothers of experimental males had somewhat more education (a mean of 5.88 on the 10-point scale) than the mothers of experimental females (5.03), whereas the mothers of comparison males (5.15) had somewhat less education than the mothers of comparison females (5.68) $(F = 5.56, p < .05)$.

Oswald intervened, to have been one of the samples in this investigation of scanning. Detailed descriptions of the tests, along with rationales for their inclusion in the battery, will be presented elsewhere in a report of the scanning study.[2] The tests will be only briefly described here.

The battery contained the following measures of intellectual ability and cognitive judgment:

12. Advanced Vocabulary Test, form V-4, a measure of the factor of verbal comprehension from the revised Kit of Reference Tests for Cognitive Factors (French, Ekstrom, & Price, 1963). In each of 36 items presented in two separately timed sections of 18 items each, S must select the correct synonym for a given word from a list of five alternative choices.

13. Mathematics Aptitude Test, form R-2, a measure of the general reasoning factor, from the revised Kit of Reference Tests (French et al., 1963). In each of 30 word problems requiring arithmetic or simple algebra, S must select the correct answer from among five choices. The items are presented in two separately timed sections of 15 problems each.

14. Gestalt Completion Test, form Cs-1, a measure of the speed of closure factor from the revised Kit of Reference Tests (French et al., 1963). In each of 20 items presented in two separately timed sections of 10 items each, S must write down as quickly as possible the name of an object portrayed in an incomplete drawing.

15. Mutilated Words Test, a measure of speed of closure developed by Thurstone (1944). In each of 51 items, a word is presented with parts of each letter missing and S must write down the complete word as quickly as possible.

16. Four-Letter Words, a measure of speed of closure developed by Thurstone (1944). S is presented with a continuous series of capital letters in 22 lines of 46 letters each and must encircle as quickly as possible all groups of four consecutive letters that spell a common English word. Both Four-Letter Words and the Mutilated Words Test described above may also reflect the factor of verbal closure isolated by Pemberton (1952).

17. Hidden Figures, a modification of the Gottschaldt figures test developed by Jackson, Messick, and Myers (1964) to measure the analytical vs. global mode of perception characterized by Witkin et al. (1962) as field independence vs. field dependence. Similar versions of this test have been used to measure the factor of flexibility of closure—Thurstone (1944), French et al. (1963). In each of 16 items, S must select which one of five simple geometrical forms is embedded in a given complex pattern.

18. Hidden Patterns Test, form Cf-2, a measure of the flexibility of closure factor from the revised Kit of Reference Tests (French et al., 1963). A single simple line figure is given and S must indicate as quickly as possible whether it is contained in each of 400 complicated patterns. Two separately timed sections of 200 items each are employed.

19. Hidden Pictures, a measure of flexibility of closure (Thurstone,

---

[2] The study of scanning, currently in progress, is being conducted jointly by the author and Harold Schiffman of Duke University.

1944) that may also reflect speed of closure, particularly with brief time limits—French (1951), Pemberton (1952). In each of three pictorial drawings of scenes involving people and objects, S must find and encircle a specified number of hidden faces or people that are concealed somewhere in the drawing. Two scores were obtained: (19a) the number of correct or keyed hidden faces encircled by S, and (19b) the number of areas circled that did not contain a keyed face, i.e., the number of "fabulated" faces (Smith & Klein, 1953). Although with looser standards and considerable imagination it would be possible to defend some of these latter unkeyed circled areas as "faces," the forms involved were generally of much poorer quality than those in the key.

20. Hidden Pictures Information, a measure of incidental memory for the content of the three drawings portrayed in the preceding Hidden Pictures Test. Free response answers are required to five specific questions about the content of each picture.

21. Shortest Road Test, form Le-2, a measure of the factor called "length estimation" from the revised Kit of Reference Tests (French et al., 1963). Each item consists of two points with three curved or jagged lines drawn between them; S must indicate the shortest of these three lines. The test contains two separately timed sections of 28 items each.

22. Nearer Point Test, form Le-3, a measure of the length estimation factor from the revised Kit of Reference Tests (French et al., 1963). Each item consists of a reference point and two dots, with some distracting lines and figures superimposed; S must indicate which dot is nearer to the reference point. The test is composed of two separately timed parts containing 30 items each.

23. Speed of Color Discrimination Test, a group-administered version of the Stroop (1935) color-word procedure consisting of (a) a color discrimination condition in which S writes as quickly as possible under each of a series of differently colored patches the first letter of the color name, and (b) an interference condition in which S again writes as quickly as possible the first letter of the color in which conflicting color names are printed (Messick, 1965). Each of the two conditions consisted of four separately timed parts, and a separate total score was obtained for each condition.

24. Perceptual Speed, Part IV of the Guilford-Zimmerman Aptitude Survey. For each of 72 items, S must indicate as quickly as possible which of five similar objects is identical to a given object.

25. Finding A's Test, form P-1, a measure of the perceptual speed factor from the revised Kit of Reference Tests (French et al., 1963). In each column of 41 words, S must mark as quickly as possible the five words containing the letter "a." The test consists of two separately timed sections of 25 columns each.

26. Spelling Test, Form 1, developed by Carlton and Diederich[3] in a

---

[3] Carlton, Sydell, & Diederich, P. B. Recognition of spelling errors in Princeton High School. Unpublished manuscript, Educational Testing Service, Princeton, N. J., 1961.

study of the 430 most commonly misspelled English words. S must indicate whether the spelling of each of 100 words is correct or incorrect.

27. Thing Categories Test, form Fi-3, a measure of the ideational fluency factor from the revised Kit of Reference Tests (French et al., 1963). S must write down as many things as he can think of that share a specified property. The test consists of two separately timed parts, one part requiring S to write down all the things that are "round" and the other all the things that are "blue."

28. Estimation Questionnaire, a procedure developed by Pettigrew (1958) to measure consistencies in the use of broad vs. narrow conceptual categories. In each of 20 items, S is informed about the average value of a specified category or dimension and must select from one set of four alternatives the largest value of the category and from another set of four alternatives the smallest value of the category. High scores indicate the use of broad categories. Since Pettigrew (1958) found that this test contained two large factors, one of which was significantly related to quantitative aptitude, a separate score was obtained for each factor by dividing the items into two groups in terms of the item loadings reported by Pettigrew.

29. Word Meaning Test, a measure of breadth of categorizing in terms of the consistent use of broad categories of word meaning (Messick & Kogan, 1965). Each of 30 items consists of a key word followed by a list of approximately 14 to 17 additional words; S must underline all of the words in the list that may be appropriately substituted for the given word in most usages. The words in each list are synonyms or analogues for the given word, but S is not informed of that fact. The score is the average number of words underlined per completed item.

30. Doodles, a measure of graphic constriction-expansiveness developed by Wallach and Gahm (1960). S is asked to draw two doodles, each on a separate sheet of paper. Graphic expansiveness vs. constriction is scored by superimposing a grid of 20 two-inch squares over each sheet; the score, which has a possible range of one to 40 for the sum of the two sheets, is the minimum number of squares covering the doodling.

31. Size estimation, a measure of accuracy in estimating the size of circles developed by Schiffman and Messick as a possible group-administered analogue of individually-administered criterion measures of scanning—Gardner et al. (1959), Gardner & Long (1962), Schlesinger (1954). Each of 30 items consists of a standard circle centered at the top of the page, with a row of five comparison circles below it; S must indicate which comparison circle is closest in size to the standard. Two scores were obtained: (a) one for accuracy in estimating the standard, and (b) one for the tendency to overestimate the standard.

32. Picture Preferences, Black and White (form B-W), a measure adapted from Schlesinger (1954) of the tendency to react affectively or indifferently to stimulus objects. In each of 60 items, a black-and-white picture is projected onto a screen and S must indicate whether he (a) likes the picture, (b) is indifferent to the picture, or (c) dislikes the

picture. Separate scores were obtained for each of these three categories of response.

33. Picture Preferences, Color (form C), a procedure similar to 32 above except that 16 colored pictures are projected. Three scores are also obtained for (a) liking the pictures, (b) feeling indifferent to the pictures, or (c) disliking the pictures.

34. Figure Choices, a forced-choice measure of preference for complexity adapted from the Barron-Welsh (1952) Art Judgment Scale (Messick & Kogan, 1965). Each of 20 items consists of a pair of drawings, one simple and one complex, and S must indicate which member of each pair he prefers most. Ten set-breaking items containing either two simple or two complex drawings were distributed throughout the test.

35. Incidental Recall, a measure of incidental memory. S is asked to write down the names of all the tests in the battery that he can remember.

The test battery also included the following personality inventory scales. Except for the measures of acquiescence and dogmatism, items from these scales were rewritten (and sometimes discarded) in order to balance each key for the number of "true" and "false" answers (Messick, 1962). See Messick and Kogan (1965) for further details. These personality items were presented to Ss in a six-point response format, but all of the derived scale scores were based upon dichotomized responses of agreement and disagreement. The tendency to use extreme categories in self-rating was scored as a separate variable to avoid confounding consistent extremity propensities with content variance (Peabody, 1962).

36. Desirability, a scale of 28 self-descriptive personality items (14 keyed True and 14 False) developed by Stricker (1963) to measure the tendency to respond desirably.

37. Saunders' (1955) ten-item Tolerance of Ambiguity scale (5T, 5F). Properties of the revised scale are described in Messick (1962).

38. Barron's (1953b) and Crutchfield's (1955) independence and yielding items (9T, 9F).

39. Barron's (1953a) Complexity-Simplicity scale (11T, 11F).

40. Fulkerson's (1958) Acquiescence scale (20T).

41. Couch and Keniston's (1960) Agreement Response Scale (15T).

42. Couch and Keniston's (1960) Agreement Response Factor items (9T, 7F).

43. Authoritarianism, a 28-item modification of the California F scale in which both the number of "true" and "false" items and the number of "extremely-worded" and "tentatively-worded" items are balanced (Clayton & Jackson, 1961).

44. Acquiescence to Extremes, the tendency to agree with the 14 extremely-worded items of variable 43.

45. Acquiescence to Tentatives, the tendency to agree with the 14 tentatively-worded items of variable 43.

46. The short form of Rokeach's (1956, 1960) Dogmatism scale (20T).

47. Saunders' (1955) Self-Sufficiency scale (5T, 5F), as revised by Messick (1962).

48. A shortened version of Barratt's (1959) Impulsiveness scale (11T, 11F).

49. Budner's (1962) Tolerance of Ambiguity scale (8T, 8F).

50. An Affective-Effective scale (5T, 5F) developed by Stice to measure artistic vs. practical interests (Messick, 1962).

51. Saunders' (1955) Anxiety scale (5T, 5F), as revised by Messick (1962).

52. The Gough-Sanford (1952) Rigidity scale (13T, 13F).

53. An Unconventionality scale (5T, 5F) developed by Stice (Messick, 1962).

54. Extremity of Self-Rating, the tendency to use extreme categories as opposed to moderate ones in endorsing 280 self-descriptive personality items presented in a six-point Likert format.

In addition, the test battery also included the group form of the Holtzman Inkblot Technique (Holtzman, Thorpe, Swartz, Herron, 1961), a word association procedure, and a collection of three early childhood memories, but these variables will be discussed in another report.

RESULTS

Differences Between Experimental and Comparison Groups

Means, standard deviations, and reliabilities of the cognitive measures are presented in Table 2 for the experimental and comparison groups separately. It would appear from an examination of mean differences in Table 2 that the effects of the assassination upon cognitive test performance were quite specific. Significantly poorer scores were obtained in the experimental group on the Hidden Patterns Test and on the Hidden Pictures Test. In addition, the experimental group responded "indifferent" to significantly more pictures in the Picture Preferences procedure than did the comparison group. The experimental group also appeared to be more constricted on the doodling measure of graphic constriction-expansiveness ($p < .07$).

It is noteworthy that the major overall effect of the assassination condition upon cognitive test performance appears primarily to implicate a single dimension of cognitive consistency, namely, the factor of flexibility of closure—Thurstone (1944), Pemberton (1952)—which bears a marked similarity to the dimension of field dependence vs. field independence or articulated vs. global cognitive style discussed by Witkin et al. (1954, 1962). Two of the three tests selected to measure this factor (Hidden Patterns and Hidden Pictures) yielded significantly lower scores in the experimental group than in the comparison group.

It is also noteworthy, however, that for the prototypal measure of this dimension, the Hidden Figures Test, a significant difference was not obtained. The difference in means on Hidden Figures also favored the comparison group, but the *t*-value was only 1.00. In an effort to clarify this apparent inconsistency, the responses to the Hidden Figures Test were examined further, and it was noted that substantially more *wrong*

Table 2 Means, standard deviations, and reliabilities of cognitive measures for the
Experimental and Comparison Groups, along with t-values from significance
tests of mean differences

Variable	Experimental Group (N = 58)			Comparison Group (N = 55)		
	Reliability[a]	Mean	σ	Reliability[a]	Mean	σ
12. Vocabulary	.65	16.64	4.34	.65	16.38	4.08
13. Math. Aptitude	.86	14.09	4.85	.86	13.31	4.57
14. Gestalt Completion	.74	12.64	4.25	.80	13.33	4.73
15. Mutilated Words	--[b]	25.60	6.09	--[b]	25.35	4.63
16. Four-Letter Words	--[b]	22.16	6.04	--[b]	24.04	9.90
17. Hidden Figures	--[b]	5.74	3.07	--[b]	6.36	3.44
18. Hidden Patterns	.89	72.16	26.48	.92	82.58	19.96
19a. Hidden Pictures	.29[c]	5.57	2.24	.63[c]	6.82	2.42
19b. Hidden Pictures, Poor Figures	--[b]	4.71	3.55	--[b]	6.00	4.34
20. Hidden Pictures Information	.62[c]	9.83	2.95	.47[c]	9.95	2.35
21. Shortest Road	.81	32.83	8.92	.83	35.47	8.71
22. Nearer Point	.89	40.10	9.67	.81	42.84	9.12
23a. Speed of Color Discrimination[e]	.94[c]	254.70	38.93	.91[c]	252.35	30.30
23b. Color-Word Interference[e]	.94[c]	197.72	66.79	.88[c]	203.75	39.46
24. Perceptual Speed	--[b]	42.74	10.38	--[b]	43.04	8.05
25. Finding A's	.86	62.95	15.90	.86	66.02	16.36
26. Spelling	.95[d]	84.40	12.99	.86[d]	84.78	8.23
27. Thing Categories	.70	21.05	6.75	.68	19.38	5.57
28a. Estimation Questionnaire, Factor I	--[b]	156.69	42.55	--[b]	156.49	43.06
28b. Estimation Questionnaire, Factor II	--[b]	156.57	52.56	--[b]	157.78	48.97
29. Word Meaning	--[b]	7.21	1.98	--[b]	7.38	2.06
30. Doodles	.72	17.19	9.00	.75	20.62	10.20
31a. Size Estimation, Accuracy	.16[d]	106.64	6.34	-.10[d]	104.96	6.82
31b. Size Estimation, Overestimation	.54[d]	150.91	11.45	.39[d]	150.96	10.88
32a. Picture Preferences B-W, Like	.76[d]	29.69	7.09	.71[d]	30.80	6.51
32b. Picture Preferences B-W, Indiff.	.90[d]	15.00	9.20	.86[d]	11.78	6.35
32c. Picture Preferences B-W, Dislike	.79[d]	15.31	6.23	.84[d]	17.42	6.52
33a. Picture Preferences C, Like	.26[d]	10.62	2.28	.41[d]	11.15	2.44
33b. Picture Preferences C, Indiff.	.42[d]	2.76	2.26	.23[d]	2.20	1.70
33c. Picture Preferences C, Dislike	.45[d]	2.62	1.86	.66[d]	2.65	2.22
34. Figure Choices	.91[d]	12.97	5.09	.90[d]	13.84	5.14
35. Incidental Recall	--[b]	7.05	1.67	--[b]	7.42	1.46

a. Unless otherwise indicated, reliability is estimated from the correlation between separately-timed halves, corrected to double length by the Spear-
Brown formula.

b. Not estimated.

c. Coefficient alpha computed from the variance of the part scores.

d. Estimated from the correlation between odd and even items, corrected double length by the Spearman-Brown formula.

e. Due to incomplete data on this test, the sample size for these values s 54 for the Experimental Group and 51 for the Comparison Group.

f. $p < .07$ $*p < .05$ $**p < .01$

answers were obtained in the experimental group than in the comparison group ($p < .01$). Several other cognitive tests for which it was appropriate to score the number of wrong answers (and in some cases the number of omits) were also examined, and the tendency observed on Hidden Figures for the experimental group to obtain substantially more wrong answers than the comparison group was found not to be a general one (*see* Table 3). Out of 13 "wrongs" and "omits" scores, the experimental group obtained higher means on six tests, and the comparison group obtained higher means on seven. In addition to Hidden Figures, significantly more wrong answers were obtained in the experimental group on only one other test, the Gestalt Completion Test, which is also a measure of closure facility but in this case as reflected in the speed of closure factor.

With respect to the consistency of cognitive measurement in the experimental and comparison groups, it should be noted that the reliabilities reported in Tables 2 and 3 are quite comparable for the two conditions and, considering the brevity of most of the tests, are generally fairly substantial.[4] Only two striking disparities appear: the reliability of Hidden Pictures is considerably lower in the experimental group than in the comparison group, whereas the reliability of the "number wrong" score on Gestalt Completion is considerably higher in the experimental group than in the comparison group. Thus, in addition to exhibiting significant mean differences between the two groups, responses to Hidden Pictures display substantially less consistency in the experimental group than in the comparison group, and the tendency to respond incorrectly to Gestalt Completion items shows much greater consistency in the experimental group.

Means, standard deviations, and reliabilities of the personality scales are presented in Table 4 for the experimental and comparison groups separately. As with the cognitive tests, the overall effects of the assassination on personality measures appear to be quite specific. On the average,

[4] As indicated in Tables 2 and 3, the reliabilities of several tests were not computed, usually because only one form was administered and the likelihood of moderate speededness would have spuriously increased split-half estimates of reliability. In a few cases where speededness was not likely, it was felt that too few items were available to warrant odd-even correlations. An indication of the reliability level of two of these tests is available from other studies: The Word Meaning Test had a corrected odd-even reliability of .97 in Messick and Kogan (1965) and Hidden Figures had an alternate form reliability of .77 in Messick and Fritzky (1963).

Table 3 Means, standard deviations, and reliabilities of "wrong" scores on the cognitive measures for the Experimental and Comparison Groups, along with t-values from significance tests of mean differences

Variable	Experimental Group (N = 58)			Comparison Group (N = 55)			t
	Reliability^a	Mean	σ	Reliability^a	Mean	σ	
12. Vocabulary, No. wrong	.81	11.57	5.62	.75	11.18	5.64	.3
13. Math. Aptitude, No. wrong	.78	5.07	3.65	.63	4.49	3.21	.8
14. Gestalt Completion, No. wrong	.86	3.02	3.24	.31	1.51	1.32	3.2
15. Mutilated Words, No. wrong	--^b	3.78	2.92	--^b	2.87	2.08	1.8
16. Four-Letter Words, No. omits	--^b	8.48	4.28	--^b	9.67	6.93	1.0
17. Hidden Figures, No. wrong	--^b	4.72	3.18	--^b	2.67	2.79	3.6
18. Hidden Patterns, No. wrong	.60	.79	1.84	.89	.95	2.08	.4
21. Shortest Road, No. wrong	.55	9.41	4.85	.74	10.96	5.72	1.5
22. Nearer Point, No. wrong	.76	9.45	5.30	.80	11.47	6.10	1.8
23a. Speed of Color Discr., omits + wrong^d	--^b	.80	1.16	--^b	1.35	2.79	1.3
23b. Color-Word Interference, omits + wrong^d	--^b	2.41	5.34	--^b	1.86	2.71	.6
25. Finding A's, No. omits	.80	7.36	8.64	.84	8.40	10.17	.5
26. Spelling, No. omits	--^b	.16	.45	--^b	.24	1.48	.3

a. Reliability estimated from the correlation between separately-timed halves, corrected to double length by the Spearman-Brown formula.

b. Not estimated.   c. $p < .07$

d. Due to incomplete data on this test, the sample size for these values was 54 for the Experimental Group and 51 for the Comparison Group.

*p < .05   **p < .01

the experimental group described itself as being significantly more yielding than the comparison group on the Barron-Crutchfield independence-yielding items and as being significantly more conventional on the Unconventionality scale. In addition, the experimental group received significantly higher scores on the Dogmatism scale and, as might be expected from the reported relation between dogmatism and extremity of opinionation (Rokeach, 1960), tended to be more extreme in expressing opinions ($p < .07$). Thus, in terms of personality scale responses the experimental group appeared to be more submissive and conventional, but also more dogmatic and polarized in expressing opinions.

With respect to the consistency of personality measurement in the experimental and comparison groups, it seems that there is more disparity in the reliabilities of personality measures in the two conditions than was the case for the cognitive tests. In addition, there appears to be some consistency in these disparities in that the reliabilities of presumed

Table 4 Means, standard deviations, and reliabilities of personality inventory measures for the Experimental and Comparison Groups, along with t-values from significance tests of mean differences

Variable	Experimental Group (N = 58)			Comparison Group (N = 55)			t
	Reliability [a]	Mean	σ	Reliability [a]	Mean	σ	
5. Desirability	.70	18.52	3.97	.59	18.76	3.26	.36
7. Saunders' Tolerance of Ambiguity	.15	4.19	1.59	.33	4.47	1.78	.88
8. BC Independence-Yielding	.18	7.19	2.02	.34	8.05	2.35	2.07*
9. Barron's Complexity-Simplicity	.48	8.17	2.72	.54	8.47	2.91	.56
0. Fulkerson's Acquiescence	.43	11.83	2.69	.35	11.18	2.61	1.28
_. Couch-Keniston Agreement Scale	.48	9.09	2.28	.25	9.22	1.93	.33
2. Couch-Keniston Agreement Factor	.58	7.55	2.61	.47	7.42	2.33	.28
3. Authoritarianism	.26	15.57	2.64	.26	14.89	2.64	1.35
. Acquiescence to Extremes	.58	6.07	2.44	.40	5.65	2.06	.97
. Acquiescence to Tentatives	.34	9.47	1.91	.43	9.31	2.07	.41
. Dogmatism	.65	11.98	3.30	.56	10.75	2.91	2.10*
. Self-Sufficiency	.64	3.36	2.11	.40	3.11	1.72	.69
. Impulsiveness	.47	12.29	2.71	.52	12.51	2.83	.41
. Budner's Tolerance of Ambiguity	.36	10.31	2.00	.41	10.51	2.05	.52
. Affective-Effective	.11	4.40	1.43	.48	4.05	1.86	1.08
. Anxiety	.61	3.81	2.25	.72	3.67	2.48	.31
. Rigidity	.64	17.00	3.62	.65	16.18	3.76	1.17
. Unconventionality	.46	2.29	1.66	.62	3.09	2.07	2.24*
. Extremity of Self-Rating	.96[b]	519.02	66.36	.97[b]	495.35	62.25	1.94[c]

    a.   Unless otherwise indicated, reliability is coefficient alpha.

    b.   Reliability estimated from the correlation between odd and even items, corrected to double length by the Spearman-Brown formula.

    c. $p < .07$ *$p < .05$

response style scales (variables 36, 40, 41, 42, 44, 45, and 54) tend to be higher in the experimental group than in the comparison group, while the reliabilities of presumed content scales (variables 37, 38, 39, 43, 46, 47, 48, 49, 50, 51, 52, and 53) tend to be higher in the comparison group than in the experimental group. Although the difference in reliabilities between the two groups was sometimes only slight (e.g., reliability of the Authoritarianism scale was .258 in the comparison group and .256 in the experimental group), there were only four reversals of this trend out of 19 scales.

Experimental Effects in Relation to Sex Differences

Means on the cognitive measures are presented in Table 5 for males and females separately within the experimental and comparison groups. Also provided separately for the two conditions is the point-biserial correlation coefficient between each cognitive measure and sex of subject (with males scored 0 and females scored 1). A point-biserial correlation coefficient significantly different from zero indicates a significant difference between the mean scores of males and females on the particular cognitive measure under consideration.

An examination of Table 5 reveals that significant sex differences favoring males were obtained in both groups on Mathematics Aptitude, Mutilated Words, Shortest Road, and Nearer Point. (On the latter three tests, a sex difference significant at the .05 level was obtained within one of the groups, and the sex difference within the other group was in the same direction and approached significance.) In addition—as in other studies, Pettigrew (1958), Wallach & Caron (1959)—males in both groups displayed significantly broader categories than females on the two factor scores from Pettigrew's (1958) Estimation Questionnaire.

Significant sex differences favoring females were obtained in both groups for measures of spelling and incidental recall. There was also a consistent tendency, which seemed much stronger in the experimental group than in the comparison group, for females to dislike more photographs than did males in the Picture Preferences procedure (variables 32c and 33c).

Sex differences such as those just described that occur with roughly the same magnitude in both the experimental and comparison groups are of little interest in the present context, except to emphasize that certain stable differences in male and female performance persist even under such distress as the assassination condition. Of considerably more interest would be differences in performance that exhibit an interaction between sex of subject and experimental conditions. An index of such interaction is provided in Table 5 by the *t*-values for the significance of differences between point-biserial correlation coefficients in the two groups. A significant *t*-value between the two groups for a particular cognitive measure in its correlation with sex indicates that the mean sex difference in one group is significantly different from the mean sex difference in the other group. Such differential performance of males and females as a function of membership in the experimental or comparison group is interpretable in the same way as a significant interaction in analysis of variance.

Only one significant *t*-value appears in Table 5, the one for the measure of ideational fluency, Thing Categories. Even though the correlation of the fluency score with sex was not significantly different from zero in either group, the sex differences in performance were reversed in the two conditions and the resulting correlation coefficients were significantly different from each other. Females exhibited approximately the same mean level of ideational fluency in the two groups, but males tended to perform at a lower level than females in the comparison group and at a higher level than females in the experimental group.[5] Although the associated *t*-values were not significant, a difference in male-female performance in the two conditions was also indicated for three other measures, for which a significant correlation with sex was obtained in one group and a negligible correlation in the other. On Hidden Patterns, both the males and females in the comparison group and the males in the experimental group all performed at comparable mean levels, but the females in the experimental group received substantially lower scores. On the doodling measure of graphic constriction-expansiveness, again the males and females in the comparison group and the males in the experimental group all achieved comparable mean levels, but the females in the experimental group appeared to be considerably more constricted. In the tendency to respond "indifferent" to black-and-white pictures, however, the comparison males and females and the experimental females displayed similar mean levels, whereas the experimental males felt indifferent toward substantially more of the pictures. Males in the experimental group, then, appeared to produce more fluent ideation and to be more indifferent in their affective reactions to photographs than males in the comparison group, whereas females maintained a comparable level on these measures in both conditions. Females in the experimental group, on the other hand, appeared more constricted in graphic expression and less facile in locating hidden patterns than females in the comparison group, while males in the two conditions maintained comparable mean levels on these measures.

Table 6 provides similar data for the personality scales; means are presented for males and females separately within the experimental and comparison groups, along with point-biserial correlations of each measure with sex and *t*-values for the significance of differences between these correlations. As can be seen in Table 6, females in both groups were significantly more anxious, more conventional, and more extreme in self-rating than males. In addition, interactions between sex of subject and experimental conditions occurred for five other measures. On the Couch-Keniston Agreement Scale, females were significantly more acquiescent than males in the comparison group, but males were more acquiescent than females in the experimental group (*t*-value for the difference between correlations of the scale with sex in the two groups was 2.64, $p < .02$). On the Self-sufficiency Scale, females described themselves as more self-sufficient than did males in the comparison group, but the reverse occurred in the experimental group (t = 2.15, $p < .05$). On the Affective-Effective Scale, females were significantly more affective than males in the comparison group, but there was a negligible sex difference in the experimental group (t = 1.87, $p < .07$). On Barron's Complexity-Simplicity Scale, no sex difference appeared in the comparison group,

[5] This interaction appears to be due primarily to the differential performance of males and females on the second subtest of Thing Categories (which requires the listing of things "blue"), where the *t*-value for the difference in the correlations with sex was 2.48 ($p < .02$). The corresponding *t*-value for the first subtest (listing things "round") was only 1.30.

Table 5 Cognitive measures
Means for males and females separately within the Experimental and Comparison Groups, along with the correlation of each variable with sex and t-values for the significance of the differences between the correlations

Variable	Experimental Group (N = 58) Means Females	Experimental Group (N = 58) Means Males	Experimental Group r with Sex[a]	Comparison Group (N = 55) Means Females	Comparison Group (N = 55) Means Males	Comparison Group r with Sex[a]	t[b] between r's
12. Vocabulary	16.48	16.84	-.04	16.61	16.15	.06	.52
13. Math. Aptitude	12.27	16.48	-.43**	11.32	15.37	-.44**	.06
14. Gestalt Completion	12.09	13.36	-.15	12.68	14.00	-.14	.05
15. Mutilated Words	24.27	27.35	-.25	23.29	27.48	-.45**	1.18
16. Four-Letter Words	22.58	21.60	.08	25.43	22.59	.14	.32
17. Hidden Figures	5.54	6.00	-.07	5.50	7.26	-.26	1.01
18. Hidden Patterns	64.52	82.24	-.33*	80.36	84.89	-.11	1.21
19a. Hidden Pictures	5.91	5.22	.17	6.68	6.96	-.06	1.20
19b. Hidden Pictures, Poor Figures	4.67	4.76	-.01	6.25	5.74	.06	.36
20. Hidden Pictures Information	9.21	10.54	-.24	9.61	10.30	-.15	.49
21. Shortest Road	31.06	35.16	-.23	32.82	38.22	-.31*	.45
22. Nearer Point	37.36	43.72	-.33*	41.00	44.74	-.21	.67
23a. Speed of Color Discrimination	258.67	249.36	.12	258.79	245.63	.23	.58
23b. Color-Word Interference	194.30	203.40	-.07	200.68	206.96	-.08	.05
24. Perceptual Speed	42.85	42.60	.01	44.32	41.70	.16	.78
25. Finding A's	65.24	59.92	.17	69.93	61.96	.24	.38
26. Spelling	90.36	76.52	.53**	87.39	82.07	.32*	1.33
27. Thing Categories	20.09	22.36	-.16	20.57	18.15	.22	1.99*
28a. Estimation Questionnaire, I	143.48	174.12	-.36**	144.61	168.81	-.28*	.46
28b. Estimation Questionnaire, II	140.00	178.44	-.36**	137.79	178.52	-.42**	.37
29. Word Meaning	7.21	7.20	.00	7.25	7.52	-.07	.36
30. Doodles	14.97	20.12	-.28*	20.79	20.44	.02	1.59
(partial)	106.03	107.44	.11	104.25	105.70	-.11	.00

a. Point biserial correlation of variable with sex (M = 0, F = 1).

b. t-values for the significance of the difference between correlation coefficients.

Table 6 Personality scales

	M	SD	r	M	SD	r	F
33b. Picture Preferences C, Indiff.	2.27	3.40	-.25	2.04	2.37	-.10	.81
33c. Picture Preferences C, Dislike	3.21	1.84	.36**	2.96	2.33	.14	1.22
34. Figure Choices	13.09	12.80	.03	14.68	12.96	.17	.73
35. Incidental Recall	7.48	6.48	.30*	7.86	6.96	.31*	.06
36. Desirability	18.91	18.00	.11	18.96	18.56	.06	.26
37. Saunders' Tolerance of Ambiguity	3.97	4.48	-.16	4.18	4.78	-.17	.06
38. BC Independence-Yielding	6.70	7.84	-.28*	8.14	7.96	.04	1.70
39. Barron's Complexity-Simplicity	7.30	9.32	-.37**	8.39	8.56	-.03	1.86^c
40. Fulkerson's Acquiescence	11.76	11.92	-.03	10.96	11.41	-.08	.26
41. Couch-Keniston Agreement Scale	8.85	9.40	-.12	9.93	8.48	.37**	2.64*
42. Couch-Keniston Agreement Factor	7.67	7.40	.05	7.89	6.93	.21	.85
43. Authoritarianism	16.03	14.96	.20	15.11	14.67	.08	.64
44. Acquiescence to Extremes	5.70	6.56	-.18	5.64	5.67	-.01	.89
45. Acquiescence to Tentatives	9.48	9.44	.01	9.25	9.37	-.03	.21
46. Dogmatism	12.00	11.96	.01	10.86	10.63	-.04	.16
47. Self-Sufficiency	3.03	3.80	-.18	3.50	2.70	.23	2.15*
48. Impulsiveness	11.97	12.72	-.14	12.29	12.74	-.08	.32
49. Budner's Tolerance of Ambiguity	10.30	10.32	-.00	10.93	10.07	.21	1.11
50. Affective-Effective	4.36	4.44	-.03	4.64	3.44	.32*	1.87^c
51. Anxiety	4.39	3.04	.30*	4.46	2.85	.33*	.18
52. Rigidity	17.48	16.36	.15	17.00	15.33	.22	.38
53. Unconventionality	1.48	3.36	-.56**	2.36	3.85	-.36**	1.32
54. Extremity of Self-Rating	538.73	493.00	.34**	520.61	469.15	.41**	.42

c. $p < .07$ *$p < .05$ **$p < .01$

but in the experimental group females favored simplicity significantly more than males did ($t = 1.86$, $p < .07$). On the Barron-Crutchfield Independence-Yielding items, a negligible sex difference occurred in the comparison group, but in the experimental group females were significantly more "yielding" than males ($t = 1.70$, $p < .10$).

Experimental Effects in Relation to Birth Order

Each of the two samples was divided into two subgroups—those subjects who were first born (including those who were an "only" child) and those subjects who were not first born. In the experimental group there were 34 first-born subjects and 24 who were not first born, and in the comparison group there were 26 first-born subjects and 29 who were not first born. Fortunately, there was a fairly even distribution of males and females within the birth-order dichotomy in both samples (the phi coefficient between sex of subject and birth order was −.10 in the experimental group and .06 in the comparison group).

Mean scores on the cognitive measures are presented in Table 7 for the first-born and not-first-born subjects separately within the experimental and comparison groups. Also provided for each group are the point-biserial correlation coefficients of each measure with birth order, along with t-values for the significance of differences between these correlations. Again, a point-biserial correlation coefficient significantly different from zero indicates a significant difference between the mean scores of first-born and later-born subjects on the particular measure in question, and a significant t-value between the point-biserial correlations obtained in the two groups indicates an interaction between birth order and experimental conditions. (Experimental effects in relation to both sex of subject and birth order as revealed in 2 x 2 x 2 factorial analyses of variance will be discussed in another, more extensive report of the present study.)

It should be noted in Table 7 that, unlike the results for sex differences, there is not a single cognitive measure for which a significant difference between first-born and later-born subjects occurred uniformly in *both* samples. For several measures, however, birth order appeared to interact with experimental conditions to produce differential scores. On the Nearer Point Test, first borns scored significantly higher than later borns in the comparison group but performed somewhat poorer than later borns in the experimental group (t-value for the difference between correlations with birth order in the two groups was 2.17, $p < .05$). On Hidden Pictures, first borns in the comparison group tended to fabulize more poor faces than did later borns, whereas first borns in the experimental group tended to fabulize fewer poor faces than did later borns ($t = 2.16$, $p < .05$). On Mutilated Words, first borns tended to score higher than later borns in the comparison group, but the reverse occurred in the experimental group ($t = 1.93$, $p < .07$). On Perceptual Speed, later borns scored higher than first borns in the comparison group and somewhat lower than first borns in the experimental group ($t = 2.00$, $p < .05$). On the doodling measure of graphic constriction-expansiveness, first borns were somewhat more expansive than later borns in the comparison group but were more constricted than later borns in the experimental condition ($t = 1.89$, $p < .07$). On Hidden Figures, first borns performed negligibly better than later borns in the comparison group but noticeably poorer than later borns in the experimental group ($t = 1.74$, $p < .10$). On Gestalt Completion, no difference appeared between first borns and later borns in the comparison group, but later borns performed significantly poorer than first borns in the experimental condition. On the Picture Preferences procedure, first borns were significantly less indifferent to the photographs in the comparison group, but in the experimental group the indifference of the first borns was at approximately the same level as that of the later borns.

It would also seem, that first borns were more indifferent in their affective reactions to stimuli, more constricted in graphic expression, more cautious in the acceptance of a stimulus as a member of a specified class (such as "faces" on Hidden Pictures), less flexible in overcoming embedding contexts (Hidden Figures), somewhat less able to achieve verbal closure (Mutilated Words), less accurate in making difficult perceptual discriminations (Nearer Point), and somewhat quicker in perceptual responsiveness (Perceptual Speed) in the experimental group than in the comparison group. Later borns, on the other hand, appeared to be somewhat more facile in reaching verbal closure (Mutilated Words) but to be slower in perceptual discrimination (Perceptual Speed) and less able to achieve perceptual closure correctly (Gestalt Completion) in the experimental group than in the comparison group (see means in Table 7).

It is also interesting to note that on several of these perceptual closure and discrimination tasks on which first borns performed more poorly in the experimental group than in the comparison group there was a slight but consistent tendency for later borns to reverse the pattern and perform better in the experimental group than in the comparison group. Such was the case for Mutilated Words, Hidden Figures, Nearer Point, Speed of Color Discrimination, Color-Word Interference, and the tendency to over-estimate in Size Estimation. At the same time, there was a slight tendency for first borns to utilize narrower categories and later borns broader categories on both factor scores of Pettigrew's Estimation Questionnaire in the experimental group than in the comparison group. There were only two perceptual tasks, Perceptual Speed and Gestalt Completion, with a suggestion of the opposite trend, that is with first borns performing somewhat better and later borns more poorly in the experimental group than in the comparison group. Both first borns and later borns tended to perform more poorly in the experimental group than in the comparison group on most of the remaining perceptual tasks (Four-Letter Words, Hidden Patterns, Hidden Pictures, Shortest Road, and Finding A's).

Similar data for the personality scales are provided in Table 8; means

Table 7 Cognitive measures
Means for first born and not first born subjects separately within the Experimental and Comparison Groups, along with the correlation of each variable with the birth order dichotomy and t-values for the significance of differences between the correlations

Variable	Experimental Group (N = 58) Means First Born (N = 34)	Not First Born (N = 24)	r with Birth Order Dichotomy [a]	Comparison Group (N = 55) Means First Born (N = 26)	Not First Born (N = 29)	r with Birth Order Dichotomy [a]	t [b] between r's
12. Vocabulary	16.65	16.63	.00	16.54	16.24	.04	.21
13. Math. Aptitude	14.50	13.50	.10	13.50	13.14	.04	.31
14. Gestalt Completion	13.68	11.17	.29*	13.38	13.28	.01	.49[c]
15. Mutilated Words	24.65	26.96	-.19	26.23	24.55	.18	1.93[c]
16. Four-Letter Words	21.82	22.63	-.07	24.50	23.62	.04	-.57
17. Hidden Figures	5.09	6.67	-.25	6.65	6.10	.08	1.74
18. Hidden Patterns	74.00	69.54	.08	82.50	82.66	-.00	.41
19a. Hidden Pictures	5.35	5.38	-.11	6.58	7.03	-.09	-.10
19b. Hidden Pictures, Poor Figures	4.12	5.54	-.20	6.96	5.14	.21	2.16*
20. Hidden Pictures, Information	10.21	9.29	.15	10.35	9.59	.16	-.05
21. Shortest Road	32.88	32.75	.01	35.54	35.41	.01	.00
22. Nearer Point	39.15	41.46	-.12	45.62	40.34	.29*	2.17*
23a. Speed of Color Discrimination	250.79	260.13	-.12	255.58	249.41	.11	1.19
23b. Color-Word Interference	189.71	210.29	-.16	202.96	204.48	-.02	.73
24. Perceptual Speed	43.76	41.29	.12	40.81	45.03	-.26	2.00*
25. Finding A's	61.32	65.25	-.12	64.58	67.31	-.08	.21
26. Spelling	83.85	85.17	-.05	83.96	85.52	-.09	.21
27. Thing Categories	20.85	21.33	-.04	19.88	18.93	.09	.67
28a. Estimation Questionnaire I	151.74	163.71	-.14	156.50	156.48	.00	.73
28b. Estimation Questionnaire II	153.82	160.46	-.06	167.35	149.21	.18	1.25
29. Word Meaning	7.24	7.17	.02	7.54	7.24	.07	.26[c]
						-.1	1.8o[c]

a. Point biserial correlation of variable with Birth Order Dichotomy (First Born = 1, Not First Born = 0).

b. t-values for the significance of the difference between correlation coefficients.

Table 8 Personality scales

33a. Picture Preferences C, Like	11.03	10.04	.21	11.12	11.17	-.01	1.16
33b. Picture Preferences C, Indiff.	2.44	3.21	-.17	1.81	2.55	-.22	.27
33c. Picture Prefereces C, Dislike	2.53	2.75	-.06	3.08	2.28	.18	1.25
34. Figure Choices	12.26	13.96	-.16	13.85	13.83	.00	.83
35. Incidental Recall	7.18	6.88	.09	7.42	7.41	.00	.47
36. Desirability	18.68	18.29	.05	18.85	18.69	.02	.16
37. Saunders' Tolerance of Ambiguity	4.26	4.08	.06	4.31	4.62	-.09	.78
38. BC Independence-Yielding	7.00	7.46	-.11	8.12	8.00	.02	.67
39. Barron's Complexity-Simplicity	8.21	8.13	.01	8.38	8.55	-.03	.21
40. Fulkerson's Acquiescence	11.65	12.08	-.08	11.04	11.31	-.05	.16
41. Couch-Keniston's Agreement Scale	8.85	9.42	-.12	9.38	9.07	.08	1.04
42. Couch-Keniston's Agreement Factor	7.29	7.92	-.12	7.31	7.52	-.04	.42
43. Authoritarianism	15.12	16.21	-.20	14.81	14.97	-.03	.89
44. Acquiescence to Extremes	5.85	6.38	-.11	6.08	5.28	.19	1.56
45. Acquiescence to Tentatives	9.56	9.33	.06	9.42	9.21	.05	.05
46. Dogmatism	12.12	11.79	.05	11.23	10.31	.16	.57
47. Self-Sufficiency	3.24	3.54	-.07	3.08	3.14	-.02	.26
48. Impulsiveness	12.06	12.63	-.10	12.69	12.34	.06	.83
49. Budner's Tolerance of Ambiguity	10.68	9.79	.22	10.27	10.72	-.11	1.73
50. Affective-Effective	4.26	4.58	-.11	4.35	3.79	.15	1.35
51. Anxiety	3.97	3.58	.08	3.58	3.76	-.04	.62
52. Rigidity	17.18	16.75	.06	15.50	16.79	-.17	1.20
53. Unconventionality	2.26	2.33	-.02	3.04	3.14	-.02	.00
54. Extremity of Self-Rating	524.15	511.75	.09	500.69	490.55	.08	.05

c. $p < .07$ *$p < .05$ **$p < .01$

are presented for first borns and later borns separately within the experimental and comparison groups, along with point-biserial correlations of each scale with birth order and t-values for the significance of differences between the correlations. It is striking that no significant differences between first borns and later borns appear in Table 8 for either sample. Only one interaction approaches significance, the one for Budner's (1962) Tolerance of Ambiguity Scale (t-value for the difference between correlations with birth order in the two groups was 1.73, $p < .10$). Later borns were slightly more tolerant of ambiguity on this scale than first borns in the comparison group but were somewhat less tolerant of ambiguity than first borns in the experimental group. It is of interest to note that according to Frenkel-Brunswik (1949) one consequence of intolerance of ambiguity is the tendency to reach perceptual closure prematurely, and later borns not only appeared more intolerant of ambiguity on the Budner scale in the experimental group than in the comparison group, but they also performed significantly poorer in the experimental group on the Gestalt Completion Test of perceptual closure (*see* Table 7).

Even though the number of older siblings and the number of younger siblings a subject has are not independent of birth order (as indicated in Table 9), correlations were computed between these two indices and all of the cognitive and personality measures to see if weights for the number of older siblings and the number of younger siblings, and hence indirectly for .family size, would alter any of the above relations with birth order as reflected in the simple "first born vs. later born" dichotomy. These correlations are presented separately for the experimental and comparison groups in Table 10 for the cognitive measures and in Table 11 for the personality scales. In both tables, t-values are also provided for the significance of the difference between the two groups in the product-moment correlation of each variable with number of older siblings and with number of younger siblings.

Most of the perceptual measures that were significantly related to

Table 9 Intercorrelations among measures of birth order and number of siblings (Experimental Group below diagonal and Comparison Group above diagonal)

Variable	8. First Born	10. No. Older Sibs.	11. No Younger Sibs.
8. First Born	--	-.70	.44
10. Number Older Siblings	-.88	--	-.35
11. Number Younger Siblings	.47	-.40	--

birth order in Table 7 also showed significant relations in the appropriate direction with one or the other of the sibling scores in Table 10, usually with a slight increase in the size of the relation. This occurred for Gestalt Completion, Mutilated Words, Hidden Figures, Hidden Pictures (poor figures), and Nearer Point. However, the significant relations with birth order reported in Table 7 for Perceptual Speed, graphic constriction-expansiveness, and indifference in picture preferences were found to be attenuated in Table 10 when the weighted scores for number of older siblings and number of younger siblings were employed. In addition, a few cognitive measures that were not significantly related to birth order in Table 7 were found to be significantly associated with one of the sibling scores in Table 10: the more older siblings, the better the performance in the experimental group on Four-Letter Words and Color-Word Interference; the more younger siblings, the higher the vocabulary score in the comparison group; the more younger siblings, the greater the tendency to prefer complexity on Figure Choices in the comparison group and to prefer simplicity in the experimental group; finally, the more younger siblings, the greater the tendency to dislike photographs in the Picture Preferences procedure in the comparison group and the smaller the tendency to dislike photographs in the experimental group.

In contrast to the general lack of relation between personality scales and birth order in Table 8, several significant relations with number of older or number of younger siblings appear in Table 11. The more older siblings, the less the acquiescence on the Couch-Keniston Agreement Scale in the comparison group and the greater the acquiescent tendency in the experimental group. The more younger siblings, the lower the authoritarianism score in the experimental group and the higher the anxiety score in the comparison group. Also, the more younger siblings, the more tolerant of ambiguity on Saunders' scale in the experimental group and the less tolerant in the comparison group. Finally, the more younger siblings, the less conventional in the experimental group and the more conventional in the comparison group.

DISCUSSION

When the subjects in the experimental condition of the present study were tested on the morning of November 23, 1963, John F. Kennedy had been dead for less than 24 hours. Lee Oswald had been apprehended but had not yet been murdered. This "Saturday was a day out of time, a day in which crowds stood mutely in the cold drizzle . . . The violence and shock of the previous day had been transmuted into the clean, precise formality of a catafalque in the East Room of the White House. . . . The few real events of Saturday seemed rather unreal, engulfed as they were in a more tangible shroud of sorrow." [6] Unless these experimental subjects were distinctly atypical, the shock and disbelief of the previous day—

[6] *Four Days*. Compiled by United Press International and American Heritage Magazine. New York: Simon and Schuster, 1964, p. 43.

Table 10 Cognitive measures
Correlations with number of older siblings and number of younger siblings separately for Experimental and Comparison Groups, along with t-values for the significance of the difference in correlations

Variable	10. Number of Older Sibs. Exp. Group	Comp. Group	t^a	11. Number of Younger Sibs. Exp. Group	Comp. Group	t^a
12. Vocabulary	.03	-.11	.72	-.02	.29*	1.65
13. Math. Aptitude	-.05	-.07	.10	.11	.18	.37
14. Gestalt Completion	-.18	-.00	.94	.30*	.19	.60
15. Mutilated Words	.23	-.17	2.10*	-.04	.30*	1.80
16. Four-Letter Words	.25	-.12	1.95[b]	-.11	.12	1.19
17. Hidden Figures	.33*	-.12	2.40*	-.17	.23	2.10*
18. Hidden Patterns	.07	-.08	.78	.04	.05	.05
19a. Hidden Pictures	.07	-.03	.52	.03	.16	.68
19b. Hidden Pictures, Poor Figures	.30*	-.14	2.33*	-.02	-.08	.31
20. Hidden Pictures, Info.	-.16	-.02	.73	.10	.01	.47
21. Shortest Road	.04	-.06	.52	-.15	-.00	.78
22. Nearer Point	.14	-.43**	3.11**	.09	.15	.32
23a. Speed of Color Discrimination	.23	-.01	1.26	-.09	.09	.93
23b. Color-Word Interference	.38**	.06	1.76	-.05	.00	.26
24. Perceptual Speed	-.09	.17	1.35	.10	-.02	.62
25. Finding A's	.11	.06	.26	-.20	.04	1.26
26. Spelling	.03	.00	.16	-.12	.15	1.41
27. Thing Categories	-.01	-.22	1.11	.10	-.07	.88
28a. Estimation Questionnaire I	.13	.03	.52	.19	-.06	1.30
28b. Estimation Questionnaire II	-.07	-.09	.10	.17	.06	.58
29. Word Meaning	.00	-.17	.89	-.07	.05	.62
30. Doodles	.21	.04	.90	-.17	.11	1.46

a. t-values for the significance of the difference between correlations (experimental group vs. comparison group).
b. p < .07   *p < .05   **p < .01

Table 11 Personality scales

33a. Picture Preferences C, Like	-.21	.07	1.47	.20	-.12	1.68
33b. Picture Preferences C, Indiff.	.18	.15	.16	-.05	-.09	.21
33c. Picture Preferences C, Dislike	.04	-.19	1.20	-.19	.19	1.99*
34. Figure Choices	.06	.03	.16	-.19	.27*	2.42*
35. Incidental Recall	-.12	-.13	.05	.04	.03	.05
36. Desirability	-.04	.11	.78	.03	-.11	.72
37. Saunders' Tolerance of Ambiguity	-.12	-.05	.37	.22	-.17	2.05*
38. BC Independence-Yielding	.04	-.10	.72	.03	-.01	.21
39. Barron's Complexity-Simplicity	-.03	-.20	.89	.22	.05	.90
40. Fulkerson's Acquiescence	.15	-.04	.99	-.19	.07	1.35
41. Couch-Keniston Agreement Scale	.15	-.30*	2.38*	-.03	.13	.83
42. Couch-Keniston Agreement Factor	.11	-.12	1.19	.01	.04	.16
43. Authoritarianism	.17	.00	.89	-.27*	-.19	.44
44. Acquiescence to Extremes	.10	-.20	1.57	.00	-.01	.05
45. Acquiescence to Tentatives	.01	.09	.41	-.15	-.15	.00
46. Dogmatism	-.02	-.03	.05	-.18	-.12	.32
47. Self-Sufficiency	.09	.07	.10	-.04	-.01	.16
48. Impulsiveness	.08	-.20	1.46	-.08	.02	.52
49. Budner's Tolerance of Ambiguity	-.17	-.01	.84	.13	.19	.32
50. Affective-Effective	.06	-.25	1.63	.00	.23	1.21
51. Anxiety	-.06	-.04	.10	.04	.27*	1.23
52. Rigidity	.02	.20	.95	-.18	-.20	.11
53. Unconventionality	.06	-.19	1.30	.13	-.23	1.89[b]
54. Extremity of Self-Rating	-.07	-.12	.26	-.20	-.13	.37

Banta (1964), Tomkins & McCarter (1965, *see* Chapter VI, Part 2 of this volume)—had given way to a cumulative awareness of the loss and to an attendent engulfment in the painful feelings of grief—sadness, guilt, shame, anger, worry, helplessness (Sheatsley & Feldman, 1964). However, these massive and intense negative affects that gripped our experimental subjects—and the nation—on the day following President Kennedy's assassination did not produce, as might have been expected, a general decrement in cognitive performance. On the contrary, the impact of this negative affect upon cognition and personality was relatively specific.

In terms of overall main effects, all three marker tests for the flexibility of perceptual closure factor were implicated, along with a prototype measure of speed of perceptual closure (experimental subjects obtained significantly lower scores on Hidden Patterns and Hidden Pictures and significantly more wrong answers on Hidden Figures and Gestalt Completion than did comparison subjects). Experimental subjects were also significantly more indifferent than comparison subjects in their affective reactions to stimuli and tended to be more constricted in graphic expression. Several significant interactions were also observed with sex of subject and with birth order, but these interactions primarily involved these same variables—measures of the two factors of speed and flexibility of perceptual closure (Gestalt Completion, Mutilated Words, Hidden Figures, Hidden Patterns, Hidden Pictures, and Nearer Point [7]), the doodling measure of graphic constriction-expansiveness, and the indifference score from the picture preferences procedure. These interactions with a simple first born vs. later born dichotomy represent remarkable consistencies in view of the considerable evidence that ordinal position has different psychological implications depending upon sex of subject, family size, and the sex of siblings—Koch (1956), Rosenberg & Sutton-Smith (1964).

The effects of the assassination on personality scales were also quite specific: experimental subjects were significantly more yielding and conventional than comparison subjects, but at the same time were more dogmatic and extreme in self-rating. Several personality scales exhibited significant interactions with sex (independence vs. yielding, complexity vs. simplicity, agreement tendency, self-sufficiency, and affective vs. effective preferences), but only one marginal interaction occurred with birth order (Budner's Tolerance of Ambiguity scale).

A consideration of possible psychological mechanisms of reaction to negative affect that might underlie these experimental differences in cognition and personality is quite complicated, primarily because of the large number of variables involved in the study. A clearer picture would emerge if the intercorrelations among the measures within each condition were taken into account and comparisons made between the two groups in terms of factor structures and differences in factor scores. Such an

---

[7] Nearer Point appears to be somewhat similar to embedded-figures measures of flexibility of closure in that the subject is required to make difficult perceptual judgments in the presence of distracting contexts.

analysis is beyond the scope of the present paper, but it has been undertaken and will be presented in a later, extended treatment of this study. For the present purposes, however, it is important that one caveat be briefly distilled from the multivariate results: The intercorrelations among the cognitive and personality measures were found to be markedly different in the two groups, as were the factor structures, suggesting the distinct possibility that performance on particular tests might be mediated by different psychological processes under the two conditions. In the absence of detailed information about consistent differences in these intercorrelations, any discussion of the experimental results reported here must remain tentative. Nevertheless, the specificity of these results would seem to permit some general comments.

A striking consistency in the pattern of significant differences occurred not only in the main effects between the two conditions but in the interactions with birth order. The generally lower scores in the experimental group on Hidden Patterns and Hidden Pictures and the specifically lower scores of first borns on Mutilated Words, Hidden Figures, and Hidden Pictures (poor figures) were attended by a significant increase in graphic constriction and in the indifference of affective reactions to stimuli. It may be that this greater graphic constriction, which is an expressive characterization of introverts and anxious extraverts (Wallach & Gahm, 1960), indicates, particularly under conditions of negative affect or anxiety, that attention has turned inward to a preoccupation with internal states, with a consequent decrease in affective response to irrelevant external stimuli and a relatively specific impoverishment of performance on cognitive and perceptual tests that require an active structuring of the stimulus field. The increase in graphic constriction in the experimental group was relatively greater for females and for first borns, which may represent a contrast for them to their typically greater social dependence—Schachter (1959), Witkin et al. (1962). The consistency of the total pattern was broken when males rather than females turned out to be more indifferent in picture preferences in the experimental condition.

Another consistency in the results warrants further comment, namely, the tendency on several tests, where first borns performed more poorly in the experimental group than in the comparison group, for later borns to perform slightly better in the experimental group than in the comparison group. This occurred on Mutilated Words, Hidden Figures, Nearer Point, and to a lesser degree on Speed of Color Discrimination and Color-Word Interference (see Table 7). The reverse trend was suggested on only two tests, Perceptual Speed and Gestalt Completion, where later borns performed more poorly in the experimental group than in the comparison group, and first borns tended to do slightly better in the experimental group than in the comparison group. It is difficult to account for both of these trends with the same mechanism. It was suggested previously that the latter tendency for the later borns to perform more poorly in the experimental group on Gestalt Completion, and to some extent on Perceptual Speed, might have been the consequence of an increased tendency to reach perceptual closure prematurely. This possibility was suggested by the concomitance of one marginal interaction between experimental conditions and birth order: later borns tended to be more intolerant of ambiguity on Budner's scale than first borns in the experimental group but slightly more tolerant of ambiguity than first borns in the comparison group (see Frenkel-Brunswik, 1949). A general tendency toward increased closure as a function of anxiety has been reported previously—Basowitz et al., (1955), Korchin & Basowitz (1954), Moffit & Stagner (1956)—but an account of the present results in these terms would require some basis for distinguishing first borns and later borns in this regard.

Although the formulation is somewhat embarrassed by the advantage displayed in the experimental group by first borns over later borns on Gestalt Completion and Perceptual Speed, the tendency on several other tests for first borns to perform more poorly and later borns somewhat better in the experimental group than in the comparison group might be a function of differential arousal levels between first borns and later borns under these conditions. Specifically, evidence has been accumulated suggesting that level of performance is related to an organism's general level of arousal by an inverted-U curve, with both low and high levels of arousal producing relatively poor performance and with optimum performance occurring at intermediate levels of arousal—Duffy (1962), Fiske & Maddi (1961). Since the concept of arousal implies a nonspecific dimension of intensity of excitation, it is usually presumed that this relation would hold for all conditions of arousal regardless of source. Although there is some indication that anxiety, as distinct from such other states of arousal as anger or concentration, may indeed be related to effectiveness of performance by an inverted-U function—Duffy (1962), Korchin (1964), Korchin et al. (1957), Longenecker (1962)—the extent to which performance is similarly related to intensity levels of specific affects, such as distress or disgust, is little known.

For purposes of relating the present results to this arousal formulation, it should be noted that first borns tend to display somewhat higher levels of arousal than later borns, particularly in evaluative situations. Although they tend to be slightly lower in IQ than later borns (Roberts, 1938), first borns tend to do slightly better in achievement (Jones, 1933; Wagner, 1940), to display somewhat more need for achievement (Sampson, 1962), and to be more competitive (Koch, 1956) than later borns. More important for the present discussion, however, first borns appear to be more sensitive to pain than later borns—Carman (1899), Jones (1933), Schachter (1959). They may be more sensitive, and may react more strongly, to the painful aspects of negative affects. Also, anxiety-provoking situations appear to arouse higher levels of anxiety in first borns than in later borns (Schachter, 1959). It would seem possible, then, that first borns might have reacted more strongly to the assassination than later borns and might have consequently reached a higher level of arousal. In the experimental condition of the present study, then, the arousal level of first borns might have been sufficiently high to produce a debilitating effect on cognitive performance, while the more moderate increase in arousal for the later borns was more likely to be in the facilitating range. That differential arousal could produce such an effect on perceptual closure tests has already been demonstrated by Longenecker (1962) who found that high arousal subjects (one group high in anxiety and another group high in achievement motivation) performed better on perceptual closure tests than low arousal subjects under non-stress conditions, but under stress conditions low arousal subjects performed better.

In most of the above discussion of the present results, it has been assumed that the nature and intensity of the affects present on the day after the assassination, as well as the manner and degree of their expression or control, were important factors in producing the cognitive and personality differences noted. In closing, some attempt will be made to support this contention by briefly summarizing some relations obtained between cognitive performance and a measure of affect expression. (These results will be described more fully in an extended treatment of the present study.) In response to one of the tasks in the test battery, subjects in both the experimental and comparison groups had written brief descriptions of their three earliest childhood recollections. These protocols were subsequently scored for the expression of eight classes of affect using a system derived from Plutchik's (1962) theory of emotions.[8] In addition, summary scores were derived for the expression of positive affect, of negative affect, and of total affect. Correlation coefficients were then computed separately for the two groups between these affect expression scores and all of the cognitive and personality measures described above. The relations of the cognitive and personality measures to the expression of specific affects were too manifold and intricate to summarize here, but the significant correlations between the cognitive tests and the composite affect scores may be easily characterized. Significant negative correlations were obtained in the experimental group between the expression of total affect (usually also the expression of positive affect but occasionally the expression of negative affect) and performance on Gestalt Completion, Four-Letter Words, Hidden Patterns, Hidden Pictures, Shortest Road, Color-Word Interference, and overestimation in Size Estimation. In addition, a significant positive correlation was obtained between the expression of negative affect and the number of poor figures on Hidden Pictures. In the comparison group, on the other hand, significant correlations were obtained for only two of these tests (Shortest Road and Hidden Patterns). Thus, for many of the perceptual tests involved in the experimental effects and interactions reported in the present study, it was found that the expression of affect in early memories was significantly associated in the experimental group with poor test performance.

[8] The author wishes to thank Dr. Ronald Wynne of Queens College for supervising the scoring of the Early Memory protocols.

SUMMARY

On Saturday, November 23, 1963, the day after John F. Kennedy had been assassinated, a six-hour battery of cognitive and personality measures was administered to a sample of 58 undergraduates at a small eastern college. Three months later, another comparable sample from the same college was administered the same battery for comparison purposes. The effects of the assassination on cognition and personality were found to be fairly specific. In terms of overall main effects, all three marker tests for flexibility of perceptual closure were implicated, along with a measure of the speed of closure factor. Experimental subjects were also found to be more indifferent than comparison subjects in their affective reactions to stimuli and tended to be more constricted in graphic expression. Several significant interactions were also observed with sex of subject and with birth order, and these interactions primarily involved these same variables—measures of the two factors of speed and flexibility of perceptual closure, of graphic constriction-expansiveness, and of indifference in affective reactions to stimuli. The effects of the assassination on personality scales were also quite specific. Experimental subjects were significantly more yielding and conventional than comparison subjects, but at the same time were more dogmatic and extreme in expressing opinions.

REFERENCES

Banta, T. The Kennedy assassination: Early thoughts and emotions. *Publ. Opin. Quart.*, 1964, *28*, 216-226.

Barratt, E. S. Anxiety and impulsiveness related to psychomotor efficiency. *Percept. mot. Skills*, 1959, 9, 191-198.

Barron, F. Complexity-simplicity as a personality dimension. *J. abnorm. soc. Psychol.*, 1953, *48* 163-172. (a)

Barron, F. Some personality correlates of independence of judgment. *J. Pers.*, 1953, *21*, 287-297. (b)

Barron, F., & Welsh, G. S. Artistic preference as a factor in personality style: its measurement by a figure-preference test. *J. Psychol.*, 1952, *33*, 199-203.

Basowitz, H., Persky, H., Korchin, S. J., & Grinker, R. R. *Anxiety and stress.* New York: McGraw-Hill, 1955.

Budner, S. Intolerance of ambiguity as a personality variable. *J. Pers.*, 1962, *30*, 29-50.

Carman, A. Pain and strength measurements of 1507 school children in Saginaw, Michigan. *Amer. J. Psychol.*, 1899, *10*, 392-398.

Clayton, Martha B., & Jackson, D. N. Equivalence range, acquiescence, and overgeneralization. *Educ. and psychol. Measmt.*, 1961, *21*, 371-382.

Couch, A., & Keniston, K. Yeasayers and naysayers: Agreeing response set as a personality variable. *J. abnorm. soc. Psychol.*, 1960, *60*, 151-174.

Crutchfield, R. S. Conformity and character. *Amer. Psychologist*, 1955, *10*, 191-198.

Duffy, Elizabeth. *Activation and behavior.* New York: Wiley, 1962.

Fiske, D. W., & Maddi, S. R. *Functions of varied experience.* Homewood, Illinois: Dorsey, 1961.

French, J. W. The description of aptitude and achievement tests in terms of rotated factors. *Psychom. Monogr. No. 5,* Chicago: University of Chicago Press, 1951.

French, J. W., Ekstrom, Ruth B., & Price, L. A. *Kit of reference tests for cognitive factors.* (Revised edition) Princeton, N.J.: Educational Testing Service, 1963.

Frenkel-Brunswik, Else. Intolerance of ambiguity as an emotional and perceptual personality variable. *J. Pers.,* 1949, *18,* 108-143.

Fulkerson, S. C. An acquiescence key for the MMPI. *USAF School of Aviation Medicine Report,* 1958, No. 58-71.

Gardner, R. W., Holtzman, P. S., Klein, G. S., Linton, H. B., & Spence, D. P. Cognitive control: A study of individual consistencies in cognitive behavior. *Psychol. Issues,* 1959, *1,* No. 4.

Gardner, R. W., & Long, R. I. Control, defence, and centration effect: A study of scanning behaviour. *Brit. J. Psychol.,* 1962, *53,* 129-140.

Gough, H. G., & Sanford, R. N. Rigidity as a psychological variable. Berkeley, University of California, Institute of Personality Assessment and Research, 1952. (Unpublished manuscript)

Holtzman, W. H., Thorpe, J. S., Swartz, J. D., & Herron, E. W. *Inkblot perception and personality.* Austin, Texas: University of Texas Press, 1961.

Jackson, D. N., Messick, S., & Myers, C. T. Evaluation of group and individual forms of embedded-figures measures of field-independence. *Educ. and psychol. Measmt.,* 1964, *24,* 177-192.

Jones, H. E. Order of birth. In C. Murchison (Ed.), *Handbook of child psychology.* (Revised edition) Worcester, Mass.: Clark University Press, 1933.

Koch, Helen L. Attitudes of children toward their peers as related to certain characteristics of their siblings. *Psychol. Monogr.: General and Applied,* 1956, *70,* No. 19.

Korchin, S. J. Anxiety and cognition. In Constance Scheerer (Ed.), *Cognitions: Theory, research, promise.* New York: Harper and Row, 1964.

Korchin, S J., & Basowitz, H. Perceptual adequacy in a life stress. *J. Psychol.,* 1954, *38,* 495-502.

Korchin, S. J., Basowitz, H., Chevalier, J. A., Grinker, R. R., Hamburg, D. A., Sabshin, M., & Persky, H. Visual discrimination and the decision process in anxiety. *Arch. Neurol. and Psychiat.,* 1957, *78,* 425-438.

Longenecker, E. D. Perceptual recognition as a function of anxiety, motivation, and the testing situation. *J. abnorm. soc. Psychol.,* 1962, *64,* 215-221.

Messick, S. Response style and content measures from personality inventories. *Educ. and psychol. Measmt.,* 1962, *22,* 41-56.

Messick, S. Cognitive interference and flexible control. Research Bulletin, Princeton, N. J.: Educational Testing Service, 1965, in preparation.

Messick, S., & Fritzky, F. J. Dimensions of analytic attitude in cognition and personality. *J. Pers.* 1963, *31,* 346-370.

Messick, S., & Kogan, N. Categorizing styles and cognitive structure. Research Bulletin, Princeton, N. J.: Educational Testing Service, 1965, in preparation.

Moffitt, J. W., & Stagner, R. Perceptual rigidity and closure as functions of anxiety. *J. abnorm. soc. Psychol.,* 1956, *52,* 354-357.

Peabody, D. Two components in bipolar scales. Direction and extremeness. *Psychol. Review,* 1962, *69,* 65-73.

Pemberton, Carol. The closure factors related to other cognitive processes. *Psychometrika*, 1952, *17*, 267-288.

Pettigrew, T. F. The measurement and correlates of category width as a cognitive variable. *J. Pers.*, 1958, *26*, 532-544.

Plutchik, R. *Emotions.* New York: Random House, 1962.

Roberts, C. S. Ordinal position and its relationship to some aspects of personality. *J. genetic Psychol.*, 1938, *53*, 173-213.

Rokeach, M. Political and religious dogmatism: An alternative to the authoritarian personality. *Psychol. Monogr.: General and Applied*, 1956, *70*, No. 18.

Rokeach, M. *The open and closed mind.* New York: Basic Books, 1960.

Rosenberg, B. G., & Sutton-Smith, B. Ordinal position and sex-role indentification. *Genetic Psychol. Monogr.*, 1964, *70*, 297-328.

Sampson, E. E. Birth order, need achievement, and conformity. *J. abnorm. soc. Psychol.*, 1962, *64*, 155-159.

Saunders, D. R. Some preliminary interpretive material for the PRI. Research Memorandum 55-15. Princeton, N. J.: Educational Testing Service, 1955.

Schachter, S. *The psychology of affiliation.* Stanford, Calif.: Stanford University Press, 1959.

Schlesinger, H. J. Cognitive attitudes in relation to susceptibility to interference. *J. Pers.*, 1954, *22*, 354-374.

Sheatsley, P. B., & Feldman, J. J. The assassination of President Kennedy: A preliminary report on public reactions and behavior. *Publ. Opin. Quart.*, 1964, *28*, 189-215.

Silverman, J. Scanning-control mechanism and "cognitive filtering" in paranoid and nonparanoid schizophrenia. *J. consul. Psychol.* 1964, *28*, 385-393.

Smith, G. J. W., & Klein, G. S. Cognitive controls in serial behavior patterns. *J. Pers.*, 1953, *22*, 188-213.

Stricker, L. J. Acquiescence and social desirability response styles, item characteristics, and conformity. *Psychol. Reports*, 1963, *12*, 319-341.

Stroop, J. R. Studies in interference in serial verbal reaction. *J. exp. Psychol.*, 1935, *18*, 643-661.

Thurstone, L. L. A factorial study of perception. *Psychom. Monogr. No. 4.* Chicago: University of Chicago Press, 1944.

Tomkins, S. S., & McCarter, R. The psychology of commitment: Part 2. Reactions to the assassination of President Kennedy. In S. S. Tomkins & C. Izard (Eds.), *Affect, cognition, and personality.* New York: Springer, 1965.

Wagner, M. E. The relation of sibling pattern to academic motivation. *Psychol. Bull.* 1940, *37*, 473. (Abstract)

Wallach, M. A., & Caron, A. J. Attribute criteriality and sex-linked conservatism as determinants of psychological similarity. *J. abnorm. soc. Psychol.*, 1959, *59*, 43-50.

Wallach, M. A., & Gahm, Ruthellen C. Personality functions of graphic constriction and expansiveness. *J. Pers.*, 1960, *28*, 73-88.

Warner, W. L., Meeker, Marchia, & Eells, K. *Social class in America: A manual of procedure for the measurement of social status.* Chicago: Science Research Associates, 1949.

Witkin, H. A., Dyk, R. B., Faterson, Hanna F., Goodenough, D. R., & Karp, S. A. *Psychological differentiation.* New York: Wiley, 1962.

Witkin, H. A., Lewis, H. B., Hertzman, M., Machover, K., Meissner, P. B., & Wapner, S. *Personality through perception.* New York: Harper, 1954.

PART THREE

AFFECT AND
SOCIAL PROCESSES

V

Some content determinants of intolerance for attitudinal inconsistency

Milton J. Rosenberg

A number of theories that have recently come to prominence view the attitude change process in terms of the arousal and reduction of inconsistency between attitude components. The larger number of these theories, though they differ from one another in certain important respects, seem to employ the same basic conceptual unit. That unit is here designated as the "attitudinal cognition" and is defined as *the perceived relationship between two affectively significant "objects."*[1] Examples of such units, or of the kinds of verbal statements from which they can be deductively drawn, are: "my beloved child is most intelligent"; "the abominable idea of bomb shelters is likely to lead us toward war"; "my good friend Alex constantly derides the perfect poems of Euphemia Clashthought."[2] If each of the three judgements incorporated in such statements is reduced to binary representation (positive or negative affect toward each of the two objects and a cognized positive or negative relationship between them)[3] the number of possible types is simply the cube value of two.

[1] In this paper, as in its precursors (Abelson & Rosenberg, 1958; Rosenberg & Abelson, 1960), "object" is used in a broadly inclusive sense: any state, person, condition, institution, action or event whose concept regularly elicits a particular affective-evaluative response from the person is an *object* of an attitude and may figure in one or more of his attitudinal cognitions. When a perceived relationship involves two objects at least one of which elicits *no* stable affect then the cognition in question is not an attitudinal one.

[2] In these and most examples in this paper object-nouns are modified by affect-expressing (i.e., evaluative) adjectives. In ordinary parlance this is usually implicit so that, for example, "my child" is taken to be "beloved." But here, for the sake of clarity, redundancy will be risked.

[3] The reduction of affects and relationships to a positive-negative code has been discussed in detail in earlier publications (Abelson & Rosenberg, 1958; Rosenberg & Abelson, 1960). Affective statements about objects can be easily and reliably coded into the positive or negative judgments they assert or imply. Perceived relations be-

This study was carried out under Contract 609(27) with the Group Psychology Branch of the Office of Naval Research.

Such writers as Heider (1946, 1958), Newcomb (1963), Cartwright & Harary (1956) and Abelson & Rosenberg (1958) agree in classifying half of these eight possible types of attitudinal cognitions as internally inconsistent (or "unbalanced") and the other four as internally consistent.[4] In the category of inconsistent attitudinal cognitions are those combinations featuring either a positive relationship between two concepts of opposite affective sign $(++-, -++)$ or a negative relationship between two concepts of similar affective sign $(+-+, ---)$. In the category of consistent cognitions are those that feature either a negative relationship between two objects of opposite affective sign $(+--, --+)$ or a positive relationship between two concepts of similar sign $(+++, -+-)$.

The authors mentioned agree further that inconsistent cognitions are more likely to arouse psychological tension than consistent cognitions and are thereby less stable, more prone to spontaneous reorganization or to reorganization guided by persuasive communications. In this sense the arousal of inconsistency within attitudinal cognitions is, in all of these theories, the basic condition for the occurrence of attitude change.

Experimental confirmations of the basic proposition that inconsistent attitudinal cognitions are comparatively unstable have been reported by Heider (1958), Jordan (1953), Newcomb (1958), Burdick & Burnes (1958), Rosenberg (1960a), Rosenberg & Abelson (1960) and others. At the same time it has occasionally been observed (Zajonc, 1960; Rosenberg, 1960b) that neither in theory nor research has there been sufficient concern with the quite frequent instance in which inconsistent attitudinal cognitions *are* tolerated and stably maintained. Indeed all of the inconsistency theories of attitude change (including, in addition to those already cited, the approaches of Festinger, 1957, and Osgood & Tannenbaum, 1955) seem inadequate in face of the compelling fact that real people are often quite accepting of illogic and inconsistency in their beliefs about attitude objects.

The future development of such theories will be aided by attempts to encompass this problem. One such attempt has been presented in an earlier publication (Rosenberg, 1960b) in which it was suggested that a number of variables may influence whether specific inconsistent attitudinal cognitions are or are not tolerated. Certain of these variables are

tween objects are classed as positive or negative depending upon whether they assert or imply conjunction or disjunction respectively. Thus words suggesting common grouping ("belongs with," "is the same as," "is part of," "is an attribute of," etc.) or positive sentiment bonds ("likes," "admires," etc.) or instrumental linking ("supports," "advocates," "helps," etc.) are all coded as positive relationships. Conversely such relational terms as "is different from," "dislikes," "opposes," etc., are coded as negative relationships.

[4] Heider, Newcomb, and Cartwright & Harary differ from Rosenberg and Abelson in that they use another representational procedure to characterize the contents of attitudinal cognitions. But translation between the two approaches is routine. Related approaches such as those of Festinger (1957) and Osgood & Tannenbaum (1955) are more truly at variance with the present treatment.

aspects of the personality of the individual, others of the situation in which he encounters and reacts to inconsistency. Yet another group of variables was suggested by the results of some studies by Rosenberg & Abelson (1960). These have to do with *content* aspects of inconsistent attitudinal cognitions themselves.

The main purposes of this chapter are: first to explicate the nature of two such content variables; then to report some findings indicating that these variables do exert strong influence upon the response to inconsistent attitudinal cognitions; and finally to develop, in the light of these findings, some new theoretical propositions about the attitude change process.

The Hedonic-Antihedonic Variable

The first of the variables to be considered concerns the hedonic or antihedonic aspect of the content of an attitudinal cognition. As employed here, "hedonic" simply denotes an attitudinal cognition that reports or forecasts *gain*, in the sense of motive-reduction; the term "antihedonic" denotes an attitudinal cognition that reports or forecasts *loss*, in the sense of the heightening or frustration of a motive.

Hedonic or antihedonic meanings seem always to be conveyed by attitudinal cognitions in which the two objects are perceived to be in either a sentiment relationship ("likes," "dislikes," etc.) or an instrumental relationship ("supports," "opposes," "fosters," "prevents," etc.). However in the case of relationships of common grouping ("belongs with," "is a part of," etc.) meanings that may be classed as hedonic or antihedonic are not always present.

Illustrative of an attitudinal cognition that is both inconsistent and hedonic is:

My hated antagonist (−) supports (+) my favorite
plan for reorganizing the department (+).

In this example an affectively negative object has positive instrumental relation to an affectively positive object. The hedonic meaning lies in the last two terms of the unit: a plus (the "favorite plan") is plussed ("supports"). The inconsistency resides in the fact that the source of "support" is a negatively evaluated object (the "hated antagonist").

Similarly:

The charlatan Paracelsus (−) always loathed (−)
those who victimized the poor (−)
and
My unpleasant neighbor (−) intends to chase away (−)
the vandals in my Japanese rock garden (−).

Though both of the cognitions are inconsistent they are also hedonic. In both instances an affectively negative object has negative relation (negative sentiment issuing from Paracelsus and negative instrumental action planned by the neighbor) to an affectively negative object.

Again the hedonic meaning lies in the last two terms of the unit: a minus (the "victimization of the poor" or the "vandals in my rock garden") is minused ("always loathed" or "chase away"). And, as in the first example, the inconsistency is due to the fact that the source of the relation is a negatively evaluated object.

What is explicated in the foregoing may be summarized in these more general terms: when an inconsistent attitudinal cognition has *direction* (i.e., when it comprises one object related toward another object by sentiment or by instrumental action) *it will be hedonic (i.e., it will convey a state of affairs representing "gain") if its content consists of a disliked object in positive relation to a positively-evaluated second object (−++) or in negative relation to a negatively-evaluated second object (−−−).*

The two remaining types of inconsistent attitudinal cognitions, ++− and +−+, may both be classified as antihedonic.

Illustrations are:

The distinguished firm of Schlag and Sons (+) have put on the market (+) a completely worthless sphygmomanometer (−)

and

The church of my choice (+) is opposed to (−) the laudable goal of desegregation (+).

In considering the last two terms in both of these examples we note that, in contrast to the earlier ones, their import is of loss (i.e., of motive frustration or heightening); and this is what renders them antihedonic. The basis of inconsistency is of course the fact that the source of loss is a positively valued object.

In general then we may say that when an inconsistent attitudinal cognition has direction *it will be antihedonic if its content consists of a liked object in positive relation to a negatively-evaluated second object (++−) or in negative relation to a positively-evaluated second object (+−+).*

We turn now to the bearing of these points upon the problem of response to inconsistency in attitudinal cognitions. There are clear grounds for assuming (as is done in all of the aforementioned inconsistency theories of attitude dynamics) that men are, to varying degrees, made uncomfortable by such inconsistency and are motivated to reduce or eliminate it.[5] However, everyday observation as well as prior research (Rosenberg & Abelson, 1960) suggest that such motivation when aroused will sometimes be opposed by competing forces.

It is here suggested that one such competing force, and a particularly important one, is the presence of hedonic, as opposed to antihedonic, meanings within the inconsistent attitudinal cognition. Specifically it is hypothesized that *reactive intolerance for inconsistency will be of lesser*

[5] For an extended theoretical discussion of this assumption see the last chapter of Rosenberg, Hovland, et al. (1960).

*intensity if the attitudinal cognition in question conveys a hedonic asser-
tion or promise of gain and of greater intensity if it conveys an antihedonic
assertion or promise of loss.* This might properly be viewed as an application to the realm of attitudinal cognition of the more common proposition
that perceptual processes often reflect a wish-fulfilling bias. However, our
concern is with reactions to established configurations of meaning (i.e.,
structured attitudes) rather than with the initial perceptual organization
of highly ambiguous material.

The Personal-General Variable

A second dimension upon which the meanings of inconsistent attitudinal cognitions may vary will be defined and illustrated by turning again
to the two examples given above of an attitudinal cognition in which two
negatively evaluated objects are seen as negatively related.

In one instance "my unpleasant neighbor" intended to chase away
"the vandals in my rock garden"; in the other the "charlatan Paracelsus"
was characterized as having "loathed those who victimized the poor."
While both of these attitudinal cognitions are hedonic in import, the
former is a more "personal" cognition than the latter; it refers directly to
an aspect of the life of the individual who holds it. To be sure the cognition about Paracelsus involves the cognizer, at least to the extent that
"Paracelsus" and "victimization of the poor" are concepts which, for him,
elicit affective response. But the matter at issue does not touch him or his
plans or problems directly. We may then label this cognition as "general,"
rather than personal, in its reference.

When will the establishment (or, for that matter, the tentative consideration) of an inconsistent attitudinal cognition arouse greater tension:
when its content is of the personal or general form? One major theoretical
consideration suggests that inconsistency of the personal type will have
greater tension-arousing potency. Adaptive overt action is guided by,
among other things, our stable affective orientations toward objects. When
these objects are inconsistently related to other objects of affective significance their affective "meanings" are rendered less stable than heretofore,
and thus our action-orientations toward them become more problematical;
habits of overt response are in danger of being invalidated. Thus if my
unpleasant neighbor is doing me a considerable favor I anticipate that in
some part I will come to view him as *less* unpleasant; and from this I may
in turn come to realize, at some level that either reaches or falls short of
articulation, that I face disorder and new decision in conducting my
further contacts with him. The consequence of such a cognitive situation
is, then, the generation of ambivalence, and ambivalence tends to disrupt
the simplicity and efficiency of action. How much such ambivalence will
bother and motivate the person must depend, at least in part, upon the
frequency and regularity with which the potentially ambivalent object
is actually encountered in response-demanding contexts.

The distinction between personal and general types of content is therefore essentially a distinction in terms of whether the object of the cognition is one which is encountered, and acted toward, with some regularity in the day-to-day life of the attitude holder. I see my neighbor often, Paracelsus never; I have more to do with the place in which I worship or the institution for which I work than with the A.M.A. or the ruler of a distant nation. Thus when my neighbor or my place of worship or my firm (or indeed "*my*" anything) is involved in some affect-laden inconsistency I am more likely to anticipate disorder and irregularity in my efforts at overt adaptation than when I am faced with a change in my conception of general objects such as Paracelsus or the A.M.A.

On the basis of these considerations it is suggested that content differences, as between personal or general reference, comprise a second variable that may influence whether or not the individual is made sufficiently uncomfortable by a particular inconsistency to undertake its reduction or elimination. It is hypothesized then that *reactive intolerance for inconsistency will be weaker if the cognition in question is of general content and greater if it is of personal content.*

Experimental Hypotheses

If, as has been suggested above, intolerance for inconsistent attitudinal cognitions is weaker when those cognitions are hedonic rather than antihedonic and when they are general rather than personal, there should be a number of observable consequences. One of these is simply that we would expect such cognitions, once established, to show less spontaneous reorganization over time. Similarly we would expect them to be less easily or fully changed through persuasive communication than cognitions that are antihedonic and/or personal in content. Another possible prediction is that attempts to *establish* new inconsistent attitudinal cognitions will be more successful if these new cognitions are hedonic rather than antihedonic and general rather than personal.

Research in this area could proceed to test these derivative predictions or it could be directed at the underlying initial theoretical propositions that are directly concerned with the degree of tension (i.e., of intolerance for inconsistency, as such) aroused in a person when he finds himself holding or tentatively entertaining an inconsistent attitudinal cognition. Deeming the latter approach the one with which an investigation of these matters might best begin, the following specific hypotheses were directly derived from the theoretical analysis that has been presented and were then put to empirical test.

Hypothesis 1. Subjects will report themselves less bothered by inconsistency within attitudinal cognitions when the content of those cognitions is hedonic and more bothered when the content is antihedonic.

Hypothesis 2. Subjects will report themselves less bothered by inconsistency within attitudinal cognitions of personal content than within those of general content.

METHOD

To test these hypotheses, and also to investigate the scope and direction of any possible interaction between the two content factors they delineate, we administered to two different groups of subjects a sixteen-item questionnaire. Each item presented a hypothetical inconsistent attitudinal cognition which the subject was to rate on a scale from 0 to 10 for the "degree to which the illogical nature of this situation bothers me." The instructions laid heavy stress upon the fact that the cognitions were to be judged for the extent to which their *inconsistency* (rather than their content) was bothersome. The exact instructions delivered to all subjects were as follows:

> We all occasionally encounter situations that perplex and confuse us because they "just don't make sense" or because they seem incongruous and violate our ideas of the way things are supposed to be related to one another. Sometimes we can say just what seems perplexing and incongruous in such a situation; sometimes it's just a feeling that we have about it. But either way such situations tend to arouse tension *simply because* they appear to us to be "puzzling," "senseless," "illogical," "mixed-up," etc.
>
> Putting all of this more simply; when we encounter such illogical situations we tend to feel actively *bothered* by them.
>
> Of course people may vary in just how much they will be *bothered* by the feeling that a particular situation is somehow incongruous and illogical. Some situations of this sort might bother them more than others. Or they might be equally bothered by all such situations. The purpose of this questionnaire is to investigate this phenomenon more closely.
>
> On the next few pages a number of different situations are described. In response to the illogical and incongruous aspects of each of these situations some people might feel greatly bothered, some moderately or only slightly bothered and some not bothered at all. We would like to get your estimate of the degree to which each of these situations would *really bother you*.
>
> Specifically here is what we want you to do: Read each separate item and right after you read it simply ask yourself to what extent would you really feel *bothered* by the fact that the situation is somehow illogical, incongruous, confusing, etc. Don't try to think through your answer. Don't try to figure out just what there is about the situation that may make it seem incongruous, puzzling, illogical, confusing, etc. Simply ask yourself: *How much would the illogical and confusing nature of this situation really bother me?* Just follow your feelings and let your immediate reaction be your guide in determining your self rating.
>
> In giving your rating use some number from 0 to 10, according to the following scale:
>
> > 0: *I would not be bothered at all* by the illogical nature of the situation.
> >
> > 1, 2, or 3: *I would be slightly bothered* by the illogical nature of the situation.
> >
> > 4, 5, 6 or 7: *I would be moderately bothered* by the illogical nature of the situation.
> >
> > 8, 9, or 10: *I would be extremely bothered* by the illogical nature of the situation.

The greater the degree to which the illogical nature of the situation bothers you, the higher the number should be.

It was assumed that variation in levels of self-reported tension arousal as between different types of hypothetical inconsistent cognitions would reflect how the S responds to such cognitions when encountered or established in his everyday experience. The use of this "how-would-you-react-if" kind of strategy made possible a degree of control over content and intensity of "stimuli" which would not otherwise have been possible.

The actual items used are reproduced and classified in Table 1. They fall into four main groups: hedonic-personal, hedonic-general, anti-hedonic-personal and antihedonic-general. Each of these groups contains two types of inconsistent cognitions; $-++$ and $---$ for the hedonic groups, both personal and general; and $+-+$ and $++-$ for the anti-hedonic groups, both personal and general; and each of these two types is represented by two separate items respectively. In addition the four items in the hedonic-personal group and the four in the hedonic-general group are matched in content with those in the antihedonic-personal and general groups respectively (see Table 1). The purpose of this parallelism was, of course, to eliminate the possibility that the predicted differences between hedonic and antihedonic inconsistencies, if obtained, could be attributed to other, uncontrolled types of content variation. A similar matching of content was not possible as between personal and general items but an effort was made to make the latter at least as clearly inconsistent in form as the personal items. The order in which the items were presented on the questionnaire was determined by a randomization procedure.

The questionnaire was administered to two separate groups: 33 male undergraduates at an eastern college and 106 female undergraduates at a large eastern city university. In the case of the latter group, and following the administration of the questionnaire, some other measures were collected as part of a larger study.

RESULTS

Only one of the male subjects and two of the females failed to fill out the questionnaire according to instructions. For all other subjects the tension ratings were tabulated and organized so as to enable analysis of variance. Table 2 reports the findings from the group of 32 males and Table 3 those drawn from the group of 104 females.

In both analyses the hedonic-antihedonic variable controls a significant proportion of the total variance in tension ratings. Thus hypothesis 1 receives strong confirmation. The effect is, as expected, in the direction of greater reported tension over inconsistency in response to the antihedonic cognitions and much less in response to the hedonic cognitions. In the case of the male sample the mean degree of reported tension for the eight

Table 1 Hypothetical inconsistent attitudinal cognitions rated by subjects

Hedonic - Personal	Antihedonic - Personal
G. L. is a fellow student (same sex as you) toward whom you have long felt extreme dislike. You learn on reliable authority that G. L. feels strong and sincere admiration and respect for you. (-++)	J. T. is a fellow student (same sex as you) toward whom you have long felt great admiration and respect. You learn on reliable authority that J. T. feels strong and sincere dislike for you. (+-+)
You have written an essay on "What I Value Most in Life." You feel that you have really written something meaningful and important and written it well. Professor X whom you dislike and disdain more than any other of your teachers reads the essay. He tells you with obvious sincerity that he found the essay "a wonderfully lucid display of mature and honest thought." (-++)	You have written an essay on "What I Value Most in Life." You feel that you have really written something meaningful and important and written it well. Professor Y whom you like and respect more than any other of your teachers reads the essay. He tells you with obvious sincerity that he found the essay "a horribly dreary piece of trashy, adolescent affectation." (+-+)
The graduate student assistant in a course you have been taking is a person whom you and all your classmates consider, with good reason, to be a loathsome and despicable person. At the end of the semester the professor who conducts the course is about to give you a failing grade. You learn on reliable authority that the assistant has interceded and that after great effort has dissuaded the professor from giving you a failing grade. (---)	The graduate student assistant in a course you have been taking is a person whom you and all your classmates consider, with good reason, to be an admirable and inspiring person. At the end of the semester the professor who conducts the course is about to give you a passing grade. You learn on reliable authority that the assistant has interceded and that after great effort has persuaded the professor to give you a failing grade. (++-)
As a second string member of a college debating team you are hoping to be included in a group that is soon to go on an international tour. You learn that the coach has decided that you will not be included. But it then develops that the undergraduate manager, whom you and your teammates have always considered a loathsome and vile person, has after great effort persuaded the coach that you should not be left behind. (---)	As a second string member of a college debating team you are hoping to be included in a group that is soon to go on an international tour. You learn that the coach has decided that you will be included. But it then develops that the undergraduate manager, whom you and your teammates have always considered an admirable and fine person, has after great effort persuaded the coach that you should be left behind. (++-)
Hedonic - General	Antihedonic - General
Unless a large sum of money can soon be found a small but very distinguished private museum will have to close down and its wonderful and unique collection be sold to pay off debts. A large and wealthy corporation that knowledgeable people rightly consider to be socially irresponsible and highly insensitive to public welfare is approached as a last expedient. That corporation contributes all the necessary funds with no strings attached	Unless a large sum of money can soon be found a small but very distinguished private museum will have to close down and its wonderful and unique collection be sold to pay off debts. A large and wealthy corporation that knowledgeable people rightly consider to be quite socially responsible and highly sensitive to public welfare is approached as a last expedient. That corporation refuses to donate any money and because

and this prevents the closing of the museum. (---)

Of all the New York theater critics there is one whose writings have convinced you that he is a particularly ignorant and insensitive lout. Now a fine play that you saw on opening night and enjoyed tremendously is about to close because it was panned by all the critics except the one you particularly dislike. But he strongly opposes its closing and largely because of the campaign he wages in his column its closing is prevented. (---)

Of all the many jazz instrumentalists you have heard one whom you really dislike is Charlie T. You read in an authoritative magazine article that Charlie is famous for respecting the rights of the musicians who work for him by paying them well and giving them a lavish share of royalty earnings. (-++)

You have a strong dislike for political dictators. You regard a certain Latin American dictator as a particularly unsavory type. You read a highly reliable series of articles showing that this same dictator has achieved wonders in improving the standard of living in his country since coming to power. (-++)

of this action the museum is forced to close down. (++-)

Of all the New York theater critics there is one whose writings have convinced you that he is particularly brilliant and perceptive. A fine play that you saw on opening night and enjoyed tremendously seems to be set for a long run because it was endorsed by all the critics except the one that you particularly admire. But he strongly opposes the play and largely because of the campaign that he wages against it in his column it is forced to close down. (++-)

Of all the many jazz instrumentalists you have heard your favorite is Benny P. You read in an authoritative magazine article that Benny is notorious for violating the rights of the musicians who work for him by underpaying them and refusing them their just share of royalty earnings. (+-+)

You have a great liking for the president of a certain Latin American country. You read a highly reliable series of articles showing that this same president since being elected has consistently opposed and blocked programs which would have vastly improved the standard of living in his country. (+-+)

antihedonic items is 5.90 and for the eight hedonic items it is 3.48. In the female sample the mean tension rating for antihedonic cognitions is 6.30 and for the hedonic cognitions it is 3.57. Similarly in the case of the matched pairs of items in each instance, and with both the male and

Table 2: Analysis of variance of "botherment at inconsistency" ratings for different types of inconsistency (male group)

Source	d.f.	Mean square	F	p
Hedonic-antihedonic	1	3042.00	80.01	< .001
Personal-general	1	1638.78	56.72	< .001
Subjects	31	136.06	——	——
Hedonic-antihedonic x personal-general	1	157.53	7.94	< .01
Hedonic-antihedonic x subjects	31	38.02	——	——
Personal-general x subjects	31	28.89	——	——
Hedonic-antihedonic x personal-general x subjects	31	19.84	——	——

female groups, the hedonic form arouses less reported tension than the antihedonic form. For instance among the female sample the item in which a disliked person is reliably reported to "feel strong admiration for you" has a mean tension rating of 3.15 while the item in which a liked person is reported to feel "strong and sincere dislike for you" has a mean rating of 6.74.

Table 3 Analysis of variance of "botherment at inconsistency" ratings for different types of inconsistency (female group)

Source	d.f.	Mean square	F	p
Hedonic-antihedonic	1	12364.97	347.82	< .001
Personal-general	1	4000.00	130.85	< .001
Subjects	103	126.50	——	——
Hedonic-antihedonic x personal-general	1	581.92	22.72	< .001
Hedonic-antihedonic x subjects	103	35.55	——	——
Personal-general x subjects	103	30.57	——	——
Hedonic-antihedonic x personal-general x subjects	103	25.61	——	——

Hypothesis 2, predicting that inconsistent attitudinal cognitions of general content will arouse less tension than those with personal content is, as Tables 2 and 3 reveal, also clearly confirmed by the present data. For the male sample the mean degree of reported tension for the eight general items is 3.80, and 5.60 for the eight personal items. For the female group the mean degree of reported tension for the eight general items is 3.20 and for the personal items it is 5.71.

Inspection of Tables 2 and 3 also shows that though both of the content factors exert highly significant influence upon the tension ratings, the hedonic-antihedonic factor is more potent than the personal-general factor. As might be expected this is reflected also in the actual rankings of the four groups of items in terms of the mean "botherment at inconsistency" scores that they elicit. Thus for the male group the mean tension score for the four antihedonic-personal items is 7.06. In descending order the remaining mean tension scores are 4.75 for the antihedonic-general items, 4.10 for the hedonic-personal items and 2.87 for the hedonic-general items.

Exactly the same ordering is obtained with the female subjects. Again the antihedonic-personal items receive the highest mean tension rating, the antihedonic-general items the next highest, the hedonic-personal items the third highest and the hedonic-general items receive the lowest mean tension rating. Respectively these mean ratings are 7.37, 5.23, 4.05, 3.09.

The significant interaction obtained in the analyses with both the male and female subjects can best be understood as reflecting this fact: the difference in the degree of tension aroused by inconsistency in antihedonic and hedonic cognitions respectively is greater when those cognitions are of personal rather than general content. Calculating from the mean tension scores for the four types of items, as reported above for male subjects, we find the following: when content is personal the mean tension for antihedonic items exceeds that for hedonic items by 2.96 points on the eleven point rating scale used to express "degree of botherment" at inconsistency; when the content of the cognitions is general rather than personal the comparable difference is 1.88 scale points. Similarly for the female subjects, when cognitive content is personal the difference between the antihedonic and hedonic means is 3.32; when cognitive content is general the comparable difference is 2.14.

Putting this in graphic terms, if we separately plot the mean tension ratings of the hedonic and antihedonic items depending upon whether they are of personal or general content, the slope resulting for the two types of personal items is steeper than that for the two types of general ones. It is this absence of parallelism that is reflected in the significant interactions reported in Tables 2 and 3.

INTERPRETATIONS OF THE DATA

The confirmation of the two hypotheses suggests in turn the validity of the theoretical analysis, presented above, from which those hypotheses were drawn. Thus the present data strengthen the credibility of this basic proposition: intolerance for inconsistency in attitudinal cognitions varies as a function of certain *content* aspects of the cognition, aspects which are *not* encompassed in any of the available inconsistency models of attitude dynamics.

But what further theoretical implications follow from the obtained significant interaction between the two content factors that have been investigated? It has been noted that this interaction reflects the fact that the differences in tension ratings between hedonic and antihedonic cognitions is greater for those that are personal, rather than general, in their content. The psychological meaning of this finding may well reside in the consideration that the hedonic or antihedonic import of a particular cognition is keyed ultimately to the person's perception of goal attainment or goal frustration for *himself*.

Issues of general content are probably often identified with, often cathected as objects relevant to the pursuit of one's personal interests or to the maintenance and expressive externalization of one's values and ideals. Thus it is not surprising that the hedonic-antihedonic variable affects the individual's comparative tolerances for inconsistent attitudinal cognitions of the general type. But with personal cognitions, in which the individual and his needs and goals are more directly and more reliably at issue, the difference between hedonic and antihedonic content would be likely to have still greater influence upon how much tension over inconsistency is aroused.[6]

Beyond these speculations over their immediate meaning, the present data, when viewed in the context of the author's general theory of attitude dynamics (Rosenberg, 1956, 1960a, 1960b), suggest some new propositions about the attitude change process. But before turning to these matters it will be useful to consider some possible critical points concerning these data and the claim that they show intolerance for intra-attitudinal inconsistency to be influenced by content variables. In discussing these critical points and the grounds for their rejection we shall also be able to introduce certain considerations that are relevant to the theoretical propositions that are presented in the last section of this chapter.

The most important of these critical points is that the subjects' ratings may not really bear upon our hypotheses as much as has been claimed. Thus it might be that, despite the instructions that preceded the questionnaire, the ratings did not so much reflect "botherment at inconsistency" as something else. The most obvious possibility would be that the subjects were mainly responding to the hedonic-antihedonic content differences; i.e., their ratings may merely have been estimates of how much they would be bothered by loss or frustration to self or others, rather than estimates of how tense they would be made by the inconsistencies *as inconsistencies*.

To rule out this possibility a separate group of 87 subjects, both male and female, took another form of the questionnaire. On this form eight of the original sixteen items (two for each of the four basic types of inconsistent cognitions) were reproduced. Eight other items were also included in randomly determined positions. Each of these was the parallel of one of the inconsistent items except that the sign of the first object was changed, rendering it consistent though equally hedonic or antihedonic and equally personal or general. An example of one such pair is:

You have a strong dislike for political dictators. You regard a certain Latin American dictator as a particularly unsavory type. You read a highly reliable series of articles showing that this same dictator has achieved wonders in improving the standard of living in his country since coming to power.

You have a great liking for the president of a certain Latin American country. You read a highly reliable series of articles showing that this same president has achieved wonders in improving the standard of living in his country since coming to power.

In this pair both cognitions are equally hedonic; the person in question has "achieved wonders" ($+$) in "improving the standard of living" ($+$). But when that person is the dictator ($-$) the cognition is inconsistent; when he is the admired president ($+$) it is consistent.

[6] Of course it should be added that there are intraindividual and interindividual differences in the extent to which general or "distant" issues may have personal significance. Indeed it might be argued that "altruism," "social responsibility," "mature citizenship" and kindred terms in the lexicon of democratic social philosophy all delineate, as an ideal, the person whose identification with the welfare of others has obliterated the distinction between the personal and large sectors of the general.

If the subjects, despite their having been told to report botherment at inconsistency, were actually responding only to the hedonic-antihedonic factor, the ratings for the items that composed each of the eight pairs would not be different since both the consistent and inconsistent items in each pair were matched in content; i.e., they were both either hedonic or antihedonic and either personal or general. However in each instance the mean ratings were significantly different, *the inconsistent cognition always receiving a higher rating than its consistent equivalent.* In effect then these additional data confirm that the questionnaire instructions received by the original subjects did succeed in establishing a set to rate the items for the degree of tension aroused by the inconsistencies that those items presented.

A second point worth considering is that the "inconsistent attitudinal cognitions" rated by the subjects were not ones they brought with them to the study; instead they were hypothetical situations and the subject was asked to judge how bothered he *would* be if he were actually to encounter them. Do such judgments actually illuminate how people respond in "real life?"

One possible answer to this objection is simply to refer to precedent. Earlier studies demonstrating the general preference for consistent rather than inconsistent attitudinal cognitions have used a similar approach; e.g., Jordan (1953), Esch, as reported in Heider (1958), Morissette (1958), McGuire (1960), Rosenberg & Abelson (1960). A more adequate argument is that the situations presented are not by any means purely hypothetical. They invoke common patterns of inconsistency, patterns that are often encountered in the lives of real persons. The comparative extents to which we are bothered by perceived inconsistency, when we actually discover that some personal or general gain is originating from a disliked source or some personal or general loss from a liked source, should be reflected with some accuracy in our judgments of hypothetical situations constructed along the same lines. Both in the present instance and in the case of many devices for personality and motivational assessment, the use of such a procedure rests upon the proposition that behavior is characterized by "response-response" lawfulness. On these grounds differences in reported botherment at inconsistency as between hypothetical cognitions that are either hedonic or antihedonic, personal or general, may be taken as reflecting differences of a similar order in the everyday attitudinal cognizing of the individuals tested.

Closely related to these speculations is a last problem that deserves consideration here. It is raised by the fact that the present data are based upon *ratings* of the degree of subjective tension aroused by various types of inconsistent attitudinal cognitions. Do such ratings, as has here been assumed, actually reflect motivation to reduce inconsistency? Or, putting this more directly, do such ratings predict the likelihood that the individual *will* in fact reduce inconsistency in similar attitudinal cognitions when he actually encounters them in "real life"?

An answer to this question is available from some additional data that have not yet been described, and that answer seems to be clearly in the affirmative. But before we present these data it will be useful to attempt a more precise delineation of the kind of basic attitude change process to which they refer.

Typically, though not universally, attitude change is achieved by getting the person to accept, or at least entertain, certain new inconsistent cognitions about the attitude object. For example, an opponent of desegregation may be propagandized to the effect that desegregation is positively related to various positive values (e.g., "desegregation is in accord with the Christian ethic"; "it will foster national unity"; "it will increase national economic productivity"). If these assertions are presented with enough persuasive force to get them accepted, then there have been implanted in the person who is opposed to desegregation a number of inconsistent attitudinal cognitions. Three possible outcomes of this sort of situation are evident: the person may simply *tolerate* the inconsistency and hold to his initial negative attitude toward desegregation; he may pursue inconsistency reduction through ultimate rejection of the new cognitions ("desegregation *won't* really foster national unity," etc.); or, when the new cognitions are difficult to reject, he may more readily achieve inconsistency reduction by changing his basic evaluation of the object "desegregation" from negative to positive. In this last case, changing the affective sign of the attitude object renders consistent all the previously inconsistent attitudinal cognitions. It is this kind of alteration in the evaluative sign of the central object that we conventionally mean when we speak of attitude change.

The question raised above, concerning the relation between ratings of botherment at inconsistency and the person's actual response to such inconsistency when directly encountered, may now be reformulated in the form of the following prediction: *attempts to produce attitude change through inconsistency arousal techniques will be more effective in persons with low self-reported tolerance for hypothetical inconsistencies than in persons with high self-reported tolerance.*

This is a prediction that can be directly and unequivocally tested. Operationally, all we need to do is take the sum of the "botherment at inconsistency" ratings obtained through the use of the present instrument, expose all Ss to an attitude change communication which presents "evidence" in support of inconsistency-generating attitudinal cognitions, determine the extent of consequent affect change toward the attitude object, and then test the relationship between the former and the latter indices.

This was done in a separate study by the author and Mrs. Lila Lowenherz. Seventy-two subjects drawn from the original group of 104 females were used in this study. For each we computed the sum of her sixteen "botherment at inconsistency" ratings. All of these subjects then received a complex communication designed to establish a number of new and favorable cognitions about a legislative proposal toward which earlier attitude measurement had shown that they held strong negative attitudes.

The arguments used were compelling ones so that inconsistent attitudinal cognitions were successfully established in most of the subjects.

Splitting the group into those who were above and below the median on the sum of their botherment at inconsistency ratings, we found that those in the higher half of the distribution showed more consistency-restoring change in their attitudes than did those in the lower half. This was evidenced in a number of ways, the simplest being that the high intolerance-for-inconsistency group showed greater change on a direct measure (administered both before and after receipt of the inconsistency arousing communication) of affective response toward the attitude object. The difference between the two groups was significant at a probability of less than .001.

In addition to their confirmatory bearing upon the prediction to which they were addressed, these data also suggest that an instrument that elicits self-reports of intolerance for hypothetical inconsistencies might possibly serve as a predictor of the individual's "general persuasibility." What seems even more likely is that this method of prediction is applicable whenever persuasion is to be attempted through direct efforts at creating intra-attitudinal inconsistency.

FURTHER PROPOSITIONS CONCERNING INCONSISTENCY AROUSAL AND ATTITUDE CHANGE

This chapter began with a review of some propositions common to a number of the consistency models of attitude change. To these it added some new propositions asserting that intolerance for inconsistent attitudinal cognitions is affected by two separate aspects of their content. Evidence serving to confirm these latter propositions was presented, and in discussing some possible alternative interpretations we had occasion to describe what is probably the most common and basic sequence of attitude change: that in which the establishment of inconsistent cognitions about the attitude object fosters a consistency-restoring shift in the affective response that it elicits.

In the context of this view of the attitude change process the present findings suggest still other new and important propositions. These concern certain differences between positive and negative attitudes when the attempt is made to change them through the creation of intra-attitudinal inconsistency. These propositions, if confirmed by further research, would add valuable detail to the theoretical view upon which the various consistency models seem to have converged.

The first of the propositions is that *the production, through persuasive communication, of intra-attitudinal inconsistency will be easier in the case of originally negative attitudes than in the case of originally positive attitudes.* This is because in the case of a negative attitude the new inconsistency-generating cognitions that one would attempt to establish would of necessity be hedonic in import; any antihedonic assertions in which a state of "loss" or "motive frustration" is linked with a negatively evaluated attitude object would be consistent with that negative evaluation. Conversely, and on the same grounds, only antihedonic cognitive assertions will generate inconsistency in the case of a positive attitude. As we have seen antihedonic inconsistency generates greater tension than hedonic inconsistency; and on this basis we would have to expect that the new cognitions required to produce inconsistency in the case of a positive attitude would be more difficult to establish, would be less readily "introjected" and more readily rejected, than those required in the case of a negative attitude.

In effect then what this suggests is that when two attitudes are opposite in sign (but equal in intensity and in personal or general reference) it will take significantly more effort and skill to produce some degree of internal inconsistency (as indexed, for example, by the *number* of inconsistent cognitions established) in the positive attitude than to produce the same degree of inconsistency in the negative attitude.

However, a second and somewhat paradoxical proposition also follows from this analysis. It is that *when equal degrees of internal inconsistency have been generated the originally positive attitude is more likely to undergo reorganization toward the negative than will the originally negative one change toward becoming positive*. This is because the antihedonic inconsistent cognitions that have been established in the case of the former are more tension-arousing than the hedonic inconsistent cognitions established in the case of the latter; and higher levels of tension over inconsistency should produce stronger motivation toward restoration of consistency through attitude change.

Crudely restated, the import of these two propositions is that, given initial equality of intensity, negative attitudes are more "penetrable" but, in final terms, less changeable than positive ones. Research addressed to testing these predictions would have to encompass not only the case of simple positive and negative attitudes but also the frequent and more complex case in which an attitude has originated through mechanisms of denial and reaction-formation and is a one-sided manifest expression of some underlying ambivalence.

Two further propositions, identical in form with the ones that have been developed, could be formulated for the case of personal as opposed to general attitudes, particularly if we assume that the attitudes in question are equal in intensity and in affective sign. Thus, it could be argued that because personal inconsistent cognitions arouse more tension than general ones, attitudes toward objects of personal significance are less readily penetrated, but once penetrated more readily changed, than attitudes toward general objects.

The propositions that have been introduced in this section, though difficult to test (and this largely because of the problem of controlling for initial intensity and complexity of attitude), can be experimentally investigated. At present some preliminary work along these lines is being planned. In general there seems to be considerable scope for extending, sharpening and deepening the propositional content of the consistency theory approach to attitude dynamics. Whether this approach will justify the interest and optimism it has so far generated (see Brown, 1962) will largely depend upon whether such further theorizing is energetically undertaken and is then submitted to appropriately inventive experimental analysis.

REFERENCES

Abelson, R. P., & Rosenberg, M. J. Symbolic psycho-logic: a model of attitudinal cognition. *Behav. Sci.*, 1958, *3*, 1-13.

Brown, R. Models of attitude change. In R. Brown, E. Galanter, E. Hess, & G. Mandler, *New directions in psychology*. New York: Holt, Rinehart, Winston, 1962.

Burdick, H. A., & Burnes, A. J. A test of "strain toward symmetry" theories. *J. abnorm. soc. Psychol.*, 1958, *57*, 367-370.

Cartwright, D., & Harary, F. Structural balance: a generalization of Heider's theory. *Psychol. Rev.*, 1956, *63*, 277-293.

Festinger, L. *A theory of cognitive dissonance*. Evanston: Row-Peterson, 1957.

Heider, F. Attitudes and cognitive organization. *J. Psychol.*, 1946, *21*, 107-112.

Heider, F. *The psychology of interpersonal relations*. New York: Wiley, 1958.

Jordan, N. Behavioral forces that are a function of attitudes and of cognitive organization. *Human Relat.*, 1953, *6*, 273-287.

Kogan, N., & Tagiuri, R. Interpersonal preference and cognitive organization. *J. abnorm. soc. Psychol.*, 1958, *56*, 113-116.

McGuire, W. J. A syllogistic analysis of cognitive relationships. In M. J. Rosenberg, C. I. Hovland, et al., *Attitude organization and change*. New Haven: Yale University Press, 1960.

Morissette, J. O. An experimental study of the theory of structural balance. *Human Relat.*, 1958, *11*, 239-254.

Newcomb, T. M. An approach to the study of communicative acts. *Psychol. Rev.*, 1953, *60*, 393-404.

Newcomb, T. M. The cognition of persons as cognizers. In R. Tagiuri & L. Petrullo (Eds.), *Person perception and interpersonal behavior*. Stanford: Stanford University Press, 1958.

Osgood, C. E., & Tannenbaum, P. H. The principle of congruity in the prediction of attitude change. *Psychol. Rev.*, 1955, *62*, 42-55.

Rosenberg, M. J. Cognitive structure and attitudinal affect. *J. abnorm. soc. Psychol.*, 1956, *53*, 367-372.

Rosenberg, M. J. Cognitive reorganization in response to the hypnotic reversal of attitudinal affect. *J. Pers.*, 1960, *28*, 39-63.   (a)

Rosenberg, M. J. An analysis of affective-cognitive consistency. In M. J. Rosenberg, C. I. Hovland, et al., *Attitude organization and change*. New Haven: Yale University Press, 1960.   (b)

Rosenberg, M. J., & Abelson, R. P. An analysis of cognitive balancing. In M. J. Rosenberg, C. I. Hovland, et al., *Attitude organization and change*. New Haven: Yale University Press, 1960.

Rosenberg, M. J., Hovland, C. I., et al., *Attitude organization and change*. New Haven: Yale University Press, 1960.

Zajonc, R. B. The concepts of balance, congruity, and dissonance. *Publ. Opin. Quart.*, 1960, *24*, 280-296.

VI

The psychology of commitment

Part 1:
The constructive role of violence and suffering for the individual and for his society

Silvan S. Tomkins

We have argued that the primary motives of man are his eight innate affects, or feelings. These are the positive affects of excitement, enjoyment and surprise, and the negative affects of distress, anger, fear, shame and contempt. These are innate. One does not learn to smile in enjoyment nor to cry in distress. However, the objects of each affect are *both* innate and learned. A baby does not learn the birth cry. It is an innate response to the excessive stimulation attendant upon being born. He will later cry when he is hungry or tired or exposed to too loud sounds. None of these are learned responses. But eventually he *will* learn to cry about many things about which he was initially unconcerned. He may learn to cry in sympathy when others are in distress, and cry. But if the crying of others may be learned to evoke one's own distress cry, so may it also be learned to evoke contempt or shame rather than sympathy. There is thus nothing under the sun which some human beings have not learned to enjoy, to fear, or to hate, to be ashamed of, or to respond to with excitement or contempt or anger. It is the innate plasticity of the affect mechanism which permits the investment of any type of affect in any type of activity or object which makes possible the great varieties of human personalities and societies. Cultural diversity rests upon the biological plasticity of the affect system in man. Puritanism, or negative affect about pleasure, and masochism, or positive affect about pain, are extreme examples of the plasticity of affect investment. The theoretical possibilities of the variety of profiles of activation, maintenance and decay of each affect are without limit. I may be very happy as a child and very sad as an adult, or conversely. I may be angry for a moment, for an hour, for a day, or always, or never. I may be frightened only occasionally or I may be anxious all my life. I may feel mildly ashamed for myself or deeply humiliated. I may feel ashamed because I have shown my feelings too publicly or because I was unable to show my feelings toward someone who needed my sympathy. In short, the object, the duration, the frequency, and the intensity of affect arousal and investment are without limit. It is this capacity of the individual to feel strongly or weakly, for a moment or for all his life, about anything under the sun and to govern himself by such motives that constitutes his essential freedom.

It is to a closer examination of the phenomenon of density of affect investment that we now turn. We have defined affect density as the product of its intensity times its duration. We will now introduce a derivative concept: ideo-perceptual-memorial-action-affect density. By this we mean the product of the intensity times the duration of all the capacities for involvement which the individual possesses. At one time his involvement may be primary ideational, at another time, primarily affective, or primarily overtly behavioral, or primarily perceptual or memorial, or any combination of these. For purposes of brevity we will henceforth refer to this as *ideo-affective density* and use the term *ideation* to refer to the variety of non-affective cognitions as well as to action. We do not mean by this to imply in any way that we regard action as a type of thinking, or in any way to blur the differences between perception, memory and thinking. We will use the term simply as a convenient abbreviation for the density of involvement of all of the critical sub-systems which together constitute a human being. Bearing in mind this special usage of the words ideo- and ideation, we will now define ideo-affective density as the product of the intensity and duration of affect and the concurrent ideation about the object of the affect. Low ideo-affective density refers to those experiences which generate little or no affect, and little or no ideation, or if the affect and ideation are intense they do not last long. High density occurs whenever the individual has both intense feelings and ideation which continue at a high level over long periods of time. In such a case there is a monopolistic capture of the individual's awareness and concern. Low and high densities represent two ends of a continuum of organizations of motive, thought and behavior which are critical for the understanding of commitment.

We wish to distinguish two gross segments of an ideo-affect density continuum—the low and high density segments. Further, we will examine some characteristic examples of each end of this continuum, so that commitment may be seen in its larger context.

Let us first consider the low end of the continuum. We distinguish two different kinds of organization both of which are characteristically low density organizations. Further, each type of organization may be primarily positive or negative in affect. One organization is *transient, casual* and the other is *recurrent, habitual*.

Consider first a transitory positive, low density ideo-affective organization. Such would be the laughter in response to a joke. The experience might be extremely enjoyable but nonetheless of very low density, because it recruited no continuing ideation or affect beyond the momentary experience. An example of a transitory negative low density ideo-affective organization would be a cut while shaving which occasioned a brief stab of pain and distress, but no further thought or feeling beyond this isolated experience. Each individual's lifetime contains thousands of such relatively casual, transient encounters. Collectively they may sum to a not inconsiderable segment of the life span. Nonetheless they constitute an aggregate of isolated components without substantial impact on the personality of the individual.

The recurrent, habitual types of low density ideo-affective organizations characteristically began with considerable intensity of affect and ideation but end with minimal involvement. Consider first the negative recurrent habitual case. Everyone learns to cross streets with minimal ideation and affect. We learn to act as if we were afraid, but we do not in fact experience any fear once we have learned how to cope successfully with such contingencies. Despite the fact that we know that there is real danger involved daily in walking across intersections and that many pedestrians are in fact killed, we exercise normal caution with minimal attention and no fear. It remains a low density ideo-affective organization, despite daily repetition over a lifetime. Successful avoidance strategies remain low density organizations because they do not generalize or spread. They do not spread just because they are successful. It should be noted that these organizations, though we have called them recurrent habitual, are far from being simple motor habits. They are small programs for processing information with relatively simple strategies, but one may nonetheless never repeat precisely the same avoidance behaviors twice in crossing the street. These simple programs generate appropriate avoidant strategies for dealing with a variety of such situations, and caution is nicely matched to the varying demands of this class of situations, with a minimum of attention and affect. Every individual, including the psychotic, possesses hundreds such avoidance and escape low density organizations. (It is a great surprise on first exposure to psychotic patients to discover as my friend Edward Engel confided to me one day, that a schizophrenic when eating soup for lunch does not put the soup into his eye!) This is not to say that crossing the street was always a low density ideo-affective organization. The earliest such experiences may well have been high adventures for the daring child, or they may have been the occasion of severe punishment at the hands of an anxious parent terrified at the sight of his toddler walking in front of a speeding automobile. Both the excitement and the pain or distress or fear which might have been suffered at the hands of a parent do not long continue. Quickly all children learn some caution in this matter and it ceases to claim either much ideation or feeling. Such attenuation of feeling and thought necessarily depend upon the success of problem solutions. Paradoxically human beings are least involved in what they can do best, when problems once solved, remain solved. Man as a successful problem solver ceases to think and to feel about successful performance and turns ideation and affect to the continuing or new, unsolved challenges.

This is so whether the original affect which powered problem solving was positive or negative. Just as we experience no terror in confronting traffic at the curb, so too with positive, low density ideo-affective organizations we experience no positive enjoyment or excitment in the daily recurrent performance which once delighted. As I finish my daily shaving I rarely puff with pride and think, "There I've done it again." I act in this case, as in crossing the street, *as if* I experienced an affect, and had a wish to achieve this goal. I do indeed achieve my intention—to shave— but the positive affect behind this ritual has long ceased to be emitted concurrently with the action. Like the low density avoidance strategy of crossing the street, it may be done daily—repeated several thousand times during a lifetime—with little or no effect on other action, or affect, or memory or perception.

HIGH DENSITY END OF CONTINUUM—NEGATIVE MONOPOLISM

What then of the high density ideo-affective organizations? By definition they can be neither transitory nor recurrent but must be enduring. Whether predominantly positive or negative in tone, they must seize the individual's feelings and thoughts and actions to the exclusion of almost all else. Consider first negative monopolism of thought and feeling. If successful and continuing problem solution is the necessary condition of the low density organization, *temporary* problem solution is the necessary condition of the negative high density organization. Consider our man on the curb. He is normally cautious but not overly concerned because his solution to the problem has always worked. But suppose that one day a passing motorist loses control of his car and seriously injures our hero. After his return from the hospital he is a bit more apprehensive than before, and now stands back a little farther from the edge of the curb than he used to. He may continue his somewhat excessive caution for some time, and, as he notes a car approaching with what appears a little too much speed, may even begin to wonder with occasional fear, whether such an accident might ever happen again. But if all goes well this increase in density of ideation and affect will pass and before long he will be indistinguishable from any other casual pedestrian. But in our tragedy all does not go well. Uncannily a drunken driver pursues our hero and he is hit again. This time it is more serious and we see the beginnings of a phobia. Our hero stations himself inside a building, peering up and down the street, before he will venture out to dare negotiate the crossing. By now his preoccupation with and fear of the deadly vehicle has grown to invade his consciousness even when he is far from the scene of potential danger. In the last act of this drama it is a bulldozer which penetrates his apparent fortress. What next? Will he be safe in the hospital? His ideation and affect have now reached a point of no return. He will henceforth generate possibilities which no reasonable man would entertain and these phantasies will evoke affects proportional to their extremity.

He will now begin negative ideo-affective creativity. Such a high density ideo-affective organization is capable of providing a lifetime of suffering and of resisting reduction through new evidence. This happens if, and only if, there has occurred a sequence of events of this type: threat, successful defense, breakdown of defense and re-emergence of threat, second successful new defense, second breakdown of defense and re-emergence of threat, third successful new defense, third breakdown of defense and re-emergence of threat, and so on, until an expectation is generated that no matter how successful a defense against a dread contingency may seem, it will prove unavailing and require yet another new defense, ad infinitum. Not only is there generated the conviction that successful defense can be successful only temporarily, but also as new and more effective defenses are generated the magnitude of the danger is inflated in the imagination of the harried one. We have defined this dynamic as a circular incremental magnification. It is circular and incremental since each new threat requires a more desperate defense and the successive breakdown of each newly improved defense generates a magnification of the nature of the threat and the concurrent affect which it evokes. We have defined such a circular incremental magnification series as a set of —+— triads in which negative affect is defended against and replaced by positive affect, but then breaks down and again produces negative affect. In comparison with the analogous low-density organization, it is the continuing uncertainty of permanent problem solution which is critical in monopolizing the individual's ideation and affect. Paradoxically it is just the fact that the individual is *not* entirely helpless in dealing with a given situation which continually magnifies both the apparent nature of the threat and his skill in coping with it. In this respect the individual may be likened to a tennis player who is first defeated by a poor opponent and who then practices sufficiently to defeat that opponent. But his triumph proves short-lived since his opponent now also improves and in turn defeats him. This then leads our hero to improve his skill so that once again he defeats his adversary, but this leads to yet another defeat when the latter improves his skill, and so on and on.

POSITIVE HIGH DENSITY IDEO-AFFECTIVE ORGANIZATION

Let us now examine the structure of the positive, high density ideo-affective organization. Instead of a series of —+— triads, here it is a series of +—+ triads which is responsible for the circular incremental magnification. Instead of increasing concern with warding off a threat, it is rather the magnification of a positive affect and the ideation about its object which is involved. Although there is negative affect sandwiched in between two positive affects in this type of triad, the individual is primarily concerned with attaining the object of positive affect. Let us consider two types of such positive ideo-affective organizations.

Psychological Addiction

First, consider what we will define as the psychological addiction. The addicted cigarette smoker will serve as an example. Individual A enjoys smoking a cigar or a cigarette after dinner. This is an unadulterated reward. At other times of the day he is unaware both of the enjoyments of smoking and of any suffering because he is not smoking. Individual B does not enjoy smoking per se, but rather uses cigarettes as a pacifier or sedative whenever he becomes distressed or anxious. Smoking at such times reduces his suffering and makes him feel better. It is not only that the function of smoking is here limited to the reduction of negative affect, but also that such negative affect arises from some source other than smoking. He is *not* disturbed simply because he is not smoking, but rather is disturbed because something else went wrong in his life. So, when everything goes well for B, he does not miss smoking, because the only function which smoking serves is to reduce other kinds of suffering. B does not think of smoking when he is not smoking—except for those occasions when he is disturbed. If he is not disturbed he has concerns other than smoking. Individual C is an addicted smoker. Like A he too enjoys smoking and like B he uses smoking to reduce all types of suffering. But here the resemblances end. C first of all is *always* aware of not smoking whenever this occurs. Second, he always responds to this awareness with negative affect which continues to increase in intensity until he can smoke. Third, he will always drop all competitors for his attention and try to get a cigarette and fourth, upon getting a cigarette and beginning to smoke he will respond with intense enjoyment at the reduction of his suffering of negative affect. Like A he enjoys smoking, and like B he also reduces his suffering by smoking, but the suffering which he *must* reduce is the suffering he experiences (and has created) just because he is not smoking. No matter how well his life goes, he is unable to be unaware of not smoking, whenever this occurs. Contrary to B he may be able to tolerate many other types of suffering without resort to sedation by smoking. So long as he has a cigarette in hand he may be quite courageous in confronting innumerable problems other than that of not smoking. B in similar circumstances might have had resort to smoking to leave the field, to sedate himself into comfort rather than to confront his problem. In addiction, too, there is circular incremental magnification produced by an ever accelerating suffering in the absence of a cigarette and an ever increasing rewarding experience of positive affect upon the reduction of the suffering of negative affect.

The hold of cigarette smoking or any other high density addiction arises from the intolerability of the ever mounting negative affect which is experienced whenever the addict attempts to break his addiction. As his suffering mounts he becomes more and more unable to tolerate the absence of smoking and extrapolates into the future a vision of an increasingly intolerable suffering, till in panic at this prospect he succumbs to his longing. It is a series of painful longings reduced by smoking which increases both the suffering of negative affect and the intensity of positive affect while smoking, in an accelerating circular incremental magnification.

Psychologically this process is similar to the mourning experience of the bereaved. The lost love object is magnified in value because of the conjoint suffering and longing which makes vivid to the bereaved his hitherto not entirely appreciated dependence on the lost love object. It is the barrier to ever again enjoying the presence of the beloved which reveals and *creates* a new appreciation. Although addiction is thereby heightened in mourning and though longing and suffering may be intensified to the point of intolerability, the mourner ultimately is freed from his heightened dependence because he is forced to endure the abstinence suffering until it no longer increases in intensity and then begins slowly to decline in intensity, until finally there is minimal suffering and no *awareness* that the lost love object has been lost. In this respect the mourner is returned to the state of someone who has been able to overcome his addiction to smoking. The addicted cigarette smoker will not willingly suffer through such abstinence suffering, because it seems to him, as to the bereaved, that he will never be able to tolerate the loss of the love object. In addiction, it should be noted, we are dealing with the lure of the familiar and the positive affect which is involved is enjoyment. It is the return to the familiar, heightened in value by the suffering of separation which creates the magic of reunion, be that reunion with an old friend, an old place or an old activity such as smoking. In contrast to commitment, as we will presently see, there is here much less involvement of exploration and of novelty and of created challenge.

Commitment

In commitment the positive high density ideo-affective organization also involves the reward of the positive affect of enjoyment, but in addition the positive affect of excitement becomes more prominent. Let us consider two examples of commitment, one characteristically abortive commitment which ends either by transformation into an addiction at somewhat less than maximal density, or ends in disenchantment; the other a high density commitment which for some extends over the entire life span. We refer in the first instance to romantic love and in the second to the committed scientist.

Consider first the *romantic lover* who intends to commit himself for life to his beloved. As we distinguished cigarette smokers, A, B, and C, we may distinguish A in this domain as one who very much enjoys his contacts with his lady friend, but who does not miss her when he is otherwise occupied. B has a lady friend he does not miss when all goes well. But he always turns to her for comfort when he becomes disturbed. She does in fact always bring him tranquility, and having been mothered back into peace of mind he is prepared again to pick up his life, and to forget his benefactress with gratitude but no regret, for the time being. Not so with C, the romantic lover. He is forever aware of the absence of his beloved, and of their enforced separation, to which he responds with intense suffering and longing. Every time he is separated he dies a little and thereby, like the true mourner, comes to appreciate more and more his dependence upon the beloved who grows increasingly desirable in her absence. Upon reunion with the beloved the intensity of his enjoyment and excitement is proportional to his prior suffering, and there is begun a circular incremental magnification. If the beloved becomes more valuable when she brings to an end the intolerable suffering and longing which preceded reunion, so much the greater will the next suffering of separation become since the beloved has by now become even more wonderful than before. Just as the nature of the threat is magnified in the negative high density series of $-+-$ triads, so here is the nature of the positive object magnified in the series of $+-+$ triads. In contrast to the ever increasing negative threat, the beloved does not necessarily continue to support indefinite magnification of her magical qualities. Romantic love imposes separation and uncertainty which increases the period of time over which longing for the love object can occur, but with the transition to the honeymoon and marriage, the prolonged intimacy and mutual exploration eventually produces a sufficient reduction in novelty and uncertainty so that excitement can no longer be indefinitely maintained. When under these conditions of continuing contact the beloved will no longer support the indefinite magnification of wonder and excitement, there may appear disenchantment or boredom, or an ideo-affective organization of reduced intensity and duration with excitement replaced by the enjoyment of the familiar and deepening relationship. But the husband will no longer miss his wife throughout the working day even though he deeply enjoys his daily reunion with her at each day's end. We have traced this potential high density ideo-affective organization, which may be short circuited by marriage, to better illuminate the nature of enduring high density commitment.

Consider next the varieties of *committed scientists* and those who are interested but not committed. Scientist A enjoys tremendously both the discovery of truth and the search for truth. He likes to putter around the laboratory. He likes to run experiments. He enjoys it when they succeed. But he is a nine-to-five scientist. When he goes home it is to another world. He does not take his scientific troubles home with him. Indeed he experiences a minimum of suffering in his role as scientist. He is in this respect like the person who loves to smoke after dinner, and like the person who enjoys the company of his lady friend, but who do not miss their enjoyment or suffer in the interim periods. Individual B, on the other hand, uses science as a sedative. Whenever he becomes depressed he turns to reading science or watching TV programs concerning the latest advances in science. However, as soon as his life becomes more rewarding, his interest in science flags, like the person who smoked to comfort himself, and like the individual who sought out his lady friend to ease his suffering, but once mothered back into peace of mind forgot his benefactress. Consider now scientist C who is committed for a lifetime to the pursuit of truth. Like the addicted smoker he is always aware of the absence of his longed-for ideal object—ultimate, permanent, truth. Like individual A, he enjoys the scientific way of life. He enjoys puttering with laboratory equipment, and with running experiments. But underlying all his enjoyment is a continuing unrest and suffering over the possibilities of error, and over the possibility of missing the main chance. When everything works as planned he is deeply excited and enjoys briefly the fruits of his labor. But his contact with truth is ordinarily as brief as it is sweet. Truth is a mistress who never gives herself completely or permanently. She must be wooed and won arduously and painfully in each encounter. With each encounter she deepens both the scientist's suffering and then his reward. It is a love affair which is never entirely and deeply consummated. Immediately following each conquest, the victory is always discovered to have been less than it appeared and the investigation must now be pursued with more skill and more energy than before.

The set of triads $+-+$ is in some respects similar to the negative set of triads $-+-$. In both cases skill must constantly be improved and in both cases the effectiveness of achieved skill is only temporary. The difference is that in the negative high density ideo-affective organization the individual is pursued by a threat, whereas in positive commitment he pursues an object of ever increasing attractiveness. In both cases circular incremental magnification is responsible for the *creation* of an idealized object. The magic of truth exists in such a magnified form only in the mind of one who will pursue truth despite increasing suffering so that each encounter becomes both more bitter and more sweet. There is minimal uncertainty in the familiar object of addiction, and there is a finite uncertainty in the romantic love affair which is almost entirely explored during the honeymoon. In the scientific commitment, however, there is sufficient continuing uncertainty so that endless circular incremental magnification of the $+-+$ triad can be sustained indefinitely if the individual has become committed. Thus a scientist who has made a major discovery and thereafter elects to rest on his laurels has ceased to be a committed scientist with high density of ideation and affect about science. It is a critical feature of high density commitment that there can be no *enduring* positive affect in having attained the pursued finite object. Rather the object is continually redefined so that a newer version of the quest can be mounted. The same dynamic appears in the pursuit of money or power. These are also capable of committing the individual to an endless insatiable quest for an object which is put out of reach almost immediately after it is attained.

COMMITTED REFORMERS

Let us turn now to yet another group of the committed—the reformer and those he reforms. Why and how do individuals and societies become committed to ideologies and to social movements? We will examine four abolitionists, Garrison, Phillips, Weld and Birney, as committed reformers. Why and how did each of these become committed to abolitionism? How did they influence others to become committed to abolitionism, or at the least to oppose the extension of slavery? It is our thesis that the same psychological dynamic underlies the commitment of the individual and the group. More particularly, we will argue that violence and suffering are critical in a democratic society, in heightening antipathy for violations of democratic values and in heightening sympathy for the victims of such violations. A radical magnification of negative feeling toward the oppressors and of positive feeling toward the oppressed is the major dynamic which powers the commitment first of the individual reformer and then of increasing numbers who are influenced by him.

Let us turn to the interpretation of abolitionism in the light of our theory of the nature of both negative and positive high density ideo-affective organizations. We will now also examine more closely just how such high density organizations are formed as well as the numerous ways in which they may fail to be sustained.

The commitment of Garrison, Phillips, Weld and Birney to abolitionism proceeded in a series of steps consistent with our general theory of commitment. The critical role of adult experience in the spiral stepwise triads of $+-+$ affects which gradually deepen commitment is underlined by the early resonance of each of these leaders to ways of life quite diverse from each other and from their future way of life. No one could have predicted with any confidence that these four young men would eventually provide the leadership for the abolitionist movement. Garrison was first attracted to writing and to politics as a way of life. Phillips led the life typical of the Boston Brahmin of his time: attendance at Harvard College, Harvard Law School and then the opening of a law practice. Weld first gave a series of lectures on mnemonics, the art of improving the memory. Birney was twice suspended from Princeton for drinking, though he was each time readmitted and graduated with honors. He, like Phillips, became a gentlemen lawyer, priming himself for a political career. After an early failure in politics he became a planter and lived the life of the young Southern aristocrat, drinking and gambling to excess. Paradoxically, of the four he was the earliest to interest himself in the slaves, but the last to commit himself to their emancipation as his way of life.

One cannot account for the abolitionist reformer on the assumption that his was a commitment such as "falling in love at first sight." None of these men knew at first that they were to commit their lives to the emancipation of the slave. Three of the four were first attracted to a career in politics. But if there is a perennial danger of exaggerating the continuity of human development, and especially the influence of the early years on the adult personality, there is also the opposite danger of exaggerating the impact of adult experience on crucial adult choices and overlooking the contribution of the early years to choices which on the surface appear to represent novelty in the experience of the adult. Our argument will stress both the continuity and the discontinuity in the development of Garrison, Phillips, Weld and Birney in their growing commitment to abolitionism.

All were early prepared and destined for leadership of a special kind, for saving the self through saving others. Each might have become a crusading politician, writer or orator or preacher. Indeed, Birney did later run as a crusading candidate for the Presidency of the United States. Weld later, because of his failing speech, did become a writer for abolitionism instead of an orator. Phillips, after the Civil War, did continue crusading for labor, for temperance, for Ireland against England, for the American Indians, and for the abolition of capital punishment. Garrison, too, after the Civil War, maintained his interest in women's rights and in temperance reform, though with much less zeal than Phillips. Therefore we must neither exaggerate the novelty of their commitment to abolitionism nor the continuity of their interest in salvation. It is to some extent a historical accident that they became abolitionists but it is not an accident that they became deeply committed to leadership for the salvation of others.

The stages in the development of their commitment to abolitionism can now be summarized. First, a resonance to the general idea of the salvation of others; second, risk is ventured on behalf of those who need to be saved; third, as a consequence of the risk which has been taken, there is punishment and suffering; fourth, as a consequence of such suffering, resonance to the original idea of the necessity of salvation is deepened and identification with the oppressed is increased as is hostility toward the oppressor; fifth, as a result of increased density of affect and ideation, there will be an increased willingness to take even greater risks and more possible punishment and more suffering; sixth, increased risk taking does evoke more punishment and more suffering; seventh, there is an increasing willingness to tolerate suffering which follows risk taking, concomitant with a proportionately increasing intensity and duration of positive affect and ideation in identification with the oppressed and with fellow abolitionists, and an increasing negative affect toward the enemy whose apparent power and undesirability is magnified as the density of affect and ideation increases. The $+ - +$ triad alternates between resonance and risk taking $(+)$, punishment and suffering $(-)$, increased densitity of positive affect and ideation $(+)$, resulting in increased risk taking $(+)$, so that the entire triad is endlessly repeated. This cumulatively deepens commitment until it reaches a point of no return—when no other way of life seems possible to the committed reformer. The spiral, composed of $+ - +$ triads, is therefore a $+ - +$, $+ - +$ set rather than a $+ - + - +$ sequence. The increased density of postive affect and ideation at the end of the $+ - +$ results in an increased positive affect invested in more *risk*, the $+$ in the next $+ - +$ triad.

It should be noted that the pathway from early resonance to final commitment is not necessarily without internal conflict. Some of the suffering comes from within as well as from the enemy. Each of these men was to suffer doubt at some point whether to give himself completely to abolitionism as a way of life.

The Original Resonance

Let us now examine the original resonance that first attracted these and other men to abolitionism. By resonance we mean the engagement of feeling and thought by any organized ideology or social movement. The fit between the individual's own loosely organized ideas and feelings, that we have called his ideo-affective posture, and the more tightly organized ideology, or social movement, need not be a very close one to induce resonance. Some men resonated to abolitionism because slavery violated their Christian faith; others because of a general sympathy for the underdog; others because of belief in the perfectibility of man; others because of a belief in the democratic assertion of the equal rights of all men, or in individualism; some were originally attracted because their own salvation required that they save others; and there were those who were attracted because they hated oppression and oppressors and some because they could not tolerate humiliation, even vicariously. The plight of the slave induced resonance for these and many other reasons.

The bases for the original resonance of Garrison, Phillips, Weld and Birney to abolitionism contained common elements and also differences. First, all four were deeply Christian. Three of the four had conversion experiences. For Garrison, Phillips and Weld, their Christianity required that they save others if they would save themselves. Each of the three had been impressed by strong, pious Christian mothers that to be good meant to do good. The fourth, Birney, had been left motherless at the age of three, and his strongest relationship was with his father who believed not only in Christian good works, but, more specifically, had along with *his* father fought to make Kentucky a free state; though they lost this fight they continued to be active against slavery. In all four families, moral and Christian zeal for the salvation of their children (and other sinners) was combined with great affection for their children. The parents provided the appropriate models for future reformers. The children were taught how to combine concern and contempt for the sinner with love for those sinners who would reform.

Second, the parents of the four had also shown a pervasive concern with public service. Garrison's mother, who was the sole provider, nursed the sick. Birney's father was politically active in favor of emancipation. Phillips' father was mayor of Boston. Weld's father was a minister. All were concerned with service to others and provided a model which predisposed their sons to resonate to any movement based on public service.

Third, all four appear to have been physically active and extroverted as children. They had abundant energy which they translated into vigorous play and into fighting with their peers. This, too, contributed to their resonance to a movement which called for direct action and face to face confrontation before large groups.

Fourth, all were exposed to, influenced by, and modeled themselves after, the great orators of their day. As Perry Miller (1961) has noted, one of the salient features of the puritans' reformation was the substitution of the sermon for the Mass. All four men were early exposed to the magic of the great orators of the day, both Christian and political. All four as young men were fluent and articulate and gave evidence of being able to hold audiences by their speaking powers. The combination of great energy, extroversion, and the power to influence others by oratorical ability predisposed them to resonate to a movement which required those who could influence others in just such ways.

Fifth, all of them were physically courageous. They had all experienced and mastered the art of fighting with their peers, so that they had a zest for combat rather than a dread of it. No one who too much feared physical combat could afford to resonate to the defense of those held in bondage by the ever present threat of force. The overly timid cannot entertain a rescue phantasy.

These are some of the characteristics which these four shared and which attracted them to abolitionism. But there were also important differences. Phillips was first attracted to the defense of abolitionism by the murder of the abolitionist Lovejoy. He was outraged, as a patrician, at the tyranny of the mob and its violation of civil liberties. He was in no sense an abolitionist at the time. He was also outraged that "gentlemen" of his own class from his own beloved Boston should form a mob and threaten the life of Garrison. He was attracted at first more by disgust at mob violence than by sympathy for the slaves. In contrast, Garrison, Birney and Weld were first attracted to the problem of slavery out of sympathy for the slave. Each resonated first not to abolitionism but to the program of the American Colonization Society of gradual emancipation with transportation of free American Negroes to Africa. Nor was even this interest salient from the outset. Although slavery interested Weld increasingly, temperance and manual labor education were his primary concerns for some time, following his initial speaking tour on the art of saving one's memory. Birney, due to his exposure to his father's and grandfather's political activity on behalf of emancipation, was earliest interested in the problem of slavery, but it was some time before he committed himself wholeheartedly to even the program of the American Colonization Society. It was to be several more years, when he was over forty, that he committed himself to abolitionism.

Garrison and Weld were soon to change the nature of their relationship to the problem of slavery. Garrison led the way with a frontal attack on the slaveholder and those who trafficked in slavery and with a denunciation of the American Colonization Society. In this he was radically to influence the entire movement, including Weld, Phillips and finally Birney. Added to sympathy for the slave was now contempt and anger both for the Southern sinners and for those Northerners who either cooperated with or were indifferent to Southern tyranny. Birney held back because he was not yet convinced that the Southern slaveholder could not be reached by reason, because he was temperamentally allergic to enthusiasm, and because he was at that time more interested in improving and preserving his beloved South than in destroying the slaveholder.

Only painfully and reluctantly was he forced to leave the South and become an abolitionist.

Garrison, in contrast, had the greatest enthusiasm for nailing the sinner to the cross, while Phillips, disgusted more with his own class than with the Southern slaveholder and responsive to the perfectibility of the lower classes, also resonated to somewhat different aspects of abolitionism. Weld, in contrast both to Phillips and Garrison, was a shy "backwoodsman" as he described himself. He was indifferent to the political action which Birney espoused, disliked politicians and all sophisticates, was suspicious of too great a reliance on "reason," was greatly troubled by exhibitionism (in contrast to Garrison who thrived on it) and was much concerned about the general problem of sin, in himself and in others, and tried to "test" himself. The resonance to abolitionism on the part of these four was prompted by both the communalities and the differences we have here examined.

The Second Stage: Risk is Ventured

So much for the first stages in the development of commitment, the resonance by which the individual is initially attracted to the new ideology. The second stage occurs when risk is first ventured following this initial resonance. Not all who are attracted will venture any risk on behalf of the ideology. Garrison was perhaps the boldest risk taker, in part because he wanted so much "to be heard" as he said. But to be heard he had not only to write but to speak in public. Early in his career he had been invited by the Congregational Societies in Boston to give the Fourth of July address at the Park Street Church. Garrison, in a letter to Jacob Horton, tells of his knees shaking in anticipation of the lecture, and a newspaper account reported that at first his voice was almost too faint to be heard, but eventually he overcame his stage fright and made a strong plea for the gradual emancipation of the slaves. Soon after this speech, however, he decided that immediate emancipation was required. He became more bold and accused a northern ship captain and ship owner of trafficking in slaves. For this he spent seven weeks in jail. It cannot be said that this was altogether painful to Garrison. He appeared to enjoy both his martyrdom and the notoriety he gained, writing to everyone and conducting interviews from his cell. Although Garrison suffered least of the four abolitionists and indeed appeared to enjoy combat, it would be a mistake to overlook the fear he experienced on numerous occasions when his life was in jeopardy from angry mobs. Indeed mob violence was a constant danger for all the abolitionists.

The Third Stage: Suffering in Consequence of Risk Taking

Garrison, Birney, Weld and Phillips continually exposed themselves to violent opposition. Each reacted somewhat differently. Garrison, though sometimes frightened, was more often delighted to be the center of attention and to respond with a crushing retort. Phillips responded

primarily with patrician contempt. Birney became depressed at the un-
reasonableness of his opposition. Weld regarded his trials as tests by
God of his mettle and worthiness. Each man was troubled in different
ways. Phillips risked and lost his status and former friends in Boston
upper class society. Weld was severely reprimanded by the Trustees and
President of the Lane (theological) Seminary for his "monomania" in
stirring the students to debate over slavery. This debate had extended
18 days and ended with a declaration in favor of immediate emancipation. After joining the American Anti-Slavery Society he toured Ohio,
converting thousands to the cause, but always facing angry mobs intent
on attacking him and breaking up his meetings. He was hurt on numerous
occasions. He considered these riots to be a test not only of his own mettle
but of all his converts. Birney's reaction to the violence his pro-Negro
activity evoked was disappointment at the intransigency of the South,
depression at the turning away of former friends and his loss of status,
chagrin and surprise at the impotence of "reason" to influence reasonable
men, considerable regret at having to leave his homeland and settle in the
North and, not least, depression over the increasing alienation between
his father and himself. Garrison clearly had least to lose and most to gain
from assuming the risks of abolitionism. He too risked his life on more
than one occasion and was badly frightened despite his zest for the fight
and his love of being the center of attention.

The Fourth Stage: Deepened Resonance, Increased Commitment

Identification with the oppressed Negro increased as did the hostility
toward the oppressor and those who were uncommitted. It should be
noted that the same characteristics which prompted the initial resonance
were also critical in creating the ability to tolerate opposition and such
negative affect as this ordinarily provokes. It was the combination of the
general wish to save and reform coupled with energetic, articulate and
courageous extroversion which diminished the sting of fear, of disappointment, and of depression at the loss of status, the loss of friends and the
threat of physical injury and possible loss of life.

All four responded to initial opposition by increased commitment.
Phillips now began to see the nobility and generosity of the Negro and of
the lower classes in general. He began to compare their nobility invid-
iously with the smugness and corruption of upper class society. Here he
found for the first time, he insisted, real and true friends. "Who are we
that we should presume to rank ourselves with those that are marshalled
in such a host? What have *we* done? Where is the sacrifice *we* have made?
Where the luxury *we* have surrendered?" (Bartlett, 1961, p. 57).

Weld also regarded the violence of the opposition as a test of the true
believer (for himself and for others): "Poor outside whitewash! The
tempest will batter it off the first stroke, and masks and veils, and sheep
clothing gone, gone at the first blast of fire. God gird us to do all valiantly

for the helpless and innocent. Blessed are they who die in the harness and are buried on the field or bleach there" (Thomas, 1950, p. 116).

Birney's initial response to the violence of the opposition was loneliness and depression. In 1834 he wrote to Weld: "I have not one helper—not one from whom I can draw sympathy, or impart joy, on this topic! . . . My nearest friends . . . think it is very silly in me to run against the world in a matter that cannot in any way do me any good . . . Even my own children . . . appear careless and indifferent—if anything rather disposed to look upon my views as chimerical and visionary . . . My nearest friends here are of the sort that are always crying out: take care of yourself—don't meddle with other people's affairs—do nothing, say nothing, get along quietly—make money" (Fladeland, 1955, p. 90). However, this did not deter Birney from again and again confronting both censure and the threat of physical violence against himself, "believing that if ever there was a time, it is now come, when our republic, and with her the cause of universal freedom is in a strait, where everything that ought to be periled by the patriot should be freely hazarded for her relief." Men must "themselves die freemen [rather] than slaves, or our Country, glorious as has been her hope, is gone forever." (Fladeland, 1955, p. 90).

Garrison too responded to opposition with increased defiance and with an increased identification with the Negro. In the first issue of *The Liberator* (*see* Ruchames, 1963) he flung his defiance in the face of the enemy:

"Assenting to the 'self-evident truth' maintained in the American Declaration of Independence, 'that all men are created equal, and endowed by their Creator with certain inalienable rights—among which are life, liberty, and the pursuit of happiness,' I shall strenuously contend for the immediate enfranchisement of our slave population. In Park Street Church, on the Fourth of July, 1829, in an address on slavery, I unreflectingly assented to the popular but pernicious doctrine of gradual abolition. I seize this opportunity to make a full and unequivocal recantation, and thus publicly to ask pardon of my God, of my country, and of my brethren, the poor slaves, for having uttered a sentiment so full of timidity, injustice and absurdity. A similar recantation, from my pen, was published in the *Genius of Universal Emancipation*, at Baltimore, in September, 1829. My conscience is now satisfied.

"I am aware, that many object to the severity of my language; but is there not cause for severity? I will be as harsh as truth, and as uncompromising as justice. On this subject, I do not wish to think, or speak, or write, with moderation. No! no! Tell a man, whose house is on fire, to give a moderate alarm; tell him to moderately rescue his wife from the hands of the ravisher; tell the mother to gradually extricate her babe from the fire into which it has fallen; but urge me not to use moderation in a cause like the present! I am in earnest. I will not equivocate—I will not excuse—I will not retreat a single inch—AND I

WILL BE HEARD. The apathy of the people is enough to make every statue leap from its pedestal, and to hasten the resurrection of the dead.

"It is pretended that I am retarding the cause of emancipation by the coarseness of my invective, and the precipitancy of my measures. The charge is not true. On this question, my influence, humble as it is, is felt at this moment to a considerable extent, and shall be felt in coming years—not perniciously, but beneficially—not as a curse, but as a blessing; and POSTERITY WILL BEAR TESTIMONY THAT I WAS RIGHT. I desire to thank God, that he enables me to disregard 'the fear of man which bringeth a snare' and to speak his truth in its simplicity and power. And here I close with this fresh dedication:

"Oppression! I have seen thee, face to face,
And met thy cruel eye and cloudy brow;
But thy soul-withering glance I fear not now—
For dread to prouder feelings doth give place,
Of deep abhorrence! Scorning the disgrace
Of slavish knees that at thy footstool bow,
I also kneel—but with far other vow
Do hail thee and thy herd of hirelings base:
I swear, while life-blood warms my throbbing veins,
Still to oppose and thwart, with heart and hand,
Thy brutalizing sway—till Afric's chains
Are burst, and Freedom rules the rescued land,
Trampling Oppression and his iron rod:
Such is the vow I take—so help me God."

In an address to an audience of Negroes he said: "It is the lowness of your estate, in the estimation of the world, which exalts you in my eyes. It is the distance that separates you from the blessings and privileges of society, which brings you so closely to my affections. It is the unmerited scorn, reproach and persecution of your persons, by those whose complexion is colored like my own, which command for you my sympathy and respect. It is the fewness of your friends—the multitude of your enemies—that induces me to stand forth in your defense" (Ruchames, 1963).

The defiance and the disgust and the disappointment with the opposition deepened early commitment, but it also raised doubts and conflicts about the wisdom of such a commitment. Phillips and Birney, who had most to lose in social position and privilege, had the most serious and prolonged reservations. Phillips, almost thirty, travelled through Europe with his invalid wife. He knew that his mother and family expected that he would return from his year abroad cleansed of his youthful enthusiasm for the radical movement. By the end of the year he had made a firm decision. He wrote to Garrison: "I recognize in some degree the truth of the assertion that associations tend to destroy individual dependence; and I have found difficulty in answering others, however clear my own mind might be, when charged with taking steps which the sober judgement of age would regret . . . with being hurried recklessly forward by the enthusiasm of the moment and the excitement of heated meetings. I am glad, therefore, to have the opportunity of holding up the cause, with all its incidents and bearings calmly before my own mind; . . . of being able to look back, cleared of all excitement, though not I hope of all enthusiasm . . . upon the course we have taken for the last few years; and . . . I am rejoiced to say that every hour of such thought convinces me more and more of the overwhelming claims our cause has in the life-long devotion of each of us" (Bartlett, 1961, pp. 73, 74).

Birney's period of doubt and indecision as we have seen was prolonged. In 1828 he had written "It (is) hard to tell what one's duty (is) toward the poor creatures; but I have made up my mind to one thing . . . I will not allow them to be treated brutally" (Birney, *Times*, p. 12). He was always concerned lest he be seduced by feeling; "Fearing the reality as well as the imputation of enthusiasm . . . each ascent that my mind made to a higher and purer moral and intellectual region, I used as a standpoint to survey very deliberately all the tract that I had left. When I remember how calmly and dispassionately my mind has proceeded from truth to truth connected with this subject (i.e., slavery) to another still higher, I feel satisfied that my conclusions are not the fruits of enthusiasm" (Birney, Letter on Colonization, p. 45).

Even after Birney had apparently firmly committed himself to abolitionism he wrote to Gerrit Smith: "I am at times greatly perplexed. To have alienated from us those with whom we [went] up from Sabbath to Sabbath to the house of God—many of our near connections and relations estranged from us, and the whole community with but here and there an exception, looking upon you as an enemy to its peace, is no small trial" (Fladeland, 1955, p. 114).

In 1837, he accepted the nomination of Secretary of the American Anti-Slavery Society. Just before his departure to New York he wrote to Lewis Tappan: "I know my own powers, I think, better than anyone else, and I fear their insufficiency for what is before me. My health is not generally so good as it was two or three years since. I am not capable of such continuous mental or physical effort as I used to be. Add to this, I have a large family of children and a sickly and dispirited wife, who is unable to control and educate them. Besides these circumstances embarrassing to myself—I apprehend, and I did from the first, that the salary I am to receive, will create some jealousy and jarring. Notwithstanding I hope for the best. Should my hope not be met I shall most cheerfully yield to circumstances that may point out to me an humbler sphere" (Fladeland, 1955, p. 160).

Nor was Birney ever to be entirely free of doubts—of his own competence—or of the effectiveness of the struggle against slavery. Six years before the end of his life, in 1851, he wrote: "I have heretofore been very earnest in my wishes and somewhat sanguine in my hopes that the North or free states would so array themselves against slavery, that it would before long be abolished; that the system would never be any stronger, and that whatever changes happened to it, would be to weaken it. I yet think, under the operation of various principles it will ultimately go out— as slavery has in Europe. But when or how it will expire, I must say I see not. It appears to me far off, that any exertion that I can make by writing or by showing it to be wrong is unnecessary and futile" (Fladeland, 1955, p. 274). Here we see the corrosion of commitment which can result from enduring and unrelenting opposition. Birney had by this time essentially withdrawn from the struggle.

For Weld the only doubts which ever assailed him were doubts about his own worthiness, his ability to control himself and to tolerate trial by fire. To his beloved Angelina Grimke had had confessed: "You know something of my structure of mind—that I am *constitutionally*, as far as emotions are concerned, a quivering mass of intensities kept in subjection only by the *rod of iron* in the strong hand of conscience and reason and never laid aside for a moment with safety" (Thomas, 1950, p. 154).

Slavery, like sex, was primarily a moral issue to Weld. "As a question of politics and national economy, I have passed it with scarce a look or a word, believing that the business of abolitionists is with the heart of the nation, rather than with its purse strings" (Thomas, 1950, p. 102). It was against conscience which he brought to bear "the accumulated pressure of myriad wrongs and woes and hoarded guilt." Weld was concerned not only about the control of sex, but also about the control of fear: "Let every abolitionist debate the matter once and for all, and settle it for himself . . . whether he can lie upon the rack—and clasp the faggot—and tread with steady step the scaffold—whether he can stand at the post of duty and having done all and suffered all, stand—and if cloven down, fall and die a martyr 'not accepting deliverance.'" (Thomas, 1950, p. 116). Whereas Phillips had been concerned with the wisdom of his choice and Birney with the nature and consequences of his choice, Weld was concerned with his ability to tolerate the inevitable consequences of the morally necessary choice.

Only Garrison suffered no serious doubts once he had embarked on his voyage "against wind and tide." As he had written in an editorial on his twenty-fifth birthday, "I am now sailing up a mighty bay with a fresh breeze and a pleasant hope—the waves are rippling merrily, and the heavens are serenely bright. I have encountered many a storm of adversity—rough, and cruel, and sudden—but not a sail has been lost nor a single leak sprung" (Merril, 1963, p. 34). Later that year after he spent seven weeks in jail he wrote: "How do I bear up under my adversities? I answer—like the oak—like the Alps—unshaken, storm-proof. Opposition, and abuse, and slander, and prejudice, and judicial tyranny, are like oil to the flame of my zeal. I am not dismayed, but bolder and more confident than ever. I say to my persecutors, 'I bid you defiance! Let the courts condemn me to fine and imprisonment for denouncing oppression: Am I to be frightened by dungeons and chains? can they humble my spirit? do I not remember that I am an American citizen? and, as a citizen, a freeman, and what is more, a being accountable to God? I will not hold my peace on the subject of African oppression. If need be, who would not die a martyr to such a cause?" (Merril, 1963, p. 39).

Engaging the Commitment of Society

Let us consider now the collective influence of the four men on their society. The same dynamic of violence and suffering which gradually deepened the commitment of the four was also responsible for engaging the commitment of others to abolitionism or at least to resistance against the extension of slavery to free soil. The violence inflicted on the early abolitionists and the suffering they endured led others to take up their cause.

The murder of the abolitionist Lovejoy and the mob action against Garrison, which had drawn Phillips into the struggle, also excited the sympathies and indignation of others. Dr. Henry Ingersoll Bowditch, a prominent physician, became an abolitionist in response to the Garrison mob: "Then it has come to this that a man cannot speak on slavery within sight of Faneuil Hall." Seeing Samuel A. Eliot, a member of the city government, he offered to help him suppress the rioters. "Instead of sustaining the idea of free speech . . . he rather intimated that the authorities, while not wishing for a mob, rather sympathized with its object which was to forcibly suppress the abolitionists. I was completely disgusted and I vowed in my heart as I left him with utter loathing, 'I am an abolitionist from this very moment'" (Lader, 1961, pp. 22-23).

Because the abolitionists were fearless, and again and again exposed themselves to the danger of physical violence they evoked widespread sympathy and respect and simultaneous indignation against those who hurt and threatened them.

After the mob destroyed Birney's press in Cincinnati and threatened his life, Salmon Chase stood openly with the abolitionists. He was to become the congressional representative of abolitionism. Chase later wrote that he "became an opponent of slavery and the slave Power while witnessing Birney's display of conviction and intelligence as he confronted the mobocrats" (Hart, 1899, p. 51).

William T. Allan's indecision between preaching Christianity or becoming an abolitionist was resolved by the same mob. Birney's own son, William, was converted to the movement by virtue of having faced the mob when it came after his father. From all over the country came letters of encouragement. Not the least of these was from the influential and widely respected New England minister, Dr. William Ellery Channing, who had previously denounced the abolitionist movement:

"I earnestly desire, my dear Sir that you and your associates will hold fast the right of free discussion by speech and the press, and, at the same time, that you will exercise it as Christians, and as friends of your race. That you, Sir, will not fail in these duties, I rejoice to believe. Accept my humble tribute of respect and admiration for your disinterestedness, for your faithfulness to your convictions, under the peculiar sacrifies to which you have been called . . . I look with scorn on the selfish greatness of this world, and with pity on the most gifted and prosperous in the struggle for office and power, but I look with reverence on the obscurest man, who suffers for the right, who is true to a good but persecuted cause" (Fladeland, 1955, p. 144).

Lewis Tappan expressed confidence that Birney would again publish the *Philanthropist*. Daniel Henshaw, a Lynn, Massachusetts, editor, called Birney "one of the noblest sons of the West" who had "dared to lift up his voice in favor of liberty when all around him seemed given over to corruption, to slavery, to moral destruction" (Fladeland, 1955, p. 145). Even Alva Woods, whom Birney had once hired as president of the University of Alabama, in his baccalaureate address expressed his deep indignation at this action by the mob.

But it was not only Garrison, Phillips, Weld and Birney who evoked violence, sympathy and indignation. There were hundreds of agents who were stoned, tarred and feathered, whipped, beaten up and in some cases killed. In addition to physical violence there was continual verbal abuse and threat of violence heaped publicly on every abolitionist. In Garrison's case a price was actually placed on his head in the South. Indeed it seems clear that without the exaggeration of Garrison's reputation by the South, his influence could never have been as great as it was.

VIOLENCE AND SUFFERING

We have argued that violence and suffering played a central role in the commitment first of the abolitionists and then in influencing general public opinion. What do we mean by violence and suffering? We refer by violence to any negative affect inflicted by someone on another, with intent to hurt; it may be an aggressive threat of physical violence, or a verbal insult. By suffering we refer to any negative affect which is instigated in the victim as a result of violence whether this be a feeling of humiliation, helpless rage, terror or distress. It is our argument that in a democratic society the impact of such violence and suffering on the observer is to arouse equally intense affect and to arouse vicarious distress, shame, fear or sympathy for the victim and anger and contempt for the aggressor. Because of this identification with the victim his ideas will tend to become more influential than before such an attack. In hierarchically organized societies, identification with the upper classes and castes will radically attenuate empathy with the victims of oppression.

Since most men in a democratic society share its values to some extent, even those who identify with the aggressor will feel a certain amount of guilt at the challenge to democratic values. Thus in the North, some of those who had identified with slaveholders and been most hostile to the abolitionists joined in lionizing them after the Civil War had ended—as if they were atoning for having identified with the "anti-democratic" position. We would argue that guilt over slavery was experienced in the South, too. There is some indirect evidence for this from the great increase in popularity of Garrison and Phillips after the Civil War. We assume that guilt over slavery was experienced in the South but that it was defended against by only half-believed exaggeration of the villainy of the victims and by exaggeration of the evils of wage "slavery" in the North.

The grounds for identification with the victim are numerous. First, the tendency to identify with any human being is quite general. Second, in a democratic society there is a taboo on inflicting hurt on anyone since it denies his equal right to life, liberty and the pursuit of happiness. Third, to the extent to which there is a tendency to identify with the aggressor, vicarious guilt is experienced, and, as a secondary reaction, sympathy for the victim is increased. Insofar as the victim is defending others (including oneself) there is, fourth, anger against the aggressor because the self is being vicariously attacked and, fifth, guilt and sympathy for the victim who is selflessly fighting the battles of others (including one's own battles).

Because of heightened identification with the victim, polarization between aggressor and victim increases; this magnifies the conflict and draws into the struggle, on both sides, thousands who would otherwise not have become involved. One half of the battle for radical social change is to increase the density of affect and ideation about the change. To look steadily at a social condition that violates the shared basic values of a society produces suffering for the society as a whole just as does the condition itself for a segment of the society. Contrary to the $+-+$ and $-+-$ triads, the Northern American citizen of the mid-nineteenth century was essentially ambivalent about slavery. He neither could approve it nor steadily disapprove it. He would have preferred to forget it. They were responsible for forcing confrontation and thereby radically increased the density of affect and ideation about the issue. This is precisely what the abolitionists made more and more difficult. Not all Americans became committed with maximum density of ideation and affect, but it is certain that the abolitionists greatly magnified the awareness and level of feeling of enemy and sympathizer alike and thereby exerted an amplified influence. The abolitionists did not permit them to look away from the ugly violation of the democratic ethos. In part they achieved this by provoking opposition and by offering themselves as victims. Thereby they evoked sympathy for themselves and their cause, and provoked anger and contempt for those who supported slavery.

The influence of the abolitionists was amplified by the growing polarization between the North and the South in their competition for the expanding frontier to the West. Again and again sectional conflict amplified the relevance and influence of their doctrine. The abolitionists converted what might have remained political issues into moral issues and thereby radically increased their influence.

As early as 1834 the American Antislavery Society encouraged all efforts to petition Congress to abolish slavery. In 1837, Congress was deluged with petitions signed by over 200,000 people. Southern congressmen, aided by Northern sympathizers, invoked a gag rule prohibiting the reception or discussion of these petitions. John Quincy Adams, unsympathetic as he had been to abolitionism, was deeply disturbed by this threat to constitutional rights and used every device to put antislavery petitions before Congress. Abolition at last had a national forum. Adams ultimately became a one-man symbol of the struggle against slavery and was indicted to be censured. Day after day "old man eloquent" held the floor in his own defense. Petitions against his censure began to pour into the house. He had suddenly, late in his life, captured the imagination of the North and become its hero. He defeated his enemies decisively. As Weld described it to his wife: "The triumph of Mr. Adams is complete. This is the first victory over the slaveholders in a body ever yet achieved since the foundation of the government and from this time their downfall takes its date" (Lader, 1961, p. 98).

The abolitionists also succeeded in converting the Fugitive Slave Law, the visit of Hoar to South Carolina, the burning of the mail in Charleston, the Dred Scott Decision, and the war with Mexico into footnotes to the abolitionist struggle. The Fugitive Slave Law of 1850 produced a very strong reaction in the North. Free Northern Negroes began an exodus to Canada. Everyone was under a potential obligation to be a slave catcher. By the 1850's, it appeared to many, for the first time, that perhaps the abolitionists had not really exaggerated the moral iniquity of the South. Many who at one time had regarded the abolitionists as the lunatic fringe were to have second thoughts when in 1854 a former slave had to be taken by force from Boston and shipped back to slavery as, ashamed and helpless, thousands were forced to look on, as their own militia guarded the prisoner against rescue. Gradually more and more Northerners came to experience the suffering of violence, at first vicariously and then more directly, until the firing on Fort Sumter suddenly galvanized all to respond in kind. War is a special case of commitment, and we would defend the position that a democratic society can commit itself to war only if it feels it has suffered violence upon itself, directly or vicariously.

The epilogue to our theory of commitment would account for the ironic necessity, one hundred years later, to repeat the struggle initiated by the abolitionists. Our history can be understood as a series of identifications with suffering against the violence which provoked it. It was widely said, before the attack on Fort Sumter, that the North could not possibly enter into war with the South. That attack produced an immediate identification with the nation which had suffered such violence. As war weariness grew, however, many in the North were prepared to relent toward the South and even to forget the issue of slavery. But the assassination of Lincoln stiffened the posture of the North once again and the North supported a severe Reconstruction against the South. Then, seeing how the South suffered violence at its hands, the North, identifying vicariously with its own victim, relented, and gave tacit consent to the reestablishment of a caste society. Now, again, we have become aware of the suffering of the Negro and are increasingly committed to rescue him.

REFERENCES

Bartlett, I. H., *Wendell Phillips, Brahmin Radical.* Boston: Beacon Press, 1961.
Birney, W. *Times.*
Birney, W. Letter on Colonization.
Fladeland, B. *James Gillespie Birney: Slaveholder to Abolitionist.* Ithaca, N.Y.: Cornell University Press, 1955.
Hart, A. B. *Salmon Portland Chase.*
Lader, L. *The Bold Brahmins.* New York: Dutton, 1961.
Merril, W. M. *Against Wind and Tide.* Cambridge: Harvard University Press, 1963.
Miller, P. *The New England Mind. The Seventeenth Century.* Boston: Beacon Press, 1961.
Ruchames, L. *The Abolitionists.* New York: Putnam, 1963.
Thomas, B. P. *Theodore Weld. Crusader for Freedom.* New Brunswick, N. J.: Rutgers University Press, 1950.

Part 2:
Reactions to the assassination
of President Kennedy

Silvan S. Tomkins
Robert McCarter
with Allison Peebles

If violence and suffering are critical in a democratic society in heightening antipathy for violations of democratic values and in heightening sympathy for the victims of such violations, then we should expect that the assassination of President Kennedy would greatly increase positive affect toward him. On the basis of the theory of commitment presented in Part 1 we would also expect both the magnitude and frequency of such shift in affect to be directly proportional to the original density of positive affect, i.e., the shift should be greatest and most frequent in those who felt most positively toward him before the assassination. Further we should expect some polarization of affect such that some of those who were most negative should become more negative. Finally, because all our respondents share the generally held values of a democratic society, we should expect among those hostile to Kennedy some evidence of guilt for identification with the aggressor, either in the form of verbally stated guilt or in the form of defensive flaunting behavior, i.e., behavior calculated to demonstrate the absence of grief.

METHOD

In an attempt to answer these questions we polled students in the senior author's undergraduate personality course on November 27th, 1963, five days after the assassination, concerning their reactions to the assassination. The number of students polled was 132. A majority of the class (170) had already left the University for the Thanksgiving holiday. Since we had not polled these students before the assassination the information they gave about changes in attitudes towards Kennedy had the disadvantage of being wholly retrospective. However, the changes appear to be consistent with those based on national polling before and after the event.

The disadvantage of the retrospective method is also attenuated by the anonymity permitted the respondent. He was told that his name was not required on his paper and that there would be no way of identifying any of the information reported. As we will see later, this permitted the communication of information which was not communicated to polling interviewers.

The questions to which written replies were requested were as follows:

1. Describe all of your reactions to the assassination of President Kennedy. (After you have finished with this, answer the following more specific questions, whether or not they appear in your own general description of all your reactions.)

172

2. Did you cry or did tears come to your eyes at any time during the period of mourning?

3. If you had to describe the total experience as one which smelled bad or as one which left a bad taste—which would it be?

4. How did you feel about Kennedy before he was assassinated? Check one of the following:

Strongly pro   Weakly pro   Indifferent   Weakly against   Strongly against

5. How do you feel now about President Kennedy? Check one of the following:

Strongly pro   Weakly pro   Indifferent   Weakly against   Strongly against

6. Did you find yourself not believing that he had been killed? If so, for how long?

RESULTS AND DISCUSSION

The major hypothesis was confirmed. There was a massive shifting of attitudes: over half of the students felt more strongly pro-Kennedy after the assassination than they had felt toward him before he was assassinated. The second prediction was partially confirmed. We predicted that the shift should be greatest and most frequent in those who felt positively toward him before the assassination. The *magnitude* of the shift was smallest for those who were originally most strongly against Kennedy, but the *percentage* of those who changed their attitudes (independent of the degree of change) did not differ significantly among those whose original attitudes ranged from strongly against to strongly pro. No matter whether one felt strongly against or for Kennedy before the assassination, over half of the students changed their attitudes in the direction of positive affect toward Kennedy. But the student was less likely to become strongly pro-Kennedy the more strongly anti-Kennedy was his original attitude. In summary, the second hypothesis was confirmed with respect to the magnitude of each change, but disconfirmed with respect to the frequency of change.

Let us now examine these changes in detail. In Figure 1 we see that the group as a whole before the assassination is biased in favor of Kennedy. 67% are originally weakly pro or strongly pro, compared with 27% strongly or weakly against and 4% indifferent. After the assassination there are 82% who are weakly pro or strongly pro, compared with 16% who are strongly or weakly against and 1.5% who remain indifferent. The most striking difference, however, is found in the increase in strongly pro feeling which rises from an original 28% to a final 56% of this sample. This occurs mainly because before the assassination the largest number (39%) of students held weakly pro attitudes towards Kennedy and if more than half of these were to change toward pro (which was the rule for almost all pre-assassination attitudes) then there was only one category remaining towards which it was possible for them to shift. The shift away from the most extreme negative attitude is also marked, though no different in frequency than from any other category. Before the assassination 13% were strongly against Kennedy and afterwards 6% remained so.

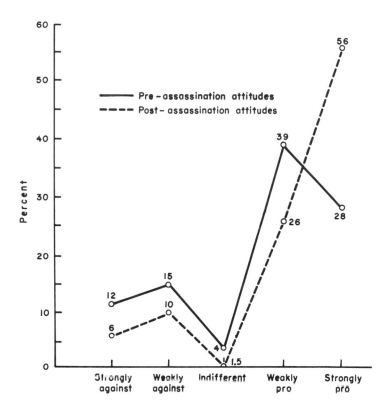

Figure 1. Pre- and post-assassination attitudes towards Kennedy of 132 Princeton students.

In Table 1 there is presented the numbers of subjects who changed from each position to each other position, and of those who did not change. In Table 2 this data has been converted into percentages for

Table 1 Numbers of subjects who changed from each position to each other position, and of those who did not change

Original position	Total in orig. position	Final position				
		Strong con	Weak con	Indifferent	Weak pro	Strong pro
Strong con	17	8	5	1	1	2
Weak con	19	0	9	0	5	5
Indifferent	6	0	0	1	3	2
Weak pro	52	0	0	0	25	27
Strong pro	37	0	0	0	0	37
Total in final position		8	14	2	34	73

those who changed from each position to every other position and the percentages of those who did not change.

Table 2 Percentages who changed to each position and percentages of those who did not change

Original position	Final position				
	Strong con	Weak con	Indifferent	Weak pro	Strong pro
Strong con	43% Unchanged	31% Change	6% Change	6% Change	12% Change
Weak con		47% Unchanged	0% Change	26% Change	26% Change
Indifferent			16% Unchanged	50% Change	34% Change
Weak pro				48% Unchanged	52% Change
Strong pro					100% Unchanged

In Table 3 the same data is expressed in terms of the numbers who changed to *any* other position, the numbers who did not change, and the percentages of those who changed.

Table 3 Percentage who changed and did not change from initial positions

Original position	Number who did not change	Number who did change	Percent change
Strong pro	37	0	0
Weak pro	24	27	53
Indifferent	1	5	83
Weak against	9	10	53
Strong against	8	9	53

The comparison of the percentage of people who change from one attitude toward another must exclude those whose original position was strongly pro. There were no changes in the negative direction against Kennedy and those most strongly pro cannot therefore indicate a more strongly pro attitude on our scale, though 5 students did volunteer the information (unasked for) that although their attitudes had originally been strongly pro-Kennedy and remained so after the assassination, that nonetheless they were now even more strongly pro-Kennedy.

When we exclude from the sample (of 132) the 37 who were originally strongly pro-Kennedy, then of the remaining 95 students, 41 (or 43%) do not change their attitudes and 54 (or 57%) do.

It should be remembered that it was theoretically possible to change in either direction but that there were no instances of changes in the negative direction.

An examination of Table 3 reveals that (exclusive of strongly pro and indifferent) there are no differences in percentage of change as a function of original position. The percentages of change are 53, 53, and 53. There were as many who shifted from strongly against, from weakly against, as from weakly for. Only among those who were originally indifferent did almost all change (5 out of 6). These latter numbers are too small to provide a sensitive test of statistical significance, but the probable significance that opinion became more intense in general is supported by an examination of Table 1 which shows not only that 5 out of 6 changed from indifference to weakly or strongly pro, but that there was only 1 case out of a possible 126 in which there was a change *to* indifference. This occurred with a subject whose pre-assassination attitude had been strongly against Kennedy. We conclude therefore that the indifferent category essentially ceases to exist under conditions of extreme violence and general suffering. Excluding the category of indifference over half the sample changes its feelings to favor Kennedy, no matter what was their original position.

Original position does make a difference but it is in the magnitude of the shift rather than its frequency. In Table 2, if we examine shifts to a strong pro position (last column) of those who were originally strongly against, 12% change to strongly pro; of those who were weakly against, 26% change to strongly pro; of those who were indifferent, 34% change to strongly pro; and of those who were weakly pro, 52% change to strongly pro. This is in part an artifact because the number of open categories possible for change toward pro steadily declines the more strongly pro a subject's initial attitude was. However, examination of the changes reveals that the most frequent single change to any single category from *any* initial position is one step. Thus from strong con to weak con there is a 31% change; from weak con to weak pro (excluding indifference) is a 26% change; from indifferent to weak pro is a 50% change; from weak pro to strong pro is a 52% change. Where the possible number of changes is greatest (from strong con) the greatest percentage of change is to the adjacent category (31%), with 6%, 6% and 12% in the succeeding categories.

All of this shift involved strong affect about Kennedy as a person. The students frequently referred to their shifts of feeling as being personal rather than political. (Sometimes both of these were reported as shifting upward together; one student described his shift as from weak against to weak for politically; and from weak pro personally to strong pro personally.) Primarily, however, the reference was personal and so stated. Only occasionally did a student refer to a significant shift in his political attitudes. This was in part a function of the fact that they were originally mostly weakly or strongly pro and there was not much room for shift.

FREE RESPONSES

The spectrum of reactions was extremely broad, ranging from defiance against sentimentalism, mild irritation at the interference with dates and other social functions, through the most intense panic, and sorrow, some on a purely personal level, some arising from a concern for the welfare of the country. Following are samples of the variation in free responses describing their reactions:

First, an example from one who was strongly against Kennedy and who remained so. In this is reflected the defiance against what is labelled the "*show*" of sorrow, which appeared primarily among the minority who were made uncomfortable by the general mourning among the Princeton undergraduates:

> No reaction for 5 minutes—no stunning. I was walking along—a guy told me, and I said 'that's too bad'—and continued back to my room which I began to clean up.
> A roomate came in & I told him & we sat around feeling sorry until the third joined us. When he heard the news he wanted to turn the radio on & blare it out—we got mad and told him to keep it low. He decided to go outside & mourn—and the 1st roommate & I were so provoked at his *show* of sorrow that we put on Surfin' Safari and started dancing around. We weren't really gay—but we did shake it up—the guys out front got mad & started calling in & finally did walk in the dorm & after a show of violence & mutual anger the stereo was turned off. Then we played tennis.

Next is the report of a student who was strongly against Kennedy and who remained so, who stresses that "it was his appointed hour to die":

> When I first heard the radio news broadcast that Kennedy had been shot I was shocked. I knew what it might mean, but I was not feeling good, bad, or indifferent about it. Later when the news of the death was announced, everyone walked around in an apparent daze. I could not believe the way people felt. I was not one of the President's biggest boosters, though I can hardly approve of shooting the man who runs our country, nor do I approve of killing anyone. It seems to me that death is a fairly commonplace thing that happens everyday, and one has to accept it no matter how close it comes.
> I was sorry that our President was dead, but no more so than I would have been for any other president. The manner of dying helps bring out the awareness of the shock, but I would have felt the same if he had died of a protracted illness. It was his appointed hour to die. Nothing could be done about it and we must accept the rules by our authority in the world beyond.

Following is another report of a student strongly against who remained so, who was concerned lest Kennedy be made into a "god":

> Sitting in the barber's chair when I heard the first broadcast come over the air my first reaction when I heard the term President was President of what. As they got more details of the shooting I just could not believe the broadcasts in fact the whole thing seemed so ridiculous that I thought it was almost funny. As the weekend wore on, I never, and still have not, felt the full impact of the President's death. I felt anger at the assassin. My reaction was sorrow for his family and my hope was that he wouldn't be made into a "god." I never agreed with his politics and don't want to see a lot of his legislation passed because of good faith to him!

Following is the report of a student who was weakly against who moved to weakly pro, who joked about the assassination with some fear that he would be overheard:

> My first thought was shock, then disbelief. I joked with someone saying that the whole thing could be a hoax but was cut short—no one jokes about such matters. Then I thought it doesn't matter; nothing can slow down the U.S. and it may do some good, Goldwater will have no one to run against him and may take '64. Then, as I saw the deep grief on so many people's faces, I began to see, the reason why. Kennedy represented the ideal American, with almost all America on his side but even he can do nothing about hate. I, and most of my friends, did not feel that mourning is valuable so most of the time we joked about the death. I felt badly when I joked about the death for fear that someone who cares would hear me.

Following is a description of the relatively mild reaction of a student who was weakly against Kennedy and who remained so:

> At first I didn't believe it, couldn't conceive it. Then when I was positive that it was true I took it very lightly without too much concern. I quickly returned to my room *after* the completion of my Friday chemistry laboratory to listen to radio reports. It seemed to me like listening to a world series game. Soon the idea sank in and for almost two days I couldn't get the idea of "Kennedy assassinated" out of my mind. I never felt remorseful or vengeful but very solemn and concerned (not really sad).

Next is a report by a student who was weakly pro and who remained so, who tried to find something "good" as a possible outcome:

> First reaction—disbelief, then anger.
> Later my anger subsided as I realized that this is one of the risks that the president has to take and I tried to find some good result which this might bring in the long run (greater nat'l unity, etc.) I felt that this would be a way that the U.S. could show the world how well it reacts and unites in time of greatest crisis. I imagine I took the assassination as somewhat of a challenge, both to myself & every other American.

Next is a report of a student who was originally strongly against who became weakly against, who concerned himself with the political consequences of the assassination and with its interference with a date:

> When I first heard the news, I didn't believe it. It stunned me, and I felt that something was in abeyance. This void remained for at least a day but was partially filled with questions about what would come next. These questions came to me within minutes after I had heard the news confirmed. I wondered about what would happen to the bills in Congress and especially what would happen in the coming election analyzing the different candidates' chances. I also felt Johnson would do as good if not better a job than Kennedy. Throughout the weekend I was interested in the developments and was in one respect angry at the whole thing because a date with a special girl I was having was clouded. Throughout the weekend I also maintained apprehensions about some of the possible results of the assassination. My sorrow was as much for the event as for the persons concerned.

Next is the weak response of a student who was weakly pro who remained so:

When my roomie and I first heard about the assassination, our mutual reaction was one of disbelief, perhaps scorn. We were entering Dillon Gym to play basketball, and a radio had been placed by the towel room. At the particular moment we entered the radio was carrying some somber, church-like music. I thought all this was some joker's idea of a way to get the student body stirred up for Dartmouth: appeal to his deep, inner needs. Just before we went to the lockers the announcer came on to say that President Kennedy was dead. I smiled. Some joke. Some other fellows were smiling, too. Perhaps this was due to translation on their part when they saw me smile or perhaps they were glad.

I first began to believe the story when someone from the lockers came to the gym floor and started to tell everyone that Kennedy was dead. Perhaps I choked a little. Then I was angry. This kind of thing just didn't happen in the U.S.

One of the fellows who were shooting around said, "Thank you, God." This sarcastic comment found an echo in my own mind. Since then my prevailing attitude has been one of bitter rationalization. I tell myself that this is not "the end of the world." I ponder the changed political picture. But I can find little emotional response in myself towards the man who died November 22, 1963.

Next is a report of a student weakly pro who remained so, who is mildly concerned about the inconvenience occasioned by the assassination:

When I first heard the news, it seemed too impossible to be true, it was unbelievable. Then I thought why was it done & who did it. I hoped it wasn't done by any foreign organizational group—for that would mean bad times ahead—possibly war.

Haven't had a chance to watch television, & radio gets a bit boring after a while, & I did too. Once I had heard all there was to hear about the death, I wished they would quit broadcasting.

I don't feel the university should have called off all the activities on Sat.— partly because I don't really think it's necessary & partly because it breaks up my Thanksgiving Vacation as I have to return this Sat. for the game.

Perhaps the reality of it all hasn't hit me yet. Its seem (sic) too pre- posterous to be true, I can't believe it, or do & don't want to.

Next is the report by a student who was originally indifferent who became weakly pro, and who stressed the consequences of the loss of the President for the country:

Did not believe the person who told me.
Anger: Person who did it should be killed.
Why would anyone shoot the President. He was probably a Russian.
How did he do it? The secret service is supposed to protect the President.
Who's going to run the country?
Will the Russians try to do something while the U.S. is confused?

Next is a reaction of a student who is self-critical because he did not give his "full self" to the assassination. He changed from weakly pro to strongly pro:

> I do not have a radio. The first I heard was from one of my former room-mates whom I was visiting. I thought he was kidding, at first, even when his roommates told me, but I finally believed them. I do not think it sunk in even then . . . death is a new experience for me; I had no precedents.
> Afterwards in greatest bewilderment I tossed the event around in my mind, looking for consequences—political, international, for Civil Rights, for the Republicans, for my own work—and considering what could be thought about the completed whole of Kennedy's life and his personality and character—and what could be thought about Johnson and what was happening to him.
> At the Chapel memorial service, and again watching the funeral for a few minutes, I did feel like crying; I think in consideration of Kennedy and the problem, burden, and consequence of leadership and power, and what happens to a nation left leaderless, and how it pays its respects. What, after all, is a nation—not a coherent simple entity—and what is a Leader of such a unit?
> For myself, I had an economics exam and a paper due this week and could not have come anywhere near finishing either if I hadn't had the extra time from the cancellation of classes and the football game. The paper still isn't done and neither is my Psych reading, though I worked the whole time. I did not have time to react to the assassination with my full self, which is very too bad.

Next is a report of a student who was strongly against who became weakly pro, on the basis of a concern for the Kennedy family rather than "for the country":

> At first, on hearing the news of Pres. Kennedy's death, I didn't believe it possible. When later I found it to be true, I was very upset and felt ex-tremely sorry for the man and his family, much more so than for the coun-try. I even had tears come to my eyes while watching the T.V. news on Fri. afternoon. Later my feelings became those of helplessness, of wanting to be able to do something to help ease the grief or rectify the wrong done. Again my feelings turned to sorrow and I must say I felt very close to the Kennedy family in their sadness. By now, Wed., most of my feelings are much less emotional to the incident, that is a great deal of my initial sorrow has been spent and I seem to be looking on now just to see what will happen next. I don't feel embittered at all, only amazed that anyone could commit such a crime, and saddened by the fact that the victim had to be a man in whom we held so much respect.

Next is the report of a student who had been weakly against who be-came weakly pro, who describes a belated awareness of the President's greatness:

> On first hearing of the news of his death, I experienced a startle. This startle immediately turned into a feeling of disbelief. I asked many different people about it in order to convince myself that it was real. Any thoughts of fear

did not enter my mind until several hours after I first heard (sic) the news. The excitement was so great that I really didn't get a chance to comprehend the consequences of the event until later. When the fear affect did enter into my mind, it was still that something like that could happen to me. I thought I was an anti-Kennedy man but it seems now like that was impossible. He is something like a painter to me in that I did not really realize how great he was until after his death. A feeling of pity also entered my mind. It was a pity for not only the immediate family but also for the whole country with myself included. I wonder what kind of country America is if things like this can happen.

Next is the report of a student originally weakly against who became strongly for him "as a courageous man":

When I first heard the news on Friday, I was deeply shocked and couldn't believe that it was true. I began to get goose-pimples and my legs felt very weak. After the initial shock, I felt myself becoming very depressed. This condition soon became mingled with a type of anger and disgust that this horrible tragic thing should have happened in America. It seemed that this should never have taken place in this country. All through the week-end, there seemed to remain this trace of disbelief. Gradually, I think that respect for the courage of the President and of Mrs. Kennedy, who proved herself to be the strongest woman that I have ever seen, became the dominant part of my thinking. This caused me to go to Washington to pay my respects. I was deeply moved by the beauty and stateliness of these ceremonies and felt that this was the greatest tribute that any man could ever get. Now, I am still very respectful for his courage and very angry that this tragic thing could have happened.

Following is the report of a student originally weakly pro who became strongly pro, who describes his first real encounter with death:

I was studying when I was told of the shooting and when it was first related to me the whole idea was so out of context that I wasn't able to fully believe or comprehend exactly what had happened. For the rest of the afternoon, despite continual exposure to radio broadcasts, etc., my primary feeling was one of disbelief. This soon became great sadness and shock, particularly was I sorry for the president's wife. Perhaps because of the constant exposure to him through the mass media, I felt as if this were a personal loss to me. I was upset over it for at least three days. I cannot remember having been so upset by someone's death ever before, even that of my grandparents. For the first time, death had been brought home to me as a reality, and not something that just happened to other people. Like most other young people, (I presume), death had had only a remote significance for me until this incident. I spent more time than I have done in the past trying to orient myself with my existence and just what the important things about life were and whether it was all worth it since we all die anyway. I further re-explored my relation to God.

At the present time, my tendency is to try and put the matter out of my mind the best I can, but every time I see a newspaper article on the event, I have a hard time to keep from crying.

Next is a report of a student originally weakly pro who became strongly pro for him as a person, who stresses the "waste" of an idealist:

I felt a sense of tragedy on hearing of the assassination. I felt a sense of absurdity because I saw Kennedy as an idealist trying to act and it seemed ridiculous for him to be killed by some lunatic. "What a goddam waste," I thought. However, besides compassion for his family, I was unable to feel much more than this sense of tragedy. I feel no personal loss; rather I felt that life seemed awfully useless when it happens that a sincere man is killed for little reason at all. I recognized that I would feel absurd if I had given my life to a certain cause and found myself suddenly struck down in the midst of trying to reach my goal. I do not feel any particular enmity toward Oswald and I have no wish to see him dead.

Next is the report of a student originally weakly pro who changed to strongly pro, who emphasizes "hate behind the sadness":

When the bulletin first came over the radio, I thought it was a joke, and was angry at the radio station and whoever might have been responsible for such a ridiculous story. Then as the reports continued my contempt turned to sudden disbelief. I couldn't comprehend that such a dynamic living figure had been shot down. The confirmed word of his death left me with a "sadness" and "emptiness" that I can't describe. Something that had been a part of me had been taken away. I began imagining all the things Mr. Kennedy might have done in the following years. I was saddened because he would no longer enjoy what so many of us who are worth so much less than he do enjoy—life. As reports concerning the assassin himself came over the wire, I felt hate that I have never truly felt before. In spite of all restraints of conscience and morals, I would gladly have taken the chance to kill the assassin with my bare hands, if he were found. I still feel the hatred. Ruby's act made no difference.

Though I was not particularly close-linked with the democratic party, and had not bothered to follow all of Kennedy's moves while he held office, my loss was no less. Throughout Friday I could see his face, smiling, as he passed through the crowds. And then the sudden look of anguish, and Jackie's cry. What will Jackie and their children do.

I still cannot fully comprehend what has happened. Things don't seem real. And there is always the hate behind the sadness.

Next is the report of a student, weakly pro who did not change, who also stresses "real hate" as well as guilt:

My first reaction was that of disbelief and scepticism. Then as the story grew more and more real I lapsed into a period when I lost part of my ability to control my actions. I was selling tickets at the time, and worked on almost by instinct, it seemed. My mind was torn away, yet I don't think there was anything concrete in the form of grief in my mind, just distraction. Later I felt moved to cry, especially when viewing pictures of the President's wife and children. I felt guilt, it seemed, at several times during the weekend—guilt because I didn't have any way to share in the suffering, I suppose. My roommate found me very silent. At several points I realized that I was experiencing real hate for the alleged assassin, and felt guilty, or disturbed, at this also. At several points I felt in need of something stable or real to hold onto, and I got a great relief out of reading Kennedy biographies in the papers and re-reading Kennedy books.

Next is a report of a student originally weakly pro who now says he is strongly pro, which stresses the shame for not feeling more sorrowful:

When I heard of it, first I didn't believe it, then I was almost amused at the novelty of it. When I heard over the radio that he had died, I felt very sorrowful, but not the same kind of sorrow as if someone close to me had died. I was ashamed at my inward reaction and tried to seem more sorrowful than I was, but now the sorrow has worn off, and I feel disappointed somehow in his loss.

Next is the report of a student originally weakly pro who became strongly pro. He emphasizes the feeling of impotence:

When first hearing of the tragedy, I stared in a combination of shock and disbelief. Though most of this feeling lingered as I listened to the radio recount Mr. Kennedy's final minutes, part of it was transformed into anger and part into an overall feeling of utter impotency. Sorrow set in when I reconstructed, in my mind, that awful scene. All of these feelings have lingered to some degree but, because of my complete inability to assist in this matter or to restore an invaluable man to life, the overriding feeling has been one of impotency and, perhaps, anger. Sorrow is easily evoked at any photograph of the late President or of the young family he leaves behind.

Next is a description by a student who was and who remained strongly pro, of an intensely personal reaction to the loss of Kennedy:

It is hard to say what I felt—panic, hate, and immediate sorrow. I sat in a large chair and listened to the radio for a long time until the president was pronounced dead. My heart was pounding furiously and my breathing was somewhat stifled. When I knew he was dead I lay on the couch with the radio on and wept for a couple of minutes. I stayed on the couch until I fell asleep utterly exhausted. I could not do anything over the week-end, so I went to Washington Sunday afternoon and came back just before dinner Monday. I tried to study Monday night, could not, so went back to my room & put on a record. I was not always thinking of the President's death but was constricted inside. It was not long after I had returned to my room when I broke down completely. Now I feel better but heavily burdened. I held a lot in store in Pres. Kennedy and it seemed that many of my hopes, confidences, and feeling of security had died with him. Now I must place them in something else.

Following is another example of a purely personal response (on the part of a Republican student) who became more "attached" to the President, changing from weakly pro to strongly pro:

My initial reaction was that it was so ludicrous it was almost funny. This merged into extreme depression which was only ended by the arrival of my date, whereupon I put it out of my mind, fairly successfully (with the help of alcohol) until Sun. nite when I was once again pretty depressed.

I felt shock not so much because the President was dead or because of the political repercussions, but mostly feeling for the President was a vital cheerful person (whom I never before had felt much affection for, being a republican). I unquestionably feel much more attached to JFK now than I did before. Mostly, though, I can now remember very little about how I felt about it a few days ago.

Next is the report of a student who was and who remained strongly pro:

At first I reacted with a NO! as though my unconscious had somehow been anxious of such a tragedy and with a strong hope at least that my ears had deceived me.

I can remember my heart pounding rapidly as I quickly turned on the radio, still hoping beyond hope that what I had heard was untrue.

The news hit me with shock, an impact that tensed my muscles and captured my full conscious attention. I felt as though I had lost my best friend and leader. There was an empty feeling as I thought only briefly & still uncomprehendingly of the loss to our country and indeed to myself.

My reaction immediately turned to profound sorrow and even grief while I still found it difficult to comprehend the fact that this man was no longer with us and that life must nevertheless go on in spite of our loss.

Everything that I did from that time onward was done with a listless feeling of loss. I could not concentrate fully on any one project with this tragedy in my mind, though still I could not comprehend it completely and felt as though sometime I would wake up finding this only a bad dream.

Next are two reports of students who were strongly pro who responded with strong religious feelings:

My reactions to the President's assassination were, I think, more extreme than most of my friends'.

At first, I didn't believe it. Then when I found he had been shot, I was dazed, but I don't believe I was yet distressed—merely shocked. When the word "assassination" came over the radio, I became numb—physically as well as mentally—and would have cried had I been alone. I remember saying, "My God" many times that afternoon. Still I was incredulous. I don't think I actually fully believed it until after the funeral.

I am not religious in the usual sense—I believe strongly in God, but don't believe in church services. Yet I felt an urgent need to go to chapel, and I attended Chapel services Saturday; I also went to chapel for personal prayer Fri., Sat., and Sunday. A friend of mine whose religious feelings are like mine went all the way to N. Y. to go to St. Patrick's Cathedral.

The aspect which upset me most was Mrs. Kennedy. Her courage was extremely moving, and every time I saw her on television and noted the expression on her face—seemingly the image of courage—I felt like crying myself.

I think I felt fear, too, as the week-end passed. When Oswald was shot, I began thinking we were all on a Merry-go-round and we were too stupid to get off before it started up again so that we had to keep buying tickets. The events reminded me of a movie, *Manchurian Candidate,* in their content and a book, *Fail-Safe*, in the speed with which they took place. In this scope, they were frightening.

Even now I feel a very strong grief over this tragedy. My shock has nothing to do with the national tragedy I don't think. I am upset by the personal tragedy which I feel and which I feel for the Kennedy family.

I should say that I did have tears in my eyes several times while watching the funeral, which, I think, saddened me far more than the funerals of some of my own relatives.

My first reaction was definitely one of disbelief. I kept hoping that an announcement would be made that this was a false report, something like the Martian Invasion scare on radio several years ago. When I finally realized that it was true that he had been shot & seriously wounded, I was shocked and could do nothing for four or five minutes I suppose. Then I began to pray as best I could (I am a Roman Catholic) although I could hardly concentrate on what I was trying to say. It was difficult to remember words of prayers that I say every day.

I remember how one of my roommates began yelling for the life of Oswald, & how he would like to give him a slow painful death. This disgusted me & I would have argued with him except that I realized this was a time for silence & not arguing.

I sat glued to the T.V. until the announcement of death was official. Then I left the room without a word to my roommates & went to church for about 20 minutes, where (sic) the real shock of what had happened finally hit me. I did not cry, but I was "choked up" as the saying goes.

The only time I took a response that might be called anger was when Oswald was shot because of the complete ignorance and poor security measures of the Dallas police. Other than this I prayed & tried to remain quiet for the entire weekend.

Next is the report of a student, strongly pro, before and after, who experienced both distress and anxiety, with the latter being experienced as a "strange feeling in the head as if my hair was standing on end." Also of interest is a concomitant increase in the rate of ideation:

After learning second hand of President Kennedy's being wounded I went back to my room and turned on the radio. On hearing them playing the "Star Spangled Banner" I realized that he had died. As I remember, I felt a strange feeling in my head as if my hair was standing on end. This is a response which I always feel whenever learning of tragedy. Naturally tears began to come to my eyes though I was far from beginning to weep. It seems that I began to think more than I normally would. Such thoughts as, why does someone have to kill if they don't agree with his views, and he was too young to die crossed my mind. It seems that I was experiencing the anguish affect except that in place of a cry I was doing excessive thinking.

Next is a student who was strongly pro and remained so, who stresses the delayed awareness of the significance of Kennedy's loss for the nation:

On last Friday after hearing the news of the death of the President my feelings were complete shock and disbelief.

As the news is now a few days old I can now accept as fact the death of Mr. Kennedy, but only after hearing about it on the radio or reading another account in the newspaper.

It will be a long time before we as a whole nation realize that we have lost a great man.

Next is a report of a student who was strongly pro, who stressed the injustice of the assassination:

Upon hearing the news from a member of our Dormitory I was disbelieving and immediately ran to my own radio.—I heard it!—Horror struck; it was only a phantasy it can't really happen because I thought it was too negative an action for my mind to comprehend. Stunned, shock, and *afraid* (of what I don't know) are the only modifiers available to describe my immediate reaction.

After hearing of the President's death I continually murmured, "but why? It isn't fair." I remember thinking all the time that *he* couldn't be killed and that it was *not* fair that such a great man should die. I believed that upon rising the next morning, all would return to normality.

The fact that the President was murdered, and not merely died of natural causes, played the determining role in activating this series of emotions.

Following is an example of a student, strongly pro before and after the assassination, who regarded it as a crime against humanity:

When President John F. Kennedy died, I experienced first a feeling of disbelief. No it just isn't possible I said to myself. How can it be? were my original thoughts.

But when I finally did come around to accepting the fact of his death I felt outraged and angry at the very injustice of the whole act. It was so uncalled for, so mean, so brutal, indeed a crime against the whole of humanity. Because Kennedy represented in his person a certain egalitarian aspiration, a clean and wholesome and just way of doing things. For such a man to be plucked instantaneously from our midst is a crime not only against all Americans but against all men the world over who aspire to high ideals and strive for Man's ultimate happiness and peace.

Finally there follows the report of a student, strongly pro originally who remained so, who describes the vulnerability of "our god":

When the assassination of President Kennedy was first reported I was greatly shocked, perhaps, at least it felt so, the greatest shock of my life. I had a sense of disbelief and doubt and yet I knew it was true. I had sort of a feeling of being lost, thinking what disaster would now befall us now the (sic) our President, the one upon whom everyone's troubles are heaped, was dead. After listening to the radio and TV the reality of the situation gradually overcame the initial incredulousness. Perhaps it was so shocking to many people in that it made death quite imminent, for even our 'god' was susceptible to it.

The idealization of Kennedy as a consequence of suffering and identification with the object of violence was noted not only by those who were strongly pro-Kennedy but also by those who were most hostile to him. As we saw before, some of these were concerned lest his martyrdom lead to the translation of his political program into law.

COMPARISON WITH OTHER POLLS

Our evidence for a general shift of attitude in the positive direction is consistent with that from other polls. Sheatsley and Feldman (1964) note that although Kennedy was elected by a little over 50%, in a poll conducted by NORC in June, 1963, 59% claimed they had favored him in 1960, and in a poll right after his death 65% claimed him as having been their preference in 1960.

Sheatsley and Feldman (1964) also report that, when asked to rate the President, a full half of the respondents called him "one of the two or three best Presidents the country ever had," and an additional 28% described him as "better than average." Only 2% termed him "somewhat below average," "one of the worst Presidents the country ever had." 97% of Negroes considered him above average, as did 90% of his white Southern supporters. Among those whites who had other political preference in 1960, 65% of Northerners and 44% of Southerners at the time of the interview called him better than average. This contrasts strongly with the last Gallup reading of the late President's popularity while he was yet alive. In a release dated November 10, it was reported that a relatively modest 59% approved of "the way Kennedy is handling his job as President," while 28% disapproved and 13% were undecided.

Further, this evidence and our own is also consistent with evidence on the increased identification which occurs when our Presidents have suffered serious defeats. Thus the Gallup polls showed a sharp rise in Eisenhower's "approval rating" after the U-2 incident and the collapse of the Paris summit meeting in 1960, and a similar increase in Kennedy's rating immediately after the "Bay of Pigs" Cuban invasion in 1961.

There is also evidence from Sheatsley and Feldman (1964) that there was a heightening of general democratic values: "75% thought some lesson had been learned, 25% specifically stating that there must be less hate and intolerance, more love and understanding, among all Americans." This is consistent with our hypothesis that violence and suffering can play a constructive role in accelerating social change and in deepening democratic values in a democratic society.

DYNAMICS OF VIOLENCE AND SUFFERING

So much for our chief hypothesis. We were also interested in the analysis of this data for any further light it might shed on the dynamics of violence and suffering in general. Let us now examine the nature of the distress response to the assassination in more detail.

Crying

In response to the question "Did you cry or did tears come to your eyes at any time during the period of mourning?" the majority, 63% (83) reported they did *not* cry and 36% (48) reported they did cry and 1% (1) did not know.

This contrasts with Sheatsley and Feldman's (1964) report on a national sample, that a majority (53%) said they cried at some time during the four-day period. They report that in the Northern, white, pro-Kennedy sub-sample 61% reported that they cried; in the Southern, white, pro-Kennedy sub-sample 53%; in the Northern, white, non-Kennedy sub-sample 42% and in the Southern, white, non-Kennedy sub-sample 34%.

In our sample, which was generally biased in favor of Kennedy, the percentage of those who say they cried (36%) is almost identical with the lowest group in the national sample—the Southern, white, non-Kennedy sub-sample (34%)—and 25 percentage points less than the Northern, white, pro-Kennedy sub-sample.

Considering the political bias in favor of Kennedy in the student group as a whole, this discrepancy might reflect greater honesty in our sample, due to the anonymity of the communication, or it might reflect a generally less intense involvement on the part of Princeton undergraduates compared with the national sample, or it might reflect the unusual severity of the taboo on crying or on admitting that one cried, peculiar to the male late adolescent.

Table 4 Percentage of students who cried among those who changed and among those who did not change

Position	Percent who cried who held position originally	Percent who cried who remained in original position	Percent who cried who changed to this position
Strong pro	57*	57*	31
Weak pro	33	37	9
Weak against	30	33	20
Strong against	26	12*	–
Indifferent	0	0	100

*Differences significant at .05 level

An examination of Table 4 reveals that it is probably none of these alternatives, since the percent of students who are originally strongly pro-Kennedy who cried is 57%, which compares favorably with the national poll sample of Northern white pro-Kennedy (61%) and with the Southern white pro-Kennedy sub-sample (53%). It should be noted that there is a strong representation of Southern whites at Princeton. Among those who say they are strongly pro-Kennedy there is a significant elevation of the percent who cried, as compared with every other group. They are most strikingly different from those who were strongly against Kennedy, and who remained so after the assassination. These cried in only 12% of the students, reliably different from all other groups. On the other hand, those who were originally strongly against (which included many who became more positively disposed after the assassination) cried in 26% of the cases, which does not differ from any other category except those who were originally and who remained strongly pro-Kennedy. Whether the distress response should be regarded as cause or effect in these relationships is not altogether clear. One might argue that the strongly pro-Kennedy group cry more because they are so strongly pro-Kennedy. But those who were strongly against Kennedy cried almost as frequently as those who were weakly against and weakly pro Kennedy (26% to 30-33%). There is clearly no strong general relationship between frequency of crying and original attitude. On the other hand, among those who were strongly against Kennedy and who remained so, there is a significant drop in percent crying. Only 12% of these cried, compared with 26% of the total original strongly anti-Kennedy group. Here it could be argued that the fact of crying *per se* helped change the strongly negative attitude or that among those strongly against, those who were most strongly against did not cry for this reason. It should be remembered that the particular occasion which evoked crying was often a surprise to the individual and was not often "political" in nature. Very frequently it was the President's young son's salute to his deceased father, or his wife's courage which evoked tears, to the surprise and against the will of the individual so seized. It is clear, however, that the most significant relationship between the distress response and the general attitude is to be found at the two ends of the scale—among those who are most strongly pro and among those who are most strongly against, and who will not change.

It is also clear that the verbal statement of moving in a direction strongly pro, or indeed to any new position, means something less than holding the position originally if we employ the percent who cried as a criterion. In each case the percent who cried who changed *to* a position was less than the percent who cried who were originally in that position, whether *they* changed or not. Thus, among those who moved to a strong pro position 31% cried whereas 57% of those originally strong pro cried. Among those who changed to a weak pro position, 9% cried compared with 30% of all who were originally weak pro, and compared with 33% who were weak pro who remained weak pro after the assassination. Among those who moved to a position of weak against there were 20% who cried compared with 30% of all who were originally weak against, and compared with 33% of those who remained weak against. None changed to strongly against, and the indifferent category appears again to have different properties, and involves numbers too small to treat statistically. However, of all seven of those who were originally indifferent, none cried, whereas the one student who changed to the indifferent category (from an originally strong against) did report tears, thus accounting for the 100% in the third column. On the other hand, if those who move to a more favorable position do not cry as often as those who originally held that position, they sometimes cry more than those who do not change their original position. Thus only 12% of those who remained strongly against Kennedy cried, compared to 26% of the total group who originally were strongly against. This may be interpreted as enjoining caution not only against overevaluating the pro feelings of those who say they became more positive, but also against overevaluating the hostility of those who say they are strongly against a man or an ideology. They would appear to include some who are die-hards and some who can be moved, emotionally, to soften their opposition, even though they do not become as strongly pro as were those who originally held that position.

In general it would appear that verbal statements of moving to more positive affect toward the victim of violence must be interpreted as falling somewhat short of the significance of the same position affirmed in the more neutral state. It would also appear that the inclusion of measures of affect in public opinion polls might add considerable sensitivity to the verbally expressed beliefs which are polled.

Let us now examine the relationship between the percent who cried and the response to the question whether the assassination left a "bad taste" or a "bad smell."

Bad Smell or Bad Taste

In response to the question "If you had to describe the total experience as one which smelled bad or as one which left a bad taste—which would it be?" 85% (112) responded "taste"; 9% (12) "smell"; 5% (7) "neither"; 1% (1) "both." This item is an indirect indicator of the left and right wing ideological posture (see Chapter III), and these results are consistent with the total test scores on these same students, which reveals that this particular group of Princeton undergraduates was the most left wing group tested by this procedure during the past several years. It should be understood that this score is not necessarily identical with a left wing political posture, since it includes a wide spectrum of ideological beliefs, ranging from beliefs about the nature of beauty, the value of the individual, attitudes toward play, toward feelings, toward children and so on.

Although the majority do not cry, there is a significant increase in not crying among the "smellers." Of those few who say the assassination leaves a bad smell, 90% (10) do not cry and 10% (1) do whereas of those who say the assassination leaves a bad taste 62% do not cry and 38% do. Since 90% of the sample are tasters it is not surprising that the percentage who cry and do not cry among them (62% and 38%) is not different from the percentage of the total sample (63% and 36%), but the percentage among the "smellers" is significantly different from the latter. The more rejecting attitude of contempt, associated with bad smells, is significantly associated with an increased percentage in not crying (90%) compared with the total sample percentage of 63%, and compared with 62% crying among the "tasters." These results are consistent with the theory presented in Chapter III that a right wing attitude is generated by a contemptuous punitive socialization of distress which minimizes the distress response in the right wing individual, and that the left wing posture is generated by a rewarding socialization of distress which results in increased sympathy either for self or for the other if either is distressed, and that the experience of distress either in the self or the other is rewarding through an increase in sympathetic intimacy between the self and the other. The model for such increased intimacy is the sympathetic parent who responds to the child's distress with loving concern rather than with contempt.

Analysis of Free Responses

An analysis of the free responses describing the general impact of the assassination revealed that those who described themselves as experiencing distress (compared with those who did not) had significantly fewer references to disbelief, defensive reactions and to denial reactions (31 no DDD to 9 references to DDD for those who mention distress, compared with 51 no DDD to 41 references to disbelief, defensive reactions or to denial for those who made no mention of distress in their free responses). It is not surprising that those who experienced no sorrow should attempt to defend against or deny sorrow.

A more interesting finding was that those who expressed distress were less likely to be concerned with the political and social consequences of the assassination. Those who mention their distress refer to political and social consequences in 3 instances and fail to do so in 37 cases, compared with those who mention no distress who refer to political and social consequences in 27 cases and fail to do so in 65 cases.

Further, those who experienced no affect, or delayed affect, were less likely to experience distress—19 instances of no distress to 2 instances of distress, compared with 73 instances of no distress to 38 instances of distress for those who did not experience delayed or little affect.

The significance of the relationship between distress and the awareness of the political and social consequences of the assassination is further illuminated by an examination of the affects which did accompany such references.

Reference to political and social consequences was significantly related, first, to the affect of surprise and, second, to the reference to feeling "numb and empty." Those who were surprised referred to political and social consequences in 23 cases, and made no reference in 52 cases, compared with those who made no mention of surprise, who referred to political and social consequences in 7 cases, and made no reference in 50 cases. The majority did not refer to political and social consequences, but those who did were also those who experienced surprise at the assassination and also numbness and emptiness. In the latter case it was 11 cases in which there were references to political and social consequences and 18 cases of no such reference, compared to 19 versus 84 for those who did not feel numb or empty.

It might be supposed from the negative correlation between distress and the mention of political and social consequences and the positive correlation between surprise and numbness and emptiness and the mention of political and social consequences, that we are dealing with the personal-impersonal dimension. Such is not the case. Surprise as well as numbness and emptiness are significantly related to a preponderance of personal over no personal references. In the case of surprise there are 33 cases of personal reference to 42 cases of no personal reference, compared with 6 cases of personal reference to 51 cases of no personal reference for those who mention no surprise.

In the case of numbness, emptiness there are 19 cases of personal reference to 10 cases of no personal reference, compared to 20 cases of personal reference to 83 cases of no personal references for those who mention no numbness, emptiness.

As might have been expected in light of these findings, there is also a significant relationship between the experience of surprise and numbness, emptiness. In the case of those who experienced surprise there were 23 cases of reference to numbness, emptiness and 52 cases of no reference, compared with 6 cases of reference to numbness, emptiness to 51 cases of no numbness, emptiness for those who mentioned no surprise.

There were in addition two other affects significantly related to surprise, but not to numbness, nor to distress. These were excitement and shame.

What shall we make of these unpredicted findings? The failure of distress to be related to "personal" references, and the correlation of these latter with surprise, numbness, and the correlation of excitement and shame with surprise first of all suggests that there is a significant relationship between the affects evoked by uncertainty (surprise and excitement) and a concern for *both* personal and remote social and political consequences (which latter also evoked shame). The numbness and emptiness, which is also associated with surprise and with personal references, suggest too that it is the destruction of a social frame of reference through sudden uncertainty which is creating shame, surprise, excitement and emptiness. In sharp contrast the distress response appears to constrict the ideation of the individual, but to be as antithetic to "emptiness" as to uncertainty and concern for the remote social and political consequences of the assassination. Grief here would appear to exclude both competing affects and competing ideation. There is a suggestion in an investigation of subjects who were tested at this time by Samuel Messick (*see* Chapter IV) that under exposure to the assassination, the earlier born showed a specific deficit in the embedded figures tests, whereas the later born showed a specific deficit in the Street Gestalt test. The latter involves passive closure, and such a deficit might result from an attempt to defend against excessive distress, from an unwillingness to immerse the self in grief. It will be remembered that distress was significantly related in our sample to the absence of disbelief, defense and denial. In the case of the first-born, on the other hand, if we assume that the rewarding socialization of distress has made passive immersion in grief a not completely negative experience, then a disability with a test such as the embedded figures test (which yields a strong field dependence score) would be the outcome of an unwillingness and an inability to take an active attitude toward distracting, extraneous information. In our descriptions it would, analogously, result in a failure to be interested in and a failure to refer to remote political and social consequences, and a reduction in the affects evoked by uncertainty (surprise and excitement) on the one hand, and in the affect evoked by identification with the welfare of the country (shame at the fact of assassination as a reflection on our country). We unfortunately do not have data on the birth order of our subjects, but the differential effect of induced distress on the cognitive functioning of subjects who differ in birth order, and in ideology, would appear to be a promising area for investigation.

The next major analysis of the data was in connection with the phenomenon of disbelief. As was apparent in the sample descriptions it was very difficult for the great majority of students to believe that the President had in fact been assassinated. In the national poll of Sheatsley and Feldman (1964) a great many volunteered the response "I couldn't believe that he was dead." "We thought it must be a joke." They also quote a Texas poll which asked, "What was your first reaction to the news of the President's assassination?" "Disbelief" and "shock" were each mentioned by 42% of the state-wide sample; 16% answered "sorrow, tears," and no other single emotion was given as first reaction by more than 10%. In a poll by Banta (1964) he reports that only 23% believed exactly what they heard, 57% were somewhat doubtful or believed only part of what they heard and 20% were completely doubtful.

In our sample 83% disbelieved the news and 23% accepted it. The reaction of disbelief is of course extremely common in mourning, and is usually more frequent in the early stages of mourning than in the later stages. We were interested in testing the hypothesis that the experience of unreality is proportional to the centrality of the loss, and the corollary that the period of time during which the individual is vulnerable to instrusions of the feeling of strangeness and unreality is proportional to the density of his original positive affect investment in the object lost. This hypothesis is based on the assumption that in grief the continuing retrieval of past information about the deceased produces surprise and the feeling of unreality each time such information is retrieved and compared with present information, as in the continuing aftereffects on land of a long voyage on board a ship. In both cases retrieval of information from the past continues to provide the imagery for the interpretation of new information, producing unsteadiness in one case, and surprise, feeling of unreality and distress in the other. As in the case of "sea-legs," the aftereffect should be proportional to the density of the former experience.

Sea legs wear off therefore much more quickly than do phantom limbs in the case of amputees.

First we examined the general relationship between the distress response and the duration of experiences of unreality and disbelief. There was no systematic relationship between distress crying and the duration of disbelief, but when we examine those who had strong pro feelings *and* who wept with those who had strong con feelings and who did *not* cry, there is a significant difference in the number of the latter who believed it immediately, when the comparison is made with the former group, and

Table 5 Percentage of total sample, and of those strongly pro and strongly con, who accepted the announcement immediately and those who did not

	Percent who did not believe announcement immediately	Percent who believed the announcement immediately
Strongly pro who cried	95	5
Total sample	83	17
Strongly against who did not cry	29	71

with the total sample. If one felt very strongly against Kennedy *and* did not cry then he was much more likely to believe upon first hearing the news, that Kennedy had indeed been assassinated. (*See* Table 5).

Banta's (1964) data is consistent with ours in showing that disbelief increased in proportion to the wish to believe. Thus the percent reporting complete belief for those not of voting age was 33%, for Republicans was 28%, for Independents was 14%, and for Democrats was 13%.

Next we examined the general relationship between the strength of belief and the duration of the period during which intrusions of feelings of unreality were experienced. The following report by a student who was originally strongly pro and who remained so is typical of this phenomenon.

> When I heard of the assassination, I, at first reacted with shock and disbelief. I then sat down in front of the television set and didn't move for the rest of the day except to eat. I really couldn't believe that something like this could happen. This was just something that happened in history, not now. I, of course, had hope that he would live, but when the announcement of his death came chills ran all through me followed by a sort of void feeling which really hasn't left yet. I felt very sad but not enough to cry. As a matter of fact, I still really can't believe that it's true. Every time I saw the casket a funny feeling came to me and every few minutes or so I would say to myself "That's Pres. Kennedy in there," with really a feeling of disbelief. It still doesn't seem right to me to hear Mr. Johnson referred to as President Johnson.

If we examine those cases in which disbelief and feelings of unreality were very brief and compare them with those who experienced such feelings for more than one day, we find that there is a significant difference only between those who were originally strongly pro-Kennedy and who did not change and all of the rest of those who did not change, no matter what their original position.

In Table 6, it will be noted that there is no difference between being

Table 6 Percentage of those with prolonged feelings of unreality over brief feelings of unreality

	Strong pro	Weak pro	Weak con	Strong con	Indifferent
Held the original position	59	20	20	20	0
Moved to the position	59	71	0	–	0

weakly pro or weakly against or even strongly against with respect to enduring feelings of unreality if there had been no change in these attitudes after the assassination. For those who remained in these positions such feelings were short-lived in contrast to those who were strongly pro-Kennedy (and therefore who could not change by our scoring procedure—but who sometimes did indicate that their feelings became more strongly pro-Kennedy). This latter is relevant because of the marked prolongation of such feelings for all of those who moved to *any* positive position, no matter what their original position. The significance of these findings is not altogether clear. We would interpret them to mean that one will be vulnerable to intrusions of feelings of unreality *either* if the original affect was very strong, or if one's affect has *become* strong in the situation (which we assume is concomitant with any change to a more positive position). These findings are in contrast to the findings on distress, where a move *to* a more pro position was accompanied by less crying than if one had originally held it (though accompanied by more crying than if one had remained in the original position). We would suggest that the evocation of strong non-distress affect (such as the syndrome of surprise, excitement, numbness, and shame) towards violence and uncertainty generally affects the cognitive frame of reference more than does the evocation of distress. On the other hand, feelings of unreality which are both cognitive and affective may be evoked, we are suggesting, *either* by distress or by strong non-distress affect. We have noted before that those who were strongly pro *and* who cried, suffered more feelings of unreality than those who were against *and* who did not cry. There is no general relationship between either distress and feelings of unreality, or between strength of feelings pro and con and feelings of unreality. But those who felt most strongly toward Kennedy did cry more and therefore had longer feelings of unreality, and those who felt strongly because they had changed to a positive attitude toward Kennedy (and who were concerned more, as we have seen, with the political and social consequences of the assassination) also had longer feelings of unreality.

SUMMARY

In summary, the major hypothesis was confirmed. Over half (57%) of our sample changed their attitudes, becoming more pro-Kennedy than they were before his assassination. Our second hypothesis was partly confirmed. The *magnitude* of shifts toward strong pro-Kennedy attitudes increased with the initial strength of pro-Kennedy attitudes. The *frequency* of shifts away from initial positions did *not* differ, however, as a function of the original positions. No matter what one's original position, over half of these attitudes shifted toward some more positive view. The indifferent category provided a special case. Only one individual remained indifferent (out of 6) and only one individual (out of a possible 126) changed to an attitude of indifference.

We also found among a few of those most hostile to Kennedy some guilt for not sharing in the generally expressed sorrow, and some defensive flaunting behavior calculated to demonstrate the absence of grief.

Further we found that the low 36% of the sample who did not cry could be accounted for in terms of the strength of their original attitudes towards Kennedy. Among those who were originally, and who remained, strongly pro-Kennedy, 57% cried, which was not too different from the percent reported in national samples among those who were pro-Kennedy. It also appeared that movements toward a more favorable position was consistently accompanied by a lower percent crying than among those who originally held that position.

Again we found that there was a significant reduction in the percent crying among those who thought the assassination left a bad smell rather than a bad taste. This is an indirect measure of the right wing ideological posture and this result is consistent with the theory presented in Chapter III.

We also found an unexpected relationship between the reference to distress (in the free responses describing the impact of the assassination) and an absence of reference to political and social consequences of the assassination. This latter was, however, correlated with the affects of surprise and numbness, emptiness; in turn, these latter affects were correlated with mention of "personal" references. Surprise and numbness were also correlated, and surprise was further correlated with shame and with excitement. We interpreted this, very tentatively, to indicate that distress excluded both ideation and the competing affects of uncertainty (excitement, surprise) and of shame. The latter we attributed to concern about the welfare of the country. We suggested that those who were concerned with uncertainty often felt numb and empty because their external social frame of reference had been seriously undermined by the assassination in comparison with those who immersed themselves and luxuriated in the communality of a nation in mourning. We related the latter posture to a rewarding distress socialization, and the former to a punitive distress socialization.

Next we examined the phenomenon of disbelief and the experience of unreality of the death of the President. On first hearing the announcement, 83% of the total sample did not believe it. Among those most strongly pro, (who also cried) this percentage was 95, and among those most strongly con (who also did not cry) this percentage was 29.

We found no general relationship between the duration of the time after the assassination during which the individual experienced feelings of unreality and either distress or strength of attitude. However, there appeared to be two independent bases for such a vulnerability. One was the intense distress of those most strongly pro-Kennedy. Compared with all others who maintained their original position, there was a significant increase in the percentage of those who were originally strongly pro-Kennedy who reported enduring feelings of unreality lasting more than a day. There was an equally great increase in such vulnerability in all of those who changed to a positive feeling toward Kennedy (whether strong pro or weak pro) no matter what their original position. It appeared that changing in the direction of positive feelings increased the feelings of unreality as much as for those whose original pro-Kennedy feelings induced severe distress.

REFERENCES

Banta, T. The Kennedy assassination: early thoughts and emotions. *Publ. Opin. Quart.*, 1964, 28, 216-226.
Sheatsley, P. B., & Feldman, J. B. The Kennedy assassination: early thoughts and emotions. *Publ. Opin. Quart.*, 1964, 28, 189-215.
Tomkins, S. S. The psychology of knowledge, this volume, chapter III.

PART FOUR

AFFECT AND
PERSONALITY CHANGE

VII Personal growth through group experience

Carroll E. Izard

The purpose of this chapter is to describe an ongoing research program on constructive change in normal personalities through group experience. We have not done formal experimentation with the groups as of this writing but we are collecting considerable data, including tape recordings of all the group sessions. This project, housed at the University Counseling Center, has a three-fold aim: (1) to offer a unique personal growth experience to college students, (2) to give graduate students in clinical psychology an opportunity to obtain experience as co-leaders in behavior effectiveness groups, and (3) to enable us to study constructive personality change and personal growth as this occurs in normal young adults through group experience. All three of these aims are important to us and they are listed in the order in which they were given priority in our program planning.

RECRUITING GROUP MEMBERS

The author visited several psychology classes and extended an invitation to students to participate in the groups. The invitation went like this:

> The principal goal of this group program is to facilitate personal growth and self-actualization. We think that some of the things that will facilitate this process will include learning more about yourself, how you really see and feel about yourself, how other people see you, and learning more about relating to other people. We do not consider this program as psychotherapy for maladjusted people. We feel that all of you fall within the normal range, but we are convinced that all normal people are capable of growth and change. We want to emphasize that the primary goal of this service is to help you become a more fully functioning person. At the same time, we want you to know that we will ask something of you in return, i.e., to

The works of G. W. Allport (1961), Gardner Murphy (1958), A. H. Maslow (1954), Arthur W. Combs and Donald Snygg (1959) were instrumental in the conception and implementation of this program, though I hasten to exempt them from any responsibility for my specific formulations. I am especially grateful to Art Combs who helped me experience *personal growth* in a graduate student group ("class" on dynamics of individual behavior) which, without him, would have settled for intellectual gains.

The research reported in this chapter was supported by Vanderbilt-ONR Contract Nonr 2149 (03), Carroll E. Izard, Principal Investigator. The opinions and conclusions do not necessarily reflect those of the United States Department of the Navy.

permit the groups to serve two other functions, a training and a research function. The training aspect will involve having a doctoral student in clinical psychology work with a staff psychologist as a co-leader. The research aspect may involve your taking some tests before and after the group sessions in order to help us understand and communicate more about how normal personalities grow and become more effective in their individual and interpersonal functioning.

During the first year of this program five groups were established. Three began in the fall semester and, of these three, one group continued intact through the second semester. The other two groups, partly because of schedule difficulties and partly because some members felt that the group had served its function for them, were reorganized with additional members who joined them at mid-year. Two new groups started in the second semester. Altogether, five groups participated for either a semester or a full year during the first year of the program. Seven new groups are in process this year. Several individuals who were group members last year, including two who were in the year-long group, returned to participate in the program this year. One member of that group entered graduate school and is now participating as a co-leader.

In this report I shall state the philosophy and principles underlying our behavior effectiveness program. I shall focus primarily on the role of the group leader, though much of what I say applies to the individual member or to effective group participation in general.

My theorizing consists for the most part in an effort to abstract principles and constructs from my direct experience with individual members and groups in the process of change. Naturally, there is the inevitable admixture of my own personality, values, and interests. The inevitability of this admixture of theory and commitment is all the more obvious in view of the fact that my personality, values, and interests were integral to my participation in the groups. Hopefully, our empirical research will add the necessary corrective to both the personality and the theory.

The data we shall present in this chapter are phenomenological in nature. We shall present the group experience directly, insofar as this can be accomplished, with excerpts from the tape-recorded sessions. We shall give a brief summary of the members' post-program evaluation reports. One member's reflections on the group sessions, together with her reaction report four months after the last meeting, will be presented in full. The last type of data is of a somewhat different order. Three members of the group who continued throughout the academic year were paid to listen and respond, ad lib, to all the tape recorded sessions of their group. This was done in the summer after the group's last meeting in May.

PHILOSOPHY AND PRINCIPLES OF THE
BEHAVIOR EFFECTIVENESS PROGRAM

The group program was begun under the assumptions that many normal people (1) are capable of becoming more fully functioning personalities, (2) desire such growth and change, and (3) will effect such development under the appropriate conditions. Inherent in these assumptions is a significant challenge to psychology. The challenge is to find the conditions under which normal people will move effectively and efficiently toward self-actualization; more specifically in relation to our program, to find what psychologists can contribute to this group experience. A still more demanding challenge is the development of an adequate theory of effective personal growth. Little enough has been done to study and understand the characteristics of structure of self-actualization (Maslow, 1954); even less has been done to explicate the process whereby normal individuals effect creative growth and change. We are not prepared to offer a definitive answer to these questions, but we are eager to continue our search. At this point we would like to set forth some of the notions which guided us in our effort to make a first approximation of the conditions which would facilitate normal personality growth and change.

Leaders and Members Participate as Persons

The most important concept in our orientation is that leaders and members must come to appreciate each other as integral human beings and not as language majors or engineering students or professors or psychologists—as open, fluid, complex, dynamic systems (persons) in process of change, not as static units in fixed relationship. Arriving at this new kind of appreciation of others requires a great deal of learning and a great deal of unlearning. For example, the average college student has to unlearn a great number of things that he does almost automatically: he brings with him to the group a host of feelings, attitudinal sets, and expectancies in relation to anyone who occupies the role of leader; he has specific sets and expectations for professors and still more specific sets and expectations regarding professors of psychology or practicing clinical pychologists. The student sees himself in a number of roles and in his early hours in the group he will behave in terms of one or more of these roles. The sets and expectancies which the participant uses in perceiving and interpreting the leader or another member we term role projection. The sets and expectancies which the individual uses in regulating his own perceptions, feelings, and responses we call role assumption.

Role projection and role assumption are in large measure automatic behaviors. As a consequence, it may be necessary for the group to confront itself directly with the problems inherent in role assumption and role projection. The most pervasive problem with which the group is confronted is that such behaviors can greatly inhibit full self-expression and communication among people at a deeper level than is customary when behavior is principally role-determined.

Leader Functions and Responsibilities

I draw a distinction between leader "roles" on the one hand and leader functions and responsibilities on the other. We have just pointed out the complex problems involved in role assumption and role projection. It is our conviction that the leader's functions are as yet very incompletely understood and in much need of clarification. Of one thing we feel certain: in describing the leader's participation we are not prescribing a role for him. This is true because we feel that the "role" (principal function, responsibility) of the leader is *being himself*, i.e., that of being the real person that he is.

I have perhaps stated the case in idealized form. It may well prove impossible for any group leader to claim exemption from role assumption and behave consistently in the presence of students or others without some of the almost automatic behaviors that characterize him in his role as professor or psychologist or psychotherapist. We are not completely convinced that role assumption is always ineffective or non-beneficial for the group. But if one must assume a role it would be beneficial for him to have full awareness of the vantage point from which he is operating, whether in the role of expert, authority figure, or therapist. At any rate, the leader must make himself available to other members as another human being. He must not only be willing, but perhaps at first even adamant, to expose his human frailties. It is expected that his strength as a human being will have every opportunity to emerge and will be more readily perceived than will his errors and weaknesses.

In considering the responsibilities of the leader in a group designed to facilitate interpersonal growth we must first consider that the leader's responsibility can be only as great as his self and his capacity for experiencing and responding permit. The leader cannot be responsible for exhibiting interpersonal warmth and empathic powers that he does not possess.

We believe that effective leadership does require the assumption of certain responsibilities and, of course, the inherent capacity to discharge these responsibilities. It is easy to agree with Rogers on the therapeutic value of positive regard, empathy, and congruence (Rogers, 1959a), but we feel that these concepts as they have been defined by Rogers are more appropriate in individual psychotherapy with neurotics than they are in facilitating personal growth of normal individuals through group experience. Although, in the kind of group experience we are describing, we feel that the presence of these qualities in a leader is growth facilitating, we do not feel that these qualities should be conceived as limiting the scope of leader behaviors in the behavior effectiveness group. This is in keeping with our belief that the leader must act on his own feelings and experience as a person, not taking refuge in procedure or technique or by swearing allegiance to theory or constructs that have symbolic meaning solely in his own realm of experiencing.

There has always been a great deal of concern over the functions and responsibilities of any individual placed in a position where he is expected to influence some change in another's personality or behavior. There has been a great deal of discussion of the responsibility of the psychotherapist in individual or group psychotherapy. There has been a great deal of research and theorizing on the role of leaders in society, business, and politics. I feel that to a large extent the whole problem of defining leader responsibility has been approached from the wrong side. Typically, responsibility has been defined only after the role of the leader and the mission of the group has been detailed. This in essence makes responsibility a *de facto* function of a number of more or less incidental and arbitrary "structural" factors external to the person of the leader. This approach makes the responsibility of the leader a function of:

1. Role assumption: the role or roles which the leader assumes not by virtue of his stature as a person but by virtue of his position, his status, and his authority.

2. Role projection: the role or roles which the members of the group project onto the leader as a function of their expectations, not of him as a person but of the position, status, and authority which accrue to the "leader."

3. Norms and values: the norms and values which individuals bring to the group as part of their socio-cultural heritage or which the group adopts to serve its immediate and long-range goals.

Certain roles, norms, and values which facilitate effective leadership for a given group may be indigenous to the leader's personality. In this case these categories of behavior may be both appropriate and effective. However, those leader behaviors which are a function of roles, norms, and values which are not indigenous to the leader's personality—not a real part of him as a person—will inhibit rather than facilitate his effectiveness in the group. For example, if a leader's behavior is a function of his "position," "authority," or "superior education," he is not functioning simply as the person he is, and is to this extent ineffective. To the degree to which the leader's behavior is a function of any of these status symbols, he is inhibiting his own competence as a responsive human being.

We are certainly not saying that a person's education as a psychologist has no place in the leadership functions in a therapy or in a behavior effectiveness group. On the contrary, we feel that those aspects of his education which have become a part of him and which are well integrated into his personality should be beneficial. To the extent that his education as a psychologist has made him a more trenchant observer of people, more appreciative of individual differences, more empathic, and more effective in communicating his understanding of another, his education and related experience will be helpful. On the other hand, education as a psychologist (or sociologist or psychiatrist or social worker) can be a definite hindrance if such education results in his adopting a system of "oughts" and "procedures" through which his personality remains comfortably or uncomfortably hidden.

What holds for roles, norms, and values holds equally for our favorite procedures and constructs. Let's assume for the moment that our most preferred theoretical framework is described as phenomenological, client centered, existential. Acceptance, reflection of feeling, unconditional posi-

tive regard, empathy, and congruence may be natural, genuine characteristics of the psychotherapist or group leader working within this
theoretical framework. On the other hand, they may influence the psychotherapist or group leader as a set of external rules, regulations, or
status symbols and result in a sterile and stifling system of "rules" and
"techniques."

In fine, the leader *emerges* as *leader*, if he does, by being more open to
experience and change, more courageous in accepting and responding
to his own and others' positive *and* negative affects, more proficient in
demonstrating empathic understanding, more effective in evoking expression of feeling and in the deepening of commitment to each other
and the group, and more proficient in integrating affect and cognition in
creative activity.

I would like to further examine some of Rogers' therapy concepts in
relation to our thinking on behavior effectiveness groups.

On Positive Regard

I am quite conscious of the fact that I tend to respond favorably to
another person when I know that he holds me in high regard. At the same
time, I am keenly conscious of the fact that when I meet another person
for the first time I have no right to expect him to hold me (a stranger) in
high regard on first encounter. I am confident that most people subscribe
to and behave in terms of these propositions—whether they be patients,
clients, or social acquaintances.

In a behavior effectiveness group I feel the leader needs to convey
something of the following attitude or set:

> I want to get to know you as a person and I am confident that I will come
> to like you if we can share experiences and get to know each other well.
> My experience has taught me that mutual sharing of personal perceptions
> and feelings generally leads to deep and meaningful relationships between
> people. Yet, in this first meeting, or in these early meetings, we must
> realize that we are human and we are imperfect. The positive regard I have
> for you now is based only partly on my impressions of you and partly on
> my attitudes and feelings toward people in general. Positive regard for the
> unique *you* must await the unfolding of the real *you*. I cannot actually like
> you as a person until I know you as a person—the real you.

This modification of the Rogerian concept of positive regard is intended
to add two dimensions to the construct as Rogers has defined it. First, we
are adding a dimension of social reality. We believe that the construct of
positive regard as Rogers defined it is an idealistic statement of a goal for
a psychotherapist conducting therapy with emotionally disturbed (typically affect-deprived) individuals. We do not feel that normal individuals
in a group experience either particularly need or desire immediate and
unfailing expression of positive regard. In fact, we feel that the delivery
of "unearned positive regard" may inhibit the development of the kind

of atmosphere that we feel is optimal for personal growth of normal individuals through group experience. We believe that the experienced service-oriented clinical psychologist may come to like and esteem other people more readily than most individuals. Yet we must function as persons in all spheres and this holds for leaders and members alike.

Second, we are adding to the Rogerian construct a dimension of challenge—a challenge to each participant (leader and member) to be himself, to be the person that he really is, to express himself and respond on the basis of his own perceptions and feelings, because it is on this basis that people grow, that relationships between people deepen, and that veridical and mutual positive regard is established. This, then, is a challenge to each person to abandon defenses, façades, and superficial roles.

On the Unconditionality of Positive Regard

Here, too, the structure and dynamics of social intercourse place some limits on a Rogerian construct. Again, the construct as Rogers has defined it is an idealistic notion that seems to me to be a concept that could exert undue restrictions on the behavior of a psychotherapist, group leader, or on anyone who felt the compulsion to comply. Is it humanly possible to continually and everlastingly express unconditional positive regard for another person? My own experience says "no" to this question. The person whom I hold in highest regard may offend me so mightily that the best I can do at a given (hopefully rare) moment is to say, "I love you, but right now I hate your guts."

In the behavior effectiveness group, I believe I would be unable to abide by the fundamental rule of behaving as the person that I am if I felt it necessary to continually hold anyone in the group in constant unconditional positive regard. For example, I believe that if a member can tolerate an expression of my hostility, this might well speed up the development of a deeper and more meaningful relationship. If I know that I can be hostile or anxious in his presence and not hurt him too badly or be hurt too badly by him, my *trust* and *respect* for him will certainly increase.

On Empathic Understanding and Its Communication

Anyone who has experienced a deep and meaningful relationship with another person knows that an essential ingredient of such a relationship is the capacity for empathy and the ability to communicate empathic understanding. I believe all psychotherapists would agree that empathy is therapeutic. Yet I believe that blind determination to be continually empathic is not the optimal operating condition in a behavior effectiveness group for normal individuals (I wonder if it is in individual or group psychotherapy or in any interpersonal relationship). I believe there are other principles and considerations that should guide our behavior in such a situation. I believe the leader's personality and behavior should communicate something of the following:

> I am deeply interested in you and your personal world, in coming as close as I can to perceiving and feeling as you do. Insofar as I succeed I can become a real part of your world, real to you so I can interact and communicate meaningfully with you. Yet I will not emerge in our relationship as a separate human being if all I do is attempt to perceive and feel as you do. *This does not mean that I want to make you over in my own image.* It does not mean that I want you to perceive and feel and value as I do. I value separateness and individuality for *you* and for *me*. Remember that my highest value in relation to people is that a person be capable himself of functioning as a separate and integral human being on the basis of his own perceptions and feelings.

On Congruence

In the concept of congruence Rogers has come closest to establishing the framework for the kind of interpersonal relating that we feel is necessary for optimal personal growth in normal personalities through group experience. Rogers conceives of congruence as the "growing edge" of his theory of psychotherapy and as such its definition and implications for the therapist's behavior are not highly structured.

To be congruent the therapist must be genuine and real in his relationship with the client. The therapist's symbolization of his own experience during the process of therapy must be accurate. If a therapist is aware only of acceptance and understanding but at a deeper level is actually experiencing anxiety or hostility he is not congruent in the relationship. The therapist must be able to symbolize both positive and negative feelings and experiences. In Rogers' (1959) last published statement of his theoretical formulation he was still struggling with the question whether the therapist should communicate to the client the accurate symbolization of his experience. Rogers stated that the therapist must express negative feelings if he finds himself so persistently focused on these feelings that his effectiveness in empathizing and expressing unconditional positive regard are greatly reduced. However, this was put forth with considerable tentativeness and Rogers summed up his position as follows:

> "Again the final answer is unknown, but a conservative answer, the one we have embodied in the theory, is that for therapy to occur the wholeness of the therapist in the relationship is primary, but a part of the congruence of the therapist must be the experience of unconditional positive regard and the experience of empathic understanding (Rogers, 1959, p. 215)."

Thus, in effect, Rogers is placing unconditional positive regard and empathic understanding as limitations on the application of the principle of congruence. By virtue of this the psychotherapist is cast into a *role*—one in which positive regard and empathic understanding are uppermost —and he is thereby restricted in his functioning as a person. He is restricted in the communication of his own feelings and experiences if these run counter to the continual expression of unconditional positive regard and empathic understanding. This may be necessary in the treatment of individuals who are themselves typically "in a state of incongruence, being vulnerable or anxious" (Rogers, 1959, p. 213). The client must be in such a state in order to meet one of Rogers' conditions of the therapeutic process. It is not strange that a sensitive therapist's keen awareness of such distress in his client would lead him to place unconditional positive regard and empathy ahead of congruence. We are not sure that this hierarchy of therapeutic principles leads to the most efficient and effective therapist-client interactions. We believe that the leader in personal growth groups for normal personalities must abandon allegiance to any fixed theory or set of principles that restrict his own personality, keep him from being the person he is.

Congruence, Confrontation, and Challenge— Integrating Affect, Cognition, and Action

We feel that the concept of congruence taken to its logical conclusion— free and open expression of perceptions, feelings, and experiences—is what is required for the development of an optimal atmosphere for change in normal personalities. Here again we think we have added an element of challenge for both leader and participant. A part of this challenge is to increase one's tolerance for the imperfections of another human being and thus to permit the wholeness of the other person to emerge and to differentiate and clarify itself.

I think that H. H. Anderson's definition of confrontation greatly enriches our understanding of the kind of interpersonal interaction that is needed for constructive change in normal personalities.

> "With the spermatozoon and the egg there is the confronting of differences. There is an interaction, or an activity-between. It is not sufficient to think, as we used to, that this confronting or activity-between represents a stimulus-response relating. Stimulus and response are terms that are too static, too slow, and too over-simplified to designate what is happening. By confronting we mean a process of relating in which the behavior or the presence of one organism makes a difference in the behavior of the other. Confronting requires another quality: it must represent a certain integrity, integerness or individuality in each organism. There is not only the fact of difference but an acting differently. The egg behaves, acts like an egg, and the spermatozoon behaves, acts like a spermatozoon. Each is biologically free to be itself. In the hypothesis that growth occurs only through the confronting and the free interplay of differences there is necessarily not only a concept of the integrity of differences, but also of action-between consistent with this biological integerness (Anderson, 1959, pp. 121-122)."

I feel that Anderson's hypothesis that "growth occurs only through the confronting and the free interplay of differences" is an excellent hypothesis that should be thoroughly tested in the operation of our therapeutic groups. It would appear that the application of the principle inherent in this hypothesis would call for a stronger statement of congruence than Rogers has embodied in his theory of psychotherapy. It would appear to confirm and support our notion that the leader in behavior effectiveness groups should operate as a fully functioning person responding openly and freely to his own feelings, perceptions, and experiences as a human being. Only in this way can all the differences among individuals in the group emerge.

Much of what we have done in describing the affects, attitudes, sets, and expectancies which characterize the effective leader apply as well to the effective group participant. It is also clear that leader behavior that follows Anderson's concept of confrontation must be integrated with our concepts of leader functions and responsibilities. A partial solution to this may be found in our notion that the feeling of responsibility for a person includes giving that person permission for self-expression, self-determination, and for achieving responsible independence and separateness. I believe, too, that for effective interaction, which results in personal growth, this kind of responsibility must not only be felt but expressed and demonstrated. How better can I express such responsibility for another person than to show him that I allow myself full self-expression, self-determination, and the right to maintain independence and separateness. From this, a new aspect of the leader's function or responsibility in the group emerges. The leader, in giving full expression to himself—his perceptions, his feelings, his experiences as a person in the group—may serve as a model and thus facilitate similar expression by the participants.

To sum up, let us say that a concept of *interpersonal difference confrontation* is emerging here. It assumes Rogerian congruence at the intrapersonal level and Andersonian confrontation at the interpersonal level. We believe that the kind of feelings and attitudes that the therapist must convey to implement this construct may be summed up like this:

> I must continue to be the person I am. I must communicate and interact with you from my personal world. Only in this way can I be real to you. I cannot deny or hide my feelings in relation to you and be myself, the real person-I-am. I am generally comfortable with and acceptant of my feelings but not always proud of them, that is, I do not always expect them to be appropriate or immediately growth inducing, or therapeutic in the conventional sense. Nevertheless, I want to be a constructive difference in your life and I want you to be a constructive difference in mine.

The Dynamics of Interpersonal Differences[1]

Psychologists of many orientations have paid homage to the ubiquity and importance of individual differences in explaining the variance of behavior, both predicted (desired effect) and unpredicted (undesired effect). I maintain that in a group whose central aim is personal growth or constructive behavior change, individual differences constitute a potent growth-inducing factor. It behooves the leader to make his *differences* immediately apparent and hence to encourage and challenge others to

[1] I know I have been influenced by the thinking of Jung (1954), Rank (1945), Johnson (1946), and Allen (1942).

express their differences. Hopefully, the leader will differ in some important growth-inducing ways, though any "healthy" differences that are free to interact are probably growth inducing *per se*.

The leader's role in facilitating expression and exploration of differences. The leader should make his differences apparent, but ideally he should not have to work at this by making conscious, deliberate responses which focus attention on differences. Such efforts may well be growth-inducing, but they may highlight the external, *objective,* or *structural* aspects of differences to the detriment of their dynamic interplay. Responses that deliberately focus attention on the external, objective features of a difference can slow down the activities which facilitate the free-wheeling confrontation of differences so necessary for the *process* of self-actualization.

Differences between one's self and another can be quite fascinating and preoccupying. Many individuals will examine and measure differences endlessly, sometimes to lay claim to a feeling of superiority and sometimes to show that the difference is trivial or even non-existent.

The interpersonal character of differences. The leader should understand that individual differences are interpersonal by nature. *Definition* of a difference by the leader (or any other individual) is necessarily incomplete. He can only give his view from his personal frame of reference. The meaning of interpersonal difference can be appreciated only through interaction of the individuals involved. Its value lies in the vigorous interplay of its divergent elements. Deliberate efforts to define a difference tend to degenerate into intellectualizing, a deadly enemy to growth-facilitating group experience.

The motivational quality of difference. Recognition of a significant interpersonal difference tends to instigate and/or amplify affects. This amplification of activity in the affect system is highly motivating. Direct affective and cognitive response to difference can lead to growth-inducing interpersonal interaction and confrontation. The studied, defining, analytic approach to (interpersonal) difference tends to stifle the affective response that needs expression. The more direct and spontaneous the individual's responses the more likely there will be movement toward integration of affect, cognition, and action.

Response to difference. Individuals (and groups) vary widely in their response to perceived difference. Some behave as though the difference is an obtruder, to be eliminated post-haste. Some members (probably rather few in number) welcome the difference and show some appreciation of its value. Some members make frequent and deliberate efforts to establish similarity between themselves and other members or within the group as a whole. Such persons seem to have a low tolerance for interpersonal difference. As a result they may: (1) fail to perceive differences, (2) perceive differences selectively, and/or (3) deny the importance of the difference. There is some evidence that need for similarity (real, perceived, or reputational) is a factor in friendship (Izard, 1960), yet there is convincing evidence that the role of similarity is sufficiently complex to raise the question as to whether *real* personality similarity is a factor in friendship between mature individuals—Izard (1963), Miller, Campbell, & Twedt (1964).

Differences, existence, and self-expression. We agree with G. W. Allport's (1961) emphasis on the vital importance of individuality and uniqueness in the psychology of personality: "That the individual is a system of patterned uniqueness is a fact" (p. 9) . . . and "Individuality is a prime characteristic of human nature" (p. 21). We feel that despite Allport's admirable championing of these critical concepts, their full significance for the science of psychology is rarely appreciated. They are even less understood and appreciated as factors in interpersonal relating.

I believe that individuality and uniqueness are key determinants of personal growth through interpersonal relating and group experience. A person's individuality is the very basis for his response to another person. It is mainly through significant interaction with others that the individual first differentiates the self that he is (his affects, cognitions) and then comes to appreciate the growth-enhancing power of differences between his self and that of others.

Accepting individuality and uniqueness as facts, we can conclude that the most effective way to maximize the confrontation and interplay of interpersonal differences is through individual self-expression. By self-expression, here, I mean an active (though not intellectualized) effort by the person to (1) discover or rediscover his affect system, (2) respond directly and immediately to his affects and to those of others, (3) further differentiate his affects, and (4) to work toward a more effective integration of affect, cognition, and action.

Once we really accept the facts of individuality and uniqueness, we can see clearly that the more the person exists and behaves as the person-he-is the more he will state and bring into play his difference from others.

The image problem. Allport (1961) has said that "the dilemma of uniqueness haunts the house of psychology" (p. 21). I believe that it haunts us as individuals and as a people. We are afraid of uniqueness in our science, so we build nomothetic nets to insure its exclusion. We are afraid of it as human beings, so we try to make every one alike. More perniciously, we try to make others over in our own image. Science's traditional search for universal laws has its parallel in the individual's search for a group (or society) where he belongs, a group that seems to demand a degree of uniformity or sameness as the price of admission. Having achieved membership (status as an individual, separate person), we strive consciously or unconsciously to make would-be members similar to us in all important ways. This is tied in with the fundamental paradox of man's *individual* and man's *social* nature. The person growing toward maturity values separateness, psychological freedom, and deep, meaningful relationships with others. A close relationship with another implies both mutual dependency and mutual responsibility, terms which typically evoke a mixture of positive and negative affects and cognitions. For example, we may want a particular person to depend on us but at the same time fear that he will become a burden, restricting our personal freedom.

One highly pervasive and ineffective "resolution" of the paradox is seen in man's attempt to make others over in his own image. This is the ultimate pseudo-solution to interpersonal difference. It enables a person to be himself without the risk of being different, separate. It enables man to falsely enjoy responsibility for another; if his ward is a responsive student he can expect to enjoy the safety of numbers: "There are and will be many like me."

We probably tend to perceive others as like ourselves when in fact they are different. This is particularly true in situations involving values of central importance to us. Such selective perception of sameness and intolerance for difference helps explain why a group (committee, staff, faculty) returns again and again to the same old problem, only to arrive at virtually the same old solution.

Sameness → Security; Difference → Originality. I want to make explicit a critical point that is implied in all that has been said in this section. The aim of interpersonal relating and group experience is *not* the resolution or compromise of differences. Rather, interpersonal interaction in the group should (1) clarify and sharpen differences, (2) encourage the emergence of new differences, and (3) maximize the creative growth that comes through the vigorous confrontation and interplay of differences. Perhaps we have a need to feel that we are like others in some rather basic ways, e.g., desire to share life and our experiences with others, to be reasonably comfortable most of the time, etc. From the satisfaction of this need there may come some elementary security and sense of well-being. But if this security becomes a goal or an *end* it will become the death-trap for individuality and creative living. Psychological security is effective only if it subserves the pursuit of individuality, an endeavor that will involve all the affects from distress and anxiety to excitement and joy. In order to enhance personal growth, group experience must facilitate the emergence and sharpening of interpersonal differences, for they are the basis of the person's uniqueness and his only hope for originality.

We would have far exceeded the limits of our vanity if we leave the impression that we have solved the great riddle that blocks personal growth and creative functioning. We do not expect the answer immediately, or the complete, final, nomothetic answer ever. Perhaps this is something each man in his own time must work out for himself. What better place to seek *personal* resolution to the paradox created by man's *individual* and *social* nature than a group where we place high value on *separateness-as-a-person* and *deep interpersonal relationships*. Perhaps in successful personal resolutions we can find some patterns that will encourage others to seek solution and maybe facilitate their effort.

Dialogues from the Group Sessions

The first type of data we shall present are excerpts from the tape recorded sessions of one of the groups. The material presented here was selected from a large pool of dialogue units established by taking four five-minute samples after 15, 30, 45, and 60 minutes of each of the twenty-six 90-minute sessions of the group. The large pool of units has the sanction of acceptable statistical sampling procedure; the selection from this pool of the specific dialogues given below was made on the basis of our judgment that they were illustrative of the personal growth process.

In the dialogues that follow, pseudonyms have been substituted for the real names of all participants; the leader and co-leader have been identified by the symbols L and CL, respectively. The letter following the session number designates the point in the meeting from which the dialogues were sampled. For example, the heading "Session 3-A" would indicate that the interactions reported were recorded during the five minutes following the first fifteen minutes of the third session; 3-B dialogues were obtained during the five minutes following the first half hour, 3-C refers to the third quarter hour; 3-D verbalizations were recorded at the end of the first hour.[2]

Session 2-B

Mitch: Well, I hope that you—one of the things that I'm afraid of, excuse me for dominating, is that I have an air of being intuitive and empathic. Yet I'm really not. And these things, you just can't cover up, I don't think. Either you really are and people know it or you're just not. I might just have an air . . . might be more pseudo-empathic than anything else and I'm afraid to look at myself and find out that that's right.

Sid (L): On the other hand, it seems to me that you have taken a rather close look at yourself and you're sort of responding and giving us some of the outcome of looking at yourself.

Mitch: Well, I hope so.

Bob (CL): I think an important point here is that what Mitch has just said was a little bit painful. I think that if we all realized that anytime we attempt to get underneath the role and really expose ourselves to anybody, it's going to be painful. And this is part of the learning we were talking about. We have to learn how to do this and when we all do it then we will feel a little more comfortable with it.

Henrietta: What good comes of exposing yourself?

Mitch: Well, like I felt I just grew a little bit. And, see, I feel a little creative . . . To myself, I feel like I've grown. I mean, when you grow it's creative, it seems to me. I don't know.

[2] Dale Johnson prepared the statistical sample for the original tapes. The dialogues for this chapter were selected from the larger sample by Robert M. Murphey, Opal Perdue, and Carroll E. Izard.

Sid (L): Can you extend that at all? Do you feel a little stronger?

Mitch: Well, here again . . . well, I get back to one of my fears—that here again I'm afraid that one of the things I might be doing is just, you know, saying "You're real close to me. You think you know something about me," and I cut it off right there or I, you know, that I might not be able to go past this first step. Do you see what I'm saying? That this is a front. It's no different from any other role, you know. That, yet I really do want to go further than that. And I think that one of the problems before was that we didn't have adequate leadership. (He is referring to a "sensitivity group" in which he participated at another university.) We did it on our own and you know there's such a point when you have to be shown by example and other ways, but, you wanted me to say about?

Sid (L): No, I was just going to check my own understanding here of you at this moment. What you're saying is that even with this looking at yourself and what you're telling us you're beginning to wonder yourself if you're still protecting yourself or something like that.

Mitch: Right, in other words, could this be just saying, "Aw, he told us everything, you know, so he's through now," I mean, uh, and here again I said that I'm afraid that I might appear warm, and I'm really trying to be, but you know, here again it's just another role and this is what was worrying me previously, that this might have been one of the reasons why that the group never really worked because it was no different from somebody else's role-playing, you know, that you're putting on a big act. So, one of the things that I really want to get out of the group is to grow—feel like I understand myself better, really get strong.

Bob (CL): This (general) question, I think, is an important one. I would ask you a (more specific) question in turn. Do you feel that it is of any value to gain a better understanding of yourself?

Henrietta: Well, I suppose it is. I don't quite understand what the value is, though. Except that you could control yourself better if you understood how you worked.

Carl: I think an existentialist would say consciousness subjugates. (Laughter from group)

Session 3-A

Bob (CL): Is it that somehow although you want to trust the other person, you just can't bring yourself to completely trust them with your feeling?

Henrietta: I don't think this has much to do with feeling. It may just be . . .

Bob (CL): I'm not sure what it does have to do with, then.

Carl: Maybe you're looking at a relationship and saying, "This is what I ought to get out of it and this is what I'm not getting out of it." No?

Henrietta: No.

Mitch: It's communication.

Henrietta: (Giggle)

Bob (CL): Yeah, but what are you trying to communicate if you're not trying to communicate feelings? This is a point that I'm hung up on. I'm not sure . . .

Mitch: Well, on the face of it, I think really it's—you don't have just an idea you want to get across—you really want—but you have to talk in terms of ideas to start off with and it just seems like that you end up in ideas and nothing else.

Henrietta: Or just plain trivial talk.

Mitch: In other words, you want to start off talking in ideas and then so they'll understand that you have a real feeling or emotion under it . . . but you get a bunch of ideas out and not really anything else. Is that it?

Henrietta: (Laugh) I don't know.

Mitch: Maybe I don't really understand.

Bob (CL): Well, from this I get the idea that everything is kept at a more superficial or trivial level.

Henrietta: Yes.

Bob (CL): And that any time you try to get a little deeper—whether it's feelings or what . . .

Henrietta: Except for the fact that we both would be aware that that was what was going on. I suppose that would be at a deeper level. Maybe if both people realized the problem.

Stephane: Have you ever talked about it?

Henrietta: Umm hmm.

Stephane: (Laugh) I didn't get this far in my situation.

Sid (L): This is real life, then, and it's current. Not history. Current event. Is there any way you can make it more explicit or—you said you would like a solution to it. I must admit I'm not quite with you yet.

Bob (CL): Perhaps in trying to give us a better understanding of the problem you will get a little better hold on it yourself. Because I think that's in a way what you're trying to get, isn't it? A little better grasp of just what is happening.

Henrietta: Yes, because I don't understand what it is.

Bob (CL): Maybe in trying to make us understand you'll understand a little better yourself.

Stephane: Well, all I know is that if we both are aware that we like each other and we both agree that we don't communicate—actually, I mean it's very superficial and trivial, I suppose.

Carl: Well, just exactly what don't you communicate?

Mitch: You don't communicate that you both like each other. I mean, you're aware of it but you can't enjoy that relationship.

Henrietta: I suppose that's it.

Session 3-C

Sid (L): Part of this is a matter of being me, let's say. The way I respond to you is part of my being myself. And if it seems harsh sometimes or unfair sometimes, wait a while. Maybe I won't be unfair all the time— maybe it will balance out. Or maybe I'm not really meaning to be unfair but it comes out this way. But, at any rate, the point is that what I am doing here is part of an effort for me to express myself and to be me in this group and I assume that true for you, too.

Henrietta: Oh, I sort of think that you're above that.

Sid (L): Above what?

Henrietta: Because you're a psychology teacher and you must have it all figured out by now. (Laughter)

Sid (L): You think I have a set pattern of what I'm going to do in this group? (Giggle from group) I have plans that I follow? Do you?

Henrietta: Not exactly that.

Sid (L): You were kidding me a little bit.

Henrietta: But I assumed that anybody who's a psychology teacher doesn't have many problems any more.

Bob (CL):   (Laughter from group). More!

Sid (L):   I don't think that's true at all. We may be different in what we're thinking of as problems, but I think that when life ceases to have problems, then you're dead.

Carl: In other words, dying ends anxiety.

Sid (L):   Yeah, and I happen to believe that. We're always trying to solve the problems that botch everything up a little bit, we may not mean the same thing by problems, but there are always things for me to worry about, me to get anxious about, and to get excited about, and to make mistakes over. It's part of living, but this is my personal view.

Carl: Yeah. I think it might be helpful for us to see what makes for spontaneity in our group.

Session 5-B

Carl: It's uh, I think it's a frustration of expectation or something like that. I come in here and I try not to overexpect of the group and I like to think that—well, it's just a time when we can sit back and think about things, you know . . . well, to objectify, for me . . . to look at the world around but to participate here—to be subjective here. But I know that it would make me feel good inside, you know, if we were discussing something that really made me get excited inside and I felt like I was learning something or teaching something or evoking something from somebody. I know I'd like that but we're not doing that very much. It's not happening to me.

Stephane: Me, too.

Henrietta: Well, I felt like it was happening to me the day that everybody was trying to help me with a problem.

Bob (CL):   Did you? I don't think you were here, Stephane, but did you agree with Henrietta's perception of that particular session?

Henrietta: It was probably individual because it was me who was concerned.

Carl: I didn't want to participate much in that, I don't think, because I felt that I was too close to Henrietta to begin with.

Bob (CL):   Are you suggesting, Henrietta, that you need to get something of yourself out where it can be . . . before the session really does this thing that Carl wants it to.

Henrietta: Well, yeah, I think you have to be.

Carl: Well, just out of curiosity, has anything further developed?

Henrietta: (Giggle) Yeah, nothing good. (Laugh from all)

Carl: Would you like to tell us about it?

Henrietta: No.

Carl: Okay.

Session 13-C

Bob (CL):   I'm rebelling against Mitch a little bit today for some reason. I don't know if you're saying—besides what Carl says—that there's a closeness without intimacy, and I keep having the feeling that for you there's got to be the intimacy . . .

Mitch: Maybe, yeah, I don't know.

Carl: I think that's a little bit too cut and dried the way you say that, Bob, but I think it's a possibility and I don't see why not. I think I tend more to try to like people than dislike them. So why shouldn't Mitch?

Bob (CL): I don't know. I feel like I can be close to someone but not really feel like they're a bosom buddy.

Mitch: Umm hmm, I can too.

Sid (L): I'm not sure that you're making sense to me. (Everyone talks)

Mitch: Well, now I have a friend that I never see, but he's a real good friend. I don't ever write him or anything else, but yet he's a real good friend.

Bob (CL): Most of my friends here, probably, at Vanderbilt . . . when I leave, you know, in the sense of being a bosom buddy and in the sense of writing and always keeping in touch and wanting to know how they're doing and what they're doing, probably not, but yet I consider myself quite close to the people here.

Mitch: It seems to me that you're putting so much emphasis on the action of writing, and all this stuff. It's really not that to me, what I'm trying to express.

Henrietta: I can't tell what it is. (Everyone talks at once)

Frank: Well, instead of going out there and trying to put it on a table and cut it apart and analyze it, let's talk it to death and talk it some more. Sometimes actions pay off.

Mitch: No, I agree—actions mean a lot, but actions grow out of the relationship but aren't the relationships . . .

Henrietta: Well, it seems to me you are trying to sort of push me into doing something which I don't really know what it is.

Mitch: No, the reason that I said what I did is that I don't think that you can understand what we're talking about unless you feel it.

Bob (CL): Yeah, Mitch doesn't want, he doesn't want you to say, "Mitch, I really love you." He just wants you to be able to sometimes say, "Mitch, I hate your guts," or something.

Mitch: Yeah!

Bob (CL): You know, just to be able to deal with it and not keep yourself out of it and reserved.

Mitch: No, to me you get off from the cognitive level and it's not there. You have to feel it.

Carl: It has bogged down. It has bogged down.

Bob (CL): What's exactly bothering you, Carl? You know I have the feeling that today you really kind of worked into this and yet when you say "Aw, it's bogging down, let's do something else," I'm really puzzled.

Session 14-A

Carl: Yeah, that's right. But I think maybe what you're trying to say is that, uh, well, I think we're both trying to say the same thing, maybe. I mean, judging by my actions, I really do give a damn or need to give a damn, okay. But there comes a point where I get scared. I don't want to give up any more power.

Sid (L): So you have to say to yourself that you don't give a damn. And you have to say to yourself, "I'm pretending and manipulating," at that point.

Carl: Yes. And I can do that effectively, too. I can say that I'm pretending and manipulating. Maybe I can't, really, no, there's not much pretense except in the way that I mean the word 'pretense.' I mean there are false pretenders and true pretenders. You know, if someone pretends to have . . . You know someone who doesn't deserve it and someone else who does. And when you take an action and you stick by it and you follow it through, then you are a true pretender.

Sid (L):   I want to apologize. I just now got your message. I was trying to talk you out of something but I wasn't—at the time—I wasn't sure what it was. I was trying to talk you out of trying to cut people off and of really believing that they had not been genuine and that you had not cared. Now I was. I was really trying to talk you out of that. I didn't . . .

Carl: Well, I think I do care. I don't start out . . .

Sid (L):   Naw, wait a minute! Don't . . . I'll feel badly if you abandon your position so easily.

Carl: I won't abandon that position. I'll elaborate on it. I mean, I start out not caring and I decide I like this person, I'll try to get closer and I start taking actions that exhibit care—you know, or that can construct back from these actions saying, this person cares. Well, this is manipulating and oh, not only manipulates the other person, manipulates me because I act and I sympathize with the actions and pretty soon I do care. I mean, I really do, but . . . And then it comes to the point where I get scared and when I get scared then I look back and I see my original motives and I say well, I have manipulated them, I've manipulated myself with these actions and I've made myself care. And perhaps I've made them care. But I can't really see whether they really do care or not, so now I'm scared. And so I don't want to give up any more power, and yet I say I'm not going to manipulate anymore.

Bob (CL):   What good is saying you don't want to manipulate anymore if you have nothing invested in the people you manipulate? If they drop you because you've been manipulating, there's nothing lost.

Carl: I can't say there's nothing lost because I do value relationships with people.

Bob (CL):   Yeah, but isn't this then an attempt to put yourself on a safe . . .

Carl: To devalue relationships. I think it's true with me.

Sid (L):   Well, it's at that point that the relationship becomes some kind of a threat to you?

Carl: Yeah.

Sid (L):   At this point you start saying . . .

Carl: Well, I start saying that because I start feeling that it's threatening me—or can be.

Sid (L):   Umm hmm.

Frank: What's this power factor in it? It's all of a sudden . . .

Carl: Knowledge is power.

Frank: Knowledge? All right . . .

Carl: And the more you sympathize with someone—the more they sympathize with you—and the more you both take actions that express the sympathy—I mean, by trial and error and everything, you learn about them and they learn about you and the problem is that you gain power over them and they gain power over you and there's nothing wrong with power as long as it isn't used—more than it should be, I mean. When someone has power over you more than you have . . .

Frank: You sound like it's a blackmail racket.

Carl: It is.

Frank: I just never thought my friends were blackmailers.

Carl: They are.

Sid (L): Would it make this a little more concrete to say "the more I reveal of myself, the more power the other person has over me"?

Carl: Umm hmm.

Session 14-B

Carl: I'm feeling hurt. I say yet, I do want to manipulate people and myself.

Henrietta: Were you talking to Frank or to Carl?

Sid (L): I was talking to Carl, when I said I think he wants to manipulate people but can't, somehow. Why does that hurt you?

Carl: I don't know.

Sid (L): It could be taken both ways, you know. It could be construed in two quite different . . .

Bob (CL): Does it hurt because Sid is perceiving the thing you brought up almost the opposite of what you intended, because it is rather novel. I got the idea that you were manipulative and you didn't like it and you wanted to change. He's suggesting that you like it and want to be even more?

Carl: Let's put it this way: I'm dissatisfied with it. It's not effective enough. (Laughter from the group)

Henrietta: Well, it's a very nice, safe position.

Carl: I mean, as long as I can maintain as much control over every situation or, you know, especially important situations, as the person I exchange with, that's fine. But when it comes to the point where I can't guarantee that I'm going to get something back or I can't guarantee that I won't get negative feedback, then I get afraid and I want to start putting out negative output.

Bob (CL): How do you react to Mitch's desire to make this group closer? How have you reacted to this?

Carl: I admire it. That's fine; that's great.

Bob (CL): But you keep yourself apart from him and you have no intention of participating.

Carl: I have intentions of trying to participate, and I have intentions of, I mean, it's a nice, productive circle; I can be sympathetic consciously and I can amplify my sympathy, I can behave a little more sympathetically than I feel, and after a while I feel a little bit more sympathetic and I just keep building it up.

Sid (L): Now we may be hung up a little bit on a word. I think I am to some extent. You asked him what he meant by manipulation and you even asked what is wrong with manipulating, and maybe we ought to try to get this down to more concrete terms in terms of our own experience. I think I do things to people sometimes in order to get them to respond.

Carl: Sure, I think that's great.

Sid (L): And I might even do some things to them to get them to respond in a particular way, so I'm not so . . .

Session 14-C

Sid (L): You see, I reacted like that because your statement's a little hostile.

Stephane: I didn't mean for it to be. Really, it wasn't.

Sid (L): Yes, you did.

Stephane: No, I don't think so.

Henrietta: That's what I don't like, Stephane . . . you see, Carl here is saying lots of things that might be embarrassing to him, but you just sit there and say, well, I don't have anything to say because you all might not understand it or you all might think it peculiar. And if we're going to do it, then I think you should too.

Stephane: I guess what I mean when I say what I said at the first of the group that I feel like too much is demanded of me.

Henrietta: Well, you don't even take the *first* step.

Carl: I'm not demanding. You can sit and listen if you want. (Laughter from the group)

Henrietta: I am, though.

Sid (L): This puts us in a real dilemma sometimes.

Carl: To get something, you have to give something.

Sid (L): Here we are, right in the middle of what we're talking about, though, in a way. The business of manipulating and wondering when to stop, see? Admittedly, I would love for you to respond sometimes, as I would for Sandra and Frank, but when do I . . . but I'm weighing losing you altogether against trying to get more from you. Did that come out right?

Stephane: Look, I ought to respond to things on just an emotional level, I mean, things Carl's saying, I feel like I understand some things completely and some things I don't understand or I have questions about, but it's not always formed into intelligent, sensible things to say.

Bob (CL): That's what you said the last time.

Sid (L): Why struggle to make things intelligent and sensible all the time?

Henrietta: Have we been saying very intelligent things?

Carl: If there's something imperfect about somebody else, we'll attack them and that's what talking is. You talk and you find out what you think, by your objections to what you say and by other people's objections to what you say and you, you know, it's just dialogue. You find out what you think eventually. Besides, I know more about what I wanted to talk about now than I did when I started talking. I had some vague idea, I don't know just what I was talking about when I first started.

Session 15-C

(Stephane is talking about leaving the group.)

Sid (L): Yeah, I think so.

Carl: Shocked, disappointed.

Stephane: Come on, be dramatic (Giggle).

Carl: We'll miss you for an hour or two.

Mitch: No, I can't say I won't miss you that much, because I don't think I will. I wish I could say that, but I just haven't gotten to feel like you're a real essential part of the group. And this is not real—I mean, I'm not trying to cut down or anything, it's just—I don't like—

Sid (L): What feeling does it brings out in you?

Mitch: I was trying to think it brings out some real definite opinions, I mean feelings, but I think it's more feelings to protect myself from saying how I failed, you know, how I hadn't, you know, how the first thing I thought about was "Oh, my God" and you know when I said I wanted to just kick you in the fanny? Well, I'm just saying maybe I was being too harsh or there are feelings just to justify my, you know, saying "Okay, good, she's left," you know, or something like that when really it isn't, I really feel hurt that you are leaving. But I think it's not because I'm going to really miss interacting with you, it's just that I'm . . . it's going to be an ever close reminder of my failure or something like that.

Henrietta: Yes, it's sort of like when we thought that we weren't capable of . . . a little bit like our responsibility didn't get fulfilled.

Carl: I'll tell you how I feel.

Stephane: I don't feel like you all weren't capable—I feel like I wasn't capable. But it doesn't particularly bother me—I'm just willing to accept it. All right, I wasn't. You know. Okay, how do you feel?

Carl: Well, there are two impulses and one, well, she's gone—well good. I can't say that I needed her, not really. It displeases me to see you go. Okay, second? I feel anger, resentment. I value the group—you don't. You cast doubts on my evaluation of the group.

Henrietta: You know, it doesn't sound very rude when you say "I feel anger, I feel resentment."

Mitch: Go ahead and finish.

Henrietta: Keep going.

Carl: Whenever . . . I'll bring a lighter along next time. And whenever I feel anger I'll light it up. And whenever I cool off, I'll put it out.

Frank: I'll bring a light bulb and every once in a while I'll flick it . . .

Mitch: I am listening.

Carl: All right, let's get back. Yeah. So, I don't really know just how I do feel, and not get nervous. I mean how, I don't know, since I've condemned these two impulses I had, one, the first one, just to reject you. That isn't the way I feel about you, I reject that feeling. I reject the anger because I see where it comes from, and I see that your evaluation of the group from your viewpoint doesn't affect my evaluation of mine.

Session 15-D

Sid (L): I want to bother you a little bit more, Bob, if I can. There's a . . . the way you react to Stephane doesn't seem to be consistent with one of the first big arguments we had in the group—about people "being themselves" being more important than achieving or changing . . .

Bob (CL): It isn't consistent, is it?

Sid (L): Yeah.

Bob (CL): Well, well, maybe it is consistent. Let's see, I'll buy it. I'll accept that but let me try to point out why I don't think it's inconsistent.

Sid (L): You gave good reasons for asking questions.

Bob (CL): Yeah, I said that, to me, to be myself in this group is to badger people that are quiet. Not badger them, but just try to get something . . .

Carl: Turn your attention on them every once in a while.

Bob (CL): Yeah, and I said that when . . . and then Stephane would each time very patiently say that she didn't have anything to say, and that was fine. I mean, I was happy then. But she was being herself there so, really, is that being inconsistent? I was being myself and she was being herself, and I am being myself when I say I expect everyone or want everyone to produce something.

Sid (L):   Maybe it's not as inconsistent as . . .

Mitch: Did you feel like we were pressing at you to talk more than you wanted to?

Stephane: Yes, I did.

Mitch: You did?

Stephane: Umm hmm.

Henrietta: Well, if that was being yourself, I mean, that's all we know to do.

Carl: Well, that's why I feel that we've . . . I've failed to some extent, because I don't think that I've been concerned enough about, ah, about getting the inside view of your feelings about, ah, not wanting to express until you have something . . . well, why not . . .

Sid (L):   And in our own way we were always finding ways to excuse Stephane or to prod her or excuse her . . . and we weren't willing just to let her participate the way she saw fit.

Henrietta: But she never saw fit to participate. (Laughter from the group)

Sid (L):   I know I'm part of all this, too. I pick at people whenever I feel like it, I guess.

Mitch: If you had to do this with another group and had the time, I mean, not with us, but just another group, would you get in again?

Stephane: No.

Session 24-A

Sid (L):   I kind of feel like, you know, in a sense you're saying we have worked together, we've done something together without placing undue restrictions on each other and without molding, without attempting, well, there were maybe some efforts to do this, but they never succeeded to the extent that they kept us from communicating. That's pretty important, I think, to me, to be able to, I mean, I think the thing I really liked about what you were saying was it was kind of flattering to me in a way because I think what you were saying was that I have remained a real person to you.

Mitch: Yes. I was just about ready to say that what you're trying to say is that. No, in other words, you made the integrity, in other words, you know, you're a real person, instead of making you my father or just somebody to discipline me or one of these other things you have answered. That's right, you did remain a real person.

Sid (L):   It's mutual too, I think, that when I do get that feeling it goes along with the feeling that you have been a very real person to me too.

Mitch: Well, I don't know . . .

Sid (L):   Well, you flattered me and I'm just talking just to get rid of it. Thank you. Well, it's mutual. It's ah, I think we both have hacked away at each other to make sure we tested out what the real person was, to some extent.

Mitch: Yeah, you know the way I look at it, I've been really cruel to you in a lot of ways.

Sid (L):   Well, not cruel, you know, but real testing. (Group all talks at once)

Sid (L): Yeah, we've both done that. Maybe it was the limits of communication, you know, here you are.

Bob (CL): It's a good American pastime. It's become a national sport. I always like that . . .

Sid (L): But this, ah, I guess I might say qualification, now, I can say to you when you arrive at this point that you can recognize that there can be negative things and there can be positive things and that there's a deeper level of communication possible.

Bob (CL): That doesn't mean that everything will always be smooth, but . . .

Sandra: Thank you for saying that.

Bob (CL): Yeah, that's right. But would you get mad?

Sid (L): But that there will be a deeper level of communication. (All talk at once)

Session 24-B

Sid (L): Henrietta, do you still look to me as a doctor, professor, speaker of wise words?

Henrietta: (Giggle) Oh, to some extent . . .

Mitch: Go ahead and say yes. You don't have to. I was going to really pounce on you if you'd said no. (Group laughter)

Sid (L): Call her a liar, huh?

Mitch: Yeah, I would, man, because (to Henrietta) you do.

Sid (L): I remember you saying that not too long ago. I just wondered if it was still a barrier between us.

Bob (CL): Do you have trouble getting close to people, Henrietta?

Henrietta: Ummm hummm.

Sid (L): That's one way of insuring distance between us, isn't it? If you keep me in my role as doctor, professor . . .

Henrietta: No, it is—but, after all, that's what you are.

Mitch: That's what I was getting at downstairs. That you're more than just rolls of—layers of the onion that you can just peel off.

Sid (L): You mean that.

Henrietta: That's not all, but it's certainly a part of it.

Sid (L): How about the other professors at Vanderbilt. Do you see me the same way that you see them?

Henrietta: No.

Sid (L): Are there differences other than just the amount of time that we've sat in a small group like this?

Henrietta: Yes, you're more of a person than some of them because you've, oh, talked to us and heard our experiences.

Mitch: The reason he would seem more a person to me is that—all right, let's say there is something under that onion other than just layer after layer. That we've peeled away a lot of those layers.

Henrietta: You misinterpreted me some, as I did you, too.

Mitch: Oh.

Henrietta: I don't see him as an onion at all . . .

Session 25-A

Sid (L): Well, I don't know, it just might have built up a while.

Frank: Why don't you answer her?

Henrietta: I hope we finish this before you get tired.

Bob (CL): It would be all right if you just sat around and cut paperdolls, but he insisted on making his inane comments.

Carl: It's not inane—it's the truth, man.

Bob (CL): No—it was inane. Let's face it.

Henrietta: I can't help . . .

Carl: It's true in this case.

Bob (CL): I've expressed my hostility. Now we can go on.

Carl: Inane, my eye. It's true, I like her.

Bob (CL): Well, we like Henrietta, too, but that doesn't mean that we're going to feel like we have to, have to protect her.

Carl: Well, I thought that it was appropriate to protect her at that time because I thought she was feeling something that it was unjust for her to feel.

Sid (L): Well, the part of it that seemed to me to be important was whether or not this was saying something to you about yourself that you weren't satisfied with or whether this was just the particular guy and the particular situation in which you felt inadequate, or miffed.

Henrietta: I don't think it was just the situation.

Sid (L): You think he was hitting a weak, he hit a vulnerable spot.

Henrietta: Yes, I know very well he was.

Sid (L): Now I'm still not real clear on what the vulnerable spot—

Henrietta: Oh, I think it's . . . oh, just like you or someone else said the the other day that I had a hard time getting close to other people and he was, well, he was rather put out about that.
well, just not open enough.

Henrietta: Um hmm.

Sid (L): Like you weren't giving enough of yourself, sort of, and were

Bob (CL): That is, you're not an outgoing, vivacious conversationalist.

Carl: She is sometimes.

Mitch: It seems like there's a difference.

Bob (CL): It may be, but—

Mitch: It seems like he was talking about your being able to put on a good show. There's a difference between being able to put on a good show and really being able to be close to somebody.

Bob (CL): Yeah, but I just wondered if this is part of, well, like last time I told Henrietta I thought she was shy and I just wondered if this is part of what she's talking about. Not being able to get close to people.

Mitch: Henrietta, is it getting close to somebody or just being able to compete with the other girls by putting on an equally good show?

Henrietta: No, I don't think it's that.

Mitch: It's really being able to have that person say "I can see that you and I don't have to talk a lot but still feel like we're saying a lot."

Session 26-A

Bob (CL): Well, Mitch said something that interests me and if you are all through . . .

Sid (L): Yeah, I think we're through with all the business for this group.

Henrietta: This sounds like a real meeting. You have business first.
(Laughter)

Bob (CL): If the old business is over, shall we get to the new business?

Mitch: What was it?

Bob (CL): That you cried a lot.

Mitch: Not a lot, I mean, I've been known to cry when I'd get upset.

Frank: Wow.

Mitch: I haven't cried in a long time. I did most of my crying in . . .

Bob (CL): Was this before you were married?

Mitch: I even cried once after I was married, too, so it's not all bliss.

Bob (CL): Well, it doesn't necessarily follow that that was the reason.

Mitch: Well, I'm just trying to figure out what it was that I was crying about. It was after seeing a movie one time. What was that fairy tale?

Henrietta: Oh, The Brothers Grimm, was that it?

Mitch: Oh, was that the name of it, I saw that, we saw that. Well something about it just touched off a lot that was built up in me. Can't remember what it was. And I cried after that. But that was last year.

Bob (CL): Well, I misunderstood you.

Mitch: No, no what I was referring to is that you said that you don't even cry when you feel like it. You feel like you'd like to. Well, I'm the exact opposite of that.

Bob (CL): Yeah, well I do cry sometimes but it's because I can't control it. I mean most of the time . . . well, I don't often feel like it but when I do I generally can control it. Do you ever cry, Sid?

Sid (L): Oh yes, I have. I do.

Bob (CL): What started this, anyhow?

Mitch: Well, you asked me about . . . you were blowing your nose or something.

Bob (CL): Well.

Mitch: And we were talking about ending the group.

A Member's Responses to the Tape Recorded Sessions[3]

Earlier in the chapter we expressed an intent to demonstrate how a member's feelings and interpersonal perceptions underwent modification as a result of group participation. If the primary aim of facilitating personal growth was effected, then one should be able to observe some amount of change in an individual's ways of viewing the world about him as the group sessions progress. Anyone reading these pages will readily appreciate the problems inherent in objectifying such an elusive construct as "feeling," but, to paraphrase Thurstone, if a feeling exists it exists in some amount, and if it exists in some amount it can be observed. From a realistic standpoint, we are painfully aware that a suitable technology for actually *seeing* a feeling is lacking, and that when we use the verb "observe" what we actually mean is that we feel that our measurement criteria permit us to make legitimate inferences with respect to the construct. The inability to touch, smell, hear, or see a feeling in no way detracts from its reality, as is sometimes implied in the literature of the logical positivists, who have exerted sizeable influence upon behavioristic psychology. The basic unit of inheritance, the gene, was for decades hypothetical construct also. Until recently, its validity was no less tenuous than that of "feeling." Technological advances in fields outside the discipline of genetics culminated in the development of electron microscopy,

[3]Prepared with the collaboration of Robert M. Murphey.

so that a gene could be "seen"; but by the time this sort of sensory validation had come about, the hypothetical, unvalidated gene had more than adequately shown its usefulness in predicting and explaining genetic phenomena, such that it was in one sense of little practical import whether the gene could be seen or not.

In an effort to describe certain changes that took place in one of the group member's verbalizations about himself (Carl), we have taken recourse to Rogers' (1959b) Scale for the Measurement of Process in Psychotherapy. This scale was devised to measure personality change in an incongruent, anxious, vulnerable person through psychotherapy. Thus, we have some misgivings as to whether we have misapplied the scale. In our analysis we show one member's progress from Stage I of the scale to Stage VII, but we doubt that Carl was ever as incongruent, anxious, or vulnerable as would be implied by this. We hope the reader will consider our "scale" analysis of the subject's personal growth as tentative and suggestive rather than definitive.

Rather than employing the scale as a means for quantifying our subject's responses, we have chosen to present Rogers' descriptions of the various scale points (as opposed to their numerical values) and to extract from the subject's report some verbalizations that seem to fit the scale descriptions. The material used in the example below, applying Rogers' scale to a technically non-therapeutic situation, was obtained in the summer after the group sessions ended, asking the subject, Carl, to listen to all the tape recorded sessions of his group and to stop the tape whenever he wished and record his thoughts and feelings.

The following exerpts from Carl's report are contrasted with what we consider to be relevant descriptive phrases in Rogers' scheme.

Selections from Rogers' Scale Description	Selections from Carl's Self-Report

Stage I

Unawareness of feeling life; strong resistance to exploring feelings; S is very distant from his subjective experiencing; a very considerable discrepancy (of which S is unaware) between experiencing and awareness; unwillingness to communicate himself; communication is about material external to self; personal constructs are extremely rigid, unrecognized as constructs, and thought of as external facts; no problems are recognized; no desire to change.	"This is a moral issue . . . the human mind is so sacred to me . . . I am intellectually involved in this discussion, evaluating what I and others said in terms of what I think of as my workable way of approaching human reality."

Stage II

Immediacy of experiencing is lacking; he seems to be afraid to move ahead on his own; desires to keep situation somewhat structured in terms of roles.

"I would have resented it out loud if it had not been that I was still afraid to impose on our leader."

Stage III

There is a freer flow of expression about self as an object; communication about self as a reflected object existing primarily in others; there is a beginning recognition that problems exist inside the individual rather than externally.

". . . I feel concern for whether or not the group 'damages' my thoughts . . . I was thinking very well, even if I wasn't as cold about life as I sounded . . . I feel stubborn and bull-headed about any argument that might develop. I don't think I really *trust completely* this approach."

Stage IV

Feelings and personal meanings are freely described; dim recognition that feelings previously denied to awareness may break through in the present but this seems to be a frightening possibility; a vague realization that a disturbing type of inner referent does exist; considerable communication of present self-related feelings; a beginning loosening of personal constructs; individual is willing to risk relating himself occasionally to others on a feeling basis.

"I feel kind of sad for Henrietta . . . My feelings aren't very strong. I just feel a little sad and wish that I could comfort her.
I have a premonition of excitement or perhaps real sympathy with someone. Something is building up to happen . . ."

Stage V

Many feelings are freely expressed in the moment of their occurrence, and thus experienced in the immediate present; feelings previously denied now tend to bubble through into awareness; feelings are sometimes experienced with immediacy; individual freely expresses present, self-related feelings; individual is concerned over his contribution to the problem; he feels that he had a definite responsibility for the problems which exist.

"I feel remorse. I am sad . . . I wished I could do something about the kind of bad we are talking about . . . I see why now it was hard for others to understand me . . . because what I said was intellectually hard to understand. However, I do find myself 'sucked into' my past self. I now sympathize with and understand the others who did not feel involved in my feelings. I feel negative towards the nasal type of voice I seem to have . . ."

Stage VI

Feelings which have been previously denied to awareness are now experienced with immediacy and acceptance; experiencing of feelings previously denied is often vivid, dramatic, and releasing for the individual; the self exists in the experience of feeling; there is a dissolving of significant personal constructs in a vivid experiencing of a feeling; the individual is living some aspect of his problem in his experiencing; he risks being himself in process in the relationship to the therapist.

"Ha, ha, ha. This is what you might call nervous laughter. Damn, I'm frustrated—two or three conversations going on at once. It's impossible to follow any one of them at all . . . Actions have power . . . The valid emotions make my actions more genuine, because they have power too. It is simplest to say that I love my behavior and emotions. I become a *true pretender* to the emotions just as an usurper king becomes a true pretender to a throne *after* he has *taken* it but not before he has taken it . . . I love Sid (Dr. Phillips), and I feel that he is being dished out a kind of necessary injustice . . ."

Stage VII

New feelings are experienced with richness and immediacy; feelings are rarely denied to awareness; the individual is able both to live in his own feelings and personal meanings and to express them as an owned and accepted aspect of himself; the individual lives comfortably in the changing flow of his experiencing; incongruence is minimal and temporary as the individual is able to live more fully and acceptantly in the process of experiencing and as he is able to symbolize and conceptualize the meanings which are implicit in the immediate moment; the self is primarily a reflexive awareness of the process of experiencing; experience is tentatively construed as having a certain meaning but this meaning is always held loosely and is checked and rechecked against further experiencing; the individual freely and openly relates to the therapist and to others on the basis of his immediate experiencing in the relationship.

"I'm jealous. They've got pie and I don't . . . I'm lonely; I want Henrietta, or Sid, or Bob to come and have a piece with *me* . . . I also feel the above is silly and funny. I feel like having a good time with somebody and making dumb, corny jokes. I just had an 'ah-ha experience,' I feel interested and involved . . . I love myself. I feel satisfied when I compare my present attitude towards involvement and personal commitment to my attitude (in the past). I still have problems. They are not the same problems. I still fear involvement and commitment, but my behavior is different. I risk myself all at once and all together now instead of a little at a time, and now and then . . . I will no longer feel guilty about not giving enough even though I might try to give more to the people I encounter. I like to laugh at Sid. I'm amused in a nervous kind of way . . . I know that . . . Mitch and I are going to have a run in, and I'm going to feel like crying. I am going to hate Mitch for a while, because he will be trying to 'put me in my place.'"

The preceding comparison between Rogers' scale point descriptions and Carl's self-report was accomplished, of course, in a completely *ex post facto* manner on our part. It is not beyond the realm of possibility that we have imposed order and perceived progress in Carl's verbalization where none exist. Hence, we have included the following comments regarding Carl's behavior from *listening and responding* reports. These were written by various people, other than the author, who were somehow associated with the group program, either as members or as listening observers.

Early sessions

"He (Carl) was an old friend of mine, but I was a little ashamed of him because he was not the kind of person I wanted him to be and I thought the group would feel the same way . . ."

"Carl . . . talked about self-consciousness in terms of existentialism, which just seemed to be so many words to me."

"Carl . . . attempts to discuss the question in a detached, academic fashion; and even though he speaks of objectifying people as a personal habit, this statement doesn't really show much self-insight. His habit seems to be based more on denial of emotions than the consciousness of emotions that he posits."

Middle sessions

"Carl is taking quite an active part . . . and is sincerely giving his personal attitude towards the topic. He reveals a certain realistic and pretty secure attitude toward his abilities and an openness to help or (seek) advice from others . . . he is not being flippant or just argumentative in the discussion as he sometimes is."

"Carl seems to be getting more at feelings. He is still intellectualizing, but he seems to be getting closer to his feelings."

Later sessions

"I can only guess at his (Carl's) feelings at this point, but I would say that one is probably a self-satisfying feeling of having really expressed how he felt . . ."

"Mitch and Julia say that they think Carl is realistically accepting himself . . ."

Members' Evaluations of the Group Experience

When asked to submit a candid written evaluation to their group experiences, fourteen of the twenty-two members who participated at least a semester responded. Six others gave oral reports, which were probably more vulnerable to bias than the written reports where the option of anonymity was offered. We shall only report that, of the six members giving oral reports, four are participating in the program again this year; one, in our judgment, had mixed feelings about the value of the group for him; and one was more negative than positive.

Of the fourteen writers, only three had been in the program both semesters. On individual's report will be presented in its entirety; the following paragraphs represent an attempt to summarize the comments of the remaining thirteen respondents.

Nine of the thirteen reports were generally high in praise for the group experience, and nine writers expressed the belief that they had, in fact, achieved some degree of personal growth. Three evaluations were predominantly negative in character, with two of the participants asserting that they had profited not at all. Some rather common complaints regarding the procedure included a lack of well-defined goals (some claimed that they were too well defined, of course), the feeling of discomfort in working through the problems relating to the leader's "role" and "status," and objections to certain aspects of the scheduling of the meetings. Personal achievements expressed were the acquisition of new friends, increased tolerance of others, improved academic performance, and greater freedom of self-expression.

Most respondents noted a feeling of satisfaction for having participated, and some desired to become (and did become) involved in future groups. Original motivations for entering the groups ranged from mild curiosity to poorly-expressed, subjective feelings of personal dissatisfaction.

We shall end this chapter with the verbatim reports of one individual. She wrote the first part of the report after one semester's participation and before we solicited the member evaluations. We think the raw data of subjective experience reported by this member speak to our aims and loosely formulated hypotheses better than any summary abstractions we might make. Yet we cannot resist saying this: the sympathetic reader will not have difficulty seeing something of the (1) discovery and differentiation of affects, (2) acceptance of and direct spontaneous response to these affects, and (3) integration of affect, cognition, and action in more creative living.

REFLECTIONS ON THE GROUP SESSIONS

I want to determine the effect of the group sessions on me and my reactions and feelings toward them. I am going to attempt to recall, and re-experience, when possible, the group interactions. I want to feel, not think, as much as possible. I hope this method will exclude my placing any kind of order when none exists. I am looking for significance to me as I am at this moment.

I see myself as I enter the group. I am a sophomore in Arts and Sciences. I stress the humanities, but my tastes run the gamut of courses and activities. I feel no specific or commanding need to enter the group. I feel capable of meeting whatever problems are presented me. Right now there is none. But there is feeling in me that I ought to join a group. Since it has been offered to me by my psychology professor, Dr. Phillips, to pass by this opportunity would leave me all too open to self-blame if something I can't handle should arise. This feeling web is a part of me I like to ignore (and after group sessions admit or discuss only as an external portion of myself). It is a general sense of conservativism, unwillingness to expose myself to a challenge, i.e., something new or something already experienced as threatening. I use an interest pattern of mine as the basis of rationalizing about joining the group: I have a curiosity about other people. I realize that this is a shallow reason, that I don't feel it. But I feel something indefinite drawing me toward the group. I try to convince myself I do not have the time. But I am so afraid I will later have to blame myself for failing to join I ask to sign up several days after the initial invitation.

Between my assignment to a group and the first Monday I attend the group I talk about it to three friends who have attended a session or are planning to do so. They seem embarrassed about admitting membership and regard it as very personal, while I try to convince them and myself that I want to join because it is a research project and because Dr. Phillips is exerting pressure on me and the class to join. I feel he would dislike me for saying this. I try to shut out more real emotions about my joining, so that what I feel is a kind of conflict that makes unexpected flames creep across my cheeks, as differing views meet at the surface of my consciousness. Because I feel shy and because of a sense of conflict, I enter the first session quite anxious and uncertain about how well I'll be able to protect myself from "the people over there." I wonder if I should be bringing some big personality problem to them like a gift, a thought which brings me a sense of irritation about their expectations.

I am going to the first session. One member of the group who is a friend of mine meets me crossing the street. We walk in. Both of us are nervous, unsure of ourselves, and (I am guessing for her) anxious. We both lack the self-confidence and direction to ask the secretary where we are to go. I am very thankful that she does not even look up when she asks us why we are here and then tells us third floor on the right. I feel a sense of easing up of anxiousness when I see Mr. Morton (he gave me guidance counseling a year ago). I know him; he is accepting and he is also nice about being the extrovert in the crowd. He can cover up my shyness. The table is too high. I feel more as though I am hanging on to a cliff edge—straining, not relaxing. It's round— clever; they're really going to force us to be a professional group. Everyone has something to play with. I wish I had my ring, or I wish I could have a cigarette. There are two counselors; they must be thinking about how anxious this bunch is. Please feel at ease. One of the counselors, Bill, introduces himself but I don't understand him. I like him for his laugh; he is going to be enjoyably goodnatured. I notice a certain tenseness around me. It is mine, it is the group's. It is Bill's tenseness, as well as Jack Morton's. When I take my turn, I am very nervous. I am surprised at the extent of my feeling, and I am afraid I am losing the little thin skin of the extrovert-me that I created painfully and carefully for situations like this where I want to impress people. I want these people to think I am mature, self-confident and friendly. I believe I really am the first and last of these three, but I wonder how I convey them? Maybe this is a situation where I can feel these people out and find a solution. Mr. Morton reads and does a monologue. I want the same freedom; I know Jack and Bill would let me have it, but the rest— they would be shocked. It is inappropriate still. Nothing that I want to remember happens. I cannot yet say why I have joined or what I want. The question bothers me. I don't think of it much after Monday night until the next Sunday. Then I wonder what they expect of me. I am glad that I have been meeting two other members of the group on campus. I feel more at ease about the group when I don't have to face what is strange, since I fear this sort of situation.

There are changes in my existence, experiences which alter my point of view. Between the second and third session, I find that the feeling of anxiety for my roommate are being supported and heightened by her actions. I have been afraid she was losing control of her ability to withstand tension and stress. Now I believe she has lost control. There are tears, a break in her past effort to conceal any strong emotion. I wonder if it is good. I think what we have read and talked about in the group concerning accepting. I think about how unskilled I am in this situation, and I realize that I am having trouble because I do not understand. I am becoming aware that I have misinterpreted the seriousness of Anne's anxiety. Now at breakfast I feel at loss; I want out, I want help for me and for Anne. She is sitting here holding her cup in one hand, the other lightly touching it, a few inches from her lips. There is no motion, no vitality in her body or face, as usual. Her eyes are focused to the right of my head just a little, and her stare is unseeing, unthinking, fixed. I am getting nervous because I do not understand. I try to break her stare, to enter her world and stare, to find out. She won't let me. For five minutes she won't let me. I feel very small, very wary, very irritated, even strange. She walks back to the room, making an effort to talk. Should I ask her what is wrong? I have given her plenty of chances and I don't want to seem intruding. I want to be included. In the room Anne sits down on her bed, fights something inside her, then breaks down, "Martha, help me, help me. What am I going to do?" I don't think at all. I say "Do you feel you need to do something? I want to help you, but I don't know what you want to do." I am beginning to see my way out. She is sobbing uncontrollably; she at first shrugs off my arm on her shoulder, then buries her head in my lap. I sit a few minutes, then move her; I make an appointment at the Counseling Center. I am so thankful to the secretary who was early, understanding, and willing to arouse Mr. Morton before the Center was really open. Anne is not capable of deciding whether she wants to see Mr. Morton. She will do as I want her to. I feel relieved, thinking I have done the right thing, that roses will bloom all over now. I am almost exhilarated as I guide Anne by the arm to the Center. She is beginning to be aware of things now. I am anxious as I wait in my room for Anne to return. I am no longer sure everything will be just fine. Anne returns. She says everything will straighten out. I feel doomed. I have not gotten Anne help yet, and she needs it this minute. I watch her show more severe signs in the next several days. When she stops confiding in me, leaves school overnight unexpectedly, and starts to be me sometimes, I get frightened and I call Dr. Phillips in desperation. He has to take my responsibility away from me. I feel relieved about Anne as I talk to him because I know that I am not really totally responsible for her, although I have wanted to feel that I am. I wanted to because I thought I could handle her problem for her. Then I found out I couldn't. Now my realization of my ability and hangover sense of responsibility combine to make me feel guilty and inadequate. I am in a web of feeling to get at the inside of me. Why wasn't I sufficient? How am I misjudging myself in thinking that I was sufficient? And specifically, what in me has been the frame and even reference point of Anne's hell in which she and I included me. I am saying to Dr. Phillips "I hate myself. What is it in me . . ." He suggests I continue in the groups and set up appointments to see Bob Hale. I am hesitant, because I am far enough knocked from my center of reference that I cannot adequately judge what will satisfy my needs. Dr. Phillips is very positive about things. It occurs to me that I must quit using up his time in hesitation. I agree to his suggestions.

The third session is different. I am worried this week. I have just been to see Dr. Phillips about what I can do to help Anne. I wanted concrete suggestions. I know he can't give me that. I am feeling some relief now because ready-or-not he is taking over some of my responsibility. I am late, the group is introducing itself member by member. I am the last one. I do not have time to get nervous. I feel a tremendous amount of energy in me which I want to release. I am glad to jabber and giggle to get it out of my system. For once I am glad to have a chance to explain my silly name. I feel as though I'm too full and have to pour myself out a little. I begin to settle down and become my beloved, shaking reserved self. Bob soon notices my shyness and says something to the effect that we're alike in that we have to be prodded to speak. We like just sitting. I like him for saying that. I don't mind admitting my shyness (since I can't hide it). I feel warm, like a separate, recognized individual inside. I am happy he said this to me. I like Bill now too because he doesn't mind making or taking a few jabs to get things started. I am surprised when his interjections get some hostility-type feedback. I begin to wonder why John, one of the members of the group, is threatened if I'm not. John gets pretty hot about things. Polly tends to be on John's side, seconding the jumping-in-with-both-feet procedure. I'm glad they're bringing in personal feelings, not book-feelings, but why aren't I feeling so strongly about it? I become afraid that I am a misfit in this situation, that my responses are inappropriate. I still feel threatened enough not to reveal my individuality. I feel closer to Bob and Bill than the others seem to, perhaps because I admire their sensitivity, perhaps because I'm trying to warm up to my future decision maker, problem solver, chief in charge of fitting the pieces together again. I don't feel they're in the group yet; they're too different. They're clinicians watching us, they're older not so much in years but in status: they aren't children. We mostly are. Yet I can't exclude them from the group because they are willing to expose themselves to us. I want to do the same thing for them.

Meanwhile I am attending private sessions. Bob, time, vacation, Anne leaving school, help me to learn that there is no *part* of me that I hate. There is no part in me. I am me. I can't single out and objectify *part* of me, like a sense of failure, and hate it. (I thought I could feel so depressd, so doomed to the tragedy of man and other elevated, pervasive-type wonderful things that I could forget my sense of failure and Anne.) That "part of me" came back into me as I regained my point of view, realizing that my lack of perception and ungodlike qualities of being unable to cure her of all her ills was an incapability. Not a failure to achieve what was in my range of capabilities. (This would have been to me an unforgiveable waste.) I feel sad, slightly depressed that Anne is gone as I near the end of the sessions. My feelings before are unrecallable; they're part of a gray-black dream that has broken and disappeared like a fever. I have been doubting my right to consume an hour of Bob's time to say "I hate myself" over and over, trying to convince myself now. But he reassures me, and I continue to see him, ending the sessions with his finally making a decision for me (not the counseling type). I feel good because I feel whole, rested, competent, and I feel I have found a friend I can trust, whose adult point of view is invaluable to me as an insurance of future support. It is with this insurance I begin to delve into the group to find meaning to it and to me.

Before we conclude the individual visits, I attend a group session where I feel highly nervous, to the point that I cannot take any length of silence without showing physical signs of tension. The muscles in the back of my neck stiffen, my palms are sweaty; I am conscious of not having loosened my hand muscles by practicing the piano today. I feel too tense to shift my legs. John notices my nervousness and breaks the silence to ask me if I liked *L'Aloutte* (which Le Treteau brought here). Bob interrupts saying he is uninterested, while Don is responding to our pointless conversation. Fair enough—only three of six care to discuss this subject. I feel childish (I unfortunately equate this word with silly) to have forced John to rescue me with that kind of small talk.

The next session brings a reaction against Bob. I just don't understand. I say nothing. I am afraid that I have misinterpreted the event. The rest seem to take a firm stand against him. I just didn't see him as being out of order. Their attack is so emotional I wonder what is really keying off such strong feeling. Or maybe I just don't understand. Because of psychology 211 and G. Allport I wonder if perhaps I'm a poor judge. I feel I'm usually highly sensitive to others. I am too cowardly to question them, too insecure, and I dislike myself for it. I feel very unworthy. I like Bob and I don't agree that he was wrong. I should say this, but I don't. Polly seems to have finished picking on Bob. She seems uninterested in John as he continues the attack. They're both good people to know; I feel very positive about them. I wonder how two personalities with the same open approach could have landed in one group.

We talk about our parents at another group session. John and Polly, two violent attackers on Bob and Bill, get into a discussion of their inadequate relationship with their parents. (I later wonder if their strong feeling on this subject was part of the intensifying factor in their attacks—friendly as they usually remained. They may have just wanted to keep their specific sensitivity area in a closet while they try to let off the pressure it is generating.) They are worrying about their parents' trying to keep strong parent-child relations and not understanding them at their level. Don emphasizes his parents are ideal. It all irritates me because I do not like to reflect on my relationship to my mom and daddy with more normal ones. I always feel in worse shape than I am. I feel and express my love for my parents. They (the group members) seem to think this inappropriate. I think it is too natural to be embarrassing. They can't conceive the difference in our upbringing. Most people don't want to think about my type of situation because they can't see similarities; they don't see Dr. Spock addressing himself to its problems. I was turned loose economically, morally, most of all an adult raised as well as my parents knew how, when I entered high school. I resent it. I appreciate it. I don't recommend the method, yet I will be eternally grateful to the freedom it allows me now. I feel insecure, isolated, because I can't find common grounds with the group. I am too aware that I am being unfair today anyway, because I am furious with Dad for pulling one of his typical forgetting stunts. I am tired of hearing them talk of their parents. It's like hearing people talk of their operations when you haven't had one. I feel left out, I resent it, but my efforts to enter by contrasting our parents fails. My pride hurts. I decide to drop out of the discussion. It is over soon, and I am glad. I leave with Polly. I like her quite a lot.

Sometimes not all of the group is present. It makes the slant of the discussion as well as content quite different. Once Bill misses a session. Bob's attitudes toward the group come through very strongly. He is very idealistic and rather specific about goals of the group. I discover a deep sincerity in him as Henry, John and I are the only others present. This time I come to accept him as a part of the group as well as a counselor. This is partly because he exposes himself more, and I appreciate him as an individual, not as a "competent counselor." I decide that this accepting would relate to Bill too (and I later test to find this is true). The sessions I have been having with Bob have given me confidence in a group situation because I feel that he has some understanding of me, that he'll be able to help me communicate how I feel to the group. I'm so afraid they'll misunderstand. My roommate is taking official steps to leave Vanderbilt. This finalizes my defeat in the race for champion minute-made counselor of the year. This leaves me a little sheepish, a little depressed because I like Anne very much; I want her to be around me very much. I want to get all this out before the group; I want their support. I want them to tell me I have dropped the whole affair on the top of too high a hill. I want them to say Anne and I are going to be friends always. Anne will be all right. Anne likes me. I want them to say they would be frightened and hurt too, if they were in my place. But I do not feel I can talk with these people about such a specific worry. It's so personal I am not sure it's really ready for sacrifice (as I perceive telling it to the group at this point). I am grateful when John brings up a good cover-up topic for me. He says, finally bluntly, he resents Henry and me for our shyness, our lack of contribution to the group. I have been feeling bad about my quietness. I feel as though I am watching these people instead of experiencing with them. I wonder if I am not dragging my heels. Should I leave the group? I am not helping it any. But I want it; I like it. I feel a sense of need that is not out of fear of the future without the group. But it is there in its weblike existence.

(Two sessions ago) Bob starts out crying failure. We meet with two absent. We wonder if John and Don won't drop out of the group. Bob expresses dissatisfaction with our lack of "progress." I want to make him feel his efforts have been worthwhile. I try very hard to be open, to expose myself. I know this is part of what he wants. The discussion is about Don and John. There is always a kind of superficial framework around our discussions—something or somebody to kick—Bill, Bob, a piece of conversation last week. I'm tired of this frame. At first it gave me a sense of safety and an aura of direction or reference to a position in which some of us felt secure and could express emotions. I like to criticize, but I feel that we're hiding now. All we have done is hide, and it's time to quit. I say this in so many words and find I am the only group member who feels any need to make such a statement. I don't need this kind of defense. My others are sufficient without it. I feel as though I am sitting there contemplating me standing back a little, a me whose inside is still protected but the numerous contrivances, "defenses" I have mustered to rally around the inner me hang unorganized, embarrassingly plain. I am seeing me without the threads of rationalization and self-lies that make me hang together in an artificially organized way. I do not like their picture of me. This is the negative, so I look at me from another point of view. I do not quite focus, yet I see me slipping around these defenses in spite of myself. I like this me much better. I can accept it without making an object of me any more; this way of looking at me is more real. Bob and Bill seem to be dropping a lot of positive reactions in my direction; so much so I wonder if they feel it will draw me out. It does help because my feelings of insecurity are mainly the superficial ones of expressing it to gain understanding. I do not question the experience of feeling—it is real and accurate at this time.

The last session is about Don and yet about all of us. John and Don return to laugh at our guessing they had quit the group. Don says he will quit because of his homework. I want to let him know how shallow I think he's being, but I feel especially reserved. I am drained from having finished two hours of tests. I am afraid to speak because I know I have been talking too slowly as a result of pain medication. Polly notices my slowness and makes a quip, since she thinks I am joking. I feel as though I will be laughed at if I say any more, and I am tired of making the effort to get a thought to the front of my mind. I settle down to listen. John and Polly begin to get inside each other. As they are communicating, they conclude they feel insecure. At this climax Don interrupts to ask for a definition of security. Bob attacks this response as inappropriate intellectualization so strongly that Don is moved to show irritation and hostility. I enjoy their give-and-take and hope Bill's very accurate (to me at least) interjections make sense to Tom. Now as usual the group situation is one of attacking, except this time it is attacking a central issue and Don is getting positive responses. Bob points out the specific, Bill puts it in context in Don's personality. Don seems at loss to understand, but he looks agitated, worried and hurt. The session ends devoted to Don. I feel omitted, but I am glad to be. I want Don to see himself. Outside the center, all except Bob and Bill stand around giving Don enough positive support that he will consider staying in the group. Polly and John keep saying they hope the sessions can help him. I want him to see it in another light. I explain to him the group is very importantant to me. I do not want it to fail. As an important part of the group he has to return. I am afraid I have said the wrong thing. I am surprised to see him start and give my eyes a sincerity check. That night he calls me and talks to me for thirty minutes on the pretext of checking on a mutual friend. He wants me to reassure him that Bob and Bill are "out of line." I might have done so a few months ago. Now I tell him as convincingly as I know how that they aren't completely wrong. The only reassurance I can give him is that he must view this criticism in light of his whole personality, that they aren't tearing him apart. I want him to come back. I feel I have been very inadequate, but I will never be just sympathetic if I can help it. It is too shallow a reaction, as I am beginning to realize.

I look at myself over this semester. I am dreading the end of these group sessions. I want them to continue next year. I am looking at why I feel so nearly completely positive about these experiences. I have just now realized the most important result: I am looking into myself because experiencing a group of this nature will inevitably lead to this. I have been looking before this time, before coming to the point that I could experience the group. Now I can see the validity of my picture of me against the background of the group. I realize that I must accept my own ability to see myself accurately, even when I may be in error. In areas like threat to my feelings that I am worth something, I see I am less accurate in self-judgment. A fear of finding nothing in me in my self-search has been removed by the group. I am becoming aware, really aware. My experiencing and inter-relating with others is richer and deeper. My whole world is becoming spring with blossoming of feeling and experiencing life around me and being aware of it. My closest friends see a change in me in the way I am frank about my feelings (at least more than I used to be; I am still very reserved). They don't all like me better for it, but some do. I am much more able to respond to them, to see them, now that I am so aware of my own feelings. One friend has been in essence alienated by my approaching nearer to her. I would guess she might feel as threatened now about experiencing herself as I was about a couple of months ago. I'm not changing, except in surface ways, as I find some of my ways of expression incongruous to my realization of deeper meanings in my life. One way of being with others has changed in a physical sense. I once was too reserved to touch a friend, even when I felt I could express what I was feeling by doing it. Now I don't mind taking a friend's hand or putting my arm around her shoulder to show her that I feel deeply. This is one gesture some girls resent, even when they will admit they feel deeply about something. I was of the same frame of mind, until I was convinced by the group, and by the reflecting it made me do, that the more freely an emotion is expressed, the more meaningful, the richer the experience.

Becoming aware and expressing my feelings has created minor problems in its wake. I used to stress consistency in behavior—the person who is intelligent and who is considered a good member of society is consistent. I took this to the extreme and set up a philosophy and ground rules for dealing with others on such a static point of view. Now my emphasis is changing. The importance of being is finding meaning in the richness of experience. As I experience, I do not go back to a set way of interpreting the situation, but I integrate it with past experience and reinterpret the past on the basis of the present. I feel free to change. Being consistent in my former framework is little more than being dead to living around me and in me. I am not trying to fill in the details of a picture in a frame. I am attempting to start with a central figure— me as I *am*—and build out and out as far as my experiences have meaning. I see my conservatism in fear of changing as choking out this richness. I am beginning to feel less fear in exploring myself; I think I can later apply it to experiencing without struggling. This kind of experiencing takes effort now; I know it will always take effort to be opened to life in this way. But it was taking a lot of effort to be closed. Despite a little feeling of fright, I am excited and determined to explore myself. I am just beginning. I hope it takes me somewhere.

Remarks Concerning the Technical Function of the Group

1. I was surprised that the group had such different meanings to different people. This is probably a result of the ambiguousness of the purposes of the group. I am coming to believe that this vagueness is a necessity to make the groups have any success.

2. Our particular group changed counselors after two sessions. This factor may have slowed the group's progress in becoming a real group, but I don't feel it hindered us.

3. Meeting with incomplete groups points up the type of interrelating that each does, giving a first key to the "kind of person I am." Attendance should be stressed, but it should be noted that no one's absence will deter the group.

4. The counselors are in the awkward position of being professionals. This is a principal reason for the reserve at the first sessions. As they become a part of the group, we quit stereotyping them and we accept them as counselors and as members. Their exposing of themselves is a necessity for this reason.

5. It is artificial to say the group is a success or the group is a failure. The fact that the group continues to meet is some measure of success. The key is whether the members of the group feel it has been for other members, although I can't apply this to one member. Then according to my basis for measuring success, the groups should continue.

6. I may change my opinion about the groups; the further removed I am in time from these sessions the better judge I think I will be of them. Will this mean anything to me in fifteen years? Would I still be in favor of their existence? I don't know.

The material below was written at my request about four months after the final group meeting. It is evidence, very convincing to me, that the process of personal growth continued over the summer.

There is a wall outside my window. It is brick, impersonal, unchanging. Last year my window was at the foot of that wall. From the window to the wall spreads out a smooth green carpet of grass, spring-green even through winter snows because of the heat seeping from the building. Always the same. A small left-to-right ripple in the flat surface. An occasional butterfly or squirrel too much in a hurry to make a change. But monotonous as that landscape was, I never thought of wanting a change. Without knowing what else I could see, I accepted the familiar for fear of a worse unknown. And then this year I moved to an end room on the second floor. I see the same walls, the same bricks that hovered over my window last year, but now they are just a footnote to a whole theme of people walking slowly on the paths below, cars turning off the street and parking and doors closing and people going to work, to play, and returning. A nurse entering the infirmary. Lights turning on in the Counseling Center. A policeman whistling "Tonight." An endless scene of endless change. A last year's corner of backdrop mushrooming into a stage bright with action. And I am audience and the light man and the heroine. In short, it is my world.

I walked into this world of life and action less than a year ago. It was a lot like climbing steps except it was harder work and I can't seem to find the end of the steps. I found this world, but I was afraid to enter. One by one all my shoring up against this world was destroyed. My desire to enter it was aroused and encouraged. Through this tearing-down, building-up process, the group sessions, I finally entered this world. This world was me. I began exploring myself, sometimes just watching, sometimes acting to test myself. I suppose it was unreasonable, or at least naive of me, but I originally thought this process of self-study would be brief and extremely painful. But there is constant change in me just as there is outside my window, and I intend to be aware of the change and to encourage and enjoy it.

A strange thing, perhaps, to say that what matters is that I am basically more aware of myself, because of the group. But that is simply the essence of it, and the result of a very difficult endeavor for me. I believe relatively few of my friends are willing or prepared to take the risk involved in introspection. Necessity, desire and ability are required by the process. One without the others would not be a wide enough base for success and conceivably could be disastrous. Necessity was provided by my environment (and it will always be so supplied). I had to alter, to change to meet its challenge, and to find out to what extent I was guilty of failure. Desire was supplied by an intense interest in people which I curiously enough decided might even extend to include me. Part was academic: if you don't know yourself, you don't know what you want, so it's impossible to make a decision. If you are reminded of this in a class three times a week, it is very difficult to forget yourself the other four days. The other part of desire to learn is curiosity, and being female I just couldn't let status quo be. It was the ability to penetrate myself that was completely absent. Then it was simply a matter of education, almost all of which I received within the special group situation. The hardest step was redirecting misinformation about myself. After that it was exhilarating to explore, to learn new things. This supplying of ability was the primary function of the group for me. I believe now it also could have provided necessity and desire, but not all three to one person. At least one must be brought to the group by the individual. And it seems to me that the most successful group would be one containing every combination of these characteristics. I feel most of the people in my group were seeking ability, which would explain some of the difficulties of our particular group.

But I'm evading the real issue. What about me? I like me a lot better, not because of change, but because I am willing to recognize more of myself and to allow myself more expression. I'm still reserved; I want to be. But I surprise myself with my courage to do what I want to do: to talk to a stranger, to shun openly what I do not want to do. Yet there is a carry-over from more timid days that I do not quite understand. I think the best example is what I might call the Left-Foot Phenomenon. Dr. Phillips, who met me at my worst emotionally, must find me completely incommunicable still. I am always disorganized when I try to talk to him, no matter how hard I try to relax. I feel perfectly at ease, I just can't appear that way. And another professor, who terrified me, still gets my old defense, sarcasm, although I feel perfectly at ease with him now. At home this summer Dad noticed that I was different but he couldn't analyze it at all. He just commented about how happy I was. Mother didn't notice it at all. Yet I know that I meet new situations quite differently. And when I get an old friend and a new one together, the conversation always ends up with stories of my shyness as compared with my present ability to "pretend to be so outgoing." If I could just understand this carry-over I might find a key to the change process itself, instead of just results.

I miss the group. I miss its members. I still find myself amused and a little irritated by a remark made during our post-mortem session at exam time. One of the counselors, yielding to the Ah-ha phenomenon, noticed I used the phrase "I feel." Quite a step forward, he seemed to think. If I could only have described to him how much, how deeply I was feeling things. The other counselor seemed a little hurt that I found it easier to write what I was feeling than to discuss it with him. I am sorry he felt that way, but that is just exactly the problem. It was impossible for me to communicate feelings then because it had been so long since I wanted to that I had lost the ability to talk about myself. It is still quite difficult, but I am practicing and learning constantly. I have spent too long trying to fit myself into a misconcept that I could rationalize. I want to constantly re-experience myself during the critical moments of the sessions because stressing one phase of myself in a crisis I see it in silhouette. A silhouette is incomplete, I know, but it is simplified enough that I can learn more about myself from it. Although I worry a great deal about things before they happen, since I'm born and bred a pessimist, I don't worry about my inadequacies in the situation. I feel capable of doing almost everything in my reach. I can laugh about what once embarrassed me. I have much more confidence in my decisions.

A girl comes to me. She talks to me as her floor counselor. She trusts me, expects me to help. I am surprised, first, because without this responsibility last year I was expected to give only sympathy. Now sympathy is unwanted; better on my part are discretion, willingness to understand, and to agree or disagree if possible. I feel so good about what I have done, both in giving advice and refusing to give it. To be able to talk with people like this is something I desire very much. To be inside, but not enmeshed in, someone's feelings. To see how many kinds of love and hate exist. To prod those who are still incapable.

Morning comes early and soft and vibrant with the sun. There is deep exhilarating solitude. To be a part of it, to put aside the rush, the heart-sickening knowledge of a mother slowly dying. To smell coffee in the early damp and hear your dog come running down to play with you. To have a nice soft laugh at how a child, me, is going to pretend to be an adult today. To look forward to living each moment. These are an indication of an inner strength and peace developing from a mutual understanding of the outer mask and the inner identity. Not a war between them. Slowly and painfully the outer mask is conceding its falseness and uselessness as my inner identity, my feelings, diffuse through me and take possession. And in the process are all the tragedies and comedies that exhilarated me and challenge me to accept what seems to be a nearly impossible environment at home. Sometimes my feelings remind me of a rhapsody, disorganized like Sibelius' *Finlandia,* with all the strength and clash and struggle and wrecking of physical environment overcome at least momentarily by a more sensitive peace coming from within, and yet understanding of sheer environmental strength. I know there is an immaturity in my exhilaration. But I want to be a child. I want to run out in the snow and pick up a handful of snow and toss it up and let it fall back on my face. I want to curl up on my window ledge and watch lightning streak through black clouds and listen for thunder to come shouting across the tallest buildings on campus. I want the excitement of the wind blowing so hard that it reminds me of a pompous violin section tuning up on opening night. I want to be a child. I want to get excited and enjoy little, common things. I don't want to lose myself in growing up. I want to learn more about myself.

REFERENCES

Allen, F. H. *Psychotherapy with children.* New York: Norton, 1942.

Allport, G. W. *Pattern and growth in personality.* New York: Holt, Rinehart & Winston, 1961.

Anderson, H. H. Creativity as personality development. In H. H. Anderson (Ed.), *Creativity and its cultivation.* New York: Harper, 1959.

Combs, A. W., & Snygg, D. *Individual behavior.* (Rev. ed.) New York: Harper, 1959.

Izard, C. E. Personality similarity and friendship. *J. abnorm. soc. Psychol.,* 1960, *61,* 47-51.

Izard, C. E. Personality similarity and friendship: a follow-up study. *J. abnorm. soc. Psychol.,* 1963, *66,* 598-600.

Johnson, W. J. *People in quandaries.* New York: Harper, 1946.

Jung, C. G. *The practice of psychotherapy.* New York: Pantheon, 1954.

Maslow, A. H. *Motivation and personality.* New York: Harper, 1954.

Miller, N., Campbell, D. T., & Twedt, H. Similarity, contrast, and complementarity in friendship choice. Mimeographed manuscript, Yale University, 1964.

Murphy, G. *Human potentialities*. New York: Basic Books, 1958.

Rank, O. *Will therapy and truth and reality*. New York: Knopf, 1945.

Rogers, C. R. A theory of therapy, personality, and interpersonal relationships, as developed in the client-centered framework. In S. Koch (Ed.), *Psychology: a study of a science*, vol. 3. New York: McGraw-Hill, 1959. (a)

Rogers, C. R. A tentative scale for the measurement of process in psychotherapy. In E. A. Rubinstein & M. B. Parloff (Eds.), *Research in psychotherapy*. Washington, D.C.: National, 1959. (b)

Cognitive aspects of affective arousal

O. J. Harvey

The aged and widespread tradition of demarcating impermeably between cognition and affectivity is currently undergoing drastic reshaping in the direction of viewing these twin facets of behavior as interdependent processes. Research during the past three decades has made it clear that intraorganismic factors may affect, and under certain conditions predominate in determining, perception, judgment and other cognitive activities. With the notable exception of a few functionally oriented psychologists, such as James (1890) and Troland (1928), it is only fairly recent, however, that serious concern has been shown for the reciprocal side of this question, the influence of cognition upon affective arousal and motive instigation, e.g., McClelland, Atkinson, Clark & Lowell (1953), Rosenberg (1956), Festinger (1957), Harvey, Hunt & Schroder (1961), Tomkins (1962), Hunt (1963).

It is chiefly with the effects of cognition on affective arousal that this chapter is concerned. While I shall assume that affective arousal always results in motive arousal, although all motivation is not necessarily preceded by affect, I will not attempt to deal with the full sequence of events and consequences from cognition, the receipt and processing of an input, through affective arousal and motive instigation to behavior connected with motive satisfaction. Rather, I shall attempt to describe briefly certain aspects of cognition and then to relate these to different qualities and intensities of affect. Following a depiction of the organism's apparent tendency toward the evolution and maintenance of a way of ordering or construing a situation, some of the "why's" underlying negative reactions to departures from the customary will be discussed briefly. The utility of one's more or less standardized modes of construal in serving as a baseline against which inputs are gauged and transformed into psychological significance will be described. Ways in which one's concepts give directionality to interpretation and response and influence affective arousal will be suggested. And lastly, some relevant but unsolved issues surrounding the influence of baseline-event incongruities will be indicated.

TENDENCY TOWARD STRUCTURE AND MAINTENANCE OF MEANING

That an individual when facing a situation of personal relevance to him will differentiate and integrate it, will somehow structure or make meaning out of it, has become one of psychology's best documented and most pervasive assumptions. While any number of labels could be, indeed have been, affixed to these more or less standardized modes of construal or interpretive predilections, we shall refer to them as *concepts*.

Once formed, concepts seem to possess as a salient characteristic resistance to change, the amount of resistance being a function of such factors as degree of commitment to or centrality of the activated concept(s) and the nature and intensity of the event pressing toward change. This tendency toward evolving a way of reading the world and of maintaining it in the face of subsequent, often discrepant, inputs disposes toward a kind of cognitive paradox involving conflict between the costs and credits of having the world too highly structured or not having it ordered enough. Although the environing world would remain in a blooming, buzzing confusion, to borrow from James (1890), probably even in a state of irrelevance and nothingness without concepts, once a way of ordering becomes established it tends to be perpetuated and to preclude seeking for or acceptance of other definitional possibilities. "Perceiving, thinking, judging and related activities are profoundly affected by—perhaps even wholly dependent upon—a pre-established system of ordering or conceptual placement . . . And yet this very dependence on a system of categories leads to a kind of conceptual closedness, reflected in a functional blindness to alternative evaluations that are not embodied in the conceptual framework employed at the moment" (Harvey & Beverly, 1961, p. 125).

In describing the "law of inhibition of instincts by habits," James (1890) pointed to some of the consequences of restricted conceptual and behavioral alternatives:

> "When objects of a certain class elicit from an animal a certain sort of reaction, it often happens that the animal becomes partial to the first specimen of the class on which it has reacted, and will not afterward react on any other specimen.

> "The selection of a particular hole to live in, of a particular mate, of a particular feeding-ground, a particular variety of diet, a particular anything, in short, out of a possible multitude, is a very wide-spread tendency among animals, even those low down in the scale . . . The rabbit will deposit its dung in the same corner; the bird makes its nest on the same bough. But each of these preferences carries with it an insensibility to *other* opportunities and occasions—an insensibility which can only be described physiologically as an inhibition of new impulses by the habit of old ones already formed . . . Few of us are adventurous in the matter of food; in fact, most of us think there is something disgusting in a bill of fare to which we are unused. Strangers, we are apt to think, cannot be worth knowing, especially if they

come from distant cities, etc. . . . And so it comes about that, witnessing this torpor, an observer of mankind might say that no *instinctive* propensity toward certain objects existed at all. It existed, but it existed *miscellaneously,* or as an instinct pure and simple, only before habit was formed. A habit, once grafted on an instinctive tendency, restricts the range of the tendency itself, and keeps us from reacting on any but the habitual object, although other objects might just as well have been chosen had they been the first-comers" (James, 1890, Vol. 2, pp. 394-395).

Such "tunnel vision" and resistance to all but a limited band of environmental impingements may be "explained" by several somewhat related but different theories.

REASONS FOR CONCEPTUAL CLOSEDNESS AND AVOIDANCE
OF DEVIANT STIMULI

As in the case of all "why's," the tendency toward "tunnel vision" and negative reactions to events and situations that depart too markedly from our habitual modes of construal and response can be "explained" by several theories that do not, as James' theory did, involve the assumption of inhibition. Four other theoretical stances that have, in one form or another, been related to conceptual fixity and negative reactions to incongruities are: (1) field theory and thermodynamics, (2) homeostasis and wisdom of the body, (3) cortical stimulation, and (4) the need for meaning and self-structure.

1. Field theory and thermodynamics. Field theory and thermodynamics, offsprings of common parents, have led to certain parallel assumptions. Most relevant to the question of conceptual maintenance is the assumption that all systems are endowed with inherent organizational tendencies which dispose toward the evolution of stable parts and toward establishment and maintenance of a state of equilibrium or synchrony among them. Incursion from external sources or malfunctioning of some intrasystem element upsets the balanced state and produces states of tension and mobilization toward restoration of harmony and equilibrium.

The notions of organization and equilibrium imply that, once it has come into being, a system is endowed with the tendency toward self-preservation, or "dynamic self-regulation," as Katz (1950) termed it. This assumption became basic to three lines of thought relevant to the present issue: the theory of psychodynamics advanced by Freud; the field theory of Gestalt psychology, especially as elaborated and popularized by Lewin; and the "wisdom of the body" or homeostasis hypothesis developed by physiology and borrowed by psychology.

Freud, with his subsystems of id, ego, and superego, was mainly concerned with ways in which the various defense mechanisms operate through unconscious means to protect the ego system from the forces disposing toward the tension state of anxiety. Lewin, more inclined toward operationalism and experimentation, focused on the effects of disequilibrium and psychic tensions produced by such situational impingements as task interruption, goal blocking, and failure to achieve at aspired levels (Lewin, 1935). Both Freud and Lewin, together with their theoretical cousins in physiology, assumed that the tension generated by threat and displacement from the steady state was resolved in ways most compatible with the welfare or functioning of the total system. Miller (1955), in his discussion of the applications of general systems theory, has expressed a derivation of this notion this way: "Systems which survive employ the least expensive defenses against stress first and increasingly more expensive ones later" (p. 528).

The impact of field theory and Lewin's thinking is evident today in such works as Festinger's (1957) theory of cognitive dissonance, in Heider's (1946, 1958) treatment of balance, in Newcomb's (1953, 1961) treatment of symmetry, in Osgood & Tannenbaum's (1955) treatment of congruity, as well as in numerous other related articles and books having to do with responses to discrepant inputs.

2. *Homeostasis and wisdom of the body.* The notion that a system mobilizes its defenses to ward off or in other ways cope with forces portending threat, too much tension and disruption, expressed commonly but in different languages by Freud and Lewin, was also central in the homeostatic doctrine of many physiologists. Upset of the equilibrium of the internal system was assumed to bring into action the necessary forces for restoration of balance. Cannon quotes Claude Bernard, whom he credits with being first to suggest that the internal environment operates in terms of equilibration, as saying: "It is the fixity of the *milieu interieur* which is the condition of the free and independent life . . . and all the vital mechanisms, however varied they may be, have only one object, that of preserving the conditions of life in the internal environment" (Cannon, 1932, p. 38).

The work of Cannon, exemplified in his monumental *Wisdom of the Body* (1932), helped to document and popularize the theory of homeostasis as a principle of system adaptation and survival. Organisms were shown to engage involuntarily and automatically in a wide range of adjustive activities in response to an upset of such internal constancies as those surrounding temperature, blood sugar, acidity, water content of the blood and lymph, oxygen, blood sodium, blood calcium, protein and other elements. As P. T. Young summarizes this work:

> "The internal conditions, as Cannon said, are not rigidly fixed, but they vary within limits according to the demand of the external environment. Thus if the existence of the total organism is threatened with an encounter with an enemy, there are prompt alterations within the internal fluid matrix that tend to assist the organism in a struggle for existence. For example, if a cat is threatened by a barking dog, there is a rise in the level of blood sugar, thus providing a source for increased energy during vigorous muscular exertion; the circulation of blood in muscles and brain is speeded up; the processes of digestion

are temporarily checked; adrenin is poured into the blood stream by the adrenal glands thus stimulating the heart and producing other adaptive changes; oxygenation is accelerated through action of the spleen, etc. All such changes prepare the cat for a life-and-death struggle in the face of a crisis. Thus internal changes meet the demands of the external conditions" (Young, 1961, p. 112).

Richter extended the principle of homeostasis to show how overt behavior facilitates the maintenance of physiochemical balance. Homeostatic imbalance is presumed to instigate behavior which compensates for the disturbance and tends to restore the steady state. Richter sought to illustrate this principle through the effects of removal of several of the ductless glands in rats. Removal of the pituitary gland, which impairs the ability of the body to generate adequate heat, resulted in the operated animals compensating by building larger and warmer nests (Richter, 1942). Adrenalectomized rats, which would normally die through the loss of sodium chloride through the urine, overcame this loss and seemingly maintained good health through marked increases in salt intake when given free access to a 3% solution of sodium chloride (Richter, 1936). Similarly, animals which had had their parathyroid glands removed were able to maintain a fairly normal life, instead of the usual weight loss, tetany and death, by taking in increased calcium when it was made freely available to them (Richter & Eckert, 1939). From these and related findings, such as the apparent tendency to avoid poisons and select proper diets in cafeteria type feedings, Richter concluded that ". . . in human beings and animals the effort to maintain a constant internal environment or homeostasis constitutes one of the most universal and powerful of all behavior urges or drives" (Richter, as quoted by Young, 1961, p. 113).

Until the recent upswing in the usage of "balance," "consonance," "congruity" and "symmetry" models, the concept of homeostasis was applied widely to a variety of psychological problems. Thus Freeman (1948) broadened the notion to include most of the traditional problems relating to motivation, or "energetics," as he preferred to term it. It was his thesis "that objective descriptions of total neuromuscular homeostasis (in terms of the interaction of isolable overt and covert part-reaction systems) offer independent and direct measures of dynamic behavior wholes which in themselves will ultimately 'outfield' the field theories of the Gestaltist, psychoanalyst, and other exponents of psychic energetics and phenomenological description" (Freeman, 1948, p. 506). Perhaps even more expansive was the effort of Stagner and Karwoski (1952) to interpret the typical issues treated in introductory psychology within the framework of the homeostatic doctrine.

3. *Cortical stimulation.* If the question "Why do man and infrahuman animals react negatively to events that deviate from what they have adapted or habituated to?" were addressed to a neurophysiological psy-

chologist or to a neo-behaviorist, his answer probably would involve some notion of arousal or activation level. Since Hebb's *Organization of Behavior* (1949) it has become increasingly more prevalent to view organisms as disposed toward maintenance of some more or less standardized and optimal level of cortical activity (see Fiske & Maddi, 1961). This "optimal," as depicted by Berlyne, for example, "will normally be some distance from both the upper and the lower extreme" (Berlyne, 1960, p. 194). Marked deviation from the optimal level of cortical arousal in either direction, toward either increased or decreased stimulation, is assumed to result in negative reaction to the input. Stimuli are generally assumed, in line with the affective arousal hypotheses of Hebb (1955) and McClelland et al. (1953), to produce maximum positive affect when they are slightly but not too discrepant from the baseline represented by the adaptation level or pooling of past experience on a particular dimension. Repeated stimulation at or near the adaptation level (AL) results in stimulus satiation and, through shifting of the AL toward the input, a less than optimal proximity to the physical value of the input. Too low a level of arousal is assumed to lead to boredom, even to hallucinations in the case of extreme sensory deprivation (Bexton, Heron & Scott, 1954), and to activity directed toward bringing in more stimulation. Hence the person or animal under stimulus satiation or less than optimal arousal should experience slightly discrepant inputs as positive, expressed in curiosity and a tendency toward exploration of its environment in search of greater stimulus complexity and novelty in order to increase its level of activation—Hebb (1955), Glanzer (1958), Berlyne (1960). The "exploratory-curiosity-manipulatory drive," suggests Hebb (p. 247) "essentially comes down to a tendency to seek varied stimulation." "The significance of this relationship," he continues, "is a phenomenon of the greatest importance for understanding motivation in higher animals. This is the *positive attraction of risk taking,* or mild fear, *and of problem solving,* or mild frustration . . ." (p. 250). Probably, as I suggested earlier, "Too varied a pattern of stimulation, too much complexity, too high a level of arousal, on the other hand, leads to efforts at reducing the stimulation by withdrawing from the different and more complex toward the simpler and the familiar, even in freezing and other strongly avoidant responses" (Harvey, 1963, p. 10).

Most of the arousal level hypotheses remain essentially theories of tension reduction (Berlyne, 1960) despite many writers in the area, including Hebb initially (1949), assuming that they were not. Instead of tissue depletions creating tension and driving behavior, as Hull (1943) and his adherents believed, the need to maintain optimal levels of arousal or stimulation has been substituted. Deviation from the optimal arousal is now seen as creating tension and discomfort, motivating the organism toward efforts at their removal. The idea that an organism is curious, seeks novelty, and explores just because of "intrinsic" factors, a view that gained a brief popularity, has been replaced fairly completely by the assumption that such behavior is instrumental to the maintenance of levels of optimal excitation, tension and arousal.

Arousal level theories, in addition to being aberrant tension reduction hypotheses, also imply a kind of homeostatic or equilibrium principle. But in these more neurophysiological notions what is being maintained has shifted from field tensions and blood chemistry balance to the optimal level of excitation in the "conceptual nervous system" (Hebb, 1955). The determinants of this assumed optimum, even at the theoretical level, remain to be worked out. The assumption appears to be that it is the volume of past stimulation *per se* that determines the adaptation level or optimal baseline. According to Glanzer, "The increase or decrease with respect to parts of the environment is a function of the difference between the average amount of information the individual is accustomed to and the current rate of flow from the environment" (1958, p. 312).

If the average volume of past stimulation or environmental inputs is the AL that determines the subjective intensity and affective consequence of a stimulus treatment, then the individual who has undergone varied and intense inputs, who has experienced a larger volume of stimulation, should, owing to a higher AL in this domain, experience less upset and negative affect in a sensory depriving condition than the person with a history of a lower volume of stimulation, whose AL, consequently, is lower and less discrepant from the low level of stimulation generated by the sensory depriving conditions. This assumption implies that the mean value of the physical intensity and variance of past stimulation serves as the immediate antecedent to behavioral and affective reactions to a homogeneous environment; that it is the magnitude of departure of subsequent input from this mean that determines its psychological weighting; and that, in keeping with the butterfly curve hypothesis, large mean-situation discrepancies should produce more negative affect than smaller, more nearly optimal, ones. Some possible shortcomings of this assumption, especially of that aspect that treats the AL or immediate precursor to response in terms of the mean of its physical attributes instead of in terms of the effects of the physical impingements upon cognitive structure, will be indicated in the next section.

4. *The need for meaning and self structure.* Negative reaction to events that depart from the habitual mode of construing them might be explained in terms of yet another theoretical alternative. A functionalist or an ethologist, without too much theoretical absurdity, might posit a biogenic need for structure; and hostility to alien events could be accounted for in terms of threat to the structure or meaning attached to the situation. The tendency to structure need not, however, be treated as a biological imperative, for, native or not, interpreting or making sense out of the situation in some way appears unquestionably essential to the prediction of recurrences and consistencies in the environing world. To cope adequately with the environment, indeed even to survive in it under certain conditions, necessitates the ability to "read" the situation with at least some

measure of veridicality. To satisfy even the simpler motives requires that the organism be capable of distinguishing relevant means-ends relationships, be able to "know" what objects or stimuli are motive relevant and be capable of delineating and engaging appropriate courses of action for their attainment. One's matrix of concepts or totality of habitual modes of construal is the vehicle through which these requisite ends are effected. Curiosity, searching, manipulation and going beyond the certain are ways in which these construal networks can be further differentiated, refined and organized into both more sensitive and more general "programs," "filters" or "metering systems." Development toward greater differentiation and integration, toward greater cognitive complexity or abstractness, renders the individual less dependent on the physical aspects of the world, more capable of transcending these both in time and space. It allows for the perception of more varied goals and more means to their attainment. It provides a more adequate means of fate control, greater independence from the pressures of the physical world, a greater mastery over what would otherwise be a capricious, unpredictable and overwhelming environment. Events that depart too far from one's conceptions of them hence portend paralysis of central aspects of one's functioning, of the apparatus through which he reads the world, interacts with and survives in it.

As we have proposed elsewhere—Harvey, Hunt & Schroder (1961), Harvey & Schroder (1963)—an individual's conceptual system, the totality of his ties to and definitions of the world, is synonymous with his self. Thus refutation of or threat to one's standardized construal of a situation would be equivalent to threat to the self, would portend negation of one's assumed means-ends relations, and, if severe enough, would render the world chaotic and unstructured, destroying in the process one's means of fate control and techniques of defining and coping with his environment.

Refutation or confirmation of some of one's many concepts, however, will produce stronger and more dramatic effects than the same treatment of others, the specific effect depending on factors to be indicated in the next section. The point being made is simply that one's cognitive makeup, comprised of a myriad of definitional components and tendencies, serves a critical function in anchoring and orienting the organism to his world and, that owing to this deep significance, one's concatenation of concepts operates to give direction to perception and behavior, provides the means of meaningful existence through mooring one in time and space, and in the capacity of a psychological yardstick functions as the baseline for affective arousal and motive instigation. The importance of maintaining stable ties to, and definitions of, the world has been demonstrated dramatically by the effects of brainwashing, marginality, sensory deprivation and other overly homogeneous environments. Without stimulus heterogeneity of some degree, no avenues are available for generating information of the environment, one is surrounded by homogeneity and meaninglessness. Without the experience of stimulus variation, growth and self-development appear retarded. Obliteration of heterogeneity, through imposition of homogeneous environments or severance of preexisting ties to the surroundings would, if extreme and lasting enough, lead to the demise and extinction of self and being.

For several theoretical reasons, however, wide variation between individuals in their reactions to homogeneous or informationally sparse environments should be expected. The assumption of such neo-behaviorists as Hebb, Berlyne, Glanzer and others, as well as most variations in adaptation-level theory, would lead to the prediction that individuals who had undergone high levels of past stimulation would be more adversely affected by a homogeneous environment, because of the larger than optimal AL-situation discrepancy, than persons who had undergone more homogeneous and lower volumes of stimulation. On the other hand, the mediational assumption that the individual's current cognitive structure rather than the mean of past stimulation is the immediate antecedent to affective arousal and behavior would lead to a considerably different prediction.

A study by Clapp (1964) is relevant to these differential predictions and, while not directly negating the assumption of the neo-behaviorists, the study indicates clearly that variations in cognitive structure related in predicted ways to affective reactions to a situation of markedly reduced external stimulation. Individuals who, among other personality and cognitive attributes, differed in concreteness-abstractness, as characterized by Harvey, Hunt & Schroder (1961) and measured by an instrument devised by Harvey (e.g., 1964) made judgments of autokinetic movement, estimated time passage, responded to the Witkin Rod and Frame Test and completed a questionnaire on affective reactions before and after disorientation. The disorientation treatment consisted of leading subjects, blindfolded and with ear-plugs engaged, to light-proofed experimental rooms over long and circuitous routes following administration of a placebo drug and other treatments aimed at generating apprehension and confusion. In addition to responding in predicted ways on the performance tasks, the more abstract subjects, according to completions of the affective arousal questionnaire, were in general less disoriented, less nervous and less negatively aroused by the treatment than were the more concrete individuals.

Unless some mediational construct is utilized, these results should not have been predicted from the construct of mean past stimulation. This latter notion would have had the subjects of higher levels of past stimulation reacting more negatively to disorientation than the individuals of lower volumes of stimulation. The use of a mediational construct, however, can both tie together the notions of past stimulation and cognitive structure and generate predictions consistent with our findings. The sequential chain might be linked together in the following gross way: more intense and varied stimulation leads to more complex mediational systems which can process or cope with a wider range of stimulus inputs before negative affect and related consequences are generated. This implies clearly, of course, that not only volume of past stimulation but other attributes of the historical inputs must be considered, such as the dimensions of range, variance et cetera.

Theoretical positions other than the four preceding ones are consistent with the tendency to keep one's conception of his world intact or one's level of arousal within certain limits of constancy. Depiction of these four should suffice, however, to indicate the wide consensus concerning the need for certainty, stability and the habitual. Actually, with little effort, the four theoretical stances could be tied together. For example, it is highly probable that an isomorphic relationship exists, if it could be found, between the structure of conceptual systems and the level of arousal sought. Both have resulted from interaction of the organism with its history of stimulation. Whether one wishes to stress the assumed neurological underpinnings or the more superordinate cognitive outcomes depends upon his purpose. Neither emphasis can be vetoed by demonstrably superior validity of the other. As a social psychologist, however, I am primarily concerned with one's cognitive makeup, particularly with one's concepts of the countless objects of experience, social and private, and how these serve as "templates," "filters," "adaptation levels," "baselines," "mediational systems," as the instruments for gauging events and responding to them. Hence in the remainder of this chapter I will attempt to discuss more directly the relationship of conceptual systems to affective arousal.

CONCEPTUAL CONFIRMATION AND REFUTATION

Together with several other writers, e.g., McClelland et al. (1953), Berlyne (1960), Haber (1958), Harvey, Hunt & Schroder (1961), Bevan (1963), Hunt (1963), we assume that the affective and behavioral consequence, the subjective intensity of a given stimulus input, is a function of its perceived discrepancy from the baseline of the recipient at the time of the impingement. We have chosen to label the perceived relationship between input and baseline as either *confirmation* or *refutation,* the former representing perception of the stimulus event as being congruent with the baseline and the latter represented by experience of the impingement as conflicting with or discrepant from the psychological referent point. In general, conceptual confirmation tends to result in positive affect, both toward self and the perceived causal agent, and, correlatively, in approach tendencies toward the agent of attributed causality. Refutation disposes toward opposite consequences, toward negative affect toward self and source and avoidance tendencies toward the perceived agent of refutation. By approach is meant the tendency to decrease the psychological distance between self and the source of confirmation; by avoidance is meant the tendency to increase the psychological distance between self and the agent of refutation. At the more concrete levels of functioning, approach and avoidance tendencies often are expressed motorically, viz., by the individual touching or in some way trying to take into itself positively cathected objects and by his trying to destroy the negatively evaluated situation, event or person or to remove himself physically from its presence. At more abstract levels of functioning, however, these behavioral predilections are more apt to be expressed symbolically, as in the attribution of positive or negative characteristics to self and/or the perceived source of confirmation and refutation. Such expressions are common consequences of interpersonal interactions and exposures to events that run counter to one's characteristic way of reading a situation. The so-called defense mechanisms, as well as other responses to concept-event disparities, are typically engaged to make a significant input conform to some central internal standards(s) or to transform the event sufficiently to minimize alteration of the mode of ordering.

While confirmation and refutation are assumed, respectively, to generate positive and negative affect among their many consequences, their specific effects depend upon several factors. The four to be discussed in this chapter include: (1) the nature of the baseline or internal referent being confirmed or refuted, (2) the direction of the input departure from the baseline, (3) the magnitude of the baseline-event disparity, and (4) the conceptual or personality structure of the respondent.

1. Nature of the baseline (What is being maintained?). Despite a wide band of agreement among representatives of diverse areas in psychology, such as psychophysics, e.g., Bevan (1963), neurophysiology, e.g., Hebb (1955), Leuba (1955), Glanzer (1958), social psychology, e.g., Harvey (1963), personality theory, e.g., McClelland et al. (1963) and general behavior theory, e.g., Berlyne (1960), that the affective and behavioral consequence of an input is a function of its proximity to or distance from some intraorganismic norm or referent, important differences exist among representatives of these several areas concerning the specific nature of this norm or subjective baseline.

The construct that has received the widest treatment as the internal referent or adaptation level (AL) is *expectancy*, the subjective probability of the occurrence or recurrence of a given consequence or outcome under given conditions. In fact, from the early work of McClelland et al. (1953), in which expectancy was posited specifically as the AL or norm against which inputs are compared or contrasted and assigned their affective weight, most of the writers dealing with baseline-event incongruities have tended to treat expectancy as the prime determinant of the effects of a given stimulus deviation or intensity.

This assumption, that expectancy is the most significant "kernel" of the possible host of factors entering into any given baseline, has led to the further assumption, owing to the nature of expectancy, that equal deviation from the baseline in either direction, above or below expectancy, produces identical affective consequences. The "butterfly curve" hypothesis, McClelland et al. (1953), Haber (1958), rests directly on this assumption. According to this hypothesis, seemingly accepted by most of the workers concerned with baseline-event disparities, an expectancy input discrepancy of zero, a complete confirmation of expectancy, should result in the negative affect of boredom; small discrepancies from this AL in either direction should produce positive affect; while large discrepancies in either direction should produce the negative affect of stress, fear and panic—McClelland et al. (1953), Haber (1958), Hebb (1955), Leuba (1955), Glanzer (1958), Berlyne (1960), Hunt (1963). Even though this version of the discrepancy hypothesis was intended as a general statement for all affective arousal, McClelland et al. (1953), even while formulating it, recognized its lack of compatibility with many cases observable from every day life. Consider, as the original authors did, the issue of flunking out of school. According to the butterfly curve hypothesis, in which expectancy serves as the prime internal referent, the individual who expected to flunk should feel good only when he came close but did not quite succeed in flunking. Were he to flunk as expected, he should feel bored; and were he to deviate from expectancy toward high achievement, he should feel very bad about it.

Relinquishment of a guiding and cognitively restricting theoretical model and openness to natural events in every day life would suggest quickly that some factor other than, or in addition to, expectancy generally operates among the internal referents affecting response to a given stimulus event. The possibility of flunking out of school, for example, not only generates certain consequences through its relationship to expectancy; it also produces affective consequences through the involvement of other internal referents such as commitment, aspiration, preference and hope. "The involvement of hope," we have suggested, "means that the subject is *evaluative*, that his interpretive schemata have good and bad poles, that events which confirm his schemata or facilitate attainment of a sought end are construed as positive and desirable while events which refute his evaluative standards are experienced as negative and something to be avoided. Thus the activation of hope or preference . . . would seem to dictate that *direction of discrepancy* as well as magnitude must be considered because deviations from expectancy of equal magnitudes could produce very different effects. Deviation from expectancy toward the achievement of hope should produce positive affect and positive construal of the causal event while deviation from expectancy of the same magnitude toward negation of hope should result in the opposite outcome" Harvey & Clapp (1965). In fact, in those cases in which hope and expectancy run counter to each other, as would obtain when one expected to flunk out of school but hoped very much he would not, the greater the refutation of expectancy, and hence the greater the confirmation of hope, the more positive should be the resulting experience. This, of course, would be in contradiction of the prediction that would be made if expectancy, which *per se* is non-evaluative and non-directional, were treated as the psychological yardstick against which impingements are gauged.

In an attempt to demonstrate that when hope is involved it makes directionality of the input important and may outweigh or combine with expectancy in producing certain effects, Harvey and Clapp (1965) exposed subjects, preassessed on self-esteem, to controlled feedback which deviated from their expectancies by one of two equal magnitudes toward either the confirmation or refutation of hope. Specifically, subjects first indicated both how they hoped and expected to be rated by another person, a relative stranger, on a list of 15 personally relevant characteristics, such as trustworthiness, morality and dependability. They also rated how they perceived self and other on the same scale. Following exposure to fictitious ratings from the other person (which deviated from their own expected ratings by either .5 or 1.5 inches on a graphic rating scale toward either confirming or refuting hope), subjects completed the self-esteem scale again. In addition they re-indicated expected and hoped-for ratings, re-rated self, re-rated the other person, and completed a three-item questionnaire that asked their degree of pleasure-disappointment and their feelings of positivity-negativity toward both self and other as a consequence of the social feedback.

The effects of the directionality of deviation from expectancy may be inferred from Table 1, in which the deviations toward hope are labeled positive and the discrepancies away from hope are labeled negative. With the exception of self-esteem and hope, which because of greater centrality

Table 1 Comparative effects of discrepancies of equal magnitude
but of different directions

| Dependent variables | Deviation (in inches) from expectancy | | | |
| | 1.5 - (-1.5) | | .5 - (-.5) | |
	x̄ Diff.	t	x̄ Diff.	t
Change in self ratings	.33	2.07*	.33	2.63**
Change in other ratings	.77	4.53**	.31	1.71*
Change in expectancy	.58	3.40**	.26	1.69*
Change in hope	.32	1.58	.19	.97
Change in self-esteem†	.33	.08	1.07	.40
Feel-toward self†	.59	1.77*	1.14	3.80**
Feel toward other†	1.45	9.60**	.93	3.36**
Disappointment†	1.94	5.16**	1.02	3.49**

*P < .05, one-tailed test

**P < .01, one-tailed test

† These four variables were measured in larger units than the other four

were expected to be not significantly influenced by the treatments, all eight dependent variables were significantly affected by the directionality of the deviation from expectancy. Changes in self ratings, other ratings and expectancy, as well as pleasure-disappointment and feelings toward self and other were significantly more positive under the positive than under the negative discrepancies. The same trend, although not significant, occurred for changes in both hope and self-esteem.

These results were interpreted to mean:

". . . that not only the magnitude of the deviation of an input from expectancy but that the direction of the discrepancy toward the confirmation or refutation of hope, also contributes significantly to the effective and behavioral consequences of an event. The fact that equivalent deviations from expectancy produced different effects depending on their relationship to hope indicates that such discrepancy hypotheses as those embodied in the notion of the butterfly curve (McClelland, et al., 1953; Haber, 1958) do not hold when aspiration and preferences are called into play. Unlike what would be predicted from the butterfly curve hypothesis, the smaller discrepancies in this study did not consistently produce more positive reactions than the larger deviations. Rather . . . the more positive discrepancy away from expectancy toward hope resulted in more positive responses than the smaller positive deviation on all dependent variables but one. At the same time, the smaller negative deviation [away from expectancy and away from hope] produced more negative reactions than the larger negative discrepancy on three of the dependent variables" (Harvey & Clapp, 1965, in press).

Even though hoped-for ends work in conjunction with expectancies, making direction of discrepancies an important variable, I do not mean to imply that hope and expectancy exhaust the list of important internal referents that in some way comprise a given subjective baseline and determine the affective consequences of a given input. More than likely a concatenation of internal factors enter into the total matrix of referents against which any input is gauged and defined. This points to the necessity of conceiving of the internal baseline in multidimensional rather than in unidimensional terms. Our emphasis on hope or preference, factors that operate so frequently in our daily lives, is aimed only at suggesting one important set of factors which, in addition to expectancy, significantly affect the impact of a stimulus event. It is even probable that many of the effects at the infrahuman level attributed to deviations from expectancy, such as the panic response of a young chimp to an anesthetized chimp or to perception of its keeper in an unfamiliar guise (Hebb, 1946), are also contaminated by preferences for certain states the animal has come to establish. It could be reasoned that the animal's need for structure and consistency in his environment, avenues through which he comes to cope with his world, leads to a commitment to, or involvement in, keeping things as they are, consonant with the expectations and habitual modes of responding. To the extent this is the case, expectancy becomes somewhat subordinate to hope, a kind of instrumentality in the attainment of a sought end.

Expectancy is defined in Webster's dictionary as "that which is expected; the object of expectation or hope." "Expect," "anticipate," and "hope," presented as synonyms, "regard some future event as about to take place. *Expect* is the strongest, and implies some ground or reason in mind for considering the event as likely to happen. To *anticipate* is to look forward to, esp. in such fashion as to realize to oneself what is to come. *Hope* adds to expectation the implication of desire; as, the accused *hopes* for an acquittal."

Thus the concept of expectancy, as used in common parlance or in more technical writing, means more than just the subjective probability of an occurrence. It is confounded by hope and desire, the operation of which give a directionality to inputs. It is possible that unless hope and desire are involved in some degree (that unless while one expects he also has a preference for a particular occurrence) no affect may be produced. This may hold in relation to aesthetics as well as simpler sensory experiences, such as temperature (Haber, 1958). It seems more clearly to obtain in relation to the preponderance of stimulus departures we encounter in our daily lives. Here, learned attitudes and values render us selective, providing us automatically with good and bad poles together with built-in directionalities. Less certain is the possibility that even our sensory experiences, pain and pleasure, and the positive and negative affect resulting from them, is at least in part determined by native, unlearned, factors that affect the AL and subsequent sensory thresholds so that the state of the organism demands or "seeks" one condition over another.

Clearly, it is important that both theoretical and methodological distinctions be made between desire and subjective probability. Until this occurs, contamination effects of one on the other cannot be extricated and specified.

2. *Direction of discrepancy.* This becomes a question only if hope or preference is included among the internal referents comprising the subjective baseline. As indicated earlier, expectancy *per se*, with related components partialled out, is non-directional, and stimulus deviations of equal magnitude above and below expectancy should, as has been hypothesized in the butterfly curve notion, have identical effects. The widespread tendency to consider expectancy as the AL has, as is appropriate from this premise, led to the general practice of considering the effects of magnitude of the baseline-event disparity and omitting from treatment the effects of the direction of stimulus deviation. However, because expectancy rarely, if ever, operates alone and in pure form, directionality of the input departure from the baseline must also be considered.

3. *Magnitude of baseline-event discrepancy.* This variable has received the widest treatment of the many factors that determine the psychological impact of a stimulus impingement. Psychophysical studies, Bevan (1963), Helson (1964), Sherif, Taub & Hovland (1958); experiments in attitude change, Goldberg (1954), Hovland & Pritzker (1957), Hovland, Harvey & Sherif (1957), Harvey, Kelley & Shapiro (1957), Harvey (1962); writings concerned with the adaptation of the organism to novel and stressful situations, Hebb (1946, 1955); as well as work on affectivity, McClelland et al. (1953) have, although often under different terminologies, been concerned with the general question of the optimal

baseline-event disparity for maximal shift of the internal norm toward the input and assimilation of it. For different theoretical reasons it might be assumed, as it has been by several writers, that the effects of increasing AL-input difference is non-linear. For example, from a purely psychophysical basis it might be expected that an event too deviant from the established "scale" or customary definitional norm would result in a break in function and the anchor, perceived as irrelevant to the scale, would cease to shift the scale in the direction of the anchor. A similar anticipation should be reached from an affective arousal point of view. When the discrepancy reaches a certain magnitude and the resulting tension and negative arousal attains a sufficient height, the subject might engage some dissociation or redefinitional process by which the deviant input would be neutralized and its impact lessened. Increased baseline-event difference beyond the magnitude at which input redefinition and/or dissociation occurred should only enhance the neutralizing tendency and reduce the likelihood of the AL being shifted in the direction of the input.

Results seem to indicate, however, that even extreme discrepancies may continue to exercise effects on shifting the baseline (concept, attitude or psychophysical scale) toward the discrepant input or anchor. For example, in several studies in persuasion in which the communication from the source has been made to deviate in graded amounts from the position of the recipient, larger discrepancies have continued to produce greater change in the recipient's position in the advocated direction—Hovland & Pritzker (1957), Goldberg (1954), Harvey, Kelley & Shapiro (1957), Harvey (1962). Complicating this picture, however, is the fact that increased discrepancies dispose toward their source being discredited, a possible manifestation of an effort to lessen the super-optimal stimulation back toward the optimal or, relatedly, to preserve one's concept of the situation as intact as possible.

Related results have been obtained in psychophysical studies in which the effects of deviant inputs in the form of extreme anchors have been examined. In an unpublished study, Bevan (1963) found extreme anchors continued to affect the scale. At the same time, there is evidence to suggest that in the case of well established scales or concepts the tendency toward distorting the anchor away from the scale increases with increased discrepancies—Harvey & Caldwell (1959), Harvey & Campbell (1963). This might be an expression of the same determinant that results in the distortion of communications away from one's own stand when they are too discrepant from it (Hovland, Harvey & Sherif, 1957).

Because most of the studies systematically varying magnitude of baseline-input discrepancy were concerned either with affective arousal or with the effect of the input on shifting the internal referent, but not simultaneously with both, it is impossible to say at this time to what extent affective quality and arousal accompany or parallel other obtained effects from disparate inputs. Obviously judgmental, affective and definitional change measures should be concurrently obtained.

Moreover, it will be impossible to establish clearly the effects of a given stimulus input, even to specify the magnitude of stimulus baseline disparity, until its relationship to the totality of internal referents, including hope, expectancy and others, are specified. Concentration solely on any one of the several possible factors affecting the subjective baseline could mean ignoring other, equally significant, ones. It is possible that ultimately some formula can be devised for weighting and properly including the totality of internal referents into a single pooled value, as Helson and others hope, so that an input can be specified in relation to one single value. It is also possible that, while theoretically plausible, this is psychologically inappropriate and that the relationship of an input to many single internal referents will simultaneously have to be indicated. We have tried to show elsewhere—Harvey, Hunt & Schroder (1961), Harvey & Schroder (1963)—that owing to the multiplicity of referent points and directional predispositions embodied in one's totality of concepts the same input may confirm one referent or concept within the total matrix of conceptual referents while simultaneously refuting others. A pooling of the many relevant internal referents might so grossly oversimplify the richness, complexity and conflict of actual cognitive and affective functioning that, while precise, it might be of questionable validity.

4. *Conceptual systems and reactions to discrepancies.* To the extent that an individual's concatenation of concepts or conceptual system actually serves as the multidimensional baseline in terms of which an input has its affective consequences, variation in the conceptual system, the "filter" or "program" through which the external impingements are processed, should produce differences in the affective and behavioral weighting assigned to common stimulus inputs. For example, an individual holding positive concepts toward some object should be affected differently by a pro-object communication or treatment from a person holding negative concepts toward the same object. Similarly, a person with a high need for external structure and certainty might be markedly upset by a stimulus situation he would perceive as highly ambiguous while an individual with a lower need for structure might perceive the same situation as so highly structured that it was constraining or boring. The individual who has become accustomed to high levels of stimulus diversity, and who presumably has evolved a highly differentiated and integrated conceptual system as a consequence, should seek more stimulation, greater diversity, more challenging situations and greater risk than individuals exposed repeatedly to stimuli of restricted ranges and diversity. In accordance with this possibility, we have found experimentally that more abstract individuals, those presumably from a developmental history of diversity and intensive exploration of their environment, are less motivated toward the resolution of dissonance or cognitive conflict than are the more concrete individuals, those presumably who have undergone prolonged restricted and structured environments in the course of their development (Harvey, 1965). Moreover, more abstract individuals, those of more differentiated and integrated conceptual systems, experience less negative

affect in the presence of highly unstructured environments than do the more cognitively simple or more concrete individuals (Clapp, 1964).

It seems quite clear, then, that the influence of both the direction and magnitude of a stimulus discrepancy are dependent on the conceptual or personality makeup of the recipient. The level of diversity, conflict, stimulation and arousal sought is in no small part a function of properties of his conceptual system, a point which, in different language, has been stressed by several preceding writers, Hebb (1955), Glanzer (1958), Hunt (1963).

IS THE SUBJECTIVE BASELINE LEARNED OR INNATE?

It has been proposed by some writers, e.g., McClelland et al. (1953), that the quality of affect is unlearned but that the conditions that elicit affective arousal, including AL-input disparities, are learned. Other writers, notably Tomkins (1962), feel that not only are affective qualities innate but that certain patterns of stimuli automatically trigger them off.

Some evidence indicates that the AL, at least in relation to the experience of pain, is largely, if not entirely, learned. Hebb (1958) reports some of the work of Melzack as showing that one dog reared in a physically and socially restricted environment, in the absence of pain-producing encounters, "repeatedly thrust his nose into a lighted match; and months later, did the same thing several times with a lighted cigar" (p. 128). Hebb concludes: "It seems certain, especially in view of the related results reported by Nissen, Chow and Semmes for a chimpanzee, that the adult's perception of pain is essentially a function of pain experience during growth—and that what we call pain is not a single sensory qualm but a complex mixture of a particular kind of synthesis with past learning and emotional disturbance" (p. 129).

On the other hand, results from an experiment by Hunt and Quay (1961) point in the direction of native AL's. In this study, addressed directly to the question of whether certain kinds of AL's are innately fixed or are modifiable through experience, one group of rats was raised in a vibratory environment while another group was reared in a stable cage. The group of animals reared in the vibrating cage "preferred" a less stable environment than did the other group of animals; but even the vibratory animals turned off the shaking of their cage at lower levels of intensity than they had undergone during development. This study suggests clearly that there are biological bases underlying some AL's at least and that these are modifiable by experience or repeated exposure only up to a point. In summarizing some of the implications of this study, Hunt (1963) concluded that ". . . rearing animals on various kinds of stimuli which typically evoke withdrawal fails to make them positive incentives for approach responses or positive reinforcers. This fact suggests that various kinds of modalities of stimulation have innate, gene-determined negative (or positive) hedonic values. Becoming 'used to' such stimulation only reduces the degree of its innate value, but it does not alter its direction or hedonic character" (p. 75).

Hunt's conclusion implies clearly that while the AL is not innately fixed there are natural limits beyond which it cannot be shifted or stretched. If true, this places limitation upon the assumption, as expressed by Glanzer (1958), for example, that the amount and kind of stimulation the organism seeks is a function of its past average of stimulation. The operation of biological limits, even though not fixed, would mean that this is not entirely correct, that the organism could be exposed repeatedly to the same stimuli, and in this sense become accustomed to or come to expect them, without shifting the internal baseline to coincide with their value. This is a further indication that in most cases the receiving organism does not neutrally and passively incorporate an input into its internal scale but, rather, in most cases the organism, by virtue of either learning or native endowment, is selective and does prefer one stimulus condition over another. This means, as stressed earlier, that the directionality of inputs as well as other of their attributes must be considered.

REFERENCES

Berlyne, D. E. *Conflict, Arousal and Curiosity.* New York: McGraw-Hill, 1960.

Bevan, W. The pooling mechanism and the phenomenon or reinforcement. In O. J. Harvey (Ed.), *Motivation and social interaction—cognitive determinants.* New York: Ronald Press, 1963.

Bexton, W. A., Heron, W., & Scott, T. H. Effects of decreased variation in the sensory environment. *Canad. J. Psychol.,* 1954, 8, 70-76.

Cannon, W. B. *The wisdom of the body.* New York: Norton, 1932.

Clapp, W. F. *Personality and reactions to unstructured environments.* M.A. Thesis, University of Colorado, 1964.

Festinger, L. *A theory of cognitive dissonance.* Evanston, Ill.: Row-Peterson, 1957.

Fiske, D. W., & Maddi, S. R. (Eds.) *Functions of varied experience.* Homewood, Ill.: Dorsey Press.

Freeman, G. L. *Energetics of human behavior.* New York: Cornell University Press, 1948.

Glanzer, M. Curiosity, exploratory drive and stimulus satiation. *Psychol. Bull.,* 1958, 55, 302-315.

Goldberg, S. C. Three situational determinants of conformity to social norms. *J. abnorm. soc. Psychol.,* 1954, 49, 325-329.

Haber, R. N. Discrepancy from adaptation level as a source of affect. *J. exp. Psychol.,* 1958, 56, 370-375.

Harvey, O. J. Personality factors in resolution of conceptual incongruities. *Sociometry,* 1962, 25, 336-352.

Harvey, O. J. Overview. In O. J. Harvey (Ed.), *Motivation and social interaction-Cognitive determinants.* New York: Ronald Press, 1963.

Harvey, O. J. Some situational and cognitive determinants of dissonance resolution. *J. pers. soc. Psychol.,* 1965, in press.

Harvey, O. J., & Beverly, G. D. Some personality correlates of concept change through role playing. *J. abnorm. soc. Psychol.,* 1961, 63, 125-130.

Harvey, O. J., & Caldwell, D. F. Assimilation and contrast phenomena in response to environmental variation. *J. Pers.* 1959, *27*, 125-135.

Harvey, O. J., & Campbell, D. T. Judgments of weight as affected by adaptation range, adaptation duration, magnitude of unlabeled anchor and judgmental language. *J. exp. Psychol.*, 1963, *65*, 12-21.

Harvey, O. J., & Clapp, W. F. Hope expectancy and reaction to the unexpected. *J. pers. soc Psychol.*, 1965, in press.

Harvey, O. J., Hunt, D. E., & Schroder, H. M. *Conceptual systems and personality organization.* New York: Wiley, 1961.

Harvey, O. J., Kelley, H. H., & Shapiro, M. Reactions to unfavorable evaluations of the self made by other persons. *J. Pers.*, 1957, *25*, 393-411.

Harvey, O. J., & Schroder, H. M. Cognitive aspects of self and motivation. In O. J. Harvey (Ed.) *Motivation and social interaction—Cognitive determinants.* New York: Ronald Press, 1963.

Hebb, D. O. On the nature of fear. *Psychol. Rev.*, 1946, *53*, 259-276.

Hebb, D. O. *The organization of behavior.* New York: Wiley, 1949.

Hebb, D. O. Drives and the CNS (conceptual nervous system) *Psychol Rev.*, 1955, *62*, 243-254.

Hebb, D. O. The mammal and his environment. In C. F. Reed, I. E. Alexander, and S. S. Tomkins (Eds.) *Psychopathology—a source book.* Cambridge: Harvard University Press, 1958.

Heider, F. Attitudes and cognitive organization. *J. Psychol.*, 1946, *21*, 107-12.

Heider, F. *The psychology of interpersonal relations.* New York: Wiley, 1958.

Helson, H. *Adaptation level theory.* New York: Harper and Row, 1964.

Hovland, C. I., & Pritzker, H. A. Extent of opinion change as a function of amount of change advocated. *J. abnorm. soc. Psychol.*, 1957, *47*, 581-588.

Hovland, C. I., Harvey, O. J., & Sherif, M. Assimilation and contrast effects in reactions to communication and attitude change. *J. abnorm. soc. Psychol.*, 1957, *55*, 244-252.

Hull, C. L. *Principles of behavior.* New York: Appleton-Century, 1943.

Hunt, J. McV. Motivation inherent in information processing and action. In O. J. Harvey (Ed), *Motivation and social interaction—Cognitive determinants.* New York: Ronald Press, 1963.

Hunt, J. McV., & Quay, H. C. Early vibratory experience and the question of innate reinforcement value of vibration and other stimuli: a limitation on the discrepancy (burnt soup) principle in motivation. *Psychol. Rev.*, 1961, *68*, 149-156.

James, W. *Principles of Psychology,* Vol. 2. New York: Holt, 1890.

Katz, D. *Gestalt psychology: its nature and significance.* Trans. by R. Tyson. New York: Ronald Press, 1950.

Leuba, C. Toward some integration of learning theories: the concept of optimal stimulation. *Psychol. Rep.*, 1955, *1*, 27-33.

Lewin, K. *A dynamic theory of personality.* New York: McGraw-Hill, 1935.

McClelland, D. C., Atkinson, J. W., Clark, R. A., & Lowell, E. L. *The achievement motive.* New York: Appleton-Century-Crofts, 1953.

Miller, J. G. Toward a general theory for the behavioral sciences. *Amer. Psychologist*, 1955, *10*, 513-531.

Newcomb, T. M. An approach to the study of communicative acts. *Psychol. Rev.*, 1953, *60*, 393-404.

Newcomb, T. M. *The acquaintance process.* New York: Holt, Rinehart and Winston, 1961.

Osgood, C. E., & Tannenbaum, P. H. The principle of congruity in prediction of attitude change. *Psychol. Rev.*, 1955, *62*, 42-55.

Richter, C. P. A behavioristic study of the activity of the rat. *Comp. Psychol. Monogr.*, 1922, 2.

Richter, C. P. Animal behavior and internal drives. *Quart. Rev. Biol.*, 1927, *2*, 307-343.

Richter, C. P. Increased salt appetite in adrenalectomized rats. *Amer. J. Physiol.*, 1936, *115*, 155-167.

Richter, C. P. Total self regulatory functions in animals and human beings. *Harvey Lecture Series*, 1942, *38*, 63-103.

Richter, C. P., & Eckert, J. F. Mineral appetite of parathyroid-ectomized rats. *Amer. J. med. Sci.*, 1939, *198*, 9-16.

Rosenberg, M. J. Cognitive structure and attitudinal affect. *J. abnorm. soc. Psychol.*, 1956, *53*, 367-372.

Sherif, M., Taub, D., & Hovland, C. I. Assimilation and contrast effects of anchoring stimuli on judgments. *J. exp. Psychol.*, 1958, *55*, 150-155.

Stagner, R., & Karwoski, T. F. *Psychology*, New York: McGraw-Hill, 1952.

Tomkins, S. S. *Affect, imagery, consciousness.* Vol. I. *The positive affects.* New York: Springer, 1962.

Troland, L. T. *The fundamentals of human motivation.* New York: Van Nostrand, 1928.

White, B. J. A variability of categories and contrast—effects in judgment. *Amer. J. Psychol.*, 1964, *77*, 231-329.

Young, P. T. *Motivation and emotion.* New York: Wiley, 1961.

PART FIVE

AFFECT AND
CHILD DEVELOPMENT

IX

Studies of sympathy

Peter B. Lenrow

Sympathy for the lot of another person is a phenomenon that has persistently attracted the attention of theorists through the ages but has largely eluded systematic understanding. How does it happen that an individual can be aware of the personal interests of a stranger and want to further those interests, even when this alliance offers no apparent rewards to the first individual? If the lot of the stranger is understood to include his hopes, fears, and self-evaluations, it may be seen that the problem of sympathy involves complex relations between affective responses of two persons. The present chapter reviews previous efforts to understand this problem and describes recent attempts to study the empirical relationships systematically.

Historically, such problems have been a central topic in philosophy, theology, and religious ministry. But theories in these disciplines have taken the form of evaluation as to how basic sympathy is in human nature and what its relative strength or scarcity in a person indicates about his worth. In psychology, particularly American psychology, relatively little attention has been given to the problem of human sympathy.

One factor discouraging the study of sympathy has been the prevalence of theoretical assumptions holding that sympathy could be reduced to far simpler or less constructive tendencies. Until recently, psychoanalytic theory assumed that sympathetic tendencies were simply transformations of sexual or aggressive strivings brought about in defense of the ego (cf. Anna Freud, 1937). This thinking led in the same direction as the assumptions of many American learning theorists that such phenomena as sympathy are derived from the operations of more basic, biological drives; cf. Miller & Dollard (1941), Dollard & Miller (1950). And since the only

The investigations by the author reviewed in this chapter were supported in part by the following sources: Laboratory of Social Relations, Harvard University, Institute of Social Sciences and Institute of Human Development, University of California, Berkeley. I am indebted particularly to Kay McGrath and Keetaek Chun for assistance in the preparation of this chapter. Mr. Chun's advice was invaluable for statistical treatment of the data.

major empirical investigation of sympathetic behavior (Lois Murphy, 1937) reported a positive correlation between aggression and sympathy in children, the status of sympathy as a secondary, derived, or defensive phenomenon seemed clear.

Fortunately, there have been theoretical developments that lessen these obstacles to the study of sympathy. Psychoanalytic theory has enlarged to encompass growth patterns in normal personality which are not simply defensive developments; cf. Erikson (1958), Lois Murphy (1962). Erikson, especially, has pointed out that the defensive patterns described by Anna Freud are only half the picture of ego functioning. On the basis of strivings that are relatively free of present conflict, the individual may develop constructive ways of relating to others which are not usefully conceived of as defensive operations. This theoretical development leaves open the question of the dynamics of sympathy, rather than generalizing from the functions of sympathy under conditions or neurotic suffering or normal defensive operations to its role in all personality development. Ideally, we would want a conceptual framework broad enough to include sympathy which is not to any large degree defensive but essentially a constructive social tendency, as well as sympathy which is essentially a means of dealing with conflicts on the part of the sympathizer and is quite indiscriminate with respect to the interest of other persons.

As for the assumption that sympathy and all other social behavior are simply a matter of habits instrumental to the gratification of biological drives, two theoretical developments have dislodged this old reductionism. White (1959, 1960) has marshalled ample evidence that drive theory must be supplemented with a concept of strivings for manipulation and control of one's environment. And Bandura (1962) has presented evidence that much social behavior is learned without external reinforcement by observation of the behavior of a model, and is subsequently generalized without external reinforcement. However, while these general theoretical advances lessen one obstacle to the study of sympathy, they do not themselves provide an alternative formulation of sympathy.

The few psychologists who have emphasized the importance of sympathy in social relations have, for their part, relied heavily on philosophical argument, anecdote, and phenomenological description; cf. Scheler (1913), Sorokin (1950), Allport (1950, 1954), Asch (1952), Maslow (1954), Heider (1958). These discussions have emphasized that the distinctive phenomena of sympathy are qualities of thought and feeling, complex dispositions, rather than specific overt actions readily susceptible to experimental manipulation. The problem of translating these descriptions into measures of overt behavior has presented a formidable obstacle to systematic study of sympathy. For example, private appreciation of and a sense of alliance with the interests of a joyful or suffering person may issue forth in behavior simply as expressions of joy or sorrow. But the sense of alliance with another person may, in the case of a response to a suffering person, take the form of an attack on the source of the other person's suffering. In such cases, the observable behavior of the sympathizer may be indistinguishable from aggressive responses to threats to the observer's own well-being. Or where an observer expresses commiseration to a sufferer, how may we distinguish the expression of a stable sympathetic tendency requiring no external rewards from a response that is primarily dependent on social approval?

Thus, while there appear to be features of the subjective experience of sympathy that are identifiable, the relation of subjective sympathy and action is complex and unclear. Given this state of affairs, one useful strategy would be to develop a theoretical formulation and a measure of sympathy as a subjective orientation to the lot of another person. The first study described in this chapter attempts to demonstrate the feasibility of such an approach.

This strategy of focusing on subjective aspects of sympathy postpones dealing with the question of how subjective sympathy is related to action. It also ignores the possibility of discovering some functional unity among a wide variety of overt actions related to sympathy. The second study described in this chapter attempts to deal with these two problems by (1) exploring a wide variety of actions in a situation constructed to be prototypic of sympathy-arousing situations, and (2) examining relations between indicators of subjective sympathy and overt actions to help an agent who is in distress.

While the studies reported in this chapter share some common theoretical framework, they are presented more as two starting points for understanding sympathy than as a smooth sequence in the development of a theory.

NEGLECTED THEORETICAL LEADS

A number of naturalistic descriptions of sympathy bear examination as a basis for a formulation of the dynamics of sympathy. We find such descriptions of the development of sympathetic tendencies in preschool years, primary-school years, and in young adulthood. Isaacs (1933) and Murphy (1937) have attempted to analyze the development of sympathy in nursery-school children. They include in their discussions of sympathy a wide range of behaviors induced by another child's distress. These include behavior that did not seem oriented to the needs of the person in distress; for example, solicitude for the sake of adult approval or intervention due to general anxiety. In addition to these frequent phenomena, both Murphy and Isaacs observed instances of sensitivity to the nature of another child's distress and supportive responses to it. Both of these writers appear to agree that such sympathy is the result of a process in which the child regards what happens to the other person as if it were happening to himself. This may then stimulate mothering behavior by the child to meet the needs that he has anticipated (Murphy, 1937, pp. 7, 319).

Let us consider first the sensitivity to distress and then the nurturant response. Murphy implies that anticipating the feelings of the other person depends on the extent to which similar experiences have befallen the observer in the past and the extent to which he tends to perceive similarities between others' situations and his own (pp. 286, 302). In young children this tendency may be due largely to a generally crude discrimination between one's own feelings and those of others.

Murphy's view thus raises the possibility that a young child's concern for distress in others is based largely on indiscriminate concern about his own security. This may account in part for the apparent instability of sympathetic tendencies in young children in contrast to more consistent and discriminating sympathy in adults. It leads to the hypothesis that as a person becomes more able to differentiate his own lot from that of others he is likely to be more discriminating in using his past experiences as a basis for anticipating what a stressful situation must be like for another person. Such a view was suggested by Freud (1922, p. 65) in discussing an instance of sympathy in an adolescent girl.

If a child anticipates that another person is distressed, to what extent will the child respond with nurturant behavior? According to Isaacs, this depends on the extent to which the child has experienced such tendencies from a parent figure in response to his own needs. Murphy points out, however, that a child may use mothering behavior to compensate for the scarcity of these pleasurable attitudes from the parent as well as to reinstate satisfying relationships.

Throughout the comments of these two writers, there appears to be much agreement on the main dynamics of sympathetic concern for others' needs. Another person's distress redintegrates the child's previous experiences of distress and his wishes for relief. Somehow, these rearoused experiences serve as cues about the distressed person's experience and set in motion actions to provide the other person with the kinds of relief the observer has *wished for* in the past. The dynamics of sympathy in children may, however, be a special case differing in important respects from sympathy in adults. It is necessary therefore to look for such differences in considering trends in later development.

Allport (1937, 1955) has emphasized the importance of investigating how the individual changes from the unsocial patterns of the infant to adult trends that include concern for others' needs. He concludes from a review of the literature that one necessary condition for such a trend is that the person receive acceptance in an affectionate environment. This permits the individual to accept himself and somehow to develop beyond the demands of his immediate needs. Allport also describes a pattern of "ego-extension" in which the individual comes to regard the satisfaction of other people's needs as important for his own sense of well-being. These concepts have much in common with those of Bridges (1931), Flugel (1945), and Maslow (1954), who also have described a pattern of ego-extension leading to increased sympathy for others' needs.

Sullivan (1953, 1954) and White (1952) go beyond this general developmental concept, ego-extension, by providing specific illustrations of the development of sensitivity to others' needs. Between the ages of eight and ten, according to Sullivan, the child begins to pay markedly greater attention to promoting the well-being of one of his several former play-mates. He treats this chum as of equally great worth as himself and devotes much effort to developing sensitivity to what matters to this other person. This development then becomes obscured by the development of interest in the opposite sex around puberty and the onset of a struggle to integrate lustful feelings with the rest of his life. In young adulthood, a trend toward increased sensitivity to others' needs again becomes prom-inent, according to White. Presumably the individual has succeeded in some measure with the problem of lust by this time. And in this later period, concern for the needs of others appears to generalize more widely than in the intense two-person relationship of preadolescence.

A particularly useful feature of the descriptions by Sullivan and White is that both include consideration of the predominant pattern of relating to others that precedes and gives way to the increase in sympathetic sensitivity. In the descriptions by both authors, the trend is from reliance on impersonal formulas for making social choices to a relatively greater concern with making one's actions appropriate to the needs of other individuals. In preadolescence, the sensitivity for a chum is a particularly striking development because it stands in such marked contrast to the primary-school child's more general habits of impersonal regulation of his social relationships. Upon entering school the child has had to struggle to develop impersonal rules in order to cope with the enlarged world of social relationships that school represents. According to Piaget (1932), he learns that the way to do things in school is not necessarily the way that benefits him particularly, nor the way things are done at home. Be-tween ages six and eight, the child finds that rules are necessary in achieving such impersonal objectives as fairness and order in work and play. Adherence to impersonal formulas appears to afford him a sense of confidence in social actions, since he can anticipate ahead of time the social consequences of actions that are guided by shared rules (cf. Asch, 1952).

The reliance on general, impersonal rules, White points out, can result in a tendency to give little attention to the needs of individuals. In adult-hood it is this long-practiced, impersonal tendency that the individual must modify to develop sensitivity to others' needs as a stable and per-vasive characteristic. White suggests that in young adults growth in sympathetic concern for others typically occurs when the person experi-ences conflict between the needs of individuals and a relatively impersonal formula for social decisions that he has relied on in the past. For example, the person becomes aware that acting on the basis of an accepted prin-ciple will produce unexpected and unwelcomed hurts to others in a particular situation.

By what processes does such conflict influence sympathy? The case studies that White uses as illustrations suggest that observation of another person in particular roles rearouses memories of concrete experiences in roles similar to those of the other person. This vicarious taking of a role like that of the other person may lead to subjective alliance with his interests and reevaluation of impersonal rules that thwart his interests. From this viewpoint, what needs to be explained for a systematic understanding of sympathy as a subjective orientation is how the individual's past experience becomes (1) readily *available* for use in interpreting others' experience, (2) organized as *relevant* to the experience of others, and (3) organized as a basis for a *favorable* attitude toward persons perceived to be in need.

HYPOTHESES CONCERNING THE DYNAMICS OF SYMPATHY IN ADULTS

Can we provide a systematic formulation of how it happens that an adult may be sympathetically disposed toward persons who are in some form of distress? Lenrow (1960, 1963) proposed that two processes underlie subjective sympathy in adults: (1) redintegration of a past emotional response by observation of a person in a similar situation or role; (2) generalization of one's positive *self*-regarding attitudes to this other person. The antecedent conditions for these hypothetical processes are proposed as follows: Redintegration is a function of affective involvement in similar roles in the past; and positive self-regard, in particular roles, is a function of positive regard from others when one has been involved in such roles in the past. Thus, affective involvement in a dependency role should increase a person's tendency to redintegrate what this experience was like when he observes another person in a similar role.[1] Depending on whether the observer has been supported or rejected for affective involvement in such roles in the past, he should redintegrate positive or negative self-regarding attitudes and generalize them to the other person who is now involved in a dependency role. Specifically, it is hypothesized that the differential effects of support or rejection for affective involvement in a role should depend on the degree of the subject's past involvement in the role.

Let us elaborate how these experiences are expected to interact as a basis for sympathy. If a person becomes affectively involved in a social relationship (e.g., a dependency role) and another person responds with positive regard for him (i.e., friendly interest), the first person develops a greater sense that the behavior, including the accompanying subjective feelings, is compatible with his being a competent, lovable person. He

---

[1] In this formulation of sympathy, affect refers to a complex response characterized subjectively by a concept that what is happening matters, positively or negatively, more or less (i.e., that how the situation turns out will be pleasant or painful for one's self-concept). Affect is characterized objectively by bodily response (e.g., glandular, neural, motoric) to events that usually produce subjective pleasure or pain. The subjective quality of particular affective experiences depends on the content of the particular situation, the particular self-concept, and the particular bodily responses.

will consequently be less motivated to inhibit or avoid rearousal of these feelings. His subsequent observation of a person in a situation (e.g., a dependency role) similar to those in which he has experienced dependency is likely to redintegrate memory traces of the subjective feelings that accompanied his dependency. He will construe the other person as having an experience like the observer has known, will feel intimately acquainted with the psychological state of the other person, and will generalize his positive self-regard to the other person.

Conversely, if a person becomes affectively involved in a role (e.g., a dependency role) and another person responds with rejection (i.e., avoidance, criticism), the subject develops a greater sense that the behavior, including the accompanying feelings, is incompatible with his being a competent, lovable person. He will consequently inhibit or avoid rearousal of these feelings. This may interfere with redintegration of these feelings in response to observation of a person in a role (e.g., a dependency role) similar to those in which he has experienced dependency feelings. Or if the memory traces of the dependency experience are redintegrated, the observer will be more likely to avoid the stimulus situation and/or to generalize to the other person the attitude he holds toward himself, namely that such feelings are incompatible with being competent and lovable. His favorable attention to and support for a person who is in a dependency role will therefore be lowered.

These considerations take for granted two hypothetical processes: Avoidance of emotional behavior perceived as incompatible with positive self-regard; and redintegration of memory traces of past emotional experiences by observation of another person in a similar role.

If a person does not become affectively involved in a role (e.g., express dependency feelings) he will subsequently have little basis in memory for feeling acquainted with the psychological state of another person he observes in a similar role. And the observer's attitudes toward himself in such roles is less likely to be generalized to the other person.

A corollary hypothesis specifies that increases in positive self-regard lead also to decreased tendency to avoid such feelings in others by means of strict adherence to impersonal roles. Hence, the antecedent conditions facilitating acceptance of dependency as compatible with positive self-regard should increase not only the absolute level of sympathetic responses but the level of sympathetic responses relative to adherence to impersonal rules.

EXPERIMENTAL DESIGN

An experiment was designed to test these hypotheses about the influence on sympathy due to (1) affective involvement in interpersonal relationships (dependency roles) analogous to the roles of individuals subsequently observed to be in distress; and (2) acceptance from one person in response to an individual's affective involvement in a role, in this case, a dependency role.

MEASURING SYMPATHY AS A SUBJECTIVE ORIENTATION

Because the writer was interested in investigating the dynamics of sympathy in young adults, the dependent measures were designed to take advantage of White's (1952) suggestion that growth in sympathetic orientations in young adults tends to occur when they experience conflict between their customary rules of conduct and needs they perceive in other individuals. If sympathetic tendencies were likely to be elicited by such conflicts, it seemed sensible to present such conflicts to subjects as stimulus material and to record their free responses.

A. Stimulus Material

Six tape-recorded narratives were prepared in each of which a social situation was described. In each situation, a person was depicted facing a conflict between action favoring people whose strivings were being thwarted and action in accordance with an impersonal rule that thwarted the individual strivings. The conflicts are summarized in Table 1. They

Table 1   Summary of social situations presented in tape-recorded narratives

1. Guards are held hostage by rioting prisoners and threatened with death unless warden yields. He doesn't.

2. Itinerant farm worker with large family to move and support is permitted to steal truck by policeman observer.

3. Dying girl in terror in hospital wants parents, who are not permitted to disturb ward with extra visits.

4. Indigent families who have completed crude winter quarters are found in violation of sanitation regulations. Inspector decides to enforce eviction but not until spring. (Filler item.)

5. Dying old woman suffering great pain and beyond relief of drugs is given a lethal dose at her request.

6. Children of Negro family are injured by bomb blast after White friend decides to ignore threats to stop socializing with the Negroes.

7. Desperate boy flees after shooting policeman in fright. Police want to shoot on sight so witness decides not to reveal boy's whereabouts.

have to do with preservation of life versus preservation of authority, relief of poverty versus duty, comfort for a sufferer versus preserving fairness and order, relief from pain versus restraint on taking a life, protection from bodily harm versus obedience to one's principles, and preservation of life versus duty. The narratives described a resolution of the conflict in favor of impersonal rules or in favor of individual needs in alternative passages. The situations were described in some detail but without affectively charged words. They were narrated in a calm, matter of fact voice. Each narrative lasted approximately one and a half minutes.

B. Instructions

These passages were presented with the rationale that they were part of a study on reports of current events. The narrative reports were characterized as dry, as if the narrator was quite distant from the events themselves. Instructions asked the subject to use his imagination to recapture what the scenes were like in real life.

The instructions were designed to evoke from the subject whatever thoughts and feelings were most salient after he imagined what the situation must have been like. By inviting free responses in a way that drew attention to neither the impersonal rules nor the persons in distress, the procedure presumably sampled verbal productions that reflected spontaneous tendencies to be concerned with the needs of others and to be concerned with the impersonal rules.

C. Content-Analysis Variables

A number of content-analysis scores were specified a priori to measure sympathetic responses and impersonal responses to the situations. Essentially, the scores weighted the extent to which the subject paid attention to and showed supportive attitudes toward the individuals in need, on the one hand, or the impersonal rules on the other hand. The scoring procedure differentiated three kinds of favorable disposition toward individuals in need. They included explicit judgments in favor of supporting the persons in need, affect supporting persons in need, and selective attention to factors favoring persons in need. Since the present chapter is concerned primarily with the role of affect in sympathy, suffice it to say that the most fruitful of these scoring categories proved to be that concerned with expression of affect supporting the persons in need. The presentation of results will therefore be confined to the measurement of sympathy as a matter of supportive affective orientation.

Affective responses were identified from the written protocols in terms of any one of the following characteristics: (1) use of emotionally-laden words showing favorable orientation to a person in need and those persons supporting him; (2) use of first-person narrative expressing the subjective experience of the person in need; (3) description elaborating on the subjective experience of the person in need. To illustrate the scoring procedure, the text of one of the stimulus narratives follows and may be compared with affective verbal response coded in the three categories and with one response that contained no affective content.

Stimulus narrative number three: "Although the nurses and doctors had been careful not to mention the fatal nature of the child's illness in her presence, the girl grew increasingly terrified that she was about to die. She cried or lay rigid for hours in her ward bed. The ward was understaffed, and the many serious cases made it impossible for her to have special attention from the nurses. In addition, visiting hours were limited to a few hours in the afternoon so that the children would not be too excited. As the girl's terror increased and her condition worsened, her parents pleaded with the doctor to let them stay by her bedside. In order to avoid upsetting the other sick children who might be disturbed by this special attention to the girl—especially children whose parents did not visit at all—the doctor decided that the parents would have to limit their visits to the regular hours."

Response containing no affective content: "Sounds like a hospital in a country of poverty and under-educated people and the doctors and nurses having too much work to do for the size of the community or the number of sick people. Or it could be a disease in which the child had to be separated or isolated from the rest."

Affective response, category (1): "The parents felt helpless as to what they could do for the child. They felt the child's terror and fear of death and had no way of eliminating it since they had not prepared the child beforehand of the danger of her condition. The parents as well as the child feared the unknown."

Affective response, category (2): "The stench of disinfectant . . . bleak white walls and the cold mask of the nurse's face . . . crazy shadows and whispers . . . waiting . . . 'Where are they?' "

Affective response, category (3): "She knew she was very sick, and she saw from the faces around her in the hospital, if not death, itself, then the cruel coldness which is death . . ."

Elaboration of legitimacy of rules. A second measure was provided by comparing the number of responses containing affect supporting persons in need with the number of responses containing explanations of what made the impersonal rules legitimate. The following verbal response illustrates consideration given to the merits of applying the rule: "The reasons for not letting the parents to see their girl were somewhat reasonable from the doctors' point of view. Doctors knew that she was going to die and there was nothing in their power to save her. To the doctors, she was already dead." The verbal response to each of the six stimulus narratives was scored for presence or absence of affect supporting persons in need and elaboration of the legitimacy of the rules. Many responses were scored as containing both categories of content. The number of responses containing affective support for persons in need, on the one hand, and elaboration of the rules, on the other hand, was summed across the six stimulus narratives. The difference between these two sums provided a measure of "net affect supporting others in need."

D. Subjects

Sixty-seven men and women sampled from a course in personality in a graduate school of education were assigned at random to the experimental treatments. The subjects were recruited to participate in three distinct phases of the research. They were assessed in class by one investigator on the sympathy measures presented as a study of reports of current events. Approximately a week later they were recruited for a second time by a second investigator from a different research organization for a study of "the usefulness of case materials in supplementing a course in personality." This provided the occasion for participation in the experimental treatments described below. This participation consisted of an hour of work with "case materials" once a week for three weeks. Approximately one week later, the original investigator again administered a form of the sympathy measures in group sessions. The rationale for this testing was to sample the subjects' behavior on a revised form of the questionnaire in order to make their data comparable to that of other groups recently tested with the new form.

EXPERIMENTAL TREATMENTS

The basic experimental manipulations were arranged in factorial design varying (1) affective involvement in dependency roles, and (2) degree of acceptance from one person in response to an individual's expression of dependency feelings. The experimental procedures used to vary these experiences all employed interpersonal relationships in which a subject and a confederate of the investigator worked together to understand the experiences of a character described in a fictitious biographical sketch presented as "case materials."

Affective involvement in dependency roles was varied as follows: In one experimental condition (the affective involvement condition), affective involvement was induced by having the subject role-play particular experiences of a character in a biographical sketch who was distressed and seeking warmth and reassurance. The subject enacted this role in relation to another character from the biographical sketch, whose role was played by a partner. In a second experimental condition (the minimal affective involvement condition), involvement of one's own feelings in dependency roles was minimized by having the subject impersonally discuss the content of the biographical sketch with his partner rather than role-play the dependency experiences in the sketch. In both the role-play and discussion variation, the partner was a confederate of the investigator posing as a research subject.

The second variable, acceptance of an individual's feelings by another person, was manipulated as follows: The partner in half of the role-play pairs and half of the discussion pairs was trained to provide a friendly, interested, reassuring attitude toward the subject throughout their association, including the subject's role play or discussion of dependency; this was called the acceptance condition. In the other half of the role-play and discussion pairs (the rejection condition), the partner provided critical or coldly indifferent attitudes toward the subject and toward the dependency which the subject role-played or discussed.

PREDICTIONS

The hypothesis that affective involvement in dependency roles contributes to subsequent sympathy for persons in distress was tested in terms of the following prediction: Subjects who are induced by means of *role play* to express dependency feelings with accepting partners will show greater increase in sympathetic response (supportive affect) to others' distress than subjects who work with the same stimulus content and accepting partners under *discussion* conditions.

The hypothesis that acceptance of one's dependency feelings by others contributes to sympathy was tested in terms of the following prediction: Subjects who are induced by role play to express dependency feelings with *accepting* partners will show greater increase in sympathetic response (supportive affect) to others' distress than subjects who role-play with *rejecting* partners.

The main hypothesis was that it is the combined effects of these two experiences that produce increase in sympathetic response to others' needs. To test this hypothesis, it was predicted that the involvement (role play versus discussion) and support (accepting versus rejecting) variables would show interaction in their effects on sympathetic response to persons in distress.

The corollary hypothesis called for a test of these predictions in terms of increase in net sympathy (support for persons in distress relative to support for rules that preclude support for the persons in need).

The dependent variables were measures of change assessed by comparing responses to the sympathy test which was administered before and after the experimental treatments. To demonstrate that the influence of the experiences in the experimental treatments was not produced by a simple transfer of habits practiced in the role play or discussion treatments, the experimental conditions and the measure of sympathy involved quite different kinds of behavior. The experimental conditions called for role-play or discussion of *dependency* experiences, whereas the sympathy measure assessed a tendency to show *support* for others in distress. The procedures made the transfer of learning still more difficult by administering the experimental conditions and the sympathy measures as two distinct and unrelated research projects. In addition to requiring transfer from practice of dependency to performance of supportive behavior, the design assured that changes in sympathy would involve generalization from a limited content to a wider range of content. Specifically, the experimental conditions dealt with people in need of warmth and reassurance in the face of loneliness, low self-esteem, and humiliation by others. The sympathy measure, on the other hand, presented people in need of protection or relief from lack of food and shelter, the acute pain of severe illness or injury, or threat of violent death.

RESULTS

An analysis of variance for unequal *n's* was performed on the measures of supportive affect sampled before the experimental treatments. The analysis demonstrated that these before-scores were independent of the variables that were to be manipulated in the experiment. A measure of increases in these scores was then obtained by subtracting the before-scores from the scores obtained approximately one week after the third experimental session. Table 2 shows the mean changes observed in sixteen experimental treatments. Increases are indicated by a positive value.

Table 2 Mean changes in affect supporting persons in distress as a function of subject involvement, partner support, and sex of subject and partner (N = 67)

| | Affective involvement in dependency role | | | |
| | High (role play) | | Minimal (discussion) | |
Partner behavior	Support A	Indifference B	Support C	Indifference D
Male subjects				
Male partners	.25 (N=4)	-1.33 (N=3)	-1.25 (N=4)	.75 (N=4)
Female partners	1.50 (N=4)	.25 (N=4)	1.40 (N=5)	0 (N=4)
Female subjects				
Male partners	1.20 (N=5)	- .20 (N=5)	-1.00 (N=4)	.50 (N=4)
Female partners	1.25 (N=4)	.20 (N=5)	.25 (N=4)	.75 (N=4)

Table 3 shows the results of an analysis of variance for change in affect supporting persons in need (distress). The predicted interaction between the subject's affective involvement in a dependency role and the partner's

Table 3 Analysis of variance for mean changes in affect supporting persons in distress as a function of subject involvement, partner support, and sex of subject and partner

Source of variance	df	Sums of squares of errors of estimate	Mean squares	F	p
Support (A)	1	.449			
Involvement (B)	1	.185			
Subject sex (C)	1	.119			
Partner sex (D)	1	2.789			
Interactions					
A x B	1	3.881	3.881	7.336	<.05
A x C	1	.198			
A x D	1	.865			
B x C	1	.297			
B x D	1	.001			
C x D	1	.483			
Error	5	2.643	.529		
Total	15	11.910			

support was found to be significant. While the involvement and support variables did not have significant independent effects, Table 6 shows that their combined effects are in the predicted direction. For the total sample, affective involvement with a supportive partner led to greater increases in supportive affect than affective involvement with an indifferent partner $(p(z=2.05)<.05)$. Affective involvement with a supportive partner also led to greater increases in supportive affect than minimal affective involvement with a supportive partner $(p(z=2.39)<.01)$.

These results support the main hypothesis that increases in subjective sympathy for a person are a function of the subject's past affective involvement in similar roles and past support from others in response to the subject's affective involvement in such roles.

Tables 4 and 5 present the results bearing on the corollary hypothesis that affective involvement in a role and support from others in response to such affective involvement should lead to increases in subjective sympathy relative to adherence to impersonal rules. No sampling bias was

Table 4 Mean changes in net affect supporting persons in distress as a function of subject involvement, partner support, and sex of subject and partner (N = 67)

| | Affective involvement in dependency role | | | |
| | High (role play) | | Minimal (discussion) | |
Partner behavior	Support A	Indifference B	Support C	Indifference D
Male subjects				
Male partners	.25 (N=4)	-1.00 (N=3)	- .50 (N=4)	.75 (N=4)
Female partners	1.50 (N=4)	.25 (N=4)	1.60 (N=5)	- .25 (N=4)
Female subjects				
Male partners	1.00 (N=5)	- .40 (N=5)	- .25 (N=4)	.50 (N=4)
Female partners	1.25 (N=4)	.20 (N=5)	.25 (N=4)	.25 (N=4)

found in an analysis of variance for the before-scores on net affect supporting persons in need. The mean changes in net affect are shown in Table 4. Table 5 shows that the predicted interaction between affect involvement and support is not significant for the measure of net affect supporting persons in need. The direction of the change is in the predicted direction, however, as shown in Table 6. For the total sample affective involvement with a supportive partner led to greater increases in net affect supporting persons in need than did affective involvement with an indifferent partner $(p(z=2.38)<.01)$. Affective involvement with a supportive partner did not lead to greater increase in this measure than minimal affective involvement with a supportive partner.

The fact that there is little evidence supporting the corollary hypothesis is probably due to the method of measuring net affect supporting persons in need. In the original study (Lenrow, 1960, 1963) the author found

Table 5 Analysis of variance for mean changes in net affect supporting persons in distress as a function of subject involvement, partner support and sex of subject and partner

Source of variance	df	Sums of squares of errors of estimate	Mean squares	F	p
Support (A)	1	1.440	1.440	3.861	n.s.
Involvement (B)	1	.031			
Subject sex (C)	1	.003			
Partner sex (D)	1	1.381			
Interactions					
A x B	1	1.626	1.626	4.359	n.s.
A x C	1	.210			
A x D	1	.766			
B x C	1	.226			
B x D	1	.250			
C x D	1	.391			
Error	5	1.864	.373		
Total	15	8.188			

support for the corollary hypothesis using measures that made use of all three categories of response related to subjective sympathy: argument, affect, and selective attention; *and* all three categories of support for impersonal rules: argument, elaboration, and selective attention. In retrospect, it appears arbitrary to coordinate elaboration of rules with affect supporting persons in need as a set of related responses to be combined in one measure. On the other hand, the test of the main hypothesis, using supportive affect as a measure isolated from the other response categories, appears to be useful in understanding the role of affect in sympathy.

It is important to question how useful is this measure of *verbal* expression of affect as an assessment of subjective sympathy. Is the instrument limited to use by people with high verbal intelligence? Is it correlated with other measures of subjective orientations that should be related to it theoretically? These questions are currently being examined in a study of a group of men and women in Peace Corps training who provide a wide range of intelligence, education, and vocational background. Preliminary results show no correlation between intelligence and the measure of affect supporting persons in need.

DISCUSSION

Bandura's work (1962) would suggest that this study confounds (1) changes in sympathy due to imitation of a model who is *observed* to support or reject dependency in another person, and (2) changes in

Table 6 Significance of differences in affect changes between treatment groups

	Predicted relative changes			
	Affective involvement with support vs.	Affective involvement with indifference	Affective involvement with support vs.	Minimal affective involvement with support
	z	n	z	n
Men and women		34		34
Affect supporting persons in need	2.05*		2.39**	
Net affect supporting persons in need	2.38**		1.07	
Women		19		17
Affect supporting persons in need	1.39		2.02*	
Net affect supporting persons in need	1.72*		1.68*	
Men		15		17
Affect supporting persons in need	1.45		n.s.	
Net affect supporting persons in need	1.45		n.s.	

*Significant at .05 level for one tail of z distribution, Mann-Whitney test

**Significant at .01 level for one tail of z distribution, Mann-Whitney test

sympathy due to *involvement* with a person whose attitudes are directed toward the subject rather than toward a third person. Hypothetically, both sets of conditions should influence the development and change of sympathy. They should be varied experimentally.

Since this study, two other systematic formulations of sympathy have become available. Both focus on aspects of parent-child relationships that are important in the development of sympathy. Both emphasize that the parent's behavior in relation to the child serves as a model that the child may emulate in dealing with others, and that the content of the parents' evaluations of the child's behavior influences the child's conceptions of what is desirable.

Tomkins (1963) has proposed how parent-child relationships influence the child's mode of managing his distress and orienting to distress in others. Parent-child relationships that are a source of mutual enjoyment permit the child to develop a sense of his own intrinsic worth and trust of others. On the other hand, relationships in which parents express contempt for the child's shortcomings in living up to parental demands impart to the child a sense of being of value only insofar as he meets standards set by authorities. Such relationships also lead to mistrust of others and intolerance for emotions in oneself and others. In the first type of relationship, distress and helplessness are occasions for expression of concern and support by parents. Under these conditions the child learns to express distress unashamedly and to adopt supportive modes of responding to distress in others. In the second type of relationship, distress and helplessness are occasions for contempt from parents. This inclines the child to suppress his own distress, to avoid distress in others, and to be contemptuous toward helplessness as a sign that a person is of little worth.

Hoffman (1963) has contributed to an understanding of sympathy in an empirical study of preschool children's consideration for others. His study illustrates the impact of the parent's behavior as a model for the child. He proposed that a child's consideration for others would be a function of the parent's expression of affection toward him, the parent's use of discipline that teaches the child to anticipate the consequences of his actions, and discipline that teaches the child to attend to the needs of others. He found that none of these variables was related to the child's consideration unless he took into account the model provided by the parent's consideration for the child's independent strivings. Parents who readily used their power to compel the child to comply with their demands did not have considerate children even if the parent showed affection and used consequence-oriented and need-oriented discipline techniques. Among parents who did not use such ready assertion of their power over the child, use of discipline emphasizing the needs of others was found to be positively correlated with how considerate the child was. Moreover, the children's considerateness was found not to be a function of inhibited behavior. Rather, it appeared to be positively related to spontaneous social interaction that was not reducible to hostility or nurturance-seeking.

A particularly interesting finding is one that bears on the question of the relationship between subjective sympathy, on the one hand, and action that supports the interests of another person, on the other hand. Hoffman found that parental affection was positively related to the child's expression of positive affect (positive tone of social contacts) but not to the child's consideration for others as expressed in helpful or tactful actions.

SUBJECTIVE SYMPATHY AND HELPFUL ACTION

A second study by the author (Lenrow, 1964) attempted to deal with the problem of relating subjective sympathy and helpful action. This study broadened the exploration of sympathy by defining sympathy as any favorable response to another person whose strivings are blocked by a barrier of some sort. This might include a supportive subjective orientation to persons in distress, action to further the interests of the distressed person, or testing of one's own effectiveness in overcoming a barrier in the path of another person, with relatively little attention to his distress.

In order to study variations in the form of sympathy, it was first necessary to devise a situation in which opportunities for sympathy were many and a great variety of behavior could be observed rather than a restricted set of responses. When pilot testing confirmed that there were marked individual differences in the form of sympathy in the situation we devised, it became possible to pursue a systematic examination of the conditions for supportive subjective response and helpful action. The present report summarizes a tentative formulation of the necessary and sufficient conditions for these forms of sympathy and an initial test of the formulation in terms of correlational data.

In order to maximize the possibility of distinguishing forms of sympathy on the basis of naturalistic observation, it was decided to study young children before their behavior repertoire, particularly their verbal repertoire, became so subtle as to thwart classification. The conceptualization of sympathy is therefore couched in terms of the behavior of preschool children but it is intended as a general model appropriate for understanding adult sympathy as well.

THEORETICAL FORMULATION

Lois Murphy's recent studies of mastery in preschool children (1962) and Robert White's case studies of competence in young adults (1963) have suggested that sympathy may play quite different roles in various coping styles. In particular, it appeared promising to study the individual's distinctive mode of sympathy as part of his general pattern for coping effectively with the environment.

The formulation of sympathy that the author developed from this perspective proposes that (1) supportive affective response to another person who expresses distress is a function of the observer's concept of distress as an occasion for help, and (2) action to overcome a barrier that thwarts another person is a function of the observer's concept that he is competent to overcome barriers. It is proposed that a necessary and sufficient condition for construing distress as an occasion for help is practice of overt expression of distress which is met by helpful responses from others. A necessary and sufficient condition for construing oneself as competent to overcome barriers is, hypothetically, practice at using one's own persistent efforts to overcome barriers that are within one's capacity to influence.

Let us elaborate this view. Assume first that overt expressions of distress are learned patterns of behavior which are strengthened by responses from others (particularly parents) that reduce the source of distress. Let us call these responses from others, helping responses. Overt expressions of distress that are met by helping responses will have an increased probability of being repeated in subsequent stressful situations. Hypothetically, help from others in response to an individual's overt expression of distress would strengthen his expectation that his overt expression of distress will be met by helping responses. With his own experience in relation to helpers as a model, he is more likely to construe overt expression of distress by another person as an occasion for help from someone.

How competent to provide help the observer will regard himself should be a function of his learned mode of coping with barriers, i.e., events that thwart his strivings. Individuals differ in their tendency to persist in the face of a barrier as contrasted with a tendency primarily to ask for help or to withdraw. The person who has developed a tendency to persist in trying to overcome barriers will be more likely to try to overcome a barrier that he identifies in the path of another person.

We may distinguish four combinations of expression of distress and patterns of coping that may develop under particular parent-child relationships. When overt expression of distress tends to be met by helping responses but the distressed person also has opportunities to learn to master problems that are not so difficult as to elicit distress, he learns both that distress is appropriately met with helping behavior and that he is competent to overcome some barriers through his efforts (alone or in collaboration with other persons). The helping responses to his overt expression of distress strengthen his tendency to express distress openly when his own coping efforts fail. Let us call this pattern *high overt expression of distress and high competence to overcome barriers.*

When overt expression of distress tends to be met by helping responses, the helper may not give the distressed person opportunities to learn to master problems that are not so difficult as to elicit distress. The helper may frequently anticipate distress when the child encounters a barrier and may help before distress occurs. In the process, he may help before the child has an opportunity to test his own competence to overcome the barrier. Such a child learns that distress is appropriately met with helping behavior but that he is not competent to overcome barriers through his efforts. The helping responses to his overt expression of distress strengthen his tendency to express distress openly in stressful situations. Let us call this pattern *high overt expression of distress and low competence to overcome barriers.*

When overt expression of distress is not met with help from others but the child has opportunities to master problems through his own efforts, he learns not to expect that distress will be met by help but that he is competent to overcome barriers. Lack of help in response to his overt expression of distress leads to low tendency to express distress openly in stress situations. This pattern is *low overt expression of distress and high competence to overcome barriers.*

When overt expression of distress is not met with help from others and the child has little opportunity to master problems through his own efforts, he learns that distress is not met by help and that he is not competent to overcome barriers. Lack of help in response to his expression of distress leads to low tendency to express distress openly in stress situations. Let us call this pattern *low overt expression of distress and low competence to overcome barriers.*

The following hypotheses were drawn from this formulation of sympathy.

1. Action to overcome a barrier in the path of another person is posi-

tively related to a disposition to persist actively in trying to overcome barriers in one's own path.

2. Supportive affective response to another person who expresses distress is positively related to a disposition to express distress overtly in stressful situations.

3. Action to overcome a barrier in the path of another person is most likely to be shown by individuals who express distress overtly in stressful situations and who also try actively to overcome barriers in their own paths.

An experiment was designed to provide preliminary tests of these hypotheses.

METHOD

In order to create a situation which presented many opportunities for sympathy and for a variety of spontaneous behavior, a puppet show procedure was devised with the collaboration of Kay McGrath, a psychology graduate student. Each child was invited by the writer to come to a room across the breezeway of a nursery school to play some new games. There he was seated at a small table in front of a large, attractively colored, cardboard puppet theater which was surrounded by standing screens. A curtain covered the stage area. The child was introduced to a hand puppet of the same sex who appeared from behind the curtain. The puppet was introduced as a real creature rather than a mere puppet, and the writer showed the child and the puppet two interesting and pleasant-sounding brass bells which they rang and handed to each other in turn. The puppet was made to appear to whisper to the writer that he wanted to give the child a present because it had been such fun to have him come over and play. The puppet then said goodby and left. The author told the child that he could watch the puppet walking home if they lifted up the curtain. He explained that he was going to go into the next room to turn on the light and get it ready for use that morning and that he would be back soon. The writer left the room as the puppet appeared on stage in a pleasantly colored scene suggesting a woods.

A prerecorded tape then presented a standard dialogue and a research assistant manipulated a number of puppets in simple actions during a fifteen minute plot. Table 7 outlines the major events in the plot. The plot was designed to present the child with a familiar social agent who encounters a barrier on his path home. The barrier is a large piece of cordwood that sticks out at one end of the stage so that it is within reach of the seated child. The hero A) identifies the log as a barrier, B) makes an effort to overcome the barrier, C) reports inadequacy to move the barrier, D) expresses distress, and E) expresses a wish for help. This sequence is repeated a second time with slight variations. The hero then meets another agent who is in a position to help but who assigns the hero a task to perform as a condition for getting help. The sequence of effort, failure, distress, and wish for help is repeated in connection with this task. In this case the barrier is distance: the hero cannot reach the twigs

Table 7 Sequence of actions in puppet show that may serve as instigating conditions for friendly or helpful responses in nursery school children:

1. Entrance of hero.
2. Hero makes effort to move barrier (log).
3. Hero reports inadequacy to move barrier.
4. Hero expresses distress.
5. Hero expresses wish for help.
6. Hero makes effort to move barrier.
7. Hero reports inadequacy to move barrier.
8. Hero expresses distress.
9. Hero expresses wish for help.
10. Cross, busy man assigns hero a task as a condition for helping hero.
11. Cross, busy man urges hero to hurry.
12. Hero makes effort to overcome barrier (distance) to perform task.
13. Hero reports inadequacy to overcome barrier.
14. Hero expresses distress.
15. Hero expresses wish for help.
16. Hero asks child (S) for help.
17. Cross, busy man withdraws his condition for help and helps hero make effort to move barrier (log).
18. Same man calls for cooperative effort.
19. Same man reports inadequacy to overcome barrier.
20. Hero expresses wish for help in finding an alternate route.
21. Hero expresses distress at isolation and helplessness.
22. Scary witch approaches hero; demands account of hero's presence there.
23. Hero asks witch for help.
24. Witch demands reward as a condition for helping hero.
25. Hero reports inadequacy to provide reward.
26. Witch changes demand to threat: something very bad might happen to hero.
27. Witch demands reward at once.
28. Hero reports inadequacy to provide reward.
29. Hero asks for help from witch.
30. Witch makes more extreme threat: you shall never leave this forest.
31. Hero expresses distress.
32. Hero expresses distress.
33. Hero expresses wish for help from someone.
34. Hero clarifies need for help (never can leave forest unless someone gives witch reward).
35. Hero expresses distress.

36. Hero asks child (S) for present as reward for witch.

37. Hero clarifies consequences of child's helping or not.

38. Hero expresses distress about permanent fate in isolation (never get home).

39. Hero expresses distress; wish to go home.

40. Good fairy enters expressing pity for hero.

41. Good fairy asks child (S) to give up present to help hero.

42. Good fairy clarifies consequences of child's (S's) help or no help.

43. Good fairy places responsibility on child for bad fate for hero.

44. Good fairy appeals to child (S) to help hero.

he is assigned to gather. They are lying scattered on the table at which the child is sitting and are easily within the child's reach. When the hero has expressed a wish for help with this task, he then faces the child and asks him directly for help. After a short pause, the other puppet comes back and reports that he has found enough twigs himself and is now ready to help move the log. After a sequence of joint effort, failure, distress and wish for help, the other puppet has to leave and suggests that perhaps someone bigger than he will help the hero. This ends the first phase of the experimental stimulus material.

A witch then appears and threatens to prevent the hero from getting out of the woods unless the hero gives the witch a present. The only present available is the one that the hero has given to the child and which was placed unopened in front of the child at the beginning of the show. The witch exits and the hero expresses distress, wishes for help, asks the child directly for his present, explains the consequences, and finally, if the child has not given up his present, a good fairy comes and asks the child to give up the present to help the hero.

The writer observed each child without his knowledge from behind a one-way mirror and returned to the room when the child gave up his present, went to the door to leave the field, or in one case, when a child appeared to be about to cry. In all cases, the writer asked the child what had been happening, suggested calling the hero on stage, did so, and invited the child to help the hero climb over the log so that he could get home. The curtain was then lowered, and the hero was called out to testify that he had gotten home. The period following the puppet show appeared to be successful in permitting each child to feel that he had taken some part in helping the hero get home, while leaving him with whatever impression he had formed as to the reality of the puppet characters.

A. Dependent Measures

The sequence of actions in the puppet show was designed to permit analysis of which children responded to what kinds of events in what ways. The author recorded all molar action on an outline of the plot (see

Table 7) for all subjects. He had no knowledge of the children's positions on the independent variables. In addition, video-tape recordings were made through the one-way mirror in the first sixteen cases in order to permit later coding of emotional behavior by several judges. The written record provided three dependent measures. Two measures of action to help another agent were presence or absence of action to help overcome a barrier (either the log or the distance to the twigs) and whether the child gave up his present to help the hero. A measure of the child's subjective orientation toward the hero was whether the child gave verbal support to the hero. This measure was obtained from the written record and the video-tape recordings. Only ten of the thirty-three children spoke to the puppet, and there was perfect agreement among three judges that eight of these children spoke supportively to the puppet. These eight children were therefore said to show verbal support.

B. Measures of Behavior in the Nursery School Setting

Children were categorized as active or passive in coping with barriers in the nursery school on the basis of written descriptions of the activity of each child over a one and one-half hour free play period. The thirty-three children were described by thirty-three different practice-teachers who were randomly assigned to a child by the head teacher according to a fixed rotation of the observer role over a six-week period. The observers were instructed to pay particular attention to what frustrating situations arose and what the child did in such situations. Two women research assistants unacquainted with the children then independently assigned the children to one of two categories on the basis of summary notes in the case of fifteen children and running descriptive accounts in the case of thirteen children. The two categories were defined as follows:

Active coping: The child persists in efforts to overcome pain, interference, or difficulty. He persists motorically or verbally in trying to have an effect on others or on objects with little seeking of help from adults. He uses his own observational, verbal, problem-solving abilities to arrive at a more satisfying status (more comfort or mastery) from his viewpoint.

Passive coping: The child makes no notable persistent effort to solve problems or overcome interference himself; or principally seeks adult help; or gives up what he is trying to do, or withdraws from difficulties; or avoids all contact with other children as stressful.

The two judges agreed in twenty-seven of thirty-three cases. The cases on which there was disagreement were arbitrarily assigned to the active coping category to make the two groups approximately equal in number. Assignment to the active coping category therefore means that there was some evidence of active coping according to at least one judge.

The child's tendency to express distress openly when confronted with stress situations was measured on the basis of ratings by two head teachers. The head teachers observed the children daily for six weeks and were presumably well situated to judge the child's general mode of handling

distress. The rating scale used independently by the judges is as follows:
Expresses distress in stressful situations—

$$
\begin{array}{ccccccc}
\text{o} & \text{o} & \text{o} & \textbf{M} & \text{o} & \text{o} & \text{o} \\
\end{array}
$$

o	o	o	M	o	o	o
1						9

(1) Inhibits expression of distress and tries to be brave, sits tight, or reassures self.

(M) Avoids source of threat and expresses distress verbally.

(9) Readily cries or flees in panic in stressful situations.

The judges' ratings were summed to provide a score for each child.

C. Sample

The children in this study were twenty boys and thirteen girls enrolled in the summer preschool at the Child Study Center of the University of California, Berkeley. Their ages ranged from three years and five months to five years and eleven months.

PREDICTIONS CONCERNING ACTION TO HELP A THWARTED AGENT

The two hypotheses concerning helpful action were subjected to empirical test in terms of the following predictions.

1. Children high in active coping with barriers in the nursery will more frequently try to overcome a barrier thwarting the puppet compared to children who cope passively in the nursery.

2. Children showing active coping *and* overt expression of distress in the nursery will more frequently try to overcome a barrier thwarting the puppet than will children showing other combinations of these variables.

RESULTS

Of the thirty-three children, thirteen helped to overcome a barrier and twenty did not. Among the thirteen children who helped to overcome a barrier, eight helped before being asked to do so directly. One anticipated distress and set out to reassure and guide the hero as soon as he identified the log as a barrier and before he had even engaged in effort to move it. A second began to help following the initial expression of distress, a third helped in response to the first expression of a wish for someone to help, a fourth began to help consistently with a barrier in response to the puppet's second effort to overcome the barrier. A fifth and a sixth child helped as soon as the task had been assigned to the hero and before the hero had begun to try to reach the twigs. A seventh responded to the puppet's statement that he would try and reach the twigs. And the eighth child responded to the hero's persistent effort to reach the twigs. The other five children who helped with a barrier responded to the hero's direct request for help in gathering the twigs following three different sequences of effort, distress, and a wish for help from some one. What order did the hypotheses bring to this data?

Table 8 shows the results concerning action to help with a barrier in the puppet show. The data are arranged in a fourfold table showing the frequency of helpful action as a function of active or passive coping and overt expression or suppression of distress in the nursery.

Table 8 shows first that the frequency of helping with a barrier was not random with respect to the two independent variables. Next, the first prediction was tested in terms of the association between the frequency

Table 8 Help with barrier in puppet show as a function of coping with barriers and expression of distress in the nursery

Coping style		Expressive style				
		Overt distress $j = 1$		Suppressed distress $j = 2$		
Active $i=1$		n_{11}	7	n_{12}	4	$n_{1.} = 11$
	$N_{11} - n_{11}$		2	$N_{12} - n_{12}$	6	
	N_{11}		9	N_{12}	10	$N_{1.} = 19$
Passive $i=2$		n_{21}	0	n_{22}	2	$n_{2.} = 2$
	$N_{21} - n_{21}$		7	$N_{22} - n_{22}$	5	
	N_{21}		7	N_{22}	7	$N_{2.} = 14$
	$n_{.1} =$		7	$n_{.2} =$	6	$n_{..} = 13$
	$N_{.1} =$		16	$N_{.2} =$	17	$N_{..} = 33$

Irrespective of the ratings on the independent variables, the outcome on the dependent variable can be only one of two (help or no help) which are mutually exclusive. Thus, for each subject we have a binomial trial. Let p_{ij} be the probability that a subject who is rated i and j will help the puppet. We have four binomial distributions to consider: $(p_{ij} + q_{ij})^{n_{ij}}$ where i = 1.2 and j = 1.2, and each having the marginal total of n_{ij} with the probability of helping p_{ij}.

Statistical tests:

1. Null hypothesis that the probability of helping the puppet is independent of the ratings on the two independent variables: $p_{11} = p_{12} = p_{21} = p_{22} = p_T$ (a constant). Result: $p (X_3^2 = 10.44) < .02$ Reject null hypothesis.

2. Null hypothesis that the probability of helping the puppet over the two expressive styles is the same irrespective of whether S is rated as having an active or passive coping style: $p_{1.} = p_{2.}$.
Result: $p (X_2^2 = 9.90) < .01$ Reject null hypothesis.

3. Null hypothesis that the probability of helping the puppet over the two coping styles is the same irrespective of whether S is rated as showing overt or suppressed distress: $p_{.1} = p_{.2}$
Result: $p (X_2^2 = 5.11) < .10$ Accept the null hypothesis.

4. Null hypothesis concerning the combination of active coping and overt distress, the "optimal condition for helping": The probability of helping the puppet under such a condition is no greater than an estimate of chance derived from the three remaining conditions: $p_{11} = p_k$
Result: $p (X_3^2 = 16.95) < .01$ Reject null hypothesis.

of helping with a barrier in the puppet show and active coping with barriers in the nursery. The prediction was confirmed (p ($X_2^2=9.90$) $<.01$), supporting the hypothesis that action to overcome a barrier in the path of another person is positively related to a disposition to persist actively in trying to overcome barriers in one's own path.

Active coping in the nursery was not found to be associated with giving up a present to help the puppet. And the two kinds of helping responses, help to overcome a barrier in the puppet show and giving up a present to help the puppet hero, were not significantly associated.

It appeared possible, however, that action to overcome a barrier in the puppet show was merely a function of general readiness to respond overtly to the puppets as agents or creatures. To check this possibility, a count was made of all overt approach and avoidance responses to the puppets other than helping responses. Only seven children did not make any approach or avoidance responses nor help the puppet. The data for the other twenty-six children were examined to provide a more rigorous test of the relationship between coping patterns in the nursery and help with the barrier in the puppet show. With this more restricted sample, the hypothesis was again supported that action to overcome a barrier in the path of another agent is positively related to a tendency to cope actively with barriers in one's own path.

What about the prediction that children who show active coping with barriers in the nursery *and* who show overt expression of distress in the nursery more frequently help the puppet to overcome a barrier than do children with the other combinations of these variables. Table 8 shows that this prediction was confirmed (p ($X_3^2=16.95$)$<.01$). This result supports the hypothesis that helpful action is a function of (1) sensitivity to distress as an occasion for help based on past distress experiences and (2) sense of competence to help based on past effectiveness in coping with barriers in one's environment.

PREDICTIONS CONCERNING SUBJECTIVE ORIENTATIONS
TO THWARTED AGENTS

The hypothesis concerning subjective aspects of sympathy for a thwarted person was as follows: Supportive affective response to another person who expresses distress is positively related to a disposition to express distress overtly in stressful situations. This hypothesis was subjected to empirical test in terms of the only readily available measure of affective response: verbal expression of support for a thwarted agent. It was predicted that children who express distress overtly in stressful nursery situations would more frequently give verbal support to the puppet who was thwarted in overcoming a barrier.

Table 9 shows the results concerning verbal expression of support as a function of active or passive coping and overt expression or suppression of distress in the nursery. First it is shown that the frequency of giving verbal support is not random with respect to the two independent variables. Table 9 then shows the results for the prediction that children who express distress overtly in the nursery will more frequently express verbal support for the puppet who is thwarted. The results confirm this prediction ($p(X_2^2 = 7.97) < .05$), supporting the hypothesis that supportive subjective response to another person who expresses distress is positively related to a disposition to express distress overtly in stressful situations.

Table 9 Verbal support for puppet as a function of coping with barriers and expression of distress in the nursery

Coping style		Expressive style					
		Overt distress $j = 1$		Suppressed distress $j = 2$			
Active $i=1$	n_{11}	5		n_{12}	0	$n_{1.} = 5$	
	$N_{11} - n_{11}$	4	$N_{12} - n_{12}$	10			
	N_{11}	9		N_{12}	10	$N_{1.} = 19$	
Passive $i=2$	n_{21}	2		n_{22}	1	$n_{2.} = 3$	
	$N_{21} - n_{21}$	5	$N_{22} - n_{22}$	6			
	N_{21}	7		N_{22}	7	$N_{2.} = 14$	
	$n_{.1} =$	7		$n_{.2} =$	1	$n_{..} = 8$	
	$N_{.1} =$	16		$N_{.2} =$	17	$N_{..} = 33$	

Irrespective of the ratings on the independent variables, the outcome on the dependent variable can be only one of two (support or no support) which are mutually exclusive. Thus, for each subject we have a binomial trial. Let p_{ij} be the probability that a subject who is rated i and j will support the puppet. We have four binomial distributions to consider: $(p_{ij} + q_{ij})^{n_{ij}}$ where i = 1.2 and j = 1.2, and each having the marginal total of n_{ij} with the probability of support of p_{ij}.

Statistical tests:

1. Null hypothesis that the probability of supporting the puppet is independent of the ratings on the two independent variables: $p_{11} = p_{12} = p_{21} = p_{22} = p_T$ (a constant). Result: $p (X_3^2 = 8.43) < .05$ Reject null hypothesis.

2. Null hypothesis that the probability of supporting the puppet over the two expressive styles i the same irrespective of whether S is rated as having an active or passive coping style: $p_{1.} = p_{2.}$. Result: $p (X_2^2 = 2.68) < .20$ Accept null hypothesis.

3. Null hypothesis that the probability of supporting the puppet over the two coping styles is the same irrespective of whether S is rated as showing overt or suppressed distress: $p_{.1} = p_{.2}$. Result: $p (X_2^2 = 7.97) < .05$ Reject the null hypothesis.

4. Null hypothesis concerning the combination of active coping and overt distress, the "optimal condition for helping": The probability of supporting the puppet under such a condition is no greater than an estimate of chance derived from the three remaining conditions: $p_{11} = p_k$. Result: $p (X_3^2 = 18.34) < .01$. Reject null hypothesis.

It was found that verbal support was not associated with help to overcome a barrier in the puppet show. Nevertheless, since verbal expression of support may influence the thwarted agent toward overcoming the barriers, the antecedents for more direct helping action were examined in relation to verbal support as well. Table 9 shows that verbal support was not associated with active coping in the nursery. However, the conditions predicted to be optimal for direct helping action, active coping and overt expression of distress in the nursery, were found to be positively associated with verbal support ($p(X_3^2=18.34)<.01$). This suggests that verbal support and direct action to help with a barrier are both functions of sensitivity to distress as an occasion for help (based on past overt expression of distress) and sense of competence to help (based on past effectiveness in overcoming barriers in one's own path).

DISCUSSION

The results suggest that verbal support is most likely to be shown by persons who are particularly sensitive to distress by virtue of experiences in which they have expressed distress overtly and received support. This agrees well with the study (Lenrow, 1960, 1963) of subjective sympathy in adults. Direct action to help overcome barriers, on the other hand, is most likely to be shown by persons who have a firm sense of competence by virtue of their past effectiveness in coping with barriers in their environment.

These findings parallel those of Hoffmann, who suggests that parental affection toward a child is correlated with the child's positive emotional orientation in the nursery but not with helpful action. Parental use of power in a way that shows respect for the child's autonomy *is* correlated with the child's helpful action. The parallel sets of evidence suggest that positive affective orientation toward a child leads to his positive affective orientation toward others; while parental behavior that provides the child with opportunities to develop a sense of competence in his own right is necessary in order for the child to take helpful action in difficult situations. It will be important to study the parental models of these children and to obtain other measures of the children's sense of competence in order to test these promising hypotheses further.

The puppet show technique appears to be highly fruitful for examining *which children* respond in a sympathetic manner and to *what events*. Of course, the test of the hypothesis concerning affective support for an agent in distress is limited to *verbal* expression of support and needs to be supplemented by detailed studies of the non-verbal expressive behavior of the children during the puppet show. Analysis of the facial and bodily expressive behavior recorded on video-tape is presently being carried out to pursue the question. This analysis may throw further light on the relation between caring and helping, that is, responding to distress as an occasion for help and taking the role of a helper.

CONCLUSIONS

The purpose of this chapter has been to demonstrate that we now have a toehold for empirical work in the domain of sympathy, rather than to marshal support for broad generalizations. Nevertheless, the two main studies summarized here suggest a common general formulation concerning sympathy. It appears that how one has come to manage his own affectively involved behavior influences his capacity to respond favorably to others' affectively involved experience. It has been suggested that this is due to two general sources. One is the models that have been provided by those who have responded to one's affectively involved behavior in the past. Here it appears to be important how they have rewarded affective involvement as well as what behavior they have provided as an example that may be imitated. The former presumably influences how willing a person is to become affectively involved vicariously in response to another person's situation. And the latter presumably influences what he does about it. A second general influence also appears to effect what he does about it, namely, how competent he has come to regard himself in taking particular roles (e.g., overcoming barriers).

The present discussion has been focused on distress as an affective experience that has far reaching effects on sensitivity to thwarted strivings in others. In order to provide a more general formulation of sympathy, it is important to include sympathy for another person's joy or hope, or indignation, or vengefulness. In the present view, one's sense of alliance with a person who was affectively involved in a joyful, hopeful, indignant, or vengeful relationship with others would depend on one's past affective involvement in such roles and the acceptance or rejection one received from significant other people at such times. This implies, of course, that there would be important individual differences in sensitivity to particular affectively involved behavior of others. In addition, it should be possible to specify differences based on common child-training practices in a culture. In our culture, where boys and girls are trained differentially to inhibit distress and anger, we may expect to find differences between men and women in their sympathy for distressed as compared to angry persons. And if parent-child relationships may have a generalized influence on how acceptable affective involvement will be regarded (Tomkins, 1963), early learned avoidance of such involvement could lead to general lack of a sense of alliance with anyone who is affectively involved.

Yet if a person shows little supportive response to someone in distress, for example, to what extent is this a function simply of inhibiting overt expression of support as compared to lack of any supportive subjective orientation? If the person can be shown to be weak on subjective supportive response, is this due to failure to *attach importance* to what matters to another person or failure to *discriminate* what matters to the other person in the first place? Clearly, these problems are in need of systematic empirical study. The fact that researchable questions are readily suggested by the findings reviewed here may provide grounds for optimism that the phenomena of sympathy are now more accessible to empirical investigation.

REFERENCES

Allport, G. W. *Personality: A psychological interpretation.* New York: Holt, 1937.

Allport, G. W. *The individual and his religion.* New York: Macmillan, 1950.

Allport, G. W. The historical background of modern social psychology. In G. Lindzey (Ed.), *Handbook of social psychology.* Vol. I. *Theory and Method.* Cambridge: Addison-Wesley, 1954.

Allport, G. W. *Becoming: Basic considerations for a psychology of personality.* New Haven: Yale University, 1955.

Asch, S. *Social psychology.* New York: Prentice-Hall, 1952.

Bandura, A. Social learning through imitation. In M. R. Jones (Ed.), *Nebraska symposium on motivation.* Lincoln, Nebraska: University of Nebraska Press, 1962.

Bridges, Katherine M. B. *The social and emotional development of the preschool child.* London: Kegan Paul, 1931.

Dollard, J., & Miller, N. *Personality and psychotherapy.* New York: McGraw-Hill, 1950.

Erikson, E. H. *Young man Luther.* New York: Norton, 1958.

Flugel, J. C. *Man, morals, and society.* New York: International Universities, 1945.

Freud, Anna. *The ego and the mechanisms of defense.* London: Hogarth, 1937.

Freud, S. *Group psychology and the analysis of the ego.* London: International Psycho-Analytical Press, 1922.

Heider, F. *The psychology of interpersonal relations.* New York: Wiley, 1958.

Hoffman, M. L. Parent discipline and the child's consideration for others. *Child Develpm.*, 1963, 34, 573-588.

Isaacs, Susan. *Social development in young children.* London: Routledge, 1933.

Lenrow, P. B. *Experimental changes in sensitivity in the needs of others.* Unpublished doctoral dissertation, Harvard University, 1960.

Lenrow, P. B. Sympathy revisited. (ms.) 1963.

Lenrow, P. B. Varieties of sympathy. (ms.) 1964.

Maslow, A. H. *Motivation and personality.* New York: Harper, 1954.

Miller, N. E., & Dollard, J. *Social learning and imitation.* New Haven: Yale University, 1941.

Murphy, Lois B. *Social behavior and child personality.* New York: Columbia University, 1937.

Murphy, Lois B. *The widening world of childhood: paths toward mastery.* New York: Basic Books, 1962.

Piaget, J. *The moral judgment of the child.* New York: Harcourt, Brace, 1932.

Scheler, M. (1913) *The nature of sympathy.* Translated by P. Heath, London: Routledge & Kegan Paul, 1954.

Sorokin, P. A. (Ed.), *Explorations in altruistic love and behavior: a symposium.* Boston: Beacon, 1950.

Sullivan, H. S. *The interpersonal theory of psychiatry.* New York: Norton, 1953.

Sullivan, H. S. *The psychiatric interview.* New York: Norton, 1954.

Suttie, I. D. *The origins of love and hate.* New York: Julian, 1935.

Tomkins, S. S. *Affect, imagery, consciousness.* Vol. II. *The negative affects.* New York: Springer, 1963.

White, R. W. *Lives in progress.* New York: Dryden, 1952.

White, R. W. Motivation reconsidered: the concept of competence. *Psychol. Rev.*, 1959, *66*, 297-333.

White, R. W. Competence and the psychosexual stages of development. In M. R. Jones (Ed.), *Nebraska symposium on motivation.* Lincoln, Nebraska: University of Nebraska, 1960. pp. 97-149.

White, R. W. Sense of interpersonal competence: two case studies and some reflections on origins. In R. W. White (Ed.), *The study of lives.* New York: Atherton, 1963.

PART SIX

AFFECT AND
FACIAL RESPONSES

X

Facial expressions as indicators of distress

Howard Leventhal
Elizabeth Sharp

The present study tests several hypotheses relating independent variables which manipulate level of stress to change in facial expressions. The investigation, which was conducted in an obstetric unit of a major hospital, was motivated in part by the desire to obtain empirical evidence that observable changes in the patient's facial reactions would prove to be valid indicators of distress.

Empirical evidence would also prove relevant to the following questions of general psychological interest: (1) Are there distinct facial changes correlated with the emotional distress produced by a specific set of circumstances? (2) Are there common stimulus attributes in facial reactions which can serve as basic cues for the perception of emotional reactions in others? (3) Will variations in the frequency of appearance of specific facial signs relate to systematic variation in a set of independent variables which are assumed to be different manipulations of the level of stress?

The role of facial and motor change in emotion is of particular interest as it has recently been suggested that variations in emotional experience are related to changes in cognitive contents associated with a common state of arousal (Schachter & Singer, 1962). Failure to locate distinctive physiological reactions for many emotions is said to cast doubt on the James-Lange position (James, 1961) that differential physical feedback is responsible for emotional experience, and to strengthen the assumption that cognition plays the central role in the differentiation of arousal states (Schachter, 1964). The cognitive formulation does not recognize, however, that the body consists of more than the viscera and endocrine

This study was supported by a grant from the U.S.P.H.S. (GN-8922). The authors wish to acknowledge the support of Dean Florence Wald and Professor Robert C. Leonard of the Yale school of Nursing throughout the period of the study. Special thanks go to Mrs. Grevilda Trembly for her careful and tireless work on the data analysis and manuscript, and to Miss Donna Diers who served as the rater in the reliability study.

A special acknowledgment must be made to the medical and nursing staffs of the Grace-New Haven Community Hospital.

systems. It ignores suggestions that motor attitudes may make an equally important contribution to differential emotional experience—Allport & Vernon (1933), Bull (1962), Plutchik (1962), Tomkins (1962). While the present study is not a direct test of this alternative hypothesis, the ability to locate common physiognomic changes in a group of subjects in a particular stress setting emphasizes the possible role of these changes for emotional experience.

The second question, the availability of cues for the perception of emotions, is a complement to the first. Though it has long been argued that we *perceive* the emotions of others, Asch (1952), Kohler (1947), observations of people's emotions are usually regarded as products of a complex judgmental process rather than a complex perceptual process. This bias seems to reflect a belief that individual differences in *stimulus* persons make it impossible to describe psychophysical relationships for the judgment of emotions. This attitude is similar to that found in the study of monocular depth perception before serious efforts were made in that area to reconceptualize the stimulus (Gibson, 1950). While the present study will hardly resolve this controversy, the location of a set of common facial expressions produced in a stress situation will support the assumption that real life settings give rise to definable facial stimuli which can serve as a basis for the perception of emotions.

On the assumption that the labor and delivery service provides a situation for observing stress reactions in pregnant women, three independent variables were chosen within this situation which were expected to be related to different intensities of stress stimulation. The variables were selected so as to be relatively independent of one another and included: (1) a situation factor (the interval of labor in which the observations were made), (2) an experiential factor (prior childbirth experience), and (3) a pre-dispositional factor (the patient's scores on the *Welch Anxiety Scale;* Welch, 1952). If specific facial signs are systematically related to these independent variables, it will provide information on the antecedents and behavioral indicators of distress.

It was expected that as labor progressed there would be an increase in the level of tension and stress experienced by the expectant mothers, which would result in increases in the frequency of facial signs of distress and a decrease in the frequency of signs of comfort.

In addition, mothers with no prior childbirth experience (primigravidae) were expected to experience greater tension than expectant mothers who have had children (multigravidae). Thus, multigravidae are likely to show fewer facial signs indicative of stress and more facial signs indicative of comfort than primigravidae. It seems reasonable to expect more signs of distress among primigravidae than multigravidae. Several mechanisms, which the hypothesis does not distinguish between, could produce the difference. For example, primigravidae might exhibit more distress signs because their longer labors produce an accumulation of distress. On the other hand, primigravidae might manifest more distress than multigravidae at equivalent stages in the process of birth because initial births introduce a greater number of, or more intense, physical changes in the reproductive apparatus. Moreover, multigravidae possess clear expectations of their potential labor experiences, e.g., pain, and this may minimize the unexpectedness (or apparent severity) of stresses, thereby reducing emotional over-reaction to the stress stimulation (Janis, 1958). (The groups used did not differ in "formal" preparation for childbirth.) The alternatives will be discussed after the results are examined.

It should also be added that the decrease in comfort over time is likely to be greater for primigravidae than for multigravidae. An interaction effect is likely since, in the initial phases of labor, the mild stress-producing stimuli should not produce a sufficient amount of discomfort to differentiate between the groups. As labor progresses, however, distress will become more intense for those mothers having their initial childbearing experience.

The third main effect anticipated was that women whose self-reports indicate relatively high amounts of anxiety and tension in their every day lives are likely to experience more distress during labor than women who report relatively little anxiety and tension. Therefore, mothers high in predispositional anxiety will more frequently exhibit signs of distress and less frequently exhibit signs of comfort than will mothers low in anxiety.

METHOD

Design and Subjects

Various aspects of facial expressions were observed during labor for two groups of women; those with prior labor experience (multigravidae) and those without (primigravidae). The observations were classified in one of four intervals of labor. The data were regrouped in order to investigate the effects of predispositional anxiety.

The setting. The research setting was the labor and delivery service of a large teaching hospital. All patients were either under the care of a private physician or registered with the University Service. Each mother was admitted to and remained in her own labor room until she was transferred to the delivery room. The expectant father was allowed to remain with his wife in labor, if the couple so desired.

Selection of sample. Observations were made for an initial sample of 100 women. To be included in the project a patient had to: (1) speak English, (2) not be a participant in another research project, (3) be in labor and show no signs of an abnormal course, and (4) not have received conduction anesthesia. If more than one mother met the sample criteria at the same time, the one clearly further along in labor was selected or, if no difference existed on this criterion, the patient with the lowest room number was selected. Though none of the 100 mothers who were asked to participate in the study refused, one asked the observer to leave during labor. Since the critical information needed to determine the duration of labor was obtained after the observations had been made (to minimize the possibility of bias in the observer), 15 cases were lost because it was impossible to obtain this datum.

Observations made after patients had had analgesia or conduction anesthesia were *not* considered comparable to observations made when the patients had not received a pain-relieving drug. Such observations were excluded from the main analysis unless they were made *no later* than five minutes after the administration of Nisental, or *no later* than fifteen minutes after the administration of Demerol and Seconal, and when they were made no less than three hours after the time of administration of any of these drugs; Musser & Bird (1959), Beckman (1958). The above rules resulted in the loss of 53 observations for 39 subjects. However, only 14 subjects were lost from the sample because all the observations made for them fell within drug intervals. The total sample, therefore, consisted of 71 patients, of whom 19 were primigravidae and 52 multigravidae.

Dependent Variables

Facial expressions. To obtain objective evidence for the hypothesis that a stress situation produces specific expressive changes for most people, it is necessary to obtain a reliable and detailed method of recording. An ideal and simple solution would be to photograph the patient's expressions. However, there are several problems with such a procedure. First, there are numerous difficulties in obtaining clearance for the installation of cameras in a hospital. Second, the introduction of cameras inevitably heightens the individual's awareness that his expressions are being recorded—unless the cameras are skillfully concealed. Concealing the equipment raises problems of ethics and obtaining permission for recording. Even if these problems can be resolved, there remains the impossibility of recording a patient's facial behavior from a *fixed* point of view. The patient cannot be immobilized and a pair of cameras would be needed to keep the loss of information to a minimum.

Therefore, the best procedure seemed to be to obtain a reliable and detailed recording method which would; (1) minimize subjective judgment on the part of the observer, and (2) make the observation itself a "flexible and natural" part of the labor setting. Using Birdwhistell's (1952) extensive work as a starting point, a relatively complete system of symbols was developed which permitted an observer to rapidly and objectively record changes in the configuration of four different regions of the face; the forehead, eyes, mouth, and nose. Thus, it was possible for a nurse to record the relevant data in the labor room without the patient being aware that her facial or other expressive actions were the object of study. Table 1 lists the items recorded for the forehead, brow and eyelid. The changes scored for the mouth, nose, and the remaining eye categories are not listed because the independent variables had no significant effects upon these indicators.

Indices of comfort and distress. Because of the limitations on the frequency with which specific acts could be observed, the symbols were combined on an *a priori basis* to form *indices of comfort* and *indices of discomfort.* The physical changes included in these indices for the forehead, brow and eyelids are listed in Table 1.

Table 1 Symbols used to score forehead, brow and eyelid behavior

Symbol	Meaning	Forehead
	Comfort	
—	1.	Smooth: (permanent thin wrinkles may or may not be present).
≋	2.	Horizontal creases or folds (wrinkled) extend across forehead.
	Discomfort	
-≋-	3.	Horizontal creases or folds in middle, smooth on either side.
⬤𝍐0	4.	Horizontal depression, grated effect, or vertical depression.
		Brow
	Comfort	
— —	1.	Brows horizontal; no ridge or depression between or over either brow.
—⌒	2.	One brow raised.
⌇⌇	3.	Slight fluttering (up and down) of one or both brows.
⌒⌒	4.	Both brows raised.
	Minor discomfort	
⌣⌣	5.	Depressions over one or both eyebrows.
⋱⋱	6.	Fluttering of brows leading to occasional V formation.
	Major discomfort	
V	7.	Medial approximation of brows with clear V formation.
s\⁄s	8.	V formation between brows and depression over one or both brows.
		Eyelids
	Comfort (normal state)	
≡≡	1.	Lids motionless except for normal blinks; no creases in upper lid if eye closed.
	Discomfort	
≋≋	2.	Fluttering (up and down movement) of upper lids.
⧗ ⧗	3.	Creases in upper lids occur without movement.
⧗⧗⎮≋≋	4.	Both (2) and (3) occur simultaneously.
= =	5.	Eyes closed with exaggerated creases of upper lids and creases surrounding eye.
⧧ ⧧	6.	Opening and closing occurs at high rates.

Schedule for observation. The patients were seen for twenty minutes at two hour intervals during labor. To insure objectivity and to minimize errors in recording, observations were made separately for each of four sections of the face: (1) forehead and brow, (2) eyes, eyelids and eyeballs, (3) mouth, and (4) nose. The restriction of observations to such narrow areas of the face was an absolute necessity as during pre-testing the observer reported that she was actually unable to "see" more than one narrow area of the face when recording. Activity in each of the four sections was recorded for a separate five minute period. The observations were made for five seconds every fifteen seconds during this interval giving the observer 10 seconds to record the observations made of the prior 5 second period. The order in which each section was observed was varied according to a regular schedule so that each of the four was observed in each position approximately an equal number of times.

Scoring. The frequency of occurrence of each symbol during the five minute interval was the score used for analysis.

Level of Stress

Interval of labor. The duration of labor was divided into intervals representing increments in level of stress stimulation. This division is based on the assumption that the amount of pain or stress increases as labor progresses. However, it is necessary to take into account the following factors: (1) that the duration of labor differs from patient to patient, and (2) that the amount of pain or stress increases more rapidly in the later stages of labor.

Each mother was questioned about the onset of contractions so as to estimate the duration of labor. This information was checked against that given to the doctor and, for each patient, the interval between onset of labor and delivery was divided into twenty segments. All observations were treated in terms of their position in one of the twenty intervals. The information on the onset of contractions, and of course the time of delivery itself, was obtained subsequent to the observations in a further effort to minimize observer bias.

A procedure was then developed to deal with the acceleration of stress stimulation in the later intervals. Hardy and Javert (1949) reported that pain intensity increases at almost an identical rate with the values of cervical dilatation. Dilatation (in centimeters) readings, obtained from the medical chart, were then plotted against intervals of labor. The resulting curves suggested an S-shaped pattern comparable to that for normal labor reported by Friedman (1959), with the rapid rise toward the last quarter of labor leveling off in the very final intervals. So that equal changes in time would be more nearly related to equal increases in stress stimulation, the values on the abscissa (intervals one through twenty) were squared making the new plot, dilatation against interval squared, nearly linear. The squared values were next grouped into four categories (from 1-100; 101-200; 201-300; 301-400) resulting in four intervals with fairly even increments in dilatation and, presumably, in level of stress stimulation.

Prior experience in labor. Mothers were classified as primigravidae or multigravidae on the basis of their obstetric histories. Their responses were kept separate in the analyses.

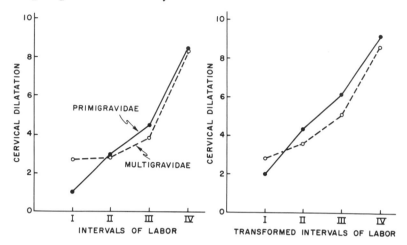

Figure 1. Effects of interval of labor and past experience upon cervical dilatation.

Predispositional anxiety levels. Predispositional anxiety levels were determined from responses to 39 items on the Welch Anxiety Scale (Welch, 1952). The questionnaire with an accompanying letter was mailed to 85 of the 88 patients two months after the completion of the experiment. (One physician objected to his patients receiving the questionnaire.) The two month delay was chosen so as to minimize the influence of the childbirth experience upon the mother's responses. Fifty-five of the 85 questionnaires (65%) were returned. The rate for the primigravidae was 83% while that for the multigravidae was 56%.

The anxiety levels were determined by dividing the distribution of scores at the median. Low scores ranged from zero to eight and high scores from nine to thirty-three.

Data Analysis

Each of the facial activity indices was treated in a 4 x 2 analysis of variance design: four intervals of labor and two subject types. The effects of predispositional anxiety were examined separately. Because of the nature of the situation in which the data was collected, it was not possible to obtain an equal number of observations for each patient or for each interval of labor. To adjust for the varying *n* in each interval an analysis of variance model for unweighted means was used (Walker & Lev, 1953). As a further check on the effect of the disproportional *n*'s chi square analyses were also conducted.

The problem of repeat measures, however, was more difficult to solve.

First, if a patient was observed more than once in the same interval of labor, her scores for the interval were averaged. However, some of the scores in different time intervals were from the same patients and therefore were not independent of one another. Because the number of observations per patient is unequal, it is exceedingly difficult to take these correlations into account.[1] One solution, omitting all cases with multiple observations, was rejected as it would seriously reduce the sample size. It appeared that the best alternative would be to assume that the observations were independent, thus leaving a relatively large sample and simplifying the analyses. If the repeated measures are positively correlated, treating them as independent scores underestimates the significance levels for duration of labor and for the interactions of duration by prior childbirth experience. Of course, if the repeated scores correlate negatively, treating them as independent will overestimate the significance levels. Therefore, for each dependent variable, high and low scores for the first versus the second half of labor were plotted for all patients observed in both halves. The responses showed positive or zero relationships and the probability tests should yield conservative estimates of the significance levels.

Because the above procedures are admittedly unorthodox, X^2 tests were also conducted as a further check on the significance of the findings. All these tests used a median split to obtain high and low scores on the indices, and divided the scores into first and second halves of labor. The tests were also done twice, once using each observation as the unit of analysis though only one score (a mean) was included for each patient in each half of labor. On the second analysis, all patients who had scores in each half of labor had one of the scores dropped at random. These analyses provide a less comprehensive picture of the data than the parametric tests and are reported in footnotes 2, 3 and 4.

RESULTS

Effects of Interval of Labor and Prior Experience in Labor

The results of the analyses of variance will only be reported for those facial measures which produced significant findings. This includes scores for the 5 forehead and brow indices and the 2 eyelid indices listed in Table 1. Thus, the significant findings represent analyses of 7 measures made up from 18 different symbol scores. On the other hand, data for 5 other indices (two eye and three mouth) and all nose symbols are omitted. The problem created by this selective procedure will be discussed later.

The results will be presented for each of the 7 indices. As several of

[1] When observations falling during medication intervals were omitted, an additional 14 patients were lost from the sample. For the remaining 71 cases, 19 primigravidae and 52 multigravidae, 11 of the primigravidae were observed once, 6 twice, and 2 three times, while 36 of the multigravidae were observed once, 13 twice, and 3 three times.

these measures are highly intercorrelated, tests will necessarily duplicate one another. This method of presentation provides, however, the clearest possible picture of the facial changes produced by stress stimulation.

Forehead. Analysis of the forehead *comfort index* showed a significant *decrement* in comfort signs as delivery neared (Figure 2: $F_{lin}=12.24$, *df* 1/92, $p<.005$). As would be expected, the forehead *distress index* shows significant increases with interval of labor, the linear trend being significant ($F=7.58$, *df* 1/92, $p<.025$). It is clear, therefore, that the increase

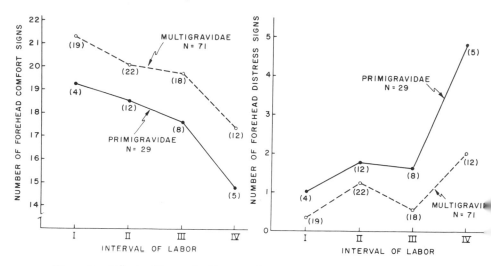

Figure 2.   Effects of interval of labor and prior experience upon forehead indices.

in stress stimulation which is assumed to occur with increased time in labor yields significant increases in those forehead reactions categorized as signs of distress.[2]

Figure 2 also shows differences as a function of prior experience in labor; primigravidae showing fewer signs of comfort ($F=6.06$, *df* 1/92, $p<.025$) and more signs of distress ($F=3.99$, *df* 1/92, $p<.05$) than multigravidae. However, unlike the *F* ratios for the duration by experience comparisons, those for prior experience may overestimate rather than underestimate the true significance levels. This occurs because the error term for testing prior experience effects, the residual between-subjects variance in a repeat measure design, would probably be larger than that used in

[2] The x^2 analysis for the forehead comfort index, comparing all scores above and below the median for early (Intervals I & II) and late labor (Intervals III & IV), was significant [Hi-comfort,, 45 early, 24 late; Lo-comfort, 12 early, 19 late; $x^2 = 5.10$; $p<.05$]. When the analysis was repeated after randomly dropping one of the two scores for all Ss with repeated measures, the result was very nearly significant ($x^2 = 3.74$; *df* 1; $p<.07$). The x^2 for the distress index was not significant, either using all observations [Hi-discomfort, 10 early, 15 late; Lo-discomfort, 47 early, 28 late; $x^2 = 3.06$; *df* 1; $p<.10$] or dropping repeated observations [$x^2 = 2.04$; n.s.].

the current analysis. Therefore, separate t and X^2 tests were computed for the prior experience factor (with repeat measures averaged). These were found to be non-significant for both indices. There also were no significant interactions of duration with prior experience.

Brow. For those observations made later in labor, significant decrements occurred in the index of brow comfort (Figure 3: $F_{lin}=27.83$, df 1/92, $p<.005$). The two indices for brow distress, that for minor signs and that for major signs of distress, showed, as expected, increases in signs of distress for observations late in labor. The effect was significant

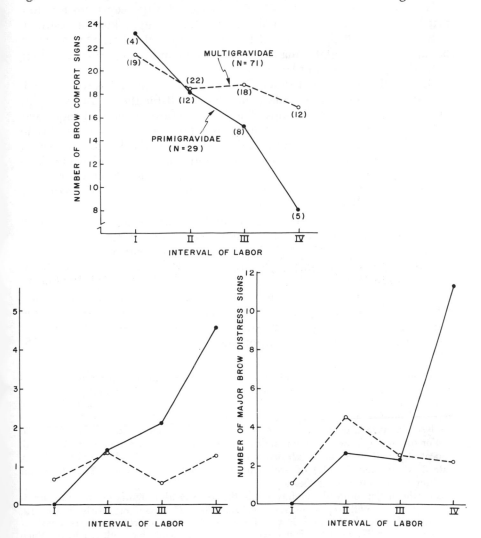

Figure 3.   Effects of interval of labor and prior experience upon brow indices.

at beyond the p=.005 level for both the minor (F_{lin}=14.480, df 1/92) and the major (F_{lin}=17.85, df 1/92) brow distress indices.

The significant linear effects of interval of labor upon the brow indices parallel the results for the forehead reactions. However, unlike the forehead indices, the brow measures showed significant interactions of duration by prior experience in labor. Thus, primigravidae showed progressively *fewer* signs of brow comfort over time than did the multigravidae (F=3.17, df 3/92, p<.05), and progressively higher scores over time for both the minor (F=3.88, df 3/92, p<.025) and the major distress indices (F=21.85, df 1/92, p<.005).[3] It can also be seen from Figure 3 that the minor brow distress index scores for primigravidae are particularly high in both the third and fourth intervals of labor. On the other hand, the scores for the major brow distress index are especially high only in the last interval of labor.

Despite the more rapid descent of the brow comfort index for primigravidae than for multigravidae, the rate of fall for the measure is quite even *within* each of the groups. The linear nature of these changes may indicate that the brow comfort index is more sensitive to variations in distress. This greater sensitivity could be due to the larger number of signs (4) comprising it. On the other hand, the more sudden and late-appearing increases for the distress signs may reflect that distress reactions, particularly those which are very intense, appear with frequency only close to delivery.

Comparisons of the brow measures by the analysis of variance showed significant differences between primigravidae and multigravidae for the comfort index (F=4.11, df 1/92, p<.05) and for both minor (F=5.61, df 1/92, p<.025) and major (F=12.85, df 1/92, p<.01) signs of brow distress. As with the forehead measures, however, neither t tests nor X^2 analyses (with repeated measures for subjects averaged) produced significant findings for the comfort or major distress index. However, the minor brow distress signs were sufficiently more numerous in primigravidae than multigravidae to approach significance (t=1.91, df 1/68, p<.07; X^2=3.21, df 1, p<.10).

[3] Using both primigravidae and multigravidae, the x^2 analyses for the brow comfort index were significant when based on all observations [Hi-comfort, 39 early, 17 late; Lo-comfort, 18 early, 26 late; x^2 = 5.84; p<.02], or when one of each pair of repeated observations was dropped at random [x^2 = 3.96; df 1; p<.05] Separate analyses for primigravidae were significant while those for multigravidae were not.

For the minor brow discomfort index the x^2 was significant for primigravidae with repeat observations included [Hi-discomfort, early 3, late 10; Lo-discomfort, early 13, late 3; x^2 = 7.60; p<.01] or excluded [x^2 = 7.93; df 1; p<.01] The effects for multigravidae were not significant.

For the major brow discomfort index the x^2 was also significant for the primigravidae either with repeat observations included [Hi-discomfort, early 4, late 10; Lo-discomfort, early 12, late 3; x^2 = 5.80; p<.02] or with repeat observations excluded [x^2 = 8.87; p<.01]. The tests were not significant for multigravidae. When primigravidae and multigravidae were combined, the x^2 with repeats dropped were usually not beyond the p<.05 level [Brow comfort x^2 = 4.94; p<.05; minor brow discomfort, x^2 = 2.94; p<.10; major brow discomfort, x^2 = 3.05; p<.10].

Eyelids. The scores for the eyelid comfort index showed a significant decrement over intervals of labor ($F_{lin}=18.336$, *df* 1/91, $p<.005$) while the complementary index of eyelid distress showed corresponding increments ($F_{lin}=11.60$, *df* 1/91, $p<.005$). Primigravidae showed the strongest changes for both decreases in comfort signs and for increases in the distress signs. However, the interactions of prior experience by interval were not significant.[4]

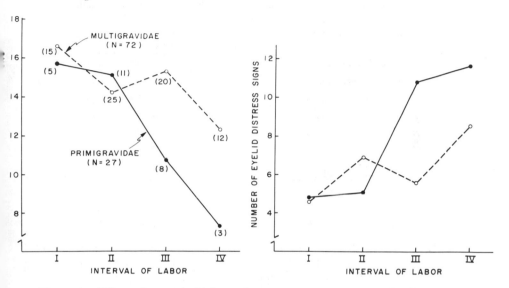

Figure 4. Effects of interval of labor and prior experience upon eyelid indices.

The analysis of variance gave a significant contrast when comparing the primigravidae and multigravidae on the comfort index ($F=4.91$, *df* 1/91, $p<.05$). However, neither *t* tests nor X^2 (with repeated scores averaged) replicated this effect.

Predispositional Anxiety

In Table 2 are the means comparing High (above the median) and Low (below the median) anxiety subjects for the indices already reported. When a subject was observed in more than one interval of labor, a mean score was used. For High anxiety subjects there were significantly *lower* comfort scores for the forehead ($F=2.08$, *n.s.*), the brow ($F=7.15$,

[4] A significant x^2 was obtained for primigravidae for the index of eyelid comfort using all observations in the first and second half of labor [*Hi*-comfort, 12 early, 2 late; *Lo*-comfort, 4 early, 9 late; $x^2 = 6.31$; $p<.02$]. For eyelid discomfort, there was no significant effect for multigravidae, but primigravidae showed more cases above the median late in labor; [*Hi*-discomfort, 5 early, 9 late; *Lo*-discomfort, 11 early, 2 late; $x^2 = 4.80$; $p<.05$]. However, when repeat scores were omitted only the test for the discomfort index (combining primigravidae and multigravidae) approached significance ($x^2 = 2.82$; $p<.10$).

$p<.01$), and the eyelid indices of comfort ($F=9.22$, $p<.01$), and significantly higher scores for the forehead ($F=5.37$, $p<.025$), the minor brow ($F=3.51$, n.s.), the major brow ($F=10.16$, $p<.01$) and the eyelid ($F=9.96$, $p<.01$) indices of distress. Thus, the facial expression scores are sensitive to differences due to *dispositional* measures of anxiety as well as to situational (interval of labor) measures of stimulus intensity.

Table 2 The effects of dispositional anxiety level on facial indicators
of comfort and discomfort

Index	High (N)	Low (N)	F	P
1. Forehead comfort	18.88 (34)	20.31 (29)	2.08	n.s.
2. Forehead discomfort	2.21 (34)	.45 (29)	5.37	.025
3. Brow comfort	17.03 (34)	21.09 (29)	7.15	.01
4. Brow minor discomfort	2.00 (34)	.94 (29)	3.51	.10
5. Brow major discomfort	4.47 (34)	.98 (29)	10.16	.01
6. Eyelid comfort	12.49 (35)	15.97 (29)	9.22	.01
7. Eyelid discomfort	8.89 (35)	4.83 (29)	9.96	.01

Selection and Independence of Dependent Measures

Prior to presenting the findings two issues were raised concerning their statistical interpretation. The first concerned the reporting only of significant results and the problem of capitalizing on chance, and the second concerned the independence of the measures.

Selection of significant findings. Data were reported for 18 symbols grouped into 7 indices while 53 symbols and 7 indices were not reported. Therefore, one might conclude that only 25% of our indicators reflected behavioral change. An examination of the non-significant categories reveals that this percentage is an extremely conservative figure. First, the nose category (based on 5 symbols) was never analysed as the nose proved to be rather unresponsive (there were few scores) and there was disagreement as to how these scores should be combined.

The two eye categories which went unreported account for 12 additional symbols. Six of these recorded the object fixated by the patient and *not* expressive changes in the eye region. The remaining 6 recorded the degree to which the eyes were open or closed. Since the eyes can be closed either when relaxed or distressed, it was no surprise that these symbols were not systematically influenced by the independent variables. Thus, 17 of the 53 unreported symbols are *irrelevant* for the question of locating significant changes in facial expression with increases in distress.

However, there were no significant effects for the mouth category, some 36 symbols which had been combined into three indices in each of two different ways. The first combination grouped the 36 symbols into those showing the corners of the mouth to be up, straight or down. The second grouping excluded those symbols with the corners up, and then classified the remaining symbols into a comfort index and a change index (changes in position of the lips with or without continuing motion of the lips). A group of the symbols comprising this change index (change in position with motion in lips) was examined separately. Since this last score is included in the change index, only *three* of the indices for mouth reactions were based on different symbols: those with corners up, those for relaxation, and those for change in lip positions. These are the only additional indices in which change could have been expected and in which change did not occur. Thus, there seems to be little reason to question the findings because they might capitalize on chance.

Independence of reported measures. Many of the correlations between the forehead, brow and eyelid indices were highly significant. As would be expected, the relationship between the comfort and distress measures was very high within each of the pairs, i.e., forehead comfort versus forehead distress, $r=-.80$, brow comfort versus brow distress (major and minor distress combined) $r=-.81$, and eyelid comfort versus eyelid distress, $r=-.89$. It is possible that these correlations are so high because they are based upon all the observations and include repeated measures on some of the same subjects. However, such correlations are the best estimates of the independence of the scores analysed in the prior sections. When each patient was assigned a mean score for each pair of the items to be inter-related, eliminating repeat measures, the magnitude of the relationships is unchanged (forehead comfort versus discomfort, $r=-.71$; brow comfort versus sum major and minor discomfort, $r=-.65$; eyelid comfort versus eyelid discomfort, $r=-.94$).

Table 3 Correlations between forehead, brow and eyelid indices

	Forehead Discomfort	Brow Comfort	Brow Discomfort	Eyelid Comfort	Eyelid Discomfort
Forehead comfort	-.80	.84	-.56	.28	-.27
(N)	(100)	(100)	(100)	(97)	(97)
Forehead discomfort		-.75	.69	-.17	.24
(N)		(100)	(100)	(97)	(97)
Brow comfort			-.81	.35	-.33
(N)			(100)	(97)	(97)
Brow discomfort				-.32	.33
(N)				(97)	(97)
Eyelid comfort					-.89
(N)					(98)

In addition to the high correlation within the index pairs, Table 3 shows high relationships between the forehead and brow measures, moderate relationships between the brow and eyelid measures and negligible relationships between the forehead and eyelid measures. The lower correlation between the eyelid and the brow and forehead indices could be due to the fact that the eyelid observations occurred at different points in the 20 minute observation schedule. However, there are several factors which suggest that the reduced correlations reflect a certain degree of intra-subject specificity in expressions of distress. First, the correlations decrease with increasing distance between the regions. Thus, disturbances in an area effect adjacent regions, but this does not necessarily carry to a more remote area. Second, when mean scores for the indices are correlated (the subject being the unit) the correlations are practically identical. Thus, the relationship depends upon the reactivity of individual subjects. One could conclude that some individuals show their stress reactions with eyelid and brow, while others respond with forehead and brow.

The correlations also suggest that the forehead and brow measures can be combined to obtain an overall significance test. Since the range of the scores was more or less the same, the distress scores were added and subtracted from the sum of the comfort measures. This analyis showed a significant effect for duration ($F_{lin}=24.12$, df 1/94, $p<.005$) and the interaction was close to significance ($F=2.45$, df 3/94, $p<.10$). A global index such as this obscures, however, the differences observed between the various indices, which are suggestive of further hypotheses concerning facial reactivity.

Medication Effects

All observations made from about 15 minutes (depending upon the drug) to 3 hours after recciving medication were excluded from the analyses. A comparison for one of the indices, major brow discomfort, was made between medicated and non-medicated observations. The mean for the medicated patients was significantly higher than that for the non-medicated patients ($\overline{X}$ medicated$=6.325$, $n=40$; $\overline{X}$ non-medicated$=3.010$, $n=100$). A significance test (ignoring that measures are repeated) suggested the difference was stable ($F=10.28$, $p<.01$). However, this finding *does not* indicate that drugs do not reduce discomfort. It may indicate that the most uncomfortable patients received medication, but the relief experienced was not sufficient to reduce their discomfort to the level of those not requiring medication. On the other hand, the medicated scores may be higher because medication was more frequent late in labor.

It is difficult to judge how the elimination of these observations affected the earlier analyses. It is possible that the increases for signs of distress late in labor were depressed since 23 observation on drugged patients were omitted in the second half of labor relative to seven in the first half. In addition, more primigravidae (21) received drugs than multigravidae (9), which would decrease the difference between these groups. The same is true for anxiety level; 19 observations on Hi-anxiety patients were omitted compared with 11 on Lo-anxiety cases. In each case, therefore, more observations were removed from the group where high scores were predicted. The pattern of loss due to drugs could, in fact, be treated as another dependent measure of stress, if we could assume that medications are given on a request basis.

Still, the loss of observations due to drugs makes it difficult to determine the form of the relationship between distress reactions and interval of labor. It is conceivable that if these patients had not received drugs their scores would have been very much higher giving even stronger findings. Of course, if primigravidae received drugs earlier in labor than did multigravidae (and there was a slight tendency in this direction), it could be that we would fail to locate the rapid increments in distress for this group. At this point it seems reasonable to suggest that conclusions concerning drug effects should wait until observations are made upon very much larger samples of expectant mothers.[5]

Reliability of the Measures of Facial Expression

Because there was only one observer during the data collection, it is important to demonstrate the reliability of the measurements. During a three-day period a second person memorized and was trained in the use of the scoring system. Ten observations were made by both raters on seven patients. The observers synchronized their observations with stop watches. Table 4 contains the number of items scored and the percent of agreement. Any disagreement, including those due to errors in synchronizing watches, etc., was counted. As can be seen from the table, agree-

Table 4 Reliability of facial expression measures

Section of face	Number		
	Scored	Agree	Percent agree
Forehead	232	215	92%
Brow	248	210	85%
Eyelids	239	163	68%
Eyes	257	188	73%
Eyeballs	294	201	68%
Mouth	312	210	67%

ment is quite high, and especially so for the categories that were significantly affected by the independent variables.

DISCUSSION

With the exception of the mouth, nose and some aspects of the eye category, the data confirm the hypotheses; i.e., there are regular changes in facial indicators with increases in stress stimulation. The signs of comfort show relatively steady decreases over time and the signs of distress

[5] Index scores for drug observations were highly variable, e.g. some distress scores being extremely low and some comfort scores extremely high.

tend to show increases, particularly in the final two intervals of labor. These respective decrements and increments tend to be more pronounced for primigravidae than multigravidae (as seen in the significant interaction effects).

Early in labor when contractions are mild, the amount of stress stimulation is insufficient to produce differences. Greater distress in primigravidae in comparison to multigravidae appears only in the presence of relatively high levels of stress stimulation. Differences between the groups were not sufficiently large through the course of labor to produce an overall main effect by t or X^2 tests.

There are a number of ways in which the interaction of prior experience and duration could come about. For example, that primigravidae show more signs of distress could be due to the fact that they are less familiar with and thus less prepared for the labor experience (Janis, 1958). As labor becomes more painful, it is possible that primigravidae become less able to make responses which control or dissipate the distress. The distress may then amplify the pain signals (Tomkins, 1962). However, it seems equally likely that the differences in distress between these groups is due to "physical" differences in labor. Changes in the reproductive organs may produce more pain at equivalent stages in labor for the primigravidae. It is also true that the final stages of labor for multigravidae are highly accelerated relative to that for primigravidae, i.e., labor is "easier." Thus, primigravidae could experience more distress in the later stages of labor due to the cumulative effect of a longer period of stimulation. In addition, it is sometimes difficult to observe multigravidae as close to delivery and at as high a level of stress stimulation as primigravidae, since, being capable of extremely rapid deliveries, multigravidae are removed from the labor room as soon as they show signs of giving birth. To check on this possibility a comparison was made of mean dilatation scores in the final interval of labor. While the scores were slightly lower for multigravidae than for primigravidae, the difference is extremely small and clearly not significant. Thus, there are no reasons to suspect that this form of subject selection produced the interaction effects.

The progression of the means for the various indices also suggests that many of the signs of distress, particularly the heavy knitting and furrowing of the brow, are elicited only when distress exceeds a minimum level or threshold. However, that some of the comfort indices (e.g., forehead comfort) showed a gradual decline indicates that changes in some expressions vary continuously with increases in stress stimulation. This suggests that for some sections of the face muscular contractions will reflect gradual changes in the level of distress, while for other sections extensive muscular contractions will not appear until relatively high levels of distress are reached. A possible example of this is seen in the behavior of the brow distress indices. The minor brow signs (depression over one or both eyebrows and fluttering of the brows with occasional V formations) showed fairly regular increments with duration, while the major brow signs (medial approximation of brows with clear V formation, and

V formation with depression over one or both brows) show an abrupt increase in frequency in the final interval of labor.

It is possible, however, that the different rates of change exhibited by the above indices reflect limitations in the method of recording. For example, for the brow indices the major signs are more intense versions of the minor signs. To the extent that the minor signs are included in but not separately scored in the major index, it would follow that the minor distress means are necessarily deflated in the third and fourth intervals and that the major distress code shows step-wise or threshold effects because it excludes the minimal changes in expression which occur between comfort and high levels of distress. It is clear, therefore, that one serious problem in this type of research is the careful specification of the dependent variables and knowledge of their relationships to one another.

Despite the problems raised concerning these indices one may still ask why there is a steady increase in the frequency of occurrence of minor signs even *after* the appearance of a significant amount of intense brow activity. That both indices increase may be due to the fact that the principal stress stimulus in labor, the contraction, has a relatively clear onset and rather quickly reaches maximal intensity. Given a cyclical stress stimulus with increasingly intense peaks, it is possible that major brow reactions are recruited by the higher stimulus peaks which appear relatively late in labor while the increase in frequency of minor reactions is due to the raising of the "average" intensity of stress stimulation between the peaks. In stress situations which are not punctuated by abrupt stimuli, one might find minor brow signs increasing with equal or greater frequency than in labor, but *no* frequent appearance of major brow reactions.

The effects of dispositional anxiety appear relatively clear: the higher the anxiety score the greater the sensitivity to stress stimuli, and the more frequent the indicators of distress.[6] Of course, the dispositional measure was administered *after* delivery, but it seems doubtful that high scores on the anxiety test were *produced* by the mothers' experience in labor. The results are affected to an unknown degree by loss of cases due to failure to reply. However, it does not appear that the loss produced a spurious relationship as an examination of the means revealed that differences between Hi and Lo anxiety Ss were similar in both multigravidae and primigravidae despite the differences between them in return rate. Another point worth mentioning is that the differences between Hi and Lo anxious women may reflect differences in their *characteristic* expressions; i.e., the analyses, simple two group comparisons, do *not* show that the differences *depend* upon the presence of a stress stimulus (see Taylor, 1956). Because of the loss of cases, an anxiety by interval by prior-experience analysis failed to clarify this question.

[6] In a personal communication Silvan Tomkins has suggested that the relationship may reflect that some of the Welch items measure proneness to distress rather than dispositional anxiety.

Despite the various criticisms we have leveled at the findings, it should be recognized that the data provide a consistent set of relationships which suggest that each of the three types of antecedent variables, situational, experiential, and dispositional, makes a significant contribution to the intensity of the distress expressions. In addition, the facial indicators appear to function as reliable indicators of this state. Therefore, we can suggest that facial signs of distress are reasonably general and provide, perhaps, the critical cues in one's body for the "awareness" of distress emotion and the cues for the judgment of distress in others. This generalization needs to be qualified in that the effects that have been recorded (especially the brow distress measures) are most clear for the primigravidae. There is a question, therefore, as to whether only primigravidae will show reactions, such as the brow-distress signs, when subjected to intense stimulation. Brow-distress signs could be specific to primigravidae if most primigravidae who have had high brow-distress scores have refused to have other children and, therefore, were *not* in our sample of multigravidae. However, if past experience with labor served to reduce both the intensity of stress stimulation and the level of emotional distress, one would not conclude that the brow signs are specific to primigravidae. Instead, one would suggest that a given level of intensity of stress stimulation is necessary to elicit these signs, that past experience reduced the intensity of stimulation, and that equating the levels of stress stimulation for these groups would cause them to respond similarly. This discussion has been restricted to the brow signs since the forehead and eyelids, while producing similar trends, failed to show significant interactions with past experience.

While the major analyses support the hypothesis that distress signs are general, the correlational data point to a degree of specificity of reaction. Thus, a patient may show a high incidence of forehead distress to a variety of stimuli, e.g., when her foot is caught in a door, when her hand is burnt while cooking, or when feeling pain during labor, while another patient might show a preponderance of eyelid distress reactions to all of these situations. Specificity in motor reactions has been demonstrated by other investigators (Goldstein, 1964). However, there is probably no need to choose between the specificity and generality positions. While the data suggest a high degree of generality, with intense distress eliciting specifiable changes in the forehead, brow and eyelid, it is also possible that some individuals will favor one or another of these locations for distress displays. Of course, the picture of expressive behavior presented here is rather simple as we have *not* examined the reactions of other body regions. Distress can also be manifested in a variety of postural tensions and the above hypotheses do not preclude that an individual might select some area other than the face as his "preferred" area for distress expressions. Further studies on the problem of choice, and the equivalence of the reactions in different response systems are needed and are being undertaken.

Another question remains concerning the specificity of the expressive changes to the *emotion of distress.* If many other emotional or motivational states produce comparable changes, then it could be asserted that increases in level of activation (Duffy, 1962) rather than distress *per se* is responsible for the expression changes. If this were so, the data would not add to the plausibility of the assumption that a particular set of facial changes are associated with particular emotions and serve as cues for emotional perception—Asch (1952), Darwin (1872), James (1961), Plutchik (1962), Tomkins (1962). To bolster this position it is necessary to conduct studies of expressive changes in a variety of emotion provoking situations. There are a number of prior studies that have attempted to identify representative changes in facial expressions with specific stimulus situations (see Woodworth & Schlosberg's 1954 review). In some of these studies, Landis (1924), Coleman (1949), there are reports indicating that highly "inappropriate" expressions, e.g., smiles, were produced to noxious stimuli. But these cases need not be accepted as evidence against the hypothesis that emotions are differentiated in facial behavior. Most of these studies were conducted in laboratory situations where the experimenter produced the stimulus (sounds, snakes, etc.,) to arouse emotion. In fact, Landis (1924) used colleagues as subjects. Thus, if emotional experience is mediated by facial expression, the "inappropriate" expression becomes a highly appropriate and deliberate technique for hiding and moderating feelings during an unpleasant "experience." Attempts to control and distort one's emotional reactions are not surprising when one is being "tested" by a fellow psychologist.

On the other hand, many studies supporting the hypothesis of regular facial changes in emotion, such as those on judging emotions from facial expressions, used posed expressions, e.g., Engen, Levy, & Schlosberg (1957), Feleky (1914), Frois-Whittman (1930), Ruckmick (1921), or drawings (Boring & Titchener, 1923). In these cases, the regularity of appearance of specific facial signs with specific emotions, and the accuracy of the judgments of expression, could be attributed to deliberate efforts to respond according to cultural stereotypes shared by both the actor and the judge.

The present study derives considerable strength, therefore, from being conducted in a natural setting where people were not asked to enact emotions and where the observer was unlikely to produce "demands" to counter the naive expression of feelings.[7] Since the recording of natural expressions of emotion provides no assurance that the expressions are specific to distress, a comparison of the present data with studies using posed expressions seemed of value. Our approach was to score the Lightfoot series of facial expressions (Engen, Levy, & Schlosberg, 1957, 1958) for the forehead and brow indicators of distress. The judge who participated in the reliability check rated the entire series of photographs, observing each picture as long as she wished. The forehead and brow

[7] Munn (1940) attempted to obtain unposed expressions from magazine photos. The degree to which he succeeded in doing so, and the representativeness of his sample of pictures, are both open to question.

signs of discomfort appeared in eleven of the forty-eight photographs rated. Eight of these eleven photographs had ratings in excess of seven on the sleep-tension (1 to 9) scale and only six other pictures in the entire series scored this high (Engen, Levy, & Schlosberg, 1958). On the circular scale of emotions four fell in the "fear and suffering" category, two in "disgust," three in "suprise," one in "love, mirth, and happiness," and one in "anger and determination."

While it is clear that the bulk of the photographs fell in the most appropriate categories, there is some scattering. It could well be that the scatter is due to the problems in the acting out of emotion. For example, Coleman (1949) found that the *mouth* region was much more likely to differentiate emotions in his stimulus persons' acted emotions than in their natural expressions of feeling, and Dunlap (1927) before him showed the lower half of the face to dominate when grouped with conflicting upper segments. If distress was aroused in the effort to act the emotions of joy or mirth (or if distress actually occurs with intense joy) and if the judging group's ratings depend primarily on lower face cues, we would expect to find distress signs in photographs placed in the joy category. We might also compare Coleman's (1949) result, that the mouth is a superior source of cues for posed expression, with the present data showing that the mouth did not discriminate changes in distress. It is conceivable that the lower part of the face is less useful as a cue to emotions in natural settings because the mouth is the servant of instrumental actions such as speaking and eating. These actions will make their own demands upon the mouth apparatus and, thereby, will obscure expressive reactions.

Regardless of the problems involved in comparing posed with unposed expressions, it is significant that both Coleman (1949) and Hanawalt (1944) have found that discriminations of *negative* emotions made solely from the upper half of the face are frequently as accurate as those made from full face expressions. On the other hand, the lower half of the face provides more reliable cues for discriminating positive emotions. This was the case with both acted and "unposed" expressions, the unposed expressions being photos from magazines (Hanawalt) and reactions to unexpected stimuli (Coleman). Hanawalt also reports some tendency to confuse unpleasant emotions with mirth and happiness due to a tendency to close the eyes in both cases. The findings are very similar to the present data where significant indicators of stress were detected solely from the upper half of the face.

Although the above evidence cannot substitute for the recording of emotional expressions in a representative sample of stimulus situations (Brunswick, 1947), the added findings with the Lightfoot series and the comparison of the present data with past findings suggest the fruitfulness of additional studies of the pattern of facial changes for different emotions. One might hope that the location of such distinctive physiognomic signs would lead to further investigations to establish a "psychophysics" of the perception of emotion and eventually lead to more rigorous investigations of the consequences of emotional reactions and perceptions for social behavior.

REFERENCES

Allport, G. W., & Vernon, P. E. *Studies in expressive movement*. New York: Macmillan, 1933.

Asch, S. E. *Social Psychology*. New York: Prentice Hall, 1952.

Beckman, H. *Drugs: Their nature, action, and use*. Philadelphia: Saunders, 1958.

Birdwhistell, R. L. *Introduction to kinesics: An annotation system for analysis of body motion and gesture*. Department of State, Foreign Service Institute, Washington, D.C., 1952.

Boring, E. G., & Titchener, E. B. A model for the demonstration of facial expression, *Amer. J. Psychol.*, 1923, *34*, 471-486.

Brunswick, E. *Systematic and representative design of psychological experiments*. Berkely, Calif.: Univer. of California Press, 1947.

Bull, N. *The body and its mind: an introduction to attitude psychology*. New York: Las Americas, 1962.

Coleman, J. C. Facial expressions of emotions. *Psychol. Monogr. 296*, 1949.

Darwin, C. *The expression of the emotions in man and animals*. London: Murray, 1872.

Duffy, E. *Activation and behavior*. New York: Wiley, 1962.

Dunlap, K. Role of eye-muscles and mouth-muscles in the expression of the emotions. *Genet. Psychol. Monogr.* 1927, *2*, 197-233.

Engen, T., Levy, N., & Schlosberg, H. A new series of facial expressions. *Amer. Psychologist*, 1957, *12*, 264-266.

Engen, T., Levy, N., & Schlosberg, H. The dimensional analysis of a new series of facial expressions. *J. exp. Psychol.*, 1958, *55*, 454.

Feleky, A. M. The expressions of emotions. *Psychol. Rev.*, 1914, *21*, 33-41.

Friedman, E. A. Graphic analysis of labor. *Bull. Amer. College Nurse-Midwifery*, 1959, *4*, No. 3 & 4, 94.

Frois-Whittman, J. The judgment of facial expression. *J. exp. Psychol.*, 1930, *13*, No. 2, 113-151.

Gibson, J. J. *The perception of the visual world*. Boston: Houghton Mifflin, 1950.

Goldstein, Iris B., Grinker, R., Heath, Helen A., Oken, D., & Shipman, W. G. Study in psychophysiology of muscle tension. *Arch. gen. Psychiat.*, 1964, *11*, 322-330.

Hanawalt, N. G. The role of the upper and the lower parts of the face as the basis for judging facial expressions. II. In posed expressions and "candid camera" pictures. *J. gen. Psychol.*, 1944, *31*, 23-36.

Hardy, J. D., & Javert, C. T. Studies in pain: measurement of pain intensity in childbirth. *J. clin. Invest.*, 1949, *28*, p. 158.

Hebb, D. O., & Thompson, W. R. The social significance of animal studies. In G. Lindzey (Ed.), *Handbook of social psychology*. Cambridge, Mass: Addison-Wesley, 1954.

James, W. *Psychology: the briefer course*. New York: Harper, 1961 (first published, 1892).

Janis, I. L. *Psychological stress*. New York: Wiley, 1958.

Jones, E. E., & Thibaut, J. W. Interaction goals as bases of inference in interpersonal perception. In Tagiuri and Petrullo (Eds.), *Person perception and interpersonal behavior*. Stanford: Stanford Univer. Press, 1958.

Köhler, W. *Gestalt psychology*. New York: Liveright, 1947.

Landis, C. Studies of emotional reactions. II. General behavior and facial expression. *J. comp. Psychol.*, 1924, *4*, 447-509.

Munn, N. L. The effect of the knowledge of the situation upon judgment of emotion from facial expressions. *J. abnorm. soc. Psychol.*, 1940, *35*, 324-328.

Musser, R. D., & Bird, J. G. *Modern pharmacology and therapeutics*. New York: Macmillan, 1959.

Plutchik, R. *The emotions: facts, theories, and a new model*. Clinton, Mass: Colonial Press, 1962.

Ruckmick, C. A. A preliminary study of the emotions. *Psychol. Monogr.*, *136*, 1921.

Schachter, S. The interaction of cognitive and physiological determinants of emotional state. In Berkowitz, L. (Ed.), *Advances in experimental social psychology*. Vol. I. New York: Acad. Press, 1964.

Schachter, S., & Singer, J. E. Cognitive, social and physiological determinants of emotional state. *Psychol. Rev.*, 1962, *69*, 379-399.

Taylor, Janet A. Drive theory and manifest anxiety. *Psychol. Bull.*, 1956, *53*, 303-320.

Tomkins, S. S. *Affect, imagery, consciousness*. Vol. I. *The positive affects*. New York: Springer, 1962.

Walker, Helen, & Lev, J. *Statistical inference*. New York: Holt, Rinehart and Winston, 1953.

Welch, G. S. An anxiety index and an internalization ratio for the MMPI. *J. consult. Psychol.*, 1952, *16*, 65-72.

Woodworth, R., & Schlosberg, H. *Experimental psychology*. New York: Holt, 1954.

XI

Affective relations and mutual glances in dyads

Ralph V. Exline
with Lewis C. Winters

The thesis that the activity of another's eyes has important affective connotations has interested literary men from antiquity to the present. Elworthy (1895) has documented the opinion that belief in the evil eye is one of the most ancient superstitions of the human race, adhered to in ancient Egypt and Babylonia, attested to in the literature of Greece and Rome; according to Tomkins (1963) it is still referred to in contemporary news dispatches.[1] Francis Bacon, in his essay "Of Envy," felt that the evil eye was caused by an excess of envy, but in addition he was willing to endow the eye with more friendly properties: "love and envy . . . both have vehement wishes, they frame themselves readily into imaginations and they come easily into the eye, especially on the presence of objects which are the points that conduce to fascination."

More recently the emphasis has been on the expressive qualities of a look. "Though we were eloquent as Demosthenes or Cicero . . . yet our skills would not equal the bewitching speech of the eyes" (Magnus, 1885). "Lips and eyes, glances and smiles are the major elements in the arsenal of expression" wrote the poet Ogden in 1961. The "speech of the eyes" is emotional speech. The intimate connection with feelings rather than impersonal ideas is suggested by Nielsen's (1962) translation of Schack's (1858) assertion that "The fine and subtle expressions and meanings of the eyes are difficult to catch in a phrase, they must be grasped with one's feelings, realized by way of imagination, seen and understood in nature."

What kinds of feelings are communicated by the use of the eyes? Bacon

[1] Tomkins reports that in 1956 an English quarterly printed the beliefs of elderly inhabitants of Somerset that the evil eye cause pigs to run wild. He also reported that an American A.P. dispatch of 1957 quoted a witness before a Congressional investigating committee as claiming that he had been hired to keep employees at work by coming ". . . in once or twice every week or so and glare at . . . employees."

The studies reported in this chapter were supported by a contract between the Group Psychology Branch of the Office of Naval Research and the University of Delaware, Contract Nonr–2285(02).

319

spoke of love and envy. We would add concern and unconcern. Love, envy, concern and unconcern describe qualities of relationships between people; one observes another's visual behavior and infers, we believe, the degree and affective sign of the other's involvement in a momentary inter-personal relationship. The involvement may range from one of great intensity to one of virtual indifference, and the sign, though perhaps not the magnitude of the affect associated with involvement, may be either positive or negative. Put differently, one learns from the behavior of the other's eyes something of the other's desire, willingness, or ability to relate emotionally to another.

ADIENCE AND AVOIDANCE

How do the eyes communicate the degree and affective quality of one's involvement with another? Obviously not, as the ancients believed, by ejaculating fascinating influences that penetrate the bodies of living creatures. The authors of this chapter believe that involvement and affect are communicated via movement or lack of movement of the eyes in the context of a given interaction situation.[2] Particularly relevant to our theme are adient and avoidant movements and the duration of fixation of the eye upon objects which can be assumed to arouse affective states within the viewer. Luborsky, Blinder, & Mackworth (1963) have shown that GSR responsivity is positively related to avoidant patterns of eye fixa-tions. Luborsky's Ss looked at "threatening" (sex and aggression) and "neutral" pictures. High GSR peaks were associated with shorter eye fixations, and Ss with the higher GSR peaks tended to look longer at the less threatening background of the pictures. Luborsky's data would thus suggest that visual avoidance is linked with the arousal of painful affect.

When the object viewed is a person who is engaged in face to face interactions with the viewer, the incidence of the exchange of mutual glances would seem to be a useful indicator of the willingness to enter into an intense interpersonal relationship. Simmel (1921) has argued that one establishes communication with another by means of the mutual glance. He believed that one's desire for union with another determined whether one sought the mutual as distinct from the oneway glance. Also relevant to the above proposition is Tomkins' argument that mutual awareness of affects occurs through mutual looking; ". . . because of the possibilities of such shared awareness there is no greater intimacy than the interocular experience." (Tomkins, 1963, p. 180).

Empirical support for these ideas is suggested by data collected by the authors in exploratory studies of factors that affect the manner in which

[2] This proposition is consistent with the view that emotion is an organizing concept referring to observable expressive manifestations over vocal, motor or autonomic nervous pathways which tend to be associated with processes of physiological arousal and states of experience felt as private (Knapp, 1963, p. 11). The observable mani-festations, Knapp argues, allow communication of physiological processes and ex-perience states to the environment.

persons look into the line of regard of another. In one study (Exline, 1963) groups of persons high in n affiliation and groups of persons low in n affiliation discussed a problem under conditions which emphasized or subdued competitive orientations toward one another. When competition was not salient those high in n affiliation engaged in significantly more mutual glances than did less affiliative subjects (and also more than did highly affiliative subjects engaged in competitive discussion). On the other hand, those groups composed of persons low in n affiliation showed a greater incidence of mutual glances under competitive conditions. The greatest incidence of mutual glances was recorded for affiliative persons in the non-competitive situation. If, as seems reasonable, we can assume that those high in n affiliation prefer a non-competitive rather than a competitive personal relationship (and vice versa), the incidence of mutual glances would seem to reflect the expected differences in willingness to relate to one another in terms of the affective modality of the situation.

A second study (Exline et al., 1965) also showed striking differences in willingness to engage in mutual glances by those who were independently judged to differ in their desire to establish warm interpersonal relations. In this case subjects were divided into two groups according to whether they indicated very strong or very weak affection and inclusion orientations toward others (Schutz, 1958). When these persons were then interviewed on personal matters by one instructed to look steadily at them during the interview, those indicating a strong affection-inclusion orientation returned the interviewer's glances significantly more often' than did those whose scale scores indicated a weak affection orientation. The striking differences in willingness to look into the line of regard of the other is indicated by the fact that the visually least active member of the affectionate group looked more steadily at the interviewer than did the most visually active member of the less affectionate group.

The results reported above suggest that personal values congruent with the kind of personal intimacy encouraged by a given interaction situation are associated with a greater incidence of shared glances. Affiliative or affectionate persons, who might be expected to seek involvement with others in contexts whose affective modality is positive or neutral, do indeed engage in more shared glances than do those who might be expected to resist becoming personally involved in such situations. Conversely, the affiliative person showed fewer mutual glances in a situation when the competitive task requirements would lead us to expect the affiliative person to be less highly motivated to become involved with others.

Thus far we have discussed mutual glances and affective involvement in terms of personal and situational factors which facilitate increased involvement. The relationship between interpersonal affect and mutual glances also can be considered in terms of factors which act to inhibit or decrease involvement. Tomkins' (1963) discussion of taboos on mutual looking suggests that the emotional involvement implicit in a mutual glance will, under certain circumstances, inhibit the desire to become involved and hence affect the incidence of such glances. "The visibility of the eyes makes them unique organs for the expression (and) communication of affects . . . to the extent to which intimacy . . . suffer(s) inhibition, there will inevitably appear taboos on interocular intimacy" (Tomkins, 1963, p. 183).

Tomkins believes that the taboo on interocular experience is a function of being taught to be ashamed of witnessing or expressing certain kinds of affect. If one is ashamed to be angry or to feel embarrassed, then he will be ashamed to look at another and be seen to be angry or embarrassed. To be ashamed of feeling is to hide the eyes lest the eyes meet and feeling stands revealed. Put another way, when involvement with another results in feelings of shame one may wish to hide or reduce the feeling by attenuating the involvement. Thus the averted gaze may serve both to hide the shame and reduce the feeling of shame by reducing the involvement.

Exline, Schuette and Gray (1965) reported data which are consistent with Tomkins' argument. One set of subjects was asked to answer personal questions designed to produce embarrassment, while a different set of subjects was asked innocuous questions about their recreational interests. The interviews were matched for length, and the amount of time the Ss returned the interviewer's gaze was compared. The results showed that Ss who were asked the less embarrassing questions looked significantly more at the interviewer when answering the questions. In casual conversation, on the other hand, the two groups of subjects did not differ in the exchange of mutual glances with the interviewer. Thus we interpreted the differences recorded during the interview as reflecting a desire to avoid an embarrassing (or shame-producing) involvement with the interviewer.

Data from the studies described would seem to provide support for the thesis that there is a predictable relationship between affective involvement and willingness to enter into mutual glances with another. Implicit in our argument to date is the assumption that if one person feels good or comfortable about relating to another he will engage in mutual glances to a greater degree than if he feels bad or uncomfortable about the relationship. Thus we assumed that a person who likes to affiliate will, when he finds himself in a situation where affiliation is possible, feel more comfortable in becoming involved with others than will: (a) a person who does not like to affiliate or (b) an affiliative person who finds himself in a situation where disagreement and other non-affiliative behaviors are likely to be required. Similarly, we assumed that any person would be more comfortable in interacting with another when the situation required the other person to ask innocuous as compared to embarrassing questions. In each of the cases described the persons assumed to feel more comfortable in the interpersonal relationship were more willing to look into the line of regard of the other.

PERSONAL ATTRACTION AND THE MUTUAL GLANCE

In neither of the previous studies described above, however, did we attempt to directly influence the sign of the affect which one person felt for another. We manipulated only the feeling about relating to another, not the feeling for the other. Since one could like another person but at the same time not like the way in which he is forced to relate to him, our data do not permit us to draw any conclusions about visual interaction and interpersonal affect per se. The remainder of this chapter will describe two studies in which the focus of interest was upon the effect which a subject's positive or negative feeling about another had upon his willingness to exchange mutual glances with the liked or disliked other.

Lambert and Lambert (1964) have used the phrase "looking into the line of regard" to describe what we have referred to as "the mutual glance." Their term more precisely describes the behavior of Ss in both studies reported in this chapter, and for the purpose of this chapter will be synonymous with the term "mutual glance."

EXPERIMENT 1: THE OBNOXIOUS INTERVIEWER AND THE MUTUAL GLANCE[3]

The general hypothesis tested in this study was that the amount of mutual glances between two persons would vary directly with the sign of the affect which characterized the relationship. The most direct test of the hypothesis would have been to locate pairs of friends and enemies and to observe the incidence of mutual glances during the time they were in one another's presence. We chose instead the more practical expedient of confronting a naive subject with an experimenter who behaved in ways designed to cause the subject to feel relatively positive or negative toward him. The expedient had two further advantages. First, it permitted us to establish three points (negative, neutral, positive) on the affect scale. Second, it gave us the opportunity to study the effect, over time, of changes of feeling upon changes in mutual glances. Thus in the laboratory we created a situation analogous to the acquaintance process in real life. Two strangers meet, interact, develop impressions of one another, and, hypothetically, act upon these impressions in ways which more or less subtly express the affective quality of their impressions. By observing and recording their mutual glances we are enabled to see if such a phenomenon provides us with one readily observable manifestation of an affective orientation toward another.

Procedure

Thirty-six male college students were recruited from freshman physical education classes required of all men. Subjects were randomly selected,

[3] The authors wish to thank David Messick and Stanley Tabasso for their assistance in the collection and analysis of data.

and excused from participation in class activities during the hour in which they participated in the study. Upon arriving at the laboratory, each S was taken to a small room equipped with a one-way vision screen and seated facing the screen. After S was comfortably seated, the experimenter (E) took a seat directly opposite S. E seated himself so that he would squarely face S at all times. The experimental procedures required E to interview S for five minutes, after which E introduced the affect induction and continued the interview for an additional five minutes. Following the second interview period, S filled out reaction forms in which he evaluated the interviewer and rated the interviewer's behavior toward and feeling about himself (S). After S completed the questionnaires E described the study, explained the purpose of the affect inductions, answered S's questions, and attempted to allay any anxiety aroused by the affect inductions. Throughout both interview periods an observer stationed behind the one-way vision screen recorded the frequency and duration of S's visual interaction with E. Figure 1 provides a schematic representation of the experimental setting.

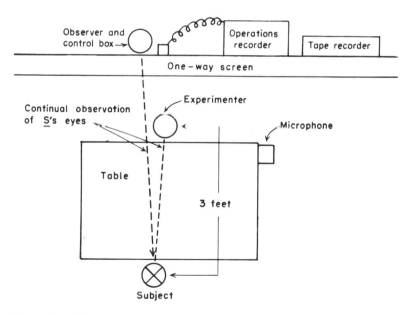

Figure 1.   Schematic representation of arrangements for the observation of mutual glances between subject and experimenter.

The procedures permitted us first to establish the operant level of Ss' willingness to engage in mutual glances, then study the effects of different affects upon Ss' "normal" behavior. By using each S as his own control, the procedure permits a more thorough investigation of the effect of positive and negative feelings on the pattern of one's visual behavior.

The specific procedures will now be more fully described.

Baseline Interview

Ss were told that the purpose of the study was to obtain information about the leisure time interests of university students. E mentioned that their remarks would be recorded on tape, then said: "O.K. Just to get started would you tell me how you usually spend your leisure time?" For the first five minutes of the interview the experimenter confined himself to listening to the subject describe his recreational interests. From time to time he would present the S with such social reinforcers as a nod, smile, a grunt of affirmation ("Uh huh") or interest ("Ummm"). The experimenter was instructed to say at least once during the interview: "That's very interesting, could you tell me more about that?" This comment was to be interjected when the experimenter sensed that the topic was one in which the student was particularly interested. (If S ran out of ideas before the end of the 5 minutes E would ask about other activities. If a second probe was required E would ask about a general area, e.g., reading, sports, social activities, not previously discussed).

The reinforcement schedule was analogous to a fixed interval schedule, a reinforcement being presented approximately every 30 seconds to the Ss in the high reinforcement condition, and every two minutes to the Ss in the low reinforcement condition. Thus in the first five minutes of the interview, Ss in the high condition received 10 reinforcements, the others only two.

(While the original interview procedures called for E to hold his expressive behavior to an absolute minimum, pre-tests showed that it was almost impossible for the interviewer to sit motionless, expressionless, and voiceless while the Ss spoke. Ss "dried up" very quickly and E had the strong impression that they were desperate to elicit some kind of a reaction from him. Since a minimum of socially reinforcing behavior seemed to be necessary to keep the interview flowing, we decided to capitalize on necessity and incorporate the variable of social reinforcement into the design. This was done in the spirit of exploration rather than prediction, for the affective properties of a given pattern of the emotionally toned expressive and non-verbal behaviors that comprise the usual operational definition of social reinforcement are not clear. The smiles and winks which please B may prove to be very irritating to C.)

As soon as the five minutes were up the experimenter signalled the ostensible close of the interview by asking the S if there was anything else he would like to mention. During this period the 30 second reinforcement schedule was continued for those in the high condition, while Ss given the low reinforcement schedule received no further reinforcements. During the interview E took no notes, but sat quietly gazing at S.

Induction of Affective Conditions

Preliminary induction (positive and negative affect). "Before you go I would like to mention the real purpose of this interview. I have been evaluating your responses to determine whether or not you impress a listener as being an intelligent and mature person. You know that people continually size you up by what you do and say, and we are interested to see how you measure up. Now I'll give you the results of my evaluation before you go, but first I will need some additional information." E then looked in a folder lying on the table saying: "There should be a form here . . . Nope—excuse me while I get one." E then left the room, returning in about 30 seconds with forms in his hand.

Positive affect. Upon returning to the laboratory E commented: "The forms were in a different folder, but I just remembered that we did not talk about an area which is of interest to many people in terms of leisure time. That is travel—Incidentally before we begin again I want you to know that you are doing very well. I have given you a very good, actually an excellent rating as to intelligence and maturity. O.K., now let's talk a little about your travel interests."

Negative affect. "The forms were in a different folder. I just remembered that we did not talk about an area which is of interest to many people in terms of leisure time. That is travel—Unh . . . before we go on, however, I think it only fair to tell you that I have given you a poor rating as to intelligence and maturity. In comparison to others I have interviewed and rated, your rating is surprisingly low. It's hard to imagine a person with your background and education making such an impression. Is this how you usually impress a listener?"[4] At this point E permitted S to respond to his question. If S agreed with the evaluation and began to cite instances of difficulties he had had in previous interpersonal relationships, E was instructed to agree with S's denigration of self, adding that he could well believe that S would have had difficulty. After making such a comment E then stated that they should talk about S's travel interests.

If S disagreed with E's evaluation, E was instructed to respond that many people deceive themselves about their faults and that he could see that S was one of those. If S persisted in his disagreement E was instructed to say that he (E) had had a lot of experience in evaluating people through interviews and that if S did not agree they would just have to recognize that their opinions differed. E was instructed to then say that it wouldn't do any good to talk about it and that they had better finish the interview.

Control condition (neutral affect). In this condition E did not refer to the evaluative purpose of the interview. Instead he used only those parts of the preliminary and affect inductions that were necessary to rationalize the continuation of the interview, keeping it standard with the affect interviews in all respects other than the induction of affect. E spoke as follows: "Before you go we need some additional information. There should be a form here." E then looked in a folder lying on the table say-

---

[4] Not one S overtly disputed E's competence to judge another on the basis of such a limited contact. Indeed, almost all Ss volunteered examples of situations in which they had demonstrated a lack of poise.

ing (as in the preliminary affect induction conditions): "There should be a form here . . . Nope . . . excuse me while I get one." E then left the room and returned in 30 seconds with the missing forms. E said: "The forms were in a different folder, but I just remembered that we did not talk about an area which is of interest to many people in terms of leisure time. That is travel. O.K., now let's talk about your travel interests."

Affect control interview. This interview was carried on for another five minutes during which time E repeated the social reinforcement schedule which he had used in the first interview period. If S ran short of ideas E suggested that S describe his travel experiences, indicate his views on the value of travel, his aspirations to travel and/or the area in which he would prefer to travel. Once again E signalled the end of the interview by asking S if there was anything else he would like to mention.

Rating scales. Upon completion of the second five-minute interview Ss were given a modification of Osgood's (1957) semantic differential to obtain their evaluation of the interviewer and of his perceived potency. Ss also marked a 20-item Likert-type scale to indicate their perception of how favorably the interviewer behaved toward and felt about them.

Bates and Cloyd (1956) have pointed out that friendliness is a strong norm of behavior among college students. The semantic differential technique was used on the assumption that it would more freely permit expression of relatively negative evaluations of the interviewer. Ss' perceptions of E were measured by means of the four adjective pairs which Osgood (1957) has found to contain the highest loadings for each of the factors of evaluation, potency and activity. The resulting twelve pairs of adjectives were arranged in a random order for presentation to the Ss.

Ten of the 20 items on the Likert-type scale were concerned with Ss' perception of how the interviewer behaved toward them while the remaining 10 items dealt with Ss' perception of E's feeling about them. In order to counteract the effects of possible response sets, half of each set of 10 items stated that the interviewer behaved or felt favorable toward S, the other half stated that E reacted negatively toward S. The critical words in each subset were roughly synonymous with one another and with the terms in the like-signed behavior or feeling sub-set. Ss were asked to state the degree of their disagreement or agreement with statements that the interviewer behaved in an encouraging, accepting, friendly, etc., way, and also that he felt sympathetic, kindly, pleasantly, etc., toward them. Similarly they were asked to state their agreement or disagreement with statements that E behaved severely, harshly, etc., and felt unfriendly, hostile, or negative toward them.

All Likert-type ratings were then converted to a unidimensional six point scale on which the high scores represented favorable behavior or feelings.

Measurement of mutual glances. E was instructed to gaze steadily at S's eyes throughout the interview. Thus, whether or not a mutual glance occurred depended on whether or not S looked back into E's eyes. S's visual behavior was recorded on an Esterline-Angus operations recorder by an observer who, screened by a one-way vision mirror, sat facing S, behind and slightly off to one side of the interviewer. Each time S looked into the line of E's regard the observer depressed a switch activating one of a set of pens. The pen traced a new course until S broke off eye contact and the observer released the switch. The procedure resulted in a continuous record of the duration of each glance as well as the frequency of mutual glances. We have used this procedure in several studies and find that even under less than perfect illumination the recordings of an experienced observer, seated behind an interviewer as described above, average better than 90% agreement with the recordings of S's glances made by the person being looked at. In view of such findings it was decided to use only one observer, thus releasing E from the distracting necessity of recording S's glances.

An index of mutual glances was obtained by dividing the total number of seconds of mutual glances by the total number of seconds which comprised the interview. Such an index does not accurately describe the pattern of mutual glances (i.e., whether S looks long and steadily or briefly but frequently into E's line of regard) but it does reflect the relative amount of time that a person spends in such behavior. The latter measure was judged to be appropriate for the purposes of this study.

Results

Effectiveness of the affect inductions. All dependent variable data,

Table 1 Summary of mean semantic differential scores categorized by affective
induction and level of social reinforcement

		Semantic differential scale					
Experimental categories	N	Evaluation		Potency		Activity	
		$\bar{x}$	σ	$\bar{x}$	σ	$\bar{x}$	σ
Affective induction							
Positive	12	21.16*	2.79	12.25	3.03	19.17	2.97
Neutral (control)	12	19.00	3.54	13.83	2.70	16.30	2.53
Negative	12	17.50	3.01	13.67	3.03	15.75	2.65
Social reinforcement							
High	18	19.78	3.66	12.22	3.34	17.78	3.34
Low	18	18.67	3.18	14.28	2.22	16.39	2.61
Affect x soc. reinforcement							
Positive-high SR	6	20.83	3.34	10.50	2.99	20.00	3.61
Positive-low SR	6	21.50	2.06	14.00	2.08	18.33	1.80
Neutral-high SR	6	19.67	4.42	14.00	2.87	18.00	2.00
Neutral-low SR	6	18.33	2.13	13.67	2.49	14.67	1.80
Negative-high SR	6	18.33	2.73	12.16	3.34	15.33	2.56
Negative-low SR	6	16.17	2.67	15.17	1.95	16.17	2.67

*Underlined means represent significant effects in the analysis of variance

whether mutual glances or questionnaire data, were analyzed in a 3 x 2 factorial design with six replications per cell. Turning first to data which are relevant to the question of whether or not the inductions had the planned effect, we see from the semantic differential data listed in Table 1 that the S's favorable evaluation of E varied directly with the positiveness of E's treatment of S. Non-treated Ss fell, as would be expected, in between the Ss in the opposed affect conditions. Table 2 shows that the effect attributable to the affect induction is significant at the .05 level.

Tables 1 and 2 also show that positively treated Ss rate E significantly higher on the activity factor, and, while E's potency (strength or threat value) does not differ significantly according to affective treatment, examination of the sub-cell means in Table 1 shows that E was rated as most potent by Ss given few social reinforcements and treated very negatively. Conversely, E was rated as least potent (threatening) by those Ss in the positive affect condition who were given many social reinforcements. (This finding was the only significant difference noted for the variable of social reinforcement as used in this study.)

Table 2 Analysis of variance of semantic differential scores of Ss given three types of affective induction under two levels of social reinforcement

Experimental variable		Semantic differential scale					
		Evaluation		Potency		Activity	
	df	MS	F	MS	F	MS	F
Affect	2	40.78	3.77*	9.09	1.06	40.09	5.38*
Social reinforcement	1	11.11	1.03	38.03	4.45*	17.36	2.33
Affect x social reinforcement	2	8.44	.78	13.03	1.52	13.20	1.77
Error	30	10.82		8.55		7.45	

*p < .05

The evaluation factor of the semantic differential has the meaning of goodness or badness. Since the behavior of E with respect to S was standardized on all dimensions but that of the affective feedback, it seems reasonable to argue that S's feeling that E is good or bad reflects an affective orientation toward E brought about by the experimental conditions. Thus we conclude that the induction was successful in creating the desired affective orientations.

Data concerning S's perception of the favorableness of E's feelings and behavior toward S (see Tables 3 and 4) provides additional support for the conclusion that the affect conditions had the desired effect on S. It is clear that Ss given the negative induction perceived E as both feeling and behaving less favorably toward S than did the positively treated Ss. The analysis of variance reported in Table 4 shows that differences in perceived favorableness of E's feeling were significant at the .01 level,

Table 3 Summary of mean perception of favorableness of interviewer's behavior and feeling by Ss, categorized as to affective inductions and social reinforcement

Experimental categories		Perception of Interviewer			
		Feeling		Behavior	
	N	$\bar{x}$	σ	$\bar{x}$	σ
Affective induction					
Positive	12	49.25	4.97	52.58	4.76
Neutral (control)	12	50.67	3.82	51.92	4.70
Negative	12	42.17	6.34	47.25	5.83
Social reinforcement					
High	18	48.06	6.00	51.83	4.78
Low	18	46.67	6.67	49.33	6.25
Affect x soc. reinforcement					
Positive high SR	6	49.67	4.96	52.33	4.78
Positive low SR	6	48.83	4.95	52.83	4.88
Neutral high SR	6	51.33	4.35	53.00	5.42
Neutral low SR	6	50.00	3.06	50.83	3.53
Negative high SR	6	43.17	5.21	50.17	3.44
Negative low SR	6	41.17	7.31	44.33	6.42

while perceptions of E's behavior reached significance at the .05 level. In both cases however the effect seemed to be due mainly to the negative treatment. Control Ss (no affect induction) rated E no less favorably than did those given the positive treatment. This point will be taken up again when we discuss the use of the line of regard.

Table 4 Summary of variance analysis of perception of interviewer by Ss given three types of affective inductions and two levels of social reinforcement

Experimental variable		Perception of interviewer			
		Feeling		Behavior	
	df	MS	F	MS	F
Affect	2	248.87	7.88**	101.34	3.58*
Social reinforcement	1	17.37	5.50	56.25	1.99
Affect x social reinforcement	2	1.02	.32	30.33	1.07
Error	30	31.57		28.31	

*p < .05
**p < .01

Mutual glances. The data support the operational hypothesis designed to test the general hypothesis concerning the relationship between affective relations and mutual glances. Mean percentages of mutual glance activity are plotted over the two interview periods in Figure 2 and listed in greater detail in Table 5. The data show that Ss who were given a

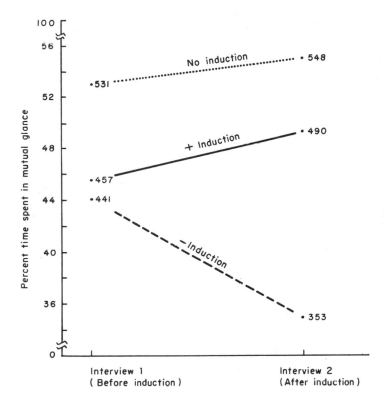

Figure 2. Percent time spent in mutual glances by experimental and control Ss in two interview periods (before and after affect induction).

negative evaluation of their performance by *E* reduced the amount to which they shared mutual glances with *E* by some 8.8% after receiving

Table 5 Mean per cent of change in mutual glances recorded after Ss, under two levels of social reinforcement received positive, negative or no affect induction (+ = increase, - = decrease)

| | Affect induction | | | | | | | |
| | Positive | | None | | Negative | | | |
Social reinforcement	x̄	N	x̄	N	x̄	N	Mean	N
High	+ .75	6	+2.17	6	- 7.00	6	-1.36	18
Low	+5.90	6	+1.33	6	-10.57	6	-1.11	18
Means for affect	+3.32	12	+1.75	12	- 8.78	12		

the negative induction. Ss given the positive induction slightly increased their mutual glances (3.3%), while those given no induction remained about the same. Results of the analysis of variance (Table 6) show the effect for the affect induction to be significant beyond the .01 level.

If we attempt to control for errors in observation and recording of the mutual glance by postulating that a change of up to 2½% in either direction is actually equivalent to no change in mutual glances from interview period 1 to period 2, changes in mutual glances can be located in a 3 x 3 matrix of change by affective induction.

Table 6 Analysis of variance of mean percent change † in mutual glances recorded after Ss under two levels of social reinforcement received affective inductions

Experimental variables	df	MS	F
Affect	2	52.01	11.36**
Social reinforcement	1	.06	.01
Affect x social reinforcement	2	8.71	1.90
Error	30	4.58	

† Actual change corrected for total possible change prior to analysis

**p < .01

The distribution of changes in mutual glance by direction and experimental conditions are graphed in Figure 3. Examination of this graph provides additional support for our operational hypothesis. We see that, even correcting for error, all 12 Ss given the negative induction looked proportionally less at E during the second interview period. Only 3 per-

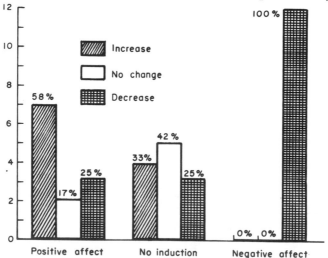

Figure 3.   Frequency of Ss in each affective condition showing increase, decrease or no change in mutual glances over two interview periods.

sons in each of the other conditions were recorded as decreasing in mutual glances and increases were recorded for 58% of those given the positive but for only 33% of those given no induction. Finally we see that no change was recorded for 42% of those given no affective treatment whereas only 8% of those given one or the other of the affective inductions did not change.

The data provide strong evidence that the affective treatments did indeed affect Ss' willingness to engage in mutual glances with their interviewer. Whether or not confirmation of the operational hypothesis proves the validity of the more general proposition depends, of course, upon how successfully the experimental procedures created the desired affects without introducing confounding variables.

Evidence was presented earlier to support the conclusion that the experimental inductions achieved the desired effects on S's feelings toward E. The question of confounding variables will be taken up in the discussion to follow. There remains, however, one more group of data relevant to the proposition that the willingness to exchange mutual glances with another is positively related to the liking one feels for the other. In spite of the fact that control Ss were given no affective induction it is understandable that they differed among themselves somewhat in the extent to which they responded favorably to E. If the general proposition is sound we would expect those control Ss who developed a favorable impression of E to maintain or increase their mutual glances with him more than would the control Ss who, for whatever reason, liked him less. On the assumption that the semantic differential evaluation factor ratings reflected Ss' relative liking or disliking for E, the mutual glances of the six Ss who evaluated E most highly were compared to the mutual glances of the remaining six. The mean difference in semantic differential evaluation between the group was 4.3 units. Those Ss who gave E the higher evaluation were found to look at him 4.07 percent more in period 2 than in period 1, whereas the remaining Ss looked at him .56 percent less. Thus even in the condition where no attempt was made to control Ss' feeling about E, those who liked him better looked at him more.

DISCUSSION

At first glance the results of this study would seem to argue against the validity of speaking of a "taboo" on mutual glances. How strong is the taboo when mutual glances were recorded during 35 to 55% of the time spent in the interviews? It is possible that the experimental procedures used may have inflated the amount of mutual glances which normally characterize visual interaction among persons. E was instructed to gaze steadily at S at all times, and a "mutual" glance was recorded whenever S returned E's gaze, whereas mutuality implies a shared activity freely entered into by both parties. E was certainly not free to avoid S, and S, upon becoming aware of E's steady surveillance, may very well have reciprocated by looking more at E than he usually would look at another.

Data from previous studies of visual interaction support the above interpretation. Where Ss were permitted to look at one another of their own volition they looked at one another only 30% of the time, and only 5% of the time was spent in mutual glances (Exline, 1963). These figures contrast with the average looking of 47% recorded in both this study and another study in which a similarly instructed interviewer was used (Exline et al., 1965). Furthermore, the fact of structuring the experimental situation as an interview rather than as a discussion may invoke different norms concerning the appropriateness of the mutual glance.

Tabooed or not, the Ss in this study showed an insignificant tendency to increase the amount to which they looked into the line of regard of another who praised them, but significantly decreased the amount to which they shared glances with a severe critic. Before asserting that these results support the proposition that one's liking for another is reflected in willingness to exchange mutual glances with him, certain limitations on the use of the data must be considered.

No women participated in this study, either as subjects or as an experimenter. Several previous studies, Exline (1961), Exline (1963), Exline et al. (1965), have shown that women exchange significantly more mutual glances than do men, but we do not know what this signifies for the relationship between their emotions and their willingness to share a mutual glance. The fact that women's mutual glances were found to be more drastically affected by competitive situations (Exline, 1963) suggests that their aversions and preferences would more markedly affect their visual orientation toward another. The point, however, requires further study.

Neither do we know how cross-sex pairings would affect the relationships between positive and negative affect and the mutual glance. Heterosexual role behaviors learned in the course of growing up in the United States might very well require that in a context of positive affect both sexes engage in cross-sex looking behavior quite different from that used when interacting with a member of their own sex. If, as Tomkins (1963) suggests, a taboo on mutual glances is a function of one's shame at becoming involved in a close personal relationship which has overtones of sexual intimacy, then the feeling of shame might be more pronounced for men with men and women with men than for a man with a woman or a woman with a woman. Thus, for example, men might seek the glance of women more aggressively (or pleadingly) than they would other males, whereas women may feel more obliged to avoid interocular contact with a male than with a female.

Since the Ss in this study were all males, the above speculations may account for the fact that those given the negative affect induction decreased their mutual glances more than those given the positive affect induction increased theirs. Also of interest is the finding that those Ss who received the positive induction without much accompanying social reinforcement from the experimenter tended to increase their mutual glances more than did those Ss who received the positive induction and much social reinforcement (see Table 5). The affective induction plus the nods and smiles of the socially reinforcing E may have created an affective overload for the male S. Again, more research is required to explore the validity of the argument.

Although we have assumed that the negative affect induction negatively influenced Ss' liking for E, it could be argued that the induction also served to shame S. E not only attacked S as being immature and inadequate but also maneuvered S into participating in the derogation of himself. The double-pronged attack may have caused S both to dislike E and feel some contempt for himself. If such were the case the resulting reduction of visual interaction may have been due to Ss' feelings of shame of self as well as feeling of dislike directed toward E. The data do not indicate whether S looked away to hide his shame, express his hostility, or both. The study next to be reported was designed to further investigate the questions raised concerning the effects of sex and possible shame upon the interrelations of affective states and the line of regard.

EXPERIMENT 2: INTERPERSONAL PREFERENCE
AND THE MUTUAL GLANCE

In this study the affects were not manipulated experimentally but were inferred from the Ss' statements of preference for one person over another. Tagiuri (1958) reports that the preferences stated by group members are more than verbal responses. Group members do better than chance in knowing who prefers whom and of the number of choices received by others in the group. This implies that "Choices have observable manifestations . . . and guessing another member's choices on the basis of these manifestations is not an act of guessing at all but is a true discrimination" (Tagiuri, 1958, p. 320). We argue that one of the readily observable manifestations of preference is that of the shared glance, and that uncoerced visual attention to another signals a desire to interact with him.

In this second study S chose one person over another after a period in which he had interacted with both persons together. To insure that the preference would be based on affective considerations, Ss were asked to choose the person whom they liked best. The procedure stressed positive affect and insured that the affect was real and not hypothetical. As will be made clear later, the pre-choice behavior of both of the potential objects of choice was designed to preclude the possibility that S would feel ashamed of himself, thus eliminating the effect of a potentially confounding variable. The dependent variable was Ss' willingness to look into the line of regard of the others both before and after the statement of preference. The validity of the proposition that, given an affective context, looking into the line of regard of the other reflects feelings of affection toward him, will be inferred from support of the following hypotheses:

Hypothesis 1. Differential affection will be directly paralleled by differential looking behavior. In operational terms, Ss will, in post- as compared with pre-choice periods, look more into the line of regard of a preferred than of a non-preferred other.

It is possible that as Ss adapt to a novel situation they reduce the amount of visual attention given to another person. Should this occur it would tend to operate against the effect of the experimental induction (preference choice) on Ss' visual behavior. Thus a control group was necessary to assess the possible impact of such an effect on the extent to which one looked into the line of regard. Although members of the control group were not asked to state a preference for one of the two others until after the experimental task was completed, it is very likely that they could come to prefer one of the confederates over the other. If the basic hypothesis concerning the relationship between positive affect and mutual glances is valid, the spontaneously developed preferences should be reflected to some degree in the visual interaction between control Ss and evaluators. Since, however, the budding preferences were not made salient or reinforced by the experimental procedures, it is likely that they developed more slowly and hence would not be expected to affect the visual behavior of control group Ss to the degree that the overt choice should, hypothetically, affect the experimental Ss' mutual glances. We therefore suggest the following corollary to Hypothesis 1:

Hypothesis 1a. Looking into the line of regard of the preferred as compared to the non-preferred other will be accentuated for Ss asked to openly choose one of the confederates, i.c., for the experimental as compared to the control Ss.

The first study described in this chapter did not permit a comparison of the two sexes. In discussing possible sex differences we suggested that socialization practices with respect to the communication and reception of positive affect might inhibit men more than women in the exchange of mutual glances with a member of their own sex. The design of the second study was to provide us with data which can be used to test the hypothesis that the male response is weaker. If positive feelings about another do affect mutual glances as predicted in Hypothesis 1, the influence of learned sex role behaviors should be reflected in a stronger effect for women than for men. Stated more concretely, the second hypothesis is:

Hypothesis 2. Females more than males will, in post- as compared with pre-choice periods, look more into the line of regard of a preferred than of a non-preferred other.

As in the case of Hypothesis 1 the validity of the corollary hypothesis (2a) concerning the visual behavior of control and experimental group members will be explored.

Procedure

Fourteen men and fourteen female students randomly drawn from the freshman class of the University of Delaware were used as subjects in this experiment. (Data of five additional Ss could not be used because three of them were acquainted with one or both of the evaluators while two Ss assigned to the experimental treatment refused to state a preference.) Ss were randomly assigned to a control or experimental group and upon arriving at the laboratory worked with two experimental confederates of their own sex.

Ss were told that they were to participate in a study of creative imagination in which their performance on a verbal story task would be evaluated both objectively and subjectively by two evaluators trained in psychological testing and experienced in administering the test used in this study. They were told that the purpose of the study was to compare Delaware students with students from other colleges. Details of the task were explained, after which the experimenter took S into the experimental room, introduced him to the evaluators, pointed out certain features of the experimental room and left, ostensibly to time the proceedings.

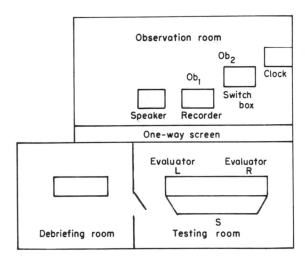

Figure 4. Floor plan and arrangement of people and apparatus. The observers were behind the one-way screen and could see and hear the S and the evaluators.

The experimental arrangements are schematically represented in Figure 4. Subjects were positioned exactly between the two evaluators and four feet distant from each one. Ss sat facing a one-way mirror behind which the observers worked unseen by the subject. Observers were approximately six feet from the S and could follow the discussion by means of sound transmitted via a microphone hidden in the experimental room. S was told that the experimenter would be behind the mirror to time the S's responses and signal the end of various sub-tasks. E then entered the observation room where he operated the timing mechanism and helped the observer record visual interaction and speech patterns.

Half way through the series of experimental tasks E returned to the room and escorted S into an adjacent room to fill out forms which were described as providing a check on the reliability of the test. At this point Ss in the experimental group were asked to state a preference for one of the two evaluators. After completing the forms S returned to the testing room to complete the task series. E returned to the observation room and continued his observations. At the end of the second period S returned to the debriefing room to fill out questionnaires describing his reactions to the experiment and the evaluators. At no time were the evaluators informed as to whether Ss were in the experimental or control groups.

The procedures outlined above permitted us to establish male and female Ss' operant level of looking into the line of regard of each evaluator, and to study the effect of the preference choice upon Ss' willingness to look at a preferred as compared to a non-preferred other of the same sex. The design required that the evaluators' behaviors be carefully standardized along several dimensions. They were required to present themselves as non-threatening yet neutral, affectively identical, and equally salient. In the sections to follow we will describe the experimental task and the evaluator behaviors designed to achieve such standardization. In addition we will describe the measurement of mutual glances and the nature of the relevant rating scales.

Experimental task and evaluator behaviors. The "creative imagination" task required S to respond to four TAT cards (Murray, 1938). S first ranked three alternatives to each of four questions about each TAT card, then for 75 seconds told a story about the picture. The four questions and alternatives for the card showing four men lying on the ground were: Who are the people in the picture? (Alternative answers: Workmen, prisoners, hoboes); Where are they? (On a farm, in a forest, etc.); What brings them here? (Taking a break, etc.); What happens next? (Separate, etc.). Variants of the above four questions, with alternatives appropriate to the picture, were used for the remaining three cards.

S was told that the evaluators would evaluate his performance after he completed his second and fourth stories. After E left the room, one of the evaluators presented the first card to S. When S finished rating the card an evaluator took S's checklist and copied the responses on his own checklist. The evaluator then passed the checklist to the other evaluator who copied it and told the S to begin his story. The presentation and collection of cards and instructions to begin the story were counterbalanced across evaluators. The evaluators' seating locations were counterbalanced across experimental and control groups. The signal to end the story was sounded by a buzzer on the timing device in the observation room.

When S finished his second story the evaluators told S which alternatives were the "most creative" answers to the questions. Each evaluator reported the answers to one half of the answers on each card (again counterbalanced) and reported as most creative the alternative S had rated either 1 or 2. Thus each evaluator reported two answers to each of the four questions, a total of four per evaluator per session. The feedback followed S's order of 1, 2, 2, 1 ranking of alternatives. In other words, the first response of both evaluators always agreed with S's first choice, the second and third responses with S's second choice, and the fourth response with S's first choice again. The sequence was repeated after the fourth story, at which time each evaluator took those questions from cards three and four which he had not reported on in giving the S evaluation of cards one and two. The nature and sequence of the evaluations are shown in Table 7.

Table 7 The sequence* in which evaluators reported as the "most creative" alternatives the first and second choices of S to the four questions for each TAT card

Question Number	Order of TAT presentation															
	Card 1				Card 2				Card 3				Card 4			
	1	2	3	4	1	2	3	4	1	2	3	4	1	2	3	4
Evaluator position																
Left*	1†	2					2	1			1	2	2	1		
Right*			1	2	2	1			1	2					2	1

*Sequence reversed each time a given evaluator sat on the left or right side of table

†Number refers to the creativity rank order given by S to alternative reported as "most creative" by E

After "scoring" S's objective choices the evaluators looked over their notes and using a 5 point rating scale marked their evaluation of S's story. S then left the experimental room for the preference induction.

When S returned to the experimental room following the preference induction the evaluators put him to work on the last two cards. The general procedures used were identical with those of the first two cards; the evaluators completed the evaluation program as shown in Table 7.

By such means the test ostensibly provided both objective and subjective measures of "creative imagination." Actually, the test merely provided a vehicle for measurement of the incidence of mutual glances between S and evaluators.

The induction of preference. Ss left the experimental room and accompanied E into an adjacent room. All Ss were first asked to re-rank their answers to the questions about the first two cards, after which they were shown that both evaluators had rated their stories as "4" on a 5 point scale of creativity. Ss in the experimental group were then asked to state which of the two evaluators they liked best. The repetition of the experimental task was presented as a check on the reliability of the test, and was introduced to provide a reason to take the control Ss out of the presence of the evaluators.

The preference induction was not an induction in the sense that we structured the situation to induce Ss to prefer one person over the other. Ss were merely required to indicate that they liked one person better than the other. We assumed that during the first two task periods Ss would either consciously or unconsciously develop weak preferences for one person over the other. Our instructions were designed to legitimize the impression, to force them to become aware of their preference and to make relatively weak preferences salient. The evaluators' behaviors described earlier were carefully designed to hold to a minimum any factors, other than preference, which would differentially attract the visual attention of the Ss. Once a S had committed himself to stating a preference for another we assumed that the chosen evaluator would be the recipient of relatively more positive affect from S.

The request itself was rationalized as giving us an indication of the ultimate effectiveness of the evaluators as psychological test administrators. Ss were told that such affectiveness depended on the tester's ability to establish rapport between himself and the testee, and that such rapport depended upon how much the tester was liked. Ss were also told that their choice would later be made known to the evaluators. They were then given a paper on which they checked which evaluator they liked the better. The amount of time each S took to make his choice was recorded by an observer located behind a one-way screen.

Experimental Ss were given the option of refusing to state a preference, though E strongly urged all to do so. Although no females exercised this option two male Ss refused to make a choice. They were allowed to complete the task but their data were not included in any of the analyses.

Measurement of mutual glances. The visual interaction of S and evaluators was recorded only during those periods in which the evaluators were instructed to look steadily at S; namely, when they listened to S telling the TAT story and when they informed S concerning the objectively most creative responses to the four questions concerning each card. Mutual glances thus were determined by whether or not S looked into the line of regard of the evaluator during the above mentioned periods.

Mutual glances were recorded by an observer positioned so as to be able to see whenever S looked into the line of regard of an evaluator (see Figure 4). Whenever this occurred the observer depressed a button-switch which recorded S's glance on an operations recorder in the manner described for the first study of this chapter. A separate switch was used for each evaluator position and thus a pen tracing of the frequency and duration of S's mutual glances with each evaluator was obtained.

Another observer similarly recorded whenever S or evaluators spoke, thus providing us with indices of mutual glances during S's speech and during his listening behavior.

Post-experimental preference ratings. On completing the final task, Ss returned to the debriefing room and marked a scale to indicate whether they felt more or less positive toward each evaluator than they had at the start of the experiment. The scale ranged from plus three to minus three with a neutral point at zero. Given a model with the letters L (left) and R (right) placed above the neutral point to indicate our assumption that Ss felt neutral about each evaluator upon first meeting them, Ss were asked to indicate their post-experiment feelings by placing the letters above the appropriate scale points on an unmarked scale.

Ss also marked a scale identical with that described above to indicate a global impression of how the two evaluators felt about one another.

Results

Since male Ss were evaluated by males and female Ss by females, the data for each sex were analyzed separately in a 2 x 2 x 2 factorial design (evaluators x preference x periods) with repeated measures of mutual glances. Previous studies, Exline (1963), Exline et al. (1965), indicated that Ss' visual behavior during their own speech differs significantly from that recorded when they listen to another speak. Separate analyses were thus made of mutual glances during Ss' speech and during the evaluators' speech.

Evaluation of experimental induction. In order to test hypotheses dealing with preference, preference should be demonstrated independently of the dependent variable measure. In other words, we must show that Ss felt more positive affect for the person they were asked to choose mid-way through the experiment. Data listed in Table 8 describe Ss' feelings toward the evaluators at the end of the experiment as compared to the beginning of the experiment.

Table 8 Mean increase in attraction of preferred and non-preferred evaluators over period of experiment

Sex	Condition	Evaluator	
		Preferred	Non-preferred
	Experimental	1.57*	.86
Male	Control	.71†	.86
	Total	1.14	.86
	Experimental	1.71	.43
Female	Control	2.19c	1.14
	Total	1.90	.78

*Scale = +3 to -3; 0 = No change

† Preference randomly assigned

c Based on Post-experimental preference

All Ss in the experimental group indicated a post-experimental preference for the evaluator whom they chose at the mid-point. Of Ss in the control group, six of seven males expressed no post-experimental preference for an evaluator while six of seven females did. Thus female Ss tended to develop spontaneous preferences when not required to, whereas men did not. For purposes of comparative analysis, one of the two evaluators was randomly designated as the preferred evaluator for each male S in the control group.

The data indicated that both male and female Ss in the experimental group (Ss who were asked to choose an evaluator during the experiment) increased in their liking for the preferred relative to the non-preferred evaluator more than did Ss in the control group (Ss who were asked to state their preference after the experiment was over). The effect of the spontaneous preference noted for females in the control group is shown by the fact that a significant F ($F=20.2$, $p<.01$, df 1/12.) was found for the evaluator effect over both experimental and control groups but not for the interaction of the choice condition and evaluator. On the other hand, the analysis of the ratings made by men produced significant F scores for both the evaluator effect ($F=12.44$, $p<.01$, df 1/12) and for the choice condition x evaluator interaction ($F=5.83$, $p<.05$, df 1/12). These data suggest that while the preference induction affected Ss in the experimental group in the intended fashion, the development of spontaneous preferences in the female control group made it less of a control group than the control group for the men.

Table 9 Mean number of seconds (out of a total of 150 seconds per period) during which male and female Ss categorized by choice or no choice conditions looked into the evaluators line of regard while speaking to them (N = 7 per mean)

Subjects	Experimental condition	Evaluator			
		Preferred		Non preferred	
		Task Period		Task Period	
		I	II	I	II
Female	Choice	21.7	37.7	23.1	13.3
	No choice	17.3*	23.9	18.9	17.7
Male	Choice	10.3	13.9	10.3	6.0
	No choice	15.3†	9.4	12.3	8.0

* Designation of preference based on Ss choice at close of experiment.

† Randomly assigned as men would not state a preference.

Preference and visual interaction. We have hypothesized that liking one person better than another will lead to a relatively greater amount of eye contact with the preferred person. In addition we suggested that the discrepancy in eye contact would be greater for women than for men. Tables 9 and 11 show the mean amounts of eye contact associated with speaking to and listening to preferred and non-preferred others. Data in Table 11 are reported in percent of looking to listening time due to the fact that the evaluators were unable to standardize the amount of time it took them to give the "objective" evaluation of Ss' work. Although Es usually took 45 to 55 seconds to read the reports, sometimes they took as little as 40 or as much as 80 seconds to give their evaluations.

The means listed in Table 9 show that women markedly increased their eye contact with the preferred and decreased their eye contact with the non-preferred evaluator over the two task periods. The effect of an early

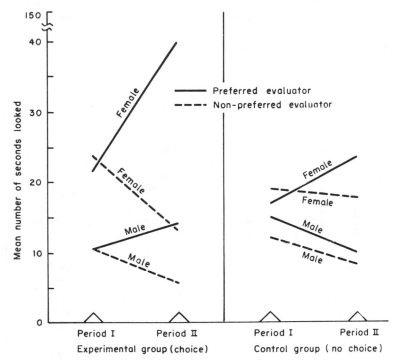

Figure 5. Increments and decrements in the number of seconds Ss looked into the line of regard of evaluators while speaking to them.

choice is also apparent, as those asked to choose during the experiment increased their eye contact with the preferred person and decreased it with the non-preferred person more than did those in the control group. These relationships are graphically represented in Figure 5. The summary of the analysis of variance listed in Table 10 indicates that the significant effects for the evaluators, evaluators by choice condition, time periods by choice conditions, and choice conditions by evaluators by time periods were significant at the .05 and .01 levels. Particularly interesting is the second-order interaction which provides substantial support for the corollary of the first hypothesis. Thus, although women in the control group developed spontaneous preferences for one or the other of the two evaluators, the effect of the formal preference induction strongly accentuated the tendency to look increasingly at the preferred one while avoiding the other.

Data for male Ss, reported in Table 9 and graphed in Figure 5, are in the direction of the hypothesis but do not reach significance. Five male Ss looked less than 5% (less than 15 out of 300 seconds) of the total interview time, thus greatly adding to the error variance.

The development of spontaneous preference by the women in the

Table 10 Summary of the analysis of variance of female S̲s̲' looking while speaking

Source	df	MS	F	p (<)
Between S̲s̲	13			
Groups	1	288.017	.47	n.s.
Error	12	612.506		
Within S̲s̲	42			
Periods	1	117.160		
Evaluators	1	665.160	9.72	.01
Groups x pds.	1	.448		
Groups x evals.	1	297.162	4.34	.05
Pds. x evals.	1	986.162	14.41	.01
Grps. x pds. x evals.	1	288.016	4.21	.05
Pooled error	36	68.434		

control group suggests that they provide a different reference point on the continuum of preference for an evaluator than do the men in the control group. If, as seems reasonable, we locate them somewhere between the undiscriminating control males and the highly discriminating experimental females (see Table 8), we find that the increment in the time at which they looked at the preferred relative to the non-preferred evaluator also falls between the two extreme groups (see Fig. 5). In fact, the comparison of liking-looking differences for all four groups show a perfect rank order correlation between group differences in increments in liking for the preferred relative to the non-preferred evaluator reported in Table 8, and differences in increments over the task periods in looking at the two evaluators reported in Table 9. Control males show decrements over time in both liking for and looking at preferred relative to non-preferred evaluators, whereas experimental males, control females, and experimental females show respectively greater increments over time in both

Table 11 Mean per cent of time S̲s̲ categorized by sex and choice condition return the glance of an evaluator while listening to him (N = 7 per mean)

Subjects	Experimental condition	Evaluator			
		Preferred		Non preferred	
		Task period		Task period	
		I	II	I	II
Female	Choice	89.7	91.6	78.6	85.1
	No choice	98.2*	92.3	89.3	89.3
Male	Choice	87.2	82.8	80.4	58.2
	No choice	79.1†	71.8	76.2	73.8

*Description of preference based on S̲s̲ choice at close of experiment

†Randomly assigned as men would not state a preference

looking at and liking for preferred relative to non-preferred evaluators. The data strongly indicate that when we speak to like sex peers we indicate our preference and our positive feelings by the direction of our glance.

Analysis of eye-contact while listening provided support for Hypothesis 1 and its corollary for male but not for female Ss. The means are listed in Table 11 and their relationships are graphically presented in Figure 6. It is clear that all men tended to reduce their visual attention to the speaker over the two periods. Those men, however, who stated their preference during the experiment reduced their eye contact with the non-preferred speaker much more (from 80% of the time in the first period to 58% in the second period) than they did with the preferred speaker (from 87% to 83% of the time). Male Ss in the control group stated no preferences even at the end of the study. In their case the preferred other was randomly assigned and it is apparent that the pattern of eye contact with "preferred" and "non-preferred" others is strikingly different from that shown by Ss in the experimental group.

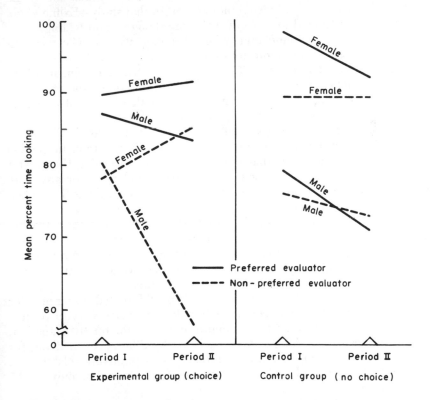

Figure 6. Increments or decrements percent time Ss looked into the line of regard of evaluators while listening to them.

The F tests showed differences attributable to the effect of evaluators ($F=25.74$) and for the interaction of conditions by evaluator (preferred - non-preferred) by task periods ($F=4.23$), to reach significance at the .01 and .05 levels, respectively. Thus the different patterns graphed in Figure 6 seem not to be random differences and the results indicate that men react to differences in postive feelings by maintaining an established level of eye contact with those they like while avoiding the eye of a less well-liked person.

Differences between the means recorded for women in the different conditions, periods, etc., were not significant. The pattern of female means appears to be different from that of the male Ss, particularly in the experimental condition, but preference for an evaluator seemed to have little effect upon whether or not a woman maintained eye contact with the speaker.

Although the differences in the women's visual behavior with the two evaluators over the two periods do not reach statistical significance, the tendency for the women in the experimental group to increase their eye contact with the non-preferred evaluator is curiously reminiscent of the results of an earlier study of visual interaction. In that study (Exline et al., 1965) Ss were instructed to conceal their true thoughts and feelings from an interviewer. It was found that, when listening, women who were instructed to conceal looked more into the line of regard of the interviewer than did women not instructed. The reverse was true for men. It would seem that factors other than interpersonal affect determine the visual behavior of the listening women. In any event Hypothesis 1 is not adequate to account for the eye contacts of the listening women.

Our hypotheses concerning sex differences cannot be statistically tested as the analyses for men and women were necessarily separate. Inspection of Figures 5 and 6 suggests that our speculations concerning the greater influence of affective phenomena on women's visual behavior are more likely to be true with respect to their behavior when speaking than when listening. It is clear from the inspection of Figure 5 that women who stated a preference for one or the other evaluator altered their looking while speaking considerably more after the choice period than did men. Similar but less marked changes which were noted in the control groups have already been interpreted as suggesting that women in the control groups developed spontaneous preferences over time.

Also of interest is the finding that one unit of differential preference for evaluators had a stronger effect upon female than male Ss with respect to the extent to which they looked more at one evaluator than another. When differences in looking at were divided by differences in liking for the evaluators, one unit of liking differences was positively related to a mean of 12.3 seconds of looking differences for women but only of 9.5 seconds for men.

Since males and females were not reacting to the same set of evaluators, the data described above cannot be used to test the general hypothesis that eye contact among women is more sensitive to changes in affective phenomena than is eye contact among men. The differential impact of female evaluators on female Ss, for example, may in subtle ways have been considerably greater than was that of male evaluators upon male Ss. The data are nevertheless consistent with the rationale of Hypothesis 2 and encourage us to search for a more definitive test.

A final point concerns the data pointing to sex differences in the overall use of the line of regard. Examination of Figures 5 and 6 graphically demonstrates sex differences in the total amount of time spent in looking at the evaluators. In addition, the finding that women looked 25% of the total time they spoke and 94% of the time they listened while men looked 16% and 82% of the time during the same activity periods is consistent with sex differences reported in previous studies of visual interaction—Exline (1963), Exline et al. (1965).

DISCUSSION

We have shown that for at least one sample of a college age population the development of positive affect for another is matched by systematic changes in the use of the line of regard. The changes, however, were not always those we had expected, for positive feelings toward another influenced women as predicted only for looking while speaking, and men as predicted only for looking while listening. The data suggest that when attention is focused on the positive quality of one's feelings for others, women express interpersonal preferences in visually active ways whereas men do so in a visually passive way. Women, that is, seem to seek out the eyes of those they like, or to whom they are momentarily attracted, whereas men do not attempt to increase their contact with the preferred so much as to avoid contact with the less preferred.

It should be emphasized that our conclusions are limited to situations in which like-sexed peers interact with others in mildly positive affective climates. Whether the specific patterns of eye contact shown by the Ss would appear in situations characterized by intense personal antagonism or intimacy, either within or across the boundaries of sex, is debatable. Neither can we state with assurance that preferences based on personal affection would determine the amount to which one looked into the line of regard of a superior when speaking or listening to him. Where it is instrumental to present oneself as confident or attentive, one may look when speaking regardless of feeling.

Even with the above restrictions on the generality of our findings, it is impressive that the minimal basis for the development of affect afforded by our procedures resulted in striking differences in eye contact with preferred and non-preferred others.[5]

[5] It is of interest to note that these differences were, in spite of the limited time and scope of interaction, readily apparent to the evaluators. Although no systematic measurements were taken the evaluators claimed that they could tell (a) whether or not S had been asked to make a choice and (b) whom S preferred. The evaluators,

The very fact of a meager basis on which to state a preference may, however, have contributed to the relatively strong effect on eye contact. Assuming the validity of our proposition that eye contact is positively related to preference, dissonance theory (Festinger, 1957) would suggest that the very difficult choice required by our procedures should lead to the divergent amounts of eye contact recorded from pre- to post-choice orientations to preferred and non-preferred evaluators (see Figures 5 and 6). Our hypothesis in itself did not require that S reduce his eye contact with the non-preferred evaluator, but dissonance theory would seem to provide a rationale for explaining the decrease which was observed.

The dissonance aroused by being required to choose one of two equally pleasant strangers may very well have created dissonance-reducing attitudes of exaggerated preference and rejection signalled in turn by marked increments and decrements of eye contact. The divergence in mutual glances in the second period might thus have been an overt expression of an unconscious dissonance-reducing mechanism.

We had hoped to test the validity of the dissonance interpretation by comparing the time taken to make a choice to differences in pre- and post-choice visual orientation toward the evaluators. Unfortunately, the time measure was rendered meaningless as a criterion of decision difficulty due to the fact that some persons re-read the experimenter's instructions whereas others did not. We do not know whether the extra reading reflected Ss' unclear understanding of the verbal instructions, methodical work habits or a desire to gain time to make a difficult decision. Thus our ideas concerning the usefulness of dissonance theory to explain the visual behaviors concomitant with choice remain speculative and untested. Future studies of this phenomenon will take into account the subjective difficulty of choice.

We believe our findings are relevant to several points raised by Tagiuri (1958) in his discussion of the perception of social preference. We refer to: (1) the observable manifestations of preference, (2) differences between covert feelings and overt statement of feelings, and (3) the speed with which one's initial positive or negative affective reaction to another takes place.

We earlier noted Tagiuri's postulate that choices have observable manifestations. Our study was based on the assumption that a relatively high level of eye contact was one such manifestation, and our data would seem to bear out the assumption.

Tagiuri has pointed to the difficulty of satisfactorily distinguishing between what one feels and what one says one feels. We suggest the looking while speaking index may provide a means of assessing the credibility of one's stated feeling of affection for another. Does the chooser, when in the presence of the choice objects, look relatively more into the line of regard of his overtly chosen one? If not, our data suggest

who had no prior knowledge of S's group assignment, based their impressions upon S's use of eye contact.

that, given the limiting conditions discussed earlier, one's stated choice may not be his true one.

It is reasonable to argue, as does Tagiuri, that we very quickly develop an affective reaction toward another person, and that such attitudes result from sets we have developed from previous experience with people "like him." We suggest that the ease with which eye contact can be made is another factor which facilitates the speedy development of an emotional reaction to a relative stranger. One can see and be seen across a crowded room filled with talking people. Thus, before a word is spoken, two persons could have engaged in considerable visual interaction with the implications for choice and rejection which we have pointed to in this study. Observe sometime the pattern of the conversations a stranger holds in a large social gathering. Once past the conversations of an introductory nature, later conversations are likely to have been preceded by an intricate pattern of visual probes and counters. Consider also your own feelings toward one who, while talking with you in a crowded room looks only at you, as compared to your feelings toward one who lets his gaze roam the faces of the passers-by. Whether or not one shares or avoids the glances of his co-conversationalist would seem to contribute much to the speedy build-up of emotional reactions within the dyad.

In conclusion, we believe that the results of both studies reported in this chapter suggest that positive and negative affects have complex but systematic effects upon the nature of visual interaction. We have interpreted our data as indicating that the impact of affective phenomena on the mutual use of the line of regard is one, in like-sexed groups, of causing men to decrease previously established levels of eye contact while leading women to vary from their operant levels in direct relation to the sign of their feeling.

An important but as yet untested question concerns whether the recipient of the glance interprets the increments and decrements of eye contact in terms of the motives we have assigned to the sender. While the evaluators' comments, reported in our study of differential preference, suggest that they do, systematic study of the target persons' interpretations of adient and avoidant glance is necessary, and will be one focus of our future research into the affective qualities of visual interaction.

REFERENCES

Bacon, Francis. *Essays and New Atlantis*. New York: Walter J. Black, 1942.
Bates, A., & Cloyd, J. S. Toward the development of operations for defining group norms and member roles. *Sociometry*, 1956, *19*, 26-39.
Elworthy, F. T. *The evil eye: the origins and practices of superstition*. London: John Murray, 1895.
Exline, R., Thibaut, J., Brannon, C., & Gumpert, P. Visual interaction in relation to machiavellianism and an unethical act. *Amer. Psychologist*, 1961, *16*, 396. (Abstract)
Exline, R. Explorations in the process of person perception: visual interaction

in relation to competition, sex and need for affiliation. *J. Pers.*, 1963, *31*, 1-20.

Exline, R., Gray, D., & Schuette, Dorothy. Visual behavior in a dyad as affected by interview content and sex of respondent. *J. pers. soc. Psychol.*, in press, 1965.

Festinger, L. *A theory of cognitive dissonance.* Evanston, Ill.: Row-Peterson, 1957.

Knapp, P. H. *Expression of the emotions in man.* New York: International Universities Press, 1963.

Lambert, W. W., & Lambert, W. E. *Social psychology.* New Jersey: Prentice-Hall, 1964.

Luborsky, L., Blinder, B., & Mackworth, N. Eye fixation and recall of pictures as a function of GSR responsivity. *Percept. Mot. Skills*, 1963, *16*, 469-483.

Magnus, H. *Die Sprache der Augen.* Wiesbaden: 1885.

Murray, H. A., et al. *Explorations in personality.* New York: Oxford Press, 1938.

Nielsen, G. *Studies in self-confrontation.* Copenhagen: Psychological Laboratory, University of Copenhagen, 1962.

Ogden, A. Looks and glances. *Harper's Bazaar*, 1961, 84+109-110.

Osgood, C. E., Suci, G. J., & Tannenbaum, P. H. *The measurement of meaning.* Urbana, Ill.: University of Illinois Press, 1957.

Schack, S. *Physiognomiske Studier.* Copenhagen: Woldike, 1858.

Schutz, W. *FIRO: A three dimensional theory of interpersonal behavior.* New York: Rinehart, 1958.

Simmel, G. Sociology of the senses: visual interaction. In R. E. Park and E. W. Burgess (Eds.), *Introduction to the science of sociology.* Chicago, Ill.: University of Chicago Press, 1921.

Tagiuri, R. Social preference and its perception. In R. Tagiuri and L. Petrullo (Eds.), *Person perception and interpersonal behavior.* Stanford, California: Stanford University Press, 1958.

Tomkins, S. S. *Affect, imagery, consciousness.* Vol. II. *The negative affects.* New York: Springer, 1963.

PART SEVEN

METHODS FOR THE STUDY
OF AFFECT AND THE JUDGMENT OF AFFECT

XII

Research with the Mood Adjective Check List

Vincent Nowlis

The concept of mood does not have an important place in contemporary psychological theory. However, dimensions or aspects of mood, when given such labels as activation, aggression, anxiety, and elation, do seem to relate to important psychological issues. The increasingly numerous investigations on such topics as arousal, stress, emotional appeals, and drug effects require a continuing search for standardized and convenient instruments for monitoring the current affective status of an individual. The Mood Adjective Check List (MACL), with its ease of administration and scoring and its broad coverage of mood states, has been used in a number of such studies. The major question at this time involves the extent to which mood as a concept and the MACL as a technique for measuring mood can serve a useful place in psychological research.

The general context within which this question can be answered is supplied by Mandler and Kessen (1959) in their discussion of the procedures by which a term, such as mood, widely used in the common language, may be reconstructed or explicated so that appropriate evaluations can be made of its actual or potential status as a technical term with respect to such standards as clarity, precision, invariance of meaning, and utility or functional relatedness to other technical terms.

An essential early part of this rehabilitation process is the meaning analysis through which we make explicit all the circumstances which elicit the terms as response in both common and scientific discourse. The resulting family of applications may yield a paradigm within which a central and restricted definition of the term may be discerned and formulated. In the widely scattered professional literature on mood the term is applied to the same features of behavior and experience to which it is applied by the layman: (1) It is applied to temporary tendencies to

Preparation of this review and the Rochester work on the MACL reported herein were supported through Contract No. Nonr-668(12), Project No. NR 171-342 between the University of Rochester and the Group Psychology Branch of the Office of Naval Research.

show or not to show certain characteristics under certain specified circumstances or to show them with greater or lesser likelihood under those circumstances. (2) Since these characteristics are often themselves dispositional in nature (such as tendencies to aggressive or anxious or dejected behavior), mood refers to higher order dispositions. (3) Mood refers to the set of the entire person and not to some one particular behavioral or motivational system. It is therefore multidimensional, since the concept of person or self is multidimensional. Mood usually also involves very broad repertoires of behavior and experience. (4) Even though mood terms are most often used when changes in a person are noted, mood does refer to constancies of behavior and experience during a certain temporal interval. (5) Finally, mood terms are often used when the determinants of the specified temporary state of the person are obscure, remote, or relatively inaccessible to manipulative control, thus emphasizing the person's bondage to internal and external controls.

Is a general definition of mood to be found in these applications? I have suggested the following: Mood is the effect on a person of his own configurations of activity (Nowlis, 1961). These configurations may be conceptualized as fundamental patterns of general functioning and orientation, such as level of activation, level of control, level of concentration, direction of social orientation, and positive (pleasant) or negative (unpleasant) general appraisal. The effect of these general patterns on the person may be mediated by cues associated with them in the life history and involves affective, cognitive, motivational, and motor responses to the cues; such responses may in turn become functionally related to the general patterns and may modify, maintain, or even instigate them. Hypotheses about the dimensions of mood can be developed from a specification of general patterns of functioning and orientation. The methods for describing or measuring the dimensions of mood can be based on an understanding of the cues and responses functionally related to each general pattern. Additional hypotheses about mood dimensions may be derived from whatever patterns these cues and responses are found to exhibit.

ADJECTIVES AND MOOD

Since mood involves the whole person and thus large repertoires of behavior and experience, it should be possible to use a wide variety of responses in studying mood, such as expressive movements, various aspects of spoken language, fluctuations in self-esteem and in the subjective estimates of the desirability and probability of uncertain future events. The MACL is based on one limited but easily accessible type of behavior, namely, the tendency of persons in our culture to apply to mood certain adjectives which complete the sentence "I feel ————." Many adjectives used to complete this sentence do not ordinarily apply to mood, such as *hungry* or *intoxicated*. But there are literally hundreds of other words which we can call mood adjectives. With appropriate instructions and test format, this large population of items provides a basis for developing an operational definition for each of several dimensions of mood which we can hypothesize and identify.

If we are to use the checking of adjectives as a basis for defining and measuring mood, we should look more closely at this type of verbal behavior. We know that the verbal responses one is disposed to make vary with mood, but we also know that all verbal responses have multiple determinants. To attempt to make the list maximally sensitive to mood and minimally sensitive to other determinants requires some analysis of what the individual does as he checks through the list and of how this compares with what he does in other situations in which he applies adjectives to his mood or to that of others. Reading the word in the list is a textual response (Skinner, 1957), that is, a verbal response which has had a long and complex reinforcement history and which also occurs in other interactions with the environment. To say "I feel angry" is a response one has learned to say when in an angry mood; its probability of occurrence is greater in that mood than in other moods. It is, as Ryle (1949) suggests, one of the many things one is disposed to do and which one sometimes finds oneself doing when in an angry mood. As the individual utters it, whether publicly or privately, its content and mode of expression may cause him for the first time to note that he is in an angry mood. Thus the utterance is frequently an avowal, admission, or declaration rather than a description; we then judge it with respect to sincerity rather than accuracy. In this context sincerity refers to the degree to which overt expression matches the concurrent private covert expression. The MACL serves as a series of prompts for avowals of mood; each word either strengthens an avowal which one is already somewhat or even strongly disposed to make or elicits a verbal response which would otherwise be extremely rare in this particular mood and which is now strengthened only by the reading of the word. As each covert textual response occurs, with its relatively constant content and its variable intonation and intensity, we assume that the individual compares his perception of the response with such standards as (1) his perception of how it usually sounds when he says it spontaneously as a sincere avowal, and (2) his perception of how much he now feels like avowing this word with sincerity and with suitable intonation and intensity. Let us also note that in everyday situations the individual may be disposed to express verbally only one aspect of mood, but that the MACL attempts to elicit within a very short period verbal behavior that applies to many aspects of mood.

The crucial technical problem is to facilitate the judgmental process in which the individual compares his perception of his private textual response with his perception of that verbal response when it was made sincerely and appropriately in the past as well as with his perception of how much he now feels like saying it in that manner. Thus everything depends on the occurrence of a single, salient textual response which can be compared with these other perceptions. Simplicity of instructions and of test format are therefore essential. To judge feelings at the moment the word is read is easier than judging average level of feelings during the day. To ask the individual to judge feelings at the moment also reduces the influence of a social desirability set, which has more influence when he is asked to report his typical mood. Still another advantage of instructions to report how one feels at the moment is that it does not inhibit inconsistency of response from one test administration to another, since some variability of mood and feeling is a familiar and accepted fact. To read a list of words related to various aspects of mood facilitates the judgmental process more than does reading a list related to only one dimension of mood, such as anxiety, since the latter more readily leads to interfering expectancies about the main interest of the test maker. To present a few options, such as *vv, v, ?, no* (Table 1), requires less difficult judgments than does presenting a Q sort, a graphic scale, or multiple-word items.

DIMENSIONS OF MOOD

In defining mood as the effect on the person of his ongoing configurations of activity, we noted that these configurations could be viewed as general patterns of function and orientation, such as level of activation, level of control, positive vs. negative social orientation, and positive vs. negative appraisal or pleasantness vs. unpleasantness. In factor analytic studies with Russel F. Green (Nowlis & Green, 1964) these four patterns were used to formulate hypotheses about four bipolar dimensions of mood. From the many adjectives applied to mood in everyday speech, a total of 120 were found which promised to provide broad definitions for the hypothesized dimensions:

Activation: active, energetic, lively, full of pep, alert, wide-awake, inspired, enthusiastic, attentive, intent, interested, concentrating, contemplative, engaged in thought, introspective, industrious, work-oriented, talkative.

Deactivation: drowsy, inactive, leisurely, sluggish, slow, dull, sleepy, tired, washed-out, bored, disinterested, careless, lazy, quiet.

Pleasantness: lighthearted, cheerful, carefree, mischievous, playful, witty, expansive, pleased, refreshed, satisfied, elated, overjoyed, delighted.

Unpleasantness: blue, downhearted, sad, sorry, fed-up, frustrated, dissatisfied, irritated, miserable.

Positive Social Orientation: lonely, cooperative, sociable, trustful, accommodating, compliant, obedient, affectionate, forgiving, full of pity, genial, kind, warmhearted.

Negative Social Orientation: aloof, detached, independent, self-centered, smug, skeptical, suspicious, defiant, rebellious, belligerent, stubborn, angry, annoyed, grouchy, sarcastic.

Control: clearthinking, decisive, effective, efficient, persuasive, resourceful, adventurous, bold, strong, vigorous, calm, optimistic, confident, secure, nonchalant, reckless, boastful, egotistic, proud.

Table 1 A short form of the Mood ACL

Each of the following words describes feelings or mood. Please use the list to describe your feelings <u>at the moment</u> you read each word. If the word definitely describes how you feel at the moment you read it, circle the double check (vv) to the right of the word. For example, if the word is <u>relaxed</u> and you are definitely feeling relaxed at the moment, circle the vv as follows:

relaxed (vv) v ? no. (This means you definitely feel relaxed at the moment.)

If the word only slightly applies to your feelings at the moment, circle the single check v as follows:

relaxed vv (v) ? no. (This means you feel slightly relaxed at the moment.)

If the word is not clear to you or you cannot decide whether or not it applies to your feelings at the moment, circle the question mark as follows:

relaxed vv v (?) no. (This means you cannot decide whether you are relaxed or not.)

If you definitely decide the word does not apply to your feelings at the moment, circle the no as follows:

relaxed vv v ? (no) (This means you are definitely not relaxed at the moment.)

Work rapidly. Your first reaction is best. Work down the first column, then go to the next. Please mark all words. This should take only a few minutes. Please begin.

angry vv v ? no	kindly vv v ? no
clutched up vv v ? no	sad vv v ? no
carefree vv v ? no	skeptical vv v ? no
elated vv v ? no	egotistic vv v ? no
concentrating vv v ? no	energetic vv v ? no
drowsy vv v ? no	rebellious vv v ? no
affectionate vv v ? no	jittery vv v ? no
regretful vv v ? no	witty vv v ? no
dubious vv v ? no	pleased vv v ? no
boastful vv v ? no	intent vv v ? no
active vv v ? no	tired vv v ? no
defiant vv v ? no	warmhearted vv v ? no
fearful vv v ? no	sorry vv v ? no
playful vv v ? no	suspicious vv v ? no
overjoyed vv v ? no	self-centered vv v ? no
engaged in thought vv v ? no	vigorous vv v ? no
sluggish vv v ? no	

Lack of Control: clutched up, dubious, helpless, uncertain, doubtful, restrained, subdued, weak, apprehensive, fearful, hesitant, insecure, jittery, self-conscious, timid, shocked, startled, ashamed, regretful.

Four other words (*careful, earnest, meticulous, serious*) were added to monitor attitude toward the test, and six others (*hungry, in pain, intoxicated, lustful, sexy, thirsty*) to monitor other feelings.

A check list consisting of these 130 words was administered to approximately 450 college men at the beginning and end of six weekly one-hour experimental sessions in a large auditorium. Different moods were induced in each session through the use of motion pictures, a frustrating hoax, and a contest for cash prizes. Five sets of data have been factor analyzed: (1) a composite set of data in which pretreatment scores in three sessions were combined; (2) pretreatment scores for the second session; (3-5) posttreatment scores for the second, third, and fourth sessions, respectively. Thirty-four of the 130 variables were eliminated from further study after an examination of response distributions, reliabilities, susceptibilities to order effects, and patterns of correlations with other variables. Ten factors were extracted by the Thurstone centroid method from each of the five matrices. Nearly all of the apparent total common variance was usually accounted for by the first nine factors; each set of nine was rotated to an oblique solution by the Pinzka-Saunders method.

In order to determine whether or not similar factors emerge from sets of data obtained when subjects are in radically different moods, we compared each set of nine rotated factors with the four other sets. It was possible to match 43 of the 45 axes across the five sets (Table 2). An axis was found *in all five sets* for four factors: A, Aggression; B, Anxiety; C, Surgency; E, Concentration. An axis was found *in four sets* for four other factors: F, Fatigue; G, Social Affection; H, Sadness; I, Skepticism. One was found *in three sets* for one factor: J, Egotism. One was found *in two sets* for two factors: D, Elation; N, Nonchalance. One of the two unmatched axes was trivial but the other unique axis was of sufficient interest to be tentatively identified as a twelfth factor, K, Vigor. Most of these matches might have been made with some confidence simply by assigning to a factor all axes on which the same variables had relatively high loadings. There were, however, 17 axes in which the words with high loadings included a few atypical variables. We therefore correlated the loadings for all 96 variables on each axis with their loadings on the other 44 axes and based all matches on the size of these r's. The median r for axes matched within a factor was 0.45; the median value of all other r's was approximately zero, with 87% of the values falling between 0.29 and −0.29.

After careful study of these 12 groups of matched axes, we selected the following 49 variables as most representative of the 12 factors:

A, Aggression (5 axes): defiant, rebellious, angry, grouchy, annoyed, fed-up.

B, Anxiety (5 axes): clutched up, fearful, jittery.

C, Surgency (5 axes): carefree, playful, witty, lively, talkative.

D, Elation (2 axes): elated, overjoyed, pleased, refreshed.

E, Concentration (5 axes): attentive, earnest, serious, contemplative, concentrating, engaged in thought, intent, introspective.

F, Fatigue (4 axes): drowsy, dull, sluggish, tired.

G, Social Affection (4 axes): affectionate, forgiving, kindly, warmhearted.

H, Sadness (4 axes): regretful, sad, sorry.

I, Skepticism (4 axes): dubious, skeptical, suspicious.
J, Egotism (3 axes): egotistic, self-centred, aloof, boastful.
K, Vigor (1 axis): active, energetic, vigorous.
N, Nonchalance (2 axes): leisurely, nonchalant.

How do these results relate to our original hypotheses? First, we had assumed that each factor would be bipolar. Actually, bipolarity was almost nonexistent in the obtained axes. For the 45 axes, the median number of variables with a loading of $+0.30$ or greater was seven; the median number with negative loading this size was zero. Thirty-five axes had no such variables with a negative loading as large as 0.30;

Table 2   Matched axes in five Green-Nowlis analyses

Factor and variable*	Highest loadings in 5 analyses	I Pre- 3+4+5	II Pre- 2	III Post-2 Hoax	IV Post-3 Comedy	V Post-4 Nuremberg
A, Aggression		Axis #1	#6	#4	#5	#6
defiant	AAAAA**	30†	50	43	39	56
rebellious	AAAAA	34	44	52	35	54
angry	-gAABA		37	37		39
grouchy	bAAbA		43	30		43
annoyed	iAA-cA		33	44		50
fed-up	aAAtA	14	37	46		45
B, Anxiety		Axis #2	#9	#1	#1	#3
clutched up	BBBbB	44	32	52	20	35
fearful	BBBbB	40	26	45	18	43
jittery	bBBtB	21	42	37		36
C, Surgency		Axis #3	#3	#5	#3	#2
carefree	CCCCC	47	36	47	52	33
playful	CCCCC	38	44	47	43	50
witty	CCcCC	48	38	28	32	35
lively	CckCC	33	24		36	30
talkative	CC-hCc	44	30		32	22
D, Elation		Axis #8	#8	None	None	None
elated	DDccC	45	30			
overjoyed	DDcCC	45	45			
pleased	DD-aCC	40	30			
refreshed	Ddccc	32	23			
E, Concentration		Axis #4	#4	#9	#4	#1
attentive	-fEEE-n		46	35	58	
earnest	EEeE-n	43	37	24	42	
serious	EEEe-n	58	44	32	28	
contemplative	EEe-cE	47	37	18		47
concentrating	EEEEe	44	59	36	47	28
engaged in tho't	EEEee	51	37	31	25	23

Table 2 continued

		Source of data				
Factor and variable*	Highest loadings in 5 analyses	I Pre- 3+4+5	II Pre- 2	III Post-2 Hoax	IV Post-3 Comedy	V Post-4 Nuremberg
intent	EEEEe	33	46	45	50	24
introspective	Eee-cE	41	23	21		39
F, Fatigue		Axis #5	#5	#2	#6	None
drowsy	FFFFg	55	52	38	50	
dull	FFFxx	32	66	30	not used	
sluggish	FFFfg	48	49	37	29	
tired	FFFFg	53	52	33	49	
G, Social Affection		Axis #6	#2	#7	None	#5
affectionate	GGGfG	52	51	50		45
forgiving	GGgfG	48	39	21		34
kindly	G-AgeG	46		28		59
warmhearted	GGGeG	43	44	39		49
H, Sadness		None	#7	#6	#2	#7
regretful	bHHhH		35	41	28	45
sad	fHHhH		39	44	21	33
sorry	bhHhH		26	39	25	44
I, Skepticism		Axis #9	#1	None	#9	#8
dubious	IiF-cB&I	32	26			43
skeptical	IIFIB&I	41	39		52	45
suspicious	IafiB	38			19	(27)
J, Egotism		Axis #7	None	#8	None	#9
egotistic	JbJA-h	45		43		
self-centered	E&JBJeJ	46		49		56
aloof	eajAJ	(22)		17		30
boastful	JaJAj	34		36		23
K, Vigor		None	None	#3	None	None
active	-f-fK-fn			31		
energetic	-f-fK-fa			30		
vigorous	-f-fK-fa			41		
N, Nonchalance		None	None	None	#7	#4
leisurely	FccNn				31	28
nonchalant	CCCNN				37	39

*Only 49 of 96 variables are included in this table

**The letters indicate the factor on which the variable had its highest loading in each analysis. Capital letters indicate values = or > than 0.30; other letters indicate values below 0.30

† Decimals omitted. The values presented are the highest loading each variable had in each rotated solution

An ampersand (&) indicates the variable had loadings = or > than 0.30 on two axes in the same matrix seven had one such variable and five had two. This result is of general interest because of the widespread assumption of bipolarity in definitions of various affective phenomena. Specifically, it suggests that aspects of mood commonly believed to be interdependently opposed to each other may be functionally independent. Thus, increases in hostility are not necessarily attended by decreases in social affection, increases in vigor not necessarily attended by decreases in fatigue, and so forth.

Failure to find bipolarity suggests that our original four hypotheses may now be viewed as eight. There is some correspondence between seven of the original hypotheses and ten of the empirical factors: Activation with K, Vigor; Deactivation with F, Fatigue; Pleasantness with C, Surgency and with D, Elation; Unpleasantness with H. Sadness; Positive Social Orientation with G, Social Affection; Negative Social Orientation with A, Aggression, with I, Skepticism, and with J, Egotism; and Lack of Control with B, Anxiety. One of the best empirical factors (E, Concentration) was not anticipated as an independent factor in the original hypotheses, nor was the poorer factor, N, Nonchalance. It appears that the empirical factors now identified can be regarded as constituting a second round of hypotheses, requiring in each case better definition and further empirical explication through factor analytic and other procedures.

CURRENT STATUS OF DIMENSIONS OF MOOD IDENTIFIED THROUGH FACTOR ANALYSIS

Between the time when the first long MACL became available and the time when the conclusions just reported were made, several other factor analytic studies were made of lists which included words wholly or partly from the first MACL. Two replications, using an early 40-word list, were done by Nowlis and Green (1964), one with navy personnel and one with college women. Borgatta (1961), using a similar 40-word list derived from the first Nowlis-Green factor analysis (1951), did two factor analyses on a large college group. Thayer (1963) performed two factor analyses on a list which included selected MACL words plus others especially chosen for his study of activation-deactivation as an aspect of mood. McNair and Lorr (1964), who have recently completed three factor analyses on large groups of neurotics, used a list (POMS) with some words from the MACL together with others from other sources. Their instructions ask "How much have you felt the way described during the past week, including today?" Clyde (1960), who used a method of sorting one-item cards into four piles, has factor analyzed a list of words (CMS) derived in part from MACL words. Reimanis (1964) has factor analyzed a set of words synonymous with some in the MACL and adapted to individuals living in a VA domiciliary. Over a long period, Cattell has factor analyzed mood-relevant sets of items which include both self-report and objective indices of behavior and experience. He believes that about 12 mood or state factors exist and that each can be shown to correspond to one of the several personality dimensions which may be said to be unstable or to fluctuate (Cattell, 1960, p. 452). There are six or seven factors which tend to appear in all these studies: Aggression, Anxiety, Concentration, Fatigue, Social Affection, and, when included in the list, Surgency. But an additional five or six factors receive sufficient support to suggest that twelve or more factors should be hypothesized and given further study in mood research. This is also the suggestion which comes from those non-factor analytic studies, to be discussed later, which have used a priori sets of words, empirically identified clusters of words, or sets of MACL words to which new words were added.

Factor A, Aggression

This factor appears in all 15 of the factor analytic studies listed in Table 3. The variables *defiant, rebellious, angry, grouchy, annoyed,* and *fed-up,* if included in the list, always tend to appear. To *angry, annoyed,*

Table 3 Factors tentatively matched across 15 studies

actor	5 Green-Nowlis analyses	2 Green-Nowlis replic.	2 Borgatta replic.	2 Thayer analyses	3 McNair-Lorr analyses	Reimanis	Matches Tests
Aggression	5 Yes	2 Yes	2 Yes	2 Yes	3 Yes	1 Yes	15/15
Anxiety	5 Yes	2 Yes	2 ?	2 Yes	3 ?	1 Yes	10/15 + 5 ?
Surgency	5 Yes	1 Yes	No Test	No Test	No Test	No Test	6/7
Elation	2 Yes	2 No	2 ?	1 Yes	No Test	1 Yes	4/12 + 2 ?
Concentration	5 Yes	2 Yes	2 Yes	2 Yes	1 Yes 2 No Test	1 ?	12/13 + 1 ?
Fatigue	4 Yes	2 Yes	2 Yes	2 Yes	3 Yes	1 Yes	14/15
Social Affection	4 Yes	2 Yes	2 Yes	1 Yes	1 Yes 2 No Test	1 No	10/13
Sadness	4 Yes	1 Yes	2 ?	2 Yes	3 ?	1 ?	7/15 + 6 ?
Skepticism	4 Yes	No Test	1 ?	2 Yes	No Test	No Test	6/9 + 1 ?
Egotism	3 Yes	1 Yes 1 ?	1 Yes	2 Yes	No Test	1 ?	7/12 + 2 ?
Vigor or general acti-vation	1 ?	2 No	No Test	2 Yes	3 Yes	1 Yes	6/13 + 1 ?
Nonchalance or general de-activation	2 ?	No Test	No Test	2 Yes	No Test	No Test	2/7 + 2 ?

and *grouchy,* McNair-Lorr add *furious* and *ready to fight* as consistent variables and label the factor, Anger-Hostility. Because of the consistency with which *defiant* and *rebellious* appeared in our analyses, we would prefer Hostility to Anger as a label; it is perhaps better than our selection, Aggression. In these studies, as in the factor analyses of more heterogeneous items performed by Cattell (1957), various items associated with aggression, annoyance, assertiveness, hostility and irritability tend to appear on other mood or state factors, such as egotism, dominance, skepticism and vigor, and on a variety of Cattell's personality factors. This need not lead us, however, to doubt that aggression-hostility is a mood factor in the domain of check list behavior, since it has been identified so consistently when lists of adjectives are factor analyzed.

Factor B, Anxiety

This factor, in some form or another, also appears in all of the studies in Table 3. The most nearly satisfactory words for Green and Nowlis were *clutched up, fearful,* and *jittery.* The pair, *startled* and *shocked,* also frequently appeared on this axis, but also moved once to an axis assigned to Factor D, Elation, and once to an axis assigned to Factor H, Sadness, and in Thayer's study to a special high-activation factor. There are a number of other words which tend to appear both in Factor B and in Factor H, such as *helpless, weak, downhearted, insecure,* and *frustrated.* These latter words correspond to the depression pole of Cattell's PUI 2, a pattern associated "with some tendency to *general* emotionality, with situations of frustration, and with a tendency to handle problems crudely, as if physiological activity were high . . . and a slowing down of all psychological tempo and output measures" (Cattell, 1960, p. 453-454). He suggests that even though anxiety and depression tend to go together statistically, they must be differentiated since they are also often characterized by independence of movement. To refine our present definition of anxiety as a mood factor obviously requires further study. McNair and Lorr (1964) find a strong factor which they call Tension-Anxiety, defined by such words as *tense, nervous, shaky,* and *on edge.* Zuckerman (1960) offers the following: *afraid, desperate, fearful, frightened, nervous, panicky, shaky, tense, terrified, upset, worrying;* he did not use factor analysis in developing this cluster. Cattell and Scheier (1961) find the following self-report variables saliently loaded on Anxiety (PUI 9): higher willingness to admit common failings, higher susceptibility to annoyance, lower ego strength, lesser confidence in untried performance, lower self-sentiment, and higher ergic tension.

Factor C, Surgency

This factor was identified late in our analyses because of its close ties with Factor D, Elation, with Factor N, Nonchalance, and occasionally with Factor G, Social Affection. Thus, it has not been adequately tested as yet in any of the replicative studies listed in Table 3. The best variables are *carefree, playful, witty, lively,* and *talkative.* It corresponds to Cattell's Source Trait F, Surgency, for which he supplies the following: *cheerful, joyous, sociable, responsive, energetic, humorous, witty, talkative, placid* (1950, p. 61). As identified in our studies, however, it is not bipolar, as is his factor, which is based on heterogeneous items. In three of our studies, Factor D, Elation, merged with Factor C. The particular variable, *lighthearted,* always had fairly high loadings on both factors when both appeared in the same rotated matrix. The little factor, N, Nonchalance, (*nonchalant, leisurely*) also tended to merge with both factors. It seems to be represented in the Cattell cluster by the word *placid,* and will be discussed later. Because of the consistency with which the first five words appeared on the same factor we suggest that Factor C should be included in any basic mood check list.

Factor D, Elation

Like Factor C, this factor was not clearly discriminated until late in our analytic studies. Its best variables are *elated, overjoyed, pleased,* and *refreshed,* plus *lighthearted* which is closely tied also to Factor C. The words all have a suffix of -ed; most of the words in the original 130-word list with this suffix had little consistency, individually, with respect to the factor on which they had a high loading in the five analyses. Perhaps such words are more often applied to dispositions which are more reactive, more ephemeral and more specific than are the dispositions usually associated with moods. In any case, we obviously need a more careful analysis which would lead to the selection of better words, such as words without the -ed suffix. We expect, however, that such words may be likely to correspond to Factor C, Surgency, words and fall on that factor. For the present, we come to the unexpected but tentative conclusion that a basic mood check list need not necessarily have variables representing elation.

Factor E, Concentration

This important factor was not directly anticipated in our original hypotheses but fortunately a number of words which had been included in the a priori definitions of the activation and control dimensions and in the special motivation cluster did emerge with consistently high loadings on axes empirically identified as Factor E. The factor also appears in all of the replicative studies. The words on the factor represent at least two allied dispositions: one cluster of words (*careful, contemplative, introspective*) suggests a reflective mood; another (*clear-thinking, decisive, efficient, attentive, earnest, serious*) suggests a positively valued, socially responsible mood of involvement; a third cluster (*concentrating, engaged in thought, intent*) seems to be correlated with both of these dispositions and is the one with the most consistently high loadings on the factor. The central idea of the factor seems to be involvement with one's thought or one's task or both.

In the McNair and Lorr study, five variables used only in their third analysis formed a factor which resembles Factor E: *able to concentrate, able to think clearly, efficient,* and with negative loadings, *forgetful* and *confused.* They interpret it either as cognitive efficiency vs. inefficiency or as a mood state characterized by effective concentration vs. bewilderment and muddleheadedness. Since their data were obtained from a single report by neurotic patients who were asked to report how they felt during the preceding week, we should retain the McNair-Lorr suggestion that their factor may, as presently defined, be based on differences in cognitive efficiency rather than on a mood state. In the Reimanis study, four words apear as Factor E: *earnest, truthful, kindly,* and *serious.* They represent the second cluster described earlier, that of socially responsible involvement with one's task or tasks.

The factor should be included in a basic MACL.

Factor F, Fatigue

We had originally hypothesized a bipolar dimension of activation-deactivation. In our original five analyses, four axes appeared on which such words as *drowsy, dull, sleepy,* and *tired* had high loadings. On three of these axes such words as *active, energetic,* and *vigorous* had negative but relatively low loadings. In one analysis these activation words formed a large, separate factor (K). The overall evidence suggested that we could be confident only about Factor F and that it was probably not bipolar. McNair and Lorr found both a fatigue factor (*tired, fatigued, worn-out, sluggish, weary, sleepy*) and a vigor-activity factor (*lively, vigorous, full of pep, active, carefree*). Reimanis also found a fatigue factor (*sleepy, tired*) and a bipolar activation factor (*active, full of pep, on the go,* versus *slow*). Thayer (1963) made repeated analyses of a check list of nineteen activation and deactivation words as well as two analyses of the MACL augmented by these special words. With both lists he consistently found four different factors apparently related to activation or deactivation or both. First, Factor F appeared as usual (*drowsy, sleepy, tired, sluggish*) but had at the negative pole the two new words *wide-awake* and *wakeful.* Secondly, a general activation factor (*full of pep, peppy, quick, active, energetic*) appeared; it will be discussed with Factor K, Vigor. Third, a general deactivation factor was consistently identified: *quiet, at rest, still, placid.* It is obviously different from Factor F and will be discussed with Factor N, Nonchalance. He also found a factor which he tentatively labelled "high activation," involving such words as *intense, stirred up* and *aroused,* but since the three words of Factor B, Anxiety, *clutched up, fearful* and *jittery,* had still higher loadings on these axes, this factor requires further general study before being interpreted as a dimension of activation.

With respect to Factor F, we can conclude that this is a dependable dimension of mood and that it should be discriminated from other factors which are also related to activation and deactivation. When it is again tested for bipolarity, such words as Thayer's *wide-awake* and *wakeful* should be included in addition to such words as *active, energetic,* and *vigorous* which probably represent Factor K.

Factor G, Social Affection

This factor derives from our original hypothesis of Positive Social Orientation. It involves, however, a more limited orientation (*affectionate, forgiving, kindly, warmhearted*) than did the original hypothesis. It appears in four of the five first analyses and in all of the replications, where it is sometimes merged with Factor D, Elation. Contrary to our expectations, words like *cooperative* and *trustful* appear on Factor E, Concentration, as often as on Factor G, while *genial* and *sociable* are very inconsistent with respect to factor identity. McNair and Lorr found in their third analysis an axis defined by *friendly, cooperative, good-natured, understanding,* and *cheerful,* a cluster which seems to represent three of our factors: C or D, Surgency or Elation; E, Concentration; and G.

There is no tendency in any of the factor analyses to develop axes with high but oppositely signed variables from both Factor G and Factor A, Aggression, refuting our original assumption of a bipolar mood dimension of positive vs. negative social orientation or, more specifically, of affection vs. hostility.

Factor H, Sadness

As with Factor F, this factor undoubtedly represents only one dimension among several that might be identified within a more general aspect of mood. Its defining words are *regretful, sad,* and *sorry,* for which an appropriate label is Sadness. These are the words which appeared with greatest consistency on the original axes assigned to this factor. Other words also appeared on those same axes but with less consistency: *downhearted, insecure, blue, lonely, full of pity,* and *frustrated;* when not in Factor H, these words fell on Factors B, Anxiety, F, Fatigue, or G, Social Affection. Obviously more hypotheses are needed to deal with such aspects of mood as depression and guilt. McNair and Lorr consistently found in their analyses a factor they call depression-dejection, defined by *worthless, helpless, unhappy, discouraged, blue, lonely,* and *gloomy.* It is similar to an a priori cluster selected by Knapp and Bahnson (1963) as an index of depression. Haefner (1956) developed a useful a priori cluster as an index of guilt (*ashamed, blameworthy, conscience stricken, contrite, guilty, regretful, remorseful, repentant,* and *sorry*). The total score for this cluster varied with the vividness with which guilt-arousing material was presented in two recordings about the effects of atomic bomb blasts. Haefner did not factor analyze his data. A guilt factor has not been identified in any of the factor analytic studies, which could be due, in part, to complete rejection of many of these words by the subjects, who were tested under conditions unlike those established by Haefner's guilt-arousing communications.

In any case, our Factor H, Sadness, and the depression-dejection factor of McNair and Lorr should be regarded as separate factors until more refined hypotheses are available.

Factor I, Skepticism

When the words *skeptical, suspicious*, and *dubious* are included in the MACL, an axis usually appears in the rotated matrix with high loadings for these words and for no others. The factor is probably worth retaining for further study and refinement. What is needed is some understanding of how suspiciousness and paranoid processes contribute to temporary general dispositions such as mood.

Factor J, Egotism

Like Factor I, Factor J usually appears as an axis with relatively few highly loaded variables. In this case, the relevant variables are *egotistic, self-centered, boastful*, and, to a lesser extent, *aloof*. Further study of the factor should explore at least three problems: (1) the antecedents which dispose one toward self-involvement rather than involvement with others or with tasks; (2) the relation of changes in self-esteem to mood; and (3) pride as mood.

Factor K, Vigor or General Activation

In discussing Factor F, Fatigue, it was noted that in one of the Green-Nowlis analyses a unique axis appeared which was tentatively labelled Vigor; the variables with high loadings were *active, energetic, vigorous, bold, strong*, and *industrious*. The vigor-activity factor of McNair and Lorr (*lively, vigorous, full of pep, active*, and *carefree*) seems to combine our Factor C, Surgency, with Factor K, while that of Reimanis is bipolar: *active, full of pep, on the go*, versus *slow*. It is in Thayer's analyses that we find the best hypothesis for this factor. He consistently found, in addition to Factor F and a factor involving general deactivation, a third factor consisting of these words: *full of pep, peppy, quick, active, energetic, lively*, and *vigorous*. Thayer calls this factor general activation.

Factor N, Nonchalance or General Deactivation

In addition to that deactivational aspect of mood represented by Factor F, Fatigue, we may postulate another aspect which refers more directly to relaxation or lack of tension. Two of the 45 axes in the five Green-Nowlis analyses were tentatively identified as Factor N; variables with high loadings on both these axes were *nonchalant, leisurely*, and *bored*. When an axis assignable to Factor N did not appear in the matrix, *nonchalant* had its highest loadings on Factor C, Surgency, as did *leisurely*, except in one instance when it appeared on Factor F, Fatigue. The variable *bored* occurred three times on Factor F. Again, in the Thayer analyses we find some clarification of this factor. His general deactivation factor is defined by the words *at rest, leisurely, quiet, nonchalant,* and *placid,* providing our best current hypothesis about this possible factor.

MOOD ADJECTIVE CHECK LIST SCORES

The empirical explication of a concept involves its introduction into experimental or other research studies which search for relations between it and other better established concepts. With mood, when measured with the MACL or most other adjective lists, we have more than one concept to explicate; indeed, there must be a concept for each of the dimensions or factors included in the list. Ideally the experimentalist, in using the list, should have a specific hypothesis about how each of his independent variables or treatments will affect each of some or all of the mood factor scores or about how each mood factor score is related to certain other response variables. This has probably never been done with a multi-factorial MACL, for a variety of reasons. In the first place, the factors, as identified in factor analytic studies, have not been well enough understood either individually or as a set to permit predictions for every factor in the list or even for most of the factors. In the second place, few if any investigators have been interested in how every one of the factor scores varied as a particular independent variable or a specific treatment was introduced. What has usually happened is: (1) the investigator introduced the list simply to find out in an exploratory way which mood factor scores would change with a particular treatment; or (2) he did have a specific hypothesis about how scores on one or two factors would change but used the entire list because it is so short, or because the inclusion of words on other factors helped to conceal his research expectancies from the subject, or because he was incidentally interested in any other changes that might be occurring; for such use the investigator often increased the number of words representing the factor in which he had special interest, in an attempt to increase the reliability of his measure; or (3) the investigator combined factor scores into composite measures, such as "euphoria" or "good mood" (e.g., Surgency plus Elation plus Activation) or "dysphoria" or "bad mood" (e.g., Sadness plus Anxiety plus Aggression).

Studies of Reliability

A problem to be faced before discussing the significance of measures of mood and of mood change is that of the reliability of the measures. The MACL is designed to provide measures of mood *change;* but its reliability in measuring change depends on the reliability of its scores in measuring mood at any given time. Since we expect mood to change within brief periods, sometimes as brief as the time taken to fill out the MACL, we cannot in principle expect perfect test-retest or even within-test reliability. We are further handicapped because so little is known about mood that there are at present few if any reliable measures of mood other than those based on verbal items, thus eliminating genuinely independent estimates of the mood measured by the MACL. Nevertheless, various estimates of reliability have been made. Despite significant preexamination-postexamination differences in some mood scores, Borgatta (1961) found in his college men test-retest r's ranging from .40 (Fatigue) to .71 (Social Affection) and in women from .07 (Fatigue) to .78 (Social Affection). Nowlis and Green (1964) included ten variables a second time among the last 30 words in a 140-word MACL and found r's for individual words to range from .52 to .80. In another of their studies (Green, 1964), 51 college men reported their momentary mood at the same time daily for periods of 25 to 60 days. When, for eleven mood factors, scores on the second MACL were correlated with those on the next to last MACL, the r's ranged from .50 (Aggression) to .75 (Depression). Furthermore, when scores within each factor for days 2, 3, 5, 7, 9, 16, 29, and 30 were intercorrelated, there was a tendency for day-to-day correlations to increase with repeated use of the MACL. Thus there may be a tendency toward stereotypy of response as a person uses the MACL daily over a long period. An alternate explanation is that practice with the test improves accuracy of response. At this time we have no way to decide between these explanations but the possibility of stereotypy of response suggests that caution is needed in interpreting the results of daily administrations of the test when frequently repeated in the same situation.

Yagi and Berkun (1961), using a population of 147 enlisted personnel, made a meticulous analysis of some aspects of reliability of the original Nowlis-Green 140-word MACL and concluded that 62% of the reports would have to be eliminated because of: (1) inconsistency in checking antonyms; (2) inconsistency in checking words on a factor (activation-deactivation) believed at that time to be bipolar; and (3) inconsistency in checking ten words repeated within the long list. Since we later found that none of these mood factors is clearly bipolar, their antonym approach cannot now be considered fully justified. Nevertheless, their conclusion that the long 140-word list needs some major modifications to be applicable to enlisted personnel is most reasonable. We should like to see the study repeated with the shorter and better standardized lists that are now available. In the Nowlis-Green studies (1964) one set of data was obtained from 167 enlisted naval personnel for a 40-word MACL. No estimates of reliability were computed but a factor analysis yielded eight factors, six of which corresponded closely to six of the basic MACL factors found for college subjects; the other two approximated two other factors secured from college data.

McNair and Lorr (1964) used instructions for their POMS list which requested judgments about typical mood during the preceding week and found test-retest r's in neurotic patients that ranged from .61 to .69

in their five factor scores, with K-R 20 estimates of internal consistency ranging from .80 to .91.

We do not know of studies which have secured estimates of the reliability of change, difference, or incremental scores derived from two administrations of the MACL, such as before and after a treatment (e.g., drug, motion picture, experimental stress) administered to change mood. Data for making such estimates are abundantly available. With respect to within-test reliability of change scores, the data shown in Table 5 for six different mood treatments show that there is a high degree of consistency in direction of change for the variables within any one factor. A difficulty which will be encountered in estimating the test-retest reliability of incremental scores stems from the fact that a second administration of a mood-inducing treatment may have weaker effects than the first administration. While this adaptation phenomenon may not be found with certain drugs, or with certain kinds of stress, it does occur with at least some motion picture films. Pomeranz (1962) presented a short anxiety-inducing film to 63 college men twice in the same long experimental session. The two presentations of the film were separated by a short period in which Ss filled out various rating scales. When compared with the initial MACL scores, scores after the first presentation of the stress film were significantly higher for Anxiety, Startle and Concentration but scores on these factors after the second presentation were actually lower than on the initial MACL, but not significantly so. As for the factors showing significant decrease in scores after the first presentation of the film (Surgency, Pleasantness, Egotism, Fatigue, Aggression, Skepticism, and Social Affection), all but the last two showed a smaller decrease after the second presentation.

The MACL and Social Desirability

In interpreting reliability estimates it is necessary to take into account the validity of the measures. In the present instance, we may ask, for example, whether our measures of mood factors are simply indirect measures of a concept already known to be measurable with a high degree of reliability, that of social desirability. It is obvious that different aspects of mood have different degrees of attractiveness. Some moods are highly valued, others are despised. The former are sought, the latter avoided; for various social reasons, one may pretend to be in a good mood, or not to be in a bad mood. Green (1964) has found that the ten factors of a 39-word MACL were widely and bimodally distributed with respect to social desirability. A total of 51 college men and 87 college women rated each of the 39 adjective on a seven-point social desirability scale from very desirable (7) to very undesirable (1). Results, as shown in Table 4, show great consistency between the male and female ratings, with four (Social Affection, Concentration, Pleasantness or Elation, and Surgency) averaging well above the null point (4) and six below that point (Depression, Anxiety, Fatigue, Skepticism, Aggression, and Egotism).

Table 4 Social desirability of 10 Mood Factors

Factor	Males	Females
Social affection (G)	6.0	6.3
Concentration (E)	5.9	6.0
Pleasantness (D)	5.3	5.5
Surgency (C)	5.1	5.3
Depression (H)	3.0	3.0
Anxiety (B)	2.5	2.4
Fatigue (F)	2.5	2.6
Skepticism (I)	2.4	2.4
Aggression (A)	2.2	2.0
Egotism (J)	2.0	2.0

When the subjects were asked to fill out the MACL according to the usual "right now I feel ————" instructions, their individual adjective scores were independent of or even negatively correlated with their ratings of the adjectives for social desirability. They were also asked to take the MACL according to (1) instructions asking how they typically felt, and (2) instructions to report a mood which would make the best possible impression on others. With the "typical mood" set, 6 of the 39 individual variables for men and 8 for women correlated with social desirability ratings, with a maximum r of .35. With the "best impression" instructions, maximum r was .50 but there were still only ten significant correlations with social desirability ratings for men and seven for women. It appears, then, that the social desirability status of a word has very little, if any, effect on how it is checked when the subject is asked to report how he feels at the moment he reads each word. This independence is based, in part, on the aforementioned fact that the individual in reporting a momentary feeling can be expected to be less involved with standards of social desirability than when he reports more enduring personal phenomena. Another reason for this independence is noted by Lazarus et al. (1962) in a passage we reproduce later in this chapter.

The MACL and Mood Change

Mood adjective check lists were used to measure mood change before analytically identified factors were available. At Rochester, a long check list was used to secure repeated reports of mood during long sessions in which administration of a drug or placebo was the main experimental treatment, Harway et al. (1953), H. H. Nowlis et al. (1953). Each drug was evaluated with respect to the individual words in the list which changed most consistently after the drug was ingested. It was sometimes possible to find a cluster of words which most clearly represented the reported mood effects of a particular drug. But with some drugs a change in the social situation produced marked changes in the adjectives showing the greatest response to the drug (Nowlis & Nowlis, 1956), a result consistent with the later findings of Schachter and Singer (1962) and others. Wendt and his colleagues (1961, 1962; Cameron & Wendt, 1964) have continued to develop a number of clusters of carefully chosen adjectives which detect the effects of specific drugs in a variety of settings with the greatest possible consistency.

When a sufficiently large number of subjects had been used, the early Rochester work did include several cluster analyses based on correlations found among the adjectives when the list was administered under non-drug conditions. Two studies at Rochester by Laties (1961) and by Haefner (1956) and one by Spence (1957) used these empirical clusters in the study of mood change. Using a 145-word list, Laties limited his measures to four clusters involving 57 adjectives: friendliness (vs. hostile aggression), elation (vs. depression), task involvement, and social initiative. Scores were significantly lower after sleep deprivation on friendliness and on social initiative; when the sleep-deprived subjects were given a combination of secobarbital sodium and amphetamine sulphate, scores on all clusters except elation increased. In a study to determine whether the Janis-Feshbach (1953) hypothesis relating attitude change to level of induced fear could be extended to level of guilt, Haefner made use of a 135-word list. He limited his measures to two of the Rochester empirical clusters (hostility and depression) plus three other clusters (guilt, fear, and general excitement), each of which was composed of adjectives "judged by clinical psychologists to be relevant to that form of emotional arousal" (1956, p. 29). Each of five different groups of 67 male college students heard a taped commentary on the effects of atomic bombs; the commentaries were designed to induce two levels of fear and two levels of guilt, effects which were successfully achieved as indicated by differential scores on the several clusters. Haefner also found, as might be expected, that each communication designed to produce a specific mood effect, such as increase in fear or guilt, also produced changes on other mood factors.

A third study using an early 145-word form of the MACL was reported by Spence (1957) who subjected five adult men and 17 adult women to failure stimulation with an anagram task. Immediately after the failure experience each subject was asked to check (one option only) those words which best describe his mood. They again filled out the check list after the experiment had been explained to them. Spence established a measure of anxiety (Anxiety Ratio) by dividing the number of words checked in a cluster of ten anxiety words by the total number of words checked in the entire list; similarly, an Elation Ratio was based on the relative number of elation words checked. Spence was not interested in how these ratios changed with failure but in how individual scores on the Anxiety and Elation Ratios after failure correlated with indices of a subject's performance on a task involving perceptual vigilance and defense. Scores on the Anxiety Ratio were found to correlate significantly with the difference between recognition thresholds for failure and control words.

A major purpose of the Nowlis and Green study (1964) was to determine whether the scores on the words found to define a factor in factor analytic studies would move coherently in the same direction when various mood treatments were presented to a large audience. Six different treatments were given to a large group of male college students who came to an auditorium on six successive Monday evenings. The 140-word list was administered before and after each experimental treatment. The number attending a session ranged from 425 to 473. On the first night we presented a documentary film, *The Face of Lincoln,* in which a a teacher-sculptor portrayed in clay the changes in the face of Lincoln during his years as president; the film ended with a moving tribute to Lincoln and his contemporary status among the peoples of the world. The second session was an aggressive hoax, in which the men were confronted with three tediously long questionnaires. After the second questionnaire had been completed we announced that with regret we had to keep them in the auditorium long beyond the expected time of dismissal, but that we wished to get a second report of mood at this time. They were, as a matter of fact, dismissed after completing this MACL and given a true explanation of our procedure that night. The hoax was successful in producing many kinds of hostile expressions. In the third session, a classic film comedy, Harold Lloyd's *The Freshman,* was shown. A documentary on the Nuremberg trials was shown on the fourth evening and a color film of a major surgical operation on the fifth. In the sixth session we held a contest, for cash prizes, for the best recall of information presented in a film about a boat trip down the Colorado through the Grand Canyon. Since we were not concerned in this study with relating the specific mood effects to special features of these films and treatments, we did not attempt to control audience reactions during the sessions but did demand silence during the checking of each list. In Table 5 the 49 variables, grouped by factor, are presented; they are the variables most consistently associated with specific factors through five factor analyses.

The post-minus-pre difference score for each variable is given for each of the six experimental treatments. In general, values equal to or greater than 0.10 are significantly different from zero in this population. Of the 294 (6 x 49) difference scores only 17 show inconsistency with other scores for variables in the same factor. All but three of these deviant scores are below the value of 0.10 and occur typically but not always when the other variables in the factor were also relatively small in size. The three most important deviations (*boastful* +.18 in session #3, *affectionate* −.15 in session #1, and *jittery* −.18 in session #2) can be partly understood as special effects due to the fact that some words take on different meanings in different contexts; but they also suggest that better sets of variables can be developed for each factor.

Since the first Nowlis-Green factor analysis appeared as an ONR Technical Report in 1957, various investigators have used these factors on later definitions of them in studies of mood change. In a study extending the Janis-Feshbach hypothesis to level of hostility, Alexander (1957) prepared three communications about governmental practices in the Union of South Africa. Although each was designed to produce a different level of hostility, only two different levels were achieved, both of which were significantly higher than that of the control group. He used variables defining the factors of Aggression, Anxiety, Pleasantness (a composite of our present Surgency and Elation), Activation-Deactivation (then thought to be bipolar), Social Affection, Depression, and Egotism. To these he added a cluster of seven words which have or would have high intensity ratings on the Buss scale for hostile words (Buss, 1961, p. 121). Scores

Table 5 Difference scores for individual variables in 12 factors in 6 different experimental sessions

Factor	One: Lincoln	Two: Hoax	Three: Comedy	Four: Nuremberg	Five: Operation	Six: Contest
A, Aggression						
defiant	-.06	.34	.02	.78	-.11	.08
rebellious	-.14	.30	.08	.69	-.11	.01
angry	-.03	.41	-.13	1.56	.00	.08
grouchy	-.24	.44	-.29	.25	-.12	.15
annoyed	-.06	.61	-.38	1.06	.03	.10
fed up	-.23	.41	-.33	.68	-.14	-.01
(Mean)	(-.13)	(.42)	(-.17)	(.84)	(-.08)	(.07)
B, Anxiety						
clutched up	-.16	.00	-.05	.48	.29	.13
fearful	.01	.02	-.01	.74	.26	.14
jittery	-.15	-.18	.04	.40	.32	.05
(Mean)	(-.10)	(-.05)	(-.01)	(.54)	(.29)	(.11)
C, Surgency						
carefree	-.37	-.10	.59	-.99	-.62	-.36
playful	-.45	-.18	.73	-1.06	-.60	-.43
witty	-.44	-.22	.38	-.94	-.62	-.42
lively	-.19	-.26	.64	-.73	-.12	-.30
talkative	-.25	-.02	.34	-.68	-.22	-.40
(Mean)	(-.34)	(-.16)	(.54)	(-.88)	(-.44)	(-.38)
D, Elation						
elated	.00	-.24	.74	-.78	-.32	-.23
overjoyed	.06	-.21	.95	-.61	-.29	-.18
pleased	.09	-.47	.84	-1.15	-.36	-.16
refreshed	-.03	-.40	.64	-.78	-.31	-.27
(Mean)	(.03)	(-.33)	(.79)	(-.83)	(-.32)	(-.21)
E, Concentration						
concentrating	.05	-.29	-.30	.45	.30	.15
engaged in thought	.20	-.21	-.43	.90	.44	.24
intent	-.01	-.24	-.10	.35	.22	.00

Table 5 Cont'd

Factor	One: Lincoln	Two: Hoax	Three: Comedy	Four: Nuremberg	Five: Operation	Six: Contest
attentive	.00	-.31	-.04	.39	.30	.06
earnest	.07	-.34	-.25	.24	.12	.04
serious	.19	-.26	-.80	.82	.49	.18
contemplative	.36	-.22	-.48	.68	.41	.13
introspective	.05	-.11	-.29	.28	.20	.01
(Mean)	(.11)	(-.21)	(-.30)	(.46)	(.27)	(.08)
F, Fatigue						
drowsy	.03	.24	-.29	-.11	-.08	.33
dull	-.11	.24	-.24	-.06	-.11	.14
sluggish	-.05	.23	-.24	-.04	-.08	.24
tired	-.08	.34	-.30	-.01	-.10	.26
(Mean)	(-.05)	(.26)	(-.27)	(-.06)	(-.09)	(.24)
G, Social affection						
affectionate	-.15	-.23	.16	-.61	-.23	-.20
forgiving	.01	-.23	-.08	-.60	-.05	-.24
kindly	.05	-.39	.20	-.70	-.09	-.20
warmhearted	.11	-.39	.31	-.74	-.22	-.26
(Mean)	(.00)	(-.31)	(.15)	(-.66)	(-.15)	(-.23)
H, Sadness						
regretful	.22	.22	-.18	1.17	.09	.14
sad	.29	.08	-.22	1.28	.13	.05
sorry	.21	-.01	-.08	1.24	.14	.06
(Mean)	(.24)	(.10)	(-.16)	(1.23)	(.12)	(.08)
I, Skepticism						
dubious	-.37	-.02	-.26	.23	-.07	.13
skeptical	-.40	.07	-.35	.19	.02	.12
suspicious	-.22	.10	-.18	.47	.01	.11
(Mean)	(-.33)	(.05)	(-.29)	(.30)	(-.01)	(.12)
J, Egotism						
egotistic	-.36	-.02	-.05	-.34	-.20	-.03
self-centered	-.23	-.01	-.14	-.27	-.15	-.02
aloof	-.11	-.61	-.13	-.20	-.18	-.08
boastful	-.22	-.01	.18	-.36	-.18	-.15
(Mean)	(-.23)	(-.16)	(-.04)	(-.29)	(-.18)	(-.07)
K, Vigor (?)						
active	-.31	-.26	.37	-.23	-.19	-.05
energetic	-.11	-.33	.41	-.24	-.22	-.28
vigorous	-.18	-.21	.39	-.18	-.14	-.12
(Mean)	(-.20)	(-.27)	(.39)	(-.22)	(-.18)	(-.15)
N, Nonchalance						
nonchalant	-.26	-.34	-.12	-.97	-.53	-.30
leisurely	-.47	-.24	-.15	-.94	-.60	-.30
(Mean)	(-.37)	(-.29)	(-.14)	(-.96)	(-.57)	(-.30)

on all mood factors except Anxiety, Concentration, and Egotism showed significant changes following the experimental communications.

In a study which examined the effect of mood change on the structure of attitudes toward consumer items, Axelrod (1963) used the same MACL factors that Alexander did but did not include the extra hostility cluster. He showed Harold Lloyd's *The Freshman* to one large audience of college women and the documentary on the Nuremberg Trials to another. Significant changes in all mood factor scores except Concentration were produced by the documentary but, unlike the male audience tested eariler, the women were not particularly moved by *The Freshman;* the only significant changes were decreases in Concentration and Depression.

C. A. Levison (1963) used the MACL in a study of the effect of mood change on social perception. Her mood factors were Aggression, Anxiety, Pleasantness, Concentration, Fatigue, Social Affection, Depression and Egotism. She presented Luis Bunuel's *Los Olvidados,* a film about poor young people in Mexico City, to 357 male college students. It produced significant changes in all mood factor scores except that for Egotism; these changes were all increases except in the case of Social Affection and Pleasantness. Levison departed from the usual four options given for each word; a seven-point graphic rating scale, anchored by the word "very" and the phrase "not at all," was presented for each adjective. This method retains most of the advantages of the four-option method. We know of no study comparing the effectiveness of the two methods.

Another study utilizing a motion picture film to induce mood change was reported by Miller (1960), who was interested in the effect of mood change on subjective estimates of the desirability and probability of uncertain future events. Here a successful effort was made to induce a happy mood by showing an audience of 186 male college students a 45-minute excerpt from the film *One Summer of Happiness.* Significant increases were found in Pleasantness, Activation, Social Affection, Nonchalance, Egotism, Startle, and Aggression together with significant decreases in Skepticism, Deactivation, Concentration, and Anxiety. Only the mean difference score for Depression was not significantly different from zero. As in C. A. Levison's study a seven-point rating scale was used for each adjective.

In the process of validating an objectively scorable apperception test of aggression, rejection, insecurity and dependency, Stricker (1960, 1962a, 1962b) presented a 27-minute film (*The Crooked Road*) which had been prepared for the Hitchcock television series and which, in a preview, had successfully had the specific effect of increasing hostility. When shown to his experimental group of 47 college students, none of whom had seen the film before, the film produced very large and significant increases for all eight words in his Aggression cluster. There was also a significant decrease in Nonchalance and in Social Affection. The 55 students who viewed an animated film (*A Short Vision*) on the effects of the atomic bomb, which was selected to increase anxiety, did not show any consistent change in mood. Those viewing a film (*From Darkness into*

Light) selected as a neutral treatment showed significant decreases on Activation and Nonchalance and no significant changes on other factor scores. Stricker has also published an interesting description (1962b) of a method for assessing difference scores. For each variable, he first uses a one-tailed binomial test to assess the significance of the proportion of subjects showing any change from prescore to postscore. For each variable which passes that test, he then uses a two-tailed sign test to assess the significance of the direction of change.

In studying the relation of the repression-sensitization dimension to reactions to stress, Pomeranz (1962) showed a 12½ minute film in color which portrayed a surgical operation on the frontal sinus, a film previously used by Alexander and Husek (1962) in standardizing their Anxiety Differential. As noted earlier, its first presentation produced very large and significant increases in scores on Anxiety as well as smaller but significant increases on Concentration and on a startle cluster, together with significant decreases on Surgency, Egotism, Pleasantness, Deactivation, Skepticism, Social Affection, and Aggression.

The studies reported above using films were done at Rochester. At the Clinical Center of the National Institutes of Health, Handlon used a modification of the MACL; subjects were asked at the end of each day to "give their impression of their general mood for the day in comparison with the previous few days." (1962, p. 159). During their first three weeks of living as paid volunteers in the research hospital, these young male and female adults showed a decrease on three dysphoric dimensions (Anxiety, Depression, Aggression) and an increase on three euphoric dimensions (Pleasantness, Social Affection, Activation). Mean urinary 17-hydroxy-corticosteroid level on the same subjects also decreased. Subjects with a high 17-OH-CS output showed a different sequence of mood changes over the initial period than did those with a low output, the latter having larger euphoric scores after the first week than the former. When subjects were shown "arousing films" (*Ox Bow Incident, High Noon,* and *A Walk in the Sun*), elevations were found in plasma 17-OH-CS levels and in factor scores on Aggression, Depression, and Anxiety. Films such as the Disney nature studies, chosen to be "bland," led to lower scores on these same mood factors and, unexpectedly, to lower 17-OH-CS levels.

The most interesting and thorough research on films and mood has been reported by Lazarus and his colleagues (1962, 1964), including Speisman (1964). As part of a long-range study of psychological stress, these investigators showed a stressor film (*Subincision*) to 35 college men and 35 college women individually. In another session each subject saw a bland control film (*Corn Farming in Iowa*). During each session, various measures of skin resistance and heart rate were made; at the end of a session, the subject completed a 96-word version of the MACL and in an interview wrote as long as he wished in reply to three questions about the film. Eight factor scores (Aggression, Anxiety, Concentration, Depression, Egotism, Activation, a reciprocal of Pleasantness and a reciprocal of Social Affection, labelled Unpleasantness and Social Unaffection, respectively) were obtained from the MACL; a large number of measures were also obtained from the written interview. The eighteen scales of the California Personality Inventory and four scales based on the Minnesota Multiphasic Personality Inventory were also scored for each subject. The stressor film, in contrast to the control film, produced larger scores on all mood factors; in decreasing order of size, these were Anxiety, Unpleasantness, Social Unaffection, Aggression, Depression, Activation, Egotism, and Concentration. The authors suggest that the five factors yielding the largest difference scores are more relevant to affect and emotion than are the three other factors. Whereas the various measures of autonomic reactivity and of the interview behavior also changed significantly with the stressor film, the correlations among the variables in all three sets of measures were extremely small. A major finding was the fact that the subjects scoring high on three CPI variables (Capacity for Status, Self-Acceptance, Communality) and on the MMPI hysterical denial subscale showed different patterns of response to stress when autonomic reactivity measures were compared with mood measures; these subjects, under the stressor film condition, had lower levels of autonomic reactivity than did others, but it was they who showed the largest increases in mood scores.

The following interpretation by these authors throws light on the relation of the MACL scores both to personality characteristics and to the social desirability set:

"The personality variables which do provide significant interactions on the Nowlis response dimensions (Cs, Sa, Hyden, and Cm) indicate self-confidence, verbal skill, an interpersonal orientation and dependability and honesty. The people involved are not only equipped to respond sensitively to an instrument like the Nowlis due to their verbal-communicative skill, but also feel constrained (due to salient traits of responsibility and honesty) to report verbally their negative reaction to those aspects of the stressor film which may be interpreted as socially unwholesome or morbid. Thus, they are also compelled to reflect their feelings on the Nowlis whereas there is no voluntary control over responses of the autonomic nervous system. Further, the qualities of honesty and responsible social action would argue against the alternative interpretation which would attribute the Nowlis response to an insincere and exploitive desire to impress the experimenter. It seems more likely that any wish to achieve a socially desirable impression in this group is obviated by the need to act responsibly on the self-report instrument. Thus, the apparent contradiction of the Nowlis and the autonomic findings seems to be a genuine difference between competing physiological and self-report systems of response and expression" (Lazarus et al., 1962, pp. 24-25).

In their two 1964 reports, the Lazarus group studied the effects of experimental alteration of cognitive appraisal on response to threat in groups of subjects identified by occupation (undergraduate students vs.

airline executives) and by strength of disposition to deny threat as measured by MMPI scales. Cognitive appraisal is altered by changing the Incision film's sound track in one study and by an introductory, prefilm statement in the other. MACL scores for Pleasantness, Depression, Social Affection, Egotism, Aggression, and Activation showed significant main effects with the sound track method and those for Pleasantness, Depression, and Concentration with the introductory statement method.

Robbins (1962) used a modified MACL with college students to measure the effects of different lengths of exposure to a fear-arousing taped communication. He added two extra clusters, one as an additional index of anxiety (*alarmed, anxious, apprehensive, concerned, disturbed, insecure, shook-up, tense, troubled, uneasy*), the other as an additional index of aggression (*angry, insulted, provoked,* etc.). Both sets of anxiety words yielded higher scores with increasing length of exposure. In the women, scores on Concentration tended to increase with length of exposure. In both groups, scores on the additional aggression cluster increased with length of exposure.

Length of stay in a novel environment has been used as an independent variable in mood studies. Handlon's study (1962) of the effects of films and of length of stay as a subject in a research hospital has already been discussed. Bass (1962) administered a 27-word, 11-factor MACL five times to a group of 30 supervisors, engineers and administrators during a ten-day sensitivity training laboratory for management. Over the ten-day period there were significant decreases in Anxiety and Skepticism. On the Sunday evening following a week-end holiday there was a significant increase in Depression accompanied by significant decreases in Concentration and Activation. At the completion of a long intergroup competition, differential effects were found for winners and losers: Concentration, winners −.01, losers +.35; Aggression, winners −.05, losers +.40; Depression, winners −.16, losers +.82; Pleasantness, winners +.40, losers −1.20; Skepticism, winners −.67, losers −.10. Sensory deprivation studies by P. K. Levison and by Murphy included use of the MACL. Levison (1959) divided a sample of 60 young men into three groups: a control group and two groups kept in an isolation chamber for 175 minutes and 280 minutes, respectively. The MACL was administered twice before and twice during isolation. To the words in the eleven mood factors Levison added a set of eight adjectives which seemed to represent some of the effects of isolation as described in previous studies: *agitated, restless, tense, confused, strange, dazed, bored,* and *miserable.* Since factor analysis of the entire list showed that these words did not fall on one axis, only individual scores on these eight words were considered. Five of them showed significant increases with length of isolation: *agitated, restless, dazed, bored,* and *miserable.* Of the mood factor scores, only Fatigue showed similar increases with length of isolation. Toward the end of each session the subject was reinforced by a series of scenic color slides during a 15-minute period of operant conditioning. This period produced significant decreases in Aggression, Fatigue, and

Depression in either the long or short group or both, together with decrease in the scores on the individual variables *restless, tense, dazed, bored,* and *miserable.* Murphy (1964) used a short MACL augmented with the eight Levison isolation words for subjects isolated for two hours. Only subjects classified as field independent on the Jackson Imbedded Figures Test showed significant increases on the set of isolation adjectives, although field dependent subjects in a postsession interview admitted to as much upset as did the field independent subjects.

Weiner and Ader (1965) used the MACL in a free operant avoidance conditioning situation in which the subject, by pressing a button, could delay for a fixed interval a shock administered at regular intervals. The subjects were medical or graduate school students who were paid volunteers. The MACL was administered at the beginning and end of two sessions; in the first session the subject was told about the experimental procedure and given the Rosenzweig Picture-Frustration Study and the Rod and Frame Test; the conditioning with shock occurred in the second session, and was followed by a postconditioning interview. Thirteen subjects learned to avoid the shock, the criterion of learning being a five minute period in which he avoided 80% or more of the scheduled shocks. Eleven subjects failed to learn; ten of these sat for one hour receiving shocks and did not press the button. Learners and nonlearners did not differ in the degree to which they expressed aggression in the postconditioning interview or in the increase in MACL Aggression during the conditioning session, but an important, unexpected finding was that ten of the 13 who learned in the conditioning session had shown either an increase or no change in MACL Aggression during the first preconditioning session, but none of the 11 nonlearners had shown an increase during that first session, with eight showing a decrease. Moreover, on the Picture-Frustraion measure the learners tended to externalize blame in a frustrating situation (Extrapunitive) while the nonlearners tended to deny the existence either of blame or of frustration (Impunitive). The authors conclude that individuals who typically express their anger are more likely to achieve in a learning situation than are those who deny either their anger or the experiences which provoke it.

In his study of activation-deactivation, Thayer (1963) used an augmented MACL to measure mood in four different activation-relevant situations: before going to sleep, at the beginning of a regular academic class, at the beginning of an examination, and after a period of performing mathematical problems interrupted several times by a loud buzzer. Mood factor scores which best discriminated among these situations were: Nonchalance, Fatigue, Vigor, Anxiety, and Concentration.

Various check lists have been used in the study of drug effects by Wendt and his colleagues (1961, 1962), Beecher (1959), Clyde (1960), and many others. We know of no drug study which has used the factor scores now available for the MACL but are now writing to the many investigators in psychopharmacology and other research areas who have requested information about and copies of the MACL.

MOOD AND PERSONALITY

Mood enters into the psychological analysis of personality in a variety of ways. Traditionally the bridge concept between these two terms is that of temperament, since temperament is defined as "the susceptibility of a person to emotional situations; the tendency to experience changes in mood" (English & English, 1958, p. 545). The test items in various standardized tests of temperament include references to all kinds of situations in which the behavioral and affective responses varying together in mood are aroused. Commonly implicit but rarely explicit in psychological literature is the assumption that dispositions may be ordered into a hierachy, Broad (1933), Nowlis (1959). As example, emotions, in contrast to emotional responses, are identified as first-order dispositions by Skinner (1953) and others. According to this scheme, mood is then considered a second-order disposition and temperament a third-order disposition. Emotion, as first-order disposition, is recurrent and of briefest duration; mood, as second-order disposition, is also recurrent, but of longer duration, while temperament is a more nearly permanent disposition. In general, the occurrence of a temporary lower order disposition depends in part on the current status of relevant higher order dispositions. The logical rules for handling hierarchical disposition terms have not yet been worked out (Berg, 1955). It is clear, however, that an adequate analysis of the interrelations among temperament, mood, and emotion will probably require some reference to a hierarchy of dispositional concepts.

Empirical studies of the relation of mood to various temperament and personality scales have used single as well as multiple samples of mood state. Green and Nowlis (Green, 1964), in the 60-day, 51-man study referred to earlier, secured daily MACL reports and, in one long terminal testing session, administered the Cattell 16PF Test, the MMPI, and the three inventories which test 13 of the Guilford temperament factors. In this session, the subjects also completed an MACL before starting each new test and were free to leave the room for as long as they wished between tests. Mean daily mood scores, with their standard deviations, were computed for each subject for the eleven mood factors retained in our present MACL plus a tentative small factor, startle. These eleven mean daily mood scores, the standard deviations for nine of the better factors, the eleven factor scores on the second MACL in the series, and the eleven factor scores on the next to last MACL in the terminal session were correlated with the 45 subtests of the five personality and temperament inventories. A total of 326 (17%) of the 1890 r's were significant. Contrary to our expectation, scores from a single MACL, whether given early in the 60-day series or on the day of personality testing, develop more correlations with the 45 subtests than do the mean scores for daily tests taken during the entire series. As shown in Table 6, the next to last MACL scores had the highest proportion of significant r's (21%) and the mean daily scores the lowest (14%). Standard deviations of the daily scores, however, yielded 73 (18%) significant r's with the personality and temperament scales. The MMPI subtests, which are not independent of each other, had the highest percentage (22%) of significant r's with various mood scores, while the Cattell 16PF subtests had the lowest (11%).

Table 6 Percentage of significant correlations between Mood Factor scores and 45 subtests of the MMPI, Cattell 16 PF test, and three Guilford inventories

	MMPI	Cattell	Guilford	Total
2nd MACL	25	10	13	16
Next to last MACL	23	15	25	21
Mean daily MACL	20	09	15	14
Standard deviation of daily MACL	20	10	25	18
Total	22	11	19	17

Two mood factors, Anxiety (B) and Sadness (H), accounted for almost half (138 or 42%) of the significant r's. Of the 360 r's between scores for these two factors and the 45 subtests, 38% were significant, a result based primarily on the fact that for the 16 MMPI scales and the 13 Guilford scales 57% and 45%, respectively, of the r's with A and H were significant. All but two of the MMPI scales (R and Ma) and all but four of the Guilford scales developed at least one significant r with either an Anxiety or Sadness mood factor score or with both. Greater specificity is found in the rest of the matrix, where about 12% of the correlations between mood scores and temperament or personality subtests are significant. Most of these correlations involve Pleasantness (approximately equivalent to our present Factor D, Elation), Surgency (C), Activation (K), and Skepticism (I); however, all of the mood factor scores, whether from a single administration, a daily mean, or a standard deviation of daily scores, develop high correlations with a number of personality and temperament subtest scores. Many of these appear where one would expect them, like MACL Surgency with Cattell Surgency, but there are intriguing surprises, like MACL Aggression with the MMPI F (Faking) scale, and a number of low correlations which one would expect to be high.

Borgatta (1961) administered an early 40-word version of the MACL to a large sample of college students, male and female, both before and after 2½ hours of "somewhat stressful work completing personality, intelligence and attitude questionnaires." Six mood factor change scores were correlated with scores on a variety of personality tests and with scores obtained through peer ratings and observation of social interaction in five-person discussion groups. Whereas the number of significant correlations between the mood scores and the ratings and observational scores obtained in the later discussion groups did not significantly exceed the number expected by chance, there were a great many correlations between mood scores and the scores on personality subtests. One of

Borgatta's mood factors, Lonely, was made up of four words: *lonely, insecure, frustrated,* and *fearful,* a cluster of words we would now interpret to represent both Factor B, Anxiety, and Factor H, Sadness. These two factors accounted for 42% of the significant correlations in the Green and Nowlis study just described. Similarly, Borgatta's Lonely factor yielded the greatest number (25) of significant correlations with the 48 subtests provided by the Guilford-Zimmerman, Cattell, Edwards, and Thurstone inventories. Both studies utilized the first two inventories and show substantial overlap in the specific subtests which correlate with this aspect of mood. Our conclusion after examining both matrices is that an adequate study of mood and temperament first requires the development of specific hypotheses linking each mood factor to specified personality and temperament dimensions. The present exploratory studies, with their unexpected but limited finding that scores derived from a single MACL, especially when given during the testing session, predict many temperament and personality subtest scores as well as the means of a series of daily MACL's, suggest that whatever the two kinds of test (MACL and personality inventory) have in common may be partly due to artifacts of test design and may initially obscure rather than clarify the problems of finding significant functional relationships between mood and temperament or personality. With our present resources, daily administration of the MACL can be expected to help in this clarification only when both daily and within-day variations in mood together with average daily mood scores are put into the analysis. Such a study might well utilize as a model the multivariate methods of Cattell (1960) who in defining anxiety as a mood state presents an empirical factor which includes introspective, questionnaire items, objective test variables, and physiological variables, designed for both P and R technique.

Korchin and Heath (1961) report a very interesting study of correlates of scores on the Mandler Autonomic Perception Questionnaire (APQ), a test which elicits reports of experiences of alteration in somatic functioning or "autonomic feedback." Through use of our original 140-item MACL (in which, however, they instructed subjects to describe how they generally felt rather than how they felt at the moment of checking the word) they found that male and female college students with high scores on the APQ also had high scores on the Anxiety and Depression factors of the MACL. Among men, high scorers on the APQ also rated themselves high on MACL Deactivation, but high-scoring women tended to rate themselves higher on *both* Activation and Deactivation. This finding led the investigators to examine the individual adjectives in the entire list in order to find those which most significantly differentiate high, median, and low APQ scorers. The high-scoring men more frequently checked such mood adjectives as *helpless, inactive, ashamed, washed-out, grouchy,* and (*not*) *wide-awake,* (*not*) *independent,* (*not*) *effective;* they present a picture of depression and futility and are defeated rather than angry. By contrast, the high scoring women more frequently checked *jittery, doubtful, shocked, insecure, full of pity, sleepy,*

belligerent, lonely, downhearted, regretful, overjoyed, and (*not*) *calm,*
thus presenting again a picture of inadequacy but now accompanied by
stronger and more labile affective responses.

The most important work on mood and personality has been done by
Wessman and Ricks (1959, 1961, 1965) and Wessman, Ricks, & Tyl
(1960). They studied the temporal co-variation of affective states in 21
Radcliffe students, who remained anonymous to the researchers, and,
a year later, in 17 Harvard students who were participating in a three-
year personality assessment program and for whom a great variety of
test and clinical information was available. Each subject filled out daily
for six weeks a set of bipolar self-rating scales dealing with various
aspects of affective experience, including some dimensions of mood
similar to those of the MACL. Since the first study led to some revision
of the scales, 51 daily measures were obtained from each male subject
and somewhat fewer for each Radcliffe student. Each of the subject's
measures over the six-week period was correlated with all of his other
measures. From six to eight factors were then extracted from each individual correlation matrix by the Thurstone complete centroid method.
The first factor was then rotated through the mean daily average score
for elation-depression and the other factors were rotated to an orthogonal
approximation of simple structure. For all subjects the first rotated factor
had two or more mood scales among its highest loadings. Typically, these
were the scales based on fullness of life, receptivity towards the environment and sociability, as well as the marker variable of elation. Other
aspects of mood, such as energy, anger, anxiety, and love, were highly
loaded on this first factor for some subjects but more often were highly
loaded on other, orthogonal factors. Two measures of mood variability,
namely, day-to-day variability and mean daily range, intercorrelated
significantly; unlike the Nowlis-Green findings, mood variability was not
related to average daily mood level.

On the basis of mean scores and variability estimates, Wessman and
Ricks divide their male subjects into the happy and unhappy and into
the stable and variable and find various personality characteristics for
each group. One of their conclusions is that personality must be measured
through time and that repeated affective measurements provide an important part of such study. Their recently completed book-length manuscript (1965) presents these findings in rich detail and also provides the
best existing review of the literature pertaining to the interrelations of
personality, mood, and affect.

CONCLUDING REMARKS

In this chapter we have found that a variety of mood scores can be
derived from the MACL and other lists of mood adjectives. Such scores
may be based on sets of words identified through factor analysis, cluster
analysis, or on the basis of a priori considerations. We have also found
that such scores correlate with many personality, situational, physiological,
and response variables, particularly when the instructions require the

subject to check each word according to how closely it applies to his feelings at the moment he reads it. Because of this abundance of empirical relationships and because of the ease and brevity of its administration, the MACL in its present form is an excellent monitoring device in experiments involving other indices of affect, emotion, mood, and response to stress. As monitor, it provides an additional informational output with minimal interference with the major phenomena specifically under study. The MACL is also useful in exploratory studies of various kinds. I cannot, however, recommend that it be used as the primary or sole index of the dependent variable or variables in a study. The three or more words which make up each MACL factor provide a crude test of only one component of all that varies in mood, a component which may be said frequently to be trivial both practically and theoretically. Yet, like changes in atmospheric pressure in the prediction of weather, that which is trivial in one way may incidentally be tied in with so many other co-varying phenomena that it can be put to important but limited use.

We had originally thought of the main dimensions of mood as different aspects of the most general orientations and functional systems of the person. But we also recognized that identifiable mood factors might also represent complex behavioral systems which temporarily become strengthened or weakened as fundamental orientations and functions change. The mood factors actually identified in our analyses and in those by others do seem to represent behavioral systems; indeed, some of these systems, like anxiety, aggression, activation, and depression, have for some period been under effective investigation by researchers with no interest at all in mood but rather in the many more interesting and salient determinants of the system. The question of what the relative contribution of mood is to the occurrence of such behavior at any moment has yet to be formulated in a researchable way. I have presented each factor empirically identified in MACL studies as an hypothesis, subject to further refinement and testing. It is of interest to note that some of these factors refer to behavioral systems which have not received much attention. As example, the large and important Factor E, Concentration, suggests a number of intriguing questions for investigation. Like aggression or anxiety, it is certainly the object of various socialization practices in many cultures. It is highly valued for both personal and social reasons, but at certain moments in the person's day or night may be eschewed. It is the least intrinsically affective mood factor and yet is frequently attended by much affect. Patterns of concentration or involvement, their content, the temporal characteristics of episodes of concentration may tell us much that is important about the person. We can just as readily speculate about the other neglected factors: Surgency, Social Affection, Egotism and Skepticism.

An inevitable question arises: Why are these factors called mood factors? By studying each factor independently can we not exhaust the domain of mood without referring at any point to mood? This question becomes particularly pertinent because of preliminary results we have obtained in our Rochester work. When subjects fill out the short MACL every fifteen minutes during a 16-hour period, the several mood factors vary more or less independently of each other. Wessman and Ricks (1965) have also shown this for a number of their mood scales when variations across days are examined. Looking at the within-day variations we must ask what the layman means when he says that someone is in a mood. Does he mean that one particular aspect of mood, comprising one factor or a few factors, is temporarily dominant? Perhaps mood, then, is not a set of second order dispositions after all but rather the inferrable ordering, in terms of momentary prepotency, of a number of basic systems of behavior and experience: aggression, anxiety, surgency, elation, concentration, social affection, fatigue, sadness, skepticism, egotism, vigor, nonchalance. Such factors, then, are mood factors insofar as their temporal fluctuations in relative strength result in variously ordered steady state patterns which assist in the understanding, prediction, and control of a person's behavior through short intervals of time. We can now also see why it can be reasonably asserted that a waking person is always in a mood, even when affective levels are very low.

The phenomena from which we infer mood have some stability through periods lasting minutes or, at the most, hours. When the relevant state continues steadily for days other terms are used or the mood is called pathological. Complex mediational processes or states of the temporal order of minutes or hours have not received as much systematic attention in research as have those of briefer or longer duration. There is a recently growing interest in other phenomena attributable to states of this same intermediate temporal span, such as the break-off phenomena, trance, the phenomena of hypnosis, and the steady states which follow the ingestion and sometimes even the subsequent complete elimination from the body of certain drugs. Peculiarly, all these states tend to involve large repertoires of behavior and experience, as does mood. Recent theories of the organization of behavior tend to focus on the mechanisms which provide the serial ordering of behavioral items through time. We also need to examine the mechanisms which provide direction and persistent affect through moderate spans of time. Theories directly or indirectly concerned with such mechanisms have been offered from the psychoanalytic viewpoint: Jacobson (1957); from the viewpoint of conflict-produced drives: Brown (1961); from the neurophysiological viewpoint: Holt (1931), Hebb (1960), John (1961), Arnold (1962); from the general theory of TOTE units, images and plans: Miller, Galanter, & Pribram (1960); and from the empirical analysis of streams of behavior: Barker (1963); and of the inherent variability of behavior: Fiske & Maddi (1961). If any further attention paid to mood phenomena contributes to our understanding of how behavior is frequently organized through temporal spans of moderate duration, mood will have become an important concept.

REFERENCES

Alexander, S. The effects of different levels of hostility on opinion change. Technical Report No. 2, Office of Naval Research: Contract No. Nonr-668 (12), 1959.

Alexander, S., & Husek, T. The anxiety differential: initial steps in the development of a measure of situational anxiety. *Educ. Psychol. Measmt.*, 1962, *22*, 325-348.

Arnold, Magda B. *Emotion and personality.* New York: Columbia University Press, 1962.

Axelrod, J. Induced moods and attitudes toward products. *J. adv. Res.*, 1963, *3*, 19-24.

Barker, R. L. *The stream of behavior.* New York: Appleton-Century-Crofts, 1963.

Bass, B. M. Mood changes in a management training laboratory. *J. appl. Psychol.*, 1962, *46*, 361-364.

Beecher, H. K. *Measurement of subjective responses.* New York: Oxford University Press, 1959.

Berg, J. A note on dispositional concepts. *Phil. & phenomenol. Res.*, 1955-56, *16*, 121-123.

Borgatta, E. F. Mood, personality, and interaction. *J. gener. Psychol.*, 1961, *64*, 105-137.

Broad, C. D. *Examination of McTaggart's philosophy.* Cambridge: Cambridge University Press, 1933.

Brown, J. S. *The motivation of behavior.* New York: McGraw-Hill, 1961.

Buss, A. H. *The psychology of aggression.* New York: Wiley, 1961.

Cameron, Jean S., & Wendt, G. R. Chemical studies of behavior: VIII. Some anomalous onset effects of benzquinamide, a "tranquilizer." *J. Psychol.*, 1964, *58*, 265-275

Cattell, R. B. *Personality: A systematic theoretical and factual study.* New York: McGraw-Hill, 1950.

Cattell, R. B. *Description and measurement of personality.* New York: World Book Co., 1957.

Cattell, R. B. The dimensional (unitary-component) measurement of anxiety, excitement, effort, stress and other mood reaction patterns. In L. Uhr & J. G. Miller (Eds.), *Drugs and behavior.* New York: Wiley, 1960.

Cattell, R. B. Personality, role, mood, and situation-perception: a unifying theory of modulators. *Psychol. Rev.*, 1963, *70*, 1-18.

Cattell, R. B., & Scheier, I. H. *The meaning and measurement of neuroticism and anxiety.* New York: Ronald, 1961.

Clyde, D. Self-ratings. In L. Uhr & J. G. Miller (Eds.), *Drugs and behavior.* New York: Wiley, 1960.

English, H. B., & English, Ava C. *A comprehensive dictionary of psychological and psychoanalytical terms.* New York: McKay, 1958.

Fiske, D. W., & Maddi, S. R. *Functions of varied experience.* Homewood, Ill.: Dorsey, 1961.

Green, R. F. The measurement of mood. Technical Report, Office of Naval Research: Contract No. Nonr-668(12), in preparation, 1964.

Haefner, D. P. Some effects of guilt-arousing and fear-arousing persuasive communications on opinion change. Technical Report No. 1, Office of Naval Research: Contract No. Nonr-668(12), 1956.

Handlon, J. H. Hormonal activity and individual responses to stresses and easements in everyday living. In R. Rilssler & N. S. Greenfield (Eds.), *Physiological correlates of psychological disorder*. Madison: University of Wisconsin Press, 1962.

Harway, Vivian T., Lanzetta, J. T., Nowlis, Helen H., Nowlis, V., & Wendt, G. R. Chemical influences on behavior: II. Development of methods and preliminary results on the effects of some drugs on emotional and social behavior. Technical Report, Office of Naval Research Project 144-060, 1953.

Hebb, D. O. The American revolution. *Amer. Psychologist*, 1960, *15*, 735-745.

Holt, E. B. *Animal drive and the learning process*. New York: Holt, Rinehart and Winston, 1931.

Jacobson, Edith. Normal and pathological moods: their nature and functions. *Psychoanalytic study of the child*. Vol. XIV. New York: International Universities Press, 1957.

Janis, I. L., & Feshbach, S. Effects of fear-arousing communications. *J. abnorm. soc. Psychol.*, 1953, *48*, 78-92.

John, E. R. Some speculations on the psychophysiology of the mind. In J. Scher (Ed.), *Toward a definition of mind*. Glencoe, Ill.: Free Press, 1961.

Knapp, P. H., & Bahnson, C. B. The emotional field: changing emotions and fantasies. *Psychosom. Med.*, 1963, *25*, 460-483.

Korchin, S. J., & Heath, Helen A. Somatic experience in the anxiety state: Some sex and personality correlates of "autonomic feedback." *J. consult. Psychol.*, 1961, *25*, 398-404.

Laties, V. G. Modification of affect, social behavior and performance by sleep deprivation and drugs. *J. psychiat. Res.*, 1961, *1*, 12-24.

Lazarus, R. S., & Alfert, Elizabeth. Short-circuiting of threat by experimentally altering cognitive appraisal. *J. abnorm. soc. Psychol.*, 1964, *69*, 195-205.

Lazarus, R. S., Speisman, J. C., Mordkoff, A. M., & Davison, L. A. A laboratory study of psychological stress produced by a motion picture film. *Psychol. Monogr.*, 1962, *76*, No. 34 (Whole No. 553).

Levison, Cathryn A. Perceived similarity and the judgment of mood in others. *J. soc. Psychol.*, 1963, *61*, 99-110.

Levison, P. K. The effects of sensory deprivation upon stimulation seeking behavior, mood, and attitude structure. Unpublished doctoral dissertation, University of Rochester, 1959.

Mandler, G. A., & Kessen, W. *The language of psychology*. New York: Wiley, 1959.

McNair, D. M., & Lorr, M. An analysis of mood in neurotics. *J. abnorm. soc. Psychol.*, 1964, *69*, 620-627.

Miller, G. A., Galanter, E., & Pribram, K. *Plans and the structure of behavior*. New York: Holt, Rinehart and Winston, 1960.

Miller, L. Subjective probability estimates as a function of attitude structure. Unpublished doctoral dissertation, University of Rochester, 1960.

Murphy, D. F. Methodological considerations in evaluating effects of suggestion and field orientation on responses to sensory deprivation. Unpublished doctoral dissertation, University of Rochester, 1964.

Myers, L. Improving the quality of education by identifying effective television teachers. Progress Report, OE 7-42-1600-173.0, December 1962.

Nowlis, Helen H., Nowlis, V., Riesen, A. H., & Wendt, G. R. Chemical influences on behavior: III. Technical Report, Office of Naval Research, Project 144-060, 1953.

Nowlis, V. The development and modification of motivational systems in personality. In M. R. Jones (Ed.), *Current theory and research in motivation.* Lincoln: University of Nebraska Press, 1953.

Nowlis, V. The experimental analysis of mood. (Abstract) XVth Int. Congr. Psychol. *Acta Psychol.*, 1959, *15*, 426.

Nowlis, V. Methods for studying mood changes produced by drugs. *Rev. de Psychol. Appliquée*, 1961, *11*, 373-386.

Nowlis, V. The concept of mood. In S. M. Farber & R. H. L. Wilson (Eds.), *Conflict and creativity.* New York: McGraw-Hill, 1963.

Nowlis, V., & Green, R. F. The experimental analysis of mood. Technical Report No. 3, Office of Naval Research: Contract No. Nonr-668(12), 1957.

Nowlis, V., & Green, R. F. Factor analytic studies of mood. Technical Report, Office of Naval Research: Contract No. Nonr-668(12). In preparation, 1964.

Nowlis, V., & Nowlis, Helen H. The analysis of mood. *N.Y. Acad. Sci.*, 1956, *65*, 345-355.

Pomeranz, D. The repression-sensitization dimension and reactions to stress. Unpublished doctoral dissertation, University of Rochester, 1962.

Reimanis, G. Personal communication. June, 1964.

Robbins, P. R. Self-reports of reactions to fear-arousing information. *Psychol. Rep.*, 1962, *11*, 761-764.

Ryle, G. *The concept of mind.* London: Hutchinson, 1949.

Schachter, S., & Singer, J. E. Cognitive, social, and physiological determinants of emotional state. *Psychol. Rev.*, 1962, *69*, 379-399.

Skinner, B. F. *Science and human behavior.* New York: Macmillan, 1953.

Skinner, B. F. *Verbal behavior.* New York: Appleton-Century-Crofts, 1957.

Speisman, J. C., Lazarus, R. S., Mordkoff, A., & Davison, L. Experimental reduction of stress based on ego-defense theory. *J. abnorm. soc. Psychol.*, 1964, *68*, 367-380.

Spence, D. P. A new look at vigilance and defense. *J. abnorm. soc. Psychol.*, 1957, *54*, 103-108.

Stricker, G. The experimental induction of mood. Technical Report No. 9, Office of Naval Research: Contract Nonr-668(12), 1961.

Stricker, G. The construction and partial validation of an objectively scorable apperception test. *J. Pers.*, 1962, *30*, 51-62. (a)

Stricker, G. An approach to assessing the meaning of "no change" in a pre-post experimental design. *J. gener. Psychol.*, 1962, *67*, 237-240. (b)

Thayer, R. E. Development and validation of a self-report adjective check list to measure activation-deactivation. Unpublished doctoral dissertation, University of Rochester, 1963.

Weiner, I. B., & Ader, R. Direction of aggression and adaptation to free operant avoidance conditioning. *J. person. soc. Psychol.*, in press, 1965.

Wendt, G. R., & Cameron, Jean S. Chemical studies of behavior: V. Procedures in drug experimentation with college students. *J. Psychol.*, 1961, *51*, 173-211.

Wendt, G. R., Cameron, Jean S., & Specht, Priscilla G. Chemical studies of behavior: VI. Placebo and dramamine as methodological controls, and effects on moods, emotions, and motivations. *J. Psychol.*, 1962, *53*, 257-279.

Wessman, A. E., & Ricks, D. F. *Mood and personality.* In pvers, Holt, Rinehart & Winston, 1965.

Wessman, A. E., & Ricks, D. F. Personality characteristics associated with mood level and variability. Paper read at East. Psychol. Ass., Philadelphia, April, 1961.

Wessman, A. E., & Ricks, D. F. *Mood and personality*. In press, Holt, Rinehart & Winston, 1965.

Wessman, A. E., Ricks, D. F., & Tyl, Mary McIlvaine. Characteristics and concomitants of mood fluctuation in college women. *J. abnorm. soc. Psychol.*, 1960, *60*, 117-126.

Yagi, K., & Berkun, M. Some problems in the reliability of the adjective check list. Paper read at West. Psychol. Ass., Seattle, June, 1961.

Zuckerman, M. The development of an affect adjective check list for the measurement of anxiety. *J. counsel. Psychol.*, 1960, *24*, 457-462.

Communication through nonverbal behavior: A source of information about an interpersonal relationship

Paul Ekman

INTRODUCTION

The interlacing of fingers, twist of a foot, slump of a shoulder, slant of a hip, curl of the lip, furrow of the brow, direction of gaze, and tilt of the head are instances of what we have called nonverbal behavior. All can occur simultaneously or separately, with or without speech, during an interaction or when an individual is alone, spontaneously or by contrivance. The concern of our study is with the communicative functions of this domain of behavior, when actions are spontaneously emitted during a verbal exchange with an immediate, emotionally-toned interpersonal relationship.

Poets and politicians, psychotherapists and playwrights, dancers and anthropologists have all provided examples of and testimonials to the rich variety of information which can be carried by interactive nonverbal behavior. The claims vary from the modest hypothesis that nonverbal cues provide qualifications about how a verbal message should be interpreted, to notions that this mode of communication escapes conscious censoring and thus reveals the "true," primitive, or repressed side of personality.

Without subscribing to the belief that body movement and facial expression are a royal road to the unconscious, or even to affect, our

This research was supported by a postdoctoral research fellowship, #MF 6092, and by a grant, #MH 07587, both from the National Institute of Mental Health, United States Public Health Service. Parts of these studies were reported at the Western Psychological Association Convention in 1962, 1963, and 1964, and at the American Psychological Association Convention, 1964.

The author is indebted to Dr. Robert Berryman, who initially encouraged this line of investigation, and to Mr. Sanford Autumn for his many criticisms and suggestions about the research design, data analysis, and interpretation. The author is grateful to Patricia W. Garlan for her editorial assistance with both the style and the content; to Joanna Bressler, who helped in the design, collection of data, and data analysis in Experiment VI and in the experiment with hospitalized depressed patients, and to Marvin Hoffman, who helped in the design, collection of data, and data analysis in Experiment VII.

decision to study *interactive* nonverbal behavior is based on the assumption that, at least in part, nonverbal behavior expresses the quality and changes of a relationship. As Bateson (1962) has suggested, this mode of expression is especially sensitive to the nuances and intricacies of how two people are getting along, despite the possibility that they, and we as observers, customarily pay little attention to this channel. Our emphasis has been on exploring what is communicated about a relationship when attention is fixed on this source alone.

Nonverbal behavior has been the subject of experimental research in psychology since the 1920's—in the early days under the rubric of expressive behavior, more recently within the framework of person-perception, emotion, and the interview. There are a number of reviews of this literature. For a recent and quite extensive review, see Klein (1963). Other recent reviews are those of Allport (1961), Bruner & Tagiuri (1954), Brengelmann (1963), and Davitz (1964). Remarkably, few of the experiments have studied *interactive* nonverbal behavior, and their relevance is limited by the setting and methods employed to elicit the nonverbal behavior.

The most popular technique has been to have actors, professional or amateur, pose certain emotions or reactions to imagined events. When individuals are so specifically instructed to send a wide range of emotions, and so strictly limited to the use of the nonverbal channel, it would appear to us that the behavior shown will be extreme or at least atypical of expressions occurring during an interpersonal transaction. Any demonstration of communication of information through nonverbal behavior in such a situation is not surprising, and is of doubtful relevance to the question of whether less artifically induced nonverbal cues communicate accurate information. The few studies which have sampled spontaneous behavior provoked the subject with novel, extreme, or bizarre stimuli, which again do not provide a picture of a person's usual nonverbal repertoire.

In either case, sampling nonverbal behavior occurring outside the context of an on-going relationship, devoid of any continuing verbal exchange, removes an important and perhaps critical constraint. Rarely do people express anger or joy unrestrictedly; usually the nature of the interpersonal relationship imposes constraints on the manner and extent of expression. A further problem with these kinds of experiments is that usually the relationship—between an experimenter giving instructions or producing novel stimuli, and a subject either acting or reacting—is blurred by the focus on task-relevant behavior.

Before discussing more recent studies which have examined spontaneous interactive nonverbal behavior, let us distinguish between two approaches, the *indicative* and the *communicative*. A nonverbal act, such as a foot tap, can be shown to be an indicator of an internal or external event, or to be a communicator of a specific item or class of information; but these are two quite different questions which entail different methods of study.

In indication, the concern is not with what a group of receivers may observe but with the relationship the experimenter is able to establish between a nonverbal act and some other class of events. Thus, the frequency of foot taps might be related to a verbal theme, or the administration of a drug, or the stress in an interview; and foot taps would then be an indicator of this other variable. Indication studies require a method of describing or recording specific classes of nonverbal activity. (See the notational system of Birdwhistell (1952); criticism of this system by Ekman (1957); more recent approaches by Buehler & Richmond (1963), Dierssen, Lorenc, & Spitalerl (1961), Jones et al. (1955, 1958, 1961), Sainesbury (1954). Studies of nonverbal indication examine only the sender within the communication system and tell us nothing directly about whether a receiver can decode any systematic information from a nonverbal indicator. For example, while foot taps might have been found to occur with greatest frequency when the sender is wistfully recalling the pleasures of early childhood, there is no reason to think that this indicator has communicative value, that the untutored receiver would infer this verbal theme, or related affect, from observing a sender tap his foot.

Communication through a nonverbal act is established only by determining whether receivers agree in their observations or in their inferences about what the act portends. Typically, a communicative study entails presenting segments of nonverbal behavior to groups of receivers who act as judges, and measuring the consistency or accuracy of their responses. Communication can be inaccurate as well as accurate; for example, if we believe that people smile only when happy, then this behavior has communicative value to receivers even if careful indicative experiments were to demonstrate that senders frequently smile under stress. Accuracy or inaccuracy of communication can be examined only if, of course, there is some independent criterion relevant to the sender's experience or his intentional attempt to communicate. Without such a criterion, communicative studies can still investigate whether a nonverbal act or series of acts provides information that is consistently interpreted (whether rightly or wrongly) or is ambiguous.

Failure to find that a nonverbal act has communicative value does not necessarily preclude the possibility that the act does have indicative value. The act may be a very strong indicator, but not familiar to the group of receivers being sampled, or perhaps not normally interpreted unless a receiver is trained to look for it. A communicative design does not provide an exhaustive sifting of what may be communicated through nonverbal behavior; it may be only a first approximation of what is potentially available.

Determination that a nonverbal act has indicative and/or communicative value does not assume that the sender intended to communicate. What the sender intends, and what the experimenter discovers through an indicative approach, or a receiver infers in a communicative study, can be completely unrelated.

Similarly, what the sender actually experiences, intentionally or non-intentionally, is not only almost impossible to determine, but is in no way necessarily equivalent to the indicative or communicative value of his nonverbal act. Resting the finger on the nose might have the communicative value to receivers, "Things smell bad." Or it might have the indicative value of occurring with greatest frequency at those moments when expert ratings of the interview typescript suggest maximal relaxation. And yet it may be that a given subject puts his finger to the side of his nose precisely at those moments when he is finished with a particular line of discourse, as an anticipatory signal that he will now ask a question.

There have been a number of recent studies of spontaneous interactive nonverbal behavior using an indicative approach. Examining clinical interviews with a patient, Dittmann (1962) found patterns of body movement indicative of the patient's mood as assessed independently by experts. More recently, Dittmann (1963) found consistencies in the pattern of body movements for each of a number of different normal subjects studied over time. Utilizing an EMG to measure body movement, Sainesbury (1955) found that the amount of movement was indicative of stress within a structured interview, of disturbance, verbal themes, and specific affects, as determined by psychiatric ratings. Exline (1963) found that amount of eye contact during interviews is indicative of reactions to embarrassing themes, or competitiveness, and bears a relationship to the sex of the subject.

Findings in comunicative studies of interviews have been more contradictory. Let us first consider two studies of interactive nonverbal behavior outside the interview situation. Investigations of experimenter bias by Rosenthal (1963a, 1963b) have found that much of the transmission of bias between experimenter and subject is carried through nonverbal cues, without awareness. At present, he is examining films of these experimenter-subject interactions to specify the particular nonverbal cues involved. Maccoby, Jecker, et al. (1964), and Jecker, Maccoby, et al. (1964) have studied students' nonverbal behavior during classroom lectures, have found nonverbal indicators of whether a student understands the lecture; and in communicative studies using teachers as receivers they have through training increased teacher accuracy in interpreting the students' behavior.

Turning now to communicative studies of nonverbal behavior within an interview, two studies varying widely in results may be cited. Mahl (1959), acting as the sole receiver, inferred with startling accuracy information about the emotional state, diagnostic classification and psychodynamic features of groups of patients being interviewed. His judgments were based solely upon observation of the nonverbal channel and then were validated by comparison with the verbal content of the interview and the case history. In marked contrast to this report is a study by Giedt (1955, 1958) which found that nonverbal cues were of little value in making clinical postdictions about four patients. Comparing judgments of an interview made on the basis of typescripts, tape-recordings, silent film, and sound film, he found that the most accurate inferences were made on the basis of the verbal cues as compared with nonverbal cues, with little improvement from a sound-film presentation of stimuli as compared to a typescript presentation of only the verbal content. The surprising results of this research raise a number of questions about the nature of the accuracy criteria, the suitability of the judgment task to the types of information which can be communicated nonverbally, the possibility that the patients photographed were not nonverbal senders, that the situation did not elicit sufficiently varied nonverbal behavior, and that the judges may not have been skilled as nonverbal receivers. Nevertheless, Giedt's study did serve to focus attention on a number of methodological considerations which directly influenced our choice of research problem and method of investigation.

Problem

In summary, then, most of the early research on expressive behavior and many of the recent studies of person-perception and affect treating nonverbal behavior were considered largely irrelevant to our interest in studying the communicative functions of nonverbal behavior spontaneously emitted during a verbal exchange in which two people have an emotional involvement in their relationship. A distinction was drawn between two kinds of approach, the indicative and the communicative. By 1959, when the present research was planned, there had been increasing evidence that spontaneous interactive nonverbal behavior is *indicative of* a number of different types of information about a person, but there was a clear contradiction between Giedt's results and Mahl's as to whether such behavior during interviews *communicates* accurate information. Our series of experiments was addressed to this discrepancy, and focused upon whether nonverbal behavior communicates accurate information about the quality of an interpersonal relationship.

The decision to study the ways in which nonverbal behavior reflects changes in a relationship was based upon the assumption that this is an important function of this communication channel, and also upon considerations as to the reasons for Giedt's failure to produce positive results about nonverbal behavior as a source of information. The two major considerations involved the sampling of the sender's behavior and the type of judgment asked of the receiver.

To provide a reasonable test of what is communicated by spontaneous nonverbal behavior, the sample should include diverse but representative pictures of the sender's nonverbal repertoire. If the sender is shown in only one mood, dealing with only one type of task, in a relationship characterized by a single relationship quality, then the receiver is deprived of the opportunity to compare and contrast possibly different nonverbal cues which might be available if mood, task, or relationship quality were sufficiently varied. The need then to sample different experiences of the sender, yet to stay within the artificial constraint of one photographing session of a single interview, led us to decide upon a standard stress interview procedure, which will be discussed shortly.

The receiver's task, the determination he is asked to make from the sender's behavior, is also crucial. Obviously, certain types of judgment task will result in one hundred percent accuracy (e.g., to determine the sender's sex), while other types of judgment task will elicit no consistent results whatsoever (e.g., to determine the sender's earliest memory). The judgment task assigned to the receiver, then, reflects the experimenter's beliefs about what may potentially be found to be communicated through nonverbal behavior. The indicative studies of Exline, Dittmann, and Sainesbury, and the writings of many theorists, in particular Sullivan (1953), suggest that what the patient is saying verbally and the nature of the relationship he is experiencing are related to his nonverbal activity. In another separate series of experiments (Ekman, 1964a), we found that there is congruence between verbal information and nonverbal information communicated at the same moment in time. Now our purpose was to move beyond the specifics of the verbal exchange, and concentrate upon whether a change in the over-all relationship between two interactants would be accurately communicated through nonverbal behavior.

Assuming that we could demonstrate that nonverbal behavior communicates accurate information about the quality of an interpersonal relationship, we were interested in investigating three further more specific questions: (1) How much of the nonverbal behavior shown during an interview actually carries consistent information; how much of the behavior is ambiguous to the receiver? Are the moments when the nonverbal activity carries information relatively rare, or is this a more continuous reiterated phenomenon? In other terms, what is the signal-to-noise ratio? (2) What specific classes of information are communicated by nonverbal behavior? How does a receiver decode a nonverbal act into some determination about the relationship between two people? Does the communication of information about the relationship depend upon some awareness of the circumstances of the interaction, or is such communication possible without most situational or contextual aids? (3) If individual senders differ in their nonverbal communicativeness, can the responses of a group of receivers serve as the basis for distinguishing between senders in the clarity of their nonverbal communicativeness?

The interview relationship is one in which the behavior of at least the interviewee is fairly spontaneous, there is an explicit communicative process, verbal behavior is the primary method of discourse, and the constraints operate against obtaining rich or extreme nonverbal records. In order to sample nonverbal behavior adequately within different interpersonal relationships, a standard interview procedure was designed in which the interviewer's attitude and behavior could be manipulated so as to permit two grossly different interactions within a short time span.

A second decision concerned the method of recording the nonverbal behavior. There are disadvantages to each of the three options: still photographs, motion pictures, and no records. Still photographs present the behavior to receivers in an artificial fashion, and are usually employed in designs in which only a few isolated slices of behavior are to be judged. Motion pictures are expensive to acquire, and often overwhelm the investigator with a mass of stimuli as complex as the original behavior, from which he must either sample only selected pieces for scrutiny or obtain judgments based on such a conglomerate mass of stimuli that it is impossible to specify how many cues, and of what type, form the basis of the receiver's judgment. If no records are made, then the receivers must be present when the behavior occurs, replication is difficult at best, and specification of what cues and how many cues served as the basis for the judgment is usually not possible.

Our decision was to record time-sample still photographs, a compromise dictated by practical considerations to limit cost but still provide a sufficient number of photographs to represent much of the behavior which occurred, and to permit us to specify how many cues and of what type communicate information. The price of this compromise, however, was that we were limited to investigating positions rather than movements, with consequent artificiality in the presentation of the sender's behavior to the receivers. Further, in studying the question of how much of the behavior shown during an interview communicates consistent or ambiguous information, we are limited by our stimulus unit of a still photograph to learning only how many of these photographic samples communicate consistent or ambiguous information.

A third decision was to photograph the entire face and body of the sender, rather than limit ourselves to recording only one portion of the sender's nonverbal activity. This decision was based on our notion that different parts of the body transmit somewhat different types of information, and therefore the receiver should have the total nonverbal message at a moment in time available.[1]

A fourth decision concerned the judgment task. The task selected was simply that judges distinguish, from photographs, the two standardized interaction patterns; in other words, judges were to determine whether a picture had been taken when the interviewer acted toward the subject in one specified way, or in the other. This task had a deceptively easy accuracy criterion which will be the subject of a much later discussion.

The fifth, and last, general decision concerned the nature of the judge population. College freshmen were chosen, not only because of their availability, but also because of our interest in determining what is communicated to a naive, untrained receiver. Results from pilot studies were in agreement with the findings reported in the literature, that experts,

[1] The usual stimulus unit was a single photograph showing all of the observable nonverbal behavior of the sender at one moment in time. By obtaining judgments for many such units, we could then determine how many of these units communicated consistent information. In other research (Ekman, 1964b) we have used a smaller stimulus unit, subdividing the single photograph into head or facial cues, and body cues, to compare the information communicated by each. But this will not be reported in this chapter. The logical next step, further to subdivide and analyze the different cues within the face and within the body, is in progress.

at least in the mental health professions, are no more and perhaps less accurate judges than college freshmen.

A number of experiments were conducted. In each of the experiments different groups of judges responded to nonverbal stimuli gathered from a series of standardized interviews. The specifics of the interview procedure, the interview participants, methods of recording the nonverbal stimuli, the judgment task and instructions to the judges are described in detail and followed by description of the individual experiments. Summaries of this material are on pages 405 and 414. After the second summary, the general discussion explores the three questions outlined (how much information is communicated, what kind of information is communicated, and how can individual differences in sending clarity be measured), and closes with a speculative discussion of the range of information which further research may show is communiated through nonverbal behavior.

EXPERIMENTS

GENERAL METHOD

Interview Procedure

A standard rather than a clinical interview was used, to better elicit contrasting affective reactions. Both the style and content of the interviewer's behavior toward the interviewee, the subject, were programmed. After an introductory affectively neutral period of ten minutes the interviewer induced a period of stress by attacking and criticizing the subject. After ten minutes the interviewer initiated a catharsis phase of ten minutes by explaining the experiment to the subject, and praising and joking with him. (The interview structure is described more fully in the Instructions to the Judges, presented below in Experiment I.)

Interview Participants

Five interviews were conducted, in which three different interviewers and five different subjects participated.[2] Two interviewers were staff research psychologists at a Veterans Administration hospital; each interviewed one psychology graduate student (Interviews A and B). The third interviewer, a senior staff research psychiatrist at a different neuropsychiatric hospital, interviewed three different psychiatric residents (Interviews C, D, and E). The interviewer in each case was in a position of some authority over the subject. The subject knew that he was participating in an experiment and that the interview would be tape-recorded and observed, but did not know that he would be photographed. The interviewer was acquainted with the general purpose of the research, and had rehearsed the interview procedure. (The five interviews will hereafter be referred to as A, B, C, D, and E.)

[2] The author is grateful for the participation of Drs. John Boswell, Enoch Calloway, Barry Decker, Irving Moelis, Joseph Rubinstein, David Saunders, Lee Wannerman, Robert Weiss.

The choice of these interview subjects, trainees in psychology and psychiatry, was dictated by ethical and methodological considerations. The stress experience is perhaps not totally unrewarding to persons who are trainees in the professional use of interview procedures; learning about this technique may partially compensate for their suffering as subjects. It was possible to utilize the knowledge of the clinical staff to select trainees

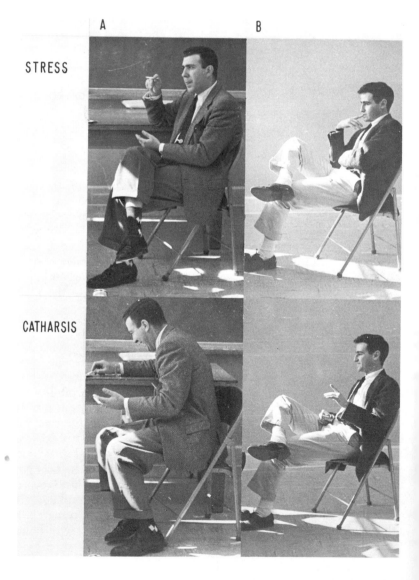

Figure 1.   Examples of photographs. Top: stress, bottom: catharsis.

able to tolerate a stress experience of this nature. The chief disadvantage of this choice was that conceivably trainees in psychology or psychiatry are less active or expressive nonverbally than most other populations, and that the constraints of being interviewed by a senior staff person might further limit the range of their nonverbal behavior. Viewed methodologically, however, such limitations were held to be advantageous, in

that they provided a more rigorous framework for obtaining positive results.

Recording Method

Photographs were taken through a one-way vision screen with a 35mm still camera. In interviews A and B the photographs showed a profile view of both interviewer and subject. In C, D, and E the photographs showed a full-face view of the subject only, with the camera aimed approximately over the interviewer's shoulder. Pictures were taken every thirty seconds during A, every fifteen seconds during B, and every five seconds during C, D, and E. (Interviews C, D, and E were recorded about a year later than A and B, when it had become evident that greater frequency of sampling was desirable, and more elaborate equipment had become available.) Examples of these photographs are shown in Figure 1, with the interviewer in A and B cut off.

Judgment Task

Judges were asked to guess whether a photograph had been taken during the stress or catharsis portion of the interview. Although it is quite possible that judges may have considered the affective experience of the subject in making their decision, it is important to note that judges were not asked to judge the subject's affect, but instead to decide during which phase of the interview a picture had been taken. The two phases were defined in the instructions primarily in terms of the nature of the relationship between interviewer and subject.

Since pilot studies had shown that judges misconstrued the word "catharsis" in the instructions, the two phases of the interview were designated as the "stress" and "final" phases. Judges saw photographs which had been randomly selected without prior inspection.

EXPERIMENTS I-IV

Experiment I

Problem. The purpose of this experiment was to determine whether nonverbal behavior communicates accurate information about two interview conditions described for the judge in terms of two different interactions between interviewer and subject. Hypothesis: Untrained judges can accurately decide whether a photograph was taken during the stress or catharsis phase of an interview.

The most stringent test of this hypothesis demanded that judgments be free of (a) the influence of practice, (b) base-line information about the subject's typical behavior, (c) comparative information about the range of behavior shown during stress and catharsis, and (d) information about sequence of positions over time. Therefore, the design restricted each judge to seeing only *one* photograph. In this form the judgment task is quite different from the usual way in which people judge others, since many of the circumstances which aid interpretation of nonverbal behavior have been eliminated. The virtue of the design is that it allows exploration of what can be learned from a minimum of nonverbal cues.

Method. A total of 48 photographs from A and B were presented to judges, half from the stress phase of the two interviews and half from the catharsis phase. Fourteen photographs were from A: all seven of the photographs taken during the catharsis phase, and seven photographs randomly selected from the 19 taken during the stress phase. Thirty-four photographs were from B: 17 randomly selected from the 40 taken during the stress phase, and 17 randomly selected from the 31 taken during the catharsis phase. The 48 photographs, showing a profile view of both interviewer and subject, were enlarged into 4 x 5" prints. A photograph was randomly assigned to each judge as he entered his classroom. Judges were given the following instructions to read:

This is a study of the way in which people are able to interpret or understand gestures, body movement, and facial expression. You will be shown a photograph which was taken during a short standardized interview. The interviewer, or Examiner, was a staff psychologist at a hospital, and the person interviewed, the Subject, was a student in training to become a psychologist. The Subject was told that he was participating in a research project on interviewing techniques and that he would be observed through a one-way vision screen and tape recorded.

Both of the interviews were standardized in that the Examiner followed a prearranged schedule of behavior designed to evoke two different emotional reactions in the Subject. After the first few minutes of getting acquainted, the Examiner became hostile and challenging, disagreeing with everything the Subject said, and continually interrupting him. With one Subject the Examiner questioned his motives for being interested in research; with the other Subject the Examiner concentrated more on the Subject's "poor" preparation for his coming examinations, and the reasons why the Subject claimed to be interested in the physiological areas of psychology. After ten minutes of the STRESSful period, the Examiner explained what he had been doing, that it had been part of the research to try to provoke the Subject and study his reactions to stress. In this FINAL period, the Examiner attempted to reassure the Subject, and generally bring about a release of tension.

In actuality, this standardized interview plan did not work out perfectly in either of the two interviews. There was some stress for the Subject throughout the interview. The FINAL phase was not completely successful in producing relief from the stress, since the Subject knew that the experiment was still continuing. Nevertheless there were some important differences between the two phases of the interview. The STRESS phase did have more overt expression of hostility and tension; and in the FINAL phase the Subject did experience some relief, at least in knowing that the worst was over.

You will be given one picture face down. Please do not look at it until you are asked to do so. When you are instructed, turn the picture over and study it. You will be allowed 20 seconds in which to make your judgment as to whether you think the picture was taken during the STRESSful or the FINAL period of the interview. At the end of the 20 seconds you will be asked to write your judgment, either the word *STRESS* or the word *FINAL* at the bottom of this page. Next to your judgment please write the number of the picture which you will find on the reverse side in the top corners.

Subjects. Forty-eight college freshmen served as judges.

Results. A total of 48 independent judgments was obtained, one for each photograph. It was assumed that if only chance factors had been operative half of the judgments would be correct. A binomial test (Siegel, 1956, p. 36) was used to evaluate the significance of the number of accurate judgments. Table 1 shows that the total number of judges who made an accurate choice across both interviews (.65) was significantly greater than would be expected by chance. When the accuracy on each interview was tested separately, the number of judges correct on A (.64) was not significant, while the number of judges correct on B (.65) was significant. (The failure to achieve significance on the judgments of A can be attributed to the small number of judges, since the proportion of correct judgments was almost identical to that obtained for B.)

Table 1   Number of J̲s̲ who made an accurate judgment

	Experiment I 48 Independent judgments Interviewer and S̲	Experiment II 48 Independent judgments S̲ alone
Total trials (A and B) (48 photos)	31*	24
Interview A trials (14 photos)	9	8
Interview B trials (34 photos)	22**	16

*p < .05
**p < .01

Discussion. These results supported the hypothesis that judges can accurately decide whether a photograph was taken during the stress or catharsis phase of an interview. Having shown both interviewer and subject in the pictures, however, we could not be sure of the extent to which accurate judgment was based on the subject's behavior, the interviewer's behavior, or inference on the part of the judges about the interaction between interviewer and subject. Experiment II was designed to address this question.

Experiment II

Problem. The purpose of this experiment was to replicate Experiment I, while limiting judges to the nonverbal behavior of only the subject. Hypothesis: Untrained judges can determine whether a photograph was taken during the stress or catharsis phase of an interview even when limited to seeing the nonverbal behavior of the subject only.

Method. The procedure was identical to that of the first experiment; the same photographs were used, except that the part of the picture showing the interviewer was covered with a cardboard mount to eliminate the interviewer's cues.

Subjects. A new group of 48 college freshmen served as judges.

Results. A total of 48 independent judgments was obtained, one for each photograph. It can be seen in Table 1 that the hypothesis was not supported, since only .50 of the judges of A and B combined made a correct choice. The difference in accuracy between Experiments I and II was evaluated by a x^2 test. While the accuracy on A was not significantly different when only the subject was shown (.58, as compared to .64 in Experiment I), the accuracy on B was less when only the subject was shown (.47, as compared to .65 in Experiment I; $p < .05$).

Discussion. It would appear from the results of Experiment II that when the interviewer's behavior is not shown, judges can no longer make accurate decisions, particularly for B. Earlier it was noted that the design employed in these experiments, allowing only one judgment of one photograph to each judge, deprived the judges of the benefits of practice, familiarity with base-line or comparative information, and sequence cues. Thus handicapped, a moderate number of judges still made a correct decision in the first experiment, although in the second experiment the further elimination of interviewer cues led to chance results. The next two experiments studied how judges' accuracy would be affected when some of these handicaps were removed.

Experiment III

Problem. The purpose of this experiment was to determine whether judges could accurately identify stress and catharsis photographs when each judge made a decision for each of a number of pictures. The procedure allowed judges the opportunity to benefit from practice, and to acquire impressions about the subject's nonverbal repertoire, specifically about the behavior shown in stress and catharsis. Since the photographs were shown in a random order, with a decision required for each picture, judges were still deprived, as they had been in the earlier experiments, of any information based on the sequence of nonverbal behavior shown in the interviews. Hypothesis: Untrained judges can accurately determine, when seeing a series of randomly selected and ordered photographs showing both interviewer and subject, whether pictures were taken during the stress or catharsis phase of an interview.

Method. The same task was employed although the procedure was modified for presentation of a series of photographs rather than one. The instructions to judges were slightly modified (in regard to the method of recording decisions). The judges as a group then saw in a random order the 48 photographs used in Experiments I and II. The pictures had been made into 35mm slides, and each was projected on a screen for twenty seconds. As in Experiment I, the pictures showed both interviewer and subject. Two versions of the answer sheet controlled for a left-right response-set bias; the word "stress" appeared at the left side of the page on one answer sheet, and at the right side on the other.

Subjects. A new group of 33 college freshmen served as judges.

Results. The number of accurate choices for each judge was tabulated. If the photographs had not systematically provided any information, accuracy scores would be expected to be symmetrically distributed at about the midpoint of the range of possible scores. A contrary distribution of accuracy scores would indicate systematic response by the independent judges to the randomly presented pictures. The statistical hypothesis was tested by applying Wilcoxon's matched-pairs signed-ranks test (Siegel, 1956, p. 75) to the differences between the accuracy score obtained for each judge and the expected midpoint; a one-tailed test was employed. (This method of testing the significance of accuracy results was employed in all of the subsequent experiments unless otherwise noted.)

The accuracy achieved on all trials and on A and B trials separately

Table 2   Results of Experiments III, IV, and V

Pictures correctly identified	Experiment III (33 Judges) Interviewer and S		Experiment IV (35 Judges) S Alone		Experiment (16 Judges) S A	
	Score	Proportion	Score	Proportion	Score	Propo
Total trials A & B (48 photos)						
Median	29.3***	.61	27.0***	.56	24.0	.50
1st quartile	27.1	.56	24.7	.51	21.7	.45
3rd quartile	32.2	.67	28.4	.59	26.2	.55
Interview A trials (14 photos)						
Median	10.1***	.72	9.7***	.69	7.5	.54
1st quartile	8.7	.62	8.2	.59	5.3	.38
3rd quartile	11.0	.79	10.7	.76	8.4	.60
Interview B trials (34 photos)						
Median	20.1***	.59	17.3	.51	16.5	.48
1st quartile	18.9	.55	16.4	.48	14.2	.42
3rd quartile	21.4	.63	18.4	.54	19.0	.56

*** $p < .001$

was significantly higher than would be expected by chance. The distribution of scores was skewed towards accuracy, particularly for interview A photographs. Table 2 shows the results for Experiment III and for the next two experiments. The median and the first and third quartiles are shown to present information about the nature of the distribution of accuracy scores. Proportions are given in addition to the actual scores, in order to facilitate comparisons between interviews A and B, where different numbers of photographs had been judged.

Discussion. Although direct comparison of the results of Experiments I and III is confused by the difference in design between requiring a single judgment and repeated judgments from each judge, descriptively it can be noted that in both of these experiments in which interviewer and subject were shown significant accuracy was achieved. Moreover, the level of accuracy over all of the photographs from the two interviews was remarkably similar in Experiment I (.65 correct) and Experiment III (.61 correct) despite the fact that the multiple judgment results of Experiment III reflect practice, familiarity with the range of behavior, etc. This similarity in results raises a number of questions about the nature of the judgment task, and how the accuracy of judgment may or may not be influenced by increased exposure of judges to nonverbal stimuli. These questions will be discussed after the first nine experiments have been presented.

The next experiment studied whether accuracy was possible if the interviewer is not shown in the photographs, but with each judge making a decision for each of a number of photographs.

Experiment IV

Problem. Experiment II had suggested that judges could not accurately decide whether a photograph was taken in the stress or catharsis phase when the pictures showed only the behavior of the subject. Experiment IV, like Experiment III, gave the judge opportunity for practice and for acquiring comparative information about the behavior shown in stress and catharsis; as in Experiment II, judges saw only the subject's behavior. Hypothesis: Untrained judges can accurately determine from a series of randomly selected and ordered photographs whether pictures were taken during the stress or catharsis phase of an interview even when limited to seeing the nonverbal behavior of the subject only.

Method. The procedure was identical to that of Experiment III except that the photographs showed only the subject's behavior.

Subjects. A new group of thirty-five college freshmen served as judges.

Results. Table 2 shows that the accuracy for the total trials and for A photographs was significant, while the accuracy for B photographs was not significant. Comparison of the results of Experiments III and IV shows that there was no difference for A, while for B there was a significant difference ($p < .01$).

DISCUSSION OF EXPERIMENTS I–IV

When accuracy across all the photographs from interviews A and B is considered, three of the four experiments provide evidence of significant accuracy in identifying the stress and catharsis phases of the interviews. The results are not nearly so uniform, however, when we consider the accuracy achieved for each of the two interviews. It is clear that these four experiments alone raise more questions than they conclusively answer, demanding additional experiments in which judges respond to photographs from new standard interviews. The emphasis of the discussion of this first set of experiments will be on these questions and the decisions they prompted for the design of additional experiments.

The accuracy level achieved seemed to have been influenced by three variables: (1) the number of persons shown in the photographs, viz., either both interviewer and subject or only subject; (2) the particular stimulus persons shown, viz., those from A or from B; (3) the method of presenting the nonverbal behavior, viz., to elicit from each judge either a single response to a single photograph or a response to each of a number of photographs.

1. When only the subject was shown, significant accuracy was found for only one of the two subjects, and only when judges rated many pictures. In contrast, the greatest accuracy was achieved when both interviewer and subject were shown. It is difficult to specify the reasons for this, since the Interviewer-Subject condition may have contained at least two types of information not present in the Subject-alone condition, and the interviewer's role may have contaminated both of them. When a judge sees both interviewer and subject he may observe something about the interplay between two people not evident when he sees either interviewer or subject separately. In addition to such clues about the interaction, the interviewer displays his own set of nonverbal cues, and the judge may look at both interviewer and subject separately and summate in some fashion his impressions of each. Interviewer and subject differed, however, in their knowledge of the experiment, the degree of their involvement, and the nature of their role. The subject did not really know what the procedure was about; he did not know the focus of the research; and his behavior was reactive to that of the interviewer, and spontaneous in the sense that he did not follow a prearranged plan. The interviewer was playing a standardized role; he knew the focus of the research; he knew what he was trying to do to the subject and how he should proceed. In comparison to the subject's actions, the interviewer's may have been more stereotyped and artificial. Since judges did best when the interviewer was shown, we are confronted with the familiar problem of posed behavior—a problem these experiments were designed to avoid. It may be that accuracy was due more to the posed behavior of the interviewer than to the more spontaneous behavior of the subject. Since our primary interest is in the latter, the decision was made to show only the subject's behavior in further experiments.

2. When we consider the results for the Subject-alone condition, a trend is evident toward better results on A than on B in Experiment II, with the difference significant in Experiment IV. It might be that the two subjects differed in their nonverbal expressiveness, that one sent more information than the other through the nonverbal channel. Intriguing as it might be to raise questions about individual differences in nonverbal communicativeness, a much simpler explanation may account for the differences in the results. Perhaps persons A and B are equally expressive in their nonverbal behavior, but their experience in the interview differed.

For example, if person A fully experienced both stress and catharsis, but person B though stressed did not experience catharsis but found the whole interview unpleasant, then judges would regard person B's "catharsis" photographs as stressful, and we, the experimenters, would call the judges wrong.

Further exploration of individual differences in nonverbal communicativeness must therefore better insure that the participants have a comparable experience. One step in this direction is to utilize the same interviewer, so that even if the subjects differ in their mode of handling the experience at least they encounter the same person.

The decision was made, therefore, to employ only one interviewer in the next series of experiments. (The consideration of whether differences in subject experience confuse a measure of nonverbal communicativeness will be presented in a later section, and a different method of measuring nonverbal sending will be offered as another solution.)

Furthermore, the new experiments were planned to permit a larger sampling of photographs than was possible with A, and a comparable number from each interview. In order to permit focus on individual differences between senders, accuracy will be reported only for judgments of each stimulus person.

3. The final decision made was to utilize the multiple (rather than single) judgment procedure in order to make more economical use of a judge population, and to build a pool of judge reactions to as many of the specific photographs from each interview as possible. Plans were made to check for benefits due to practice; data on practice effects in these experiments will be reported later, with analysis of practice effects on the subsequent experiments.

EXPERIMENTS V-IX

Before proceeding to the experiments with Interviews C, D, and E, one more experiment relevant to A and B was needed to explore and, if possible, refute the notion that the results were derived from a factor extraneous to our fundamental hypothesis. The task for the judges in the first four experiments was specified as identifying the stress and catharsis phases of an interview from nonverbal cues. Since stress had always preceded catharsis, it might be argued that judge accuracy was not based on the linking of nonverbal cues to the stress and catharsis phases of the interview as such, but more simply on recognition of nonverbal behavior typical of the start or end of any interview. Accordingly, Experiment V was conducted to determine whether judges could accurately identify photographs taken at the beginning and end of an interview if they were told nothing about the nature of the interaction. The procedure was identical to that of Experiment IV except that the instructions omitted any mention of the stress and catharsis phases, and instead stated that in a standard interview the interviewer had acted one way at the start and a different way at the end. Judges were asked to decide whether photographs were taken in the first or second part of the interview. The results, shown in Table 2, indicate that accuracy was not significant, and demonstrate that the accuracy in Experiment IV was dependent at least in part upon the judges' cognizance of the stress-catharsis interview relationship.

Experiment VI

Problem. The purpose of this experiment was to determine whether, with a larger sampling of nonverbal behavior from two new interviews, results from the earlier experiments would be replicated to provide further evidence that nonverbal behavior communicates accurate information about two interview conditions. Hypothesis: Untrained judges can accurately determine whether randomly selected and ordered photographs were taken during the stress or catharsis phase of standard interviews.

Method. Twenty photographs were randomly selected from the stress phase and 20 from the catharsis phase of Interview C; the same was done for Interview D. The photographs from each interview were arranged in a random sequence. Judges were shown all 40 photographs of one subject, and then the 40 photographs of the other subject. Judges were randomly assigned to two groups; group one responded first to person C and then to person D, while group two had the reverse order. In all other respects the procedure was identical to that of Experiment IV.

Subjects. A new group of 49 college freshmen served as judges.

Results. Since there were no differences in the accuracy scores achieved by judges who had seen person C first and those who had seen person D first, the scores for the two groups were combined. The obtained accuracy scores reached significance for both C photographs and D photographs. Table 3 shows, however, that the median number of pictures of person C accurately identified was only slightly above .50 correct. The photographs of person D were identified with significantly greater accuracy than those of person C ($x^2=16.41$, $p<.001$). The distribution of scores was skewed towards accuracy for person D.

Discussion. These results closely replicate the findings reported for Experiment IV, despite the difference in persons shown in the photographs and the use of new groups of judges. It might be noted, further, that a year elapsed between the first four experiments and Experiment VI; thus, the judge population and other time-related factors could vary.

Once again, as in Experiment IV, there is a difference in the level of judge accuracy on the two persons. The accuracy level for C is almost the same as for B, while A and D seem to elicit a higher level of accuracy. Examination of the interview typescript and inspection of the photographs suggested that the subject in C experienced less catharsis and was more uncomfortable throughout the interview than the subject in D. Thus, again, the question of individual differences arose. In the discussion of the results for all the experiments, this question will be explored.

Table 3 Results of Experiments VI, VII, VIII, and IX
Multiple judgment procedure

ctures correctly entified	Experiment VI (49 Judges) 40 Photos of C 40 Photos of D		Experiment VII (70 Judges) 36 Photos of D 36 Photos of E		Experiment VIII (40 Judges) 60 Photos of D 60 Photos of E		Experiment IX (74 Judges) 100 Photos of E	
	Score	Proportion	Score	Proportion	Score	Proportion	Score	Proportion
terview C								
Median	21.0*	.52	- - -	- - -	- - -	- - -	- - -	- - -
st quartile	18.8	.47	- - -	- - -	- - -	- - -	- - -	- - -
rd quartile	22.8	.57	- - -	- - -	- - -	- - -	- - -	- - -
erview D								
Median	25.7***	.64	21.9***	.61	39.2***	.65	- - -	- - -
st quartile	23.0	.58	19.6	.54	35.8	.60	- - -	- - -
rd quartile	27.2	.68	23.8	.66	43.0	.72	- - -	- - -
terview E								
Median	- - -	- - -	21.8***	.61	38.8***	.65	68.0***	.68
st quartile	- - -	- - -	20.9	.58	36.5	.61	63.4	.63
rd quartile	- - -	- - -	23.6	.66	41.5	.69	72.1	.72

* $p < .05$
* $p < .001$

Experiment VII

Problem. The purpose of this experiment was to replicate the findings on D and extend the findings to another subject, the subject in E. Hypothesis: Untrained judges can accurately determine whether a randomly selected and ordered series of photographs were taken during the stress or catharsis phase of an interview.

Method. Thirty-six photographs were randomly selected from D, 36 from E. The procedure was identical to that of Experiment VI.

Subjects. A new group of 70 college freshmen served as judges; half viewed E first, then D; half followed the reverse order.

Results. Again there was no significant difference between those judges who had seen E first and those who had seen D first, and the scores for the two groups of judges were combined. The obtained accuracy scores were significant for person D and for person E photographs, and there was no difference in accuracy on the two subjects. Table 3 presents these results.

Discussion. The results on person D replicate the earlier results on this person; the results on person E are quite similar to those reported for persons D and A.

Experiment VIII

Problem. This experiment was designed to explore judge ability to interpret the behavior of different persons, a problem to be discussed in a later section. It is reported here only as a replication of Experiment VII. Hypothesis: Untrained judges can accurately determine whether randomly selected and ordered photographs were taken from the stress or the catharsis phase of an interview.

Method. The procedure was identical to that of Experiment VII except that a new group of photographs was randomly selected from D and E, and 60 pictures, rather than 36, were chosen from each interview.

Subjects. A new group of 40 night-school students served as judges.

Results. Again there was no difference in the accuracy scores of those who saw E first and those who saw D first, and the results were combined. The obtained accuracy was significant for photographs of D and E. Table 3 shows these results.

Discussion. These results closely replicate the earlier findings. The findings on D have been quite consistent across the different independent groups of judges, and for different randomly selected samples of photographs in Experiments VI, VII, and VIII. The same is true for E in Experiments VII and VIII.

Experiment IX

Problem. This experiment addressed the problem of stability of judgment of nonverbal behavior over time. The problem will be discussed later, but part of the results are reported here as a final replication of this series of experiments. Hypothesis: Untrained judges can accurately determine whether randomly selected and ordered photographs were taken during the stress or the catharsis phase of an interview.

Method. The procedure was identical to that of Experiment VIII except that only photographs of E were shown. A new sample of 100 photographs was randomly selected, and judgments were made twice by each judge, with a four-day interval between trials. Two different randomly determined orders of presentation were employed.

Subjects. A new group of 74 college freshmen served as judges.

Results. The results for the first testing are shown in Table 3. Again, E was accurately judged, replicating the results of Experiments VII and VIII.

Discussion. This experiment replicated the accuracy results on E. That is, the same general level of accuracy was achieved on E in Experiments VII, VIII, and IX. It should be noted that for each experiment a different sample of photographs was randomly selected from the interviews, and a different group of students served as judges.

These experiments did vary in the absolute number of photographs shown to judges, and it appears that the median number of photographs correctly identified slightly increased as the size of the photograph sample increased. For person E the increase was as follows:

in Experiment VII the 36 photographs gave a median accuracy of .61; in Experiment VIII the 60 photographs gave a median accuracy of .65; in Experiment IX the 100 photographs gave a median accuracy of .68. The increase was as follows for person D:

in Experiment VII the 36 photographs gave a median accuracy of .61; in Experiment VI the 40 photographs gave a median accuracy of .64; in Experiment VIII the 60 photographs gave a median accuracy of .65. While the increases in accuracy are small, they show at least that any loss which might be due to fatigue associated with making an increased number of judgments is more than counteracted by the benefits associated with seeing a larger sample of interview behavior. The benefits, practice effects and the opportunity to acquire ideas about the subjects' range of behavior, made possible by the use of many photographs, will be discussed next.

FURTHER ANALYSIS OF EXPERIMENTS III-IX

The data from Experiments III-IX were further analyzed to examine the influence of practice on accuracy, and the ability of a judge to achieve significant accuracy for more than one stimulus person (interview subject).

Practice Effects

With the use of the procedure in which judges gave separate responses to many photographs, in Experiments III-IX, it seemed reasonable to expect that there might be some increments in accuracy over trials as a result of practice in performing the judgment task. Such a possibility was explored by comparing a judge's accuracy on the first third of the trials with his accuracy on the next third of the trials. The judgments of the last third were not included, since any benefits due to practice might possibly have been counteracted by fatigue or boredom toward the end of the procedure. A Wilcoxon matched-pairs signed-ranks test was performed on the difference for each judge between his first-third and second-third accuracy scores, employing a two-tailed significance test. Table 4 shows these data; results are not given for person A, because fourteen trials did not provide enough judgments for measuring practice effects, nor for Experiment V, because in that experiment the judgment task concerned interview chronology rather than the stress and catharsis phases.

The results were inconsistent. In some experiments the increase in accuracy scores was not only statistically significant but substantial in size; for example, in Experiment III the increase in accuracy on B was 20 proportion points, and in Experiment VII the increase in accuracy on E was ten proportion points. On the other hand, significant decreases in accuracy also occurred, even with the same stimulus person in different experiments; for both persons D and E, accuracy significantly increased in one experiment, significantly decreased in another experiment; and there was the further inconsistency that in the same experiment in which

Table 4 Practice Effects

Experiment	Stimulus persons	Number of trials in each third	Median first third trials	Median second third trials	p
III	B	11	4.85	7.05	< .001
IV	B	11	4.81	5.85	< .05
VI	C	13	6.45	5.55	> .10
	D	13	8.88	7.88	< .05
VII	D	12	7.00	6.85	> .10
	E	12	6.00	7.14	< .001
VIII	D	20	11.80	14.50	< .001
	E	20	12.14	11.10	< .05
IX	E	30	19.00	19.50	< .05

judgments of D increased, judgments of E decreased. The inconsistency of these results on possible practice effects is in marked contrast to the consistency of the accuracy scores across all trials noted for the different stimulus persons across the various experiments.

Our interpretation of this confusing state of affairs is that, while practice may have an effect, the effect is probably contaminated by differences in the difficulty of judging particular photographs. It should be remembered that a different random selection of photographs of each stimulus person was used in each of Experiments VI-IX. Thus, the inconsistent results for a given stimulus person may be due to differences in the degree of difficulty represented by the particular selection and ordering of two sets of photographs; in one experiment the first third might have been more difficult to judge, while in another experiment the second third might have been more difficult. The results on person B were consistent in Experiments III and IV, in which the same photographs in the same order were shown.

A check was made to determine whether an equal number of stress and catharsis photographs had been presented in the first-third and second-third of the trials in the various experiments, since a differential rate of guessing either response might have led to greater or lesser accuracy if the two types of photographs were unequally distributed. But they were not. Further, practice effects were again measured for each experiment to compare the first ten trials with the last ten trials, and almost identical results to those reported in Table 4 were obtained. Thus, we conclude that it was not possible to determine whether an increase in accuracy results from practice over trials.

Judge Ability Across Stimulus Persons

These experiments were not designed for studying the characteristics of the good and bad judge of nonverbal behavior, nor were they chiefly intended to demonstrate that judging ability is consistent across different stimulus persons. This latter point, however, does raise some relevant questions about the nature of nonverbal communication. How much overlap is there in the repertoire of nonverbal cues—specific facial expressions or body positions—of two different persons? Does the same nonverbal cue have the same meaning in the repertoire of two different persons?

A procedure for establishing similarities in accuracy for a given judge across different stimulus persons (interview subjects) would be to correlate his accuracy scores on two stimulus persons. There are three possible outcomes, supporting one or more interpretations. If similar nonverbal cues are displayed by different stimulus persons and have the same meaning for both persons, then a judge who can decipher one person's nonverbal behavior could do so with another's, and the correlation coefficient for judge accuracy on any two people should be positive. If the nonverbal cues shown by two stimulus persons are dissimilar, but a judge is familiar with the meanings of the two distinct sets of cues, then again he would score similarly on both persons, and the correlation coefficient would again be positive. If two sets of nonverbal cues are dissimilar and the judge is familiar with only one of the types, then positive or negative results on one stimulus person would not predict a judge's ability to interpret the behavior of another, and the correlation would not be significant. If different stimulus persons display some of the same nonverbal cues, but these cues have different meanings for the different stimulus persons, then a judge who applies the same standards of interpretation to a given cue whenever it appears will be correct for one person and incorrect for another person, and the correlation will be negative.

This is not meant to be an exhaustive list, but rather an indication of some of the questions which could be raised by a study of judge ability across different stimulus persons. Unfortunately, as we shall soon see, the data from the present experiments do not very well lend themselves to this type of analysis.

The correlations of judges' accuracy on different stimulus persons is reported in Table 5 for Experiments III, IV, VI, VII, and VIII. Before Experiment VIII was designed, the distribution of accuracy scores in the other experiments was examined to explore the reasons for the low correlations. These distributions of accuracy scores are quite skewed and limited in range; almost all of the judges scored correctly on between .55 and .75 of the photographs. Such a limit on the distribution of scores would of course greatly restrict the size of any correlation coefficient between two sets of accuracy scores. Experiment VIII was designed to overcome this limitation. A larger sample of photographs of each interview subject was shown, and the judge population, night-school students, was selected because of their greater heterogeneity as compared to daytime students. The median age for the judges in Experiments I-VII was 21.5, with an inter-quartile range of less than two years; the median age for the judges in Experiment VIII was 31.3, with an inter-quartile range of about seven years. These efforts to enhance the correlation coefficient seem to have been modestly successful; the largest correlation coefficient achieved was in this experiment.

Table 5   Correlations between accuracy scores on different Ss

Experiment	Number of judges	Stimulus persons shown	Rank order correlation
III	33	A & B	.319*
IV	35	A & B	.233
VI	49	C & D	.269
VII	70	D & E	.217
VIII	40	D & E	.44**

*p < .05
**p < .01

The data from these nine experiments suggest that there is a positive correlation in judging ability across stimulus persons. The questions outlined earlier would be more meaningfully studied with a test which not only yields a greater range of accuracy scores, but, more importantly, which presents the nonverbal behavior of stimulus persons systematically selected for their differences in personal characteristics. Work presently in progress is exploring judges' reactions to photographs of different psychiatric groups.

SUMMARY OF EXPERIMENTS IV-IX

Experiments IV-IX differed from the earlier experiments in some features of their design. Experiments I and III showed both interviewer and subject; Experiments I and II required only one judgment from a judge for one photograph. Experiments IV-IX all showed only the subject, and all required a judgment for each of many photographs from each judge.

Summary of method. In Experiments IV-IX judges in every case saw a number of randomly selected and ordered photographs of each stimulus person they judged, and in every case saw only the subject without the interviewer. Viewing time for each photograph was twenty seconds, during which time judges wrote their decision as to whether the picture had been taken during the stress or catharsis phase of the interview which had been described generally in the instructions. The actual number of photographs shown varied for the five interviews from 14 to

100. Across all of the experiments judgments were obtained on a total of 14 photographs of A, 34 photographs of B, 40 of C, 100 of D, and 120 of E. Photographs were selected in every case in a random fashion without prior inspection of the pictures; in most of the experiments a new random sample was selected each time a particular interview was to be shown.

Summary of judge population. Independent groups of judges viewed the photographs. In every experiment except one these were freshmen psychology students; in Experiment VIII a more heterogeneous group of night-school psychology students served as judges. In all, 35 judges responded to photographs of A, 35 judged B, 49 judged C, 159 judged D, and 184 judged E.

Summary of results. Significant accuracy was achieved for at least one of the stimulus persons judged in all of the experiments except Experiment V, which was designed as a control experiment and was not expected to produce accuracy. Significant accuracy was achieved on four of the five stimulus persons judged, although for one of the four, person C, the level of accuracy was just above the chance level. The levels of accuracy were quite similar on persons A, D, and E; the median proportion of photographs accurately judged ranged from .69 on A, to .61, .64, and .65 on D, and .61, .65, and .68 on E. The results on persons D and E were replicated across three independent groups of judges, who in each case responded to a different random sample of photographs.

The accuracy results were similar for B and C, and differed from the three interviews just described in that either slight but significant or nonsignificant accuracy levels were obtained. The median proportion of photographs correctly identified was .51 for B and .52 for C.

Practice effects were evaluated; results were inconclusive.

In two of the nine experiments a significant low-to-moderate correlation in judge accuracy among the different stimulus persons was obtained. In the other experiments the correlations were also positive, but not significant.

GENERAL DISCUSSION

With the establishment of the proposition that nonverbal behavior as shown in still photographs provides accurate information to observers about the two phases of a standard interview, many questions are raised: (A) How much of the nonverbal behavior shown during an interview actually communicates information? (B) What kind of information does nonverbal behavior provide? (C) What might account for the differences in judge accuracy between stimulus persons; or, do differences in judge accuracy reflect differences in the nonverbal communicativeness of individual stimulus persons, and if so, what do such differences mean? (In discussing these questions data from two new series of experiments will be introduced.)

A. THE AMOUNT OF NONVERBAL BEHAVIOR
COMMUNICATING INFORMATION

Most generally phrased, our concern is with how rich nonverbal behavior is as a source of information. But, there are two aspects to this question: *what different kinds* of information may be learned from a given sample of nonverbal behavior, and *how much* of the behavior sampled actually communicates systematic information of any kind. This latter question will be discussed first, and can be stated operationally as *how many* of the photographs provided information relevant to the judgment task. In answering this question we will draw a distinction between photographs which elicited from the judges substantial agreement, regardless of accuracy, and photographs about which judges usually disagreed. The former will be defined as pictures which provide *consistent* information, and the latter will be considered as *ambiguous* photographs.

In deciding how much of the nonverbal behavior communicated information we will consider the following: (1) the ratio of consistent to ambiguous photographs; (2) the meaning of inaccuracy; (3) a new experiment which studied a further question to be raised in the second section.

1. Do most of the photographs convey consistent or ambiguous information?

The levels of accuracy in the first nine experiments can be cited in support of either of two contradictory hypotheses: that most of the photographs were ambiguous, and that most of the photographs communicated consistent information.

On the hypothesis that most of the pictures were ambiguous, it might be argued that, since the median proportion of correct indentification never reached .75, judges were responding in a chance fashion to *most* of the pictures and correctly identifying only those few which do carry clear information, thus raising the median accuracy level from .50 to .60-.70. On the hypothesis that most of the pictures carried consistent information, the moderate level of the median proportion correct can be attributed to most of the photographs carrying either *consistently inaccurate* or *consistently accurate* information, thus canceling each other out, in part.

In the discussion to follow, a *consistent photograph* is one to which the majority of judges gave the *same* designation, whether "stress" or "final," whether accurately or inaccurately in terms of the task. An *ambiguous photograph* is one about which there was considerable disagreement. Boundaries were arbitrarily set, as follows: consistent photographs were those which were either correctly identified or incorrectly identified by more than 60% of the judges. Consistently accurate photographs were those which more than 60% of the judges correctly identified; consistently inaccurate photographs were those which less than 40% of the judges correctly identified. The boundaries of the criterion for ambiguity were set at ten percentage points on either side of .50, around the point at which half the responses to a given picture were "stress," and half were "final." Figure 2 shows examples of consistent and ambiguous photographs.

The data from Experiments IV-IX were further analyzed in order to provide a basis for choosing between the two hypotheses as to whether

Figure 2. Examples of consistent and ambiguous photographs.

most of the photographs communicated consistent or ambiguous information. The first analysis compared the responses of different groups of judges to the same sets of photographs to determine through a rank order correlation whether the photographs maintained their same relative position in terms of the proportion of judges accurate on each picture. The judges who had viewed the photographs in Experiments IV, VI, VII and VIII were randomly assigned to two subgroups; the proportion of correct responses to each photograph was calculated for each subgroup and a Spearman rank-order correlation (Siegel, 1956, p. 202) was performed. The correlations, shown in Table 6, are generally high, indicating that the photographs tend to remain in the same relative position in terms of accuracy of identification when viewed by different groups of judges. These results are interpreted as providing some support for the hypothesis that most of the photographs carry consistent information. If most of the photographs were in fact ambiguous, certainly it would be unlikely that they would maintain the same relative standing when judged by different groups.

Table 6   Rank order correlation between proportion of correct responses to each photo

Experiment	Interview	Number of judges within each group	Rank order corre- lation by photo
IV	A	17 and 18	.81
	B	17 and 18	.87
VI	C	25 and 24	.73
	D	25 and 24	.84
VII	D	35 and 35	.86
	E	35 and 35	.88
VIII	D	20 and 20	.63
	E	20 and 20	.85
IX	E	100 test-retest	.92

All of the correlations are significant beyond .001 level of confidence.

The data from Experiment IX allowed examination of another type of consistency: consistency over time for the same set of judges. In Experiment IX the same group of judges viewed the same pictures on two occasions separated by four days. A Spearman rank-order correlation was performed between the numbers of correct responses to each photograph on the two time occasions. This correlation is higher than the others reported in Table 6, probably because this was the only instance in which the same judges viewed the same pictures.[3] This correlation was interpreted as also supporting the hypothesis that most of the pictures provide consistent information. The reasoning is that, if most of the pictures were ambiguous, they could not be expected to maintain so well their relative

[3] Although less relevant to the problem under discussion, it might be mentioned that Experiment IX also offered the opportunity to establish whether judges maintained the same relative level of accuracy over time. Thus, a rank order correlation was also computed on the basis of the number of photographs accurately identified by each judge on the two time occasions. This Rho was .60, $p < .001$, showing a moderate stability on judge performance.

position when judged on two different occasions by the same judges.

Another approach to the problem was to examine the distribution of scores for each interview to find the numbers of photographs judged consistently accurately, consistently inaccurately, and ambiguously, according to the criterion previously described. The number of judges correct on each photograph was tabulated. The proportions of correct identifications were calculated by totaling the correct judgments for each photograph across all experiments in which it had been viewed and dividing the sum by the total number of judges who had seen the picture. A frequency distribution was drawn, grouping these proportions of correct identifications into ten-point intervals. The frequency of photographs within each interval was then converted .into a proportion of the total number of photographs for which judgments had been obtained; this step was necessary to adjust for the considerable divergence in the

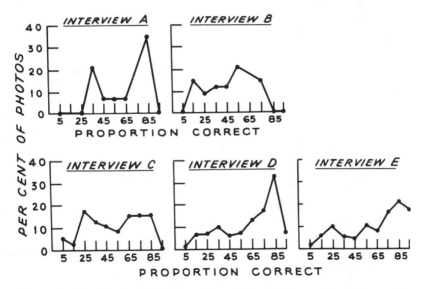

Figure 3.   Distribution of photographs within each interview in terms of the proportion of judges who correctly identified each of the pictures.

numbers of photographs judged from each interview. Figure 3 shows these data, which bear directly on the choice between the two hypotheses under discussion. If most of the photographs were ambiguous, we should expect distributions symmetrically centered around the .50 level of correct identification, with the greatest concentration near the .50 level. Clearly, this is not the case. The figure shows that some photographs were inaccurately judged (below .40), some were in the ambiguous range, and many were accurately judged (above .60), thus supporting the hypothesis that most of the pictures provided consistent information. These data have been summarized in Table 7. (From both Table 7 and Figure 3

Table 7 Ambiguity - Consistency

Interview	Number of photos for each interview	Ambiguous photos (41 to 60% of Js correct)	Consistent Photos		Accurate and inaccurate
			Accurate (61 to 100% of Js correct)	Inaccurate (0 to 40% of Js correct)	
		%	%	%	%
A	14	14	65	21	86
B	34	32	32	36	68
C	40	17	45	38	83
D	100	11	67	22	89
E	120	15	63	22	85

it is evident that there were differences among the stimulus persons in the five interviews; these data will be further examined later in the discussion.)

2. *What does inaccuracy mean?*

In the course of establishing that the majority of the photographs communicated consistent information, we have discovered that some of the pictures in each interview were consistently inaccurately interpreted. Now, the question is, how do we interpret this phenomenon?

The accuracy criterion was simply that judges correctly identify the phase when a picture was taken. Accuracy, therefore, depended in some part on the success of the standard interview procedure, on the interviewer's eliciting two quite distinct reactions from the subject during the two phases.

Even if we assume such success, inaccuracy could still occur in two ways. Particular expressions reflective of a phase for a particular stimulus person might be peculiar to him, and in fact might connote just the opposite experience to most observers. For example, a slouching posture shown during stress might be a habitual uncomfortable response for a given stimulus person, and yet be usually, but inaccurately by our criterion, judged as a cathartic response. Another possibility is that at certain moments a subject may have tried to disguise his feelings or conceal them from the interviewer, and his masking cues might have misled the judges. For example, a subject's hands carefully folded in his lap during stress might have been read by judges as a poised or relaxed nonverbal cue, and incorrectly called catharsis. Thus, both possible idiosyncracies in the subject and possible attempts to mask his actual experience could account for inaccuracy.

If, to these sources of possible confusion arising from the subject, we add the possibility that the interview procedure was not successful in eliciting two quite distinct reactions in the subjects, or in all subjects, then we must consider a different kind of inaccuracy—one which is at·

tributable to a limitation in the experimental control of the interview. Discussions with the participants after the interview, their responses to their own photographs, and our own reading of the typescripts, all suggest that the standard interview format was not completely successful. It appears that the subject's experience was not unidimensional within each phase. For example, it seems likely that there were moments during the stress phase when the subject felt he had temporarily avoided attack, or obtained the upper hand, and that these experiences as captured by the photographs appeared to judges to be part of the catharsis phase. Similarly, moments during the catharsis phase when the subject introspected about his behavior during stress, or wondered why the interview was still continuing, might have been stressful for him, and been regarded by judges as part of the stress phase.

It is doubtful that experimental manipulations of a standard stress interview can completely control for a subject's repertoire of defensive tactics to meet the interviewer's assault, or for the interviewer's failure in a particular line of inquiry to evoke a particular feeling in a subject. We may conclude that the inaccuracy results reflect, at least in part, this lack of complete experimental control over the subject's experience. Therefore, we must not interpret inaccuracy as evidence that the nonverbal behavior necessarily provides wrong or misleading information.

3. *Does accuracy increase if judgments are based on more nonverbal cues?*

It is possible that accuracy might have been substantially improved if short bursts of motion picture film had been shown instead of still photographs, so that judges could observe movement in addition to positions, and stimuli more closely resembling behavior ordinarily seen. In a recently completed doctoral dissertation on the training of judges to interpret nonverbal behavior, Hoffman (1964) used as his stimuli five-second bursts of motion picture film. He employed a stress interview procedure patterned after ours, with four different subjects and the same judgment task of guessing whether each stimulus unit was from the stress or catharsis phase of the interview. Thus, our experiments are comparable except that Hoffman's showed 24 frames per second for five seconds and ours showed one frame. The accuracy obtained by Hoffman's judges was remarkably similar to that reported here; prior to training, the average accuracy across all judges across all four stimulus persons was .56 of the photographs correctly identified, with a range of average accuracy of .48 to .64. Clearly, for this judgment task short motion picture film bursts yield no greater accuracy than the still photograph.

Another feature of both designs, however, might account for our obtaining only moderate accuracy. Judges were forced to respond to behavior presented completely out of context. Possibly, inaccurate judgments could be avoided with an experimental design which shows to judges a larger parcel of consecutive behavior, thus permitting them to disregard a set of cues which are inconsistent with the general tenor of the experience. Certainly, in usual interactions many more nonverbal cues are available to observers than are shown in either a split-second photograph *or* five seconds of motion picture film shown out of a larger temporal context. More typically, a given nonverbal cue is seen in the context of behavior which precedes and follows it, and observers can evaluate the behavior within that framework. An experiment was therefore designed which differed from the previous nine in that it provided judges with a substantially increased and sequential sample of nonverbal behavior.

Experiment X

Problem. The purpose of this experiment was to determine whether the addition of sequential context cues would increase accurate judgment. Hypothesis: Providing judges with all of the photographs from a single interview phase will lead to higher accuracy levels than have previously been found.

Method. The instructions and procedure were the same as those of the earlier experiments with the following exceptions. Judges were shown all of the photographs from a single phase of the interview in succession, with each picture projected for five seconds. After seeing all of the photographs from a phase, judges recorded their decision—viz., whether the pictures were of the stress or catharsis phase. When making their judgment they did not know that they would next see all of the photographs from the other phase. Before seeing the other set of photographs they were told that, when they had seen the second set, they would again judge the *first* set of pictures. They were specifically instructed to write down a second decision about the *first* series of photographs, and not to change their first answer; moreover, they were told that there was no need to be consistent, that their second answer could be the same as or different from their first answer.

Photographs from D and E were shown because the earlier studies produced good results with these interviews, and because fairly extensive photographic records of each were available: 80 photographs were shown of person D during stress, 80 during catharsis; 74 photographs were shown of person E during stress, 74 during catharsis. There were four experimental groups; half saw D, half saw E; half saw the stress phase first, half the catharsis phase.

Judges. Undergraduates from upper division psychology courses served as judges. Since this experiment was conducted with summer school students, the range of age was greater than in any of the judge samples reported earlier; in order to obtain a more comparable age group, persons over 30 years of age were discarded from the data analysis. Forty-four judges remained of D, 32 of E.

Results. Table 8 shows the results for the first and second decisions. The hypothesis pertained only to the first decision, for which the judges had seen all of the photographs from an entire interview phase, but only from one phase. The prediction was that the accuracy level would be

Table 8 Results of Experiment X

Interview	Number of Js	Number (and proproportion) of Js accurate first decision	second decision
D	44	28 (.636)	38 (.864)
E	32	19 (.594)	23 (.719)

greater than was found in the previous experiments where no sequential cues were available. There had been considerable variation in the design of the first nine experiments, however, and none of them allows an exact comparison in which all variables could be held constant except for that of sequential cues. Table 9 compares the experiments on six aspects of their design.[4]

Experiment II is comparable with Experiment X in that both showed only the subject, required only one judgment from each judge, and

[4] Although not directly relevant to the problem under discussion, the data from Experiment X can be analyzed to yield some ideas about comparative accuracy on the two phases of the interview. The reader may have wondered why there has been no such presentation of results for the stress and catharsis photographs separately in the earlier experiments. The reason is that such an analysis would be quite unsound, since the judges' rate of guessing either stress or catharsis would confuse the interpretation of such results. If, for example, a judge guessed stress most of the time, he would obtain higher accuracy on stress than on catharsis photographs, although, it should be noted, that such a guess rate would not contaminate the accuracy measure across all photographs. Inspection of the data from the first nine experiments did reveal that most judges guessed stress more frequently than catharsis; whether this is because the pictures are more stressful than cathartic, or because of response set is unknown. Experiment X is not entirely free of this problem, but at least judges have responded to only one set of photographs, either stress or catharsis. These data have been relegated to a footnote, however, since the judges' stress guess rate could still cause a difficulty in interpretation, and if our interest had been to study the differences between the two phases a more elaborate design would have been necessary in which the judges' guess rate was first assessed, and the subjects matched on this basis.

The differences in the accuracy on the two phases in Experiment X, in any case are not particularly impressive. For Interview D, .70 of the judges were accurate on stress, .58 on catharsis; for Interview E, .59 were accurate on stress, .60 on cartharsis. These results were found on the first decision made in Experiment X, and it appears that there is a trend toward more accurate judgment of stress for Interview D, but not for Interview E. The results found for the second decision are .95 of the judges correct on stress, .79 correct for cartharsis on Interview D; .76 correct on stress, .67 correct for catharsis on Interview E. While stress appears to be more correctly identified by more judges on both D and E, interpretation is further confounded by the fact that when they made the second decision judges had seen both phases of the interview, and differential accuracy may be due to order effects, willingness to change one's mind, etc. These data have been presented more to satisfy any curiosity about why stress and catharsis have not been separately analyzed than because of the substantive value of these results.

Table 9 Features of the designs of the experiments

Experiment	Stimulus persons shown in photos	Interviews judged	Number of photos shown of each stimulus person to each judge	Judgments Pictures	Each judge sees photos from one or both interview phases	Absolute number of judgments by each judge
I	Interviewer & S̲	A & B	1	1/1	One phase	1
II	S̲ only	A & B	1	1/1	One phase	1
III	Interviewer & S̲	A & B	14 A 34 B	1/1	Both phases	48
IV	S̲ only	A & B	14 A 34 B	1/1	Both phases	48
VI	S̲ only	C & D	40 C 40 D	1/1	Both phases	80
VII	S̲ only	D & E	36 D 36 E	1/1	Both phases	72
VIII	S̲ only	D & E	60 D 60 E	1/1	Both phases	120
IX	S̲ only	E	100 E	1/1	Both phases	100
X (First decision)	S̲ only	D & E	80 D 74 E	1/80 1/74	One phase	1

showed each judge only one phase of the interview; the two differed in that Experiment X provided not only sequential cues but also a larger number of pictures and a different interview sample. The results for Experiment II show that .58 of the judges of A and .47 of the judges of B correctly identified the interview phase, as compared to Experiment X, in which .64 of the judges of D and .59 of the judges of E correctly identified the interview phase. This difference in accuracy is misleading, however. It reflects the generally low accuracy of the judgments of person B. Since Experiment X had excluded persons who had been poorly judged (viz., person C), a more appropriate comparison would also exclude the results on person B. If only the results on person A from Experiment II are compared with the results from Experiment X, the accuracy difference is no longer very great.

Experiment VI-IX are comparable with Experiment X in that the same stimulus persons were shown, and many photographs were shown of each stimulus person; they differed in that Experiment X provided not only sequential cues but also showed only one phase to a judge and required only one judgment from each judge. The differences in accuracy are not striking. The median accuracy ranged from .61 to .65 of the photographs of person D correctly identified in Experiments VI, VII, and VIII, as compared to .64 in Experiment X. For person E, the median accuracy ranged from .61 to .68 in Experiments VII, VIII, and IX, as compared to .59 in Experiment X. Thus, the comparison of the results on the first decision in Experiment X with the results on the earlier experiments does *not* support the hypothesis that accuracy is greater when sequential cues are available to judges.

When the judges in Experiment X had seen the other phase of the interview, their second decision was better than their first. For D the accuracy level of the second decision, .86 judges correct, is considerably higher than that of the earlier experiments on D photographs.

Discussion. Common sense would suggest that adding more information, in particular providing clues about sequence of nonverbal behavior and its context, would increase accuracy; and yet this was not found to be so. The earlier discussion of the meaning of inaccuracy may help to explain this unexpected result. We interpreted the experiences of stress and catharsis as being not unidimensional, in that there was some overlap between the two phases which, when perceived by judges, led them to mis-identify certain pictures. This interpretation implies that nonverbal behavior may not only reflect an individual's gross affect changes, such as from stress to catharsis, but may also be fairly sensitive to and track the more moment-to-moment changes in an individual's handling of each experience. If the experience represented in the photographs is not unique or pure, then such momentary tracking may be faithfully reflecting the many features within the experience.

When a judge responds to many photographs singly he has no awareness of any of the contradictory elements within an interview phase; when he sees a smile during stress, for example, he does not know that it may have been preceded and/or followed by a terrible frown; he simply calls the photograph *cathartic* without any awareness of a problem—and his judgment is scored as inaccurate. When judges are shown an entire interview phase, they may benefit from context or sequence cues, but at the expense of having to contend with some of the seemingly contradictory messages sent within one interview phase. Admittedly, this is an ex post facto explanation, but it appears to be a reasonable one, and data from a new series of interviews lend some credence to it.

These new interviews were conducted with female patients hospitalized with a severe depression. Each patient was photographed at the time of admission to the hospital and again after some weeks of treatment shortly before discharge when she had made at least a partial recovery. Judges saw one entire interview and then were asked to decide whether the interview occurred when the patient was depressed or remitted. (The design was similar to that of Experiment X; but in these new experiments a judge saw only one interview and made one decision.) For this sample of depressed patients the mood experienced is quite uniform within an interview, the depression intense and durable, and so we could expect that judges would not be exposed to many contradictory or varied nonverbal messages within an interview. In the two experiments conducted to date, more than 90% of the judges correctly identified the interviews. The question of whether nonverbal behavior expresses momentary changes in an individual's mood will be discussed again in the following section about the kinds of information communicated by nonverbal behavior.

Experiment X does show, however, that when a judge sees the two contrasting sets of stimuli (both the stress and catharsis phases of the interview) his second decision is considerably better than his first. Showing both phases of the interview, in addition to providing more comparative information, also informs judges that there was overlap between the two phases and thus may give a better basis for evaluating contradictions within each phase. (It can be noted that there was more improvement on D than on F; this difference is consistent with data from Experiment XI, to be presented later, which show that there was more similarity during the two phases in the behavior of person E than of person D.)

The reader may have some interest in the comparative value of a design like that of Experiment X, in which a judgment is based on seeing many photographs in sequence, and a design like that of Experiments III-IX, where judges respond to each of many single photographs shown out of order. While all of the experiments are artificial in that only nonverbal behavior is presented, judges are removed from the interaction, and still pictures rather than motion pictures are the basic stimuli, Experiment X is a little more akin to the more usual observation situation in that at least the behavior was shown in sequence, and the behavior sampled from an entire interview phase was presented. It is interesting to note that this advantage of being somewhat more true to life may be vitiated by our ignorance of the way in which people arrive at an interpretation of nonverbal behavior in ordinary interactions. That is, in an ordinary life situation, when persons observe a segment of nonverbal behavior we cannot know whether (1) the observer *utilizes all of the cues,* either by making definite judgments of each cue, summing them up and concluding "That man is stressed," or by making tentative partial interpretations, moment by moment, subject to modification by each succeeding cue; or (2) the observer *utilizes only a few cues,* either because others do not carry information or because the observer does not observe what information is there.

Showing a large amount of nonverbal behavior can be informative of how observers respond in more usual situations; some notions can be gained about the upper limits of accuracy, for example. But such a procedure does not help answer the question which has been discussed throughout this section of the paper. With a design like that of Experiment X it is impossible to resolve the question of how much of the nonverbal behavior carries consistent information; for if the observer responds to a mass of nonverbal behavior he could be picking up many separate cues from each photograph, all of which carry some information, or he could just as well be completely in the dark about most of the photographs and basing his judgment on a few consistently communicating pictures. Thus, while the procedure in Experiment X is more true to life, the procedure of obtaining judgments of more limited samples provides a better answer to the question of how much of the nonverbal behavior shown during an interview communicates consistent information. It should be noted that "the size" of the more limited sample, whether still photograph or a few seconds of motion picture film, is not the relevant issue. The critical point is that the design be one in which judges must react to many separate slices of nonverbal behavior rather than to a conglomerate mass.

A second advantage of the design followed in the earlier experiments is that it allows study of the relationship between judgments and particular facial expressions and body positions shown. With the proposition now substantially established that judges respond systematically to nonverbal cues, it would be valuable to link judgments to particular nonverbal configurations, particularly if these apply to more than one stimulus person. Such analysis of these stress interviews and judgments is presently in progress.

B. THE KINDS OF INFORMATION COMMUNICATED BY NONVERBAL BEHAVIOR

In the preceding section we have seen that most of the nonverbal behavior shown during an interview communicates consistent information to observers. Our focus now shifts to an attempt to specify the types of information revealed by nonverbal behavior. Most generally, we are concerned with what an observer can learn from nonverbal behavior; specifically, our question is what were the kinds of information provided by the photographs which allowed judges to identify the stress and catharsis phases.

In most interpersonal settings, even those in which one person's role is defined as that of observer, nonverbal cues are not seen in isolation. The observer has verbal (content of a spoken message), vocal (voice quality), olfactory, and perhaps even tactile cues available concurrently with the nonverbal behavior (facial expressions, body movements and positions). The observer's knowledge of the situation, his expectations about the normative behavior for that situation, aid in his interpretation of the stimulus person's behavior. Yet with so many different possible sources of information available, it is difficult to determine what each source may contribute to any judgment, unless some are held constant or eliminated. In evaluating nonverbal behavior as a source of information we have eliminated verbal and vocal cues, and have held constant the observers' knowledge of the situation as given in the single set of instructions. Yet having given observers this information in the instructions about the situation makes it impossible to specify exactly what type of information they were utilizing in reaching their stress-catharsis judgment.

Judges had been specifically instructed to guess when the pictures had been taken. The terms *stress* and *final* were not defined as emotional experiences of the subject, per se, but were explained by a description of the interviewer's behavior in the two phases and how this may have affected the subject. Obviously the nonverbal cues shown in the pictures did not directly transmit the information *stress* or *final*, but this response of the judge represented an end point in a decisional chain in which he evaluated the cues in the photographs and then translated this evaluation into the terms dictated by the experiment: *stress* or *final*. A judge's basis for this evaluation remains unknown, although at least three possibilities will be mentioned.

A judge knew what the interviewer was trying to do in each phase, and may have evaluated each photograph by thinking, "Does this look as if the interviewer has just attacked the subject's motivation for choosing his vocation, or as if the interviewer has just apologized for his behavior during stress?" The judge could also have made some inferences about the subject's affect, and approached each photograph with the question, "Does this look as if the subject is angry, hurt or apprehensive, or does it look as if the subject is relieved, relaxed and happy?" Another basis for evaluation would entail inferences about the relationship between interviewer and subject during the two phases; a judge might have thought, "Does this look as if they are distant or close; is the subject alert and paying attention, or withdrawn and uninterested?" Thus, three possible bases of evaluation may be distinguished: knowledge of the interviewer's behavior given in the instructions, inferences about the subject's affect, and inferences about the relationship between interviewer and subject. These three bases are not independent, but may have been used jointly by a judge, may each have been used by different judges, or may each have been used by the same judge when viewing different photographs.

The fact that the instructions gave the purpose of the interview, and an account of some of the interviewer's behavior and some of the subject's reactions, makes it impossible to specify which of these classes of information were linked to the nonverbal cues in identifying the stress and catharsis pictures. The experiment now to be introduced, however, eliminated any reference to any aspect of the interview and avoided mention even of the fact that an interview had been conducted, in an attempt to focus upon whether nonverbal behavior provides one specific class of information, affect.

Experiment XI

Problem. The major purpose of this experiment was to determine whether affect ratings of the photographs would differ between stress and catharsis pictures. By avoiding mention of the fact that the photographs were taken during an interview, Experiment XI tested whether nonverbal behavior alone, free of any aids in interpretation from knowledge of situational context, provides information about a person's affect which reflects the experiences we attempted to induce during the stress interviews. Thus this experiment parallels many of the past studies in the literature of the judgment of emotion. But, in place of the criterion of whether judge ratings match the intent of an actor to pose an emotion, our criterion was whether judge ratings of emotion differed for the two different interview phases.

A second purpose of this experiment was to verify the distinction drawn previously, between consistently accurate, ambiguous, and consistently inaccurate photographs. Where photographs were randomly selected from the stress and catharsis phases of the interview, we could expect all three types of photographs to be represented. A difference in the affect ratings between stress and catharsis photographs randomly selected could be anticipated, but because of the presence of ambiguous and inaccurate photographs the difference should not be large. Where, however, only consistently accurate photographs were selected, then the difference in the affect ratings should be much larger.

Hypotheses: (1) Judge ratings of affect shown in the photographs will differ for the stress and catharsis photographs. (2) There will be a larger difference in affect ratings between stress and catharsis photographs selected from the consistently accurate category than from a sample of the two phases randomly selected from the entire range of photographs.

Method. This experiment is one of a series of studies (Ekman, 1964b), not to be presented here, utilizing Schlosberg's three dimensions of emotional expression to study the differences in communication between head and body cues.

Two samples of photographs were selected for ratings: a representative and a highly communicative sample. The representative sample was obtained by selecting 12 photographs at random from each of the five stress interviews: six of the pictures were taken from the stress phase, six from the catharsis phase. The 60 pictures from the five interviews were arranged into a randomly determined sequence. The highly communicative sample was composed of photographs for which more than 80% of the judges in the first nine experiments had correctly identified the interview phase; if more than one group of judges had seen a picture, then only pictures which met this criterion for each group of judges were chosen. Six pictures each from A, B, and C met this criterion; the twelve highest pictures within this criterion were chosen from D, and E; in each case half were stress and half catharsis photographs. Thus, the highly communicative sample was composed of 42 consistently accurate pictures; they were arranged in a randomly determined sequence for presentation to judges.

Judges rated each photograph on three nine-point scales: from pleasant to unpleasant, from tension to sleep, and from attention to rejection. Schlosberg's definitions of the three dimensions were used *verbatim* as follows:

Pleasantness-Unpleasantness. You are to rate each picture on a 9 point scale where 1 indicates that the person in the photograph is feeling about as UNPLEASANT or unhappy as imaginable, and 9 indicates the maximum PLEASANTNESS.

Attention-Rejection. You are to rate each picture on a 9 point scale where 9 indicates that the person in the photograph is feeling the maximum ATTENTION, as if the person is making every effort to see something. A rating of 1 indicates that the person is feeling the maximum REJECTION, as if the person is trying to shut out or keep out any stimulation. Inattention is not the true opposite of attention, but occupies a position of about 5, midway between ATTENTION and REJECTION.

Sleep-Tension. You are to rate each picture on a 9 point scale where 1 indicates that the person in the photograph is feeling the complete relaxation of SLEEP, whereas 1 would be given to the most 'emotional' expression you can imagine, in which the person is very excited and shows maximum TENSION.

Schlosberg has suggested that these three scales represent the basic dimensions of emotional expression; his definitions of the scales and other aspects of his procedure were followed. Judges saw the photographs three times, rating each photograph on one of the scales during each presentation. The order in which the dimensions were considered by the judges was balanced. The individual photographs were shown for twenty seconds each during each presentation.

There was a slight overlap between these two photographs samples. About 10% of the representative sample was also included in the highly communicative sample.

Subjects. Twenty-six college freshmen served as judges of the representative sample of 60 photographs; seventeen college freshmen judged the communicative sample of 42 photographs.

Results. The judgments were analyzed by first obtaining a median rating for each judge across all of the stress photographs from the five interviews, the same for the catharsis photographs, and the difference between the two medians. A Wilcoxon matched-pairs signed-ranks test was then performed on the difference scores for all judges. This analysis was performed separately for the judges who viewed the representative sample and those who viewed the highly communicative sample. Table 10 summarizes these data, showing the median stress score across all stress photographs and across all judges, a similarly derived score for catharsis, and the median difference between the two. For both representative and communicative samples there was a significant difference on Pleasantness-Unpleasantness dimension ratings and on Attention-Rejection ratings, and no difference on Sleep-Tension ratings.

It is reasonable that *stress* was rated as more unpleasant than was *catharsis*, and as more "rejecting" than "attentive." However, the Attention-Rejection findings are questionable in that a high intercorrelation was found between Attention-Rejection ratings and Pleasantness-Unpleasantness ratings, and the difference obtained was small. The lack of difference between stress and catharsis photographs on Sleep-Tension ratings we have interpreted as signifying that the intensity of the affect states experienced during stress and catharsis was not different. Thus, the results shown in Table 10 support the first hypothesis on the Pleasantness-Unpleasantness dimension that there would be a difference in affect ratings for the stress and catharsis photographs, and the second hypothesis, that this difference would be larger for the highly communicative sample than for the representative sample.

Table 10   Median ratings of stress and catharsis in a representative and a
communicative sample of photos in Experiment XI

Sample:	Pleasant (9) - Unpleasant (1)		Attention (9) - Rejection (1)		Sleep (1) - Tension (9)	
	Repr.	Comm.	Repr.	Comm.	Repr.	Comm.
Stress photos	4.33	3.89	5.93	5.75	5.60	4.75
Catharsis photos	5.68	6.89	6.27	6.43	5.61	4.88
Difference (catharsis-stress)	+1.25***	+3.00***	+.34***	+.68*	+.01	+.13

* p < .05
*** p < .001

The data were further analyzed in order to examine the responses to
each individual photograph from each interview. The median and interquartile range on the pleasantness scale was calculated for each individual photograph across all judges who had viewed that picture. Figure 4
shows these data for the representative sample, Figure 5 for the highly
communicative sample. The difference predicted in the second hypothesis between the ratings on the representative and the highly communicative sample can be easily seen by comparing these two figures.

Discussion. This experiment differed from the others in that judges
were deprived of any knowledge of the context within which the nonverbal behavior occurred, and were required to judge the affect of the
stimulus person rather than guess when the pictures were taken. The
fact that judges ascribed different affect to the pictures from the two

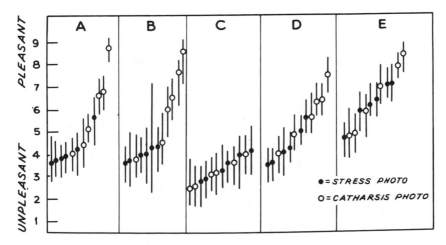

Figure 4.   Median and interquartile range on pleasantness for each photograph in
each interview for the random sample.

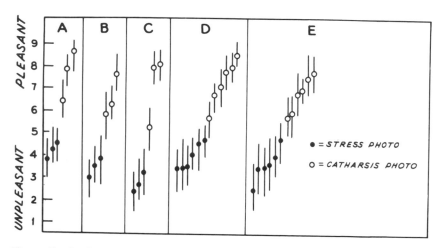

Figure 5.   Median and interquartile range on pleasantness for each photograph in each interview for the highly communicative sample.

interview phases without any knowledge of the interview strengthens our conclusion that nonverbal behavior communicates accurate information. Experiment XI has shown that judges are able to interpret affect accurately from photographs without any knowledge of the situation, with the criterion of accuracy specifying that judge ratings of affect differ in an expected fashion for the two phases of the interview. It may be that other types of information, in addition to affectual, are communicated by nonverbal behavior, and that these other types were also utilized by the judges. A later discussion will introduce a speculative formulation about the range of classes of information communicable by nonverbal behavior.

Experiment XI served also to further verify that there were differences between the consistently accurate, ambiguous, and consistently inaccurate photograph categories. As had been predicted, there was a much greater difference in the affect ratings of the highly communicative sample (the consistently accurate photographs) than of the representative sample (containing inaccurate and ambiguous pictures as well as accurate ones).

A further verification of the distinction drawn between consistently accurate, ambiguous, and consistently inaccurate photographs was made by examining the Pleasantness-Unpleasantness ratings and the percentage of correct identification for the stress/catharsis task for each of the photographs in Experiment XI. There was an almost perfect linear relationship, such that with the stress photographs the ratings moved from Pleasantness to Unpleasantness as the percentage of correct identification varied from 0 to 100%. In like fashion, the ratings of the catharsis photographs moved from Unpleasantness to Pleasantness as the percentage of correct identification varied from 0 to 100%.

Figures 4 and 5, showing the results for each individual photograph from each interview, draw our attention again to the differences found for the different stimulus persons in the five interviews. These data will be discussed next.

C. INDIVIDUAL DIFFERENCES IN NONVERBAL BEHAVIOR

The differences in results for the five stimulus persons will now be considered, to establish that the differences obtained can be attributed to actual differences between individuals in the clarity of their nonverbal communicativeness.

In the discussion of Tables 2 and 3 it was noted that low levels of accuracy were achieved for persons B and C, in contrast to A, D, and E. These differences were statistically significant.

In the discussion of Experiments I-IV, differences in the actual interview experience were raised as a possible explanation of such results. The interview experience might have been different for at least two reasons: either the interviewer's tactics varied, or the stimulus persons differed in their method of handling him. If the interviewer was too harsh during stress, and lost his knack of bringing about catharsis, then the subject's experience would have been uniformly stressful and judges would not have been able to differentiate the photographs even if the nonverbal behavior clearly carried the message about the experience. Similarly, if the interviewer could not bring himself to attack, then a subject's experience would have been rather non-stressful throughout, and again, even if the nonverbal behavior clearly reflected the subject's experience, judges would not have been able to differentiate the pictures from the two phases. Even if we assume that the interviewer performed similarly in all five interviews, the subject's method of handling the experience might have differed. If, for example, a subject was very well defended, accustomed to such assaults and skilled in parrying the interviewer, then his experience during stress might not have been very unpleasant, and again judges would have had difficulty identifying stress and catharsis pictures. Finally, if a stimulus person lacked resilience, or was vulnerable to attack, then the whole experience might have been miserable, and again judges would not have accurately identified the photographs.

In order to interpret the results on the five stimulus persons as due to some variable associated with clarity of nonverbal communication, we must find a measure which will reflect only differences in nonverbal sending, not these possible differences in the interview experience. One solution is to analyze the consistency versus ambiguity of information communicated, rather than accuracy. The consistency measure, as indicated earlier, is not contaminated by differences in the interview experience, since inaccurate photographs (i.e., stress photographs called catharsis and vice versa) are also considered consistent. The consistency measure, it may be recalled, was based on judge responses to each photograph. Pictures which elicited between 40 and 60% correct identifications were labeled ambiguous; all other pictures were considered consistent, accurate or inaccurate. In Table 7 the proportions of consistent and ambiguous photographs for the five interviews were shown.

A uniformly stressful or uniformly cathartic interview experience would be reflected in a relatively high consistently inaccurate score, but would not contaminate the ambiguous category. Table 7 shows that Interview C had no more ambiguous photographs than the other interviews; instead the low level of accuracy achieved in the experiments seems to be due to the large number of consistently inaccurate photographs. In Interview B, on the other hand, not only does the stimulus person seem to have had a different interview experience (as shown in the proportion of inaccurate photographs), but more of his photographs were ambiguous than any of the others.

The greater ambiguity of stimulus person B's nonverbal behavior can also be inferred from the data in Experiment XI, shown in Figures 4 and 5. Both the median and the interquartile ranges for each of twelve photographs are shown on the Pleasantness-Unpleasantness scale for each of the five interviews. The medians reflect possible differences in individual experience within the interviews, and will be discussed below. The interquartile ranges, however, tell us how great was the spread of interpretation by judges for each of the pictures seen. We should expect that the interquartile ranges on B would be higher than the others, since we have noted that on the stress/catharsis task his behavior was more ambiguous. Inspection of Figures 4 and 5 shows that this is the case.

It is possible that the absolute median value might limit the size of the interquartile ranges, and therefore the best comparison of the interviews would hold the median value constant. Table 11 shows the average interquartile range for each interview, when only photographs with a median between three and five are considered from all interviews. This range of score values was chosen because it approaches the middle of the Pleasantness-Unpleasantness scale, and because it maximized the number of photographs which could be considered from each interview. As expected, B's photographs resulted in the largest average interquartile range.

The median values on the five interviews can serve to clarify some of our earlier impressions about the differences in interview experience among the five stimulus persons. Person B, whose behavior we have found to be most ambiguous, still received a number of different Pleasantness-Unpleasantness ratings, and most of his stress photographs were rated as

Table 11 Average inter-quartile range of photos between 3 and 5 on pleasantness-unpleasantness

	A	B	C	D	E
Number of photos	7	8	8	6	3
Average inter-quartile range	1.79	2.38	1.83	1.65	1.82

more *unpleasant* than his catharsis pictures. Person C, however, was rated as feeling uniformly *unpleasant;* there was no difference in the ratings of his stress and catharsis pictures. Finally we might note that person E was generally more highly rated as feeling *pleasant* than anyone else; even many of the photographs from the stress phase were rated as *pleasant.* What we are now considering is not how ambiguous the behavior was, not the spread of interpretations of any given photograph, but instead the range of different affects observed. While persons C and E are rated quite differently from the others, one as being typically *unpleasant* and the other as *pleasant,* we can not determine whether this represents a baseline difference in affect between the two, or in their method of handling the experience, or in the interviewer's behavior.

There is no theoretical import in having shown that person B's nonverbal behavior is ambiguous; the stimulus persons were not selected on any personality variable, and five persons is too small a sample for drawing inferences about personality variables associated with nonverbal communicativeness. We have, however, shown two methods for evaluating individual differences in nonverbal communication: consistency/ambiguity of information communicated with a dichotomous judgment, and average interquartile range on a scale judgment of affect. These measures could be applied to the nonverbal behavior of individuals selected according to a personality variable.

CONCLUSIONS

Our question for study was defined in the introduction as whether nonverbal behavior communicates accurate information about the quality of an interpersonal relationship; and, more specifically, as whether a change in the overall relationship between two interactants would be accurately communicated through nonverbal behavior. The experiments reported and discussed have provided the basis for a positive answer. This finding allows us to infer two propositions: (1) that nonverbal behavior systematically changes as a function of a gross modification in the quality of the relationship between two people; and (2) that such nonverbal behavior is communicative and can in part be accurately understood. The judges' accuracy on the first nine experiments would not have been possible unless both of these propositions are true. If there had been no systematic changes in the nonverbal behavior of the five stimulus persons, then judges would have performed no better than chance. The fact that these were unsophisticated receivers, with no prior experience in observing stress interviews, shows that the behavior which occurred in these standardized interviews is not unique to the laboratory or to these particular stimulus persons. Accuracy required that the particular body positions and facial expressions shown in the photographs be familiar to the receiver, and similarly interpreted by a number of such observers.

With reference to the literature reviewed at the outset of this paper, our findings are in general agreement with the findings of Dittmann, Exline,

Sainesbury, Rosenthal, Maccoby, Jecker et al., and Mahl, all of whom have found that spontaneous interactive nonverbal behavior either indicates or communicates information about a class of events, such as mood, diagnostic features, understanding, verbal content, experimenter bias, psychodynamics. Our research has added the evidence that nonverbal behavior can accurately communicate information relevant to a gross change in the relationship between the interactants. In light of the earlier research on expressive behavior, which suggested that accurate information depended in large part on some knowledge of the situational context within which the behavior was emitted (e.g., Munn, 1940), the results of Experiment XI are worthy of particular note. Accurate communication through nonverbal behavior, measured by predicted differences in affect ratings of behavior in the two parts of the interview, is possible without any knowledge about any feature of the situational context.

Most of the samples of nonverbal behavior were found to communicate consistent information to receivers. This would not be entirely surprising if the behavior had been posed, or the sender had known that he should so act that at some later time others could interpret his behavior when limited to the nonverbal channel alone; but this was not the case. Instead our statement that most of the nonverbal behavior emitted is not ambiguous, but rather carries consistent information, pertains to the more usual circumstances of interpersonal behavior—when individuals are behaving spontaneously and concentrating in large part on the verbal dialogue. The ratio of consistent to ambiguous information communicated to a group of receivers was noted as one method of discriminating between senders which is relatively free of many of the artifacts usually associated with reliance solely on a measure of consistently accurate information. A second method of measuring individual differences in clarity of nonverbal communicativeness was described and applied to the data. This measure, the average interquartile range on scales of affect, utilizes a different response system which permits an assessment of the spread in receiver interpretations of a given sender's nonverbal behavior, again relatively free of some of the artifacts more usually found in reliance upon accuracy scores.

In considering what specific information may be communicated by the photographs which would allow accurate identification of the interview phase, a number of possibilities were outlined, and evidence was obtained that at least one of the classes of information, impressions about affect, is communicated by spontaneous nonverbal behavior. Importantly, these affect ratings relate to the circumstances of the interpersonal relationship, even though those circumstances are not known by the persons who make the affect judgments. But, there are many other routes, many other possible classes of information, which may have been communicated by the nonverbal behavior to permit judges' accurate determinations. This chapter will close with a speculative formulation of the classes of information which may be communicated by nonverbal behavior.

A FORMULATION OF CLASSES OF INFORMATION COMMUNICATED BY NONVERBAL BEHAVIOR

In most situations nonverbal behavior is seen in the context of some knowledge of the situation and awareness of the concomitant verbal behavior. Though sometimes the verbal behavior is not heard by the observer, some features of the situation in which the behavior was emitted are usually known to him. Very rarely in real life is nonverbal behavior observed without any knowledge of the situation; usually in seeing another person's nonverbal cues we also learn something about his situation, and it is only in experiments that an observer is given the opportunity to judge nonverbal cues without having any other knowledge. Our discussion will consider: (A) what the observer can learn when he is completely deprived of any cues other than nonverbal ones, in order to establish a base line about what may be contributed by this source alone; (B) how these classes of information are interpreted when the observer does know something about the situation; and (C) how nonverbal behavior can function in relation to a verbal message.

Before proceeding, it might be wise to restate our use of the term *communication*. The communicative value of a nonverbal act is established by determining that a group of receivers will similarly interpret the sender's behavior. To say that the sender's nonverbal act is then communicative does not imply that the sender intended to communicate, nor does it imply that the communication is in any way accurate, for the receivers may be foolish, prejudiced or for some other reason may have completely misunderstood the significance of the act; but the act nevertheless communicates, since they, the receivers, show agreement in their interpretation of it. In no sense do we assume that there is any equivalence between the nonverbal cue and that which it communicates; while scratching the head may be found to communicate nervousness or anxiety or contemplation, there is no reason to suppose that head scratching is necessarily equivalent to, an attribute of, or an expression of any of these states. So cautioned, let us proceed with our discussion.

A. CLASSES OF INFORMATION FROM NONVERBAL BEHAVIOR ALONE

Affect: Experiment XI showed that nonverbal behavior alone can provide accurate information about affect. One interpretation of the results from Experiment X would be that nonverbal behavior may sensitively track moment-to-moment changes in affect.

Verbal-symbolic: Nonverbal behavior may provide publicly understood symbolic information through what are usually called gestures. The distinctive feature of a gesture is that the nonverbal act usually means very little in and of itself, but arbitrarily or by analogy has been assigned a precise symbolic meaning. It is because of this clearly accepted verbal translation that we have labeled this class of information as verbal-symbolic.

Psychodynamic and diagnostic clues: The reports of gifted clinicians suggest that nonverbal behavior may provide symbolic information which is private, rather than public, in that it is recognized and interpreted only by rather special observers. Mahl (1959), for example, was able to infer marital problems from a patient's play with her wedding ring, or problems in managing aggressive impulses from hand clasping positions.

Instrumental acts: Nonverbal behavior is directly involved in the pursuit of certain instrumental activities even when an individual sits in a chair, and provides information that the person is tying his shoe, or scratching his head, or smoking.

Portrayals, dramatizations, reenactments: Nonverbal behavior can be used to act out in miniature or in detail a past, present, or future event.

Demography: Visual appearance, although at times deceptive, rather clearly states the age, sex, and perhaps through dress the social status of an individual. While not precisely demographic, related information about intelligence, aesthetic quality, values and occupation can be inferred from nonverbal behavior.

Style: The rate, rhythm and type of bodily activity can lead to inferences about expressiveness and temperament.

This list is not meant to be exhaustive, but to suggest some different kinds of information which may be communicated by nonverbal behavior. Obviously no claim is made that nonverbal behavior provides accurate information about each class of information, although it is probable that through the operation of stereotypes a reasonable amount of *consistent* information is communicated about each.

In some cases we have linked specific forms of nonverbal behavior to a particular category of information, and it is conceivable that this might be more systematically explicated. The problem is a difficult one, especially since a given cue can provide more than one type of information; e.g., an instrumental act may tell us not only what a person is doing at the moment, but also about his affect and perhaps about his psychodynamics.

B. ADDITIONAL INFORMATION AVAILABLE WHEN NONVERBAL BEHAVIOR IS INTERPRETED WITHIN KNOWLEDGE OF THE SITUATIONAL CONTEXT

If the observer also knows something about the situation in which the behavior occurred, then more specific inferences can be drawn within each of the classes of information. Usually the observer has such knowledge available, even if he cannot hear the verbal communication. There are many situations in which there is a shared intent to communicate, but the situation prevents verbal exchange: hitch-hiker and motorist, pilot and landing crew, charade player and audience, hunters stalking prey, etc.

If extensive communication is necessary, then gestures, improvised forms of verbal-symbolic behavior, portrayals, and instrumental acts will predominate. There are other situations in which the sender is not talking, does not intend to communicate to the observer, or is involved in an exchange with another person, where the observer can see but not hear. An example is the hidden observer; or the visual eavesdropper watching a conversation across the room at a cocktail party; or the therapist trying to understand the mute or resistant patient. In such situations the observer will attempt to utilize all of the classes of information available, although such typically intention-based categories as verbal-symbolic and portrayals will not be present.

We will consider only interpersonal situations, exploring first how the observer's interpretations of nonverbal behavior may be aided by knowledge of an abstract aspect of an interpersonal relationship: whether it is representative or atypical of the stimulus person's relationships.

If the nonverbal cues provide information about affect, and we also know that the situation is one typical of a person's interpersonal relationships, then it is possible to draw further inferences about his general level of satisfaction, and his usual or enduring moods. If, for example, we note that he looks sad, and we also believe that we have seen a representative sample of his usual affective reactions in his interactions, inferences could be drawn about the presence of a depressive disorder. Probably closely related to affect is information about the *quality of the interpersonal relationship*—whether it is close or distant, whether the person is involved and interested or detached and withdrawn. Knowledge about these two classes of information, affect and relationship quality, can lead to further inferences about the person's typical *role*—whether he is compliant or assertive, pliable or rigid, open or defensive, dominant or submissive, etc. If the observer knows that the sample of behavior shown is typical of the stimulus person's relationships, then such information about relationship quality and role can lead to further judgments about the general tenor of his interpersonal relationships, and related personality formulations based on assumptions about these relationships.

If the role of the other participant is known, whether that of spouse, employer, stress interviewer, etc., then many more specific inferences can be drawn from the classes of information provided by nonverbal cues. Information about affect can tell how satisfied the person is in his marital adjustment or work situation, what moods characterize his friendships, etc. Similarly, information about relationship quality can suggest that he is distant with employers but close with spouse, or any other such possibility. And finally, information about interpersonal role could suggest subservience with employer but dominance with wife as the typical roles.

To summarize, knowledge of the situation within which nonverbal behavior is emitted can greatly expand the interpretations of nonverbal cues. If it is known that the nonverbal behavior occurred during an interpersonal relationship, two new classes of information can be inferred from nonverbal behavior—*relationship quality* and *role*. If the observer knows that the sample of nonverbal behavior is representative of the stimulus person's usual relationships, then information about affect, relationship quality, and role can lead to more specific inferences about adjustment in different types of interactions, and formulations about the general style of interpersonal relationships and associated psychodynamic and diagnostic features.

C. HOW NONVERBAL BEHAVIOR MAY PROVIDE INFORMATION
RELATED TO VERBAL BEHAVIOR

In other research, also based on the stress interviews (Ekman, 1964a), we have shown that a very specific moment-to-moment relationship between verbal and nonverbal cues can be accurately recognized by an observer. The relationship between these two channels of communication is complex; nonverbal behavior can serve a variety of communicative functions in relation to verbal behavior. Seven functions will be considered here: (1) repeating, (2) contradicting, (3) substituting for a verbal message; (4) reflecting the person's feeling about his verbal statement; (5) reflecting changes in the relationship; (6) accenting parts of the verbal message; and (7) maintaining the communicative flow.

Nonverbal behavior can simply *repeat* the substance of a verbal message. If the verbal behavior describes an affective reaction, the nonverbal behavior can repeat the affect. If the verbal behavior describes a certain event or course of action, the nonverbal behavior can be an action portrayal of the event or action. Gestures can also repeat some aspect of the verbal message. These nonverbal repetitions of verbal messages can serve to emphasize the message; their exaggeration or understatement or lack of appearance can lead to inferences about style, e.g., expressiveness, warmth.

Nonverbal behavior can directly *contradict* the content of the verbal message. The most obvious case is an affect shown nonverbally which directly contradicts the verbal message. Other information carried by nonverbal behavior can also contradict the verbal message. The person who says "yes" and shakes his head "no" provides an instance of a gesture contradicting a verbal message. The individual who verbally states his control over a situation and nonverbally drops what he is holding, trips, etc., provides an instance of instrumental actions contradicting a verbal message. Such nonverbal contradictions of verbal behavior can lead to further inferences about areas of conflict and attempts to inhibit or control communication.

Nonverbal behavior can also be a *substitute* for a specific word or phrase in a verbal message. A nonverbal expression of affect can replace the verbal statement and be directly embedded in a verbal message describing how the person feels. Similarly, instrumental acts, gestures, portrayals, can all be used as substitutes for part of a verbal message.

Nonverbal communication can indicate a person's *feeling about his verbal statement;* e.g., shyness, embarrassment, pride, can all serve to qualify what is being stated verbally. In a similar way, nonverbal cues pertaining to the relationship quality can be informative of how *changes in the relationship* are affecting or being affected by the verbal level of discourse. A change in posture in a chair from a relaxed to a more formal or stiff position, while a patient verbally states a highly charged theme, might be communicating that the relationship is bordering on more tender areas and the sender wishes to retreat to a more stereotypical superficial relationship. Certain actions, usually of the head or hands, can be used rhythmically to *accent* or underline certain words. Certain rather minimal nonverbal cues, head nods, eye movements, shifting of position, can serve to *maintain the communicative flow.* These nonverbal cues serve to signal when the speaker needs feedback from the receiver, when he is nearly finished speaking and will allow the receiver a chance to communicate verbally; from the receiver they can indicate that he agrees and the sender need not stop his line of discourse, that he cannot wait much longer to get in his own ideas, etc.

To summarize, seven classes of information communicated by non-verbal behavior alone are presented: affect; verbal-symbolic; psychodynamic and diagnostic clues; instrumental acts; portrayals; demography; style. If the observer also knows that the behavior was emitted during an interpersonal relationship, then nonverbal cues may also communicate information about the relationship quality and the stimulus person's role. Further knowledge of how representative the behavior is, and the role of the other participant in the relationship, can lead to interpreting from nonverbal cues information about the nature and style of interpersonal relationships. Finally, most of the classes of information provided by nonverbal behavior can serve to repeat, contradict, or substitute for a verbal message, as well as accent certain words, maintain the communicative flow, reflect changes in the relationship in association with particular verbal messages and indicate a person's feeling about his verbal statement.

REFERENCES

Allport, G. *Pattern and growth in personality.* Chapter 19. New York: Wolf-Rinehart, 1961.

Bateson, G. Personal communication. 1962.

Birdwhistell, R. L. *Introduction to kinesics.* Louisville: University of Louisville Press, 1952.

Brengelmann, J. C. Expressive movements and abnormal behavior. In H. J. Eysenck (Ed.), *Handbook of abnormal psychology.* New York: Basic Books, 1963.

Bruner, J. S., & Tagiuri, R. The perception of people. In G. Lindzey (Ed.), *Handbook of social psychology.* Cambridge: Addison-Wesley, 1954.

Buehler, R. E., & Richmond, Jo F. Interpersonal communication behavior analysis: a research method. *J. Communic.,* 1963, *13*, 3, 146-155.

Davitz, J. R. (Ed.) *The communication of emotional meaning.* New York: McGraw-Hill, 1964.

Dierssen, G., Lorenc, M., & Spitalerl, R. M. A new method for graphic study of human movements. *Neurology*, 1961, *11*, 610-618.

Dittmann, A. T. The relationship between body movements and moods in interviews. *J. consult. Psychol.*, 1962, *26*, 5, 480.

Dittmann, A. T. Personal communication. 1963.

Ekman, P. A methodological discussion of nonverbal behavior. *J. Psychol.*, 1957, *43*, 141-149.

Ekman, P. Body position, facial expression and verbal behavior during interviews. *J. abnorm. soc. Psychol.*, 1964a, *68*, 3, 295-301.

Ekman, P. A comparison of the information communicated by head and body cues. Paper read at American Psychological Association Convention, 1964b.

Exline, R. V. Explorations in process of person perception: visual interaction in relationship to competition, sex, and need for affiliation. *J. Pers.*, 1963, *31*, 1.

Giedt, F. H. Comparison of visual, content and auditory cues in interviewing. *J. consult. Psychol.*, 1955, *19*, 6, 407-416.

Giedt, F. H. Cues associated with accurate and inaccurate interview impressions. *Psychiatry*, 1958, *21*, 4, 405-409.

Hoffman, M. The effects of training on the judgment of non-verbal behavior. An experimental study. Doctoral dissertation. Harvard University, Cambridge, Mass., 1964.

Jecker, J., Maccoby, N., Breitrose, H., & Rose, E. Teacher accuracy in assessing cognitive visual feedback from students. *J. appl. Psychol.*, 1964, in press.

Jones, F. P., & Narva, M. Interrupted light photography to record the effect of changes in the poise of the head upon patterns of movement and posture in man. *J. Psychol.*, 1955, *40*, 125-131.

Jones, F. P., O'Connell, D. N., & Hanson, J. A. Color coated multiple image photography for studying related rates of movement. *J. Psychol.*, 1958, *45*, 247-251.

Jones, F. P., & Hanson, J. A. Time-space pattern in a gross body movement. *Percept. mot. Skills*, 1961, *12*, 35-41.

Klein, Z. E. The nonverbal communication of feelings: a review of the literature. Unpublished manuscript, 1963.

Maccoby, N., Jecker, J., Breitrose, H., & Rose, E. Sound film recordings in improving classroom communications; experimental studies in nonverbal communication. Report, Institute for Communication Research, Stanford University, 1964.

Mahl, G., Danet, B., & Norton, Nea. Reflection of major personality characteristics in gestures and body movements. *Amer. Psychologist*, 1959, *7*, 357.

Munn, N. L. The effect of knowledge of the situation upon judgment of emotion from facial expressions. *J. abnorm. soc. Psychol.*, 1940, *35*, 324-338.

Rosenthal, R. Experimenter attributes as determinants of subjects' responses. *J. proj. Tech.*, 1963(a), *27*, 3, 324-331.

Rosenthal, R. On the social psychology of the psychological experiment: the experimenter's hypothesis as unintended determinant of experimental results. *Amer. Scientist*, June 1963 (b), *51*, 2, 268-283.

Sainesbury, P. A method of recording spontaneous movements by time-sampling motion pictures. *J. Ment. Sci.*, 1954, *100*, 742-748.

Sainesbury, P. Gestural movement during psychiatric interview. *Psychosom. Med.*, 1955, *17*, 458-469.

Siegel, S. *Nonparametric statistics for the behavioral sciences.* New York: McGraw-Hill, 1956.

Sullivan, H. S. *The interpersonal theory of psychiatry.* New York: Norton, 1953.

PART EIGHT

DISCUSSION

XIV Discussion

Gardner Murphy

I

This volume represents an effort, through well-planned experimental research, to give an enhanced dignity and meaning to the concept of affect in systematic scientific psychology.

It could well be asked how it came about that all these varied papers, representing such a wide range of interests, appear together. Why do we have an excellent study of group dynamics combined with a study of sympathy in children, and with a study of the reward and punishment value of pleasant-unpleasant pictures? The answer lies in the three facts: 1) There is a general spread of interest in the affective life; 2) t. ere are organizing or coagulating centers, persons like Silvan Tomkins, interested in drawing attention and giving more explicit focus to the broad trend; 3) there are eager experimentalists who are responsive both to the broad trend and to the imaginative integrator. This volume, though not *by* Silvan Tomkins, indeed representing but little of his own, bears the mark of his interest and his organizational flair, and it will quite properly be referred to by our generation in these terms.

Since the reader has doubtless read, in his own selective and interpretative fashion, the materials offered here, it would be a waste of time to recapitulate the contributors' concepts and methods. Probably what is more appropriate is an evaluation of what is being done in the affectivity research area as represented by this book, an attempt to pinpoint the significance of studies of affect, and an effort to gauge where such work may be tending.

The classical problems of affect—problems of the experienced quality of the various feelings and emotions, their phylogenetic and ontogenetic origins, the conditions of their excitation and development, their relations to cognitive and conative processes, to personality and social life— are directly represented, or touched upon in passing, by one or more of the current studies. The volume is a reasonably representative portrayal of the kinds of problems in affectivity that concern psychologists today. The contributors are modern experimental, clinical, and physiological

444

psychologists who aim to meet a high scientific standard, and to portray solid findings which will command respect. They seek *objectivity*.

But the problem of the nature of "objectivity" hardly comes up at all in connection with the material presented. In Izard's discussion of group dynamics (Chapter VII) and in the brief references to an existential view of one's own distress (Leventhal and Sharp, Chapter X), there is a little that might arouse discontent among those who believe that visually apprehended pointer readings are the only solid basis for modern science; but there is very little of this kind of "non-objective" material in the book. Yet the authors evidently are quite concerned that their criteria of scientific reality shall be clean and severe, and the question of the *nature of objectivity* in such studies is surely something which a discussant is expected to discuss.

II

We might begin with the problem of objectivity by suggesting a few simple notes on the psychology of scanning. At the seashore we scan the horizon for incoming vessels, or the sky for impending storms. If there is any reason to doubt the adequacy of the observations, we set up on our seashore the telescope, the anemometers, or other gear necessary to reduce the unreliability of naked eye observations and calculated guesses. We soon find, however, that under certain circumstances the weather-beaten observers who know that particular beach well are more useful in predicting the probable arrival of visible shipping and the arrival of storms than the best present physical equipment, and gear, can yield. We then have a nice question as to what is "objective." The term is frequently used to mean "based upon exteroceptive information." Frequently, however, it means "independent of individual likelihood of error," and error is reduced by the use of multiple independent observers. It is frequently surprising, but useful, to note that observations which have very high reliability or "objectivity" in the *latter* sense have little or nothing of the qualities implied in the *former* use of the term; and that exteroceptively given information may quite frequently turn out to be very misleading when judged by a standard of objectivity which allows scope for freedom and the use of a rich variety of individual observational material.

But we might go on to another kind of scanning. Suppose that while on the same beach you listen for the sound of whistling buoys or of the ominous roar which bespeaks a distant but rapidly approaching danger by air and water. Here the information is still exteroceptive, but at rather a poor level of dependability.

Smell and taste would be useful in certain cases in which particles make their impact upon receptors under known conditions which are rarely realized, though of course much used in certain specialized problems which come up in biological research, especially biochemistry. The sense of touch is traditionally one that we rely on. In fact, for the sheer identification of the presence of a known object, touch is often ranked first in objectivity. But it is too coarse-grained (even when we think of two point thresholds on fingertips or the tip of the tongue) to be used as a serious gauge where the eye, or particularly the augmented eye, utilizing microscope, telescope, or spectroscope, enriches and more fully specifies the nature of the pattern presented by nature. In general, we use a combination of exteroceptors when we want the most complete evidence, and the evidence least likely to be contradicted by further evidence or by the test of prediction.

III

But we have said nothing so far about the interoceptors. Why not? Is there evidence that interoceptors are always inferior to exteroceptors when we must scan for necessary information, or having found the object sought, must make an accurate report? When we come to think of it, we realize that amazingly there is little good evidence to show how far interoceptive information may be reliably used. The experienced clinician may at times be able to tell from the patient's description of "how he feels" what the toxic or other pathogenic agent may be, though he usually gets as much supplementary information from temperature, etc., as he can. Still there are cases where he needs to know how much it hurts at some point inside, or whether there are certain queasy feelings which, despite our poor vocabulary for such matters, he can interpret as the layman cannot. Experimental psychologists have done extraordinarily little with these internal scanning and specifying processes. We simply do not know how good they are as reality indicators. It is worth the experimental time of a band of experimentalists, however, to locate such information. It is quite likely, for example, in the new worlds of ataractic and of psychedelic drugs, that the person can tell us an extraordinary amount which is specific to the effects of particular drugs and that a better yardstick for certain drug effects can be obtained by reports on enteroception than any other method known. In aviation—and with a vengeance in space travel—we are certainly getting all sorts of queer new input from the viscera as well as from other parts of the body. It behooves us to try to learn how to understand. This will mean that the scanning of such interoceptive input will be a very important part of the research on adaptation to conditions of jet and space flight.

But what we are now suggesting regarding investigation of the scanning of interoceptive cues is much more palpably significant and needs much more emphasis when it comes to *proprioceptive* cues. Here it is not a question of the shortage of experimental evidence; for there has been over several decades a reasonably respectable investigation of the accuracy of proprioceptive information from movements of limbs— evidence brought into physiological relation to known input from striped muscles, and especially from tendons and joints, and an accelerating investigation of input from the external eye muscles meaningfully related to visual scanning, centration, shifts of attention, and other problems in "physiological psychology." Indeed we do not use the exteroceptive information alone, but regularly combine it, as well as we know how, with proprioceptive information. Proprioceptive and vestibular information can, of course, also be used without relying upon vision or other exteroceptive sources of information. A number of important lines of work in contemporary physiological optics make use of input from the striped musculature under various conditions of body tilting, and the sensory-tonic investigations of Werner, Wapner, and their associates underscore the importance of striped muscle cues for the general psychology of space perception. The uses of modern forms of curare, freed from some of its disturbing side effects, are even playing an important part in the investigation of basic learning processes, as in the work of Solomon. Interference with proprioceptive feedback in clinical cases with proprioceptive defects can be meaningfully brought into relation to interrupted visual feedback in a manner helping us to understand the combined use of vision and proprioception in motor learning.

All of this strongly suggests that there is a vast amount of important information from inside the body which must be taken seriously if we are to talk about "objectivity" in either of the two senses defined above. We can no longer say that information has to be exteroceptively based in order to be taken seriously by science; in fact, it is likely that the extended use of proprioception will soon be followed by the extended use of interoception when it comes to getting systematic knowledge of what goes on inside the body. This is surely a psychologist's concern to the same degree as is his knowledge of what goes on in his visible performance; ultimately an organismic psychology will have to be ready to use all the functional information it can get. It cannot afford to turn up its nose at systematically planned information gathering and processing simply because the information is not of exteroceptive origin.

IV

Now it seems probable that exactly the same line of logic will soon be appropriate as we learn to investigate *affect*. The affects certainly are not now available to exteroceptive scanning, but affect and exteroceptive information can be studied conjointly. Modern devices, such as those of Lisina in the Soviet Union, have thrown the internal, vegetative changes in panel form upon a screen where the subject can himself observe what is going on inside him. There often is good isomorphism, spatially and temporally, between certain internal patterns and those which are exteroceptively perceptible on the panel. It would make little sense to say that one kind of information is objectively scientific, the other not, when each is isomorphic with the other, and when the subject can learn to report on the internally given pattern, just as he can learn to report on the externally given pattern. The affective upheavals, whether they be equated with physiological upheavals or not, are plainly matters of importance to a psychology which wants to observe with the highest level of accuracy and objectivity attainable.

Much confusion has prevailed for several decades as a result of the felt need of many observers to say, in relation to enteroception and affect, that the scientific datum is the "verbal report." In mature sciences such as physics and chemistry, where one turns observations into both verbal and numerical form, there is no tendency to say that the verbal report of the event *is the only event studied by science.* An almost infinite variety of verbal reports can be offered, but none of them is the central datum which the physicist is concerned with. He is concerned rather with the realities to which the report refers by one or another direct or indirect method. This is not far from the world of "hypothetical constructs" and "intervening variables." But instead of apologizing for dealing with that which is not directly apprehended through the exteroceptors, the physicist or chemist takes it as a matter of course that much which is real and important is not capable of such exteroceptive observation. In observations of the electron, for example, (or the gene) it is sufficient that the reality of the entity be defined by a series of processes which make its presence known. Actually the psychologist dealing with such non-exteroceptively given material is considerably better off than the physicist or chemist, because he has not only indirect but also direct evidence from his own observations. He can usually sit in the chair where his subject sat, and get the datum not only by the indirect, but also by the direct method. Affect, then, is in considerable degree at a higher level of scientific observability and knowability than is the world of the very small physico-chemical events not directly observable by electron microscopes.

It is, of course, certain that the resolving power of such internal observation is typically crude. The primary problem is to train observers and learn what level of dependability their observations can achieve, first in terms of inter-judge agreement, and second in terms of isomorphic congruence with physiological measures in those instances in which one can work back and forth from the observer's level—the phenomenological level—and the physiologist's level. Often the resolving power of the physiological device will be finer than that of the observer of interoceptive processes, in which case the physiological can often act as pacemaker in improving the resolving power of interoception. Hefferline has already shown that visual observation can in this way act as pacemaker for the training of proprioceptive observation. The subject watches an outside panel which tells him how far open his mouth is at a given moment, and learns to ascertain quite precisely from *masseter jaw muscle* input how far open his mouth "feels," and can then open it to the refined specifications of the experimenter. The process of training the observer in both qualitative and quantitative reports upon his own internal processes would apparently be of the same general sort, but with limits of trainability which are at present simply unknown. If observations are not offered in a more refined form than is needed for the level of analysis required, we already have sufficiently good observations to distinguish gross affective states—what William James called the "coarser emotions." They are perhaps comparable in discriminability to gross variation of light and dark, warm and cool, "surprising" versus "startling" news, etc.

The matter takes on a new guise when we take into account Schachter's observations that the same physiological upheaval may be apprehended, classified, and named differently by different persons, or by the same person upon different occasions; the same upheaval may be called annoyance or anxiety or rage. Obviously, the lines of investigation of internal scanning will have to take into account both the cruder, coarser, or more "sensory" aspects of the inner input and the higher-level perceptual-cognitive responses to this input, as shown in the Schachter experiments.

V

Thus the logic of scanning and reporting upon their sensations, based on input from the interior of the body, appears to differ in no respect from scanning and reporting upon affect. Just as pain sensitivity, as one explores the skin, can be directly compared with warm or cold or surface or deep touch sensitivity, so pain, strain, ache, etc. from the *interior* may be compared with such sensory qualities as the warm and cold derived from warm and cold drinks, etc. One classical theory of affect, associated in the modern age with the name of Titchener, is that affects are essentially sensory in quality. If so, the whole thesis developed above regarding the observability of interoceptive sensations would apply also to the observability of affect. The point need not, however, be labored. It is an empirical question, not yet settled by clear-cut experimental evidence, whether the qualities of the internal input can all be resolved to sensory qualities, just as it is uncertain whether physiological and neuroanatomical evidence will show the affective life to be a sensory life in the full sense of the term. These empirical questions will be resolved in the next generation with the same devoted attention that has been given to the immediate confrontation and introspective-phenomenological description of the exteroceptive life. Indeed, several studies were made, even in Titchener's era, of the types of internal sensations to which we are referring, and doubtless many more would have been made if the instrumental possibilities of the sort already quoted from Lisina had existed.

VI

The question is not to be prejudged as to whether the higher structural possibilities at the level of perception, judgment, and cognition generally exist likewise for the interoceptive types of experience. It seems to be self-evident that sight and hearing give the richest structural and architectonic possibilities, as the estheticians usually insist. Maybe this is a function of the amount of care and consensual validation which men in society typically give to things which they can directly compare with one another. Maybe when they get to the point of comparing their experiences of the fragrance of perfumes in the same manner, they will pass on to the study of affect in the same analytical and synthetic spirit.

This, of course, sounds "not quite decent." We can check with one another the exquisite qualities of a Mozart quartet, but only poets will describe the inner resonance to Mozart or to daffodils, and it is a rare poet indeed who has the courage or effrontery to tell us the actual inner quality of his own interoceptive response. Perhaps he cannot; perhaps, however, he can, but does not push his scanning and analytical powers to the point where he would turn himself inside out and make himself too nakedly and patently observable to all.

The taboo on the revelation of the interoceptive world may in fact be paralleled by an equally deep taboo even on one's own inner confrontation of it. But in the last half of this century we are entering an era of rather shameless self-analysis, as is evident everywhere from the taboo-collapsing processes of psychoanalysis, modern poetry, cross-cultural revelations of the self, and inside-outside panels in the laboratory, and the whole gamut of modern medical and physical scientific devices for looking inside. The meaning of the term "inside," as used by the physicist, is different from the term "inside" as used here, but the one leads to the other. Indeed each will act as pacemaker to the other; and just as the use of exteroceptive panels will help us to observe more clearly what is going on at our own phenomenological level, so vice versa more and more refined phenomenological observation will draw attention to physically observable *events for which we had not been looking*. When this has occurred, we shall have come full circle from the ancient animism in which we find in nature what is really going on in ourselves, to one in which we find in ourselves the reflected-back images of what we perceive exteroceptively in the outside world.

Here again is an empirical question. Can we find within ourselves that which resonates isomorphically to what is going on in another person, as in the studies of sympathy presented here by Lenrow (Chapter IX), and look out to see what degree of isomorphism there may be between our experiences and the spatial or temporal patterns of the world which give rise to them? It is true that the taboo goes very deep; and in addition to the taboo as such there also may be intrinsic reasons why direct observation of the affective life is hard. From an evolutionary point of view, we have to note that attention has always been given primarily to the outer events confronting an organism, and that the upheaval within could not be directly attended to without diverting one from the external task. Such evolutionary arguments are usually double-edged swords, however, since it may turn out, as observation becomes more and more skilled, that we can carry out the subtle affective adjustments required in modern life *more effectively* if we have learned to observe and to understand them.

VII

It is not quite enough to get rid of the naive physicalism which makes bodily responses more "real" than conscious responses, or which finds it possible to observe physical events but not to observe conscious events. There is also a deeply ingrained dualism, not identical with Descartes' soul acting on body and body acting on soul, yet almost as confusing. Just as the modern physician working with the concepts of psychosomatic medicine may say that an unconscious conflict *causes* a hypertension, so the psychologist may be tempted to say that an affect *causes* a train of action. In fact I find, at several points in the present volume, lapses into this kind of language in which the affect is regarded as the primary or essential component in a motive series, the motive series being conceived in physiological or broadly defined organic terms. The affect that is referred to, however, in these passages appears to be the affect as directly known; that is, it is phenomenological affect. To make it a *cause* of a physiological train is perilously close to a Cartesian dualism. It might seem long-winded to make use of a more careful expression, "the response of which the affect is an aspect," but it would be worth the trouble. At several other points in this volume the problem of the relation of conscious affect to total response of the organism is muted or evaded, as, for example, in the study of the pain of childbirth (Chapter X) in which there is a hint that it is the increasing intensity of the *pain* that gives rise to the increasing facial indicators, whereas surely what is meant is that the total stress, of which the pain is simply an aspect, activates more and more intense response of the facial musculature.

Rosenberg's paper on "Attitudinal Inconsistency" (Chapter V) can be viewed as an interesting modernization of the old problem of "mixed affects," to which Titchener gave his attention (the question whether one can have a positive and negative affect at the same time), and more broadly of the Wundtian problem of the hierarchial structure of the affective life. Though the problem has its esoteric aspects, it bears directly on the question of the stability or instability of the affective structures, and therefore has direct implications for education and for communication theory at large. Rosenberg's paper is representative also of a broad modern trend towards the integrated study of cognition and affect. Having done honor to one process and then to the other, psychology has been moving into a study of "affecto-cognitive" structures as well as of "affecto-motor" structures. Extraordinarily interesting in this connection is Harvey's study (Chapter VIII) of the role of cognitive structure upon the arousal mechanisms—part of the problems of the way in which the apprehension of a situation gives it affective meaning. These forms of commerce between cognition and affect traverse two-way streets. Indeed we might have learned long ago from Sherrington that the central nervous system is so constructed as to make interactions of cognitive, affective, and motor components inevitable. In any modern adaptation level theory, it becomes clear that it is not only within one modality or one form of experience that the existing base line helps us to determine the response to the impact of a new stimulus. Expectancy and hope, readiness and set are concepts here of increasing importance predetermining the size and nature of the gap between what we are ready for and what we encounter; and a psychology of gaps begins to appear to be related to and expressed by the "dissonance theory" of today, on the one hand, and the Lewinian conception of a discrepancy between our present functioning level and the levels to which we aspire.

The continuing dualism of our everyday speech is shown by our habit of hooking together all the "physiological indicators," and comparing them individually or collectively against the quality or intensity or duration of the direct personal experience. We conceive ourselves to be comparing physiological versus psychological levels or response or physiological versus psychological types of processes. Actually, a little chart (Figure 1) might make clear some of the typical interrelations

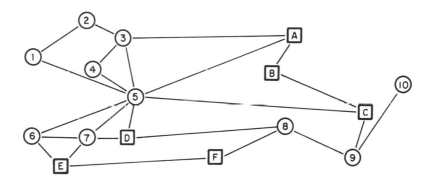

Figure 1.   Hypothetical relations of some "physiological" and some "affective" observations. *Numbers*: observations of physiological responses. *Letters*: observations of attributes of experienced affect.

between various "physiological" and various "psychological" kinds of evidence. They would show that while certain psychological items do hang together with certain other psychological items, some of them hang together much better with certain physiological indicators; in the same way, the physiological indicators are not a massive team or total, hanging consistently together, but a variety of somewhat independent components, some of which hang together well with one another, and some of which hang together with certain psychological indicators. The cross articulation of the two systems shows that there is really one system, not two. Indeed some of the natural clusters of events bind tightly together certain "psychological" and certain "physiological" classes of evidence which are core realities to be investigated, while at the periphery there are certain psychological items which do not agree very well with anything else and, likewise, certain physiological indicators that do not agree well with anything else. The dualistic habit, the "mental versus physical" way of looking at matters, has merely confused us.

In the excellent experimental work of Ekman (Chapter XIII) on the communication of affect through various types of non-verbal behavior, we have a good synthesis of evidence of various sorts regarding the feeling tone existing between persons. It is rather tantalizing, perhaps, in its avoidance of a direct confrontation of affect. In the same manner the very rewarding problem of the tendency of people to seek one another's eyes or to look away from them, the exchange of "mutual glances," is beautifully pursued by Exline and Winters (Chapter XI). In these and in several other studies, I find excellent integrated approaches to the affective life with perhaps a little of the tendency on the part of the investigators themselves to exchange "mutual glances" with one another and with their psychological problem rather than willingness to confront (or to stare "out of countenance") the basic psychological issues which come up when affect is dealt with experientially as well as externally. In Messick's study (Chapter IV) we have many apparent results of affect upon cognition and personality, but have no sure way of knowing what kind of affects triggered these responses.

Affect is certainly more "respectable" as an aspect of personality than as an aspect of a psychophysiological response or a momentary social situation, and it is not surprising that in Nowlis' study (Chapter XII) of moods when the time dimension, the longitudinal aspect, is considered, there is a sustained confrontation of the problem. Mood is classically the more enduring affective aspect of personality, and just as the studies of sympathy in children (Chapter IX) deal both with momentary and with developmental and changing reflections of the affect life, so the more stable and persistent aspects are well specified in the Nowlis devices for the measurement of moods and their interrelations.

VIII

So my conclusion is that there is much good material on affect here, and that it advances our understanding of the interrelation of evidence from physiological, developmental, and phenomenological sources.

I do not feel that the result is very well integrated, primarily because modern research in affect is itself poorly integrated. The reason lies in the fragmentation of man which has been heralded by a confused use of the term "objective," and the reluctance to see the affective life in an evolutionary perspective in which experienced affect is a vital aspect of the confrontation of and the adaptation to the environment.

The *effort* at integration, as much for the book as for the man, is a sign of health.

INDEX